Codes for Detecting and Correcting Unidirectional Errors

CODES FOR DETECTING AND CORRECTING UNIDIRECTIONAL ERRORS

MARIO BLAUM

IEEE Computer Society Press
Los Alamitos, California

Washington • Brussels • Tokyo

Library of Congress Cataloging-in-Publication Data

Blaum, Mario, 1951-
Codes for detecting and correcting unidirectional errors / Mario Blaum.
p. cm. -- (IEEE Computer Society Press reprint collection)
Includes bibliographical references (p.).
ISBN 0-8186-4180-0 (paper). -- ISBN 0-8186-4182-7 (case). -- ISBN 0-8186-4181-9 (m/f)
1. Fault-tolerant computing. 2. Debugging in computer science.
I. Title. II. Series.
QA76.9.F38B48 1993
005.7 ' 2 -- dc20 CIP 93-17499

Published by the
IEEE Computer Society Press
10662 Los Vaqueros Circle
PO Box 3014
Los Alamitos, CA 90720-1264

IEEE Computer Society Press Order Number 4182-03
Library of Congress Number 93-17499
ISBN 0-8186-4181-9 (microfiche)
ISBN 0-8186-4182-7 (case)

Additional copies can be ordered from

IEEE Computer Society Press
Customer Service Center
10662 Los Vaqueros Circle
PO Box 3014
Los Alamitos, CA 90720-1264

IEEE Computer Society
13, avenue de l'Aquilon
B-1200 Brussels
BELGIUM

IEEE Computer Society
Ooshima Building
2-19-1 Minami-Aoyama
Minato-ku, Tokyo 107
JAPAN

Technical editor: Murali Varanasi
Editorial production: Robert Werner
Copy editing: Henry Ayling
Cover design by Joseph Daigle/Schenk-Daigle Studios
Printed in the United States of America by Braun-Brumfield, Inc.

THE INSTITUTE OF ELECTRICAL AND
ELECTRONICS ENGINEERS, INC.

PREFACE

Most error-correcting/detecting codes deal with symmetric errors;[1-6] a transmitted 0 may be received as a 1 (denoted as a $0 \rightarrow 1$ error), or a transmitted 1 may be received as a 0 (denoted as a $1 \rightarrow 0$ error). However, applications exist in which errors tend to be either asymmetrical or unidirectional. We categorize errors as asymmetrical if only one error type occurs — for example, $0 \rightarrow 1$.[6,7] Numerous researchers have studied codes for correcting asymmetrical errors.[7-18] Unidirectional errors differ slightly from asymmetric errors; we say that unidirectional errors have occurred when all errors are either of type $0 \rightarrow 1$, or of type $1 \rightarrow 0$. In other words, both error types are possible, but only one type occurs in a code word. Unidirectional errors have been observed in VLSI computer memories. Polarity changes may affect several bits; consequently, bits that have been stored as 0's can be read as 1's, and bits that have been stored as 1's can be read as 0's.[19] Many papers on codes dealing with unidirectional errors have been published since the early 80's, especially after the pioneering work of Bose, Pradhan, and Rao.[20-23]

The papers that I have assembled herein best represent state-of-the-art research in the theory and practice of codes correcting or detecting unidirectional errors. I have included not only those papers giving the best results in each subject related to unidirectional errors, but also those having historical or pedagogical value for readers. I have grouped this volume's seven chapters according to topics of interest; each chapter begins with a brief introduction to the papers selected.

This book was prepared for (1) engineers working in computer memory technologies and VLSI design, (2) researchers working in the general area of error control codes for computer applications, and (3) graduate students needing access to such material, which is not covered by most books on error-correcting codes — the only exception being Rao and Fujiwara, who briefly address the topic (unidirectional errors).[6]

THE CONTENTS

Chapter 1 presents four papers of historical and pedagogical interest. They provide a good introduction to the topic (including its applications).

Chapter 2 addresses the detection of unidirectional errors and should interest engineers and mathematicians alike, since a close relationship abides between codes detecting unidirectional errors and the combinatorics of finite sets.[24]

Chapter 3 focuses on the correction of unidirectional errors. The necessary and sufficient conditions for these codes are complex and the codes are difficult to construct. Known constructions and bounds are mainly combinatorial, so this chapter contains more theoretical than practical material.

Chapter 4 provides results on codes correcting a limited number of symmetric errors, and detecting either all unidirectional errors or a limited number exceeding the number of correctable symmetric errors. The necessary and sufficient conditions for these codes are simpler than for the pure correction of unidirectional errors, and efficient constructions were obtained. This chapter should interest engineers and mathematicians; in VLSI applications, polarity changes may cause many unidirectional errors that cannot be corrected but must be detected. At the same time, we may want to retain a limited error-correcting capability. From the theoretical viewpoint, a close relationship exists between t-error-correcting, all-unidirectional-error-detecting (AUED) codes, and generalizations of Sperner's lemma.[25,26] Readers will also find upper and lower bounds of interest.

Chapter 5 presents codes for detecting and correcting different combinations of symmetric and unidirectional errors together with necessary and sufficient conditions, and also addresses the connection with combinatorics of finite sets.

Chapter 6 identifies codes for detecting and correcting unidirectional errors when these errors occur in bursts — a common event in VLSI applications.

Finally, Chapter 7 deals with codes for correcting and detecting unidirectional byte errors, with potential applications in page-oriented computer memories.

ACKNOWLEDGMENTS

I would like to thank the following colleagues and friends: Khaled Abdel-Ghaffar, Bella Bose, Jehoshua Bruck, Dhiraj Pradhan, Yuichi Saitoh, Paul Siegel, Henk van Tilborg, Jos Weber, Zhen Zhang — and also this volume's Technical Editor, Murali Varanasi, and the anonymous IEEE Computer Society Press referees for their valuable comments during the review of my manuscript. Among other contributions, they pointed out several mistakes and embarrassing omissions in the original text.

I also want to thank CS Press Editorial Director Henry Ayling and Production Editor Robert Werner for their outstanding editing of this volume's final draft. Technical errors or omissions, if any, are my responsibility.

Mario Blaum
May 7, 1993

TABLE OF CONTENTS

CHAPTER 1: UNIDIRECTIONAL ERRORS

This chapter presents four papers of considerable introductory value. The first, by Fujiwara and Pradhan, is a tutorial on error-correcting codes utilized in computer memories. Although codes dealing with unidirectional errors are a subset of this paper, readers seeking an introduction to the field will profit from reading the entire paper because it places unidirectional errors in the more general context of fault tolerance for computer memories. Our references provide additional information on this topic.[27,28]

Pradhan was one of the first to describe the occurrence of unidirectional errors in the context of computer memories. In particular, he discusses constructions of codes that can correct a few symmetric errors and detect numerous unidirectional errors. Pradhan proves the necessary and sufficient conditions for these codes (see also Chapter 4).

Bose and Rao effectively introduce the theory of codes for detecting and correcting unidirectional errors. They also give constructions of single error-correcting/all-unidirectional-error-detecting codes, introducing the group theoretic method. This technique was also used in a recent paper by Zhang and Tu.[29]

Matsuzawa and Fujiwara present a coding technique for masking unidirectional line faults. Designers of fault-tolerant computer memories will find the authors' detailed discussion of the engineering problem valuable.

Elsewhere, Bose provides more information regarding early work on unidirectional errors.[20]

Error-Control Coding in Computers

Eiji Fujiwara, Tokyo Institute of Technology
Dhiraj K. Pradhan, University of Massachusetts*

Imaginative use of low-level error-control techniques can offset the need for massive high-level redundancy. This article covers the application of codes in actual systems.

Sophisticated error-correcting codes, now commonplace in both commercial and noncommercial computers, contribute substantially to achieving dependable, reliable systems. Prime examples can be found in a wide variety of applications, including codes for high-speed and mass memories and even for processors.

Coding for computers is a distinct discipline that, unlike coding for communications, must satisfy very restrictive speed, power, and area constraints.[1,2] For the codes to be useful, any increase in computing speed demands a corresponding increase in the encoding and decoding speed. Therefore, high-speed VLSI implementation of encoders and decoders is a major engineering concern. But speed is not the only concern; reliability is equally important. Since encoders and decoders use the same technology as the unit the code protects, they cannot be assumed to be fault-free. Consequently, fault-tolerant implementation of encoders and decoders is also a topic of importance.

In computer coding, we can sometimes rely on a priori information about error location. For example, single-parity codes are not useful in communications but can be quite useful in computers. In a RAM, fault location can be determined by running diagnostics. Once the location of the error is known, the bit can be treated as an erasure and corrected by a single-parity code. Thus, coding for computers does not always require new, sophisticated codes; a clever use of simple, existing codes may do the job as well.

Another, newer application of error-correcting codes is yield improvement.[2,3] As we approach RAM chips of 16 megabits and beyond, random cell defects will be a major source of yield detraction. The conventional spare-row-and-column techniques will be of limited use. But on-chip coding could provide both benefits: protection against cell defects and protection against soft errors.

This article, intended for readers with basic knowledge in coding, surveys codes used in actual systems.

Error control in high-speed memories

Because high-speed caches and main memories are prone to soft errors, error-correcting codes are used in their design and, more recently, in the design of on-chip memories. For a code to be useful for high-speed memories, its structure must permit rapid, parallel encoding and decoding. The complexity of the parity check circuit used in the encoder and decoder can be a major factor in determining speed. By examining the structure of the parity check matrix, known as the **H** matrix, we can estimate the complexity of the parity check circuit.

For example, consider a length-6 code, $n = 6$, with three information bits, $k = 3$, and

*This work was performed while Pradhan was visiting Japan under a Japan Society for Promotion of Science fellowship.

Reprinted from *Computer*, July 1990, pp. 63-72.

0-8186-4182-7/93 $3.00 © 1990 IEEE

three check bits, $r = 3$. The two **H** matrices below provide the same error-correcting capability. Since all columns of the **H** matrix are distinct, the code can correct all single errors, but the parity check circuit for $\mathbf{H_1}$ is less complex than that for $\mathbf{H_2}$. $\mathbf{H_1}$ requires only three 2-input XOR gates to compute the parity checks, whereas $\mathbf{H_2}$ needs two 2-input XORs to compute c_0 and c_1 and one 3-input XOR to compute c_2. Because of the 3-input XOR gate, the encoder and decoder using $\mathbf{H_2}$ will be slower, as well as more complex.

$$\mathbf{H_1} = \begin{array}{c} \begin{matrix} d_0 & d_1 & d_2 & c_0 & c_1 & c_2 \end{matrix} \\ \begin{bmatrix} 1 & 0 & 1 & 1 & 0 & 0 \\ 0 & 1 & 1 & 0 & 1 & 0 \\ 1 & 1 & 0 & 0 & 0 & 1 \end{bmatrix} \end{array}$$

$$c_0 = d_0 \oplus d_2$$
$$c_1 = d_1 \oplus d_2$$
$$c_2 = d_0 \oplus d_1$$

$$\mathbf{H_2} = \begin{array}{c} \begin{matrix} d_0 & d_1 & d_2 & c_0 & c_1 & c_2 \end{matrix} \\ \begin{bmatrix} 1 & 0 & 1 & 1 & 0 & 0 \\ 1 & 1 & 0 & 0 & 1 & 0 \\ 1 & 1 & 1 & 0 & 0 & 1 \end{bmatrix} \end{array}$$

$$c_0 = d_0 \oplus d_2$$
$$c_1 = d_0 \oplus d_1$$
$$c_2 = d_0 \oplus d_1 \oplus d_2$$

Basically, the number of 1's in the **H** matrix determines the overall complexity of the parity check circuit. The fewer the number of 1's, the less complex the circuit. Also, the slowest parity check circuit corresponds to the row with the maximum number of 1's. Therefore, it is important to keep both the number of 1's overall and the number of 1's in any row to a minimum.

Bit error-correcting error-detecting codes. In high-speed memories, single-bit error-correcting and double-bit error-detecting codes (SEC-DED codes) are most commonly used. This is because many semiconductor RAM chips are organized for one bit of data output at a time; therefore, any failure in one chip manifests itself as one bit in error.

Hsiao codes. Let's consider the two odd-weight r-tuples. Here, weight refers to the number of 1's. Note that the sum of two odd-weight r-tuples is an even-weight r-tuple. Because of this property, an SEC-DED code with r check bits can be constructed. Here, the **H** matrix consists of odd-weight column vectors. Thus, the double-bit error syndrome is an even-weight r-tuple and is distinguished from the single-bit error syndrome, which is an odd-weight r-tuple. This code is different from the original *Hamming SEC-DED code*, whose **H** matrix has an all-1 row vector in addition to the SEC code **H** matrix.

The Hsiao class of codes[4] is optimal because it has a minimum number of 1's in the **H** matrix, which makes the encoding/decoding circuit simple. To obtain a high-speed encoding/decoding circuit, the number of 1's in each row is equal or as close as possible to the average number. The maximum code length is equal to the maximum number of r-tuples of odd weight and thus $n = 2^{r-1}$.

Figure 1 is a simple example of this class of code and its parallel decoding circuit. Figure 2 is an example of the **H** matrix for the (72, 64) SEC-DED code with code length $n = 72$, information bits $k = 64$, and check bits $r = n - k = 8$.

For any SEC-DED code, the probability of miscorrection when triple or more errors occur must be minimal. A miscorrection here refers to an erroneous decoding that results in an erroneous corrected word. For example, for the code in Figure 1, a triple error in an all-1 code word 11111111 can produce 11111000. This will be miscorrected as a single error, and the decoder will output the erroneous code word 11101000.

For the code in Figure 2, simulation gives a 43.72 percent probability of detected triple errors and a 99.19 percent probability of detected quadruple errors. On the other hand, a non-odd-weight-column code having the same code parameters has a 24.0 ~ 43.5 percent probability of detecting triple errors and a 98.90 ~ 99.18 percent probability of detecting quadruple errors.

These results show that odd-weight-column SEC-DED codes have two practical advantages: encoder/decoder simplicity and lower probability of erroneous decoding. These codes are therefore widely used, for example, in IBM, Cray, and Tandem systems. Commercially available parallel error-detection-and-correction ICs are based on these codes.

Error control for multiple-bit errors. High-density memory chips create new reliability problems. One example is the alpha particle problem in high-density semiconductor RAM chips. These soft errors may line up with existing hard errors, giving rise to multiple errors that are not correctable with SEC-DED codes.

The direct method for correcting multiple errors is to use multiple-error-correcting codes. Therefore, random *double-bit error-correcting (DEC) codes* are becoming increasingly important. The well-known *BCH code*,[1] constructed using finite-field theory, and the *majority-logic decodable code* are viable candidates for double error correction in memory. But these codes require twice as many check bits as the SEC-DED codes, and the decoding is ensuingly more complex.

To solve the above problems, low-cost techniques using extensions of SEC-DED codes have been proposed. These techniques use *erasure correction* for errors whose location is already known a priori. This location information enables a distance-4 code (SEC-DED code) to correct up to three erasures. In a different method based on *address skewing*,[1] multiple errors on the same address are dispersed as single errors in different addresses. These single errors can then be corrected. Another technique for multiple error correction is the *read-retry technique*.[1] In this technique, repeated read cycles are used to eliminate the soft errors. *Sparing* replaces a defective component with a spare one. This *masking* of hard faults requires some additional memory read and write operations for detection and correction.

Byte error-correcting/detecting codes. Certain high-density semiconductor memory chips are organized b bits wide. If a failure occurs, the resulting word read-out is likely to have a b-bit block (byte) in error. In this kind of application, it is desirable to have an error-correcting code capable of correcting/detecting byte errors as well as bit errors.

Byte error-correcting codes. The **H** matrix for a single-byte error-correcting code is constructed as follows: Choose as columns of the **H** matrix all the nonzero r-tuples of elements from a finite field F, in particular, from Galois field $GF(2^b)$, such that no column of **H** is a multiple of another column. Thus, every pair of columns is linearly independent, and there is a minimum Hamming distance-3 for the code. The code, known as *SbEC code*,[1] is capable of correcting all single b-bit byte errors.

Implementing this type of code requires transforming the **H** matrix over $GF(2^b)$ to a binary form. By using a binary primitive polynomial, $g(x)$ of degree b, we can define a nonsingular matrix **T**, expressed as a $(b \times b)$ binary matrix.[1] The set of these matrices is a field that is isomorphic to $GF(2^b)$. Therefore, the elements of $GF(2^b)$

Information bits				*Check bits*			
d_0	d_1	d_2	d_3	c_0	c_1	c_2	c_3

$$\mathbf{H} = \left[\begin{array}{cccc|cccc} 1 & 1 & 1 & 0 & 1 & 0 & 0 & 0 \\ 1 & 1 & 0 & 1 & 0 & 1 & 0 & 0 \\ 1 & 0 & 1 & 1 & 0 & 0 & 1 & 0 \\ 0 & 1 & 1 & 1 & 0 & 0 & 0 & 1 \end{array}\right]$$

Memory readout word: $D = [d_0, d_1, d_2, d_3, c_0, c_1, c_2, c_3]$

Syndrome: $S = D \cdot \mathbf{H}^T \, [s_0, s_1, s_2, s_3]$

$$s_0 = d_0 \oplus d_1 \oplus d_2 \oplus c_0$$
$$s_1 = d_0 \oplus d_1 \oplus d_3 \oplus c_1$$
$$s_2 = d_0 \oplus d_2 \oplus d_3 \oplus c_2$$
$$s_4 = d_1 \oplus d_2 \oplus d_3 \oplus c_3$$

$\oplus$: modulo 2 addition

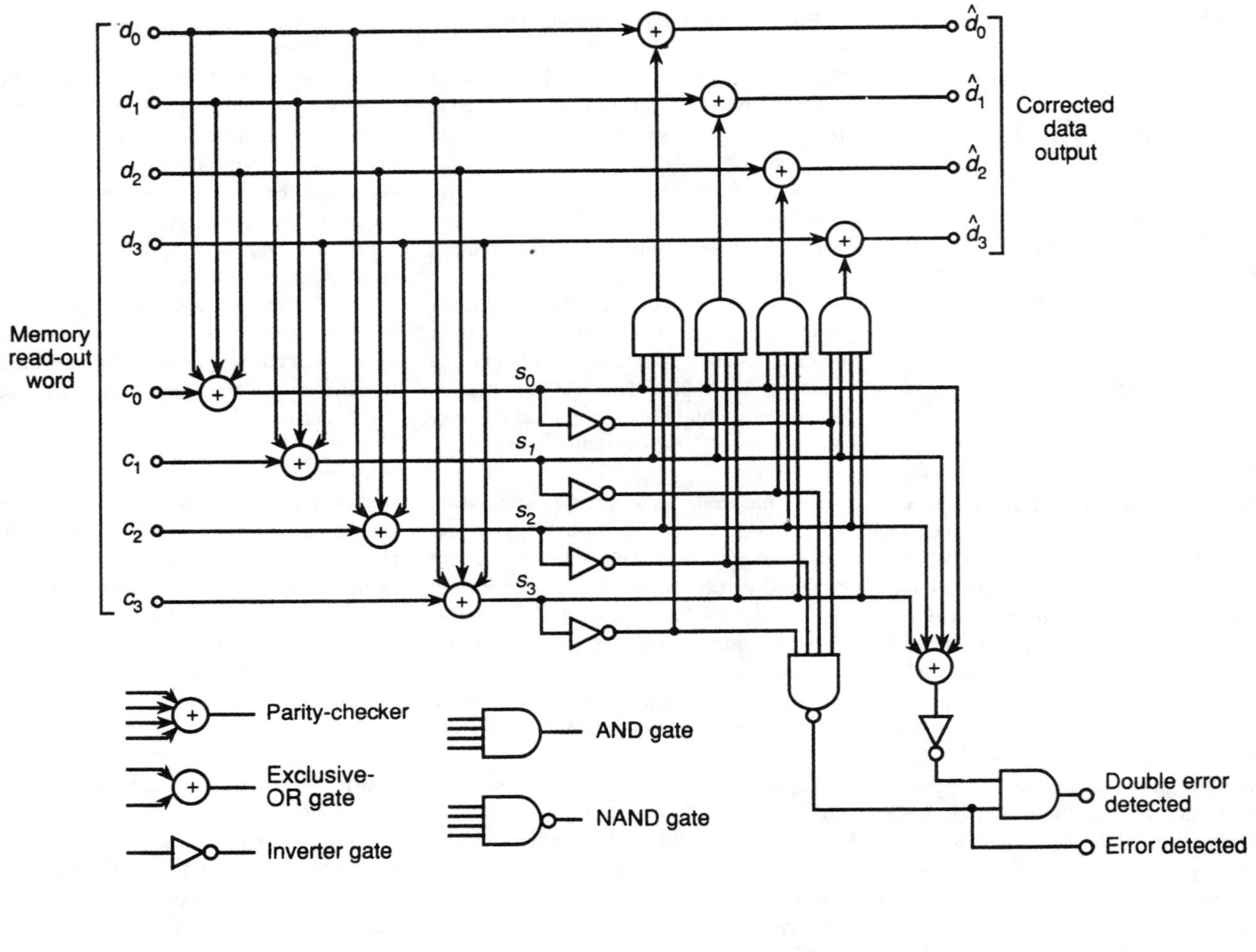

Figure 1. A simple odd-weight-column code and its parallel decoding circuit.

Byte	1								2								3							
Bit	0	1	2	3	4	5	6	7	8	9	10	11	12	13	14	15	16	17	18	19	20	21	22	23
S_0	1	1	1	1	1	1	1	1			1			1	1			1			1			1
S_1	1	1	1						1	1	1	1	1	1	1	1			1			1	1	
S_2				1	1	1			1	1	1						1	1	1	1	1	1	1	1
S_3				1			1	1				1	1	1			1	1	1					
S_4				1								1			1	1				1	1	1		
S_5	1			1								1								1			1	1
S_6		1			1			1	1			1								1				
S_7			1			1	1			1			1			1	1			1				

Byte	4								5								6							
Bit	24	25	26	27	28	29	30	31	32	33	34	35	36	37	38	39	40	41	42	43	44	45	46	47
S_0	1			1								1								1			1	1
S_1		1			1			1	1			1								1				
S_2			1			1	1			1			1			1	1			1				
S_3	1	1	1	1	1	1	1	1			1			1	1			1			1			1
S_4	1	1	1						1	1	1	1	1	1	1	1			1			1	1	
S_5				1	1	1			1	1	1						1	1	1	1	1	1	1	1
S_6				1			1	1				1	1	1			1	1	1					
S_7				1								1			1	1				1	1	1		

Byte	7								8								Check							
Bit	48	49	50	51	52	53	54	55	56	57	58	59	60	61	62	63	C_0	C_1	C_2	C_3	C_4	C_5	C_6	C_7
S_0				1	1	1			1	1	1						1							
S_1				1			1	1				1	1	1				1						
S_2				1								1			1	1			1					
S_3	1			1								1								1				
S_4		1			1			1	1			1									1			
S_5			1			1	1			1			1			1						1		
S_6	1	1	1	1	1	1	1	1			1			1	1								1	
S_7	1	1	1						1	1	1	1	1	1	1	1								1

Figure 2. An H matrix for the (72, 64) SEC-DED code.

$$
\mathbf{H} = \left[\begin{array}{cccccc|ccc}
\mathbf{I} & \mathbf{I} & & \mathbf{I} & & \mathbf{I} & \mathbf{I} & & \\
\mathbf{I} & \mathbf{T} & \cdots & \mathbf{T}^{i} & \cdots & \mathbf{T}^{2^b-2} & & \mathbf{I} & \\
\mathbf{I} & \mathbf{T}^{2} & & \mathbf{T}^{2i} & & \mathbf{T}^{2(2^b-2)} & & & \mathbf{I}
\end{array}\right]
$$

Figure 3. S*b*EC-D*b*ED extension of Reed-Solomon code.

can be expressed as $\{\mathbf{0}, \mathbf{T}, \mathbf{T}^2, \mathbf{T}^3, \ldots, \mathbf{T}^{2^b-2}, \mathbf{T}^{2^b-1} = \mathbf{I}\}$, where $\mathbf{I}$ is the $(b \times b)$ identity matrix and $\mathbf{0}$ is the $(b \times b)$ zero matrix.

The symbols n and k denote the code length and the information length, respectively, of this type of code over $GF(2^b)$. The derived S*b*EC code is an (N,K) code in binary form, where $N = n \cdot b$ and $K = k \cdot b$. Similarly, the number of check bits is $R = r \cdot b = (n - k) \cdot b$. The maximum length (in bits) of this Hamming-type code is given by $N_{\mathbf{H}} = b \cdot n = b \cdot (2^{br} - 1)/(2^b - 1)$.

Fujiwara[5] has derived a new type of S*b*EC code that has an odd-weight column characteristic. This type of code over $GF(2^b)$, in general, satisfies the following condition for every distinct column vector having r elements in the $\mathbf{H}$ matrix:

$$\sum_{i=0}^{r-1} h_{i,j} = I,$$

for columns $j = 0, 1, \cdots, n - 1$

where $h_{i,j}$ is the ith element ($\in GF(2^b)$) in the jth column vector, I is an identity element in $GF(2^b)$, and Σ means summation in $GF(2^b)$. It is easily proved that the corresponding binary converted form of the $\mathbf{H}$ matrix has an odd-weight column characteristic over the binary field. No two columns are identical, and no column is all-0 or a multiple of another column. Therefore, two distinct columns are a linearly independent pair, and the code is at least distance-3. The maximum code bit length of the Fujiwara code is $N_F = b \cdot 2^{b(r-1)}$. For $b = 1$, this is equivalent to the odd-weight-column SEC-DED code and therefore includes it. Another important feature of this code is its error-detection capability for certain double-byte errors. That is, the code can always detect two byte errors, E_i and E_j $(i \neq j)$, provided their error patterns E_i and E_j are equal.

Because S*b*EC codes do not guarantee detection of random double-bit, spanning over double-byte, errors, these codes are not used in computer systems. Instead, computers use single b-bit byte error-correcting and double b-bit byte error-detecting codes, called *SbEC-DbED codes*. Reed-Solomon codes are a general class of codes of any distance-d over $GF(q)$, from which, as a special case, we can derive S*b*EC-D*b*ED codes of distance-4 over $GF(2^b)$. The proposed extension appends three columns to the $\mathbf{H}$ matrix of the distance-4 R-S codes. The $\mathbf{H}$ matrix in Figure 3 shows this extended code, where $\{\mathbf{0}, \mathbf{T}, \mathbf{T}^2, \ldots, \mathbf{T}^{2^b-2}, \mathbf{T}^{2^b-1} = \mathbf{I}\} \in GF(2^b)$. The bit length of the code is equal to $b(2^b + 2)$. Therefore, such codes do not exist for information lengths of $k = 64$ and 128 with byte lengths of $b = 2$, 3, and 4.

Kaneda and Fujiwara* have proposed a class of S*b*EC-D*b*ED codes having arbitrary code and byte length. First, the $\mathbf{H}$ matrix shown in Figure 3 is converted to an $\mathbf{H}$ matrix whose first row is an all-$\mathbf{I}$ vector. We can write the converted matrix $\mathbf{H}_1$ as

$$\mathbf{H}_1 = \begin{bmatrix} \mathbf{I} & \mathbf{I} & \mathbf{I} & \ldots & \mathbf{I} \\ \mathbf{h}_0 & \mathbf{h}_1 & \mathbf{h}_2 & \ldots & \mathbf{h}_{n_1-1} \end{bmatrix}$$

where $\mathbf{h}_0, \mathbf{h}_1, \ldots, \mathbf{h}_{n_1-1}$ are column vectors with two elements each, where $n_1 \leq 2^b + 2$. Using the above defined matrix $\mathbf{H}_1$ of an (N_1, N_1-R_1) S*b*EC-D*b*ED code, where $N_1 = n_1 \cdot b$ and $R_1 = r_1 \cdot b$, the following $\mathbf{H}$ matrix is an S*b*EC-D*b*ED code of length $(n_1 \times n_2)$ bytes with $(r_1 + r_2 - 1)$ check bytes:

$$\mathbf{H} = \left[\begin{array}{c|c|c|c} \mathbf{H}_2 & \mathbf{H}_2 & \cdots & \mathbf{H}_2 \\ \mathbf{h}_0\mathbf{h}_0 \cdots \mathbf{h}_0\mathbf{h}_0 & \mathbf{h}_1\mathbf{h}_1 \cdots \mathbf{h}_1 & \cdots & \mathbf{h}_{n_1-1}\,\mathbf{h}_{n_1-1} \cdots \mathbf{h}_{n_1-1} \end{array}\right]$$

*Kaneda and Fujiwara's work is described in Rao and Fujiwara,[1] a recent and comprehensive secondary reference. See the additional reading list at the end of this article for publication information regarding Kaneda and Fujiwara, as well as for several other original sources.

$$
\mathbf{H} = \left[\begin{array}{cccccccc|cccccccc|ccc}
I & I & I & I & I & I & I & I & & & & & & & & & I & & \\
 & & & & & & & & I & I & I & I & I & I & I & I & & I & \\
I & T^1 & T^2 & T^3 & T^4 & T^5 & T^6 & T^7 & I & T^2 & T^4 & T^6 & T^8 & T^{10} & T^{12} & T^{14} & & & I \\
I & T^2 & T^4 & T^6 & T^8 & T^{10} & T^{12} & T^{14} & I & T^1 & T^2 & T^3 & T^4 & T^5 & T^6 & T^7 & & & & I
\end{array}\right]
$$

Module 0 | Module 1 | Check part

Figure 4. The (80, 64) S4EC-D4ED code used in the Fujitsu 380/382 system.

H =

1000	0010	1000	1111	0100	0000	0001	0010	1000	0010	1000	1111	1111	0001	0100	0001	1001	0100
0110	0100	1111	1100	0100	0010	1000	0001	1100	1000	0011	0100	1000	0010	1101	1000	0010	1000
1001	1101	1010	0001	0001	0011	1100	0001	0001	0000	1000	0011	0100	1100	1000	1000	1101	0010
0001	1000	0010	1000	1100	1000	0101	0010	0100	1111	0010	0101	0001	0110	0010	0100	1011	0001
0010	1000	0100	1000	0010	0100	0001	0101	1001	0100	1111	0010	0010	0011	1010	1001	0100	0011
1100	0100	0100	0010	0010	0001	0100	1000	0010	0011	1100	0100	1000	1001	0001	1100	1111	0101
0011	0001	0001	1011	1010	0010	0010	0100	0110	0001	0010	1100	0011	1000	1111	0000	1000	0010
0100	0001	0001	0100	1000	0001	1000	0110	0011	1100	1111	1000	0100	0100	1000	1111	0001	0100

Figure 5. Code used in the Fujitsu M-780 system.

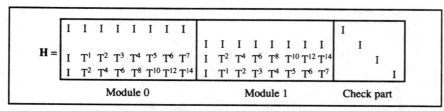

Here, $\mathbf{H}_2$ is a nonconverted **H** matrix of an (N_2, N_2-R_2) SbEC-DbED code, where $N_2 = n_2 \cdot b$ and $R_2 = r_2 \cdot b$.

An interesting type of SbEC-DbED code is the modularized code. Figure 4 is an example of the (80,64) S4EC-D4ED modularized code used in the Fujitsu-380/382 system. The matrix **T** is derived from the primitive polynomial $g(x) = x^4 + x + 1$. The code structure gives a modularized organization to the encoding/decoding circuit such that the entire circuit can be constructed from the same two subcircuits corresponding to module 0 and module 1 in the figure.

Byte error-detecting SEC-DED codes. A further extension is a class of codes to detect single-byte errors, as well as correct single-bit errors and detect double-bit errors. *SEC-DED-SbED codes* can be attractive, since they require only a small increase in redundancy. These codes have been studied extensively,[1] but the "best" code to meet the upper bound on code length for an arbitrary byte length b has yet to be found. However, we can realize an SEC-DED-S4ED code of $r = 8$ check bits corresponding to the SEC-DED code (with $K = 64$ information bits). This type of code has already found application in the Fujitsu M-780 system,[6] which employs 64K × 4-bit high-speed static RAM chips in the main memory units. Figure 5 shows the adopted code, possessing the odd-weight column characteristic and eight bits of error-detection capability over any two bytes, with $K = 64$ and $r = 8$.

Table 1 lists the codes used in the high-speed memories of some commercial systems. Figure 6 shows the estimated gate count of the decoding circuit and the decoding speed for those codes.

Table 1. Check-bit lengths of codes for high-speed memories with information-bit lengths of k = 32, 64, and 128.

Code Class	Check-bit length, where $k = 32$	$k = 64$	$k = 128$
SEC	6	7	8
SEC-DED	7	8	9
DEC			
BCH-based	12~16	14~18	16~23
Majority-logic decodable	16~24	22~32	31~48
SEC-DED-SbED			
$b = 4$	7	8	9
$b = 8$	10	10	11
SbEC			
$b = 4$	8	12	12
$b = 8$	16	16	16
SbEC-DbED			
$b = 4$	12	16	16
$b = 8$	24	24	24

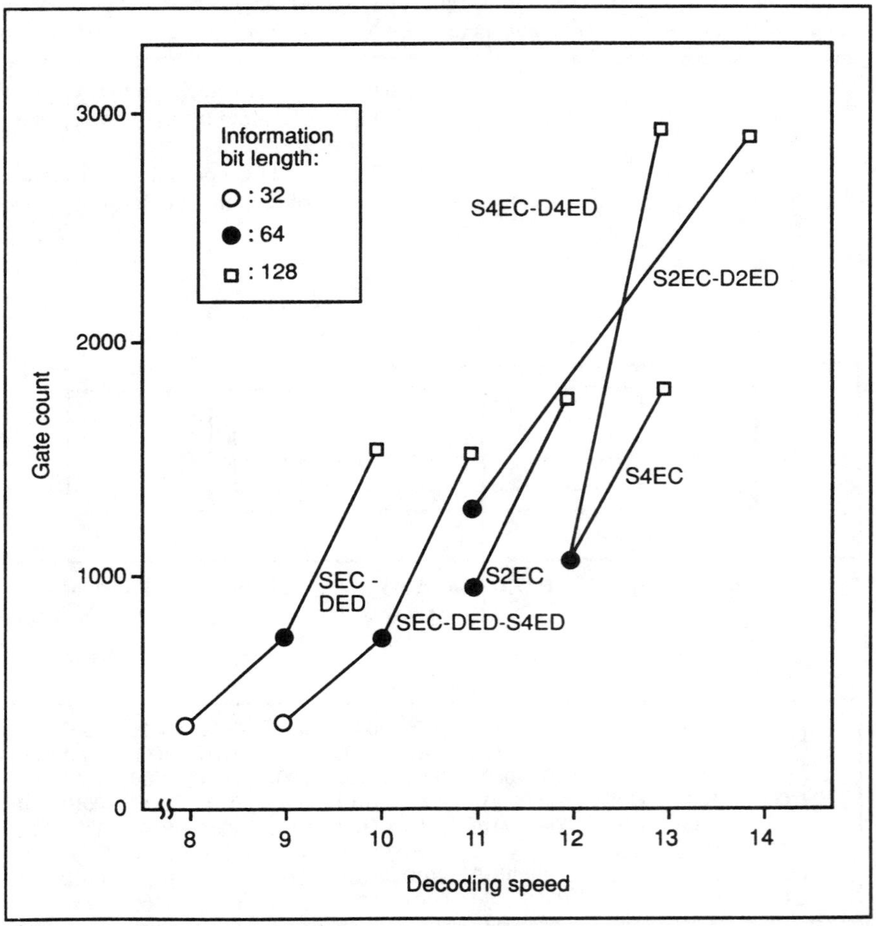

Figure 6. Decoder gate counts and speeds for the high-speed memory codes.

Error control in mass memories

Characteristic problems with magnetic tapes and disks and optical disks include burst errors, caused by defects and dust particles on the recording surfaces, and random errors, caused by noise in the read/write heads. The above-described R-S byte error-correcting/detecting codes, interleaved with other codes and using erasure correction techniques, handle these problems quite effectively.

Tape memory codes. Magnetic tapes are widely used in computer systems. The half-inch, nine-track tape system is par-

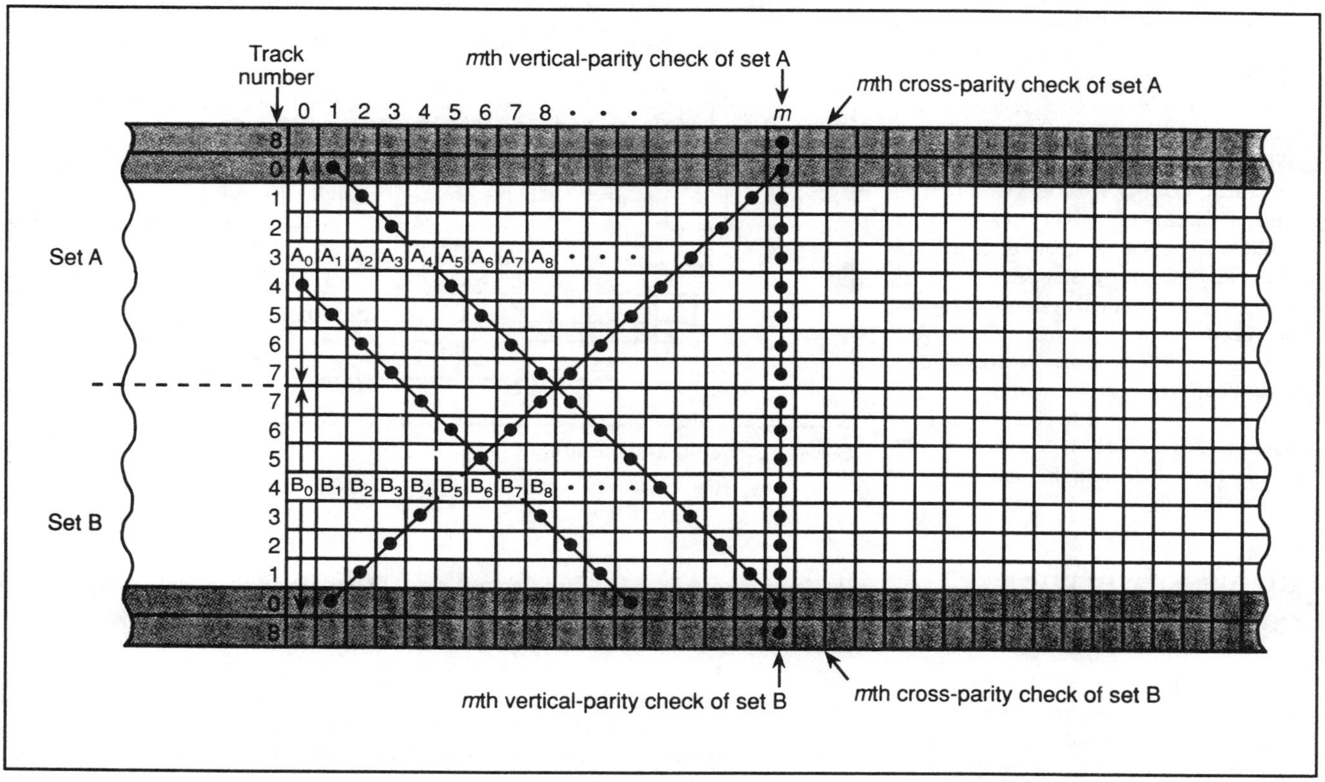

Figure 7. Data format encoded in AXP code for the 18-track high-density subsystem.

ticularly prevalent and has evolved through extensive use. Errors in magnetic tape recording are primarily due to defects on the magnetic media or to variations in head-media separation in the presence of dust particles. Such errors often affect as many as 100 bits at a time, depending on recording density. Because of increased bit densities and tape speeds, tape systems require more sophisticated error-correction codes. Newer coding schemes include the so-called *optimal rectangular code (ORC)* for 6,250-bits-per-inch nine-track tape units and the *adaptive cross-parity (AXP) code* for higher density, 18-track units.

ORC is designed to correct any single-track or (given erasure pointers) any double-track error in the tape. ORC code words have a rectangular format, and check bits are located on two orthogonal sides of the rectangle. ORC is generated using S8EC R-S codes.

The AXP code,[7] included in a class of convolutional codes, possesses a simple block structure compared to ORC, which is based on vertical and cross-parity checks. In this coding scheme, the 18 tracks are divided into two sets, each consisting of seven data tracks and two check tracks. Figure 7 shows the data format grouped into two sets. Set A consists of nine parallel tracks, and set B consists of the remaining nine parallel tracks. In this figure, the two sets are shown side by side with a symmetrically ordered track arrangement. Each check bit in track 0 of set A and set B provides a cross-parity check along the diagonal, with positive slope and negative slope, respectively, involving bits from both sets. Each check bit in track 8 of set A and set B is a vertical parity over the bits of the same position, m in sets A and B. The encoding and decoding equations, that is, the four parity equations, are all simple. The erroneous track can be identified by the external pointers. Using these pointers, up to four erroneous tracks spanning over two sets, or up to three erroneous tracks in one set, can be corrected.

Disk memory codes. Magnetic disk memory has played an important role in high-speed, large-capacity file memory for many years. As with magnetic tape systems, burst errors predominate. Most errors are related to imperfections on disk surfaces or surface irregularities. The remaining errors are mostly due to heads, which are susceptible to random noise-induced errors. The disk has a higher rotation speed and, consequently, a higher data rate than tape. Hence, its sensing circuit design must allow for greater tolerance. In recent disk systems, the *interleaved R-S code* has replaced the Fire burst-error-correcting code. Apart from these, other important recovery techniques such as *defect skip, alternate data block*, and *reread* are used to enhance reliability and data integrity.

Digital optical disks are a relatively new technology for storing data. Each disk is coated with special materials. Reading and writing are performed using a laser. Almost all errors are related to imperfections in the disk, and the remaining errors result from focusing shift in recording or random noise in reading. Therefore, this medium requires both burst-error-correcting and random-error-correcting facilities.

Compact disc (CD) digital audio systems[8] adopted a new code design technique, *cross-interleaved R-S code*. CIRC is a new class of doubly encoded codes in which the second R-S code encodes the cross-interleaved outputs of the first encoded R-S code.

The digital data-storage system called *compact disc ROM* (CD-ROM) has almost 540-megabyte capacity on one disk. CD-ROMs use doubly encoded R-S SbEC and cyclic redundancy check (CRC) codes in addition to CIRC. The two R-S codes used are (26,24) and (45,43) codes over $GF(2^8)$. Thus, the data is effectively quadruply encoded. If CRC is also included, then data is effectively quintuply encoded.

Two types of optical systems, the *write-once read-many optical disk* (CD-WORM) and the *writable or erasable optical disk*, have been popular in computer mass memories. These memories use a large distance (distance-17) R-S code with 120- to 140-byte code length, interleaved to degree 4 to 10.

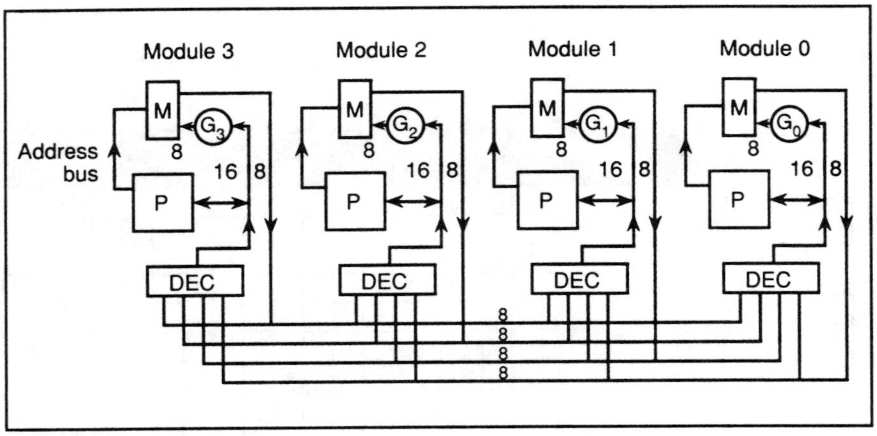

Figure 8. The (4, 2) computer.

Processor error control

In 1972, Pradhan and Reddy[9] showed that parity code using redundancy of the order duplication could achieve effective error control. This theoretical prediction that only duplication can achieve error correction in processors[9] has been realized in some sense in the (4,2) computer.[10] Figure 8 illustrates this concept, which is already seeing use as a commercial product, the Philips S2500 switching system.

The S2500 uses four processor-memory pairs. Each processor is 16 bits wide, but the memory is only 8 bits wide. Therefore, there is fourfold redundancy in the processor but only twofold redundancy in the memory. The 16-bit output of each processor is encoded into a (4,2) version of $GF(2^8)$ R-S code, yielding a 32-bit code. This code can correct any single 8-bit byte. The output of each processor is encoded by separate encoders. Each encoder produces only 8 bits of the 32-bit code word. The memory associated with the *i*th processor stores the *i*th byte; therefore, the encoder for the *i*th processor produces the 8 bits corresponding to the *i*th byte. In other words, the first processor's memory stores the first byte, the second processor's the second byte, and so on.

On the read operation, all four bytes are fetched from the memory and decoded by the decoder, which can correct any single byte in error or any double-bit error in two different bytes. It may be noted that a single processor or memory failure affects only a single byte in the code word; thus, the system can tolerate failure of any single processor-memory pair. In addition, the code can correct single-byte-erasure and single-bit errors. Thus, one can remove a processor-memory pair for repair and continue to operate the system using error-erasure decoding. Any subsequent single-bit-error will get corrected.

This use of coding in processor error control is quite attractive. The only real drawback is that, since the address lines to the memory are not encoded, no error correction takes place on a write operation. In general, we believe that, by using nontraditional approaches such as the one described above, parity check codes can provide effective processor error control. Their use will eliminate the need for code conversion and its associated delay in memory-to-processor transfer, thus providing uniform error control.

Unidirectional error-control codes

Unidirectional error codes have found recent applications in 4-megabit VLSI ROMs by NTT and large-area LCDs for defect tolerance[3] by NTT and have, therefore, been the focus of recent research. Unidirectional errors[11] are defined as a class of errors where the mode of errors is presumed to be either 1 to 0 or 0 to 1 in a particular code word. However, no prior knowledge of which type of error may occur is assumed. Therefore, in a particular transmission, the receiver may receive two successive words with two different types of errors, but any individual word may have only 1 to 0 or 0 to 1 errors. (This should not be confused with asymmetric errors where all code words are presumed to have the same type of errors and the type is known beforehand.)

Fundamentals. Codes specifically designed for unidirectional errors are receiving limited but growing attention.[12-16] One of the assumptions in developing these codes is that errors induced by transient and intermittent faults are limited either to a small number of symmetric errors or to an unbounded number of unidirectional errors. Consequently, much of the research has been devoted to developing codes that can correct t symmetric errors and detect all unidirectional errors. The assumption here is that these faults cause a small number of symmetric errors that need to be corrected, whereas faults that cause an unbounded number of unidirectional errors need to be detected.

The basic framework[11] for these codes shows that for a code to correct t symmetric errors and detect all unidirectional errors, the code must have a minimum asymmetric semidistance of $(t + 1)$.* Asymmetric semidistance can be defined as follows: Given two vectors **X** and **Y**, let $d_{10}(\mathbf{X},\mathbf{Y})$ represent the number of positions in which **X** is 1 and **Y** is 0. Unlike Hamming distance, $d_{10}(\mathbf{X},\mathbf{Y})$ need not be equal to $d_{01}(\mathbf{X},\mathbf{Y})$. For example, $\mathbf{X} = 0110$ and $\mathbf{Y} = 1000$, $d_{10}(\mathbf{X},\mathbf{Y}) = 2$ and $d_{10}(\mathbf{Y},\mathbf{X}) = 1$. The minimum asymmetric semidistance Δ is defined as

$$\Delta = \min\{d_{10}(\mathbf{X},\mathbf{Y}) \mid \mathbf{X},\mathbf{Y} \in C\}$$

Consider the code described in Tables 2 and 3. Using odd and even parity to achieve $\Delta = 2$, the code can correct all single errors and detect all unidirectional errors. Al-

*This result was derived independently by Pradhan,[11] as well as by Bose and Rao (see additional reading list).

Table 2. A random error-correcting and unidirectional error-detecting code.

Information Bits (Positions 1,2)		Check Bits (Positions 3-6)			
d_0	d_1	c_0	c_1	c_2	c_3
0	0	1	1	0	1
0	1	1	0	1	0
1	0	0	1	1	0
1	1	0	0	0	1

$c_0 = d_0 \oplus 1$ $c_2 = d_0 \oplus d_1$
$c_1 = d_1 \oplus 1$ $c_3 = d_0 \oplus d_1 \oplus 1$
(c_0, c_1, and c_3 are odd parities.)

Table 3. Syndrome bits and error positions.

S_0	S_1	S_2	S_3	Bit in Error
0	0	0	0	None
1	0	1	1	1
0	1	1	1	2
1	0	0	0	3
0	1	0	0	4
0	0	1	0	5
0	0	0	1	6
All other combinations				Multiple unidirectional error detection

$S_0 = c_0 \oplus d_0 \oplus 1$ $S_2 = c_2 \oplus d_0 \oplus d_1$
$S_0 = c_1 \oplus d_1 \oplus 1$ $S_2 = c_3 \oplus d_0 \oplus d_1 \oplus 1$

Table 4. Code length (n) of some single-error-correcting and all known unidirectional-error-detecting codes.

Information Bit Length (k)	Pradhan[11] 1980	Bose and Pradhan[13] 1982	Nikolos et al.[15] 1986	Kundu and Reddy[16] 1990
12	25	27	25	24
15	30	30	28	27
16	35	31	29	29
30	54	48	46	45
32	60	50	48	47
62	108	83	81	79
63	100	84	82	80
64	105	85	83	81
120	171	141	139	138
126	190	149	147	145
256	342	281	280	277

Table 5. Best known t-error-correcting and all unidirectional-error-correcting codes by Bruck and Blaum.[14]

$t = 2$		$t = 3$		$t = 4$	
k	n	k	n	k	n
6	19	4	19	38	76
20	38	11	29	98	145
50	73	15	39	222	275
112	139	44	75		
222	252	105	142		
	214	255			
	483	529			

though this odd/even parity technique has not yet been generalized, two different techniques have been formulated to derive such codes.

For nonsystematic codes, the basic technique is to extract from a set of constant-weight code words a subset that has the desired Δ. For systematic codes,[11] the basic technique is to combine two different forms of redundancy, one for symmetric error correction and the other for unidirectional error detection. The original combining technique did not produce efficient codes, but it was modified and has become the basis of many ingenious techniques that produce a large class of very efficient codes. However, constructing codes that meet the bound derived by Bose and Pradhan[13] remains an elusive goal. The bound states that the number of check bits required to correct t errors and detect all unidirectional errors is bounded from below by $\mathbf{O}((t+1)\log k)$, but the codes discovered so far require about $\mathbf{O}((2t+1)\log k)$ check bits. Table 4 compares certain single-error-correcting and all unidirectional-error-detecting codes; Table 5 presents some of the best multiple-error-correcting and all the unidirectional-error-detecting codes known at the time of writing this article.[14]

Another area not yet fully explored is multivalued unidirectional error codes, where the code alphabets are over q-ary symbols. Here, the unidirectional error is defined as an error that either increases or decreases the component values. Bose and Pradhan[13] have presented an optimal class of unidirectional multivalued error-detecting codes, but other generalizations have not been explored.

The following is an example of a real-world application of a unidirectional code.[3]

Application to masking asymmetric line faults. Unidirectional code has found a real-world application in VLSI microprocessors, where the bus line area increases as the processor word length increases. Since these lines connect circuit elements, line faults or defects seriously affect LSI chip yield and reliability. Unidirectional error codes have been applied in NTT 4-megabit VLSI ROMs[3] to mask these asymmetric line faults (defects in the address bus lines), without the need for additional circuits such as error decoders.

Short-circuit and open-circuit defects in bus lines change the signal line to one of several levels — high, medium, or low. By controlling the bus driver and the bus terminal gate, however, the level of the faulty

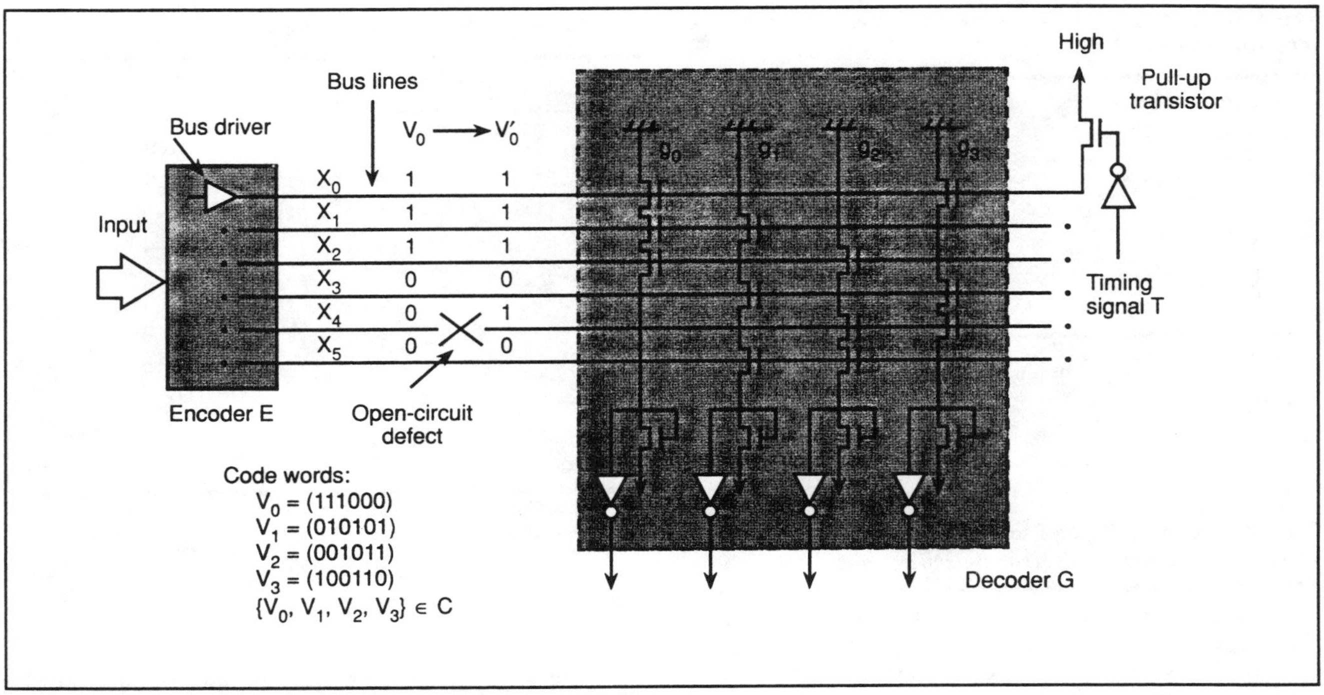

Figure 9. Circuit for masking single, unidirectional "0" errors on bus lines.

line can always be made either high or low. For open-circuit defects in the bus lines, adding a pull-up transistor at the tip of the bus line makes the isolated part of the line electrically high. For short-circuit defects, the bus drivers can be designed to maintain a high level on all bridged lines. The driver makes its output impedance high when the input signal level is low. Such a fail-safe design achieves asymmetry in errors. It makes the probability of "1" errors (1 becoming 0) extremely small compared to "0" errors (0 becoming 1). Thus, we'll concentrate on "0" errors. These asymmetric errors can be masked by new coding techniques.

Figure 9 shows a bus line circuit that can mask single "0" errors. The decoder G consists of AND gates g_0 to g_3, corresponding to code words V_0 to V_3 in code C. Because each gate has transistors at the bus line where the element in the code word is "1," the gate is only activated by receipt of the corresponding code word.

The circuit in Figure 9 works correctly even if there is a single asymmetric "0" error in the bus lines. We assume that the input information is given and then encoded into code word $V_0 = (111000)$, and we also assume that one "0" error occurs in the fifth line, x_4. The code word V_0 is changed to $V_0' = (111010)$. However, AND gate g_0, which would be activated only by V_0 if there were no fault, is activated because V_0' has 1's at the positions where V_0 has 1's — that is, $x_0 = x_1 = x_2 = 1$. The other AND gates, g_1 to g_3 cannot be activated for V_0' because V_0' has at least one 0 at a position where V_1 to V_3 have 1's — that is, x_3 for V_1 and V_3 and x_5 for V_2. Hence, one asymmetric line fault never causes faulty activation and can be masked.

In general, when "0" errors change the code word Y to Y', any other code word, say X, in C has to satisfy the condition $X\overline{Y'} \neq 0$. This causes the bus line circuit to work correctly. This condition shows that there are one or more cases where X has 1 at the position where Y' has 0. From this, it can be easily proven that a code C with $\Delta = t + 1$ can mask t asymmetric errors.

As implementation costs for error-control coding continue to decrease, we expect more and more applications to be found. Indeed, the development of cost-effective low-level techniques may offset the need for massive high-level redundancy.[12] Therefore, the major challenge of the future is developing an integrated design framework where we can study the various trade-offs between low-level and high-level redundancy techniques. ■

Acknowledgment

The work reported here was supported in part by the Air Force Office of Scientific Research (88-0205) and the National Science Foundation (88-05586).

References

1. T.R.N. Rao and E. Fujiwara, *Error-Control Coding for Computer Systems*, Prentice Hall, Englewood Cliffs, N.J., 1989.
2. N. Jarwala, and D.K. Pradhan, "Cost Analysis of On-Chip Error Control Coding for Fault-Tolerant Computers," *Proc. FTCS-17*, Computer Society Press, Los Alamitos, Calif., Order No. 778 (microfiche only), July 1987, pp. 278-283.
3. K. Matsuzawa and E. Fujiwara, "Masking Asymmetric Line Faults Using Semi-Distance Codes," *Proc. FTCS-18*, Computer Society Press, Los Alamitos, Calif., Order No. 867 (microfiche only), 1988, pp. 354-359.
4. M.Y. Hsiao, "A Class of Optimal Minimum Odd-Weight-Column SEC-DED Codes," *IBM J. R&D*, Vol. 14, July 1970, pp. 395-401.
5. E. Fujiwara, "Odd-Weight-Column *b*-Adjacent Error-Correcting Codes," *Trans. Inst. Elect. Comm. Eng., Japan*, Vol. E61, 1978, pp. 781-787.

6. T. Tsuchimoto et al., "A Large Computer System M-780," in Japanese, Nikkei Electronics, 396, June 1986, pp. 179-209.

7. A.M. Patel, "Adaptive Cross-Parity (AXP) Code for a High-Density Magnetic Tape Subsystem," *IBM J. R&D*, Vol. 29, Dec. 1985, pp. 546-562.

8. T. Doi et al., "Cross-Interleave Code for Error Correction of Digital Audio Systems," *Proc. 64th AES Convention*, Nov. 1979.

9. D.K. Pradhan and S.M. Reddy, "Error Control Techniques for Logic Processors," *IEEE Trans. Computers*, Vol. C-21, No. 12, Dec. 1972, pp. 1,331-1,337.

10. T. Krol, "N,K Concept Fault-Tolerance," *IEEE Trans. Computers*, Vol. C-35, No. 4, Apr. 1986, pp. 339-349.

11. D.K. Pradhan, "A New Class of Error-Correcting/Detecting Codes for Fault-Tolerant Computer Applications," *IEEE Trans. Computers*, Vol. C-29, No. 6, June 1980, pp. 471-481.

12. D.K. Pradhan, ed., *Fault-Tolerant Computing: Theory and Techniques*, Prentice Hall, Englewood Cliffs, N.J., 1986.

13. B. Bose and D.K. Pradhan, "Optimal Unidirectional Error Detecting/Correcting Codes," *IEEE Trans. Computers*, Vol. C-31, No. 6, June 1982, pp. 564-568.

14. J. Bruck and M. Blaum, "Some New EC/AUED Codes," *Proc. FTCS-19*, Computer Society Press, Los Alamitos, Calif., Order No. 1959, June 1989, pp. 208-215.

15. D. Nikolos, N. Gaitanis, and G. Philokyprou, "Systematic *t*-error Correcting/All Unidirectional Error Detecting Codes," *IEEE Trans. Computers*, Vol. C-35, No. 5, May 1986, pp. 394-402.

16. S. Kundu and S.M. Reddy, "On Symmetric Error Correcting Codes and All Unidirectional Error Detecting Codes," *IEEE Trans. Computers*, Vol. C-39, No. 6, June 1990.

Additional reading

Blaum, M., "Systematic Unidirectional Error Detecting Codes," *IEEE Trans. Computers*, Vol. C-37, No. 4, Apr. 1988, pp. 453-457.

Blaum, M., and van Tilborg, "On *t* Error Correcting/All Unidirectional Error Detecting Codes," *IEEE Trans. Computers*, Vol. 38, No. 11, Nov. 1989, pp. 1493-1501.

Boinck and van Tilborg, "Constructions and Bounds for Systematic *t*EC/AUED Codes," submitted to *IEEE Trans. on Inf. Theory.*

Bose, B., "Burst Unidirectional Error Detecting Codes," *IEEE Trans. Computers*, Vol. C-35, No. 4, Apr. 1988, pp. 350-353.

Bose, B., "On Systematic SEC/MUED Code," *Proc. FTCS-11*, Computer Society Press, Los Alamitos, Calif., Order No. 350 (microfiche only), June 1981, pp. 265-267.

Bose, B., "Unidirectional Error Correction/Detection for VLSI Memory," *Digest 11th Int'l Symp. Computer Architecture*, Computer Society Press, Los Alamitos, Calif., Order No. 538 (microfiche only), June 1984, pp. 242-244.

Bose, B., and D.J. Lin, "Systematic Unidirectional Error Detecting Codes," *IEEE Trans. Computers*, Vol. C-34, No. 11, Nov. 1985, pp. 1,026-1,032.

Bose, B., and T.R.N. Rao, "Theory of Unidirectional Error Correcting/Detecting Codes," *IEEE Trans. Computers*, Vol. C-31, No. 6, June 1982, pp. 521-530.

Bossen, D.C., "*b*-Adjacent Error Correction," *IBM J. R&D*, Vol. 14, July 1970, pp. 402-408.

Bossen, D.C., and M.Y. Hsiao, "A System Solution to the Memory Soft-Error Problem," *IBM J. R&D*, Vol. 24, May 1980, pp. 390-397.

Chen, C.L., "Byte-Oriented Error-Correcting Codes for Semiconductor Memory Systems," *IEEE Trans. Computers*, Vol. C-35, No. 7, July 1986, pp. 646-648.

Dunning, L.A., "SEC-BED-DED Codes for Error Control in Byte-Organized Memory Systems," *IEEE Trans. Computers*, Vol. C-34, No. 6, June 1985, pp. 557-562.

Ikeno, K., and G. Nakamura, "Constant-Weight Codes," in Japanese, *Trans. Inst. Elect. Comm. Eng., Japan*, Vol. 54-A, July 1971, pp. 410-417.

Imai, H., ed., *Essentials of Error-Control Coding Techniques*, Academic Press, 1990.

Kaneda, S., "A Class of Odd-Weight-Column SEC-DED-SbED Codes for Memory System Applications," *IEEE Trans. Computers*, Vol. C-33, No. 8, Aug. 1984, pp. 737-739.

Kaneda, S., and E. Fujiwara, "Single Byte Error Correcting-Double Byte Error Detecting Codes for Memory Systems," *IEEE Trans. Computers*, Vol. C-31, No. 7, July 1982, pp. 596-602.

Lin, D.J., and B. Bose, "The Theory and Design of *t*-Error Correcting and $d(d<t)$-Unidirectional Error Detecting Codes," *IEEE Trans. Computers*, Vol. C-37, No. 4, Apr. 1988, pp. 433-439.

Pradhan, D.K., and J.J. Stiffler, "Error-Correcting Codes and Self-Checking Circuits," *Computer*, Vol. 13, No. 3, Mar. 1980, pp. 27-37.

Sakai, S., et al., "A Defect-Tolerant Technology for an Active-Matrix LCD Integrated with Peripheral Circuits," *SID 88 Digest*, Society for Information Display, Playa del Rey, Calif., 1988, pp. 400-403.

Weber, de Vroedt, and Broekee, "Bounds and Constructions for Codes Correcting Unidirectional Errors," *IEEE Trans. Inf. Theory*, Vol. 35, No. 4, July 1989, pp. 797-810.

Eiji Fujiwara has been an associate professor in the Department of Computer Science at the Tokyo Institute of Technology since October 1988. Before that he was with Nippon Telegraph and Telephone's Electrical Communication Laboratories, where he was engaged in designing and developing DIPS-1 and DIPS-11 computer systems and in fault-tolerant computing research. Fujiwara's research interests are error-correcting codes, fault-tolerant memory, self-checking logic, VLSI testing, VLSI defect-tolerant techniques, and expert systems. He is a coauthor of *Error Control Coding for Computer Systems* (Prentice Hall, 1989) and of *Essentials of Error-Correcting Coding Techniques* (Academic Press, 1990).

He received BS, MS, and Dr. Eng. degrees in electronic engineering from the Tokyo Institute of Technology in 1968, 1970, and 1981. He is a member of the IEEE, IEICE Japan, and the Information Processing Society of Japan.

Fujiwara's address is Dept. of Computer Science, Tokyo Institute of Technology, 2-12-1 Ookayama, Meguro-ku, Tokyo 152, Japan.

Dhiraj K. Pradhan is a professor in the Department of Electrical and Computer Engineering at the University of Massachusetts, Amherst. He has been involved in fault-tolerant computing and parallel processing research since receiving his PhD in 1972, presenting numerous papers and publishing extensively in journals. Pradhan was guest editor of special issues on fault-tolerant computing of *IEEE Transactions on Computers* and *Computer*, published in April 1986 and March 1980, respectively, and a coauthor and editor of *Fault-Tolerant Computing: Theory and Techniques*, Volumes I and II (Prentice Hall, 1986). Currently, he is an editor for several journals.

Pradhan holds an MS degree from Brown University and a PhD from the University of Iowa. He is a fellow of the IEEE.

Pradhan's address is Electrical and Computer Engineering, University of Massachusetts, Amherst, MA 01003.

A New Class of Error-Correcting/Detecting Codes for Fault-Tolerant Computer Applications

DHIRAJ K. PRADHAN, MEMBER, IEEE

***Abstract*—Separable error-correcting/detecting codes are developed that provide protection against combinations of both unidirectional and random errors. Specifically, codes are presented which can both: 1) correct (detect) some t random errors, and 2) detect any number of unidirectional errors which may also contain t or fewer random errors. Necessary and sufficient conditions for the existence of these codes are also developed. Decoding algorithms for these codes are presented, and implementations of the algorithms are also discussed.**

The codes presented provide certain unique error control capabilities in that they are effective against both transient and solid faults that occur in real time in certain integrated circuits. Furthermore, these codes are *systematic* and, therefore, they have a wide-ranging potential, such as being useful in both processors and storage.

The codes are specifically suited for fault-tolerant logic built out of memory, read-only memories, certain mass memories, etc.

***Index Terms*—Coset codes, decoder logic, error correction, error detection, erasure decoding, mass memories, multiple errors, multiple faults, random errors, read-only memories, self-checking, shift register memories, transient faults, TSC checkers, two-rail checkers, unidirectional errors.**

I. Introduction

IN this paper, certain new error-correcting/detecting codes, as well as their decoding algorithms, are presented. These codes are useful for combinations of both unidirectional [7] and random [3] errors; in addition, they have particular relevance in fault-tolerant designs that tolerate transient [2] as well as solid [1] faults in real time.

There is a twofold objective to this paper. First, we have sought to develop certain basic results—results which will provide the groundwork for further research and extensions. Second, we have presented certain codes along with their decoding algorithms which will be shown to have potential applications in the design of fault-tolerant computers. Following is a discussion of some of the practical and theoretical significances of the results presented in this paper.

The codes presented here provide certain unique error control capabilities. They are able to correct (detect) t random errors, and also simultaneously detect any number of additional errors which may contain both unidirectional and random errors. These codes are especially useful in their ability to protect against both transient and solid faults and are developed with specific applications in mind. Some of these applications include the design of fault-tolerant processors, built by using logic from memory; [16] read-only memories for control store [5], [9]; mass memories, such as shift register memories [6]; and magnetic recording memories [6]. Also, the codes are of interest in the design of fault-tolerant-failsafe logic [4].

These proposed codes are *systematic* (separable), and it is important to note that separable codes have significant advantages over nonseparable codes. Although nonseparable codes have found certain applications [5], they still have only a very limited use. Only separable codes, for instance, can be used for encoding such items as addresses, operands, certain microinstructions, etc. [15]. (Therefore, as an example, for a code to be useful in the design of both processors and storage systems, it really must be separable. It might be pointed out that a particular advantage in using the same code—uniform coding—throughout a computer is that the need for code conversion is eliminated.)

In addition to the codes presented here, several theoretical results, as well as decoding algorithms for the codes, are also developed. These theoretical results are important because they provide a basic understanding of the structure of these codes.

One interesting possible application that could be extended from the results of this paper is seen in the design of fault-tolerant computers that use ROM's and PLA's [16], [18]. The development of computers that use logic designed from memory is fast becoming increasingly attractive, especially since the rapid advancement in LSI. This fact has particular significance to fault-tolerant computer design. The basic reason behind this is chiefly that the regularity of memory makes it amenable to sophisticated fault-tolerant techniques, such as the use of error-correcting codes and self-checking checkers [11], [12]. Some of the designs discussed in this paper will further provide some viable examples.

This paper is organized into the following main sections. In Section II, different error patterns that are caused by transient and solid faults are characterized. Based on these, various new error control approaches are proposed. These approaches provide a wide diversity in the degree of error protection they offer. Section III develops necessary and sufficient conditions for the existence of codes that are precisely suited for the different error control approaches discussed in Section II. These

Manuscript received August 15, 1979; revised January 25, 1980. This work was supported by AFOSR Contract F49620-79-C-0119.

The author is with the School of Engineering, Oakland University, Rochester, MI 48063.

0-8186-4182-7/93 $3.00 © 1980 IEEE

conditions reveal some insight into the basic structure of the codes; they also provide the framework for the construction of the codes in the next section as well. Section IV presents the techniques for the actual construction of the codes which are suitable for the different types of error control proposed. In Section V, decoding algorithms for these codes are developed. Section VI discusses implementations of these algorithms, some of which are shown to be totally self-checking.

II. Formulation of Error Control Approaches

In the following, two different types of errors—unidirectional and random errors—are defined; these form the basis for the formulation of different error control approaches proposed later.

Definition: A set of errors is said to be *unidirectional* if it consists of either 1 to 0 or 0 to 1 errors, and not both.

Definition: A set of errors is said to be *random* if no specific relationship among the errors exists (such as their being unidirectional, restricted to contiguous bits, etc.).

Many faults that commonly occur in integrated circuits cause unidirectional errors [8]. Included here are those faults that affect address decoders, word lines, power supply, read/write circuits, etc. [5]–[9], [18]. For example, it can be shown that a single stuck-at, cross-point, or bridging fault [19] in PLA's produce only unidirectional errors at the outputs. Furthermore, bursty errors, that are due to failures in certain storage devices are likely to be unidirectional, as well.

A likely source of random errors is transient faults (faults that occur momentarily) and single faults. The number of random errors is usually limited. On the other hand, the number of unidirectional errors, caused by the above-mentioned faults, can be fairly large. Since: 1) many faults cause unidirectional errors, and 2) transient faults constitute the majority of real-time faults [2], it is imperative that effective error control mechanisms be developed to provide protection against both unidirectional and random errors.

Protection against errors can be achieved by means of error detection and/or correction. Error detection provides the only means of error control for unidirectional errors. This is because the errors are not necessarily limited and, hence, cannot be easily corrected.

On the other hand, error correction is particularly suited for random errors, especially those that are caused by transient faults. This follows from the following observations.

1) Transient faults are environmentally induced, or caused by components working near the limit of their tolerance. This makes them particularly hard to diagnose. Therefore, dynamic redundancy techniques, such as switching to standby spare and rollback, are less suitable, since all that is needed may be to restore the correct information, instead of discarding physical components. Consequently, this makes error detection less desirable than error correction for transient faults.

2) The number of errors produced by transient faults is likely to be limited in number because of the short duration of these faults. This makes efficient error correction feasible.

Thus, a combination of random error correction along with unidirectional error detection may prove to be more effective when there is the likelihood of both transient and solid faults (as usually is the case).

Based on the above discussions, the following error control approaches are proposed. These are presented in order of their protection capabilities, i.e., A1 provides the least amount of protection, on through A4, which provides the most. (Also, A3 and A4 are more effective than A1 and A2 for transient faults.)

A1: Detection of: 1) all patterns of t or fewer random errors, and 2) any number of errors if they are unidirectional.

A2: Detection of all error patterns that consist of a *combination* of t or fewer random errors along with any number of unidirectional errors. (The difference between approaches 1 and 2 is that in A2, we do not assume that if the number of errors exceeds t, they are all unidirectional.)

A3: 1) Correction of all patterns of t or fewer random errors, and 2) detection of $(t + 1)$ or more errors if they are all unidirectional.

A4: 1) Correction of t or fewer random errors, and 2) detection of $(t + 1)$ or more errors if they contain, *at most*, t random errors.

The following example illustrates the different approaches further.

Example 1: Let

$$X = 111000,$$

$$X_1 = 000000,$$

$$X_2 = 011100,$$

and

$$X_3 = 001111.$$

Let X represent the correct vector, and let X_1, X_2, and X_3 represent three erroneous vectors that result from errors ϵ_1, ϵ_2, ϵ_3 in X, respectively.

The pattern ϵ_1 consists of three errors which are unidirectional; the pattern ϵ_2 consists of two errors which are random; and the pattern ϵ_3 consists of five errors, and these five errors can be interpreted as a combination of two random errors and three unidirectional errors.

Table I describes the effectiveness of different Ai's for different ϵ_i's, assuming that $t = 2$.

In the next section, a set of necessary and sufficient conditions are developed for codes that will meet the error control requirements specified in different Ai's.

III. Necessary and Sufficient Conditions

A binary code C constitutes a subset of the set of 2^n binary n-tuples where n is referred to as the block length of the code. A code is said to be linear if, for every pair of codewords, $(X, Y) \in C$, the bit-by-bit ex-or sum of X and Y, $(X \oplus Y)$, also belongs to C. (Otherwise, the code is said to be nonlinear.)

Thus, any linear code must contain $X \oplus X$, which is the all-0 codeword.

Let the number of codewords in C be M. A code C is said to be systematic (separable) if, for every i, $0 \leq i \leq M - 1$, there exists a codeword $X \in C$ in which the binary number i

TABLE I
RELATIONSHIP BETWEEN Ai'S AND ϵ_i'S FOR $t = 2$

	A1	A2	A3	A4
ϵ_1	*D*	*D*	*D*	*D*
ϵ_2	*D*	*D*	*C*	*C*
ϵ_3	*F*	*D*	*F*	*D*

D—Detection. *C*—Correction. *F*—Failure.

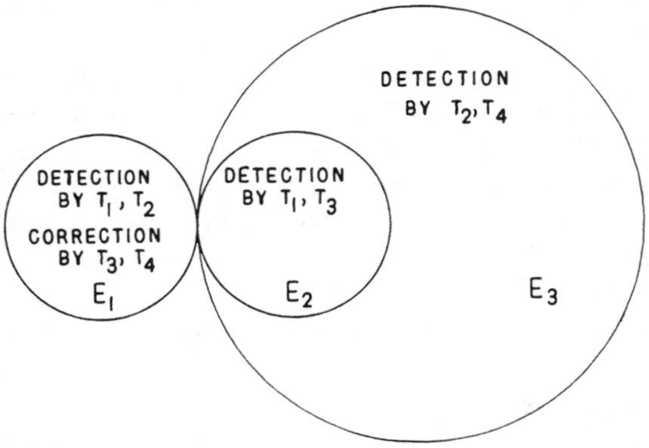

Fig. 1. Error control capabilities of different codes.

appears in the first (some) k positions in X. One can obtain a systematic code from a separable code by performing a permutation on the coordinates. If $M = 2^k$ for some k, then k is said to be the number of information bits in the code.

Definition: Let Ti denote any code C that meets the error control requirements specified in Ai, $1 \leq i \leq 4$.

Fig. 1 illustrates the varying degrees of error control capabilities provided by the $T1$, $T2$, $T3$, and $T4$ codes defined above.

In this figure, the following holds.

E_1 denotes the set of all possible combinations of t or fewer random errors.

E_2 denotes the set of all possible combinations of $(t + 1)$ or more errors which are unidirectional.

E_3 denotes the set of all possible combinations of those $(t + 1)$ or more errors which contain t or fewer random errors along with any number of unidirectional errors.

(It may be noted that E_2 is a proper subset of E_3. This set, E_3, can also be defined as union of E_{30} and E_{31} where $E_{30}(E_{31})$ consist of all error patterns which contain, at most, t, 0 to 1 (1 to 0) errors along with any number of 1 to 0 (0 to 1) errors.)

Since any single error is also a unidirectional error, the only $T1$ codes that are of interest are those with $t > 1$. On the other hand, for $T2$, $T3$, and $T4$ codes, the case of $t = 1$ is also significant. To date, no technique exists to construct systematic $T1(t > 1)$, $T2$, $T3$, and $T4$ codes.

In this section, the general theory underlying these Ti codes is developed.

First, it may be noted that any unidirectional error-detecting code cannot contain the all 0 codeword. This implies that Ti codes *cannot* be *linear*.

However, a class of codes does exist that is related to linear codes; these are known as coset codes [3] which do not contain the all 0 codeword. (These coset codes are derived from linear codes: a fixed vector is added to each codeword in a linear code.) This, therefore, poses a natural question, and that is whether Ti codes can be coset codes. The following provides an example of a $T3$ code which *is* a coset code. This example also serves to introduce one of the results presented later.

Example 2: The code C, shown below, is a linear systematic (6, 2) code with a minimum distance of 4.

$$C = \left\{ \begin{array}{cc|cccc} \multicolumn{2}{c|}{\text{Information Bits}} & \multicolumn{4}{c}{\text{Check Bits}} \\ x_1 & x_2 & x_3 & x_4 & x_5 & x_6 \\ 0 & 0 & 0 & 0 & 0 & 0 \\ 0 & 1 & 0 & 1 & 1 & 1 \\ 1 & 0 & 1 & 0 & 1 & 1 \\ 1 & 1 & 1 & 1 & 0 & 0 \end{array} \right\}$$

The code C^1, shown below, is a coset code derived from C.

$$C^1 = \left\{ \begin{array}{cc|cccc} \multicolumn{2}{c|}{\text{Information Bits}} & \multicolumn{4}{c}{\text{Check Bits}} \\ y_1 & y_2 & y_3 & y_4 & y_5 & y_6 \\ 0 & 0 & 1 & 1 & 0 & 1 \\ 0 & 1 & 1 & 0 & 1 & 0 \\ 1 & 0 & 0 & 1 & 1 & 0 \\ 1 & 1 & 0 & 0 & 0 & 1 \end{array} \right\}$$

The following shows that C^1 is a $T3$ code with $t = 1$, i.e., it corrects all single errors and detects all multiple errors *if* they are all unidirectional.

The following equations describe the relationships between the check bits $\{y_3, y_4, y_5, y_6\}$ and the information bits $\{y_1, y_2\}$:

$$y_3 = y_1 \oplus 1$$

$$y_4 = y_2 \oplus 1$$

$$y_5 = y_1 \oplus y_2$$

$$y_6 = y_1 \oplus y_2 \oplus 1.$$

(Note that check bits y_3, y_4, and y_6 are odd parities.)

Let (s_1, s_2, s_3, s_4) be the four error syndrome bits as given below.

$$s_1 = y_3 \oplus y_1 \oplus 1$$

$$s_2 = y_4 \oplus y_2 \oplus 1$$

$$s_3 = y_5 \oplus y_1 \oplus y_2$$

$$s_4 = y_6 \oplus y_1 \oplus y_2 \oplus 1.$$

The correspondence between error patterns and different syndrome bit combinations is shown in Table II.

Now it may be further noted that the above code, C^1, is *also* a $T2$ code with $t = 1$. Therefore, all error patterns which are combinations of single random errors along with any number of unidirectional errors are also detectable. In other words, any error pattern ϵ which contains single 0 to 1 (1 to 0) errors along with any number of 1 to 0 (0 to 1) errors can be detected as well by the same code C^1.

As an example, consider the codeword 110001 in C^1. A

TABLE II
ERROR PATTERNS AND SYNDROME BIT COMBINATIONS

s_1	s_2	s_3	s_4	Bit in Error
0	0	0	0	None
1	0	1	1	y_1
0	1	1	1	y_2
1	0	0	0	y_3
0	1	0	0	y_4
0	0	1	0	y_5
0	0	0	1	y_6
0	0	1	1	Multiple Unidirectional Error
0	1	0	1	Multiple Unidirectional Error
0	1	1	0	Multiple Unidirectional Error
1	0	0	1	Multiple Unidirectional Error
1	0	1	0	Multiple Unidirectional Error
1	1	0	0	Multiple Unidirectional Error
1	1	0	1	Multiple Unidirectional Error
1	1	1	0	Multiple Unidirectional Error
1	1	1	1	Multiple Unidirectional Error

single error in y_2 along with unidirectional errors in y_3, y_4, y_5 will result in the vector 101111. This will produce the error syndrome 1001 which *is* detectable.

In the following, results are developed that yield insight into the structure of these Ti codes. Also, it is shown that $T2$ codes are indeed equivalent to $T3$ codes in general.

Definition: Let $d(X, Y)$ represent the Hamming distance between two codewords X and Y.

Definition: The minimum distance of the code C denoted as $d_{\min}$, is the $\{\min d(X, Y) | X, Y \in C \text{ and } X \neq Y\}$.

Definition: Let $d_{01}(X, Y)(d_{10}(X, Y))$ represent the number of places in which X equals 0(1) and Y equals 1(0).

(The notations d_{01} and d_{10} were introduced in [12], and sometimes refer to asymmetric distances.)

In the following, we introduce a new concept in minimum distance to be used in developing our results.

Definition: The minimum asymmetric distance of code C, denoted as $d_{a\min}$, is the $\min \{\min \{d_{01}(X, Y)\}, \min \{d_{10}(X, Y)\} | \text{ where } X, Y \in C, \text{ and } X \neq Y\}$.

In the following example, we illustrate the above definitions.

Example 3: Let C constitute three codewords, $X = 11000$, $Y = 00110$, and $Z = 10101$.

The various distances between these codewords are given in Table III.

TABLE III
VARIOUS DISTANCES BETWEEN CODEWORDS

Distance	Codeword Pair (X, Y)	(X, Z)	(Y, Z)
d	4	3	3
d_{10}	2	1	1
d_{01}	2	2	2

Thus,

$$d_{\min} = \min (4, 3, 3) = 3$$

$$d_{\max} = \max (4, 3, 3) = 4$$

and

$$d_{a\min} = \min (\min (2, 1, 1), \min (2, 2, 2)) = 1.$$

It can be seen that C^1 in Example 2 has $d_{a\min} = 2$.

Lemma 1: For any code C, there exists a pair of codewords $X, Y \in C$ for which $d_{10}(X, Y) = d_{a\min}$.

Proof: The proof follows from the observation that $d_{10}(X, Y) = d_{01}(Y, X)$ for all $X, Y \in C$. Q.E.D.

Lemma 2: For any code C, $d_{\min} \geq 2\, d_{a\min}$.

Proof: Proof follows from the observation that $d(X, Y) = d_{10}(X, Y) + d_{01}(X, Y)$. Q.E.D.

The following is a formulation of a known result [12] in terms of $d_{a\min}$.

Lemma 3: A code C can detect all unidirectional errors if and only if $d_{a\min} \geq 1$.

Theorem 1: A code C is a $T1$ code if and only if $d_{a\min} \geq 1$ and $d_{\min} \geq t + 1$.

Proof: The proof is a direct consequence of Lemma 3 and the fact that to detect t-errors, one needs $d_{\min} \geq t + 1$. Q.E.D.

Theorem 2: A code C is

1) a $T2$ code if and only if $d_{a\min} \geq t + 1$
2) a $T3$ code if and only if $d_{a\min} \geq t + 1$
3) a $T4$ code if and only if $d_{a\min} \geq 2t + 1$.

Proof: Proof given in the Appendix.

The following is an interesting consequence of the above theorem, and confirms the observation made in Example 2.

Corollary 1: A $T2$ code is also a $T3$ code and vice versa.

In addition, the following observations may be made regarding the above-derived conditions.

a) All codes except $T1$ codes require $d_{a\min} > 1$. As it will be seen in the next section, achieving $d_{a\min} > 1$ requires sophisticated code construction techniques.

b) The required minimum distance ($d_{\min}$) of $T4$ codes is equal to $(4t + 2)$, which is two times that required for a code that corrects only t-random errors.

IV. TECHNIQUES TO CONSTRUCT CODES

In this section, we present two code construction techniques. The first is for $T1$ codes and is relatively straightforward. The second technique is for the construction of $T2$, $T3$, and $T4$ codes and requires a more sophisticated approach. These two techniques produce *systematic* codes.

Construction of T1 Codes

The following technique involves concatenation of two codes so as to produce a $T1$ code. Let k be the number of information bits, and let t be the required error-detection capability of the desired $T1$ code.

Step 1: Select an (n_1, k_1) code C_1 for which $k_1 = k$ and $d_{\min} = t + 1$. Encode the k information bits into a codeword in this code.

Step 2: Select an (n_2, k_2) Berger code[1] C_2 for which $k_2 = n_1$. Encode the codeword in Step 1 into a codeword in this code.

[1] The Berger code [10] consists of 2^k words for some k. The codewords are the 2^k binary k-tuples, augmented by $\log_2 (k + 1)$ check bits. These check bits represent the number of 0's that appear in the original k-bit segment.

TABLE IV
*T*1 CODES

k	n	
	$t = 2$	$t = 3$
4	10	12
11	19	21
26	36	38
57 (57)	69 (68)	71 (70)
120 (108)	134 (122)	136 (124)
502 (360)	520 (378)	522 (380)

The length of the final codeword is $n = n_2$. What becomes readily apparent is the following.

1) The above technique indeed produces a $T1$ code.

2) The number of redundant bits in the codeword is equal to $n_1 - k + \log n_1$.[2]

3) The above two steps can be interchanged.

The parameters shown in Table IV for a set of $T1$ codes, where $t = 2$ and $t = 3$, are derived by using distance-3 and distance-4 Hamming codes as C_1 codes.

A possible application of these codes can be seen in ROM control stores of PDP 11/40, IBM 370/168, and Nanodata QM1. The sizes of control words in these machines, respectively, are 56, 108, and 360 bits. In order to suit the control word sizes, the codes given in the above table can be modified by deleting information bits. These modified codes are shown in the parentheses in Table IV.

Construction of T2, T3, and T4 Codes

In the following, we develop a technique for constructing codes which achieve a specified $d_{amin} > 1$ as required for $T2$, $T3$, and $T4$ codes. This technique is based on the principle of construction of iterated codes. We therefore first review the construction of iterated codes before presenting our technique.

The construction of iterated codes can be best described in terms of the matrix shown in Fig. 2. These codes are designed by using two linear codes C_1 and C_2. If C_1 and C_2 are (n_1, k_1) and (n_2, k_2) codes, respectively, then the resulting iterated code is an $(n_1 n_2, k_1 k_2)$ code.

The encoding process is as follows. The $k_1 k_2$ information bits are arranged in terms of a $k_1 \times k_2$ matrix. The k_1 rows are encoded as codewords in C_2, and then the resulting n_2 columns are encoded as codewords in C_1. If the codes C_1 and C_2 are both linear, then: 1) this process is interchangeable in that it does not matter whether we encode the rows or columns first, and 2) the minimum distance of the product code is the product of the minimum distances of C_1 and C_2.

The technique described below for the construction of $T2$–$T4$ codes uses two separable codes. There are some fundamental differences between these codes and the conventional iterated codes for which C_1 and C_2 both are linear codes. (See Remark 1 at the end of this section.)

[2] Hereafter, $\log x$ represents $\log_2 x$.

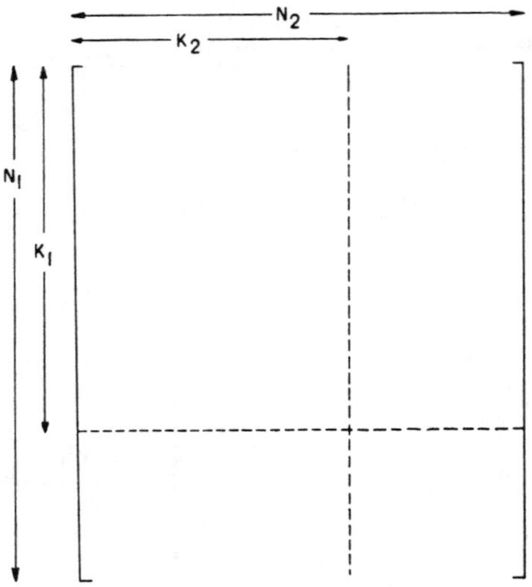

Fig. 2. Iterated code construction.

In the following, it is assumed that the number of information bits k to be encoded is not a prime number. Thus, let $k = k_1 k_2$ for some k_1 and k_2.

Construction Technique:

Step 1: Encode the k_1 rows using an (n_2, k_2) linear error-correcting code. This (n_2, k_2) code must have its minimum distance d_r equal to d_{amin}, the minimum asymmetric distance of the code to be constructed. The resulting matrix will be a $k_1 \times n_2$ matrix.

Step 2: Now encode the n_2 columns into codewords in a Berger code. The resulting matrix will be an $n_1 \times n_2$ matrix where $n_1 = k_1 + \log(k_1 + 1)$, as shown in Fig. 3.

The bits in the $n_1 \times n_2$ matrix represent the codeword. The code is systematic where the information bits are available in the first k_1 rows and the first k_2 columns.

Example 4: Let $k = 6$ and let the desired $d_{amin} = 2$. Thus, one can select $k_1 = 3$ and $k_2 = 2$. The single parity code has a minimum distance of 2. Therefore, the row code may be selected as this single parity code. In the following, we illustrate the construction of this code for a given combination of six information bits. In (a), these six bits are arranged into a 3×2 matrix. In (b), the column of single parity bits is added. Finally, in (c), the columns are encoded into codewords in the Berger code. (Note that the last row is not an even parity codeword.)

$$\begin{bmatrix} 0 & 0 \\ 1 & 0 \\ 1 & 1 \end{bmatrix}$$

(a) Information bits arranged in a matrix.

$$\begin{bmatrix} 0 & 0 & 0 \\ 1 & 0 & 1 \\ 1 & 1 & 0 \end{bmatrix}$$

(b) Rows encoded into single parity code.

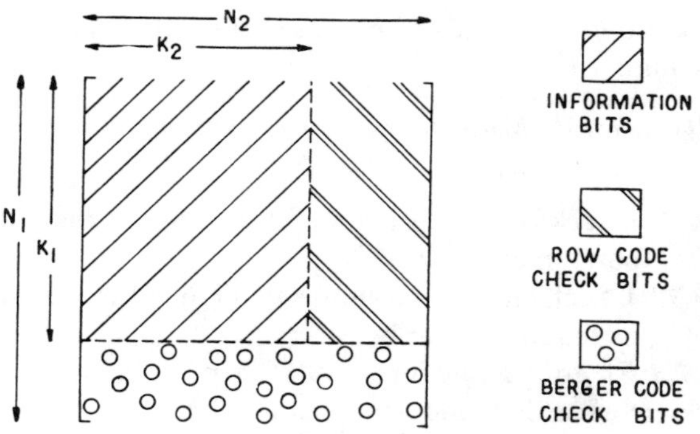

Fig. 3. Complete codeword in Step 2.

$$\begin{bmatrix} 0 & 0 & 0 \\ 1 & 0 & 1 \\ 1 & 1 & 0 \\ \hdashline 0 & 1 & 1 \\ 1 & 0 & 0 \end{bmatrix}$$

(c) Columns encoded into Berger code.

Theorem 3: The above technique results in a code which has $d_{amin} = d_r$ where d_r represents the d_{min} of the row code.

Proof: Consider two distinct codewords X and Y. These codewords must differ in at least one information position. Let this position be in the ith row of the matrices that represent X and Y. Note that $1 \leq i \leq k_1$. Now consider these two ith rows for X and Y. Since the row code has a minimum distance d_r, these two ith rows must differ in at least d_r places. Let these positions be denoted as $j_1, j_2, \cdots, j_h$ where $h \geq d_r$.

Consider the $j_1, j_2, \cdots, j_h$th columns of the two matrices that represent the codewords X and Y. Let these columns be x_{js} and y_{js}, $1 \leq s \leq h$. These columns are all codewords in the Berger code and $x_{js} \neq y_{js}$, $1 \leq s \leq h$. Therefore, one has $d_{10}(x_{js}, y_{js}) \geq 1$ and $d_{01}(x_{js}, y_{js}) \geq 1$ for all s, $1 \leq s \leq h$.

Since

$$d_{01}(X, Y) \geq \sum_{s=1}^{h} d_{01}(x_{js}, y_{js}),$$

and

$$d_{10}(X, Y) \geq \sum_{s=1}^{h} d_{10}(x_{js}, y_{js}),$$

one has

$$d_{01}(X, Y) \geq h \text{ and } d_{10}(X, Y) \geq h.$$

Thus, $d_{amin} \geq d_r$, the minimum distance of the row code.

Q.E.D.

The following is a direct consequence of Theorems 2 and 3.

Theorem 4: The above-described technique results in

a) a $T2$ code with $t = d_r - 1$,

b) a $T3$ code with $t = d_r - 1$, and

c) a $T4$ code with $t = [d_r - 1/2]$ where d_r is the d_{min} of the row code used, and where $[x]$ represents the largest integer that is smaller than or equal to x.

Remarks:

1) The differences between the code constructed here and the iterated codes where both column and row codes are linear as follows.

a) The bottom $(n_1 - k_1)$ rows here are not necessarily codewords in the selected row codes.

b) The two codewords that may result from: 1) encoding rows first and columns next, and 2) encoding columns first and rows next are not necessarily the same codewords here.

2) It may be noted that the column code is a fixed code, whereas the selection of the row code is a function of the type of code one wishes to construct, as well as a function of the desired t needed to be achieved.

3) For a given k, a large number of possibilities exist for selecting k_1, k_2. Given a particular code as the row code, there is an optimum choice of k_1, k_2 which provides minimum redundancy.

For example, given any k, in order to construct a code which has $d_{amin} = 2$, one may select the row code as the single parity code. The optimum combination of (k_1, k_2) can be found by selecting that particular pair (k_1, k_2) where $n = (k_1 + 1)(k_2 + \log k_2)$ is minimum and $k = k_1 k_2$. As an illustration, $k = 105$; the optimum selection is $k_1 = 7$ and $k_2 = 15$.

4) As yet, no upper bounds or existence bounds are available for the systematic $T2$–$T4$ codes presented in this section. It would be important to discover such bounds because this would provide insight into the limitations of the efficiency of these and other potential codes.

5) The repetition code (equivalently, the replication technique) which provides a useful basis for evaluating the efficiency of coding schemes in general is not applicable here. This is because repetition codes *cannot* provide the type of error control described here.

One of the practical advantages of these codes presented here is the existence of fast-decoding algorithms—which are developed in the next section.

V. Decoding Algorithms

The decoding algorithms for $T1$ and $T2$ codes consist of procedures to detect errors. These procedures result in the indication of the presence or absence of errors. (In the presence of errors, the k information bits are disregarded.)

The decoding of $T3$ and $T4$ codes involves both error correction as well as error detection. These decoding algorithms produce the correct information bits if there are no errors in the codeword or if the error present is correctable. On the other hand, if an error is detected which is not correctable, then the information bits are disregarded.

As it will be seen here, error correction, along with error detection, requires more involved steps than just error detection.

A. T1 Codes

The error-detection procedure for these codes is fairly straightforward. This procedure involves the following two steps: 1) checking for unidirectional errors in the entire word by using the Berger code error-detection procedure, and 2) checking for random errors in the first n_1 bits by using the error-detection procedure for the chosen code C_1. These two steps can be performed in parallel. As will be seen later, this error-detection procedure can be implemented by a totally self-checking circuit.

B. T2 Codes

Since these $T2$ codes are error-detecting codes only, the decoding procedure is also simple. This procedure requires checking for errors in the top k_1 rows, as well as in all of the n_2 columns of the codeword matrix. The errors in the top k_1 rows can be detected by computing the syndromes and checking whether or not they are nonzero. The errors in the columns are detected by using the error-detection procedure for Berger codes. The k information bits are decoded when no error is detected.

C. T3 Codes

$T3$ codes are capable of correcting t random errors, as well as detecting all unidirectional errors. In the following, we present two versions of the decoding algorithm; the first one is for $t = 1$, and the second is for any arbitrary t. (This second algorithm which performs multiple error correction requires error erasure decoding, whereas the implementation of the first algorithm, which performs single error correction, is relatively simple.)

Algorithm A (Single Error Correction/Unidirectional Error Detection)

A1: Check the top k_1 rows for errors. Let the number of rows found in error be e_1.

A2: Check all of the n_2 columns in error. Let the number of columns found in error be e_2.

A3: If $e_1 = 0$ and $e_2 = 0$ or 1, then there are no errors in the top k_1 rows, and hence, the k information bits contained in the codeword are the correct bits.

A4: If $e_1 = e_2 = 1$, then there is a single error in the information bits. This error is located at the intersection of the row and column found to be in error. The correct information bits are obtained by complementing this erroneous bit.

A5: If e_1 and e_2 have any value other than the values mentioned in A3 and A4, then there is a multiple error and it cannot be corrected. The information bits, therefore, have to be disregarded

Error-Erasure Decoding Algorithm for Multiple-Error Correction

Next we present the decoding for *multiple* error correction. This requires *error-erasure* decoding. An erasure represents a missing bit from a codeword whose location is known. A code with a minimum distance $d_{\min}$ can correct [3] any combination of e_x errors and e_y (1) provided that

$$2e_x + e_y + 1 \leq d_{\min}. \tag{1}$$

This error-erasure correction requires the following simple steps. First, 0's are placed in all the positions which have erasures. Decoding is attempted on this vector using the error-correcting decoder for this code. If decoding fails, then 1's are placed in all the positions which have erasures. Decoding is again attempted on this vector. The decoding must succeed now if the errors and erasures are bounded by the above-given inequality (1).

Algorithm B (Multiple Error Correction/Unidirectional Error Detection)

B1: Check the first k_1 rows for errors. Let the number of rows found in error be e_1.

B2: Check all the n_2 columns for errors. Let the number of columns found in error be e_2.

B3: If $e_1 > t$ and/or $e_2 > t$, then the number of errors present exceeds t, and hence, cannot be corrected. Therefore, disregard the k information bits and indicate error detection.

B4: If $e_1 \leq t$ and $e_2 \leq t$, then the errors contained are correctable by the following procedure.

Consider the e_1 e_2 positions which are at the intersection of the e_1 rows and e_2 columns in error. Assume that these positions as erasures. Next perform error-erasure decoding on the e_1 rows found to be in error.

The following example illustrates the above algorithm.

Example 5: Consider the codeword matrix shown in Fig. 4(a). This codeword has three random errors and is a codeword in a $T3$ code for which $t = 3$. The three errors are in the second and third rows, as shown in Fig. 4(a). The row code is a distance-4 code. Therefore, the row code is capable of correcting *single* errors *as well as* detecting *double* errors, *or* just detecting *triple* errors.

In Step B1, we will check first the top $k_1 = 3$ rows, and find both the second and third rows in error. Therefore, e_1 will be assigned the value 2. Next, in Step B2, we will check all of the six columns for errors. This will indicate that only the fifth column is in error. (The double error in the fourth column is not detected by the Berger code.) Thus, e_2 will be assigned a value 1. Since $e_1 \leq 3$ and $e_2 \leq 3$, the procedure in Step B4 will be carried out. The two bits which are at the intersection of the fifth column and the second and third rows will be assumed to be erasures, as shown in Fig. 4(b). Next, error-erasure decoding is performed on the second and third rows. This decoding involves the following operations. First, decoding is attempted by assuming x as 0. With $x = 0$, both the second and third rows will now contain double errors, and hence, the decoding will fail indicating double error detection. This is because the code cannot correct double errors and can only detect them. Since the decoding failed, x will now be assumed to be 1 instead, and decoding will be attempted again. This time, decoding will succeed since both of the rows now contain only single errors. The triple error is now corrected and the information bits are error-free.

Proof of Validity of Algorithm B: First, it may be noted that when $e_1 > t$ or $e_2 > t$, there are at least $(t + 1)$ or more errors, and hence, these errors cannot be corrected. Therefore, to prove the validity of Algorithm B, one only has to show that the algorithm produces correct k information bits when: 1) $e_1 \leq t$ and $e_2 \leq t$, and 2) there are at most t random errors or any number of unidirectional errors.

First, let us consider the latter case when there are only unidirectional errors. Since the column code can detect any number of unidirectional errors, these errors must be confined

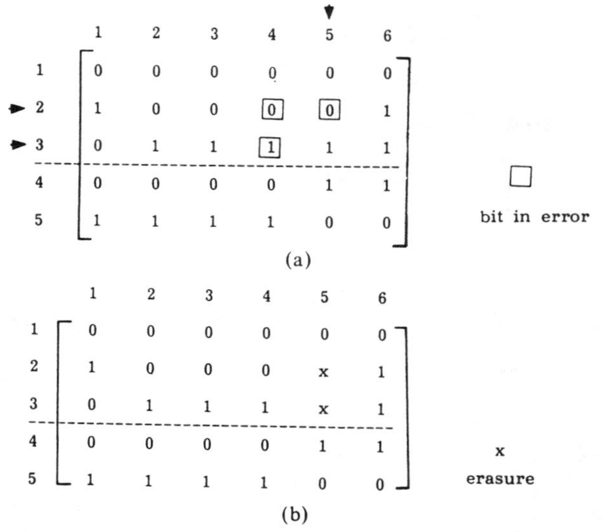

Fig. 4. (a) A codeword with three errors. (b) Codeword with erasures in suspected erroneous positions.

to the e_2 columns found in error. Furthermore, it may be seen that the unidirectional errors in the top k_1 rows must also be confined only to the e_1 rows found in error. This follows from the observation that $e_2 \leq t$ and that the row code can detect up to any t random errors. Thus, it may be seen that errors in the top k_1 rows are confined to the e_1e_2 positions which are assumed to be erasures. Thus, these errors are corrected since the row code can correct up to t erasures and $e_2 \leq t$.

Now let us consider the other case when there are t or fewer random errors. It may be noted that we need to only consider the case when these random errors are not confined to the e_2 columns found in error. This follows from the observation that the case when these errors are all confined to the e_2 columns found in error is equivalent to the above case of unidirectional errors.

Let us assume that there are p random errors, $p \leq t$. Let $p = p_1 + p_2$ where p_1 represents those errors that are confined to the e_2 columns found in error and where p_2 represents the remaining errors that occur outside these e_2 columns. Let these p_2 errors occur in $j_1, j_2, \cdots, j_m$th columns. Thus, each row may contain at most m errors, in addition to the e_2 erasures in Step B4. The following two observations may be made about these p_2 errors that lie in these m columns. First, the portion of these p_2 errors which occurs in the top k_1 rows must be confined to the e_1 rows *already* found to be in error. This follows from the fact that $p_2 \leq t$ and t is the error-detection capability of the row code. Therefore, these errors cannot occur in a row and they go undetected. Second, each one of the m columns which contains these p_2 errors must contain at least two errors each. This follows from the fact that the column code can detect any single error; therefore, if an error in a column is to be undetectable, it must consist of least two errors. Thus, one has $m \leq p_2/2$. Since $e_2 \leq p_1$, one has

$$e_2 + 2m \leq p_1 + p_2 \leq t. \tag{2}$$

Each one of the e_1 rows in error has a combination of at most m errors and e_2 erasures. From 1) and 2), it follows that the row code is capable of correcting these. Thus, in Step B4, all these errors are guaranteed to be corrected. Q.E.D.

D. *T4 Codes*

The decoding of $T4$ codes for multiple error correction is an open problem. However, for single error correction, Algorithm A is also valid for $T4$ codes.

In the next section we discuss implementation of these algorithms. (It may be noted that it would be preferable to incorporate any error-correcting/detecting logic into the device itself. This would mimimize the need for additional pins.)

VI. Implementation of Decoding Algorithms

One of the key differences in the uses of codes in fault-tolerant computer applications as opposed to those in communications applications is in the implementation of the encoding/decoding circuitry [18]. In fault-tolerant computers, the encoding/decoding circuitry forms an integral part of the medium (device) to be monitored by the code. Therefore, this circuitry has to be faster and more reliable.

In this section, techniques to implement various decoding algorithms presented earlier are discussed. As it will be seen here, the error-detecting circuits can be designed to be totally self-checking. The error-correcting circuits can also be made partly self-checking by using self-checking implementations of some of the steps in the algorithms. Self-checking circuits are designed in such a way that they are tested *on-line* during normal operation of the circuit. A fault in these circuits never produces an incorrect output without the fault *itself* being detected. Thus, these self-checking circuits provide one possible way to eliminate "hard-core."

A totally self-checking (TSC) error-detection circuit for an error-detecting code is referred to as a TSC checker. TSC checker designs for $T1$ and $T2$ codes are presented in Sections VI-A and B that follow.

A. *T1 Codes*

The error-detection circuit for these codes may be implemented to be totally self-checking as delineated in Fig. 5. This is possible because TSC checkers are already available for Berger codes [13] and most linear codes [1], [14] such as Hamming codes.

The two checkers shown in the first level of Fig. 4 can be designed to be TSC. The outputs of each of these checkers form a 1-out-of-2 code in the absence of any errors in the input's codewords. These pairs of outputs can be combined by a so-called two-rail checker [11], [1] as shown. The outputs of the two-rail checker will be {01, 10} in the absence of any error in the codeword. On the other hand, an erroneous codeword will produce either 00 or 11 as the output. By appropriate design of the checkers in the first level, it is possible to ensure that the two-rail checker receives as inputs all of the four possible input combinations {0101, 0110, 1001, 1010} during normal operation (that is, with the codeword inputs being error-free). This is sufficient to guarantee that the two-rail checker is TSC, which in turn makes the complete error detection circuit also TSC.

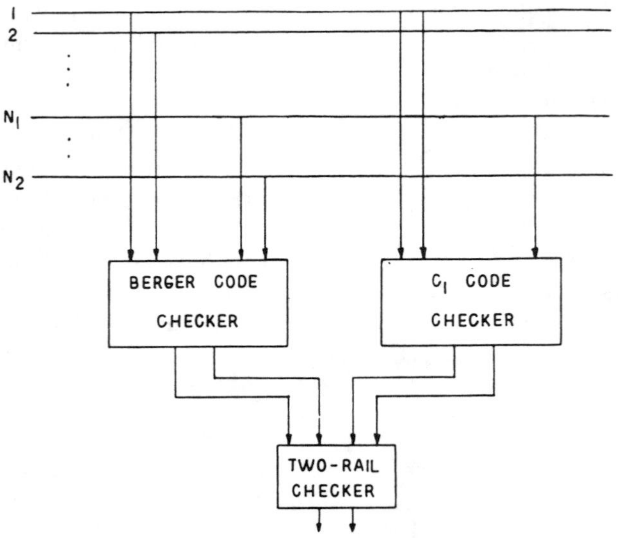

Fig. 5. TSC checker design for $T1$ codes.

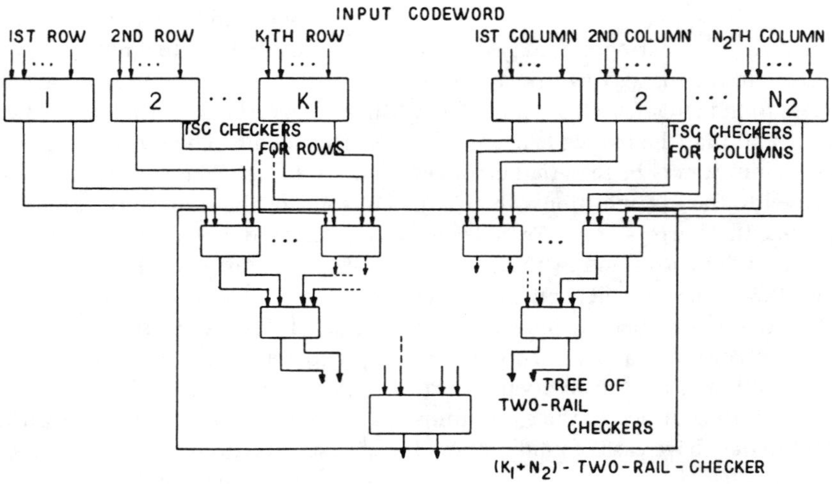

Fig. 6. TSC checker design for $T2$ codes.

B. T2 Codes

The error-detection circuit for $T2$ codes may also be implemented as a TSC checker, as explained below.

A design of this circuit is shown in Fig. 6. This design consists of two levels of checkers. In the first level, a group of k_1 TSC checkers and a group of n_2 TSC checkers check for errors in the top k_1 rows and n_2 columns (of the matrix), respectively. This can be done in parallel, as shown. The outputs of these checkers then form the inputs to a $(k_1 + n_2)$-two-rail checker, as shown in the figure. This two-rail checker is a tree network of two-two-rail checkers, also as illustrated in the figure. It combines the $(k_1 + n_2)$-two-rail inputs in pairs to produce a two-rail output in $\log (k_1 + n_2)$ levels. The total design is TSC, provided each individual two-two-rail checker receives all the four possible input combinations {0101, 0110, 1001, 1010} during normal operation.

C. T3 Codes

Algorithm A: A possible implementation of the algorithm is shown in Fig. 7. The k_1 rows and n_2 columns are checked for errors in the first level. These circuits simply compute the syndromes and produce a 1 output if there is an error detected and a 0 output otherwise. The k_1 outputs of k_1 row code detection circuits are then fed to a 1-out-of-k_1 checker [1]. Similarly, the n_2 outputs of the column code detection circuits are fed to a 1-out-of-n_2 checker. The outputs of each of the checkers are either 01 or 10 if there is exactly one 1 in its inputs. A 01 or 10 output will thus indicate a single row/column in error. On the other hand, 00 at the outputs of this checker indicates that there are no 1's at the inputs of the checker. Thus, a 00 output will indicate the absence of any error. Finally, a 11 output from the checkers indicates that there is more than one 1 at its inputs. This thus indicates more than one row/column in error.

The outputs of these two 1-out-of-m type checkers are monitored by a decision logic which is designed to produce a 1 output when one or both of the 1-out-of-m type checkers produces 11 outputs, thus indicating multiple error.

The single error correction can be easily performed by using an AND gate and an EXOR gate for each information bit, as shown in the figure. The outputs of the two error detection

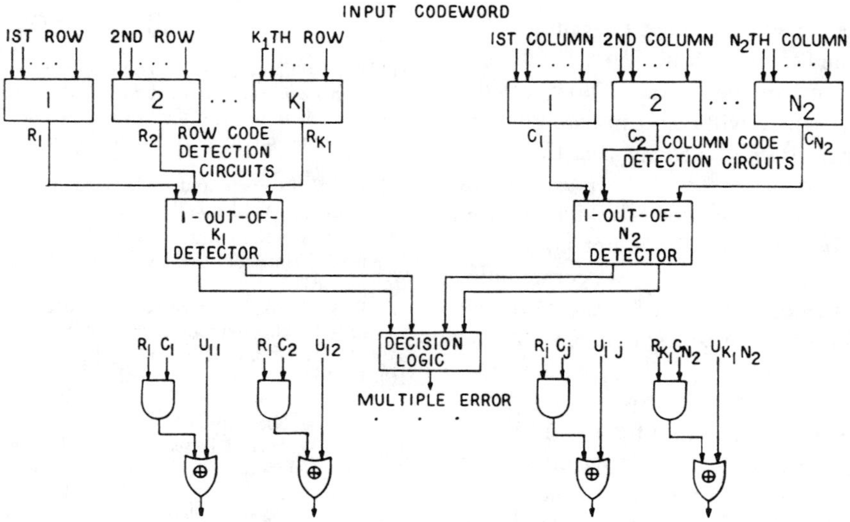

Fig. 7. Single error-correcting decoder for $T3$ codes.

circuits that correspond to the ith row and the jth column are ANDed and then EXORed with the ijth information bit. The output of this AND gate will be 1 if an error is detected in the bit u_{ij} appearing at the intersection of the ith row and the jth column.

Algorithm B: This algorithm can be implemented by adapting the circuit for Algorithm A. In this, instead of 1-out-of-m type checkers, one would need t-out-of-m type checkers and a more sophisticated error-correction logic.

VII. Conclusion

Several results have been presented that led to the development of error-correcting/detecting codes—codes which provide protection against both random and unidirectional errors. It is important to point out that these codes are unique because they not only are systematic, but also are the only known codes which provide this form of specialized protection. Decoding algorithms have also been developed, and their implementations are discussed as well. The error-erasure decoding algorithm developed here might prove to be of some special significance.

(It is our belief that the $T3$ codes for $t = 1$ are probably of the most practical interest. This is chiefly based on the fact that these codes provide adequate protection against both random and unidirectional errors and are easy to decode.)

It may be pointed out that the results and the codes presented here constitute an initial framework upon which further research may be carried out. (Independent work, to construct similar codes by using arithmetic codes, is currently being performed by Bose and Rao [17] and Bose [20].)

A class of coset codes has been constructed by the author which is analogous to that described in Example 2. These codes have not been detailed in this paper as they are not as efficient as those discussed here in Section IV. However, it should be noted that the coset code approach may have potential that needs to be further investigated.

Appendix

Definition: Let X^t represent the Hamming sphere of radius t around a codeword X.

Proof of Theorem 2:

Necessity: The proof is by contradiction.

1) Let C be a $T2$ code with $d_{a\min}$ equal to t. Thus, from Lemma 1, there exists some $X, Y \in C$ for which $d_{10}(X, Y) = t$. Let $d_{01}(X, Y) = s$; one has $s \geq t$.

Consider an error pattern ϵ which changes the codeword X to the codeword Y. This error pattern ϵ obviously cannot be detectable. But ϵ consists of t 1 to 0 errors and s 0 to 1 errors. Thus, ϵ can be interpreted as consisting of a combination of t random errors and s unidirectional errors. By the definition of $T2$ codes, ϵ *must* be detectable. Hence, this is a contradiction.

2) Let C be a $T3$ code with $d_{a\min} = t$. Thus, using Lemma 1 again, there exists some $X, Y \in C$ for which $d_{10}(X, Y) = t$ and $d_{01}(X, Y) = s$ with $s \geq t$. First, it may be noted that $s = t$ implies that $d(X, Y) = 2t$. This makes t random error correction *impossible.* But $T3$ codes *are* capable of t random error correction; therefore, we have the contradiction. In the following, we consider the cases $s > t$.

Let ϵ_1 be a t-error pattern which changes t 1's in X to 0's. Let these t errors be in precisely those t positions in which X is 1 and Y is 0. Let this error ϵ_1 in X result in the vector Z.

Now consider an s-error pattern which changes s 1's in Y to 0's. Let these s errors occur in exactly those s positions in which X is 0 and Y is 1. It can be readily seen that this error, ϵ_2, also results in the changing of Y to Z, the same vector that is produced by ϵ_1 in X. This implies that the code *cannot* correct ϵ_1 *as well as* detect ϵ_2. This is a contradiction since $T3$ codes by definition can correct t random errors, such as ϵ_1, as well as detect all unidirectional errors, such as ϵ_2.

3) Let C be a $T4$ code with $d_{a\min} = 2t$. Thus, again using Lemma 1, there exist some two codewords $X, Y \in C$ for which $d_{10}(X, Y) = 2t$ and $d_{01}(X, Y) = s$ with $s \geq 2t$.

Let ϵ_1 be a t-error pattern which changes t 1's in X to 0's. Let these t errors be confined to those $2t$ positions in which X is 1 and Y is 0. Let ϵ_1 in X produce the vector Z. Now consider a different error pattern ϵ_2 which will result in changing the codeword Y to the vector Z. It can be easily seen that error pattern ϵ_2 is composed of t 0 to 1 errors and s 1 to 0 errors. Thus, ϵ_2 can be interpreted as a combination of t random errors and s unidirectional errors. Obviously, it is not possible to detect ϵ_2 as well as at the same time correct ϵ_1—a combination of t errors. But *both* the detection of ϵ_2 as well as the correction of ϵ_1 are within the capability of $T4$ codes; hence, we have a contradiction.

Sufficiency:

1) To prove this, one has to show that for any $X, Y \in C$, $X \neq Y$, one cannot change any $Z \in X^t$ to Y with only unidirectional errors in Z. This, in turn, requires that $d_{10}(Z, Y) \geq 1$, and $d_{01}(Z, Y) \geq 1$ must be satisfied. Using triangular inequality, one has

$$d_{10}(X, Z) + d_{10}(Z, W) + d_{10}(W, Y) \geq d_{10}(X, Y). \quad \text{(A1)}$$

Thus, $d_{10}(X, Z) + d_{10}(Z, Y) \geq t + 1$ since $d_{10}(X, Y) \geq t + 1$. Furthermore, $d_{10}(X, Z) \leq t$, and hence, it follows that $d_{10}(Z, Y) \geq 1$. Similarly, it can be shown that $d_{01}(Z, Y) \geq 1$.

2) This can be established by showing that for any pair of codewords $X, Y \in C, X \neq Y$, the following is satisfied.

a) $d(X, Y) \geq 2t + 1$.

b) If $Z \in X^t$, then $d_{10}(Z, Y) \geq 1$ and $d_{01}(Z, Y) \geq 1$.

Condition a) guarantees the error-correction capability, whereas condition b) guarantees error-detection capability in addition to the correction capability.

Inequality a) follows from that given in Lemma 2. The proof for condition b) is available in the proof of 1).

3) To prove this, one has to show that given any two codewords X, Y, any combination of at most t-random errors along with any number of unidirectional errors cannot change Y to Z where $Z \in X^t$. It can be seen that this is also equivalent to proving that for any $Z \in X^t$ and for any $W \in Y^t$, both $d_{10}(Z, W) \geq 1$ and $d_{01}(Z, W) \geq 1$.

$$d_{10}(X, Z) + d_{10}(Z, W) + d_{10}(W, Y) \geq d_{10}(X, Y). \quad \text{(A1)}$$

Since

$$d_{10}(X, Y) \geq 2t + 1,$$

$$d_{10}(X, Z) \leq t,$$

and

$$d_{10}(W, Y) \leq t,$$

one has

$$d_{10}(Z, W) \geq 1,$$

using (A1).

Similarly, it can also be shown that $d_{01}(Z, W) \geq 1$.

Q.E.D.

References

[1] J. F. Wakerly, *Error Detecting Codes, Self-Checking Circuits and Applications.* Amsterdam: North-Holland, 1978.

[2] M. Ball and F. Hardie, "Effects and detection of intermittent failures in digital circuits," in *AFIPS Conf. Proc.*, vol. 35, 1969, pp. 329–335.

[3] W. W. Peterson and E. J. Weldon, *Error Correcting Codes.* Cambridge, MA: M.I.T. Press, 1972.

[4] D. K. Pradhan and S. M. Reddy, "Fault-tolerant-failsafe logic networks," in *Proc. IEEE COMPCON*, San Francisco, CA, Mar. 1977, pp. 361–363.

[5] R. W. Cook, W. H. Sisson, T. F. Storey, and W. W. Toy, "Design of a self-checking microprogram controls," *IEEE Trans. Comput.*, vol. C-22, pp. 255–262, Mar. 1973.

[6] B. Parhami and A. Avizienis, "Detection of storage in mass memories using low-cost arithmetic error codes," *IEEE Trans. Comput.*, vol. C-27, pp. 302–308, Apr. 1978.

[7] J. F. Wakerly, "Detection of unidirectional multiple errors using low cost arithmetic codes," *IEEE Trans. Comput.*, vol. C-24, pp. 210–212, Feb. 1975.

[8] R. M. Sahani, "Reliability of integrated circuits," in *Proc. IEEE Int. Comput. Group Conf.*, Washington, DC, June 1970, pp. 213–219.

[9] M. Diaz and J. Moreira de Souza, "Design of self-checking microprogrammed controls," in *Dig. FTCS-5*, Paris, France, pp. 137–142.

[10] J. M. Berger, "A role or error detection codes for asymmetric channels," *Inform. Contr.*, vol. 4, pp. 68–73, Mar. 1961.

[11] W. C. Carter and P. R. Schneider, "Design of dynamically checked computers," in *IFIP Congr.*, vol. 2, Edinburgh, Scotland, 1968, pp. 878–883.

[12] D. A. Anderson, "Design of self-checking digital networks using coding techniques," Univ. Illinois, Urbana, CSL Rep. R-527, Oct. 1971.

[13] M. A. Marouf and A. D. Friedman, "Design of self-checking checkers for Berger codes," in *Dig. 1978 Int. Symp. Fault-Tolerant Computing*, Tolouse, France, June 1978, pp. 179–184.

[14] M. J. Ashjee and S. M. Reddy, "On totally self-checking checkers for separable codes," in *Proc. 1976 FTCS*, June 1976, pp. 151–156.

[15] A. S. Tenanbaum, *Structured Computer Organization.* Englewood Cliffs, NJ: Prentice-Hall, 1976.

[16] C. G. Bell, J. C. Mudge, and J. E. McNamara, "Technology progress in logic and memories," *Comput. Eng.*, Digital Press, 1978.

[17] B. Bose and T. R. N. Rao, Southern Methodist Univ., Dallas, TX, Internal Rep., 1979.

[18] D. K. Pradhan and J. J. Stiffler, "Error correcting codes and self-checking circuits in fault-tolerant computers," *IEEE Computer* (*Special Issue on Fault Tolerant Computing*), Mar. 1980 pp. 27–37.

[19] S. J. Hong, private communication.

[20] B. Bose, "Theory and design of unidirectional error codes," Ph.D. dissertation, Dep. Comput. Sci., Southern Methodist Univ., Dallas, TX, to be published.

Dhiraj K. Pradhan (S'70–M'72) was born on December 1, 1948, in Orissa, India. He received the M.S. degree in electrical engineering from Brown University, Providence, RI, in 1970 and the Ph.D. degree, also in electrical engineering, from the University of Iowa, Ames, in 1972.

He was a member of the Computer Science Faculty at the University of Regina, Canada, and has held positions as Staff Engineer at the IBM Corporation and as a Visiting Associate Professor at Wayne State University, Detroit, MI, and Stanford University, Stanford, CA. He is currently an Associate Professor in the School of Engineering, Oakland University, Rochester, MI. His publication record is extensive, with work done in the areas of fault-tolerant computing, parallel processing, database systems, and switching theory.

Dr. Pradhan was the Guest Editor of a Special Issue on Fault-Tolerant Computing published in the IEEE Transactions on Computers.

Theory of Unidirectional Error Correcting/Detecting Codes

BELLA BOSE, MEMBER, IEEE, AND THAMMAVARAM R. N. RAO, SENIOR MEMBER, IEEE

***Abstract*—In this paper we present some basic theory on unidirectional error correcting/detecting codes. We define symmetric, asymmetric, and unidirectional error classes and proceed to derive the necessary and sufficient conditions for a binary code to be unidirectional error correcting/detecting.**

As of practical importance, we derive two new classes of single-error correcting and all unidirectional-error detecting (SEC–AUED) codes.

***Index Terms*—Asymmetric distance, asymmetric error, constant weight vectors, Hamming distance, SEC–AUED codes, symmetric error, unidirectional error.**

I. INTRODUCTION

ERROR correcting/detecting codes have been extensively discussed for improving the reliability of computer systems and communication networks [1]–[10]. Most of the theories on random error correcting/detecting codes have been developed under the fault assumption of symmetric errors in the data bits. The most likely faults in some of the recently developed LSI memories are of unidirectional type (i.e., all bit failures are in the same direction) rather than symmetric type [11]–[15]. For example, Cook *et al.* [11] have analyzed the nature of faults in integrated circuits and come to the following conclusion.

"... any number of bits may fail but they all fail in the same direction, either s-a-1 or s-a-0. Both no access and multiple access of words from a memory cause unidirectional errors. Also, most failures on a chip that affect multiple bits on that chip, e.g., power failures, tend to affect all parallel bits in the same direction ..." Also in a shift register type memory system a permanent failure in one of the registers results a constant 0 or 1 output from that shift register [14]. The unidirectional failure properties of some of these LSI memories have provided the basis for a new direction of study in coding theory and fault-tolerant computing.

The theory we developed here is only for binary block codes. In Section II we first make a clear distinction among symmetric, unidirectional, and asymmetric errors. In Section III, by using the parameter $N(X, Y)$ (which is the number of $1 \rightarrow 0$ crossovers from X to Y), we establish the necessary and sufficient conditions on binary block codes for unidirectional error correction/detection. In Sections IV and V two methods of constructing single error correcting and all unidirectional error detecting (SEC–AUED) codes are given. In method I we select a suitable subset of the constant weight vectors to form the SEC–AUED code. While designing the fail-safe network Pradhan and Reddy [25] have independently given a method of designing the SEC–AUED code. They have also taken all the constant weight vectors from the Hamming distance 4 code. For the SEC–AUED codes constructed by their method or by the method I proposed here, no efficient encoding/decoding algorithm is known and also these codes are nonsystematic.

In method II we append an appropriate $\left\lfloor \frac{r}{2} \right\rfloor$-out-of-$r$ vector to each of the w-out-of-n vector to form the SEC–AUED code where $\binom{r}{\left\lfloor \frac{r}{2} \right\rfloor} \geq n$. When the information is originally in the form of constant weight vectors, this code could be called systematic. For certain values of w and n we prove that the code is optimal. When the information part contains all possible 2^k tuples, where k is the number of information bits, an efficient encoding/decoding algorithm is devised [26] and will be given in a subsequent paper.

(By taking the product of linear code and Berger code, Pradhan [31] has recently given systematic SEC–AUED codes. The number of check bits for this product code will be $(k_1 + 1) \lceil \log (k_2 + 1) \rceil + k_2$, where $k = k_1 k_2$ is the number of information bits. Even though the codes presented here and in [29] are nonsystematic, the number of check bits for these codes are less than or equal to $\left\lceil \frac{3}{2} \log n \right\rceil + 1$, where n is the length of the code words. Also, it is proved [26] that any systematic SEC–AUED code requires at least $2 \log k \approx 2 \log n$ check bits. Hence, the information rate of the code presented here is higher than that of any optimal systematic SEC–AUED codes.)

Manuscript received September 4, 1980; revised August 10, 1981. This work was supported by the Office of Naval Research under Grant N00014-77-C-0455.

B. Bose is with the Department of Computer Sciences, Oregon State University, Corvallis, OR 97331.

T. R. N. Rao is with the Department of Computer Science, University of Southwestern Louisiana, Lafayette, LA 70504.

0-8186-4182-7/93 $3.00 © 1982 IEEE

II. Symmetric, Asymmetric, and Unidirectional Errors

In this section, we first make a clear distinction among symmetric, asymmetric, and unidirectional errors and then briefly review the error correcting/detecting capabilities of binary block codes for symmetric and asymmetric errors. In the sequel we will refer to the transition $0 \rightarrow 1$ as 0-error and to the transition $1 \rightarrow 0$ as 1-error. Using these types of errors we define the following error classes.

Symmetric Errors: If both 0-errors and 1-errors appear in a received word with equal probability then the channel is called symmetric channel and the errors are called symmetric type.

Asymmetric Errors: In an ideal asymmetric channel only one type of error can occur and the error type is known *a priori*. We call such errors here asymmetric type.

Unidirectional Errors: If both 1-errors and 0-errors can occur in the received words, but in any particular word all errors are of one type, then they are called unidirectional errors.

The following remarks will help clarify further.

If we assume that the errors are of symmetric type, then the probabilities of occurrence of 0-errors and 1-errors are equally likely. A channel model that is commonly used for symmetric random errors is the binary symmetric channel [1]–[6] and it can be characterized as shown in Fig. 1. Note that in this case the $1 \rightarrow 0$ crossover probability is the same as the $0 \rightarrow 1$ crossover probability.

If we assume that only asymmetric 1-errors can occur in the code words, then this implies that the probability of occurrence of 0-errors is zero. This type of channel is called ideal binary asymmetric channel and it can be characterized as shown in Fig. 2. p is the $1 \rightarrow 0$ crossover probability and $\in$ is the $0 \rightarrow 1$ crossover probability. $\in$ is equal to 0 for ideal case.

Finally, if we assume the errors are of unidirectional nature, then this implies that the occurrence of 0-errors and 1-errors is equally likely, but the probability of occurrence of both 0-errors and 1-errors in any particular received word is zero.

In the following paragraphs we briefly review the error correcting capabilities of binary block codes for symmetric and asymmetric errors. We start with the following concept.

Let X and Y be two n-tuples over $GF(2) = \{0, 1\}$. We denote the number of $1 \rightarrow 0$ crossovers from X to Y by $N(X, Y)$.

For example, when $X = (110110)$ and $Y = (001110)$, then $N(X, Y) = 2$ and $N(Y, X) = 1$. Note that in general $N(X, Y) \neq N(Y, X)$.

It is well known that the concept of Hamming distance [1]–[6] is useful in discussing the symmetric error correcting/detecting abilities of codes. This is defined below.

Definition 1: The Hamming distance between two n-tuples X and Y, denoted by $D(X, Y)$, is defined as the number of positions in which the two words differ.

In terms of $1 \rightarrow 0$ crossovers, we can express the Hamming distance between two n-tuples X and Y as

$$D(X, Y) = N(X, Y) + N(Y, X). \qquad (1)$$

The following theorems give symmetric error correcting/detecting capabilities of binary block codes [1].

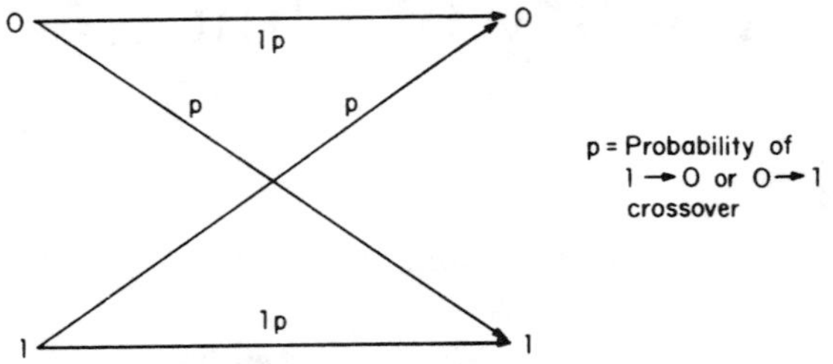

Fig. 1. Binary symmetric channel.

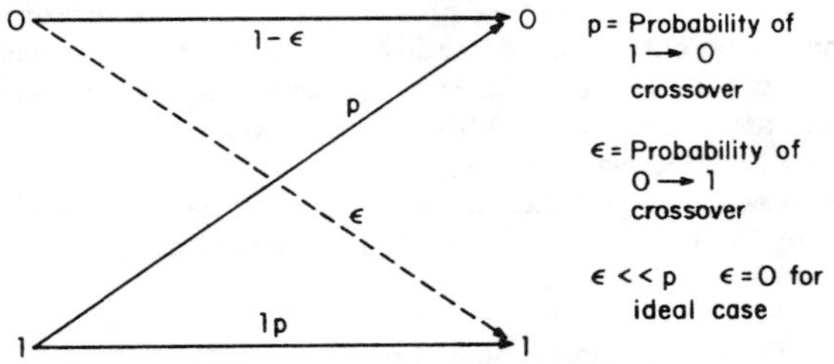

Fig. 2. Binary asymmetric channel.

Theorem 1: A code C is capable of detecting t or fewer errors iff the minimum Hamming distance of the code is at least $t + 1$.

Theorem 2: A code C is capable of correcting t or fewer errors iff the minimum Hamming distance of the code is at least $2t + 1$.

Theorem 3: A code C is capable of correcting t or fewer errors and detecting up to d $(d \geq t)$ errors iff the minimum Hamming distance of the code C is at least $t + d + 1$.

Block codes for symmetric error correction/detection are extensively discussed in [1]–[6].

Rao and Chawla [17] and Anderson [12] have defined "asymmetric distance" with reference to the asymmetric error correcting capabilities of binary block codes as follows.

Definition 2 [12], [17], [22]: The asymmetric distance between two n-tuples X and Y denoted by $D_a(X, Y)$ is defined as the maximum number of $1 \rightarrow 0$ crossovers from X to Y or from Y to X, i.e.,

$$D_a(X, Y) = \max\,[N(X, Y), N(Y, X)]. \qquad (2)$$

It is shown in [17] that the asymmetric distance is a metric.

The following theorem gives the asymmetric error correcting capabilities of binary codes [12], [17].

Theorem 4: A binary code C with minimum asymmetric distance d_a is capable of correcting $d_a - 1$ or fewer asymmetric 1-errors (or 0-errors).

Note that $D(X, Y) = d$ implies $D_a(X, Y) \geq \left\lfloor \frac{d+1}{2} \right\rfloor$, where $\lfloor r \rfloor$ denotes the integer part of r. We know that a code C with minimum Hamming distance $2t + 1$ is capable of correcting t or fewer symmetric errors. For this code C the minimum asymmetric distance will be at least $t + 1$, and hence C is capable of correcting t or fewer asymmetric errors. Since the condition required for asymmetric error correction is less restrictive than for symmetric error correction, it is expected that for a given length n, a t-asymmetric error correcting code to have more code words (i.e., higher information rate) than a

t-symmetric error correcting code. Single asymmetric error correcting codes having information rates better than single symmetric error correcting codes have been derived in [17]–[22].

III. Necessary and Sufficient Conditions for Unidirectional Error Correction/Detection

In this section by using the parameter $N(X, Y)$, the number of $1 \rightarrow 0$ crossovers from X to Y, we establish the necessary and sufficient conditions for unidirectional error correction/detection. We start with the following definition.

Definition 3: A vector $X = (x_1 x_2 \cdots x_n)$ is said to cover another vector $Y = (y_1 y_2 \cdots y_n)$ if for all i, $y_i = 1$ implies $x_i = 1$. Then we write $Y \leq X$.

If $X \nleq Y$ and $Y \nleq X$, then these vectors are said to be "unordered." If $X \leq Y$ or $Y \leq X$, then they are said to be an "ordered pair."

For example, when $X_1 = (1011)$ and $Y_1 = (1001)$, then $Y_1 \leq X_1$ (i.e., X_1 covers Y_1). On the other hand, the vectors $X_2 = (1010)$ and $Y_2 = (0110)$ are unordered since $X_2 \nleq Y_2$ and $Y_2 \nleq X_2$.

Note that the vectors X and Y are unordered iff $N(X, Y) \geq 1$ and $N(Y, X) \geq 1$. Also, if X and Y are ordered pair, then the asymmetric distance and Hamming distance between them are equal, i.e., if

$$X \leq Y \text{ or } Y \leq X$$

then

$$D(X, Y) = D_a(X, Y). \tag{3}$$

It is well known that Berger codes [23], [24] and m-out-of-n codes are capable of detecting multiple unidirectional errors. For completeness we prove the following theorem which gives the necessary and sufficient conditions for unidirectional error detection.

Theorem 5: A code C is capable of detecting all unidirectional errors iff every pair of code words is unordered, i.e.,

$$\text{for all distinct } X, Y \in C$$
$$N(X, Y) \geq 1 \text{ and } N(Y, X) \geq 1. \tag{4}$$

Proof: For all distinct $X, Y \in C$, $N(X, Y) \geq 1$ and $N(Y, X) \geq 1$. Hence, we have the following form in at least two positions, say i and j of X and Y.

$$\begin{aligned} &\quad\;\; i \qquad\; j \\ X &= (\ldots 0 \ldots\ldots 1 \ldots) \\ Y &= (\ldots 1 \ldots\ldots 0 \ldots). \end{aligned}$$

Any vector obtained from X due to 1-errors differs from Y in position i, and any vector obtained from X due to 0-errors differs from Y in position j.

Conversely, if there exists X and Y in C such that $N(X, Y) \geq 1$ and $N(Y, X) = 0$, than 1-errors [0-errors] in the positions where X differs from Y can transform X to Y [Y to X]. These errors are undetectable.

The other important results established in this section are given in the following three theorems. The proofs are given in the Appendix.

Theorem 6: A code C is capable of correcting t or fewer unidirectional errors iff the following condition holds.

For all distinct $X, Y \in C$

$$\begin{aligned} D_a(X, Y) = D(X, Y) &\geq 2t + 1 \qquad \text{for } X \text{ and } Y \text{ an ordered pair} \\ D_a(X, Y) &\geq t + 1 \qquad \text{otherwise.} \end{aligned} \tag{5}$$

Theorem 7: A code C is capable of correcting t or fewer unidirectional errors and detecting all ($t + 1$ or more) unidirectional errors iff the following condition (6) holds.

For all $X, Y \in C$

$$N(X, Y) \geq t + 1 \text{ and } N(Y, X) \geq t + 1. \tag{6}$$

A stronger result for the code C with the property (6) is given in the following theorem.

Theorem 8: For all distinct $X, Y \in C$ if $N(X, Y) \geq t + 1$ and $N(Y, X) \geq t + 1$, then C is capable of correcting t or fewer symmetric errors, detecting $t + 1$ symmetric errors and also detecting all ($t + 2$ or more) unidirectional errors.

A similar theorem without proof is given by Pradhan and Reddy in [16]. Before proceeding to the next section, it is worthwhile to make some remarks regarding Theorem 6. First, note that there is no difference between single symmetric errors and single unidirectional errors. Second, it is obvious that a code C capable of correcting up to t symmetric errors is also capable of correcting up to t unidirectional errors. Since the condition required for unidirectional error correction is less restrictive than for symmetric error correction, we can expect for a given length n, a t-unidirectional error correcting code to have more code words than a t-symmetric error correcting code. For example, consider the set of code words $C = \{0111, 1000\}$. The minimum Hamming distance of this code is 4 and so it can correct only single symmetric errors (and detect double symmetric errors). However, we can see from the following decoding table that it can correct up to 2 unidirectional errors.

Code Words	0111	1000
Single Errors	1111	0000
	0011	1100
	0101	1010
	0110	1001
2-Unidirectional Errors	0001	1110
	0010	1101
	0100	1011

At this point the problem of constructing t-unidirectional error correcting codes having information rates better than that of t-symmetric error correcting codes is still an open research question.

IV. Group Theoretic SEC–AUED Codes

In this section we design a class of codes which is capable of correcting single errors and detecting all (more than one) unidirectional errors. We call these codes group theoretic single error correcting and all unidirectional error detecting (SEC–AUED) codes. The method used here is an extension of the one used by Constantine and Rao [22]. A second method of designing SEC–AUED codes is discussed in Section V. Even though the information rate of the latter class of codes is slightly less than the former one, we can have a better encoding and decoding method for the latter one. We also derive some theoretical upper and lower bounds for the number of code words.

A. Description of Group Theoretic SEC–AUED Codes

The codes described here are constant weight codes with minimum Hamming distance 4. Corollary 1 gives the single error correcting and multiple unidirectional error detecting properties of these codes.

Lemma 1: A constant weight code C, with minimum Hamming distance $2t + 2$ is capable of correcting t-symmetric errors and detecting all unidirectional errors.

Proof: Since C is a constant weight code, for all distinct $X, Y \in C$, $N(X, Y) = N(Y, X)$. Furthermore, $D(X, Y) = N(X, Y) + N(Y, X) = 2N(X, Y) \geq 2t + 2$. Therefore, $N(X, Y) \geq t + 1$. Hence, by Theorem 8 the code C is capable of correcting t-symmetric errors and detecting all unidirectional errors.

Corollary 1: A constant weight code C with minimum Hamming distance 4 is capable of correcting single errors and detecting all unidirectional errors.

Proof: The proof of this corollary follows from Lemma 1 by putting $t = 1$.

Best *et al.* [27] have given bounds for the maximum number of code words $M_{\max}$, with length n ($n \leq 24$) and minimum Hamming distance d ($d \leq 10$). $M_{\max}$ for $d = 4$ is of interest to us and it can be seen from [27] that of all constant weight codes $\left\lfloor \frac{n}{2} \right\rfloor$ out of n codes have the highest information rates. Hence, in generating constant weight SEC–AUED codes, we take the value of the constant weight as $\left\lfloor \frac{n}{2} \right\rfloor$, where n is the length of the code words. In the following paragraphs we give a systematic way of designing SEC–AUED codes for any given length n.

Let G be an additive Abelian group of order n having elements $\{g_1, g_2 \cdots g_n\}$ where g_1 is the identity element. Let $B = \{0, 1\}$. Consider the set $V = \{v/v \in B^n\}$, i.e., V is the set of all binary n-tuples. Then

$$|V| = 2^n.$$

We define a function $T: V \rightarrow G$ such that

$$T(v) = T((a_1, a_2 \cdots a_n)) = \sum_{i=1}^{n} a_i g_i \tag{7}$$

where

$$a_i g_i = \begin{cases} g_1 & \text{for } a_i = 0 \\ g_i & \text{for } a_i = 1. \end{cases} \tag{8}$$

The operation of summation in (7) is the group operation.

Now consider the set V', where $V' = \{u/u \in B^n$ and u has w $(n - 2 \geq w \geq 2)$ 1's and $n - w$ 0's$\}$. Note that $|V'| = \binom{n}{w} = \frac{n!}{w!n - w!}$.

The function T defined above will partition the set V' of $\binom{n}{w}$ elements into n mutually disjoint subsets, i.e.,

$$V' = V_1 \cup V_2 \cup \cdots V_n$$

and

$$V_i \cap V_j = \varnothing \qquad i, j = 1, 2 \cdots n \quad i \neq j \tag{9}$$

where the set V_j is defined as follows:

$$V_j = \left\{ v = (a_1 a_2 \cdots a_n) \in V' \Big/ \sum_{i=1}^{n} a_i g_i = g_j \right\}. \tag{10}$$

The following example illustrates the construction of such a set using the additive group of $GF(2^3)$.

Example 1: The addition table of $GF(2^3)$ is given below.

	g_1	g_2	g_3	g_4	g_5	g_6	g_7	g_8
$+$	0	1	x	x^2	$1+x$	$1+x^2$	$x+x^2$	$1+x+x^2$
0	0	1	x	x^2	$1+x$	$1+x^2$	$x+x^2$	$1+x+x^2$
1	1	0	$1+x$	$1+x^2$	x	x^2	$1+x+x^2$	$x+x^2$
x	x	$1+x$	0	$x+x^2$	1	$1+x+x^2$	x^2	$1+x^2$
x^2	x^2	$1+x^2$	$x+x^2$	0	$1+x+x^2$	1	x	$1+x$
$1+x$	$1+x$	x	1	$1+x+x^2$	0	$x+x^2$	$1+x^2$	x^2
$1+x^2$	$1+x^2$	x^2	$1+x+x^2$	1	$x+x^2$	0	$1+x$	x
$x+x^2$	$x+x^2$	$1+x+x^2$	x^2	x	$1+x^2$	$1+x$	0	1
$1+x+x^2$	$1+x+x^2$	$x+x^2$	$1+x^2$	$1+x$	x^2	x	1	0

The 14 vectors in the set V_1 are shown below.

		0	1	x	x^2	$1+x$	$1+x^2$	$x+x^2$	$1+x+x^2$
X_1	=	0	1	1	1	0	0	0	1
X_2	=	0	1	1	0	0	1	1	0
X_3	=	0	1	0	1	1	0	1	0
X_4	=	0	1	0	0	1	1	0	1
X_5	=	0	0	1	1	1	1	0	0
X_6	=	0	0	1	0	1	0	1	1
X_7	=	0	0	0	1	0	1	1	1

X_8	=	1	1	1	0	1	0	0	0
X_9	=	1	1	0	1	0	1	0	0
X_{10}	=	1	1	0	0	0	0	1	1
X_{11}	=	1	0	1	1	0	0	1	0
X_{12}	=	1	0	1	0	0	1	0	1
X_{13}	=	1	0	0	1	1	0	0	1
X_{14}	=	1	1	0	0	1	1	1	0

Every vector $X_i = (a_1a_2a_3a_4a_5a_6a_7a_8) \in V_1$ has the property

$$\sum_{i=1}^{8} a_i g_i = g_1 = 0.$$

The other sets $V_2, V_3 \cdots V_8$ can be constructed similarly.

The following lemma is a direct consequence of the property (9).

Lemma 2: At least one of the sets $V_1, V_2 \cdots V_n$ has cardinality greater than or equal to $\frac{\binom{n}{w}}{n}$, i.e.,

$$V_i \geq \frac{\binom{n}{w}}{n} \qquad \text{for some } i = 1, 2, \cdots n. \tag{11}$$

Next, we will consider one of the partitions V_i, induced by G in the set of vectors V' and establish the following important result in constructing the SEC–AUED code.

Theorem 9: Each of the set V_i satisfies the following condition (12). For distinct $X, Y \in V_i$

$$N(X, Y) \geq 2 \text{ and } N(Y, X) \geq 2. \tag{12}$$

Proof: Suppose there exists two vectors X_1 and Y_1 in V_i such that $N(X_1, Y_1) = 1$. Since the weight of each vector is same, the following condition is the only alternative:

$$X_1 = (a_1a_2 \cdots a_{k-1}1\, a_{k+1} \cdots a_{l-1}0\, a_{l}-1 \cdots a_n)$$
$$Y_1 = (a_1a_2 \cdots a_{k-1}0\, a_{k+1} \cdots a_{l-1}1\, a_{l+1} \cdots a_n)$$

where $k \neq l$ and $k, l \in \{1, 2, \cdots n\}$.

Since $X_1, Y_1 \in V_i$, we will have

$$\sum_{\substack{j=1\\ j\neq k\\ j\neq l}}^{n} a_j g_j + g_k = \sum_{\substack{j=1\\ j\neq k\\ j\neq l}}^{n} a_j g_j + g_l = g_i. \tag{13}$$

Hence, we get

$$g_k = g_l = g_i - \sum_{\substack{j=1\\ j\neq k\\ j\neq l}}^{n} a_j g_j. \tag{14}$$

This gives the contradiction because $g_k \neq g_l$ for $k \neq l$. Hence, for distinct $X_1, Y_1 \in V_i$ $N(X_1, Y_1) \geq 2$ and $N(Y_1, X_1) \geq 2$.

By consequence of Theorems 8 and 9, one can easily see that the sets of vectors $V_1, V_2, \cdots V_n$ individually can be used as SEC–AUED codes.

We explain below how the error correction/detection process can be implemented for the above SEC–AUED code. An ordering of the elements in the group G is presupposed for the purposes of uniquely determining the faulty position.

Let the set of vectors V_i constitute the SEC–AUED code. Let us assume that the number of 1's in each code word is w where $w \geq 2$. Suppose that a 0-error occurs in a code word $X \in V_i$ resulting in the word $X' = (a_1a_2 \cdots a_n)$ such that

$$\sum_{j=1}^{n} a_j g_j = g_l. \tag{15}$$

Then the number of 1's in the word X' will be $w + 1$, and hence the existence of 0-error in X' is immediately known. The position r in error can be located by

$$g_r = g_l - g_i. \tag{16}$$

Thus, r is determined and therefore correction can be implemented.

On the other hand, if a 1-error occurs in a code word $Y \in V_i$, resulting into a word $Y' = (b_1b_2 \cdots b_n)$ such that

$$\sum_{j=1}^{n} b_j g_j = g_m \tag{17}$$

then the number of 1's in the word Y' will be $w - 1$ and the existence of a 1-error in Y' is immediately known. The position s in error can be located by $g_s = g_i - g_m$. Once s is obtained, error correction can be implemented.

Finally, if more than one 0-errors occur in any word $Z \in V_i$, then the number of 1's in the received word will be greater than $w + 1$ and if more than one 1-errors occur in any code word $Z \in V_i$, then the number of 1's in the received word will be less than $w - 1$. In both cases all unidirectional errors can be detected.

The following example illustrates the above concept.

Example 2: Consider the set of code words given in the Example 1. Suppose that a message $X' = 00110001$ is received. The existence of 1-error in X' is evident because the weight of X' is only 3. Also $T(X') = x + x^2 + (1 + x + x^2) = 1$ and $0 - 1 = 1 = g_2$, which implies the second bit of X' is in error. Hence, the transmitted code word is (01110001).

On the other hand, if the received message is $Y' = 1111\ 0001$, then the existence of 0-error is evident because the weight of Y' is 5. Since $T(Y') = 0.1 + 1.1\ 1.x + 1.(1 + x + x^2) = 0 = 0 + 0 = g_1$, the first bit of Y' is in error. Hence, the transmitted message is (0111 0001).

B. Bounds on the Size of the Code

One of the aspects of coding theory is to obtain codes with as high information rate as possible. That is, we wish to have the cardinality of the code to approach the theoretical maximum which we denote by $M_{\max}$. For the group theoretic SEC–AUED codes, at present time, we do not have a closed formula to find out $M_{\max}$. For a particular group G of order n, to find out $M_{\max}$ in the group theoretic SEC–AUED code two important points need further investigation.

1) What should be optimal value of w, the number of 1's in the code words, and

2) Which subset V_i has the highest cardinality?

From Lemma 2 we can see that one of the V_i's has cardinality greater than or equal to $\frac{\binom{n}{w}}{n}$. Since $\binom{n}{w}$ is maximum when $w = \left\lfloor \frac{n}{2} \right\rfloor$, and also from the tables in [27] M is maximum when $w = \left\lfloor \frac{n}{2} \right\rfloor$, we conjecture that M will be maximum for $w = \left\lfloor \frac{n}{2} \right\rfloor$ or $\left\lceil \frac{n}{2} \right\rceil$. The second question is still an open problem.

In the following lemma we give an asymptotic lower bound for M, the number of code words in the group theoretic SEC–AUED code.

Lemma 3: For large values of n, the number of code words M in a group theoretic SEC–AUED code is given by the following bound:

$$M \geq \frac{\sqrt{2}}{\sqrt{\pi}} \frac{2^n}{n^{3/2}}. \tag{18}$$

Proof: By Lemma 3

$$M \geq \frac{\binom{n}{w}}{n}$$

where n is the length and w is the weight of the code words.

When $w = \left\lfloor \frac{n}{2} \right\rfloor$ we will have

$$M \geq \left(\begin{array}{c} n \\ \left\lfloor \frac{n}{2} \right\rfloor \end{array} \right) \Big/ n.$$

By using stirling approximation for factorial function $\left(\text{i.e., } n! = \sqrt{2\pi n}\left(\frac{n}{e}\right)^n \text{ for large } n\right)$, we will have

$$M \geq \frac{\sqrt{2}}{\sqrt{\pi}} \frac{2^n}{n^{3/2}}.$$

This completes the proof.

Corollary 2: The number of redundant bits required for the group theoretic SEC–AUED code is less than $\lceil 3/2 \log_2 n \rceil + 1$.

Proof: From Lemma 3 we know the number of code words M is given by

$$M \geq \sqrt{2/\pi}\,(2^n/n^{\frac{3}{2}}).$$

Hence

$$\log_2 M \geq n - \tfrac{3}{2}\log_2 n + \tfrac{1}{2} = \tfrac{1}{2}\log \pi.$$

Then

$$n - \log_2 M < \tfrac{3}{2}\log_2 n + 1.$$

Hence the corollary is proved.

V. SEC–AUED Code Design—Method II

In this section we give a second method of designing the SEC–AUED codes. Even though the information rate of these codes is slightly less than the one presented in Section IV, we can have a better encoding/decoding algorithm for the codes presented here [26].

The format of the code C is shown below. In the first n bits of the code C, we take all possible w-out-of-n vectors where $w \geq 2$. To each of the

w 1's	$\left\lfloor \frac{r}{2} \right\rfloor$ 1's
n	r

w-out-of-n vectors, an appropriate $\left\lfloor \frac{r}{2} \right\rfloor$-out-of-$r$ vector is appended such that the resultant vectors form the SEC–AUED code. We call the first n bits with weight w as the first part of the code word and the next r bits with weight $\left\lfloor \frac{r}{2} \right\rfloor$ as the second part of the code word. If the data words are constant weight vectors, which is the case in some applications [11], [28], then the code described here can be considered as a systematic one.

First, note that if X_1 and Y_1 are any two distinct w-out-of-n vectors, then we will have $N(X_1, Y_1) \geq 1$ and $N(Y_1, X_1) \geq 1$. Additional $\left\lfloor \frac{r}{2} \right\rfloor$-out-of-$r$ vectors are added in order to satisfy the conditions given in the Theorem 8, i.e., for all $X, Y \in C$, $N(X, Y) \geq 2$ and $N(Y, X) \geq 2$. The complete description of the code construction is given below.

Let V' be the set of w-out-of-n vectors. Let $G = \{g_1 g_2 \cdots g_n\}$ be an additive Abelian group. In our case we take $G = \{0, 1, 2, \cdots n - 1\}$ with the additive operation as the mod n addition. Let T be a function from V' the set w-out-of-n vectors to G as defined in (7) and (8), i.e.,

$$V' = V_0 \, U \, V_1 \, U \cdots V_{n-1} \tag{19}$$

and

$$V_i \cap V_j = \phi \qquad \text{for } i, j = 0, 1 \cdots n - \text{ and } i \neq j.$$

We now describe how the additional $\left\lfloor \frac{r}{2} \right\rfloor$-out-of-$r$ vectors are to be appended.

Let r be the smallest integer such that $\left(\begin{array}{c} r \\ \left\lfloor \frac{r}{2} \right\rfloor \end{array} \right) \geq n$, and U be the set of $\left\lfloor \frac{r}{2} \right\rfloor$-out-of-$r$ vectors. Define an arbitrary one to one function f from G to U, i.e.,

$$f\colon G \rightarrow U \text{ such that if } f(i) = f(j) \text{ then } i = j.$$

Now the code words are formed as follows. Let v be a w-out-of-n vector with $T(v) = j$ and $f(j) = u$. Then concatenate the vector u with the vector v to form the code word. The following example explains these concepts.

Example 3: Let V' be the set of all 3-out-of-6 vectors. Hence, $n = 6$, $w = 3$, and $|V'| = 20$. The Abelian group G will be $\{0, 1, 2, 3, 4, 5\}$ with additive operation as mod 6 addition.

We want to choose the smallest r such that $\binom{r}{\left\lfloor \frac{r}{2} \right\rfloor} \geq n = 6.$

Then r must be 4. So the set U will be 2-out-of-4 vectors. Let us define the function $f\colon G \rightarrow U$ as follows.

$$f(0) = 0011, f(1) = 0101\; f(2) = 0110$$

$$f(3) = 1001\; f(4) = 1010\; f(5) = 1100.$$

Then we will have the following set C, of code words.

$T(X) = j$,	012	345	$f(j)$
0	000	111	0011
5	001	011	1100
4	001	101	1010
3	001	110	1001
4	010	011	1010
3	010	101	1001
2	010	110	0110
2	011	001	0110
1	011	010	0101
0	011	100	0011
3	100	011	1001
2	100	101	0110
1	100	110	0101
1	101	001	0101
0	101	010	0011
5	101	100	1100
0	110	001	0011
5	110	010	1100
4	110	100	1010
3	111	000	1001

(columns 012 and 345): All possible 3-out-of-6 vectors

(column $f(j)$): Appended 2-out-of-4 vectors

Note that the code described above is also a constant weight one. The number of code words in C will be $\binom{n}{w}$. Since $\binom{n}{w}$ is maximum for $w = \left\lfloor \frac{n}{2} \right\rfloor$, we can take the weight of the first part of the code words as $\left\lfloor \frac{n}{2} \right\rfloor$ to get maximum information rate. The following theorem gives the SEC–AUED property of the code.

Theorem 10: The code C described above satisfies the following condition. For all

$$X, Y \in C\; N(X, Y) \geq 2$$

and

$$N(Y, X) \geq 2. \tag{20}$$

Proof: Let $X = X_1X_2$ be any code word in C where X_1 corresponds to the w-out-of-n vector part and X_2 corresponds to the $\left\lfloor \frac{r}{2} \right\rfloor$-out-of-$r$ vector part. For any two distinct code words $X = X_1X_2$ and $Y = Y_1Y_2$ in C, let $T(X_1) = i$ and $T(Y_1) = j$. If $i = j$ then $X_2 = Y_2$ and by Theorem 9 $N(X, Y) = N(X_1, Y_1) \geq 2$ and $N(Y, X) = N(Y_1, X_1) \geq 2$. If $i \neq j$ then $X_2 \neq Y_2$ and hence $N(X_2, Y_2) \geq 1$ and $N(Y_2, X_2) \geq 1$. Hence, $N(X, Y) = N(X_1, Y_1) + N(X_2, Y_2) \geq 2$ and $N(Y, X) = N(Y_1, X_1) + N(Y_2, X_2) \geq 2$. In both cases the theorem is valid.

We explain below how error correction and detection process can be implemented. Let C be the SEC–AUED code. For any $X \in C$ let $X = X_1X_2$, where $X_1 = (a_0a_1 \cdots a_{n-1})$ is the w-out-of-n vector with $w \geq 1$, and $X_2 = (b_1b_2 \cdots b_r)$ is the appropriate $\left\lfloor \frac{r}{2} \right\rfloor$-out-of-$r$ vector. Suppose that a 0-error occurs in the X_1 part of the code word $X = X_1X_2 \in C$ resulting into a word $X' = X'X'_2 = (a_0a_1a_2 \cdots a_{n-1}b_1b_2 \cdots b_n)$ such that

$$\sum_{j=0}^{n-1} ja_j \equiv l \bmod n.$$

Then the number of 1's in X_1' and X_2' will be, respectively, $w + 1$ and $\left\lfloor \frac{r}{2} \right\rfloor$. Hence, the existence of a 0-error in the X_1' part is immediately known. Let $f^{-1}(X_2') = f^{-1}(X_2) = i$. Now the position p in error can be located by

$$p = l - i.$$

Once p is known, bit a_p is completed to get the correct word.

On the other hand, suppose that an 1-error occurs in X_1 part of $X = X_1X_2 \in C$ resulting into a word $X'' = X_2'' = (d_0d_1d_2 \cdots d_{n-1}\, e_1e_2 \cdots e_r)$ such that

$$\sum_{j=0}^{n-1} jd_j \bmod n = l_1.$$

Then the number of 1's in X_1'' and X_2'' will be $w - 1$ and $\left\lfloor \frac{r}{2} \right\rfloor$, respectively, and the existence of a 1-error in X_1'' part is immediately known. Again $f^{-1}(X_2'') = f^{-1}(X_2) = i$. The position q in error can be located by

$$q = i - l_1.$$

Hence, the bit a_q can be complemented to get the correct word.

If a single error occurs in Y_2 part of $Y = Y_1Y_2 \in C$ resulting into a vector $Y' = Y_1'Y_2' = (a_0a_1 \cdots a_{n-1}b_1b_2 \cdots b_r)$ such that $\sum_{j=0}^{n-1} ja_j \equiv i \bmod n$ then the number of 1's in Y_2' will differ from

$\lfloor \frac{r}{2} \rfloor$ by one. Hence, the existence of a single error in Y_2' part is known. Since there is no error in Y_1' part, the correct part of Y_2' can be obtained by using the function f as $f(i) = Y_2$.

If multiple 1-errors occur in a code word $X \in C$, then the number of 1's in the erroneous word X' will be less than $w + \lfloor \frac{r}{2} \rfloor - 1$ and if multiple 0-errors occur in a code word $X \in C$, then the number of 1's in the erroneous word will be greater than $w + \lfloor \frac{r}{2} \rfloor + 1$. In both cases the unidirectional errors can be detected.

We give the following example to illustrate these concepts.

Example 4: Let C be the set of code words as given in Example 3. Let 000011 0011 be the received word. Since the number of 1's in the first 6 bits is only 2, the existence of 1-error is obvious. Therefore

$$(j + 4.1 + 5.1) \equiv (f^{-1}(0011) \equiv 0 \bmod 6.$$

Hence, $j \equiv -9 \equiv 3 \bmod 6$. Therefore, the correct word is 000111 0011.

On the other hand if (001111 0011) is the received word, then the existence of 1-error in one of the first 6 bits is known. Then the erroneous bit j can be found out from

$$(1.2 + 1.3 + 1.4 + 1.5) - f^{-1}(0011) \equiv 14 - 0 \equiv 2 \pmod 6.$$

Then the correct word is 000111 0011.

If (000111 1011) is the received word, then the existence of a single error in one of the last 4 bits is known because the number of 1's in this part is 3 instead of 2. Since $f(1.3 + 1.4 + 1.5) = f(0) = 0011$, the correct word must be 000111 0011. Finally, if multiple unidirectional errors occur in a code word it can be easily detected by finding the weight of the received vector.

The information rate of the code presented here is slightly less than the one presented in Section IV. It is straightforward to note that the redundancy will be minimum when $w = \lfloor \frac{n}{2} \rfloor$, and r is the smallest integer such that $\binom{r}{\lfloor r/2 \rfloor} \geq n$. Then the number of the code words will be $\binom{n}{\lfloor n/2 \rfloor}$ and the length of the code words is $\mathbf{n} = n + r$. For large n we can easily prove that the number of redundant bits in this code is $\frac{1}{2} \log n + r$. For an example, if we want to encode a 16 bits of information to SEC–AUED code, we can easily calculate that the second method requires 25 bits and the first method requires 24 bits for the length. Hence, the information rate of the codes constructed by method II is comparable to that of the codes constructed by method I.

A. Optimality of the Code

When the data (informations) are constant weight vectors, the SEC–AUED code constructed by method II can be considered as a systematic one. In this case, the code is optimal for certain values of w and n. The following theorem given by Freiman [24] is useful in order to establish our result. Here unordered codes refer to unidirectional error detecting codes.

Theorem 11 [24]*:* Among all unorder codes of length n, the $\lfloor \frac{n}{2} \rfloor$-out-of-$n$ or $\lceil \frac{n}{2} \rceil$-out-of-$n$ codes give minimum redundancy.

Lemmas 12 and 13 give the lower bound for the number of check bits.

Lemma 4: When the data are w-out-of-n vectors with $1 \leq w \leq \lfloor \frac{n}{2} \rfloor$, then any systematic SEC–AUED code requires at least r check bits where r satisfies the equation $\binom{r}{\lfloor r/2 \rfloor} \geq (n - w + 1)$.

Proof: Consider the following $(n - w + 1)$ information symbols.

$n - w$	w
$000 \cdots 000$	$111 \cdots 111$
$000 \cdots 001$	$011 \cdots 111$
$000 \cdots 010$	$011 \cdots 111$
$100 \cdots 000$	$011 \cdots 111$

The check symbols for these information symbols must all be unordered. Otherwise the code does not satisfy the condition given in Theorem 8. Hence, by Theorem 11 the code requires at least r check bits, where

$$\binom{r}{\lfloor r/2 \rfloor} \geq n - w + 1.$$

When $w > \lfloor \frac{n}{2} \rfloor$ we can prove the following lemma similar to the above one.

Lemma 5: When the data are w-out-of-n vectors with $n > w > \lfloor \frac{n}{2} \rfloor$, any systematic SEC–AUED code requires at least r check bits, where $\binom{r}{\lfloor r/2 \rfloor} \geq w + 1$.

From the above two lemmas we have the following result.

Theorem 12: For any integer r such that $\binom{r}{\lfloor r/2 \rfloor} \geq n$ and

$\binom{r-1}{\left\lfloor \frac{r}{2} \right\rfloor} < \max(n - w + 1, w + 1)$ the proposed code is optimal.

Proof: We have $\binom{r-1}{\left\lfloor \frac{r}{2} \right\rfloor} < \max(n - w + 1, w + 1)$ and hence by Lemmas 4 and 5 the required number of check bits for the code will be greater than or equal to r. Since $\binom{r}{\left\lfloor \frac{r}{2} \right\rfloor} \geq n$ the proposed code uses exactly r check bits and hence the code is optimal.

A stronger result of the above theorem is given below.

Theorem 13: When $n = \binom{2s}{s}$ or $n = \binom{2s}{s} - 1$, then the proposed code is optimal for all values of w in the range $1 \leq w \leq n - 1$.

Proof: Since $\binom{2s}{s} = n$ we have $\binom{2s-1}{s} = \frac{n}{2} < \frac{n}{2} + 1$ and $\max(n - w + 1, w + 1) > \frac{n}{2}$. Therefore, the optimality of the code follows from Lemmas 4 and 5.

From the above theorem we can see that the code is optimal for $n = 5, 6, 19, 20, 69, 70$, etc., with $1 \leq w < n$.

VI. Conclusion

In this paper the unidirectional error correcting/detecting capabilities of binary block codes are discussed. Two methods of designing SEC–AUED codes are given. In the first method we take a subset of constant weight vectors with Hamming distance 4 to form the SEC–AUED code. Although it is not known that the subset of $\left\lfloor \frac{n}{2} \right\rfloor$-out-of-$n$ vectors with distance 4 gives the maximum number of SEC–AUED code words, Graham and Sloane have proved [30] that method I gives almost the maximum possible number of distance 4 constant weight code words for large values of n.

The second method is an extension to the first one. When the information symbols are constant weight vectors the code generated by method II could be considered as a systematic one. In this case we proved that the code is optimal for certain values of w and n. When the data are all possible 2^k-tuples, k is the number of information bits, we can use the encoding/decoding method discussed in [26].

Appendix

Here we give the outlines of the proofs for Theorems 6–8 and the complete proofs can be seen in [26] and [29].

Outline of the Proof for Theorem 6

Let S_{z1} and S_{z0} refer to the set of all vectors obtained from a code word Z due to t or fewer (possibly zero) 1-errors and 0-errors. Let $S_z = S_{z1} \cup S_{z0}$. Let X and Y be any two code words. Then we have to prove $S_x \cap S_y = \phi$. If they are ordered pair then $D(X, Y) \geq 2t + 1$ and hence the condition $S_x \cap S_y = \phi$ can be proved easily. If they are unordered then $D_a(X, Y) \geq t + 1$. Also, $S_x \cap S_y = (S_{x0} \cup S_{x1}) \cap (S_{y0} \cup S_{y1}) = (S_{x0} \cap S_{y0}) \cup (S_{x0} \cap S_{y1}) \cup (S_{x1} \cap S_{y0}) \cup (S_{x1} \cap S_{y1})$. We can prove each of the term $S_{xi} \cup S_{yj} = \phi$, where $, j \in \{0, 1\}$ and hence the first part of the theorem is valid.

Conversely, if any $X, Y \in C$ and they are an ordered pair with $D(X, Y) \leq 2t$ or if they are unordered pair with $D_a(X, Y) \leq t$ then we can prove $S_x \cup S_y \neq \phi$.

Outline of the Proof for Theorem 7

Let S_z be as defined before. Let Q_z be the set of all vectors obtained from z due to $t + 1$ or more unidirectional errors. Let Q be the set of all vectors obtained from all code words in C due to $t + 1$ or more unidirectional errors, i.e.,

$$Q = Q_x \cup Q_y \cdots.$$

If X and Y are any two code words then we have to prove the following two conditions:

$$S_x \cap S_y = \phi$$

and

$$S_x \cap Q = \phi.$$

The proof for the first condition is the same as before. The second condition can be written as

$$S_x \cap Q = S_x \cap (Q_x \cup Q_y \cup \cdots) = (S_x \cap Q_x) \cup (S_x \cap Q_y) \cup \cdots.$$

We can prove that each of the terms is empty and the first part of the theorem is valid.

Conversely, if X and Y are two code words in C such that $N(X, Y) \leq t$, then we can prove $S_x \cap Q_y \neq \phi$.

The proof of Theorem 8 is almost identical to the above proof.

Acknowledgment

The authors would like to thank the anonymous referees for their valuable comments.

References

[1] R. W. Hamming, "Error detecting and error correcting codes," *Bell Syst. Tech. J.*, vol. 29, pp. 147–160, Apr. 1950.
[2] W. W. Peterson and E. J. Weldon, *Error Correcting Codes.* Cambridge, MA: MIT Press, 1972.
[3] E. R. Berlekamp, *Algebraic Coding Theory.* New York: McGraw-Hill, 1968.
[4] ——, *Key Papers in the Development of Coding Theory.* New York: IEEE Press, 1974.
[5] S. Lin, *An Introduction to Error-Correcting Codes.* Englewood Cliffs, NJ: Prentice-Hall, 1970.
[6] N. J. A. Sloane and F. J. MacWilliams, *The Theory of Error Correcting Codes.* Amsterdam, The Netherlands: North-Holland, 1978.
[7] T. R. N. Rao, *Error Coding for Arithmetic Processors.* New York: Academic, 1974.
[8] F. F. Sellers, M. Y. Hsiao, and L. W. Bearnson, *Error Detecting Logic for Digital Computers.* New York: McGraw-Hill, 1968.

[9] J. F. Wakerly, *Error Detecting Codes, Self-Checking Circuits and Applications.* Amsterdam, The Netherlands: North-Holland, 1978.
[10] S. M. Reddy, "A class of linear codes for error control in byte-per-card organized memory systems," *IEEE Trans. Comput.*, vol. C-27, pp. 481-482, June 1978.
[11] R. W. Cook, W. H. Sisson, T. G. Stoney, and W. N. Toy, "Design of self-checking microprogram control," *IEEE Trans. Comput.*, vol. C-22, pp. 255-262, Mar. 1973.
[12] D. A. Anderson, "Design of self-checking digital networks using coding techniques," Univ. of Illinois, Urbana, CSL Rep. R-527, Oct. 1971.
[13] R. W. Sahni, "Reliability of integration circuits," in *Proc. IEEE Int. Comput. Group Conf.*, Washington, DC, June 1970, pp. 213-219.
[14] B. Parhami and A. Avizienis, "Detection of storage errors in mass memories using low-cost arithmetic error codes," *IEEE Trans. Comput.*, vol. C-27, pp. 302-308, Apr. 1978.
[15] D. K. Pradhan and J. J. Stiffler, "Error correcting codes and self-checking circuits in fault-tolerant computers," *Computer*, pp. 27-37, Mar. 1980.
[16] D. K. Pradhan and S. M. Reddy, "Fault tolerant-failsafe logic networks," in *Proc. IEEE COMPCON*, San Francisco, CA, Mar. 1977, pp. 361-363.
[17] T. R. N. Rao and A. S. Chawla, "Asymmetric error codes for some LSI semiconductor memories," in *Proc. Annu. Southeastern Symp. on Syst. Theory*, Mar. 1975, pp. 170-171.
[18] W. K. Kim and C. V. Freiman, "Single error correction codes for asymmetric channels," *IRE Trans. Inform. Theory*, pp. 62-66, June 1959.
[19] R. R. Varshamov, "Some features of linear codes that correct asymmetric errors," *Cybern. Contr. Theory*, vol. 9, pp. 538-540, Jan. 1965; also in *Dokl. Adad. Nauk SSSR*, vol. 157, pp. 546-548, July 1964.
[20] ——, "On the theory of asymmetric codes," *Cybern. Contr. Theory*, vol. 10, pp. 901-903, Apr. 1966; also in *Dokl. Akad. Nauk SSSR*, vol. 164, pp. 757-760, Oct. 1965.
[21] ——, "A class of codes for asymmetric channels and a problem from additive theory of numbers," *IEEE Trans. Inform. Theory*, vol. IT-19, pp. 92-95, Jan. 1973.
[22] S. D. Constantin and T. R. N. Rao, "Group theoretic codes for binary asymmetric channels," *Inform. Contr.*, vol. 40, pp. 20-26, Jan. 1979.
[23] J. M. Berger, "A note on error detecting codes for asymmetric channels," *Inform. Contr.*, vol. 4, pp. 68-73, Mar. 1961.
[24] C. V. Freiman, "Optimal error detection codes for completely asymmetric binary channel," *Inform. Contr.*, vol. 5, pp. 64-71, Mar. 1962.
[25] B. Bose and T. R. N. Rao., "Unidirectional error codes for shift register memories," presented at Int. Symp. on Fault-Tolerant Comput., Japan, Oct. 1980; and Dep. Comput. Sci. Eng., Southern Methodist Univ., Dallas, TX, Tech. Rep. CS 7917, Dec. 1979.
[26] B. Bose, "The theory and design of unidirectional error codes," Ph.D. dissertation, Southern Methodist Univ., Dallas, TX, May 1980.
[27] M. R. Best *et al.*, "Bounds for binary codes of length less than 25," *IEEE Trans. Inform. Theory*, vol. IT-24, pp. 81-93, Jan. 1978.
[28] W. H. Kautz and B. Elspas, "Single error-correcting codes for constant-weight data words," *IEEE Trans. Inform. Theory*, vol. IT-11, pp. 132-141, Jan. 1965.
[29] B. Bose and T. R. N. Rao, "On the theory of unidirectional error correcting/detecting codes," Dep. Comput. Sci. Eng., Southern Methodist Univ., Dallas, TX, CS 7817, Sept. 1978; and presented at Int. Symp. on Inform. Theory, Grignano, Italy, June 1979.
[30] R. L. Graham and N. J. A. Sloane, "Lower bounds for constant weight codes," *IEEE Trans. Inform. Theory*, vol. IT-26, pp. 37-43, Jan. 1980.
[31] D. K. Pradhan, "A new class of error-correcting/detecting codes for fault-tolerant computer applications," *IEEE Trans. Comput.*, vol. C-29, pp. 471-481, June 1980.

Bella Bose (S'77-M'80) received the B.E. degree in electrical engineering from Madras University in 1973, the M.E. degree in electrical engineering from the Indian Institute of Science, Bangalore, India, in 1975, and the M.S. and Ph.D. degrees in computer science from Southern Methodist University, Dallas, TX, in 1979 and 1980, respectively.

From September 1975 to December 1976 he was an Instructor in the Department of Electrical Engineering, Birla Institute of Technology and Science. Presently, he is an Assistant Professor in the Department of Computer Science, Oregon State University, Corvallis. His current research interests includes fault-tolerant computing, coding theory, computer architecture, and algorithm analysis.

Dr. Bose is a member of the Association for Computing Machinery.

Thammavaram R. N. Rao (S'62-M'67-SM'76) received the B.S. degree in physics from Andhra University, India in 1952, the D.I.I.Sc. degree from the Indian Institute of Science, Bangalore, India, in 1955, and the M.S. and Ph.D. degrees in electrical engineering from the University of Michigan, Ann Arbor, in 1961 and 1964, respectively.

He was a member of the Technical Staff of Bell Laboratories, Holmdel, NJ from 1964 to 1966, where he worked on the development of Electronic Switching System No. 1. He was also with the Department of Electrical Engineering, University of Maryland, College Park, from 1966 to 1975, and the Department of Computer Science, Southern Methodist University, Dallas, TX from 1975 to 1980. Presently, he is a Professor of Computer Science at the University of Southwestern Lousiana, Lafayette. His interests are in computer architecture, computer arithmetic, fault-tolerant computing, and coding theory.

Dr. Rao served as Distinguished Visitor of the IEEE Computer Society from 1972 to 1973. He is the author of *Error Coding for Arithmetic Processors* (New York: Academic, 1974).

MASKING ASYMMETRIC LINE FAULTS USING SEMI-DISTANCE CODES

Kazumitsu MATSUZAWA and Eiji FUJIWARA

NTT Communications and Information Processing Laboratories
Musashino-shi, Tokyo 180, Japan

Abstract

This paper proposes a new masking method for asymmetric line faults in LSIs using semi-distance codes, a class of non-linear codes. Faults caused by open or short circuit defects in line areas of LSIs can be made asymmetric by controlling the bus driver and the bus terminal gates. The conditions required for codes to mask these faults are clarified and the codes satisfying these conditions for random faults and adjacent faults, caused by line bridging defects, are constructed by using a new concept of semi-distance. This masking technique has the advantage that no additional circuits, such as error decoders, are needed. The codes have been applied to the bus lines in the address decoders of the 4-Mbit ROMs to improve fabrication yield of the LSIs.

1. INTRODUCTION

The use of error control codes, to achieve highly reliable computer systems or to improve fabrication yields of LSIs, is becoming an important design technique. Error correcting/detecting codes are used extensively in modern computer systems, especially in memory units [HSIA81].

The theory of symmetric error codes has been well developed [PETE72], where symmetric errors mean that both 1 → 0 and 0 → 1 errors can occur simultaneously in a single word. On the other hand, codes for unidirectional errors or asymmetric errors have been studied for VLSI memory systems or logic systems. Unidirectional errors have 0 → 1 or 1 → 0 errors, but both types of error do not appear simultaneously in a single word. Asymmetric errors have only one type of errors, say 0 → 1; the other type of errors, say 1 → 0, will never occur in any word. Thus, it is clear that asymmetric errors are a subclass of unidirectional errors, which in turn are a subclass of the symmetric errors.

The well-known unidirectional error detecting codes are nonsystematic constant-weight codes [FREI62] and systematic Berger codes [BERG61], which detect all unidirectional errors in a word. Recently, systematic t-unidirectional error detecting codes [DONG84] [BOSE85] [JHA87] and burst unidirectional error detecting codes [BOSE86] have been proposed. Furthermore, extended unidirectional error codes such as single symmetric error correcting and all unidirectional error detecting (SEC-AUED) codes [BOSE82a] [ITOH82], and more generally, t-error correcting and all unidirectional error detecting (tEC-AUED) codes [PRAD80] [BOSE82b] [NIKO86] have been proposed.

As for asymmetric error codes, there have been single asymmetric error correcting (SAEC) codes based on the theory of the Abelian group [CONS79], and codes based on a new concept of semi-distance, called semi-distance codes [IKEN71] [NAEM71] [NAKA72].

These unidirectional and asymmetric error codes have been proposed for power supply failure, stuck-at faults in shift register memories [BOSE84], and self-checking logic systems (using constant-weight codes or Berger codes [ANDE73] [MARO78] [NANY85]). Recently, optical communication where the signal is a definite photon number has been popular as a new communication technology. This communication channel is asymmetric, so using efficient asymmetric error codes should be considered [MCEL81] [BERG86] [HIRO86].

This paper proposes a unique application of these types of error codes to masking asymmetric faults in bus lines in LSIs whose open or short circuit faults have already been made asymmetric by controlling the bus driver and the bus terminal gates. The paper proposes an extended theory for masking these asymmetric errors, and demonstrates a practical application of these types of code to address bus lines in ROM LSIs.

Section 2 shows the principle of masking line faults using asymmetric error codes. Section 3 discusses codes that can mask these asymmetric faults, and evolves a theory of semi-distance codes. Section 4 shows code construction based on the theory in section 3 and proposes a new type of code, adjacent asymmetric error masking code. Section 5 demonstrates an application of the proposed codes to masking bus lines faults in ROM LSIs, and evaluates improvements in LSI yield.

2. MASKING ASYMMETRIC LINE FAULTS

In recent microprocessor LSIs, the area of bus lines has been increasing as word bit length increases. These lines commonly connect circuit elements, e.g., processing elements and memory elements. Therefore, defects or faults in these lines seriously influence the LSI yield and reliability.

Figure 1 shows a typical model of the bus line circuit. Information signals are sent on parallel bus lines. Several circuit elements, shown in Fig. 1 as circuit A to circuit X, which operate function such as AND and selection, work at positions on the bus lines to obtain the information from all or part of these lines. For example, in a memory address decoder of RAM or ROM LSIs, address information is sent on address bus lines, and only one decoder gate (AND gate), i.e., only one circuit element, is activated according to the information for a memory unit. In

Reprinted from *Proceedings FTCS-18*, 1988, pp. 354-359.

0-8186-4182-7/93 $3.00 © 1988 IEEE

this model, since the bus lines are often very long and occupy large chip areas in LSIs, the bus lines are vulnerable to manufacturing defects or noise. Therefore, technologies which tolerate these defects or faults are necessary to improve LSI yield and reliability.

Figure 2 shows a bus line circuit with defect masking, which consists of bus lines **L**, encoder **E**, and circuit elements, d_0 to d_{m-1}. Input information **I** is encoded into a code **C** by the encoder **E**, and then **C** is sent to the bus line **L**. The code **C** is designed to tolerate bus line faults. Each circuit element acts to mask these line faults as well as to operate the function that is originally required. Therefore, we call set of these circuit elements as decoder **D**. Finally, we can get correct outputs of this bus line circuit.

In the bus lines **L**, short-circuit and open-circuit defects often occur. These defects change the signal line into several levels, i.e., high, low, or medium. However, by controlling the bus driver and the bus terminal gate the level of faulty line can always be made either high or low. For example, for open-circuit defects in the bus lines, a pull-up transistor is added at the tip of the bus line to make the isolated part of the line electrically high. For short-circuit defects in the bus lines, the bus drivers are designed to maintain a high level on all bridged lines.

Figure 3 shows an example of the bus line circuit which can always maintain the faulty line at a high level even in the presence of open-circuit defects in a bus line. First, the timing signal T is set to a low level, and then the bus line is charged up to a high level by the bus terminal gate. Next, T is turned to a high level, and therefore the bus line level is fixed as the input signal level by the driver. Even if there is an open-circuit defect in the bus line, the isolated part of the line, i.e., the part from the open-circuit defect point to the end of the line, maintains a high level. This is due to current supplied from the bus terminal gate.

For short-circuit defects, the bus driver is designed to work in two steps. In the first step, the driver discharges the bus line. In the second step, the driver charges the bus line when the input signal level is high. When the level is low, the driver makes its output impedance high to maintain the bus line at a low level. Therefore, even if there is a short-circuit defect in the bus lines, the bridged lines are always charged up by the driver, i.e., maintained at a high level.

Such a fail-safe design achieves asymmetry in errors. The probability of '1'-errors ('1' becoming '0' errors) is made extremely small compared with '0'-errors ('0' becoming '1' errors). These defects can also make the line level only low by controlling the construction of the bus driver and the bus terminal gates. In this paper, we will mainly concentrate on '0'-errors.

These asymmetric faults can be masked by new coding techniques. Figure 4 illustrates an example of a bus line circuit which can mask single asymmetric '0'-errors in the bus lines. The decoder **D** consists of AND gates d_0 to d_3 corresponding to codewords V_0 to V_3 in code **C**, i.e., $\{V_0, V_1, V_2, V_3\} \in C$. Because each gate has transistors at the bus line where the element of the codeword is '1', the gate is only activated by receiving the corresponding codeword. In this paper, we consider the circuit elements of this bus line circuit, e.g., decoder gates d_0 to d_3, as AND gates.

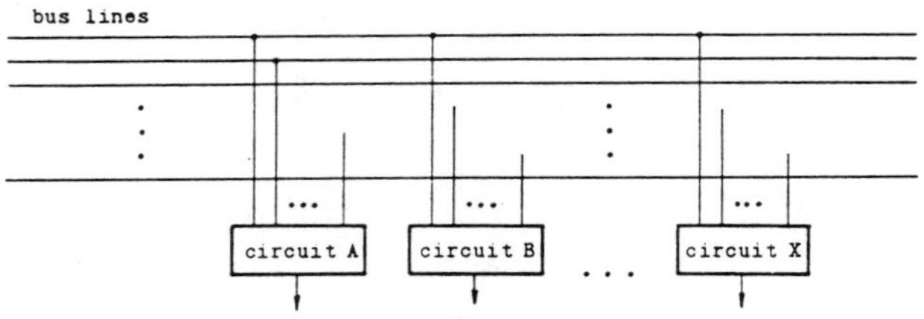

Figure 1. A typical model of bus line circuit

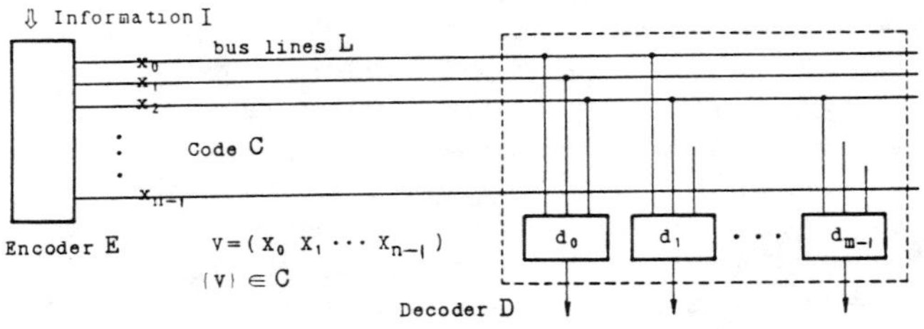

Figure 2. A bus line circuit with defect masking coding

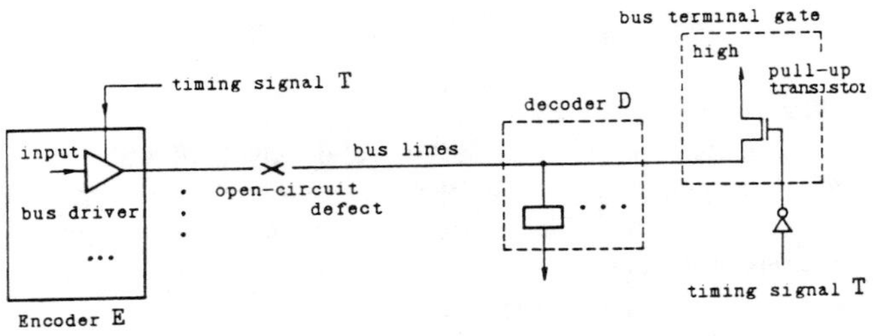

Figure 3. An example of an open-circuit defect in a bus line

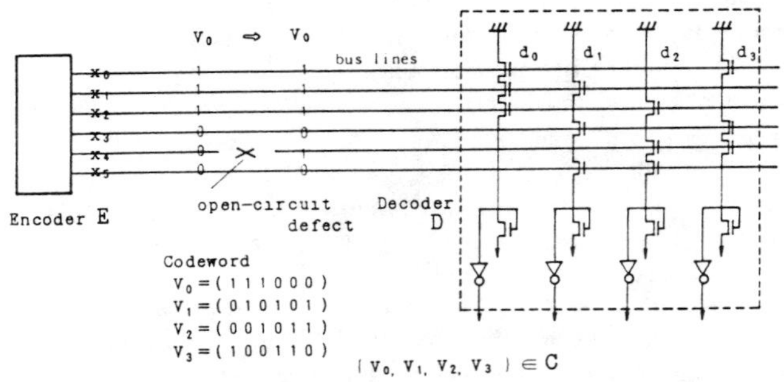

Figure 4. An example of a masking single asymmetric fault

This circuit can work correctly, even if there is a single asymmetric '0'-error in the bus lines. For example, we assume that information I is given and then encoded into codeword V_0 = (1 1 1 0 0 0). Furthermore, we assume that one '0'-error occurs in the fifth line x_4. The codeword V_0 is changed into V_0' = (1 1 1 0 1 0). However, only one AND gate d_0, which would originally be activated only by V_0 if there is no fault, is activated, because V_0' has '1's at the positions where V_0 has '1's, i.e., $x_0 = x_1 = x_2 =$'1'. The other AND gates d_1 to d_3 cannot be activated for V_0', because V_0' has at least one '0' at the position where V_1 to V_3 have '1', i.e., x_3 for V_1, V_3 and x_5 for V_2. Hence one asymmetric line fault never causes faulty activation and therefore it can be masked.

If the code C includes other words, for example, V_4 = (1 1 0 0 1 0) or V_5 = (1 0 1 0 1 0), the AND gates corresponding to these words are activated by V_0' incorrectly. This is because V_0' always has '1's at the positions where these words have '1's. V_4 or V_5 are said to be covered by V_0', or V_0' covers V_4 or V_5.

In general, when '0'-errors change the codeword Y into Y', any other codeword, say X, in C has to satisfy the next condition. This causes the bus line circuit to work correctly.

$$X \cdot \overline{Y'} \neq 0 \qquad (2\text{-}1)$$

This equation shows that there are one or more cases where X has '1' at the position where Y' has '0'.

Generally, since the bus lines are coded into an asymmetric error masking code, no wrong circuit output is given even in the presence of bus faults. This masking technique has the big advantage that no additional circuits, except for bus terminal gates and additional bus lines, are needed for masking these faults. That is, the output of the bus line circuit is always correct, in spite of errors, without explicitly using an error correction circuit.

3. SEMI-DISTANCE CODES

We introduce a new concept of semi-distance that fits to the condition shown in Eq. (2-1) in the previous section, and the codes, called semi-distance codes, based on the concept. Further, we extend the codes to error masking codes that can mask unidirectional errors as well as asymmetric errors.

Let arbitrary two n-tuple words in a set C be shown as follows:

$$X = (x_0, x_1, \ldots\ldots, x_{n-1})$$
$$Y = (y_0, y_1, \ldots\ldots, y_{n-1})$$

Definition 1 [IKEN71]:

The semi-distance d_s of any two different words X and Y in C is defined as:

$$d_s(X, Y) = \sum_{\substack{i=0 \\ X,\, Y \in C}}^{n-1} x_i \cdot \overline{y_i}. \qquad (3\text{-}1)$$

Theorem 1 [IKEN 71]:

The semi-distance d_s satisfies the following relations for any different words X, Y and Z in C :

(1) $d_s(X, X) = 0$

(2) $d_s(X, Y) \geq 0$

(3) $d_s(X, Y) + d_s(Y, Z) \geq d_s(X, Z)$

(4) If $d_s(X, Y) = d_s(Y, X) = 0$, then X = Y.

Although d_s itself is not a distance under the above relations, it clearly satisfies the concept of distance if the following condition is added.

(5) $d_s(X, Y) = d_s(Y, X)$

The semi-distance defined in above Eq. (3-1) just fits to the condition of Eq. (2-1) considered in the previous section.

As for relation between the Hamming distance $d_H(X, Y)$ and the semi-distance $d_s(X, Y)$, we have the following properties:

Property 1: $d_H(X, Y) = d_s(X, Y) + d_s(Y, X)$

Property 2: If $d_s(X, Y) = d_s(Y, X)$, then $d_H(X, Y) = 2 \cdot d_s(X, Y) = 2 \cdot d_s(Y, X)$, and X, Y are constant-weight words.

Property 3: $d_s(X, Y) = d_s(\overline{Y}, \overline{X})$

Definition 2 [IKEN71]:

The minimum semi-distance d_{sm} of any two words X and Y in C is defined as

$$d_{sm} = \min \{ d_s(X, Y) \}$$

Definition 3 [IKEN71]

The semi-distance code with d_{sm} is defined as the set of words, C, having minimum semi-distance d_{sm}.

Definition 4:

A code C is defined as an error masking code, more exactly as an asymmetric '0'-error masking code, if for all X $\in$ C, the erroneous word X', i. e., X' = X $\oplus$ E, E: '0'-error (0→1 error) pattern, never covers any other codewords in C.

It is apparent that we can also define an asymmetric '1'-error masking code for '1'-error (1→0 error) pattern.

Theorem 2:

A code C with d_{sm} = t can mask (t − 1) asymmetric errors.

This can be easily proved from the example below.

Example 1:

The following set of words is equal to the semi-distance code with a code length of 10 and d_{sm} = 3:

V_0 = (1 1 1 1 1 0 0 0 0 0) V_3 = (0 0 0 1 1 1 1 0 1 0)
V_1 = (1 1 0 0 0 1 1 1 0 0) V_4 = (0 1 0 1 0 0 0 1 1 1)
V_2 = (1 0 1 0 0 1 0 0 1 1) V_5 = (0 0 1 0 1 0 1 1 0 1)

Assume that there are double asymmetric erros in V_2, for example, two '0'-errors ('0' becoming '1' errors) at the fifth and the eighth bits of the codeword V_2, i.e., $V_2' = V_2 \oplus E$ = (1 0 1 0 1 1 0 1 1 1), where error pattern E = (0 0 0 0 1 0 0 1 0 0). The word V_2' never covers any other codewords, i.e., $V_2' \not> V_0, V_1, V_3, V_4, V_5$. Therefore even if there are double asymmetric errors at any bit places in the codeword, the resultant word, i.e., erroneous word, does not cover any other codewords. This relation holds for all codewords in the above set. Hence, the semi-distance code with d_{sm} = 3 can mask random double asymmetric errors ('0'-errors). Therefore, this code is called a double asymmetric error ('0'-error) masking code.

In the above example, we can see that the erroneous word with two '1'-errors ('1' becoming '0' errors) is never covered by any other codewords. From this, we will consider the relationship between the codes that can mask asymmetric errors and the codes that can mask unidirectional errors.

Theorem 3:

A semi-distance code C with d_{sm} = t can mask (t −1) unidirectional errors.

Proof: Consider two codewords $X = (x_0, x_1, \ldots, x_{n-1})$ and $Y = (y_0, y_1, \ldots, y_{n-1})$ in C. We can assume that $d_s(X, Y)$ = t and $d_s(Y, X)$ = t + a, a ≥ 0, without loss of generality. Even if there exist (t − 1) '0'-errors in Y, Y never covers X. Also even if there exist (t − 1) '1'-errors in X, X is never covered by Y.

These are due to $d_s(X, Y) = t$. For other cases of $(t - 1)$ '0'-errors and '1'-errors, these relations are apparently valid because $d_s(Y, X) = t + a, a \geq 0$. This proves the above proposition. Q.E.D.

From these theorems, the semi-distance code with $d_{sm} = t$ can mask $(t - 1)$ unidirectional errors as well as $(t - 1)$ asymmetric errors.

4. CODE CONSTRUCTION

Systematic implementation of the semi-distance codes has been proposed by using the concept of block deisgn (BIBD), Hadamard Matrices, finite projective geometries, Mathieu groups, and orthogonal arrays [IKEN71] [NAEM71]. These are non-systematic constant-weight codes.

Constant-weight semi-distance codes are conjectured to be optimal in the sense that they have a maximum number of codewords [NAKA72]. From this standpoint, in this paper, we will concentrate on the implementation of the constant-weight semi-distance codes.

We have to clarify the code conditions necessary for masking line faults economically and with better yield.

1. To minimize the number of transistors in the decoder of the bus line circuit shown in Fig. 4, the codes should have minimum weight.
2. To minimize the number of bus lines, the number of codewords should be maximum.
3. Consideration is needed about the fault cases of bridging faults in the bus lines that cause to adjacent asymmetric errors.

The optimal codes that satisfy conditions 1 and 2 have minimum weight and the maximum number of codewords. In condition 3, we will also have to consider another type of code, adjacent asymmetric error masking codes which also satisfy conditions 1 and 2. Hence we will investigate the codes with minimum weight which mask two types of asymmetric errors, i.e., random single asymmetric errors and adjacent asymmetric errors.

(1) Random Asymmetric Error Masking Codes

Let $N(n, w, t)$ denote the number of codewords of a semi-distance code with length n, constant-weight w and $d_{sm} = t$.

Theorem 4 [IKEN71]:

The maximum number of codewords of the $d_{sm} = 2$ semi-distance codes with constant-weight w $(w \leq [n/2])$ is given by

$$N_{max}(n, w, 2) = {}_nC_w/(n - w + 1), \qquad (4\text{-}1)$$

where $[z]$ is the largest integer less than or equal to z, and ${}_xC_y$ expresses the combinations of y taken out of x.

Table 1 shows N_{max} for n and w. N_{max} can apparently be made maximum for $w = [n/2]$. According to conditions 1 and 2, we have to choose the optimum code in the table that has minimum weight and a large enough number of codewords.

Figure 5 shows some examples of the semi-distance code with $d_{sm} = 2$.

We can also derive the semi-distance codes with $d_{sm} = 2$ from the Hamming codes. The number of codewords of the Hamming code with $d_H = 4$ and weight w, i.e., Hamming distance four code with constant-weight w, is given from the weight distribution or the weight spectrum of the code [PETE72] by

$$N(n, w, d_{sm}=2) = \{ {}_nC_w + (n - 1)\, {}_wC_w/2 \} /n. \qquad (4\text{-}2)$$

The ratio of $N(n, w, d_{sm}=2)$ of Eq. (4-2) to N_{max} of Eq. (4-1) tends to 1/2 as n gets larger, i.e., $\lim_{n \to \infty} \{ N(n, w, d_{sm}=2)/N_{max} \} = 1/2$.

Table 1. Maximum number of codewords $N_{max}(n,W,2)$

n \ w	2	3	4	5	6	7	8
4	2	-	-	-	-	-	-
5	2	-	-	-	-	-	-
6	3	5	-	-	-	-	-
7	3	7	-	-	-	-	-
8	4	9	14	-	-	-	-
9	4	12	21	-	-	-	-
10	5	15	30	42	-	-	-
11	5	18	41	66	-	-	-
12	6	22	55	99	132	-	-
13	6	26	71	143	214	-	-
14	7	30	91	200	333	429	-
15	7	35	113	273	500	715	-
16	8	40	140	364	728	1144	1430

$n = 7, w = 3$

V_0 = (1110000)
V_1 = (1001100)
V_2 = (1000011)
V_3 = (0101010)
V_4 = (0100101)
V_5 = (0011001)
V_6 = (0010110)

$n = 8, w = 4$

V_0 = (11110000)
V_1 = (00001111)
V_2 = (11001100)
V_3 = (00110011)
V_4 = (11000011)
V_5 = (00111100)
V_6 = (10101010)
V_7 = (01010101)
V_8 = (10100101)
V_9 = (01011010)
V_{10} = (10011010)
V_{11} = (01100110)
V_{12} = (10010110)
V_{13} = (01101001)

$n = 10, w = 5$

V_0 = (1100100101)
V_1 = (1010001110)
V_2 = (1001010011)
V_3 = (0110110010)
V_4 = (0101011100)
V_5 = (0011101001)
V_6 = (1100011010)
V_7 = (1010110001)
V_8 = (1001101100)
V_9 = (0110001101)
V_{10} = (0101100011)
V_{11} = (0011010110)
V_{12} = (1011100010)
V_{13} = (1101001001)
V_{14} = (1110010100)
V_{15} = (0001110101)
V_{16} = (0010011011)
V_{17} = (0100101110)
V_{18} = (0111010001)
V_{19} = (0001111010)
V_{20} = (0010100111)
V_{21} = (1101000110)
V_{22} = (1110101000)
V_{23} = (1000011101)
V_{24} = (0001001111)
V_{25} = (0111100100)
V_{26} = (0100111001)
V_{27} = (1011011000)
V_{28} = (1000110110)
V_{29} = (1110000011)
V_{30} = (0010111100)
V_{31} = (0100010111)
V_{32} = (0111001010)
V_{33} = (1000101011)
V_{34} = (1011000101)
V_{35} = (1101110000)

Figure 5. Some examples of semi-distance codes with $d_{sm} = 2$

(2) Adjacent Asymmetric Error Masking Codes

First, with using an easy example of the adjacent assymmetric error masking codes, we will clarify how an adjacent asymmetric error influences the codeword. The following set of codewords expresses an adjacent asymmetric error masking code with $n = 5$ and $w = 2$.

V_0 = (1 0 1 0 0) V_2 = (0 0 1 0 1)
V_1 = (0 1 0 1 0) V_3 = (1 0 0 0 1)

If there is a bridging '0'-error (a single short '0'-error) at the third and the second bits in V_2, then the erroneous word will be $V_2{}'$ = (0 $\underline{1}$ 1 0 1), that is, the second bit '0', adjacent to the third bit

'1', is changed to '1'. In general, a bridging '0'-error changes the bit, which is adjacent to the original bit having '1', from '0' to '1'. In this example, the erroneous word V_2' never covers any other words. This holds for the cases at any bit position with a value of '1' in the codeword.

The theoretical derivation of this type of codes is not yet established. We obtained these by computer search. Table 2 shows the number of codewords obtained to date. The numbers marked with * are the maximum numbers of codewords and the others are still being calculated. As a result, we can get a larger number of codewords with smaller weight, compared to those of the random asymmetric error masking codes shown in Table 1. This property suits our previously mentioned requirements.

Examples of the codes obtained are shown in Fig. 6. It should be noted that these codes are asymmetric error ('0'-error) masking codes, not unidirectional error masking codes.

5. APPLICATION TO ROM FOR YIELD IMPROVEMENT

The masking method proposed in this paper has been applied to 4-Mbit ROM LSIs, used as KANJI character generator. Since this LSI is fabricated on a very large chip, i.e., 34×21 mm^2, effective defect-tolerant technologies are needed to improve fabrication yield [KOHD86] [KIKU86].

Figure 7 shows a photomicrograph of the ROM, which has comparatively long address bus lines. Bus line defects are tolerated by applying defect tolerant address decoders with asymmetric error masking codes to two bus line circuits in the ROM. One circuit is for 1-out-of-16 memory unit selection, and the other circuit is for 1-out-of-32 word line selection. The bus lines are designed to make the defects asymmetric, i.e., the level of faulty line is always high (see section 2).

For masking single asymmetric faults, the code with $d_{sm} = 2$ is needed. The number of codewords should be equal to or larger than the number of circuit outputs, i.e., 16 and 32 in the above bus line circuits. The codeword length and the weight should be small in order to reduce the number of bus lines and transistors. According to the fault analysis of this ROM, the probability of short-circuit faults to adjacent bus lines is larger than the probability of random short-circuit faults or open-circuit faults. Therefore, the adjacent asymmetric error masking codes, i.e., the code with n=9 and w=2 for memory unit selection and the code with n=10 and w=4 for word line selection, can be chosen from Table 2. These codes are shown in Fig. 6.

In general, $2 \times m$ bus lines are necessary to select one out of $M=2^m$ outputs in ordinary bus line circuits, e.g., address decoders. This is because ordinary m and its complement m signal lines are needed. Therefore, 8 bus lines are needed to select one out of 16 circuit outputs, and 10 bus lines are needed to select one out of 32 circuit outputs. Table 3 compares the number of bus lines for M in ordinary bus line circuits with the number of bus lines in defect-tolerant bus line circuits having random asymmetric error masking codes with d_{sm}. It should be noted that there are cases, marked with * in the table, in which the number of bus lines in defect-tolerant bus line circuits is smaller than that in ordinary bus line circuits. This technique can also be applied to PLA AND plane, considering that the output number of PLA input decoders can be reduced.

Table 2. Number of codewords of the adjacent asymmetric error masking codes

n \ w	2	3	4	5	6
4	2*	.	.	.	.
5	4*	2*	.	.	.
6	6*	4*	.	.	.
7	9*	7*	7*	.	.
8	12*	11*	14	.	.
9	16*	15	20	16	.
10	20*	23	33	29	.
11	25*	33	50	50	46
12	30*	49	73	81	89

*: maximum number of codewords

n = 9 and w = 2	n = 10 and w = 4	
V_0 = (101000000)	V_0 = (1111000000)	V_{16} = (0110100001)
V_1 = (010100000)	V_1 = (1100110000)	V_{17} = (0110011000)
V_2 = (001010000)	V_2 = (1100001100)	V_{18} = (0101101000)
V_3 = (000101000)	V_3 = (1100000011)	V_{19} = (0101100010)
V_4 = (000010100)	V_4 = (1010101000)	V_{20} = (0101010100)
V_5 = (000001010)	V_5 = (1010100010)	V_{21} = (0101010001)
V_6 = (000000101)	V_6 = (1010010100)	V_{22} = (0101000101)
V_7 = (100010000)	V_7 = (1010100001)	V_{23} = (0011110000)
V_8 = (010001000)	V_8 = (1010001010)	V_{24} = (0011001100)
V_9 = (001000100)	V_9 = (1010000101)	V_{25} = (0011000011)
V_{10} = (000100010)	V_{10} = (1001100100)	V_{26} = (0010101010)
V_{11} = (000010001)	V_{11} = (1001100001)	V_{27} = (0010010101)
V_{12} = (100000100)	V_{12} = (1001011000)	V_{28} = (0001101001)
V_{13} = (010000010)	V_{13} = (1000101010)	V_{29} = (0001011010)
V_{14} = (001000001)	V_{14} = (1000010101)	V_{30} = (0000111100)
V_{15} = (100000001)	V_{15} = (0110100100)	V_{31} = (0000110011)
		V_{32} = (0000001111)

Figure 6. Examples of adjacent asymmetric error ('0'-error) masking codes

maximum length bus lines (10 + 9 lines)

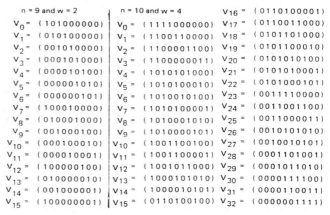

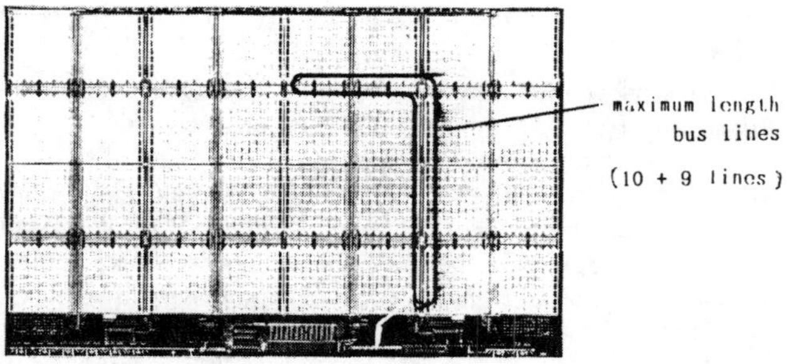

Figure 7. Photomicrograph of the 4-Mbit ROM (34x21mm^2)

Table 3. Comparison of the number of bus lines

Number of circuit outputs M (k=1024)		16	32	64	128	256	512	1k	2k	4k	8k	16k
Number of bus line in ordinary bus line circuit		8	10	12	14	16	18	20	22	24	26	28
Number of bus lines in defect-tolerant bus line circuit	Code with d_{sm}= 2	9	10	11*	12*	14*	15*	16*	17*	18*	19*	20*
	d_{sm}= 3	11	12	14	15	16	18	19*	20*	21*	22*	23*
	d_{sm} 4	14	15	16	18	19	20	21	22	24	25*	26*

In the defect-tolerant bus line circuit, an encoder is needed to encode the input information. As area of the encoder is less than 1% of that of the bus lines, defects in the encoder only slightly influence the total yield of the LSI chip.

We will now investigate yield improvement of the defect-tolerant bus line circuit. We assume that defects occur according to a Poisson distribution. Furthermore, we assume that the LSI yield with area A′ is p′. Then yield p of an LSI with area A can be expressed as

$$p = p'^{\,A/A'}. \qquad (5\text{-}1)$$

Let P be the yield of the defect-tolerant bus line circuit with asymmetric error codes which have length n and minimum semi-distance d_{sm}. Let p′ be the yield of the ordinary bus line circuit with n′=2m bus lines. Then P can be expressed as follows:

$$P = \left(\sum_{i=0}^{d_{sm}-1} {}_{n}C_{i}\, p^{n-i} (1-p)^{i} \right) p^{nr} \qquad (5\text{-}2)$$

where $p = p'^{1/n'}$, and r is the ratio of the area of the encoder to that of the bus lines.

Figure 8 shows the yield of a defect tolerant bus line circuit with codes that have parameters n=10, w=4, and d_{sm}=2 against the yield of an ordinary bus line circuit with n′=10. This figure shows that the yield of the defect-tolerant bus line circuit is superior to the yield of the ordinary bus line circuit in the range of $r \leq 0.5$. For example, the yield can be improved by 30% at the point r=0.1 and p′=0.5 of the ordinary bus line circuit.

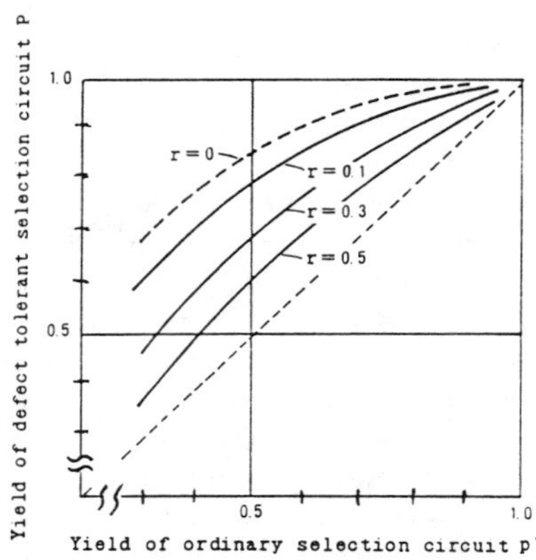

Figure 8. Yield of the bus line circuit by using defect masking method

6. CONCLUSION

This paper has proposed a unique application of asymmetric error codes to fault toleration in bus lines. Faults caused by open or short circuit defects in these lines can be made asymmetric by controlling the bus drivers and the bus terminal gates. These asymmetric faults are tolerated by using new codes based on a concept of semi-distance.

This paper introduces the semi-distance code and extends this as the error masking code. The semi-distance code with d_{sm} = t is shown to mask (t − 1) unidirectional errors as well as (t − 1) asymmetric errors. To mask bridging bus line faults, this paper has shown the necessity of adjacent asymmetric error masking codes. Some optimal codes are proposed and these are actually applied to address bus lines in ROM LSIs, and are also applicable to PLAs.

The masking technique proposed in this paper has the unique feature that no error correction circuits are needed, and therefore additional circuits are very small.

Theoretical analysis and the systematic derivation of adjacent asymmetric error masking codes remain as future studies.

ACKNOWLEDGMENT

The authors would like to express their gratitude to Professor F.P. Preparata of University of Illinois for his comments on the use of the constant-weight distance-four Hamming code for short-circuit protection.

REFERENCE

[ANDE73] D.A. Anderson and G. Metze, 'Design of Totally Self-Checking Check Circuits for m-Out-of-n Codes,' IEEE Trans. Comput., vol. C-22, pp.263-269, Mar. 1973

[BERG61] J.M. Berger, 'A Note on Error Detecting Codes for Asymmetric Channels,' Inform. & Contr., vol. 4, pp. 68-73, Mar. 1961

[BERG86] E.E. Bergmann, A.M. Odlyzko and S.H. Sangani, 'Half Weight Block Codes for Optical Communication,' AT&T Tech. J., vol. 65, pp. 85-93, May/June 1986

[BOSE82a] B. Bose and T.R.N. Rao, 'Theory of Unidirectional Error Correcting/Detecting Codes,' IEEE Trans. Comput., vol. C-31, pp. 521-530, June 1982

[BOSE82b] B. Bose and D.K. Pradhan, 'Optimal Unidirectional Error Detecting/Correcting Codes,' IEEE Trans. Comput., vol. C-31, pp. 564-568, June 1982

[BOSE84] B. Bose and T.R.N. Rao, 'Unidirectional Error Codes for Shift-Register Memories,' IEEE Trans. Comput., vol. C-33, pp. 575-578, June 1984

[BOSE85] B. Bose and D.J. Lin, 'Systematic Unidirectional Error-Detecting Codes,' IEEE Trans. Comput., vol. C-34, pp. 1026-1032, Nov., 1985

[BOSE86] B. Bose, 'Burst Unidirectional Error-Detecting Codes,' IEEE Trans. Comput., vol. C-35, pp. 350-353, April 1986

[CONS79] S.D. Constantin and T.R.N. Rao, 'On the Theory of Binary Asymmetric Error Correcting Codes,' Infor. & Contr., vol. 40, pp. 20-26, Jan. 1979

[DONG84] H. Dong, 'Modified Berger Codes for Detection of Unidirectional Errors,' IEEE Trans. Comput. vol. C-33, pp. 572-575, June 1984

[FREI62] C.V. Freiman, 'Optimal Error Detection Codes for Completely Asymmetirc Binary Channels,' Infor. & Contr., vol. 5, pp. 64-71, 1962

[HIRO86] O. Hirota, K. Yamazaki, M. Nakagawa and M. Ohya, 'Properties of Error Correcting Code Using Photon Pulse' Trans. IECE Japan, vol. E69, pp. 917-919, Sept., 1986

[HSIA81] M.Y. Hsiao, W.C. Carter, J.W. Thomas and W.R. Stringfellow, 'Reliability, Availability and Serviceability of IBM Computer Systems: A Quarter Century of Progress,' IBM J. Res. Develop., vol. 25, pp. 453-465, Sept., 1981

[IKEN71] K. Ikeno and G. Nakamura, 'Constant-Weight Codes,' (in Japanese) Trans. IECE Japan, vol. 54-A, pp. 410-417, July 1971

[ITOH82] H. Itoh and M. Nakamichi, 'A Construction of Single Error Correcting and Multiple Unidirectional Error Detecting Codes,' (in Japanese) Trans. IECE Japan, vol. J65-A, pp. 934-941, Sept., 1982

[JHA87] N.K. Jha and M.B. Vora, 'A Systematic Code for Detecting t-Unidirectional Errors,' Dig., 17th Annu. Int. Symp. Fault-Tolerant Comput., pp. 96-101, 1987

[KIKU86] H. Kikuchi, K. Matsuzawa and S. Kohda, 'A Study of Defect-Tolerant Technologies in Wafer-Scale Integrated ROMs,' Paper of Technical Group FTS86-12, IECE Japan, Sept., 1986

[KOHD86] S. Kohda, K. Masuda, K. Matsuzawa and Y. Kitano, 'A Giant Chip Multigate Transistor ROM Circuit Design,' IEEE J. of Solid-State Circuit, vol. SC-21, no. 5, pp. 713-719, Oct., 1986

[MARO78] M.A. Marouf and A.D. Friedman, 'Design of Self-Checking Checkers for Berger Codes,' Dig., 8th Annu. Int. Symp. Fault-Tolerant Comput., pp. 179-184, 1978

[MCEL81] R.J. McEliece, 'Practical Codes for Photon Communication,' IEEE Trans. Infor. Theory, vol. IT-27, no. 4, pp. 393-398, July 1981

[NAEM71] K. Naemura, G. Nakamura and N. Ikeno, 'Constant-Weight Codes and Block Designs,' (in Japanese) Trans. IECE Japan, vol. 54-A, pp. 671-678, Dec., 1971

[NAKA72] G. Nakamura, N. Ikeno and K. Naemura, 'Optimality of Constant-Weight Codes,' (in Japanese) Trans. IECE Japan, vol. 55-A, pp. 354-359, July 1972

[NANY85] T. Nanya and T. Kawamura, 'Error Secure/Error Propagating Concept and Its Application to the Design of Strongly Fault Secure Processors,' Dig., 15th Annu. Int. Symp. Fault-Tolerant Comput., pp. 396-401, June 1985

[NIKO86] D. Nikolos, N. Gaitanis and G. Philokyprou, 'Systematic t-Error Correcting/All Unidirectional Error Detecting Codes,' IEEE Trans. Comput., vol. C-35, pp. 394-402, May 1986

[PETE72] W.W. Peterson and E.J. Weldon, Jr., Error Correcting Codes, Second Edition, MIT Press 1972

[PRAD80] D.K. Pradhan, 'A New Class of Error-Correcting/Detecting Codes for Fault-Tolerant Computer Applications,' IEEE Trans. Comput., vol. C-29, pp. 471-481, June 1980

CHAPTER 2: CODES FOR DETECTING UNIDIRECTIONAL ERRORS

This chapter addresses codes for detecting unidirectional errors, a problem equivalent to finding a maximal collection of unordered sets. For example, consider a binary vector $\mathbf{X} = a_1, a_2, \ldots, a_n$. The set of coordinates in which **X** is 1 is called the support of **X**. For example, if **X** = 1 1 0 0 1, then the support of **X** is {1,2,5}. We say that a vector **X** is contained in a vector **Y** (notation, $\mathbf{X} \subseteq \mathbf{Y}$) if the support of **X** is contained in the support of **Y**. For instance, if **X** is the vector above and **Y** = 1 1 1 0 1, then $\mathbf{X} \subseteq \mathbf{Y}$. This discussion enables us to define unidirectional errors simply: Assume that **X** is a transmitted vector and **Y** is a received vector corresponding to the transmission of **X**. We say that **X** has suffered unidirectional errors if (and only if) either $\mathbf{X} \subseteq \mathbf{Y}$ or $\mathbf{Y} \subseteq \mathbf{X}$. It is clear from this definition that, if we want to construct a code that can detect all unidirectional errors, then no code word can be contained in another code word. Given two vectors — **X** and **Y** — we categorize **X** and **Y** as unordered if neither is contained in the other. We categorize a code as unordered if any two code words are unordered. Therefore, a code is AUED if (and only if) it is unordered.

This said, the question naturally follows — What is an unordered code of length n and maximal size? Which is equivalent to asking — What is a collection of unordered subsets of $1,2,\ldots,n$ of maximal size (a collection of unordered subsets is usually called an "antichain")? Sperner answered this question in 1928:[30] An antichain of maximal size is given either by all the subsets of cardinality $\lfloor \frac{n}{2} \rfloor$ or by all the subsets of cardinality $\lceil \frac{n}{2} \rceil$ (given a number x, $\lfloor x \rfloor$ denotes the largest integer smaller than or equal to x, and $\lceil x \rceil$ the smallest integer larger than or equal to x). In vector terminology, an optimal unordered code is given by all the vectors of (Hamming) weight $\lfloor \frac{n}{2} \rfloor$ (or by all the vectors of weight $\lceil \frac{n}{2} \rceil$). The vector set of weight $\lfloor \frac{n}{2} \rfloor$ is commonly called the set of balanced vectors of weight $\lfloor \frac{n}{2} \rfloor$. Our references identify more detailed reading for some proofs of Sperner's theorem and its generalizations (in particular, Anderson's first chapter).[24] In applications, however, encoding a set of vectors into the set of balanced vectors is difficult. One approach for constructing AUED codes uses systematic codes (also called separable codes by some authors). A systematic code has r redundant bits separated from k information bits. In AUED codes, we want to add redundancy to k information bits such that the resulting code is unordered.

That problem was solved by Berger, whose result is contained in this chapter's first paper. Berger's construction is fairly simple: Redundancy is shown as the number of 0's in the information portion, written as a binary number. For example, if k=7, the information vector 1 0 0 1 0 1 1 is encoded as 1 0 0 1 0 1 1 0 1 1.

Freiman proves that Berger's construction is optimal, in the sense that the redundancy obtained using Berger's procedure is the shortest one that "unorders" the k information bits. Notice that the redundancy is in the order of $\log_2 k$ bits. Our references cite other work on Berger code types,[31,32] in addition to a generalization of Berger's code over Z_q (the digit set $\{0,1,\ldots,q-1\}$.[21]

Borden constructs an optimal code that can detect up to t unidirectional (or asymmetric) errors — an interesting theoretical result that we can view as a natural generalization of Sperner's lemma, which gives an optimal code for detecting all unidirectional errors. The author also considers extensions to the q-ary asymmetric channel introduced in 1973 by Varshamov.[33]

Bose and Lin studied the same problem as Borden — but from the viewpoint of systematic codes, which are more application relevant. The optimality of the Bose-Lin construction (in the Berger sense) is still an open problem. Our references cite related work and other papers dealing with the detection of unidirectional errors in applications.[34-37]

For certain applications, we might want to encode an information vector into a balanced vector. For example, balanced vectors may be used to keep data integrity in optical disks against hostile changes of information.[38] Other applications are in state assignments for fault-tolerant sequential circuit design,[39] fiber optics,[40,41] and magnetic recording.[40] Another recent application addresses noise reduction in VLSI systems.[42]

Knuth concludes Chapter 2 with a general method for encoding an information vector into a balanced vector by using a set of control vectors. Knuth's code redundancy resembles the redundancy of Berger codes. Knuth's set of control vectors is optimal, in the sense that it contains no smaller set of balancing vectors.[43] Knuth gives a serial decoding scheme with $k=2^r$ information bits and r redundant bits, and a parallel decoding scheme with $k=2^r-r-1$ information bits and r redundant bits. Bose improves on Knuth's results, presenting r redundant bits, a serial decoding scheme with $k=2^{r+1}-(r+2)$ information bits, and a parallel scheme with $k=2^r$ bits.[44] Our references provide more detail on this topic,[45,46] and also more work on balanced codes with error correction.[47-49]

A Note on Error Detection Codes for Asymmetric Channels

J. M. Berger

IBM Advanced Systems Development Division, Ossining Laboratory, Yorktown Heights, N. Y.

Some new codes are described which are separable and are perfect error detection codes in a completely asymmetric channel. Some results are given of comparisons between one simple form of the code in which the check bits correspond to the sum of ones in the information bits and the four out of eight code. The new code is found to compare favorably in error detection capability in several cases. In addition, some more complex codes of this type are indicated.

I. INTRODUCTION

Recently the fixed weight codes, notably the four out of eight, have been adopted as transmission codes in some communication systems. One of the main reasons given for their adoption has been their advantages in a communication channel that is asymmetric to a large degree, because in a completely asymmetric channel, the fixed weight code is a perfect error detecting code. A completely asymmetric channel is one in which only one type of error occurs, either only zeroes converted to ones or only ones converted to zeros. In a binary symmetric channel (i.e., both types of errors equally likely), the fixed weight codes will detect all odd numbers of errors and will only fail to detect those even errors that correspond to an interchange of zeros with ones, i.e., a zero being changed into a one compensated by a one in the same code word being changed into a zero. For a given word length, the optimum fixed weight code also has in general more valid code word combinations than does a separable code of equivalent error detection ability.

The major disadvantage of the fixed weight code is the fact that it is nonseparable, where by separability we mean that the bits containing the information to be transmitted and the bits provided for error detection are distinct. In the fixed weight code, it is the pattern that provides the error detection facility and as such, short of a code conversion, it is impossible to separate off the redundant bits. The result of this lack of separability is that effectively, the information bits of the code and the error detection capability are inextricably bound up together and modification of the code in a system cannot be simply made. For example, in the typical use of a fixed weight code, the basic alphabet of the system would first be established and then the appropriate fixed weight code with a sufficient number of valid code word combinations would be selected, each fixed weight code word then corresponding to a particular symbol in the alphabet. The disadvantage of this type of assignment arises in the case where it is customary to transmit a string of symbols. Since the redundancy is already in each symbol, it is not possible to take advantage of the economies that would be allowed by coding over the whole string of symbols. Thus, it appears that a separable code has the advantages over a nonseparable code of greater flexibility in the system and the possibility of greater economy, particularly in coding over large blocks of information. The question remains as to whether this relative advantage can be maintained in an asymmetric channel.

It is our purpose here to describe some codes that are separable and which also detect all possible errors in a completely asymmetric channel. We will describe one simple such code in detail and give the results of comparison of some of its features with a fixed weight code. We will then indicate some other codes of this type that can be constructed and that have some additional properties.

II. DESCRIPTION OF SUM CODES

We consider a set of $n - k$ information bits and k check bits. We form the binary number corresponding to the number of ones in the $n - k$ information bits and take the binary complement of each digit in this number; i.e., change all zeros to ones and all ones to zeros. This resultant binary number is the k check bits.[1] (As an alternative, we might use for the k check bits the binary number that corresponds to the sum of the zeroes in the $n - k$ information bits. This is fully equivalent and might be simpler to implement.) Thus, k is equal to the smallest integer that contains $\log_2 (n - k)$. The $n - k$ information bits are any

[1] This particular code has been independently suggested by H. J. Smith, Jr. and also C. Freiman in private communications.

string of bits that are decided upon. They might be one six-bit character, in which case $k = 3$; they might be six eight-bit characters, in which case $k = 6$, etc. As a particular example, consider the case for $n = 9$, $k = 3$. One such valid code word would be,

k check	$n - k$ information bits
(100	011010)

We will indicate these codes by the symbol $\Sigma(k, n - k)$.

In the completely asymmetric channel, either only ones are changed to zeros or vice versa. Consider first ones changed to zeros. Then, the number of ones in the information bits must (if an error occurs) decrease; therefore, the number, which is the sum of the received ones and which must check with the number represented by the check bits, is smaller. In the received k check bits each digit is again complemented and the resultant binary number is used for comparison. If ones had been changed to zeros in transmission, the received k bits would have more zeros and the resultant binary number after complementation would have more ones and would necessarily be larger than the original check sum. Thus, for this type of error, the sum derived from the received information bits is always smaller than the number representing the sum derived from the check bits, if any errors occur. In a similar fashion, all errors will be detected if the nature of the error is to change zeros into ones. In Table I, a detailed example of the complete process is given. Thus, it may be seen that for any $n - k$ information bits, with the k check bits chosen in the above described manner, this code will provide complete error detection for the fully asymmetric channel.

In any other channel this code will detect all single errors and a large fraction of the multiple errors. If we assume that errors are independent and all code words are equally likely, it is a simple matter to compute the expected numbers of undetected errors for these sum codes as well

TABLE I

1. Information bits to be transmitted	011010
2. Binary form of sum of ones	011
3. Complemented form of sum	100
4. Transmitted word	100 011010
5. Received word with two errors	000 001010
6. Sum formed from information bits	010
7. Sum formed from complement of check bits	111

TABLE II[a]

AVERAGE NUMBER OF UNDETECTABLE ERROR PATTERNS IN SYMMETRIC CHANNEL

Type of Error Pattern	Type of Code		
	$\Sigma(3, 6)$	$\Sigma(3, 7)$	4 out of 8
Independent double error	10.5	14	16
Independent triple error	1.97	—	0
Burst of length two	3	3.5	4
Burst of length three	2.68	—	3.4

[a] Note that by a burst of length n, we mean any error pattern of length n in which both the first and nth bits are in error.

as for the four out of eight fixed weight code. An indication of the relative merits of the sum codes is provided by the results of some such calculations for the symmetric channel that are given in Table II.

It is interesting to note that even though more double errors can occur in the $\Sigma(3, 6)$ code word (there are nine bits compared to eight in the 4/8), there are considerably fewer undetectable double errors possible, i.e., 10.5 on the average compared to 16. This relative advantage is maintained very closely for any degree of asymmetry. A similar result is observed for the $\Sigma(3, 7)$ code.

It is apparent that as n increases, the sum codes will become relatively less efficient than the corresponding string of four out of eight code words with respect to undetectable double errors. The crossover point is near the point of equal redundancy. For example, in the symmetric channel, the $\Sigma(4, 12)$ code has 39 expected undetectable errors, while two consecutive four out of eight code words have 32 undetectable double errors. However, for large n, the sum code will have considerably less redundancy and will still be a perfect error detecting code in the fully asymmetric channel.

III. UTILIZATION OF SUM CODES

It would therefore appear that the sum code might be best utilized in two possible cases. The first case might be the situation in which one has a start-stop operation, or, in general, where it is convenient to check character by character. There, a $\Sigma(3, 6)$ or $\Sigma(3, 7)$ code might be used in preference to a fixed weight code since it does afford some additional protection and has the advantage of separability. The second case in which its use might be valid is that in which long records are customarily transmitted. There, a sum code might be applied over the entire record where each character in the record has a compact binary representation, i.e., a dense binary character set. Since the protection afforded by the sum code would be less than that obtained by a string of four out of eight characters, for greater reliability, a supplementary cyclic code might be applied. Inasmuch as the redundancy of the sum code increases only as $\log_2$ of the number of information bits, it would be possible to get considerably better protection than the 4/8 code provides and still achieve a considerable savings in channel utilization. For example, a card-type record of about 480 bits would require 9 sum check bits while the 4/8 code would have about 160 check bits. A cyclic code used in addition and employing 20 or fewer bits would almost certainly provide greater protection than the 4/8 code. The use of the sum code in either instance is only justified if the channel can be expected to be considerably asymmetrical. Otherwise, purely cyclic codes can be expected to be superior.

IV. OTHER CODES

It is possible to construct other codes, of similar character to the sum code earlier described, that have some additional features and which are still perfect error detection codes in the completely asymmetric channel. For example, consider a code in which each bit position of the information word has distinct weights associated with it, none of these weights corresponding to any power of two. The check bits are now formed by the sum of the weights that correspond to bit positions occupied by ones. The sum formed is expressed as a binary number and, as before, each bit is complemented before transmission. Explicitly, the sequence of weights corresponding to the successive information bits would be as follows: 3, 5, 6, 7, 9, 10, 11, 12, 13, 14, 15, 17, etc. This code would now do all that the previously described sum codes do and, in addition, would detect all double errors. It requires, however, approximately twice the number of check bits required by the simple sum code since in this case the number of check bits necessary is the smallest integer larger than $\log_2 \{[(n + \mu)(n + \mu + 1)/2] - 2\mu + 1\}$, where n is the number of information bits and μ is determined from the relation $2^{\mu-1} < n + \mu < 2^{\mu}$. As an example, consider the information word (0110100001). The sum of the weights, using the sequence above, is 34 and with $n = 10$, $\mu = 4$, the number of check bits required is 7. The binary representation of the check sum is (0100010). The finally transmitted sequence is (1011101 0110100001). Just as before, in the totally asymmetric channel, all errors will be detected for exactly the same reasons. In addition, in a channel of any symmetry, all double errors as well as all single errors will be detected. To show this, consider the following cases which exhaust all possibilities: (a) The two errors occur within the check positions. This is obviously detected since the received formed sum and check sum cannot possibly check since, with each check bit position effectively weighted by a distinct power of two, it is impossible with two errors to receive the correct check sum. (b) The two errors occur within the information bits. Again, since each weight is distinct, no two errors can cancel each other's effect on the formed sum. (c) One error in the check bits and one error in the information bits. The error in the check bits can effect that sum by the addition or subtraction of some power of two, but no weight in the information bits is a power of two, hence the two errors cannot compensate each other.

It is undoubtedly possible to construct similar codes which will also detect quadruple errors, etc. The construction of such codes becomes increasingly more complex and does not seem warranted at this time. For example, in order to detect two sets of compensating errors, that is, two zeros changed to ones and two ones changed to zeros, the requirement to be satisfied by the multipliers now is that the difference between any two multipliers be distinct. There does not seem to be any simple way to generate such a sequence. In addition, other restrictions have to be imposed in order that the entire formed word be protected.

V. SUMMARY

The codes that have been described here have been designed to be separable codes that are also perfect error detection codes in a completely asymmetric channel. The major purpose has been to demonstrate that this major feature of the fixed weight codes can also be achieved with separable codes so that advantage may be taken of the asymmetry of a channel while still maintaining the flexibility and compatibility associated with separable codes. We have shown that these sum codes can compete favorably in their error detecting capability with the four out of eight fixed weight codes in several instances. We have also indicated extensions of the sum codes that increase their error detection abilities at the cost of greater redundancy.

Received: November 22, 1960.

Optimal Error Detection Codes for Completely Asymmetric Binary Channels*

C. V. Freiman

IBM Research, P.O. Box 218, Yorktown Heights, New York

The $(n/2)$-out-of-n code is proved to be the least redundant binary block code which permits the detection of all errors in completely asymmetric channels. It is then proved that the sum code of Berger, Smith, and Freiman is the least redundant of all separable codes of this type. The redundancies of the sum and $(n/2)$-out-of-n codes are then compared and it is shown that the former is asymptotically twice as redundant as the latter. An efficient method of constructing separable codes which detect up to a given number, but not all, asymmetric errors is included as an appendix.

I. INTRODUCTION

Berger (1961) has recently introduced a class of separable binary block codes which, like the nonseparable m-out-of-n codes,[1] permits perfect error detection in completely asymmetric channels. These separable codes were termed *sum codes* by Berger and he offered the following as one method by which they could be constructed.

> Take the redundant positions of a code word to contain the binary representation of the number of 0's found in that code-word's message positions.[2]

Thus, the code words of a sum code of three message positions would

* Submitted in partial fulfillment of the requirements for the degree of Doctor of Engineering Science in the Faculty of Engineering, Columbia University.

[1] An n-position binary sequence is a code word of an *m-out-of-n-code* if, and only if, it contains exactly m 1's. In a *separable code*, k of a code word's n positions are specified arbitrarily by an independent message source. Only the remaining $n - k$ positions may be used for coding purposes.

[2] This method—or one complementary to it—of constructing separable perfect asymmetric error detection codes was developed independently and concurrently by Berger (1961), Smith (1960), and the present author.

be:

000	11
001	10
010	10
100	10
011	01
101	01
110	01
111	00.

The sum code's detection properties may easily be verified by observing that, whenever only a code word's 0's (1's) are affected by errors, the number of 0's among the message positions of the resulting sequence will be less (greater) than the number indicated by the redundant positions of that sequence.

In what follows, we shall first prove that the $(n/2)$-out-of-n-code[3] is the least redundant of all block codes which permit the perfect detection of errors in completely asymmetric channels. We shall then prove that no separable perfect asymmetric error detection code exists which is less redundant than the sum code. The redundancies of comparable sum and $(n/2)$-out-of-n codes will then be considered and it will be shown that the former is asymptotically twice as redundant as the latter. A brief discussion of separable codes which detect up to a given number, but not all, asymmetric errors is found as Appendix A at the conclusion of the paper.

It is desirable to introduce several definitions and observations before proceeding with the proof that the $(n/2)$-out-of-n code is of maximum efficiency. We shall view the set of all binary sequences of n positions as a partially ordered system with respect to the following ordering relation. A sequence s is said to *include* a sequence r (denoted $s \supset r$) if and only if s contains a 1 in every position where r contains a 1 and $s \neq r$. (For example, $1110 \supset 0110$ but $1110 \not\supset 0001$.) We say that s *covers*[4] r if $s \supset r$ and no sequence t exists such that $s \supset t \supset r$. Finally, we will term a subset of n-position sequences a *chain* whenever it is true that for any pair of sequences of the subset, x and y, either $x \supset y$ or $x \subset y$.

[3] When $n = 2m + 1$, the $(n/2)$-out-of-n code is taken as either the m-out-of-n code or the $(m + 1)$-out-of-n code.

[4] The nomenclature is that of Birkhoff (1948).

We now observe that for a code to permit perfect error detection in a completely asymmetric channel it is necessary and sufficient that no code word include another. Or, alternatively stated, that no pair of code words form a chain. This leads us to refer to any binary block code which permits perfect asymmetric error detection as a *chainless code*.[5]

II. $(n/2)$-OUT-OF-n CODES

Use will be made of the following lemmas in proving that the $(n/2)$-out-of-n code contains the greatest number of code words (and hence is least redundant) of all chainless codes. Note that all sequences referred to are of n positions and that the *weight* of a binary sequence is the number of 1's it contains.

LEMMA I. *Let f be the number of sequences in any nonempty set F of binary sequences of weight w where $0 \leqq w < [n/2]$.*[6] *Let g be the number of sequences in G, the set of all sequences which cover at least one sequence of F. Then $g > f$.*

PROOF: We observe that each sequence of G is of weight $w + 1$ and that any sequence of weight $w + 1$ covers $w + 1$ sequences of weight w, while any sequence of weight w is covered by $n - w$ sequences of weight $w + 1$. We then consider h, the number elements in the set of all ordered pairs (a, b) where $a \in F$ and $b \in G$. Since every sequence which covers any element of F is in G, we have

$$h = f(n - w). \tag{1}$$

It is not necessarily true that every sequence covered by an element of G is in F, however, and thus

$$h \leqq g(w + 1). \tag{2}$$

It follows that

$$f \leqq g \times \frac{w + 1}{n - w} \tag{3}$$

[5] Note that a more general channel model for which a chainless code permits perfect error detection is that in which errors may affect either a code word's 1's or its 0's, but not both. Completely asymmetric channels, of course, are special cases of these *block-asymmetric channels*.

[6] [] denotes "the integer part of" while {} denotes "the least integer not less than."

as $n - w > 0$. The factor $(w + 1)/(n - w)$ is always less than 1 for $w < [n/2]$ and thus

$$f \leqq g \times \frac{w+1}{n-w} < g. \tag{4}$$

LEMMA I′. *Let f be the number of sequences in any nonempty set F of binary sequences of weight w where $\{n/2\} < w \leqq n$. Let g be the number of sequences in G, the set of all sequences covered by at least one element of F. Then $g > f$.*
Note that Lemma I′ may be considered a corollary to Lemma I as it reduces to Lemma I when all sequences are complemented.

THEOREM I. *If $n = 2m$, no other chainless code contains as many code words as the m-out-of-n code. If $n = 2m + 1$, the only chainless code which contains as many code words as the m-out-of-n code is the $(m + 1)$-out-of-n code.*

PROOF: (a) We first consider the case $n = 2m$. Let C be any chainless code with some code words of weight other than m. If C contains code words of weight $<m$, replace all those of least weight by the set of all sequences which cover at least one of these least-weight code words. The new code is easily seen to be chainless and, by Lemma I, contains more code words than C. Continue this process until a code C^* is obtained such that none of its code words is of weight $<m$. (If the original code C contains no code words of weight $<m$, take C to be C^*.) If C^* contains code words of weight $>m$, replace all those of greatest weight by the set of all sequences which are covered by at least one of these greatest-weight code words. Again, the new code is chainless and, by Lemma I′ contains more code words than C^*. Continue this process until a code C^{**} is obtained such that all of its code words are of weight m. (If C^* contains no code words of weight $>m$, take C^* to be C^{**}.)

Since it is impossible for C and C^{**} to be the same code, we have shown that any chainless code containing some code words of weight other than m can be replaced by a chainless code of more code words—each of weight m. It only remains to note that the m-out-of-n code contains all sequences of weight m and hence is the chainless code with the largest possible number of code words.

(b) In the case of $n = 2m + 1$, we take C to be any chainless code other than the m-out-of-n code or the $(m + 1)$-out-of-n code. By a process of code replacement similar to that in (a) above, we obtain C^{**}, a chainless code all of whose code words are either of weight m

or of weight $m + 1$. The code C^{**} either contains more code words than C or is the code C itself. We now prove that C^{**} can contain no more than

$$\binom{2m+1}{m} = \binom{2m+1}{m+1}$$

code words and that, for C^{**} to contain $\binom{2m+1}{m}$ code words, it must be either the m-out-of-n code or the $(m + 1)$-out-of-n code.

Let f_m and f_{m+1} represent the number of code words in C^{**} of weight m and $m + 1$, respectively. Arguments similar to those used in the proof of Lemma I enable us to state that the number of sequences of weight m covered by a code word of weight $m + 1$ is not less than f_{m+1}. As none of these covered sequences may be a code word, it follows that

$$f_m \leqq \binom{2m+1}{m} - f_{m+1} \tag{5}$$

which proves that C^{**} contains no more than $\binom{2m+1}{m}$ code words. If C^{**} is to contain $\binom{2m+1}{m}$ code words, then a count of ordered pairs—again as in the proof of Lemma I—shows that each of the f_{m+1} noncode words of weight m is covered only by code words of weight $m + 1$. Thus, starting with a code word of weight $m + 1$, changing any of its 1's to 0 will yield a noncode word of weight m and any subsequent change of a 0 to 1 will always yield a code word of weight $m + 1$. But, it is clear that any sequence of weight $m + 1$ can be generated by a succession of such alternate changes of 0's and 1's. It follows that, if $f_{m+1} > 0$, f_{m+1} must equal $\binom{2m+1}{m}$. In this manner we have shown that for any chainless code to contain $\binom{2m+1}{m}$ code words it must be either the m-out-of-n code or the $(m + 1)$-out-of-n code.

III. SUM CODES

In this section we restrict our attention to separable chainless codes of k message positions. The first k positions of any code word are taken to be message positions and the contents of these positions shall be referred to as that code word's *prefix*. Similarly, the contents of the redundant positions shall be referred to as the code word's *suffix*. Note that each of the 2^k code words has a unique prefix and that suffixes must be assigned in such a manner as to make the over-all code chainless. For economy, of course, suffixes should be of the smallest possible number of positions.

THEOREM II. *No separable chainless code of k message positions exists which is less redundant than the sum code of k message positions.*

PROOF: The number of redundant positions required by a sum code of k message positions is easily seen to be $\{\log_2(k+1)\}$ as the number of 0's found in message positions varies from zero to k. It remains to be shown that any separable chainless code of k message positions must use at least $\{\log_2(k+1)\}$ redundant positions.

Consider the following $k + 1$ prefixes

$$\underbrace{\begin{matrix} 000 \cdots 0000 \\ 000 \cdots 0001 \\ 000 \cdots \quad 11 \\ 000 \cdots \;\; 111 \\ 000 \cdots 1111 \\ \vdots \\ 011 \cdots 1111 \\ 111 \cdots 1111. \end{matrix}}_{k \text{ positions}}$$

Were the same suffix to be used with any two of the above prefixes, the resulting pair of code words would form a chain. Therefore, at least $k + 1$ different suffixes must be used and the smallest possible number of redundant positions is seen to be $\{\log_2(k+1)\}$.

IV. RELATIVE REDUNDANCY

We define the redundancy R of a block code to be

$$R = \frac{n - \log_2(\text{number of code words})}{n}. \tag{6}$$

(For separable codes, of course, this reduces to $(n - k)/n$). Table I contains the redundancy of both the $(n/2)$-out-of-n code $(R_{n/2})$ and the sum code (R_{sum}) as well as their ratio for certain small values of n. Stirling's formula may be used to show that the asymptotic behavior

TABLE I

n	$R_{n/2}$	R_{sum}	$R_{n/2}/R_{sum}$
2	0.50	0.50	1.00
4	0.35	0.50	0.70
5	0.33	0.40	0.81
7	0.27	0.43	0.62
8	0.23	0.37	0.62
9	0.22	0.33	0.67
10	0.20	0.30	0.67
12	0.18	0.33	0.54
16	0.145	0.250	0.58
32	0.088	0.156	0.56
38	0.078	0.158	0.49
64	0.052	0.094	0.55
128	0.030	0.055	0.55
256	0.017	0.031	0.54
512	0.009	0.018	0.54
1024	0.005	0.010	0.53

of this ratio of redundancies is given by

$$\frac{R_{n/2}}{R_{sum}} \sim \frac{\log_2(n\pi/2)}{2\{\log_2 n\}}. \tag{7}$$

From this we see that, as n increases, the ratio of redundancies tends to oscillate about 0.5 with ever decreasing amplitude.

APPENDIX A

Let us briefly consider separable codes of k message positions which are required to detect up to a asymmetric errors where $1 < a < k$.[7] It is easy to show that at least $\{\log_2(a + 1)\}$ redundant positions must be used. It is not sufficient, however, to simply represent the number of message position 0's mod$(a + 1)$ as a binary number in the redundant positions. For example, if $a = 3$ and $k = 4$, we would obtain the following as two of our code words:

0000 00
0001 11.

Clearly this is inadmissible.

[7] Among all codes which detect up to a asymmetric errors, it would appear that one which uses all sequences of weights $[n/2] \pm i(a + 1)$ $(i = 0, 1, 2, \ldots)$ as code words is least redundant.

If a chainless code is used to represent the mod $(a + 1)$ count of the message position 0's, however, the over-all code does protect against up to a asymmetric errors. Thus, if $a = 5$, and $k > 15$, the code words of a 2-out-of-4 code might well be used to represent the mod 6 count of 0's. Such a use of chainless codes does not prove optimal for large a, but for many cases of interest this method does result in minimum redundancy.

RECEIVED: October 26, 1961.

REFERENCES

BERGER, J. M., (1961), A note on error detection codes for asymmetric channels. *Inform. and Control* **4**, 68–73.

BIRKHOFF, G., (1948), "Lattice Theory." American Mathematical Society, New York.

SMITH, H. J., JR., (1960), private communication.

Optimal Asymmetric Error Detecting Codes

J. MARTIN BORDEN

Department of Mathematical Sciences, Worcester Polytechnic Institute, Worcester, Massachusetts 01609

Some of the properties of codes capable of detecting errors when used on a binary asymmetric (or Z) channel are examined and in fact the maximum cardinality codes are determined. These results are extended to the q-ary asymmetric channel introduced by Varshamov (1973), *IEEE Trans. Inform. Theory* **19**, 92–95).

I. PROPERTIES OF ASYMMETRIC ERROR DETECTING CODES

The binary asymmetric channel, also called the Z channel, has the property that a transmitted 0 is always received correctly ($0 \to 0$), but a transmitted 1 may be received as a 0 or a 1 ($1 \to 0$ or $1 \to 1$). This channel model frequently arises, for example, in optical communication systems, where photons may fail to be detected ($1 \to 0$) but the creation of spurious photons ($0 \to 1$) is impossible. Here we study block codes C of length n which are capable of detecting the occurrence of any pattern of e or fewer asymmetric errors ($1 \to 0$). For C to be able to do this it is necessary and sufficient that whenever a codeword $\underline{x}$ of C is changed to a word $\underline{y}$ by e or fewer asymmetric errors, then $\underline{y}$ is not a codeword of C. Hence a decoder determines the presence of errors by the reception of a noncodeword. For example, any constant weight code detects any number of asymmetric errors: a received word contains errors if and only if it has weight less than the weight of a codeword. In Section II we prove that maximal cardinality asymmetric error detecting codes are obtained by taking the collection of all length n words having certain weights (depending on e), but here we simply examine some of the properties of error detecting codes for the Z channel.

Let $\underline{x}$ and $\underline{y}$ be binary n-tuples. We say $\underline{x} \geqslant \underline{y}$ if the inequality is valid for each component of $\underline{x}$ and $\underline{y}$. If neither $\underline{x} \geqslant \underline{y}$ nor $\underline{y} \geqslant \underline{x}$ in this partial ordering, then $\underline{x}$ and $\underline{y}$ are said to be incomparable. In any case, define $\underline{x} \backslash \underline{y}$ to be the binary n-tuple whose ith component is 1 if and only if $x_i = 1$ and $y_i = 0$; regard $\underline{x}$ and $\underline{y}$ as indicator functions on an n-set to see that this is simply a set difference. Let $|\underline{x}|$ denote the Hamming weight of $\underline{x}$, that is, the real sum of the components of $\underline{x}$.

Reprinted from *Information and Control*, Vol. 53, April 1982, pp. 66-73.

Evidently, if $\underset{\sim}{x}$ is transmitted along the Z channel and $\underset{\sim}{y}$ is received, then $\underset{\sim}{x} \geqslant \underset{\sim}{y}$. The proof of the following theorem is immediate from the above discussion:

THEOREM 1. *Code C detects all patterns of e or fewer asymmetric errors if and only if whenever distinct codewords $\underset{\sim}{x}$ and $\underset{\sim}{x}'$ of C satisfy $\underset{\sim}{x} \geqslant \underset{\sim}{x}'$ they also satisfy $|\underset{\sim}{x} \backslash \underset{\sim}{x}'| \geqslant e+1$.*

It is interesting to compare this requirement with the combinatorial requirements arising in other coding problems. Write

$$\partial(C) = \min\{|\underset{\sim}{x} \backslash \underset{\sim}{x}'| : \underset{\sim}{x}, \underset{\sim}{x}' \in C, \underset{\sim}{x} \geqslant \underset{\sim}{x}', \text{and } \underset{\sim}{x} \neq \underset{\sim}{x}'\},$$

with the understanding that if all pairs of distinct codewords of C are incomparable, then $\partial(C) = n+1$. Theorem 1 states that C detects $\partial(C)-1$ asymmetric errors. Let us write $M(\underset{\sim}{x}, \underset{\sim}{x}')$ and $m(\underset{\sim}{x}, \underset{\sim}{x}')$, respectively, for the maximum and minimum values of $|\underset{\sim}{x} \backslash \underset{\sim}{x}'|$ and $|\underset{\sim}{x}' \backslash \underset{\sim}{x}|$. The asymmetric distance between $\underset{\sim}{x}$ and $\underset{\sim}{x}'$ is $d_a(\underset{\sim}{x}, \underset{\sim}{x}') = M(\underset{\sim}{x}, \underset{\sim}{x}')$ and the Hamming distance between $\underset{\sim}{x}$ and $\underset{\sim}{x}'$ is $d(\underset{\sim}{x}, \underset{\sim}{x}') = M(\underset{\sim}{x}, \underset{\sim}{x}') + m(\underset{\sim}{x}, \underset{\sim}{x}')$. We write $d_a(C)$ and $d(C)$ for the minimum value of these distances taken over all pairs of distinct codewords. The following facts are well known: C corrects e asymmetric errors if $d_a(C) \geqslant e+1$ (see, e.g., Constantin and Rao (1979)), C detects e symmetric errors ($1 \to 0$ or $0 \to 1$) if $d(C) \geqslant e+1$, and C corrects e symmetric errors if $d(C) \geqslant 2e+1$. It is thus obvious that any code that can detect (correct) e symmetric errors can also detect (correct) e asymmetric errors. For linear codes we have a partial converse.

COROLLARY. *A linear code C detects e asymmetric errors if and only if C detects e symmetric errors.*

Proof. We need only prove the "only if" and for this it is sufficient to prove that $\partial(C) \leqslant d(C)$. Suppose $\underset{\sim}{x}$ and $\underset{\sim}{x}'$ in C satisfy $d(\underset{\sim}{x}, \underset{\sim}{x}') = d(C)$. Since C is linear, $\underset{\sim}{0}$ and $\underset{\sim}{x} + \underset{\sim}{x}'$ lie in C and thus $\partial(C) \leqslant |\underset{\sim}{x} + \underset{\sim}{x}' \backslash \underset{\sim}{0}| = d(\underset{\sim}{x}, \underset{\sim}{x}') = d(C)$. Q.E.D.

Perhaps what is more interesting is that unlike the situation in coding for symmetric errors, asymmetric error detecting codes and asymmetric error correcting codes require different combinatorial structures. Indeed, for asymmetric error detection we require that $d_a(\underset{\sim}{x}, \underset{\sim}{x}')$ be large only when $\underset{\sim}{x}$ and $\underset{\sim}{x}'$ are comparable.

It is possible to generalize Theorem 1 to include both cases of symmetric and asymmetric error detection. Suppose we desire a code C capable of detecting e_{10} errors of type $1 \to 0$ and e_{01} errors of type $0 \to 1$. Let E and e be the maximum and minimum of e_{10} and e_{01}. It is easy to check that C will have the desired property if for all pairs of distinct codewords $\underset{\sim}{x}$ and $\underset{\sim}{x}'$ we have $M(\underline{x}, \underline{x}') > E$ or $m(\underline{x}, \underline{x}') > e$. This requirement reduces to Theorem 1 when $e_{01} = 0$ and to the requirement for symmetric error detection when $e_{01} + e_{10}$ is fixed. Note that an error detecting code for the Z channel will perform equally as well when used on an "inverted Z" channel, where only errors of the type $0 \rightarrow 1$ occur.

Sometimes a code with a mixture of error correcting and error detecting abilities is desired; we might wish to correct e errors and detect f errors (where $e < f$). We examine a curious channel, the unidirectional channel with unknown direction of drift (UCUD), that will never be seen in practice, but which is a hybrid of the binary symmetric channel (BSC) and the Z channel. It turns out that codes designed to correct errors when used on the UCUD have a mixture of error detecting and correcting abilities when used on the Z channel. We imagine the UCUD as a channel that, prior to the transmission of each codeword, randomly chooses to send the codeword along either a Z channel or an inverted Z channel; we do not know the outcome of this selection. It is important to realize that the UCUD does not choose an asymmetric channel and then maintain this same choice for the transmission of all later codewords; nor, at the other extreme, does the UCUD randomly choose a channel before the transmission of each bit. The UCUD chooses a direction of drift before transmitting each codeword.

THEOREM 2. *Properties* (1) *and* (2) *are equivalent and are implied by* (3). *If C is assumed to be linear, then all three properties are equivalent.*

(1) *C corrects e errors when used on the* UCUD.

(2) *C corrects e errors and detects* 2*e errors when used on the Z channel.*

(3) *C corrects e errors when used on the* BSC.

Proof. We confine ourselves to proving the equivalence of (1) and (2) since the remainder of the theorem is a straightforward consequence of definitions and the corollary to Theorem 1.

Property (1) implies (2). If (1) holds, then C can certainly correct e errors when used on the Z channel, so we need to prove that C detects $2e$ asymmetric errors, that is, $\partial(C) \geqslant 2e + 1$. Let $\underline{x}$ and $\underline{x}'$ be in C with $\underline{x} \geqslant \underline{x}'$ and $|\underline{x} \backslash \underline{x}'| = t$, say. Let $\underline{y}$ be chosen to have $\lceil t/2 \rceil$ ones and $\lfloor t/2 \rfloor$ zeros in the coordinates where $\underline{x}$ and $\underline{x}'$ disagree, and let the remaining coordinates of $\underline{y}$ agree with those of $\underline{x}$. Then $\underline{y}$ can be received when either $\underline{x}$ or $\underline{x}'$ is transmitted on the UCUD after an occurrence of no more then $\lceil t/2 \rceil$ errors. Thus C fails to correct $\lceil t/2 \rceil$ errors on the UCUD, so that by (1), $\lceil t/2 \rceil \geqslant e + 1$. Hence, $t \geqslant 2e + 1$, which implies $\partial(C) \geqslant 2e + 1$.

Property (2) implies (1). Suppose that a codeword of C has been transmitted along the UCUD and after an occurrence of no more than e

errors the word $\underset{\sim}{y}$ is received. We show that (2) implies that $\underset{\sim}{y}$ is uniquely decodable. Since C corrects e errors of type $1 \to 0$, there exists at most one codeword $\underset{\sim}{x}$ such that $\underset{\sim}{x} \geqslant \underset{\sim}{y}$ and $|\underset{\sim}{x} \backslash \underset{\sim}{y}| \leqslant e$. However, a code correcting e errors of type $1 \to 0$ also corrects e errors of type $0 \to 1$ (see, e.g., Constantin and Rao (1979)) and so by the same reasoning there exists at most one codeword $\underset{\sim}{x}'$ such that $\underset{\sim}{y} \geqslant \underset{\sim}{x}'$ and $|\underset{\sim}{y} \backslash \underset{\sim}{x}'| \leqslant e$. One of the words $\underset{\sim}{x}$ or $\underset{\sim}{x}'$ must exist and be the transmitted codeword. However, $\underset{\sim}{x}$ and $\underset{\sim}{x}'$ cannot both exist and be distinct, for otherwise $\underset{\sim}{x} \geqslant \underset{\sim}{x}'$ and $|\underset{\sim}{x} \backslash \underset{\sim}{x}'| = |\underset{\sim}{x} \backslash \underset{\sim}{y}| + |\underset{\sim}{y} \backslash \underset{\sim}{x}'| \leqslant 2e$, contradicting the fact that $\partial(C) \geqslant 2e + 1$. Therefore $\underset{\sim}{y}$ can be uniquely decoded as the codeword comparable with $\underset{\sim}{y}$ and having asymmetric distance from $\underset{\sim}{y}$ not exceeding e. Q.E.D.

II. Optimal Codes

We write $B(n, e)$ for the maximum number of codewords in any length n binary code capable of detecting e (or fewer) asymmetric errors. In this section we determine $B(n, e)$ and show that the result readily generalizes to the q-ary asymmetric channels discussed by Varshamov (1973) and other authors.

We have already remarked that a constant weight code can detect any number of asymmetric errors and so, for example, $B(n, n) \geqslant \binom{n}{\lfloor n/2 \rfloor}$, the number of words of weight $\lfloor n/2 \rfloor$. Freiman (1962) proved that equality obtains in this estimate; in doing so he reproved a classical theorem of Sperner (1928) which asserts exactly this fact: the maximal number of incomparable binary n-tuples is attained by taking all words of weight $\lfloor n/2 \rfloor$ (or $\lceil n/2 \rceil$). Here we evaluate $B(n, e)$ by making use of a generalization of Sperner's theorem due to Kleitman (1974).

To state Kleitman's theorem requires further terminology. Let S be a partially ordered set. A subset of S is said to be a chain if it contains no incomparable elements; a chain is maximal if it is not a proper subset of any other chain. The set S itself may be a chain in which case the elements of S are linearly ordered. Suppose $S_1, \ldots, S_n$ are chains and let S be the Cartesian product $S = S_1 \times \cdots \times S_n$. Then S can be partially ordered in a natural way by letting $(s_1, \ldots, s_n) \leqslant (t_1, \ldots, t_n)$ mean that the relation holds in each component. In this case where S is a product of chains there is a well-defined rank function: for each $\underset{\sim}{x} \in S$, the rank of $\underset{\sim}{x}$ is the maximum number of elements in any chain that contains only elements strictly less than $\underset{\sim}{x}$. The example of present interest is where S is the set of binary n-tuples, each $S_i = \{0, 1\}$, and the rank of $\underset{\sim}{x}$ is $|\underset{\sim}{x}|$. A maximal chain γ in S may be expressed as an array $\gamma = (\underset{\sim}{0}, \underset{\sim}{x}_1, \ldots, \underset{\sim}{x}_{n-1}, \underset{\sim}{1})$, where $\underset{\sim}{x}_i \leqslant \underset{\sim}{x}_{i+1}$ and $|\underset{\sim}{x}_i| = i$.

As proved by Hsieh and Kleitman (1973), any partially ordered set which is expressible as a product of chains possesses the so-called LYM property (or equivalently, the normalized matching property: see Kleitman (1974)). This means that there exists a nonempty list of maximal chains from the partial order such that for any w each of the elements of rank w appear in the same number of chains. Thus, if there are L chains in the list and $n(w)$ elements of rank w in the poset then each element of rank w appears in $L/n(w)$ of the chains.

Suppose that P denotes a property that a subset of a partial order may enjoy. We will say that P is inheritable if whenever a set C enjoys P so does every subset of C. For example, the property of containing only incomparable elements is inheritable.

We now can state Kleitman's result.

THEOREM 3. *Suppose a partially ordered set possesses the* LYM *property and has $n(w)$ elements of rank w. Let C be any subset of the partial order which enjoys an inheritable property P. Then we can upper bound the cardinality of C as*

$$|C| \leqslant \max_{\gamma} \sum_{\underset{\sim}{x} \in \gamma} n(|\underset{\sim}{x}|),$$

where the maximum is taken over all chains γ which enjoy property P.

Proof. Suppose $(\gamma_1, \gamma_2, \ldots, \gamma_L)$ is the list of chains given by the LYM property. Write each of these chains as a column of elements from the partial order to obtain a matrix $(\underset{\sim}{x}_{ij})$. We place a uniform probability distribution p on those elements in the matrix which also belong to C, that is,

$$\begin{aligned} p(\underset{\sim}{x}_{ij}) &= 0, \qquad \text{if} \quad \underset{\sim}{x}_{ij} \notin C, \\ &= k, \qquad \text{if} \quad \underset{\sim}{x}_{ij} \in C, \end{aligned}$$

where k is a suitable constant. Since an element $x \in C$ appears $L/n(|\underset{\sim}{x}|)$ times in a row of this matrix we obtain a distribution on the elements of the partial order

$$\begin{aligned} p(\underset{\sim}{x}) &= 0, \qquad &\text{if} \quad \underset{\sim}{x} \notin C, \\ &= kL/n(|\underset{\sim}{x}|), \qquad &\text{if} \quad \underset{\sim}{x} \in C. \end{aligned}$$

Thus, the expected value of $n(|\underset{\sim}{x}|)$ is

$$E(n(|\underset{\sim}{x}|)) = \sum_{\underset{\sim}{x} \in C} kL = kL\,|C|.$$

On the other hand, from the matrix point of view,

$$\begin{aligned}
E(n(|\underline{x}|)) &= \sum \{kn(|\underline{x}_{ij}|) : \underline{x}_{ij} \in C\} \\
&= kL \cdot \frac{1}{L} \sum_{j=1}^{L} \sum_{\underline{x} \in \gamma_j \cap C} n(|\underline{x}|) \\
&= kL \operatorname*{average}_{\gamma_j} \sum_{\underline{x} \in \gamma_j \cap C} n(|\underline{x}|)) \\
&\leqslant kL \max_{\gamma_j} \sum_{\underline{x} \in \gamma_j \cap C} n(|\underline{x}|) \\
&\leqslant kL \max_{\gamma} \sum_{\underline{x} \in \gamma} n(|\underline{x}|).
\end{aligned}$$

The last inequality, in which γ is an arbitrary chain enjoying P, follows since the previous maximum involves chains $\gamma_j \cap C$, each of which enjoys the inheritable property P. Q.E.D.

We now use Theorem 3 to evaluate $B(n, e)$. Actually, an equivalent result was proved by Katona (1972) in a different context and by different methods.

THEOREM 4. *The code C consisting of all length n words whose weight is congruent to $\lfloor n/2 \rfloor$ modulo $(e + 1)$ attains $B(n, e)$. Thus,*

$$B(n, e) = \sum_{w = \lfloor n/2 \rfloor \mathrm{mod}(e+1)} \binom{n}{w}.$$

Proof. Suppose code C_1 attains $B(n, e)$. Since C_1 detects e asymmetric errors, any subset of C_1 also detects e errors, that is, comparable elements must differ in weight (rank) by at least $e + 1$. Applying Theorem 3, we see that

$$B(n, e) = |C_1| \leqslant \max_{\gamma} \sum_{\underline{x} \in \gamma} \binom{n}{|\underline{x}|},$$

where the maximum is taken over all chains γ such that any two elements of γ differ in weight by at least $e + 1$. It is now clear that

$$B(n, e) \leqslant \max_{t} \sum_{w = t\, \mathrm{mod}(e+1)} \binom{n}{w}.$$

The numbers $\binom{n}{w}$ are unimodal and symmetric, that is, $\binom{n}{i} < \binom{n}{j}$ if $i < j \leqslant n/2$ and $\binom{n}{w} = \binom{n}{n-w}$. Hence the maximum occurs when $t = \lfloor n/2 \rfloor$ (or $\lceil n/2 \rceil$). Code C of the theorem detects e errors and attains this bound. Q.E.D.

By a routine Fourier analysis (see, e.g., Knuth, 1968) we have for even n,

$$B(n, e) = \frac{2^n}{e+1} \sum_{k=0}^{e} \cos^n \left(\frac{k\pi}{e+1}\right),$$

and for odd n, $B(n, e) = \frac{1}{2}B(n+1, e)$. For example,

$$\begin{aligned} B(n, 2) &= (2^n + 2)/3 && \text{for even } n, \\ &= (2^n + 1)/3 && \text{for odd } n; \end{aligned}$$

and

$$\begin{aligned} B(n, 3) &= 2^{n-2} + 2^{(n-2)/2} && \text{for even } n, \\ &= 2^{n-2} + 2^{(n-3)/2} && \text{for odd } n. \end{aligned}$$

Note that the density of a maximal e error detecting code among the 2^n possible words is quite large, slightly larger than $1/(e+1)$. Also, decoding these codes is very easy: only the weight of a received word must be checked. However, these codes are generally not systematic, which may be desirable in practice. Berger (1961) constructed a family of codes detecting all asymmetric errors, but which have fewer than $\binom{n}{\lfloor n/2 \rfloor}$ codewords. We do not know of a systematic construction for e asymmetric error detecting codes. One place where this might not be of concern is in the coding of control operations, where the weight of a codeword could signal that a certain set of commands be called, and the 1's positions of a codeword could signal subset of these commands should be executed.

We look at error detecting codes for the q-ary asymmetric channel. This channel, first studied by Varshamov (1973), has the property that whenever a q-ary word $\underset{\sim}{x}$ is transmitted the possible received words are those q-ary $\underset{\sim}{y}$ such that $\underset{\sim}{x} \geqslant \underset{\sim}{y}$ (where the inequality is interpreted componentwise). We write $\underset{\sim}{x} \backslash \underset{\sim}{y}$ for the word whose ith component is $\max\{0, x_i - y_i\}$ and $|\underset{\sim}{x}|$ for the real sum of the components of $\underset{\sim}{x}$. When $\underset{\sim}{x}$ is transmitted and $\underset{\sim}{y}$ is received, we say that $|\underset{\sim}{x} \backslash \underset{\sim}{y}|$ asymmetric errors have occured (e.g., $(3, 1) \rightarrow (1, 0)$ counts as 3 errors). It is easy to see that even with this new interpretation, Theorem 1 remains valid. Note that the q-ary n-tuples can be viewed as a product of chains $\{0, 1, \ldots, q-1\}$ and that the rank of $\underset{\sim}{x}$ is again $|\underset{\sim}{x}|$. Let $B_q(n, e)$ be the maximum number of codewords in a length n code capable of detecting e errors on the q-ary asymmetric channel.

THEOREM 5. *The code C consisting of all q-ary words $\underset{\sim}{x}$ whose rank $\underset{\sim}{x}$ is congruent to $\lfloor n(q-1)/2 \rfloor$ modulo $(e+1)$ attains $B_q(n, e)$. Thus,*

$$B_q(n, e) = \sum_{w \equiv \lfloor n(q-1)/2 \rfloor \bmod (e+1)} P_q(w, n),$$

where $P_q(w, n)$ denotes the number of q-ary n-tuples of rank w.

Proof. The proof parallels the proof of Theorem 4 in every detail except that it is not entirely obvious that the numbers $P_q(w, n)$ are unimodal and symmetric about $n(q-1)/2$. Observe that

$$P_q(w, n+1) = P_q(w, n) + P_q(w-1, n) + \cdots + P_q(w-(q-1), n)$$

since a length $n+1$ word of rank w may be formed by juxtaposing a letter i, $0 \leqslant i \leqslant q-1$, with a length n word of rank $w-i$. Using this recurrence and the trivial fact that $P_q(w, 1) = 1$ for $0 \leqslant w \leqslant q-1$ we deduce that

$$\sum_{w=0}^{n(q-1)} P_q(w, n) z^w = (1 + z + z^2 + \cdots + z^{q-1})^n.$$

From this it is evident (or may be proved simply by induction) that $P_q(i, n) < P_q(j, n)$ whenever $i < j < n(q-1)/2$ and that $P_q(w, n) = P_q(n(q-1) - w, n)$. Q.E.D.

Acknowledgment

Much of this material appeared in my doctoral dissertation and I wish to thank Professor R. J. McEliece for his help and guidance.

References

Berger, J. M. (1961), A note on error detection codes for asymmetric channels, *Inform. and Contr.* **4**, 68–73.

Constantin, S. D. and Rao, T. R. N. (1979), On the theory of binary asymmetric error correcting codes, *Inform. and Contr.* **40**, 20–36.

Freiman, C. V. (1962), Optimal error detection codes for completely asymmetric binary channels, *Inform. and Contr.* **5**, 64–71.

Hsieh, W. N. and Kleitman, D. J. (1973), Normalized matching in direct products of partial orders, *Stud. Appl. Math.* **52**, 285–289.

Katona, G. (1972), Families of subsets having no subset containing another with small difference, *Nieuw Arch. Wisk.* (3) **20**, 54–67.

Kleinman, D. J. (1974), On an extremal property of antichains in partial orders, the LYM property and some of its implications and applications, in "Combinatorics" (M. Hall, Jr. and J. H. Van Lint, Eds.), pp. 277–290, Math Centre Tracts 55, Amsterdam.

Knuth, D. E. (1968), "The Art of Computer Programming," Vol. 1, pp. 70 and 486, Addison–Wesley, Reading, Mass.

Sperner, E. (1928), Ein Satz über Untermengen einer endlichen Menge, *Math. Z.* **27**, 544–548.

Varshamov, R. R. (1973), A class of codes for asymmetric channels and a problem from the additive theory of numbers, *IEEE Trans. Inform. Theory* **19**, 92–95.

Systematic Unidirectional Error-Detecting Codes

BELLA BOSE, MEMBER, IEEE, AND DER JEI LIN

Abstract —**The theory and design of systematic t-unidirectional error-detecting codes are developed. Optimal systematic codes capable of detecting 2, 3, and 6 unidirectional errors using 2, 3, and 4 check bits, respectively, are given. For $r \geq 5$ where r is the number of check bits, the systematic codes described here can detect up to $5 \cdot 2^{r-4} + r - 4$ unidirectional errors. Encoding/decoding methods for these codes are also investigated.**

Index Terms —**Asymmetric errors, decoder, encoder, Hamming distance, self-checking checker, symmetric errors, unidirectional errors.**

I. Introduction

It is desirable, and sometimes vital, that data in a computer system must be reliable when written into memory, stored, read from memory, communicated, or manipulated. The complexity of modern computers makes it impractical to depend solely on reliable components and devices for reliable operation. Some redundancy is needed for detection and/or correction of errors, which will invariably occur as information is being stored, transferred, or manipulated.

An extensive theory of symmetric error-control coding has been developed [1]–[4], where symmetric errors are those in which $1 \rightarrow 0$ and $0 \rightarrow 1$ errors are equally likely in a data word. However, the error statistics in some of the recently developed VLSI circuits are of unidirectional type [5]–[7], meaning both $1 \rightarrow 0$ and $0 \rightarrow 1$ errors are possible in data words, but in any particular word all the errors are of the same type.

The only known unidirectional error-detecting codes are nonsystematic constant weight codes and systematic Berger–Freiman codes [8], [9], which detect all unidirectional errors in a data word. In systematic codes the information bits are separately identified from the check bits. The advantage of systematic codes is that the encoding/decoding and data manipulation can be done in parallel.

When not all 2^k information symbols occur in a code, where k is the number of information bits, Smith [18] has proposed systematic codes which need fewer check bits than the Berger–Freiman codes. Again, these codes detect all unidirectional errors in a codeword.

When all unidirectional errors in a data word need to be detected, both $\lfloor n/2 \rfloor$-out-of-n codes, Berger–Freiman codes and the codes proposed by Smith are all optimal, but when a fixed t-errors need to be detected, this is not the case. This can be seen from the theory and codes presented in this paper. In [10], the author has given modified Berger codes to detect 2^i, $i = 2, 3, 4, \cdots$ unidirectional errors. The number of check bits needed to detect 2^i errors is $i + \lceil \log_2(i + 1) \rceil$. Even for these cases, the codes presented here have higher error-detecting capabilities.

The unidirectional codes presented in this paper have the following characteristics.

1) The codes are systematic; i.e., the check bits can be separately identified from the information bits. The advantage of systematic codes is that the encoding/decoding and data manipulation can be done in parallel.

2) Unlike t-symmetric error-detecting codes the t-unidirectional error-detecting codes need only a fixed number of check bits *independent of the number of information bits*. Furthermore, the number of check bits needed for t-unidirectional error detection is less than the number for t-symmetric error detection.

3) The parallel encoding/decoding circuits for these codes are easy to implement, and thus these codes are suitable for high-speed computer systems.

4) The codes are optimal or near optimal.

5) The totally self-checking (TSC) checkers for these codes are easy to design.

The paper is organized as follows. The unidirectional error-detecting capabilities of binary block codes are established in Section II. A new class of systematic codes, with 2, 3, and 4 check bits, capable of detecting, respectively, 2, 3, and 6 unidirectional errors is described in Section III. These codes are optimal. Codes capable of detecting up to $5 \cdot 2^{r-4} + r - 4$ unidirectional errors, using $r \geq 5$ check bits, are also given. The codes need simple encoding/decoding circuits, and these are described in Section IV.

Another interesting paper on unidirectional error detecting codes is by Borden [11], where he proved that among all t-unidirectional error-detecting codes of length n, the set of codewords with weight $\lfloor n/2 \rfloor \bmod (t + 1)$ forms the optimal code. However, these are nonsystematic codes.

Research in the direction of unidirectional error correction and detection is discussed in [15], [19]–[22].

II. Unidirectional Error-Detecting Capabilities of Binary Block Codes

The main results of this section are given in Theorems 2.2 and 2.3. Before that, some definitions and notations are described.

The types of error statistics which occur in memory, logic, and arithmetic units are many and varied. However, we can broadly classify them as symmetric, asymmetric, and unidirectional errors.

Symmetric errors: The error statistics are said to be sym-

Manuscript received April 20, 1984; revised May 5, 1985. This research was supported by the National Science Foundation under Grants ECS-8307450 and DMC-8421104.

The authors are with the Department of Computer Science, Oregon State University, Corvallis, OR 97331.

0-8186-4182-7/93 $3.00 © 1985 IEEE

metric when both $1 \rightarrow 0$ and $0 \rightarrow 1$ errors can occur simultaneously in a data word.

Asymmetric errors: When the errors in a data word are only one type, say $1 \rightarrow 0$, these error statistics are called asymmetric. In this case the other type of errors, say $0 \rightarrow 1$, will never occur in any data word.

Unidirectional errors: When the error statistics in a data word are $0 \rightarrow 1$ or $1 \rightarrow 0$ errors, but both the types of errors do not appear simultaneously in a word, these are called unidirectional errors. In this case the data word has only $0 \rightarrow 1$ errors or only $1 \rightarrow 0$ errors, but the decoder does not know *a priori* the type of errors.

From the above definitions it is clear that the asymmetric error class is a subclass of the unidirectional error class, which in turn is a subclass of the symmetric error class. Thus, any code capable of correcting/detecting t-symmetric errors is also capable of correcting/detecting t-unidirectional or t-asymmetric errors, and any code capable of correcting/detecting t-unidirectional errors is also capable of correcting/detecting t-asymmetric errors. However, the converse may not be true. In fact, there are t-asymmetric error-correcting codes with higher information rate than that of t-symmetric error-correcting codes [12]–[14]. However, it is not known whether there exist unidirectional error-correcting codes having higher information rate than that of symmetric error codes [15].

Hamming distance is useful in studying the symmetric error-correcting/detecting capabilities of codes, where the Hamming distance between any two words is the number of positions in which they differ. For example, the Hamming distance between $X = (11001)$ and $Y = (01100)$ is 3. The following well-known theorem describes the symmetric error-detecting capabilities of binary block codes.

Theorem 2.1: (Hamming) A code C is capable of detecting t-symmetric errors if and only if the minimum Hamming distance of the code is at least $t + 1$.

In the sequel, a t-symmetric error-detecting code is called a t-symmetric code. Thus, as discussed before, a t-symmetric code is also a t-unidirectional and t-asymmetric code. Moreover, a t-unidirectional code is also a t-asymmetric code. Surprisingly, in the case of asymmetric and unidirectional errors, the converse is also true; i.e., a code C capable of detecting t-asymmetric errors is also capable of detecting t-unidirectional errors. This is proved below in Theorem 2.2, which also describes the asymmetric error-detecting capabilities of binary block codes. Before that, we need the following definitions.

A word $X = (x_1 x_2 \cdots x_n)$ is said to *cover* another word $Y = (y_1 y_2 \cdots y_n)$ whenever $y_i = 1$, $x_i = 1$, for all $i = 1, 2, \cdots, n$. When neither covers the other, they are called unordered. For example, $X = (11011)$ covers $Y = (10001)$, whereas $Z = (00111)$ and X are unordered. X covers Y is written as $Y \leq X$.

Further, a set of n distinct vectors $X1, X2, \cdots, Xn$ is called a *maximal cover* of length n whenever $Xi \leq X(i + 1)$ and there exists no Y which is distinct from Xi and $X(i + 1)$ such that $Xi \leq Y \leq X(i + 1)$ for $i = 1, 2, \cdots, n - 1$. For example, the set $\{0000, 0001, 0011, 0111, 1111\}$ is a maximal cover of length 5.

Theorem 2.2: A code C is capable of detecting t-asymmetric errors if and only if the following condition is true. For all $X, Y \varepsilon C$, either X and Y are unordered or $d(X, Y) \geq t + 1$ when one covers the other, where $d(X, Y)$ is the Hamming distance between X and Y. Further, a code capable of detecting t-asymmetric errors is also capable of detecting t-unidirectional errors.

Proof: We can assume that the asymmetric errors are of $1 \rightarrow 0$ type. Consider two codewords, $X = (x_1 x_2 \cdots x_n)$ and $Y = (y_1 y_2 \cdots y_n)$ in C. When they are unordered, there exists x_i, x_j, y_i, and y_j such that $x_i = 1$, $x_j = 0$, $y_i = 0$, and $y_j = 1$ where $1 \leq i, j \leq n$. Suppose $X' = (x_1' x_2' \cdots x_n')$ is a word obtained from X due to t or fewer $1 \rightarrow 0$ errors. Then X' and Y differ at location j. Thus, any t or less $1 \rightarrow 0$ errors in X will not transfer X to Y. Further, when X and Y are ordered, then $d(X, Y) \geq t + 1$. Again, any t or less $1 \rightarrow 0$ errors in X will not transfer X to Y. Conversely, when X covers Y and $d(X, Y) \leq t$, then the $1 \rightarrow 0$ errors in the bits where X differs from Y will transfer X to Y.

Now we prove that C is also capable of detecting t-unidirectional errors. Consider any two codewords $X, Y \varepsilon C$. When they are unordered, then there exists x_i, x_j, y_i, and y_j such that $x_i = 1$, $x_j = 0$, $y_i = 0$, and $y_j = 1$. When X' is a vector obtained from X due to t or fewer $1 \rightarrow 0$ errors, then X' differs from Y at location j, and when X'' is a vector obtained from X due to t or fewer $0 \rightarrow 1$ errors, then X'' differs from Y at location i. Further, when they are ordered, say X covers Y, the Hamming distance between them is at least $t + 1$. Thus, neither t or fewer $1 \rightarrow 0$ errors in X nor $0 \rightarrow 1$ errors in Y can transfer one to the other. □

By consequence of Theorem 2.2, it is clear that the conditions required for t-unidirectional errors are the same as those of t-asymmetric errors. For completeness, the unidirectional error-detecting capability of block codes is stated below.

Theorem 2.3: A code C is capable of detecting t-unidirectional errors if and only if the following condition is valid.

For all $X, Y \varepsilon C$, either X and Y are unordered or $d(X, Y) \geq t + 1$ when one covers the other.

Thus, in order to show that a code is capable of detecting t-unidirectional errors, it is sufficient to prove that C is capable of detecting t-asymmetric, say $1 \rightarrow 0$, errors, and we use this approach in this paper.

III. Code Construction

The unidirectional error-detecting codes developed in this section are systematic codes; i.e., the information bits are separately identified from the check bits. Berger codes given in [8] are also systematic unidirectional codes which detect all unidirectional errors in the information and the check symbols. The number of check bits r required for these codes is $\lceil \log_2(k + 1) \rceil$ where k is the number of information bits. Further, these are optimal codes. Thus, when the number of information bits k is less than 2^r where r is the number of check bits, Berger codes are superior to any t-unidirectional error-detecting codes. Hence, in this paper we assume that the number of information bits k is greater than $2^r - 1$.

For convenience, the code construction techniques are described by taking three cases. Double and triple error-detecting codes, which require 2 and 3 check bits, respectively, are described in Section III-A. Six error-detecting codes with 4 check bits are given in Section III-B. All these codes are shown to be optimal. For $r \geq 5$, the number of check bits, the codes designed in Section III-C detect up to $5 \cdot 2^{r-4} + r - 4$ errors.

Before describing the code construction techniques let us briefly consider the case of single error. Obviously, there is no difference between single symmetric error and single unidirectional error. Thus, a single check bit odd or even parity codes can be used to detect single unidirectional error. Later it is shown that a systematic code with 1 check bit cannot detect 2 unidirectional errors. Thus, single bit parity codes are also optimal single unidirectional error-detecting codes.

The following notations are used in this paper.

k	number of information bits,
r	number of check bits,
$n = k + r$	length of the code,
$k0$	number of 0's in the information bits,
$k1$	number of 1's in the information bits.

In the rest of this paper unidirectional errors will be referred to simply as errors, unless otherwise specified.

A. Double and Triple Error-Detecting Codes

As we mentioned before, double and triple error-detecting codes described here need 2 and 3 check bits, respectively, independent of the number of information bits. The check symbol CS for each codeword is generated as follows. Count the number of 0's in the information symbol and take mod 2^r; i.e., CS $= k0$ mod 4 in the case of double error-detecting codes and CS $= k0$ mod 8 in the case of triple error-detecting codes. (Another way of generating the check symbol CS is as follows. Count the number of 1's in the information symbol, take modulo 2^r, and complement the bits; i.e., CS $= 3 - (k1$ mod 4) in the case of double error-detecting codes and CS $= 7 - (k1$ mod 8) in the case of triple error-detecting codes.)

We will show that these codes satisfy the conditions described in Theorem 2.3. First, double error-detecting codes are considered. Suppose X and Y are any two codewords. If the information parts of X and Y are unordered, then obviously X and Y are unordered. On the other hand, if the information part of X covers that of Y and the Hamming distance between the information symbols is exactly 1, then either the check symbol of Y covers that of X or the check symbols are unordered, thus making X and Y unordered; or the check symbol of Y is 00 and that of X is 11, thus making $d(X, Y) = 3$. Further, if the information part of X covers that of Y and the distance between these information parts is exactly 2, then the check symbols are distinct, and thus $d(X, Y) \geq 3$.

For example, let the number of information bits be 8. Then the check symbols for the following set of information symbols, which is a maximal cover of length 9, are shown below.

Information bits		Check bits
0000	0000	00
0000	0001	11
0000	0011	10
0000	0111	01
0000	1111	00
0001	1111	11
0011	1111	10
0111	1111	01
1111	1111	00

Any two codewords, which are unordered in their information part, satisfy the conditions given in Theorem 2.3 trivially. Therefore, only ordered sets of information symbols are considered. In the above set, as the weight of the information symbols, which are a maximal cover, increases, the check symbols repeat themselves in a sequence of $\cdots$, 11, 10, 01, 00, 11, 10, $\cdots$, etc. Thus, any two codewords, say X and Y, are either unordered or $d(X, Y) \geq 3$.

For triple error-detecting codes also we need to consider only the information symbols which are a maximal cover. In this case, as the weight of information symbols increases, the repetitive sequence of check symbols is $\cdots$, 111, 110, 101, 100, 011, 010, 001, 000, 111, 110, $\cdots$. Thus, it can be seen that any two codewords X and Y are either unordered or $d(X, Y) \geq 4$.

Another way of proving the code capability is as follows. Let X be a codeword with check symbol CS and X' be the received word with check symbol CS$'$. Let CS$''$ be equal to the number of 0's modulo 8 in the information part of X'. For an error-free codeword CS$'$ = CS$''$ = CS. Suppose there are $p \leq 3$ errors, say $1 \rightarrow 0$ type, in the codeword. When the errors are confined to the information part, CS$''$ = (CS $+ p$) mod 8 $\neq$ CS$'$ = CS because $p \leq 3$. When the errors are only in the check part, CS$'$ = CS $- q$ where $1 \leq q \leq 7$. This is because there are only 3 check bits, and even if $p \leq 3$ errors occur, the change in the check value can be at most 7. Thus, CS = CS$''$ $\neq$ CS$'$ = (CS $- q$) mod 8. Further, when the errors are spread over, with p_1 errors in the information part and p_2 errors in the check part such that $p_1 + p_2 \leq 3$, CS$''$ = (CS $+ p_1$) mod 8 and CS$'$ = CS $- q_2$ where q_2 is the binary number with p_2 1's at the error positions of the check part. Again, CS$''$ $\neq$ CS$'$ because $p_1 + q_2 \neq 0$ mod 8. If $p_1 = 1$, then q_2 must be 7, thus there would have to be 4 errors, 1 in the information part and 3 in the check part. Similarly, if $p_1 = 2$, then $q_2 = 6$, and when $p_1 = 3$, then $q_2 = 5$. Thus, there must be at least 4 errors in order to get $p_1 + q_2 = 0$ mod 8. Thus, the code is capable of detecting 3 errors.

The optimality of the codes is considered in the following theorem.

Theorem 3.1: Any t-error-detecting systematic code where t = 2, 3, or 4 requires at least t check bits. Thus, the single, double, and triple error-detecting codes described above are optimal.

Proof: In a double error-detecting code, the three check symbols, for the set of information symbols {00 · · · 000, 00· · ·001, 00 · · · 011}, which is a maximal cover of length 3, must be distinct. If any two check symbols are equal, then the Hamming distance between these two codewords can be at most 2. Therefore, we need at least $\lceil \log_2 3 \rceil = 2$ check bits to detect double errors. In other words, at most 1 error can be detected using 1 check bit, and thus the single bit parity codes are optimal.

Consider the following set of information symbols, which is a maximal cover of length 4, in a triple error-detecting code.

00 · · · 0000
00 · · · 0001
00 · · · 0011
00 · · · 0111

The check symbols must be distinct. Suppose only 2 check bits are used. Then 00 cannot be a check symbol for the first three information symbols. If it were, the corresponding codeword would have been covered by the next codeword and the distance between them would be at most 3. Further, 00 cannot be a check symbol for the last word either. This is because the codeword with information part 00 · · · 01111 would cover the fourth codeword and the distance would be at most 3. Thus, we are left with only three distinct check symbols {11, 10, 01}, and they are not sufficient. Therefore, we need at least 3 check bits to detect 3 errors, or at most 2 errors can be detected using 2 check bits. Thus, the double error-detecting codes described above are optimal.

Next we try to construct four error-detecting codes using 3 check bits. Then 000 and 111 cannot be check symbols for any of the information symbols. This can be shown by a similar argument discussed in the last paragraph. Thus, only six check symbols are left. Suppose weight 1, say 001, is a check for some information symbol. Then consider the set of information symbols, which are a maximal cover of length 4, with this information symbol as the first element. Without loss of generality we can take the following symbols.

Information Part	Check Part
· · · 0000	001
· · · 0001	--0
· · · 0011	--0
· · · 0111	--0

The check symbols must all be distinct. Moreover, the least significant bit of the last three check symbols must be 0. If it were 1, then either the distance between the codewords would become less than 5 or we would be forced to use 111 as the check symbol. But we have proved that 111 cannot be used as a check symbol. Thus, we are left with {010, 100, 110} for the last three information symbols. From the above argument it can be further noted that no two weight-1 symbols can appear as check symbols for two information symbols which have a distance between them of exactly 1. If they were, we would be forced to use 000 as one of the check symbols. Thus, whatever way we assign {010, 100, 110} for the last three information symbols, two consecutive information symbols will have two check symbols with weight 1. Thus, we need at least 4 check bits to detect 4 errors; i.e., we can detect at most 3 errors with 3 check bits, and thus the triple error-detecting codes described above are optimal. □

B. Error-Detecting Codes with 4 Check Bits

The codes described here can detect up to 6 errors, and these codes are also optimal.

The check symbol CS for a given word is generated as follows. Count the number of 0's in the information symbol and take mod 8. This number will be in the range between 0 and 7. Express this number in 4 bit binary. Then the most significant bit will be 0. Add 4, which in binary is 0100, to this number to get the check symbol; i.e., CS = $(k0 \bmod 8) + 4$ where $k0 \bmod 8$ and 4 are 4 bit binary numbers.

In other words, count the number of 0's in the information symbol and take mod 8. Let this number in binary be $b_2b_1b_0$. Then the check symbol $a_3a_2a_1a_0$ is given by $a_3 = b_2, a_2 = \overline{b}_2, a_1 = b_1, a_0 = b_0$ or $a_3 = \overline{b}_2, a_2 = b_2, a_1 = b_1, a_0 = b_0$.

For example, let the number of information bits be 24. Then the check symbols for the given set of maximal cover information symbols are shown below.

24 bit information symbols		Check symbols
0 · · · 00000	0000	0100
0 · · · 00000	0001	1011
0 · · · 00000	0011	1010
0 · · · 00000	0111	1001
0 · · · 00000	1111	1000
0 · · · 00001	1111	0111
0 · · · 00011	1111	0110
0 · · · 00111	1111	0101
0 · · · 01111	1111	0100
0 · · · 11111	1111	1011

The check bits $a_3a_2a_1a_0$ are divided into two parts of 2 bits each, a_3a_2 and a_1a_0. a_3a_2 can take either 01 or 10, whereas a_1a_0 can take all four possible combinations, namely, {11, 10, 01, 00}. Thus, the check symbols are divided into two groups with {1011, 1010, 1001, 1000} in group 1 and {0111, 0110, 0101, 0100} in group 2. Any eight codewords, which are a maximal cover with respect to their information symbols, will have all these eight symbols as their checks. These codewords can also be divided into two groups, depending upon whether the check symbol is from group 1 or 2.

Any two codewords X and Y which are in different groups are unordered because $a_3a_2 = 10$ in one case and $a_3a_2 = 01$ in the other case. Within one group of four codewords, whenever the information symbol of one codeword X covers that of the other codeword Y we get three possibilities — 1) check symbol of Y covers that of X, 2) the check symbols of X and Y are unordered, and 3) check symbol of X covers that of Y. Whenever 1) and 2) occur, X and Y will be unordered, whereas when 3) occurs, $d(X, Y)$ will be at least 7.

In the above example, where $k = 24$, the tenth codeword, whose check symbol is 1011, covers the fifth codeword, whose check symbol is 1000. Moreover, the fifth codeword is the first codeword from the bottom, covered by the ninth codeword. The Hamming distance between these two codewords is 7 because the information symbols and the check symbols differ in 5 and 2 bits, respectively. It is not difficult to show that the Hamming distance between any two codewords X and Y where X covers Y will be at least 7. Thus, the code is capable of detecting 6 errors.

The following theorem establishes the optimality of the 4 check bit codes described above.

Theorem 3.2: Any systematic code that detects 7 errors requires at least 5 check bits, if $k \geq 20$. Thus, the six error-detecting codes which use 4 check bits are optimal if $k \geq 20$.

Proof: It is sufficient to prove this theorem for the case $k = 20$. Let $X_0 = I_0 C_0$, $X_1 = I_1 C_1, \cdots, X_{20} = I_{20} C_{20}$ be 21 codewords with the information parts $I_0 = 0 \cdots 0$, $I_1 = 0 \cdots 01$, $I_2 = 0 \cdots 011, \cdots, I_{19} = 01 \cdots 1$, and $I_{20} = 1 \cdots 1$, forming a maximal cover of length 21. If there exists a code which uses only 4 check bits and detects 7 errors, then there is a proper assignment to check symbol C_i's such that either X_i and X_j are unordered or $d(X_i, X_j) \geq 8$ for all $i \neq j$ and $0 \leq i, j \leq 20$. We want to show that there is no such assignment.

Obviously, 1111 and 0000 can only be assigned to C_0 and C_{20}, respectively.

Now we want to show that none of C_1 through C_9 has weight 1. Let us consider $C_i, C_{i+1}, \cdots, C_{i+10}$ where $1 \leq i$, $i + 10 \leq 19$. If C_i has weight 1, say 0001, then C_{i+1} through C_{i+5} must be of the form ---0. Otherwise, $d(X_i, X_{i+j}) < 8$ for some $1 \leq j \leq 5$. In addition, C_{i+6} has to be of the form ---0, too. Otherwise, C_{i+6} must have weight 3, say 0111. Then there are only four possible assignments 1110, 1100, 1010, and 1000 to C_{i+1} through C_{i+5}, which is impossible since C_{i+1} through C_{i+5} have to be distinct. Now consider C_{i+7}. If it is of the form ---0, then 0001 is the only possible assignment to C_{i+8}. Thus, there is no proper assignment to C_{i+9} since C_{i+4} through C_{i+8} contain all four weight-1 symbols, 1000, 0100, 0010, and 0001. Hence, C_{i+7} must be of the form ---1. Obviously, the weight of C_{i+7} must be 2, say $C_{i+7} = 0011$. Then 1000 and 0100 must appear in C_{i+4} through C_{i+6}. This forces C_{i+8}, C_{i+9}, and C_{i+10} to be of the form 00--. Then there are only two possible assignments 0010 and 0001 to C_{i+8}, C_{i+9}, and C_{i+10} which are impossible.

Therefore, C_i cannot be of weight 1. That is, none of C_1 through C_9 has weight 1.

Similarly, none of C_{11} through C_{19} has weight 3.

Next, using these consequences, we can show that C_{10}, C_{11}, C_{12} cannot have weight 1, too. Suppose the weight of C_i, where $i = 10, 11, 12$, is 1, say 0001. Then, using the same argument as before, we can prove that C_{i+1} through C_{i+6} must be of the form ---0. But none of C_{i+1} through C_{i+6} has weight 3, and thus 1000, 0100, and 0010 must appear among them. This forces C_{i+7} to be of the form 000-. Further, 0001 cannot be assigned to C_{i+7}.

Therefore, C_{10}, C_{11}, and C_{12} cannot have weight 1.

Similarly, C_8, C_9, and C_{10} cannot have weight 3.

By these consequences, C_8 through C_{12} must all have weight 2; and none of these can be assigned to C_5 through C_7. Thus, at least two of C_5 through C_7 will have weight 3. Observing that any two weight-3 symbols cover five weight-2 symbols, we know that there are at most two weight-3 symbols and at most one weight-2 symbol which can be assigned to C_1 through C_4, which is impossible.

Thus, we have proved the theorem. □

Note: When $16 \leq k \leq 19$, we do have codes which detect more than 6 errors using 4 check bits; i.e., when $k = 16, 17, 18$, and 19 we have codes that detect 9, 8, 7, and 7 errors, respectively.

Furthermore, all these can be proved to be optimal. But no simple implementations like the one we designed for detecting 6 errors have been found yet for these codes.

C. Error-Detecting Codes with More than 4 Check Bits

Method 1: Let $(a_{r-1}, a_{r-2}, \cdots, a_0)$ be the r bit check symbol where $r \geq 5$. We can again divide the check bits into two parts with $a_{r-1}a_{r-2}$ in the first part and the remaining $r - 2$ bits in the other part. The 2 most significant bits can take only 01 and 10, whereas the next $r - 2$ bits can take all 2^{r-2} possible binary $(r - 2)$ tuples. Thus, the number of check symbols will be $2 \times 2^{r-2} = 2^{r-1}$. The check symbols can be generated as follows.

Count the number of 0's in the information symbol and take modulo 2^{r-1}. Express this number in terms of an r bit binary number. The most significant bit of this number will be 0. Add 2^{r-2} to this number; i.e., CS $= (k0 \bmod 2^{r-1}) + 2^{r-2}$ where $k0 \bmod 2^{r-1}$ and 2^{r-2} are r bits long, even though $r - 1$ bits are sufficient.

For example, when $r = 5$, there will be 16 check symbols. The repetitive check symbol sequence for the information symbols, which are a maximal cover, will be $\cdots$, 10111, 10110, 10101, 10100, 10011, 10010, 10001, 10000, 01111, 01110, 01101, 01100, 01011, 01010, 01001, 01000, $\cdots$.

It can be verified that the codes described above can detect up to $2^{r-2} + r - 2$ errors.

Even though the encoding/decoding methods, which are described in the next section, are simpler for these codes, their error-detecting capabilities are less efficient than that of the codes given below.

Method 2: Instead of dividing the check bits into two parts of 2 bits and $r - 2$ bits, in this method they are divided into two parts of 4 bits and $r - 4$ bits. The first 4 bits take any one of the 2-out-of-4 vectors, namely, 0011, 0101, 0110, 1001, 1010, or 1100, whereas the last $r - 4$ bits take any one among the 2^{r-4} binary $(r - 4)$ tuples. Thus, there are $6 \times 2^{r-4}$ distinct check symbols. Let CS$' \equiv ko \bmod (6 \times 2^{r-4})$. Thus, CS$'$ is $(r - 1)$ bits long. The 3 most significant bits of CS$'$ can be $\{000, 001, 010, 011, 100, 101\}$ in binary or $\{0, 1, 2, 3, 4, 5\}$ in decimal. Now define any one-to-one function f from $\{0, 1, 2, 3, 4, 5\}$ to 2-out-of-4 code. One simple function is $f(i) \leq f(j)$ for $i < j$ where $0 \leq i, j \leq 5$; i.e.,

$f(000) = 0011$, $f(001) = 0101$, $f(010) = 0110$, $f(011) = 1001$, $f(100) = 1010$, and $f(101) = 1100$. The concatenation of these 2-out-of-4 codes to the least $r - 4$ bits of CS′ gives the check symbol CS.

For example, let $r = 5$. Consider maximal cover information symbols of length 12. Let the number of 0's in the first information symbol be 11 mod 12. Then the check symbols appear in the following sequence.

	Information part			Check part
$X0$	···0000	0000	0000	11001
$X1$	···0000	0000	0001	11000
$X2$	···0000	0000	0011	10101
$X3$	···0000	0000	0111	10100
$X4$	···0000	0000	1111	10011
$X5$	···0000	0001	1111	10010
$X6$	···0000	0011	1111	01101
$X7$	···0000	0111	1111	01100
$X8$	···0000	1111	1111	01011
$X9$	···0001	1111	1111	01010
$X10$	···0011	1111	1111	00111
$X11$	···0111	1111	1111	00110

In any collection of $5 \times 2^{r-4}$ codewords whose information symbols are a maximal cover, every pair of codewords is unordered. Further, whenever a codeword X covers another codeword Y, then it can be verified that $d(X, Y) \geq 5 \cdot 2^{r-4} + r - 3$. Thus, these codes are capable of detecting $5 \cdot 2^{r-4} + r - 4$ errors. When $r = 5$, the codes designed by both Methods 1 and 2 detect 11 errors. But, when $r \geq 6$, $5 \cdot 2^{r-4} + r - 4 > 2^{r-2} + r - 2$, and thus the codes designed by Method 2 are superior.

The error-detecting capabilities of codes designed by both methods are tabulated in Table I.

Even though at the present time we do not have a proof for the optimality of these codes, we feel that these are either optimal or close to optimal. For example, we could prove that any code with 5 check bits can detect at most 12 errors, whereas the proposed code here detects up to 11 errors. The optimality problem is under investigation, and the results will be given in a future correspondence.

TABLE I
MAXIMUM NUMBER OF ERRORS DETECTED BY CODES DESIGNED BY METHODS 1 AND 2

Number of Check Bits, r	No. of Errors Detected	
	Method 1	Method 2
5	11	11
6	20	22
7	37	43
8	70	84
9	135	165
10	264	326
11	521	647
12	1034	1288

IV. ENCODING/DECODING OF THE CODES

In all codes presented in this paper, the check symbols are given by $k0$ mod m where m is some appropriate integer. Thus, in order to generate the check symbol at the encoder side, we need a circuit which counts the number of 0's mod m. To verify whether the received word is error free, again we need to count the number of 0's mod m in the received word and compare this with the received check symbol. If they match, then the received codeword is error free; otherwise, there must be some error.

In a sequential encoding/decoding method a simple mod m counter, which increments for every input 0, is all we need. However, in a computer system where the data transfer rate is on the order of hundreds of kilobits per second, we need a faster encoding/decoding technique.

When m is a power of 2, which is true for codes, with r, the number of check bits, greater than or equal to 5 (by Method 1) and equal to 2, 3, and 4, the 0 counter circuit can be implemented using a tree-type r bit 2's complement adder circuit. For simplicity, let k be a power of 2 and the bits be in the complemented form. At the first level the bits are added using $(k/2)$ 1 bit adders, so that we get 2 bit output. At the second level these 2 bit numbers are added using $(k/2^2)$ 2 bit input and 3 bit output adders, and so on, until we get r bit output numbers at level $r - 1$. From then on we need to add these r bit numbers using r bit adders. The carry from the most significant bit can be ignored. An example is shown in Fig. 1 to generate $k0$ mod 4 for the double error-detecting code with $k = 8$.

For the codes designed by Method 1 in Section III-C, where $r \geq 5$, we can generate $r - 1$ bits $X_{r-2}, X_{r-3}, \cdots, X_0$ using the technique described above. Then the r check bits $a_{r-1}, a_{r-2}, \cdots, a_0$ are given by $a_{r-1} = X_{r-2}$, $a_{r-2} = \overline{X}_{r-2}$, and $a_i = X_i$ for $i = 0, 1, 2, \cdots, r - 3$.

For the codes designed by Method 2 in Section III-C, first we need to generate ko mod$(6 \times 2^{r-4})$ where $r \geq 5$. In a sequential encoding a simple modulo $6 \times 2^{r-4}$ counter can be used to find this value. The second method of generating ko mod$(6 \times 2^{r-4})$ is to use a tree of adders similar to the one we described above, but with some minor modifications. i bit adders (two i bit inputs and one $(i + 1)$ bit output) are used for levels $i = 1, 2, 3, \cdots, r - 3$. For levels $r - 2$, $r - 1, \cdots, \lceil \log_2 k \rceil$, modulo$(6 \times 2^{r-4})$ adders are used to add two $(r - 1)$ bit numbers to get one $(r - 1)$ number. This circuit is much faster than the sequential encoding.

After generating ko mod$(6 \times 2^{r-4})$ we need to translate the 3 most significant bits to a 2-out-of-4 code as described by the one-to-one function f. To implement this, an appropriate combinational circuit with 3 inputs and 4 outputs, corresponding to function f, can be designed.

When a conventional checker is used at the decoder side, these checkers form the "hard core." Any fault at the checker is not tolerated and may result in disaster. In order to reduce this hard-core problem, TSC checkers are introduced [7].

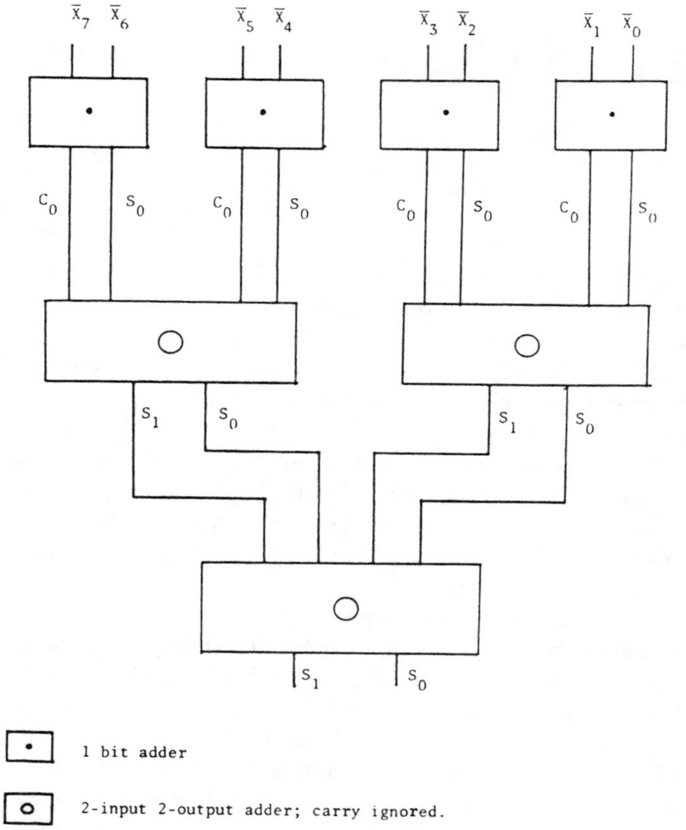

Fig. 1. Check symbol generator circuit for double error-detecting code with $k = 8$.

These TSC checkers not only detect errors in the data word but also detect faults in the checker circuits. Further properties of TSC circuits can be found in [7], [16], [17]. The TSC checkers for the codes presented here will be given in a future correspondence.

V. Conclusion

In this paper, we described the theory and design of t-unidirectional error-detecting codes. Unlike t-symmetric error-detecting codes, where the number of check bits grows proportionately to the number of information bits, a t-unidirectional error-detecting code needs a fixed number of check bits, independent of the number of information bits. The codes presented here are optimal or near optimal, and the encoder/decoder circuits are simple to implement.

References

[1] E. R. Berlekamp, *Algebraic Coding Theory.* New York: McGraw-Hill, 1968.

[2] S. Lin, *An Introduction to Error-Correcting Codes.* Englewood Cliffs, NJ: Prentice-Hall, 1970.

[3] W. W. Peterson and E. J. Weldon, *Error Correcting Codes.* Cambridge, MA: M.I.T. Press, 1972.

[4] N. J. A. Sloane and F. J. MacWilliams, *The Theory of Error Correcting Codes.* Amsterdam, The Netherlands: North-Holland, 1977.

[5] R. W. Cook *et al.*, "Design of self-checking microprogram control," *IEEE Trans. Comput.*, vol. C-22, pp. 255–262, Mar. 1973.

[6] D. K. Pradhan and J. J. Stiffler, "Error correcting codes and self-checking circuits in fault-tolerant computers," *IEEE Computer*, vol. 13, pp. 27–37, Mar. 1980.

[7] D. A. Anderson and G. Metze, "Design of totally self-checking circuits for *m*-out-of-*n* codes," *IEEE Trans. Comput.*, vol. C-22, pp. 263–269, Mar. 1973.

[8] J. M. Berger, "A note on error detecting codes for asymmetric channels," *Inform. Contr.*, vol. 4, pp. 68–73, Mar. 1961.

[9] C. V. Freiman, "Optimal error detection codes for completely asymmetric binary channels," *Inform. Contr.*, vol. 5, pp. 64–71, Mar. 1962.

[10] H. Dong, "Modified Berger codes for detection of unidirectional errors," in *Dig. Papers, 12th Int. Symp. Fault-Tolerant Comput.*, June 1982, pp. 317–320.

[11] J. M. Borden, "Optimal asymmetric error detecting codes," *Inform. Contr.*, to appear.

[12] R. R. Varshamov, "A class of codes for asymmetric channels and a problem from additive theory of numbers," *IEEE Trans. Inform. Theory*, vol. IT-19, pp. 92–95, Jan. 1973.

[13] S. D. Constantin and T. R. N. Rao, "On the theory of binary asymmetric error correcting codes," *Inform. Contr.*, vol. 40, pp. 20–26, Jan. 1979.

[14] B. Bose and S. Cunningham, "Systematic and multiple asymmetric error correcting codes," *IEEE Trans. Inform. Theory*, to appear.

[15] B. Bose and T. R. N. Rao, "Theory of unidirectional error correcting/detecting codes," *IEEE Trans. Comput.*, vol. C-31, pp. 521–530, June 1982.

[16] J. F. Wakerly, *Error Detecting Codes, Self-Checking Circuits and Applications.* Amsterdam, The Netherlands: North-Holland, 1978.

[17] B. Bose and D. J. Lin, "PLA implementation of *k*-out-of-*n* code TSC checker," *IEEE Trans. Comput.*, vol. C-33, pp. 583–588, June 1984.

[18] J. E. Smith, "On separable unordered codes," *IEEE Trans. Comput.*, vol. C-33, pp. 741–743, Aug. 1984.

[19] D. K. Pradhan, "A new class of error correcting/detecting codes for fault-tolerant computer applications," *IEEE Trans. Comput.*, vol. C-29, pp. 471–481, June 1980.

[20] B. Bose, "On systematic SEC–MUED codes," in *Dig. Papers, 11th Int. Symp. Fault-Tolerant Comput.*, June 1981, pp. 265–267.

[21] B. Bose and D. K. Pradhan, "Optimal unidirectional error detecting/correcting codes," *IEEE Trans. Comput.*, vol. C-31, pp. 564–568, June 1982.

[22] D. Nikolos, N. Gaitanis, and G. Philokyprou, "Systematic error correcting and all unidirectional error detecting codes starting from cyclic AN codes," in *Dig. Papers, 14th Int. Conf. Fault-Tolerant Comput.*, June 1984, pp. 318–323.

Bella Bose (S'78–M'79) received the B.E. degree in electrical engineering from Madras University in 1973, the M.E. degree in electrical engineering from the Indian Institute of Science, Bangalore, India, in 1975, and the M.S. and Ph.D. degrees in computer science from Southern Methodist University, Dallas, TX, in 1979 and 1980, respectively.

From September 1975 to December 1976 he was an Instructor in the Department of Electrical Engineering, Birla Institute of Technology and Science. Presently, he is an Associate Professor in the Department of Computer Science, Oregon State University, Corvallis. His current research interests include fault-tolerant computing, coding theory, computer architecture, and algorithm analysis.

Dr. Bose is a member of the Association for Computing Machinery.

Der Jei Lin received the B.S. and M.A. degrees in mathematics from Fu-Jen University, Taipei, Taiwan, and Oakland University, Rochester, MI, respectively, and is currently working towards the Ph.D. degree in computer science at Oregon State University, Corvallis.

His research interests include coding theory, combinatorics, the design and analysis of algorithms, and cryptography.

Efficient Balanced Codes

DONALD E. KNUTH, HONORARY MEMBER, IEEE

***Abstract*—Coding schemes in which each codeword contains equally many zeros and ones are constructed in such a way that they can be efficiently encoded and decoded.**

A BINARY word of length m can be called *balanced* if it contains exactly $\lfloor m/2 \rfloor$ ones and $\lceil m/2 \rceil$ zeros. Let us say that a *balanced code* with n information bits and p parity bits is a set of 2^n balanced binary words, each of length $n+p$.

Balanced codes have the property that no codeword is "contained" in another; that is, the positions of the ones in one codeword will never be a subset of the positions of the ones in a different codeword. This property makes balanced codes attractive for certain applications, such as the encoding of unchangeable data on a laser disk [2]. Conversely, if we wish to form as many binary words of length m as possible with the property that no word is contained in another, Sperner's lemma [3] tells us that we can do no better than to construct the set of all balanced words of length m.

A balanced code is *efficient* if there is a very simple way to encode and decode n-bit numbers. In other words, we want to find a one-to-one correspondence between the set of all n-bit binary words and the set of all $(n+p)$-bit codewords such that, if w corresponds to w', we can rapidly compute w' from w and vice versa. Furthermore, we want p to be very small compared with n, so that the code is efficient in its use of space as well as time. For example, it is trivial to construct a balanced code with n information bits and n parity bits by simply letting the binary word w correspond to the codeword $w' = w\overline{w}$, where $\overline{w}$ is the complement of w. Encoding and decoding is clearly efficient in this case, but memory space is being wasted.

Let $M(m) = \binom{m}{\lfloor m/2 \rfloor}$ be the total number of balanced binary words of length m. To have a balanced code with n information bits, we clearly need to have enough parity bits p so that $M(n+p) \geq 2^n$. Stirling's approximation tells us that

$$\log M(m) = m - \frac{1}{2}\log m - \frac{1}{2}\log\frac{\pi}{2} - \frac{\epsilon(m)}{m},$$

where $0 \leq \epsilon(m) \leq 1.25/\ln 2 < 1.81$; all logarithms here have radix 2, and the constant $1/2 \log \pi/2$ is approximately 0.326. Therefore, in particular, we must have $p > 1/2 \log n + 0.326$ in any balanced code.

The purpose of this correspondence is to describe a balanced code with 2^p information bits and p parity bits, for which serial encoding and decoding is especially simple. This means, for example, that 256-b words can be encoded efficiently with only eight parity bits, obtaining 264-b balanced words; thus the percentage of memory devoted to overhead in order to satisfy the balance constraint is only $8/264 = 3.03$ percent.

A similar scheme that allows efficient *parallel* decoding and efficient serial encoding is also described. The parallel method for n information bits takes roughly $\log n + 1/2 \log\log n$ parity bits in its simplest form, and the $1/2 \log\log n$ term can be replaced by 1 at the expense of additional complexity. For example, a balanced code with 256 information bits and nine parity bits will be constructed explicitly. This code has the property that the 256-b word w corresponds to a balanced 265-b codeword $w' = uw^{(k)}$, where $w^{(k)}$ denotes w with its first k bits complemented and where the 9-b prefix u determines k. It is clearly possible to determine w quickly from w' in such a code.

A Simple Parallel Scheme

Let $\nu(w)$ be the total number of ones in the binary word w, let $\nu_k(w)$ be the number of ones in the first k bits of w, and let $w^{(k)}$ be the word w with its first k bits complemented. For example, if $w = 0111010110$, we have $\nu(w) = 6$, $\nu_4(w) = 3$, and $w^{(4)} = 1000010110$. Since $k - \nu_k(w)$ of the first k bits of w are zeros, we have

$$\nu(w^{(k)}) = \nu(w) + k - 2\nu_k(w).$$

This relation is the key to all the coding schemes that will be described in the following.

If w has length n and if we let $\sigma_k(w)$ stand for $\nu(w^{(k)})$, the quantity $\sigma_k(w)$ changes by ± 1 when k increases by one, so it describes a "random walk" from $\sigma_0(w) = \nu(w)$ to $\sigma_n(w) = n - \nu(w)$.

Now comes the point: the value $\lfloor n/2 \rfloor$ lies in the closed interval between ν and $n - \nu$ for all integers ν; hence a k always exists such that $\sigma_k(w) = \lfloor n/2 \rfloor$. In other words, every word w can be associated with at least one k such that $w^{(k)}$ is balanced. If we encode k in a balanced word u of length p, and if n and p are not both odd, we can let w correspond to the balanced codeword $uw^{(k)}$. If n and p are both odd, we can use a similar construction, but the

Manuscript received November 12, 1984; revised July 8, 1985. This work was supported in part by the National Science Foundation under Grant DCR-83-00984.

The author is with the Computer Science Department, Stanford University, Stanford, CA 94305.

IEEE Log Number 8406080.

0-8186-4182-7/93 $3.00 © 1986 IEEE

value of k should be chosen so that $\sigma_k(w) = \lceil n/2 \rceil$; then again $uw^{(k)}$ will be balanced.

For example, suppose that we want a balanced code of this sort having eight information bits. Every 8-b word w defines at least one value of k such that $w^{(k)}$ is balanced; we never need to use $k = 8$, so we can assume that $0 \le k < 8$. If we arbitrarily choose eight balanced words $(u_0, \cdots, u_7)$ of length five, we can represent w by the balanced word $u_k w^{(k)}$. (Such a choice of u's is possible since $M(5) = 10 > 8$.) This gives a code with eight information bits and five parity bits. Parallel decoding is easy, because k is determined from u_k by table-lookup; then w is $w^{(k)(k)}$. Serial encoding is also easy because we can determine k by computing $\sigma_k(w)$ for $k = 0, 1, \cdots$ until finding $\sigma_k(w) = 4$.

A similar scheme gives a balanced code with 256 information bits and 11 parity bits, because $M(11) > 256$. In general, this approach works with n information bits and p parity bits whenever $M(p) \ge 2\lceil n/2 \rceil$.

A Simple Serial Scheme

We can decrease the number of parity bits in the previous construction by using all the bits of u. The idea is to encode w as $uw^{(k)}$ for some u and k, as before, but u does not have to be balanced; any imbalance in u will be compensated by a corresponding imbalance in $w^{(k)}$. For example, when $n = 4$ and $p = 2$ we can simply let $k = 0$ when $0 < \nu(w) < 4$; if $\nu(w) = 1, 2, 3$ we can let $u = 11, 01, 00$, respectively. The remaining two cases $w = 0000$ and $w = 1111$ are handled by letting $k = 2$ and $u = 10$.

When $n = 8$ and $p = 3$, an exhaustive analysis shows that no similar scheme exists in which k is determined by u; however, we can construct a code in which u is determined by $\nu(w)$ as follows:

$\nu(w)$	u	s	$\nu(w)$	u	s	$\nu(w)$	u	s
0	001	4	3	101	3	6	111	2
1	011	3	4	100	4	7	110	3
2	010	4	5	000	5	8	001	4.

The word $uw^{(k)}$ will be balanced in this case if and only if $\nu(uw^{(k)}) = \nu(u) + \sigma_k(w) = \lfloor 11/2 \rfloor = 5$; this happens if and only if $\sigma_k(w) = s$, where the values of s have been tabulated. Since $\sigma_k(w)$ runs from $\nu(n)$ to $n - \nu(n)$, it is easy to verify in each case that some value of k will make $\sigma_k(w) = s$. The code is defined by choosing the smallest such k.

To decode this scheme, that is, to deduce w given $uw^{(k)} = uv$, we first determine $\nu(w)$ from u. Then we find the smallest k such that $\sigma_k(v) = \nu(w)$. This is the value of k for which $v = w^{(k)}$. (Why? Because the value of k used in the encoding clearly has this property. Furthermore, if $w = v^{(k)}$ and if $\sigma_{k'}(v) = \sigma_k(v)$ for some $k' < k$, then $\nu(v^{(k')}) = \nu(v^{(k)})$; hence $\nu_k(v) = \nu_{k'}(v) + (k - k')/2$; hence $\nu_k(w) = \nu_{k'}(w) + (k - k')/2$ and $\sigma'_k(w) = \sigma_k(w)$, contradicting the minimality of k. We are essentially applying the "reflection principle" of [1].)

One complication exists, however: two different values of $\nu(w)$ correspond to the same value of u, namely, $u = 001$ has both $\nu(w) = 0$ and $\nu(w) = 8$. This is not really a difficulty, because it arises only for the two words $w = 00000000$ and 11111111 (when we know that $k = 4$); but it is an annoying anomaly. The best way to avoid it is to consider only the values of $\sigma_k(v)$ modulo 8 when decoding. We know $\nu(w)$ mod 8, so we choose the smallest k such that $\sigma_k(v) \equiv \nu(w)$ (modulo 8).

Incidentally, there is no balanced code with $n = 8$ and $p = 2$, since $M(10) = 252$ is less than 256. Therefore, the balanced code just defined is optimum for $n = 8$.

A similar balanced code can be constructed with p parity bits and $n = 2^p$ information bits, for all $p \ge 3$, as follows. For $0 \le l < n$, let u_l be a p-bit word such that the number

$$s_l = n/2 + \lfloor p/2 \rfloor \nu(u_l)$$

lies between l and $n - l$, inclusive. This should be a permutation of the p-bit words; that is, $l \ne l'$ should imply that $u_l \ne u_{l'}$. An n-bit word w is then encoded as $u_l w^{(k)}$, where $l = \nu(w)$ mod n and where k is minimal such that $\sigma_k(w) \equiv s_l$ (modulo n). An $(n + p)$-bit word $w' = uv$ is decoded as $v^{(k)}$, where k is minimal such that $\sigma_k(v) \equiv l$ (modulo n) and where l is determined by the condition $u = u_l$.

It remains to specify the correspondence between l and u_l. Since p is much smaller than n, the choice is delicate only when l is near $n/2$. It is not difficult to find a mapping that assigns the balanced words to values of l near $n/2$; the rest of the codes are essentially arbitrary.

For example, let $p = 8$ and $n = 256$. We want to permute the 8-b words u_{128+t} for $-128 \le t < 128$ in such a way that $0 \le t + \nu(u_{128+t}) - 4 \le 2t$ when $t \ge 0$ and $0 \ge t + \nu(u_{128+t}) - 4 \ge 2t$ when $t < 0$. The inequalities are always valid when $|t| \ge 4$, so the choice of u_l is important only when $124 < l < 132$. A suitable mapping is obtained by letting $u_l = a_l b_l$, where a_l is the 4-b binary representation of $(l + 8)$ mod 16 and b_l is the 4-b binary representation of

$$\left(\tfrac{1}{16}(l - 120 - a_l) + \bar{a}_l\right) \bmod 16.$$

If $120 \le l < 136$ this make $b_l = \bar{a}_l$; hence u_l is balanced. Conversely, it is easy to deduce l from a given pair of 4-b words ab:

$$l = (120 + a + 16((b - \bar{a}) \bmod 16)) \bmod 256.$$

An Optimized Parallel Scheme

We have now constructed two balanced codes with $n = 256$; one has $p = 11$ parity bits to allow parallel decoding, and the other has $p = 8$ parity bits to allow serial decoding. The author has been unable to construct a parallel decoder for such schemes when $n = 256$ and $p = 8$, but the following method gives parallel decoding when $p = 9$ and in general whenever $n = 2^{p-1}$.

The idea is to choose l words $(u_1, \cdots, u_l)$ of p bits each and to choose l values $(k_1, \cdots, k_l)$ in the range $0 \le k_j \le n$

such that every random walk

$$(0, \sigma_0(w)), (1, \sigma_1(w)), \cdots, (n, \sigma_n(w)) \qquad (*)$$

is guaranteed to pass through one of the points

$$P_j = \left(k_j, \lfloor (n+p)/2 \rfloor - \nu(u_j)\right)$$

for some j. We can then encode w as the balanced word $u_j w^{(k_j)}$. Parallel decoding is possible since the p-bit parity word u determines the extent of complementation.

We shall choose the u's and k's in such a way that $\nu(u_{j+1}) - \nu(u_j) = 0$ or 1 and $k_{j+1} - k_j = 1 - (\nu(u_{j+1}) - \nu(u_j))$. This means that $P_{j+1} - P_j$ is always either $(1,0)$ or $(0,-1)$. For example, when $p = 3$ and $n = 4$, we can let the pairs (k_j, u_j) be

$$(0,001) \quad (1,010) \quad (2,100) \quad (2,011) \quad (3,101) \quad (4,110)$$

so that the points P_j are

$$(0,2) \quad (1,2) \quad (2,2) \quad (2,1) \quad (3,1) \quad (4,1).$$

We shall also choose $k_1 = 0$ and $k_l = n$, so that any random walk $(*)$ must lie entirely "above" or "below" the set of P's.

Let $P_1 = (0, M)$ and $P_l = (n, m)$ be the extreme points. If $(*)$ does not intersect the set $\{P_1, \cdots, P_l\}$, we must have either $(\sigma_0(w) > M$ and $\sigma_n(w) > m)$ or $(\sigma_0(w) < M$ and $\sigma_n(w) < m)$. Since $\sigma_0(w) + \sigma_n(w) = n$, this cannot happen unless $n > M + m + 2$ or $n \le M + m - 2$. Therefore, it suffices to design the construction so that $|M + m - n| \le 1$.

A moment's thought now makes it clear what to do: we list all p-bit numbers u in any order such that the weights $\nu(v)$ are nondecreasing, then we choose $l = n + h + 1$ of these near the "middle" of the sequence such that $\nu(u_l) - \nu(u_1) = h$ for some h. For example, the case $p = 3$ worked out earlier has $h = 1$ and $l = 6$. When $p = 9$ there are 126 u's of weight four and 126 of weight five; we can take $h = 3$, $l = 260$, starting with any four words $(u_1, \cdots, u_4)$ of weight three, then $(u_5, \cdots, u_{130})$ of weight four, then $(u_{131}, \cdots, u_{256})$ of weight five, and $(u_{257}, \cdots, u_{260})$ of weight six. In this case $n = 256$, $M = \lfloor 265/2 \rfloor - 3 = 129$, $m = \lfloor 265/2 \rfloor - 6 = 126$; hence $M + m = n - 1$ and we have achieved our objective. It is not difficult to verify that the method works for all $p \ge 3$: when p is odd, h will be odd, and we will have $M = (n + h - 1)/2$, $m = (n - h - 1)/2$, but when p is even, h will be even and we will have $M = (n+h)/2$, $m = (n-h)/2$.

The method just described does not depend in any essential way on the assumption that n is a power of two. We can use it, in fact, to transmit as many as $2^p - p - 1$ information bits if we let $l = 2^p$.

Acknowledgment

The author wishes to thank an anonymous referee for several penetrating observations that substantially improved this correspondence.

References

[1] D. André, "Solution directe du problème resolu par M. Bertrand," *Comptes Rendus*, Acad. Sci. Paris, vol. 105, pp. 436–437, 1887.

[2] E. L. Leiss, "Data integrity in digital optical disks," *IEEE Trans. Comput.*, vol. C-33, pp. 818–827, 1984.

[3] E. Sperner, "Ein Satz über Untermengen einer endlichen Menge," *Math. Zeitschrift*, vol. 27, pp. 544–548, 1928.

CHAPTER 3: CODES FOR CORRECTING UNIDIRECTIONAL ERRORS

This chapter focuses on the study of codes that correct unidirectional errors — a difficult topic, since conditions for correcting unidirectional errors are more complicated than conditions for codes correcting t errors and detecting all unidirectional errors (which is covered in Chapter 4). The known constructions are mainly combinatorial and more of theoretical than of practical interest. Engineers dealing with a limited number of unidirectional errors and fairly large block codes will certainly use traditional error-correcting codes,[1,2] since no known practical codes can correct unidirectional errors nor have a better information rate than traditional codes.

Weber, de Vroedt, and Boekee introduce codes correcting unidirectional errors, as well as necessary and sufficient conditions, code constructions, and upper bounds. The authors introduce a distance (denoted d_3 in their paper) that enables us to define the unidirectional correction capability of a code as a function of d_3 (as the Hamming distance of a code defines its symmetric error-correcting capability). In other words, a code C can correct up to t unidirectional errors if (and only if) $d_3 \geq 2t+1$. Interested readers will find further reading in our references.[50,51]

Saitoh, Yamaguchi, and Imai discuss constructions of codes correcting asymmetric and unidirectional errors (and thus, lower bounds), using two programs based on a greedy algorithm. The authors present tables with the number of code words for correcting three, four, five, and six errors and lengths from 14 to 23.

Etzion concludes Chapter 3 with further constructions of asymmetric and unidirectional correction codes, using various methods. Again, results are tabulated for blocks of length up to 23 and, in general, are better than those contained in the previous paper.

Our references contain further reading on these topics.[52]

Bounds and Constructions for Codes Correcting Unidirectional Errors

JACOBUS H. WEBER, STUDENT MEMBER, IEEE, CORNELIS DE VROEDT, AND DICK E. BOEKEE

Abstract—We first give a brief introduction on the theory of codes correcting unidirectional errors in connection with symmetric and asymmetric error-correcting codes. Upper bounds on the size of a code of length n correcting t or fewer unidirectional errors are then derived. Methods in which codes correcting up to t unidirectional errors are constructed by expurgating t-fold asymmetric error correcting codes or by expurgating and puncturing t-fold symmetric error correcting codes are also presented. Finally, tables summarizing some results on the size of optimal unidirectional error-correcting codes which follow from these bounds and constructions are given.

I. Introduction

We consider coding systems with a binary memoryless channel and use a binary block code C of length n ($C \subseteq (\mathrm{GF}(2))^n = V$). We will hereafter refer to the transition $0 \to 1$ as a 0-error and to the transition $1 \to 0$ as a 1-error. Most classes of codes have been designed for use on symmetric channels on which 0-errors and 1-errors occur with equal probability (*symmetric errors*). However, in certain applications, such as optical communications, the error probability from 1 to 0 is significantly higher than the error probability from 0 to 1. These applications can be modeled by an asymmetric channel on which only 1-errors can occur (*asymmetric errors*). Further, some of the recently developed VLSI memory systems behave like a unidirectional channel, on which, even though both $1 \to 0$ and $0 \to 1$ errors are possible, all errors are of the same type in a single data word (*unidirectional errors*). In this paper we are interested in codes correcting errors of the latter type.

We first define the error types just mentioned in a more formal way. For any $\boldsymbol{u} = (u_1, u_2, \cdots, u_n) \in V$ and $\boldsymbol{v} \in (v_1, v_2, \cdots, v_n) \in V$, let $N(\boldsymbol{u}, \boldsymbol{v})$ denote the number of coordinates where $\boldsymbol{u}$ is 0 and $\boldsymbol{v}$ is 1 ($N(\boldsymbol{u}, \boldsymbol{v}) = |\{ i | u_i = 0 \wedge v_i = 1\}|$). We say that the vector $\boldsymbol{u}$ is covered by the vector $\boldsymbol{v}$ if $N(\boldsymbol{v}, \boldsymbol{u}) = 0$ (notation: $\boldsymbol{v} \geq \boldsymbol{u}$).

Manuscript received January 14, 1988; revised June 15, 1988. This paper was presented in part at the 1988 IEEE International Symposium on Information Theory, Kobe, Japan, June 19–24, 1988, and at the 1988 Beijing International Workshop on Information Theory, Beijing, People's Republic of China, July 3–7, 1988.

J. H. Weber and D. E. Boekee are with the Delft University of Technology, Department of Electrical Engineering, Information Theory Group, P.O. Box 5031, 2600 GA Delft, The Netherlands.

C. de Vroedt is with the Delft University of Technology, Department of Mathematics and Informatics, P.O Box 356, 2600 AJ Delft, The Netherlands.

IEEE Log Number 8929039.

Definition 1: Assume that we transmit a vector $\boldsymbol{e} \in V$ and receive a vector $\boldsymbol{f} \in V$.

a) We say that $\boldsymbol{e}$ has suffered t *symmetric* or *random errors* if

$$N(\boldsymbol{e}, \boldsymbol{f}) + N(\boldsymbol{f}, \boldsymbol{e}) = t.$$

b) We say that $\boldsymbol{e}$ has suffered t *asymmetric errors* if

$$N(\boldsymbol{e}, \boldsymbol{f}) = 0 \wedge N(\boldsymbol{f}, \boldsymbol{e}) = t.$$

c) We say that $\boldsymbol{e}$ has suffered t *unidirectional errors* if

$$(N(\boldsymbol{e}, \boldsymbol{f}) = 0 \wedge N(\boldsymbol{f}, \boldsymbol{e}) = t) \vee (N(\boldsymbol{e}, \boldsymbol{f}) = t \wedge N(\boldsymbol{f}, \boldsymbol{e}) = 0).$$

Example 1: Let $n = 12$ and

$$\boldsymbol{e} = 111111000000$$
$$f_1 = 110000100000$$
$$f_2 = 111100000000$$
$$f_3 = 111111000001.$$

a) When sending $\boldsymbol{e}$ over a channel which may cause errors of the symmetric type, it is possible to receive $f_1(t = 5)$, $f_2(t = 2)$, or $f_3(t = 1)$.

b) When sending $\boldsymbol{e}$ over a channel which may only cause errors of the asymmetric type, it is possible to receive $f_2(t = 2)$ but impossible to receive f_1 or f_3.

c) When sending $\boldsymbol{e}$ over a channel which may only cause errors of the unidirectional type, it is possible to receive $f_2(t = 2)$ or $f_3(t = 1)$ but impossible to receive f_1.

Codes correcting symmetric errors have been studied extensively. We only mention the excellent book of MacWilliams and Sloane [11] which includes a list of more than 1000 references. The theory of asymmetric error-correcting codes is less well developed. A bibliography has been given by Kløve in [10]. As far as we know, codes correcting unidirectional errors have hardly been studied at all. Bose and Rao [4, theorem 6] have given a necessary and sufficient condition for a code to be unidirectional error correcting. Several authors have studied codes that can correct up to t random errors and detect more than t unidirectional errors [2]–[4], [12], [14].

Of course, symmetric error-correcting codes can also be used to correct unidirectional errors. However, it is likely that codes correcting up to t unidirectional errors can be constructed which contain more codewords than corresponding codes of the same length correcting up to t symmetric errors.

0-8186-4182-7/93 $3.00 © 1989 IEEE

To study the error-correcting capability of a code C, we define three distances $d_i(\boldsymbol{u}, \boldsymbol{v})$ between $\boldsymbol{u} \in V$ and $\boldsymbol{v} \in V (i = 1, 2, 3)$.

Definition 2: Let $\boldsymbol{u} \in V$ and $\boldsymbol{v} \in V$, then

a) $d_1(\boldsymbol{u}, \boldsymbol{v}) = N(\boldsymbol{u}, \boldsymbol{v}) + N(\boldsymbol{v}, \boldsymbol{u})$

b) $d_2(\boldsymbol{u}, \boldsymbol{v}) = 2\max\{N(\boldsymbol{u}, \boldsymbol{v}), N(\boldsymbol{v}, \boldsymbol{u})\}$

c) $$d_3(\boldsymbol{u}, \boldsymbol{v}) = \begin{cases} d_1(\boldsymbol{u}, \boldsymbol{v}), \text{ if } N(\boldsymbol{u}, \boldsymbol{v}) = 0 \vee N(\boldsymbol{v}, \boldsymbol{u}) = 0 \\ d_2(\boldsymbol{u}, \boldsymbol{v}), \text{ if } N(\boldsymbol{u}, \boldsymbol{v}) > 0 \wedge N(\boldsymbol{v}, \boldsymbol{u}) > 0 \end{cases}.$$

It is obvious that $d_1(\boldsymbol{u}, \boldsymbol{v}) \le d_3(\boldsymbol{u}, \boldsymbol{v}) \le d_2(\boldsymbol{u}, \boldsymbol{v})$ for all $\boldsymbol{u}, \boldsymbol{v} \in V$. The Hamming distance $d_1(\boldsymbol{u}, \boldsymbol{v})$ is related to the distance $d_2(\boldsymbol{u}, \boldsymbol{v})$ by

$$d_2(\boldsymbol{u}, \boldsymbol{v}) = d_1(\boldsymbol{u}, \boldsymbol{v}) + |w(\boldsymbol{u}) - w(\boldsymbol{v})|$$

where $w(\boldsymbol{u}) = |\{i | u_i = 1\}|$, the weight of the vector $\boldsymbol{u}$. If $w(\boldsymbol{u}) = w(\boldsymbol{v})$, then $d_1(\boldsymbol{u}, \boldsymbol{v}) = d_2(\boldsymbol{u}, \boldsymbol{v}) = d_3(\boldsymbol{u}, \boldsymbol{v})$.

Example 2: Let

$$\boldsymbol{a} = 111111000000$$
$$\boldsymbol{b} = 110000000000$$
$$\boldsymbol{c} = 101010101010.$$

Then

$$d_1(\boldsymbol{a}, \boldsymbol{b}) = 4 \qquad d_2(\boldsymbol{a}, \boldsymbol{b}) = 8 \qquad d_3(\boldsymbol{a}, \boldsymbol{b}) = d_1(\boldsymbol{a}, \boldsymbol{b}) = 4$$
$$d_1(\boldsymbol{a}, \boldsymbol{c}) = 6 \qquad d_2(\boldsymbol{a}, \boldsymbol{c}) = 6 \qquad d_3(\boldsymbol{a}, \boldsymbol{c}) = d_2(\boldsymbol{a}, \boldsymbol{c}) = 6$$
$$d_1(\boldsymbol{b}, \boldsymbol{c}) = 6 \qquad d_2(\boldsymbol{b}, \boldsymbol{c}) = 10 \quad d_3(\boldsymbol{b}, \boldsymbol{c}) = d_2(\boldsymbol{b}, \boldsymbol{c}) = 10.$$

As usual we call a distance function d: $V \times V \to \mathbb{Z}$ a *metric* on V if it satisfies the following four conditions for all $\boldsymbol{u}, \boldsymbol{v}, \boldsymbol{w} \in V$:

1) $d(\boldsymbol{u}, \boldsymbol{v}) \ge 0$

2) $d(\boldsymbol{u}, \boldsymbol{v}) = 0 \Leftrightarrow \boldsymbol{u} = \boldsymbol{v}$

3) $d(\boldsymbol{u}, \boldsymbol{v}) = d(\boldsymbol{v}, \boldsymbol{u})$

4) $d(\boldsymbol{u}, \boldsymbol{v}) + d(\boldsymbol{v}, \boldsymbol{w}) \ge d(\boldsymbol{u}, \boldsymbol{w})$ (triangle inequality).

It can easily be checked that $d_1(\boldsymbol{u}, \boldsymbol{v})$ and $d_2(\boldsymbol{u}, \boldsymbol{v})$ are both metrics on $V = (\mathrm{GF}(2))^n$. Note that $d_3(\boldsymbol{u}, \boldsymbol{v})$ does satisfy the conditions 1)–3), but it is not a metric on $(\mathrm{GF}(2))^n$ (for $n \ge 3$), since it does not satisfy the triangle inequality, as can be seen from the next example ($n = 3$):

$$d_3(110,100) + d_3(100,001) = 1 + 2 = 3 < 4 = d_3(110,001).$$

For a code C we also define three distances $d_i (i = 1,2,3)$.

Definition 3: Let $C \subseteq V$; then

$$d_i = \min\{d_i(\boldsymbol{u}, \boldsymbol{v}) | \boldsymbol{u}, \boldsymbol{v} \in C, \boldsymbol{u} \ne \boldsymbol{v}\}, \qquad \text{for } i = 1,2,3.$$

Again, it is obvious that $d_1 \le d_3 \le d_2$ for all codes C.

Example 3: Let C be the code of length 8 containing the following four codewords:

$$c_1 = 10000000$$
$$c_2 = 01110000$$
$$c_3 = 00001110$$
$$c_4 = 11101101.$$

For this code $d_1 = 4$, $d_2 = 6$, and $d_3 = 5$.

The following theorem gives necessary and sufficient conditions for the error-correcting capability of a code. The theorem simply recasts several well-known results in accordance with our notation.

Theorem 1: Let C be a code of length n with distances $d_i (i = 1,2,3)$. Then

a) C can correct t or fewer symmetric errors if and only if (iff) $d_1 \ge 2t + 1$ [11];

b) C can correct t or fewer asymmetric errors iff $d_2 \ge 2t + 1$ [10];

c) C can correct t or fewer unidirectional errors iff $d_3 \ge 2t + 1$ [4].

For the sake of completeness we include a proof of Theorem 1c) in Appendix I.

Let $A_1(n, t)$ denote the maximum number of codewords in a code of length n correcting t or fewer symmetric errors. Similarly, let $A_2(n, t)$ and $A_3(n, t)$ denote the maximum number of codewords in a code of length n correcting t or fewer asymmetric/unidirectional errors. In this paper we study upper and lower bounds on $A_3(n, t)$. Since any code of length n correcting up to t symmetric errors is also capable of correcting up to t unidirectional errors, and any code of length n correcting up to t unidirectional errors is also capable of correcting up to t asymmetric errors, it follows that $A_1(n, t) \le A_3(n, t) \le A_2(n, t)$ for $n \ge t \ge 1$. Further, a single symmetric error is necessarily unidirectional. Hence $A_3(n,1) = A_1(n,1)$ for $n \ge 1$.

In Section II we give an upper bound on $A_3(n, t)$ which can be found by solving an integer programming problem. Two other upper bounds on $A_3(n, t)$ are derived in Section III. These bounds make use of known upper bounds on $A_1(n, t)$.

Lower bounds on $A_3(n, t)$ can be obtained by constructing codes. In Section IV we derive lower bounds on $A_3(n, t)$ for $1 \le t \le n \le 2t + 3$ which equal the best known upper bounds. Hence the problem of determining $A_3(n, t)$ is solved for these cases. In Section V we present construction methods in which a code correcting up to t unidirectional errors is constructed by expurgating a code correcting up to t asymmetric errors, or by expurgating and puncturing a code correcting up to t symmetric errors. In Section VI we construct unidirectional error-correcting codes, by applying both the methods of Section V and trial and error.

Finally, tables of bounds on $A_i(n, t)$ (for $1 \le i \le 3$, $1 \le t \le 4$, $t \le n \le 23$) are provided in Section VII. In this final section we also summarize the main results of this paper.

Many of the techniques used to derive the results on unidirectional error-correcting codes in this paper resemble techniques which were used to derive similar results on asymmetric error-correcting codes. These latter techniques were adapted in such a way that they became suitable for the unidirectional case. The results of this paper reinforce the idea that the unidirectional error-correcting behavior of codes is in many respects strictly between the symmetric and the asymmetric error-correcting behavior.

II. Integer Programming Bound

In [7] Goldbaum obtained upper bounds on $A_2(n,t)$ by solving an integer programming problem. These bounds were improved by Delsarte and Piret [6], Kløve [9], and Weber *et al.* [20] by adding more constraints to this integer programming problem. These integer programming bounds give the best possible or best known upper bound on $A_2(n,t)$ for many (small) values of n and t.

Since $A_3(n,t) \le A_2(n,t)$, the aforementioned bounds are also upper bounds on $A_3(n,t)$. However, we can improve these bounds for some values of n and t by adapting some of the constraints to the unidirectional case. This is done in Theorems 2–4. The new integer programming problem is then stated in Theorem 5.

We first introduce some notation. Let C be a code of length n ($C \subseteq (\mathrm{GF}(2))^n = V$). A_i denotes the number of codewords of weight i in C ($A_i = |\{\boldsymbol{c} \in C | w(\boldsymbol{c}) = i\}|$ for $i = 0,1,\cdots,n$). V_i denotes the subset of V containing all the vectors of length n and weight i ($V_i = \{\boldsymbol{v} \in V | w(\boldsymbol{v}) = i\}$ for $i = 0,1,\cdots,n$). $H_i(\boldsymbol{v})$ denotes all the vectors of V_i which cover $\boldsymbol{v}$ or are covered by $\boldsymbol{v}$ ($H_i(\boldsymbol{v}) = \{\boldsymbol{a} \in V_i | \boldsymbol{a} \ge \boldsymbol{v}\}$ if $w(\boldsymbol{v}) \le i$, $H_i(\boldsymbol{v}) = \{\boldsymbol{a} \in V_i | \boldsymbol{v} \ge \boldsymbol{a}\}$ if $w(\boldsymbol{v}) > i$, for $i = 0,1,\cdots,n$ and $\boldsymbol{v} \in V$). Hence $|H_i(\boldsymbol{v})| = \binom{n - w(\boldsymbol{v})}{i - w(\boldsymbol{v})}$ if $w(\boldsymbol{v}) \le i$, and $|H_i(\boldsymbol{v})| = \binom{w(\boldsymbol{v})}{i}$ if $w(\boldsymbol{v}) > i$. $A(n,d,w)$denotes the maximum number of binary vectors of length n, Hamming distance (d_1) at least d apart, and constant weight w. $A_U(n,d,w)$ and $A_L(n,d,w)$ denote upper and lower bounds, respectively, on $A(n,d,w)$. Some tables of bounds on $A(n,d,w)$ can be found in [1], [8], [11], and [15]. $T(w_1,n_1,w_2,n_2,d)$ denotes the maximum number of binary vectors of length $n_1 + n_2$, Hamming distance at least d apart, where each vector has exactly w_1 1's in the first n_1 coordinates and exactly w_2 1's in the last n_2 coordinates. $T_U(w_1,n_1,w_2,n_2,d)$ and $T_L(w_1,n_1,w_2,n_2,d)$ denote upper and lower bounds, respectively, on $T(w_1,n_1,w_2,n_2,d)$. Tables of bounds on $T(w_1,n_1,w_2,n_2,d)$ can be found in [1]. Finally, we define

$$
\begin{aligned}
G(n,t,w) &= \binom{w+t+1}{t+1} - \binom{2t+1}{t+1} A(w+t+1, 2t+2, 2t+1) \\
&\quad - \sum_{j=1}^{t} T(w, w+t+1, j, n-w-t-1, 2t+2)
\end{aligned}
$$

for $0 \le w \le n-t-1$ and $1 \le t \le n$. $G_L(n,t,w)$ denotes a lower bound on $G(n,t,w)$, which can be obtained by replacing $A(w+t+1,2t+2,2t+1)$ and $T(w,w+t+1,j,n-w-t-1,2t+2)$ in the definition of $G(n,t,w)$ by upper bounds $A_U(w+t+1,2t+2,2t+1)$ and $T_U(w,w+t+1,j,n-w-t-1,2t+2)$, respectively:

$$
\begin{aligned}
G_L(n,t,w) &= \binom{w+t+1}{t+1} - \binom{2t+1}{t+1} A_U(w+t+1, 2t+2, 2t+1) \\
&\quad - \sum_{j=1}^{t} T_U(w, w+t+1, j, n-w-t-1, 2t+2).
\end{aligned}
$$

In [6, theorem 4] Delsarte and Piret derived conditions on the numbers A_i in a code correcting asymmetric errors by using some simple counting arguments. We first use similar arguments to derive conditions on the numbers A_i in a code correcting unidirectional errors.

Theorem 2: In a code C of length n with $d_3 \ge 2t+1$ the numbers A_i satisfy

$$\sum_{j=0}^{t} \binom{n-w+j}{j} A_{w-j} + \sum_{j=1}^{t} \binom{w+j}{j} A_{w+j} \le \binom{n}{w}$$

for $w = 0,1,\cdots,n$.

Proof: Let $U_1 = \{\boldsymbol{a} \in C | w+1 \le w(\boldsymbol{a}) \le w+t\}$ and $U_2 = \{\boldsymbol{a} \in C | w-t \le w(\boldsymbol{a}) \le w\}$.

a) Let $\boldsymbol{u}_1, \boldsymbol{u}_2 \in U_1, \boldsymbol{u}_1 \ne \boldsymbol{u}_2$. Suppose $\exists \boldsymbol{x} \in V_w$: $\boldsymbol{x} \in H_w(\boldsymbol{u}_1) \cap H_w(\boldsymbol{u}_2)$; then we may assume without loss of generality that $\boldsymbol{u}_1$, $\boldsymbol{u}_2$, and $\boldsymbol{x}$ resemble the following three vectors:

$$
\begin{array}{cccccc}
\boldsymbol{u}_1: & 11\cdots1 & 11\cdots1 & 11\cdots1 & 00\cdots0 & 00\cdots0 \\
\boldsymbol{u}_2: & 11\cdots1 & 11\cdots1 & 00\cdots0 & 11\cdots1 & 00\cdots0 \\
\boldsymbol{x}: & 11\cdots1 & 00\cdots0 & 00\cdots0 & 00\cdots0 & 00\cdots0 \\
 & \leftrightarrow & \leftrightarrow & \leftrightarrow & \leftrightarrow & \leftrightarrow \\
 & \mathrm{a} & \mathrm{b} & \mathrm{c} & \mathrm{d} & \mathrm{e}
\end{array}
$$

with $a+b+c+d+e=n$, $a=w$, $b+c \le t$, and $b+d \le t$. We distinguish between two cases:

1) $c = 0 \vee d = 0$: $d_3(\boldsymbol{u}_1,\boldsymbol{u}_2) = d_1(\boldsymbol{u}_1,\boldsymbol{u}_2)$
$= \max\{c,d\} \le t < 2t+1$

2) $c > 0 \wedge d > 0$: $d_3(\boldsymbol{u}_1,\boldsymbol{u}_2) = d_2(\boldsymbol{u}_1,\boldsymbol{u}_2)$
$= 2\max\{c,d\} \le 2t < 2t+1$.

This contradicts $d_3 \ge 2t+1$. Hence $H_w(\boldsymbol{u}_1) \cap H_w(\boldsymbol{u}_2) = \varnothing$.

b) Let $\boldsymbol{u}_1 \in U_1$, $\boldsymbol{u}_2 \in U_2$. Suppose $\exists \boldsymbol{x} \in V_w$: $\boldsymbol{x} \in H_w(\boldsymbol{u}_1) \cap H_w(\boldsymbol{u}_2)$; then $\boldsymbol{u}_1 \ge \boldsymbol{x} \ge \boldsymbol{u}_2$. Hence $d_3(\boldsymbol{u}_1,\boldsymbol{u}_2) = d_1(\boldsymbol{u}_1,\boldsymbol{u}_2) = w(\boldsymbol{u}_1) - w(\boldsymbol{u}_2) \le 2t < 2t+1$. This contradicts $d_3 \ge 2t+1$. Hence $H_w(\boldsymbol{u}_1) \cap H_w(\boldsymbol{u}_2) = \varnothing$.

c) Let $\boldsymbol{u}_1, \boldsymbol{u}_2 \in U_2$, $\boldsymbol{u}_1 \ne \boldsymbol{u}_2$. Proceeding as in a), we can prove that $H_w(\boldsymbol{u}_1) \cap H_w(\boldsymbol{u}_2) = \varnothing$.

From a)–c) it follows that

$$
\begin{aligned}
\binom{n}{w} = |V_w| &\ge \left| \left\{ \bigcup_{\boldsymbol{u} \in U_1} H_w(\boldsymbol{u}) \right\} \cup \left\{ \bigcup_{\boldsymbol{u} \in U_2} H_w(\boldsymbol{u}) \right\} \right| \\
&= \left| \left\{ \bigcup_{\boldsymbol{u} \in U_1} H_w(\boldsymbol{u}) \right\} \right| + \left| \left\{ \bigcup_{\boldsymbol{u} \in U_2} H_w(\boldsymbol{u}) \right\} \right| \\
&\quad - \left| \left\{ \bigcup_{\boldsymbol{u} \in U_1} H_w(\boldsymbol{u}) \right\} \cap \left\{ \bigcup_{\boldsymbol{u} \in U_2} H_w(\boldsymbol{u}) \right\} \right| \\
&= \sum_{\boldsymbol{u} \in U_1} |H_w(\boldsymbol{u})| + \sum_{\boldsymbol{u} \in U_2} |H_w(\boldsymbol{u})| - |\varnothing| \\
&= \sum_{j=0}^{t} \binom{n-w+j}{j} A_{w-j} + \sum_{j=1}^{t} \binom{w+j}{j} A_{w+j}. \qquad \square
\end{aligned}
$$

In [20, theorems 2.2–2.6] the conditions of Delsarte and Piret were sharpened using some more advanced counting arguments. We now use similar arguments to sharpen the conditions in Theorem 2.

Theorem 3: In a code C of length n with $d_3 \geq 2t+1$ the numbers A_i satisfy

$$\sum_{j=0}^{t} \binom{n-w+j}{j} A_{w-j} + \sum_{j=1}^{t} \binom{w+j}{j} A_{w+j} + \frac{G_L(n,t,w)}{\left\lfloor \frac{n-w}{t+1} \right\rfloor} A_{w+t+1} \leq \binom{n}{w}$$

for $w = 0, 1, \cdots, n-t-1$.

Proof: Let $U = \{a \in C | w-t \leq w(a) \leq w+t\}$, $U_1 = \{a \in C | w+1 \leq w(a) \leq w+t\}$, $U_{21} = \{a \in C | w-t+1 \leq w(a) \leq w\}$, $U_{22} = \{a \in C | w(a) = w-t\}$, and $Z = \{a \in C | w(a) = w+t+1\}$.

a) Let $u_1, u_2 \in U$, $u_1 \neq u_2$. In the proof of Theorem 2 it was shown that $H_w(u_1) \cap H_w(u_2) = \varnothing$.

b) Let $u \in U_{21}$ and $z \in Z$. Suppose $\exists x \in V_w$: $x \in H_w(u) \cap H_w(z)$; then $z \geq x \geq u$. Hence $d_3(u,z) = d_1(u,z) = w(z) - w(u) \leq 2t < 2t+1$. This contradicts $d_3 \geq 2t+1$. Hence $H_w(u) \cap H_w(z) = \varnothing$.

c) Let $u \in U_{22}$ and $z \in Z$, $N(z,u) > 0$. Suppose $\exists x \in V_w$: $x \in H_w(u) \cap H_w(z)$; then $z \geq x \geq u$. This contradicts $N(z,u) > 0$. Hence $H_w(u) \cap H_w(z) = \varnothing$.

d) Let $u \in U_{22}$ and $z \in Z$, $N(z,u) = 0$. If $x \in H_w(u) \cap H_w(z)$, then we may assume without loss of generality that u, z, and x resemble the following three vectors:

z:	$11\cdots1$	$11\cdots1$	$11\cdots1$	$00\cdots0$
x:	$11\cdots1$	$11\cdots1$	$00\cdots0$	$00\cdots0$
u:	$11\cdots1$	$00\cdots0$	$00\cdots0$	$00\cdots0$.
	$\leftrightarrow$	$\leftrightarrow$	$\leftrightarrow$	$\leftrightarrow$
	$w-t$	t	$t+1$	$n-w-t-1$

Hence $|H_w(u) \cap H_w(z)| = |\{x \in V_w | z \geq x \geq u\}| = \binom{2t+1}{t+1}$.

e) Let $z \in Z$. Consider the codewords of weight $w-t$ which are covered by z. After deleting those coordinates for which $z_i = 0$, these codewords form a constant weight code of length $w+t+1$, weight $w-t$, and Hamming distance at least $2t+2$. Hence $|\{u \in U_{22} | z \geq u\}| \leq A(w+t+1, 2t+2, w-t) \leq A_U(w+t+1, 2t+2, 2t+1)$.

f) Let $u \in U_1$ and $z \in Z$. Suppose $N(z,u) = 0$; then $d_3(z,u) = d_1(z,u) = w(z) - w(u) \leq t < 2t+1$. This contradicts $d_3 \geq 2t+1$. Hence $N(z,u) > 0$.

g) Let $u \in U_1$ and $z \in Z$, $d_3(u,z) = d_2(u,z) = 2t+2+2k$. Without loss of generality we may assume that u and z resemble the following vectors:

z:	$11\cdots1$	$11\cdots1$	$00\cdots0$	$00\cdots0$
u:	$11\cdots1$	$00\cdots0$	$11\cdots1$	$00\cdots0$
	$\leftrightarrow$	$\leftrightarrow$	$\leftrightarrow$	$\leftrightarrow$
	$w-k$	$t+1+k$	$k+j$	$n-w-t-1-k-j$

where $j \in \{1, 2, \cdots, t\}$. Hence

$$|H_w(u) \cap H_w(z)| = |\{x \in V_w | z \geq x \wedge u \geq x\}| = \begin{cases} 1, & \text{if } k = 0 \\ 0, & \text{if } k > 0 \end{cases}.$$

h) Let $z \in Z$. Consider the sets of codewords $W_j = \{a \in U \cap V_{w+j} | d_3(a,z) = 2t+2\}$ for $j = 1, 2, \cdots, t$. For all $u, u_1, u_2 \in W_j$, $u_1 \neq u_2$:

$$|\{i | u_i = 1 \wedge z_i = 1\}| = w$$
$$|\{i | z_i = 1\}| = w+t+1$$
$$|\{i | u_i = 1 \wedge z_i = 0\}| = j$$
$$|\{i | z_i = 0\}| = n-w-t-1$$
$$d_1(u_1,u_2) = d_2(u_1,u_2) - |w(u_1) - w(u_2)| = d_2(u_1,u_2) = d_3(u_1,u_2) \geq 2t+2.$$

Hence

$$\left|\{a \in U \cap V_{w+j} | d_3(a,z) = 2t+2\}\right| \leq T(w, w+t+1, j, n-w-t-1, 2t+2) \leq T_U(w, w+t+1, j, n-w-t-1, 2t+2),$$

for $j = 1, 2, \cdots, t$.

i) Let $a \in V_w$. Consider the codewords of weight $w+t+1$ covering a. After deleting those coordinates for which $a_i = 1$, these codewords form a constant weight code of length $n-w$, weight $t+1$, and Hamming distance at least $2t+2$. Hence

$$|\{z \in Z | z \geq a\}| \leq A(n-w, 2t+2, t+1) = \left\lfloor \frac{n-w}{t+1} \right\rfloor.$$

Next consider the following subset X of V_w:

$$X = V_w \setminus \Big\{ \bigcup_{u \in U} H_w(u) \Big\}.$$

Let $z_1, z_2, \cdots, z_{A_{w+t+1}}$ be the elements of Z. For each z_i we define a subset X_i of X:

$$X_i = H_w(z_i) \cap X, \qquad \text{for } i = 1, 2, \cdots, A_{w+t+1}.$$

From a)–i) it follows that

1) $$|X| = \binom{n}{w} - \sum_{j=0}^{t} \binom{n-w+j}{j} A_{w-j} - \sum_{j=1}^{t} \binom{w+j}{j} A_{w+j};$$

2) $$\begin{aligned} |X_i| &= |H_w(z_i)| - \Big|H_w(z_i) \cap \Big\{ \bigcup_{u \in U} H_w(u) \Big\}\Big| \\ &= \binom{w+t+1}{t+1} - \sum_{\substack{u \in U_{22} \\ z_i \geq u}} \binom{2t+1}{t+1} - \sum_{\substack{u \in U_1 \\ d_3(u,z_i) = 2t+2}} 1 \\ &\geq \binom{w+t+1}{t+1} - \binom{2t+1}{t+1} A_U(w+t+1, 2t+2, 2t+1) \\ &\quad - \sum_{j=1}^{t} T_U(w, w+t+1, j, n-w-t-1, 2t+2) \\ &= G_L(n,t,w), \qquad \text{for all } i; \end{aligned}$$

3) $$|\{i | a \in X_i\}| = |\{z_i \in Z | z_i \geq a\}| \leq \left\lfloor \frac{n-w}{t+1} \right\rfloor,$$

for all $a \in X$.

From 1)–3) it follows that

$$G_L(n,t,w)\cdot A_{w+t+1} \le \sum_{i=1}^{A_{w+t+1}} \sum_{a\in X_i} 1 = \sum_{a\in X} \sum_{\substack{i=1\\ a\in X_i}}^{A_{w+t+1}} 1$$

$$\le \left\{ \binom{n}{w} - \sum_{j=0}^{t} \binom{n-w+j}{j} A_{w-j} - \sum_{j=1}^{t} \binom{w+j}{j} A_{w+j} \right\} \left\lfloor \frac{n-w}{t+1} \right\rfloor . \quad \square$$

When $G_L(n,t,w)$ is positive, it is clear that Theorem 3 gives a stronger condition on the weights of a code C than the corresponding condition which follows from Theorem 2. When $G_L(n,t,w)$ is nonpositive, the condition which follows from Theorem 3 does not improve on the one from Theorem 2.

Theorem 4: In a code C of length n with $d_3 \ge 2t+1$ the numbers A_i satisfy

$$\frac{G_L(n,t,n-w)}{\left\lfloor \frac{w}{t+1} \right\rfloor} A_{w-t-1} + \sum_{j=0}^{t} \binom{n-w+j}{j} A_{w-j} + \sum_{j=1}^{t} \binom{w+j}{j} A_{w+j} \le \binom{n}{w}$$

for $w = t+1,\ t+2, \cdots, n$.

Proof: This theorem can be proved in the same way as Theorem 3. □

Theorem 5: For $n \ge t \ge 1$ let

$$J_U(n,t) = \max \sum_{r=0}^{n} z_r$$

where the maximum is taken over the following constraints:

1) the z_r are nonnegative integers;

2) a) $\sum_{j=w-s}^{w} A_L(s,2t+2,w-j) z_j \le A_U(n+s,2t+2,w)$

for $s = 0,1,\cdots,w$ and $w = 0,1,\cdots,n$;

b) $\sum_{j=w-s}^{w} A_L(s,2t+2,w-j) z_{n-j} \le A_U(n+s,2t+2,w)$

for $s = 0,1,\cdots,w$ and $w = 0,1,\cdots,n$;

3) a) $\sum_{j=0}^{t} \binom{n-w+j}{j} z_{w-j} + \sum_{j=1}^{t} \binom{w+j}{j} z_{w+j} \le \binom{n}{w}$

for $w = 0,1,\cdots,n$;

b) $\sum_{j=0}^{t} \binom{n-w+j}{j} z_{w-j} + \sum_{j=1}^{t} \binom{w+j}{j} z_{w+j} + \frac{G_L(n,t,w)}{\left\lfloor \frac{n-w}{t+1} \right\rfloor} z_{w+t+1} \le \binom{n}{w}$

for $w = 0,1,\cdots,n-t-1$;

c) $\frac{G_L(n,t,n-w)}{\left\lfloor \frac{w}{t+1} \right\rfloor} z_{w-t-1} + \sum_{j=0}^{t} \binom{n-w+j}{j} z_{w-j} + \sum_{j=1}^{t} \binom{w+j}{j} z_{w+j} \le \binom{n}{w}$

for $w = t+1, t+2, \cdots, n$.

Then

$$A_3(n,t) \le J_U(n,t).$$

Proof: Let C be a code of length n with $d_3 \ge 2t+1$, which contains $A_3(n,t)$ codewords. Let z_r be the number of codewords in C of weight $r (z_r = |\{c \in C | w(c) = r\}|$ for $r = 0,1,\cdots,n)$. Hence the z_r satisfy 1). Since $d_2 \ge d_3 \ge 2t+1$, the z_r satisfy 2) according to Kløve ([9]). From Theorems 2–4 in this section it follows that the z_r also satisfy 3). Thus

$$A_3(n,t) = |C| = \sum_{r=0}^{n} z_r \le J_U(n,t). \qquad \square$$

Note that the value of $J_U(n,t)$ depends on the values of $A_L(s,2t+2,w-j)$, $A_U(n+s,2t+2,w)$, $T_U(w,w+t+1,j,n-w-t-1,2t+2)$, etc. To obtain the best upper bounds on $A_3(n,t)$, take the largest known value for each lower bound and the smallest known value for each upper bound. Knowledge of these bounds can affect the value of $J_U(n,t)$.

We shall now illustrate this integer programming bound $J_U(n,t)$ by considering the case $n = 12$ and $t = 3$. We then have the following:

1) $z_0 + z_1 + z_2 + z_3 \le 1$ ($w = 3$ and $s = 3$ in constraint 2a));
2) $z_4 \le 3$ ($w = 4$ and $s = 0$ in constraint 2a));
3) $12z_0 + z_1 + 2z_2 + 3z_3 + 4z_4 \le 12$ ($w = 1$ in constraint 3a));
4) $z_5 + z_6 \le 4$ ($w = 6$ and $s = 1$ in constraint 2a));
5) $z_7 + z_8 \le 3$ ($w = 8$ and $s = 1$ in constraint 2a));
6) $z_9 + z_{10} + z_{11} + z_{12} \le 1$ ($w = 12$ and $s = 3$ in constraint 2a)).

From 1)–3) it follows that $z_0 + z_1 + z_2 + z_3 + z_4 \le 3$. Hence

$$A_3(12,3) \le (z_0+z_1+z_2+z_3+z_4) + (z_5+z_6) + (z_7+z_8) + (z_9+z_{10}+z_{11}+z_{12})$$
$$\le 3+4+3+1 = 11.$$

III. Other Upper Bounds

In [10] the Borden bounds on $A_2(n,t)$ were presented. These bounds are stated in the next two theorems.

Theorem 6 (Borden): $A_2(n,t) \le (t+1)A_1(n,t)$ for $n \ge t \ge 1$.

Theorem 7 (Borden): $A_2(n,t) \le A_1(n+t,t)$ for $n \ge t \ge 1$.

Using arguments similar to Borden's we can sharpen these bounds for the unidirectional case. The bound corresponding to the first Borden bound (Theorem 6) is given in Theorem 8, and the bound corresponding to the second Borden bound (Theorem 7) is given in Theorem 9. Lemma 1 is used to prove Theorem 9.

Theorem 8: $A_3(n,t) \le tA_1(n,t)$ for $n \ge t \ge 1$.

Proof: Let C be a code of length n with $d_3 \ge 2t+1$ and $|C| = A_3(n,t)$. Define

$$S_r = \{ \boldsymbol{x} \in C | w(\boldsymbol{x}) \equiv 2r \pmod{2t} \vee w(\boldsymbol{x}) \equiv 2r+1 \pmod{2t} \}, \quad \text{for } r = 0,1,\cdots,t-1.$$

We shall prove that each S_r is a code with $d_1 \ge 2t+1$. Let $\boldsymbol{u}, \boldsymbol{v} \in S_r$, $\boldsymbol{u} \ne \boldsymbol{v}$, $w(\boldsymbol{v}) \ge w(\boldsymbol{u})$.

a) *The case $N(\boldsymbol{v},\boldsymbol{u}) > 0$:* Note that either $w(\boldsymbol{v}) - w(\boldsymbol{u}) \le 1$ or $w(\boldsymbol{v}) - w(\boldsymbol{u}) \ge 2t-1$:

i) The case $w(\boldsymbol{v}) - w(\boldsymbol{u}) \le 1$: since $d_2(\boldsymbol{v},\boldsymbol{u}) \ge d_3(\boldsymbol{v},\boldsymbol{u}) \ge 2t+1$ and $d_2(\boldsymbol{v},\boldsymbol{u})$ is even, it follows that $d_2(\boldsymbol{v},\boldsymbol{u}) \ge 2t+2$; hence

$$d_1(\boldsymbol{v},\boldsymbol{u}) = d_2(\boldsymbol{v},\boldsymbol{u}) - (w(\boldsymbol{v}) - w(\boldsymbol{u})) \ge 2t+2-1 = 2t+1;$$

ii) the case $w(\boldsymbol{v}) - w(\boldsymbol{u}) \ge 2t-1$: since $N(\boldsymbol{u},\boldsymbol{v}) - N(\boldsymbol{v},\boldsymbol{u}) \ge 2t-1$ and $N(\boldsymbol{v},\boldsymbol{u}) \ge 1$, it follows that

$$d_1(\boldsymbol{v},\boldsymbol{u}) = N(\boldsymbol{u},\boldsymbol{v}) + N(\boldsymbol{v},\boldsymbol{u}) \ge 2t-1+2N(\boldsymbol{v},\boldsymbol{u}) \ge 2t+1.$$

b) *The case $N(\boldsymbol{v},\boldsymbol{u}) = 0$:*

$$d_1(\boldsymbol{v},\boldsymbol{u}) = d_3(\boldsymbol{v},\boldsymbol{u}) \ge 2t+1.$$

In conclusion, each S_r is a code of length n with $d_1 \ge 2t+1$, and thus

$$|S_r| \le A_1(n,t), \quad \text{for all } r = 0,1,\cdots,t-1.$$

Hence

$$A_3(n,t) = |C| = \sum_{r=0}^{t-1} |S_r| \le tA_1(n,t). \qquad \Box$$

Definition 4: Let $i \in \{1,2,3,\cdots\}$. Then we define the function $\boldsymbol{u}_i$: $\mathbb{Z} \to (\mathrm{GF}(2))^i$ by

$$\boldsymbol{u}_i(w) = (s(w), s(w+1),\cdots,s(w+i-1))$$

where

$$s(w) = \begin{cases} 0, & \text{if } w \equiv 0,1,\cdots,i \pmod{2i+2} \\ 1, & \text{if } w \equiv i+1, i+2,\cdots,2i+1 \pmod{2i+2} \end{cases}.$$

Example 4: Let $i = 3$. Then

$$\boldsymbol{u}_3(0) = 000$$
$$\boldsymbol{u}_3(1) = 000$$
$$\boldsymbol{u}_3(2) = 001$$
$$\boldsymbol{u}_3(3) = 011$$
$$\boldsymbol{u}_3(4) = 111$$
$$\boldsymbol{u}_3(5) = 111$$
$$\boldsymbol{u}_3(6) = 110$$
$$\boldsymbol{u}_3(7) = 100$$
$$\boldsymbol{u}_3(w) = \boldsymbol{u}_3(w-8), \quad \text{for all } w \in \mathbb{Z}.$$

Lemma 1 (Borden): Let $i \in \{1,2,3,\cdots\}$. Then

a) $d_1(\boldsymbol{u}_i(x), \boldsymbol{u}_i(y)) + d_1(\boldsymbol{u}_i(x+i+1), \boldsymbol{u}_i(y)) = i$, for any integers x and y;

b) $y - x - 1 \le d_1(\boldsymbol{u}_i(x), \boldsymbol{u}_i(y)) \le y - x$, for any integers x and y such that $x \le y \le x+i+1$.

Proof: The proof is straightforward. An outline of the proof can be found in [10]. $\Box$

Theorem 9: $A_3(n,t) \le A_1(n+t-1,t)$ for $n \ge t \ge 1$.

Proof: From Theorem 8 it follows that the theorem holds for $t = 1$. Let $t \in \{2,3,4,\cdots\}$. Let C be a code of length n with $d_3 \ge 2t+1$ and size $A_3(n,t)$. Let $\boldsymbol{u}_{t-1}$: $\mathbb{Z} \to (\mathrm{GF}(2))^{t-1}$ be defined as in Definition 4. We now construct a code D of length $n+t-1$ by lengthening each codeword $\boldsymbol{c}$ of C with $\boldsymbol{u}_{t-1}(w(\boldsymbol{c}))$:

$$D = \{ (\boldsymbol{c}, \boldsymbol{u}_{t-1}(w(\boldsymbol{c}))) | \boldsymbol{c} \in C \}.$$

We shall prove that D is a code correcting up to t symmetric errors.

Let $\boldsymbol{c}_1, \boldsymbol{c}_2 \in C$, $\boldsymbol{c}_1 \ne \boldsymbol{c}_2$, $w(\boldsymbol{c}_1) \ge w(\boldsymbol{c}_2)$. We distinguish between two cases: A) $N(\boldsymbol{c}_1,\boldsymbol{c}_2) > 0$, and B) $N(\boldsymbol{c}_1,\boldsymbol{c}_2) = 0$.

A) The case $N(\boldsymbol{c}_1,\boldsymbol{c}_2) > 0$: In this case $N(\boldsymbol{c}_2,\boldsymbol{c}_1) = d_2(\boldsymbol{c}_1,\boldsymbol{c}_2)/2 = d_3(\boldsymbol{c}_1,\boldsymbol{c}_2)/2 \ge t+1$ and $N(\boldsymbol{c}_1,\boldsymbol{c}_2) \ge 1$. We have

$$\begin{aligned} d_1((\boldsymbol{c}_1, \boldsymbol{u}_{t-1}(w(\boldsymbol{c}_1))), (\boldsymbol{c}_2, \boldsymbol{u}_{t-1}(w(\boldsymbol{c}_2)))) &= d_1(\boldsymbol{c}_1,\boldsymbol{c}_2) + d_1(\boldsymbol{u}_{t-1}(w(\boldsymbol{c}_1)), \boldsymbol{u}_{t-1}(w(\boldsymbol{c}_2))) \\ &= N(\boldsymbol{c}_1,\boldsymbol{c}_2) + N(\boldsymbol{c}_2,\boldsymbol{c}_1) \\ &\quad + d_1(\boldsymbol{u}_{t-1}(w(\boldsymbol{c}_1)), \boldsymbol{u}_{t-1}(w(\boldsymbol{c}_2))). \end{aligned}$$

1) *The case $N(\boldsymbol{c}_1,\boldsymbol{c}_2) + N(\boldsymbol{c}_2,\boldsymbol{c}_1) \ge 2t+1$:* Then

$$d_1((\boldsymbol{c}_1, \boldsymbol{u}_{t-1}(w(\boldsymbol{c}_1))), (\boldsymbol{c}_2, \boldsymbol{u}_{t-1}(w(\boldsymbol{c}_2)))) \ge N(\boldsymbol{c}_1,\boldsymbol{c}_2) + N(\boldsymbol{c}_2,\boldsymbol{c}_1) \ge 2t+1.$$

2) *The case $N(\boldsymbol{c}_1,\boldsymbol{c}_2) + N(\boldsymbol{c}_2,\boldsymbol{c}_1) \le 2t$:* Then $N(\boldsymbol{c}_1,\boldsymbol{c}_2) \le 2t - N(\boldsymbol{c}_2,\boldsymbol{c}_1) \le 2t-(t+1) = t-1$ and $0 \le N(\boldsymbol{c}_2,\boldsymbol{c}_1) - N(\boldsymbol{c}_1,\boldsymbol{c}_2) \le 2t - 2N(\boldsymbol{c}_1,\boldsymbol{c}_2) \le 2t-2$.

a) If $0 \le N(\boldsymbol{c}_2,\boldsymbol{c}_1) - N(\boldsymbol{c}_1,\boldsymbol{c}_2) \le t$, then $w(\boldsymbol{c}_2) \le w(\boldsymbol{c}_1) \le w(\boldsymbol{c}_2) + t$. Hence it follows from Lemma 1 that

$$\begin{aligned} d_1(\boldsymbol{u}_{t-1}(w(\boldsymbol{c}_1)), \boldsymbol{u}_{t-1}(w(\boldsymbol{c}_2))) &\ge w(\boldsymbol{c}_1) - w(\boldsymbol{c}_2) - 1 \\ &= N(\boldsymbol{c}_2,\boldsymbol{c}_1) - N(\boldsymbol{c}_1,\boldsymbol{c}_2) - 1 \\ &= 2N(\boldsymbol{c}_2,\boldsymbol{c}_1) - 1 - N(\boldsymbol{c}_1,\boldsymbol{c}_2) - N(\boldsymbol{c}_2,\boldsymbol{c}_1) \\ &\ge 2t+2-1 - N(\boldsymbol{c}_1,\boldsymbol{c}_2) - N(\boldsymbol{c}_2,\boldsymbol{c}_1) \\ &= 2t+1 - N(\boldsymbol{c}_1,\boldsymbol{c}_2) - N(\boldsymbol{c}_2,\boldsymbol{c}_1). \end{aligned}$$

b) If $t+1 \le N(\boldsymbol{c}_2,\boldsymbol{c}_1) - N(\boldsymbol{c}_1,\boldsymbol{c}_2) \le 2t-2$, then $w(\boldsymbol{c}_2) + t + 1 \le w(\boldsymbol{c}_1) \le w(\boldsymbol{c}_2) + 2t - 2$. Hence $w(\boldsymbol{c}_2) \le w(\boldsymbol{c}_1) - t - 1 \le w(\boldsymbol{c}_2) + t - 3$, and so $w(\boldsymbol{c}_2) \le w(\boldsymbol{c}_1) - t \le w(\boldsymbol{c}_2) + t$.

Hence it follows from Lemma 1 that

$$\begin{aligned} d_1(\boldsymbol{u}_{t-1}(w(\boldsymbol{c}_1)), \boldsymbol{u}_{t-1}(w(\boldsymbol{c}_2))) &= t-1-d_1(\boldsymbol{u}_{t-1}(w(\boldsymbol{c}_1)-t), \boldsymbol{u}_{t-1}(w(\boldsymbol{c}_2))) \\ &\geq t-1-(w(\boldsymbol{c}_1)-t-w(\boldsymbol{c}_2)) \\ &= 2t-1-(w(\boldsymbol{c}_1)-w(\boldsymbol{c}_2)) \\ &= 2t-1-(N(\boldsymbol{c}_2,\boldsymbol{c}_1)-N(\boldsymbol{c}_1,\boldsymbol{c}_2)) \\ &= 2t-1-N(\boldsymbol{c}_2,\boldsymbol{c}_1)+N(\boldsymbol{c}_1,\boldsymbol{c}_2) \\ &= 2t-1-N(\boldsymbol{c}_2,\boldsymbol{c}_1)-N(\boldsymbol{c}_1,\boldsymbol{c}_2)+2N(\boldsymbol{c}_1,\boldsymbol{c}_2) \\ &\geq 2t+1-N(\boldsymbol{c}_2,\boldsymbol{c}_1)-N(\boldsymbol{c}_1,\boldsymbol{c}_2). \end{aligned}$$

From 2a) and 2b) it follows that

$$\begin{aligned} d_1((\boldsymbol{c}_1, \boldsymbol{u}_{t-1}(w(\boldsymbol{c}_1))), (\boldsymbol{c}_2, \boldsymbol{u}_{t-1}(w(\boldsymbol{c}_2)))) &= N(\boldsymbol{c}_1,\boldsymbol{c}_2)+N(\boldsymbol{c}_2,\boldsymbol{c}_1) \\ &\quad + d_1(\boldsymbol{u}_{t-1}(w(\boldsymbol{c}_1)), \boldsymbol{u}_{t-1}(w(\boldsymbol{c}_2))) \\ &\geq N(\boldsymbol{c}_1,\boldsymbol{c}_2)+N(\boldsymbol{c}_2,\boldsymbol{c}_1)+2t+1 \\ &\quad - N(\boldsymbol{c}_1,\boldsymbol{c}_2)-N(\boldsymbol{c}_2,\boldsymbol{c}_1) \\ &= 2t+1. \end{aligned}$$

B) The case $N(\boldsymbol{c}_1, \boldsymbol{c}_2) = 0$: In this case

$$d_1((\boldsymbol{c}_1, \boldsymbol{u}_{t-1}(w(\boldsymbol{c}_1))), (\boldsymbol{c}_2, \boldsymbol{u}_{t-1}(w(\boldsymbol{c}_2)))) \geq d_1(\boldsymbol{c}_1,\boldsymbol{c}_2) = d_3(\boldsymbol{c}_1,\boldsymbol{c}_2) \geq 2t+1.$$

From A) and B) it follows that

$$d_1((\boldsymbol{c}_1, \boldsymbol{u}_{t-1}(w(\boldsymbol{c}_1))), (\boldsymbol{c}_2, \boldsymbol{u}_{t-1}(w(\boldsymbol{c}_2)))) \geq 2t+1, \quad \text{for all } \boldsymbol{c}_1, \boldsymbol{c}_2 \in C (\boldsymbol{c}_1 \neq \boldsymbol{c}_2).$$

Hence D is a code of length $n+t-1$ correcting up to t symmetric errors. In conclusion,

$$A_3(n,t) = |C| = |D| \leq A_1(n+t-1,t). \qquad \square$$

IV. $A_3(n,t)$ for Relatively Small n

In this section we give the exact values of $A_3(n,t)$ for $1 \leq t \leq n \leq 2t+3$ (Theorem 10). These results are derived by constructing codes of length n correcting up to t unidirectional errors, the sizes of which reach the best corresponding upper bounds from the previous sections.

Theorem 10:

a) $A_3(n,t) = 1$ for $t \leq n \leq t+1$ and $t = 1,2,3,\cdots$.

b) $A_3(n,t) = 2$ for $t+2 \leq n \leq 2t+2$ and $t = 1,2,3,\cdots$.

c) $A_3(2t+3,t) = 4$ for $t = 1,2,3,\cdots$.

Proof: a) The code of length t containing only the all-zero word corrects up to t unidirectional errors; thus $A_3(t,t) \geq 1$. From Theorem 9 it follows that $A_3(t+1,t) \leq A_1(2t,t) = 1$. Hence $1 \leq A_3(t,t) \leq A_3(t+1,t) \leq 1$.

b) The code of length $t+2$ containing the two codewords $100\cdots0 = 10^{t+1}$ and $011\cdots1 = 01^{t+1}$ corrects up to t unidirectional errors since $d_3 = d_2 = 2t+2$. Hence $A_3(t+2,t) \geq 2$. From Theorem 9 it follows that $A_3(2t+2,t) \leq A_1(3t+1,t) = 2$. Hence $2 \leq A_3(t+2,t) \leq A_3(t+3,t) \leq \cdots \leq A_3(2t+2,t) \leq 2$.

c) The code of length $2t+3$ containing the four codewords 1100^t0^t, 0011^t0^t, 0110^t1^t, and 1001^t1^t corrects up to t unidirectional errors since $d_3 = 2t+2$. Hence $A_3(2t+3,t) \geq 4$. From b) it follows that $A_3(2t+3,t) \leq 2A_3(2t+2,t) = 4$. Hence $4 \leq A_3(2t+3,t) \leq 4$. $\square$

The results of Theorem 10 are shown in Table I (for $t \geq 2$) and Table VII (for $t = 1$), where we have also included the corresponding results for $A_1(n,t)$ and $A_2(n,t)$.

TABLE I

$A_i(n,t)$ for $i = 1,2,3$, $t \leq n \leq 2t+3$, and $t = 2,3,4,\cdots$

n	$A_1(n,t)$	$A_3(n,t)$	$A_2(n,t)$
t	1	1	1
$t+1$	1	1	2
$t+2$	1	2	2
⋮	⋮	⋮	⋮
$2t$	1	2	2
$2t+1$	2	2	2
$2t+2$	2	2	4
$2t+3$	2	4	4

V. Construction Methods

In this section we present two construction methods for unidirectional error-correcting codes. In Construction Method A, codes of length n correcting up to t unidirectional errors are obtained by expurgating a code of the same length correcting up to t asymmetric errors ($1 \leq t \leq n$). In Construction Method B codes of length $n-m$ correcting up to t unidirectional errors are obtained by expurgating and puncturing a code of length n correcting up to t symmetric errors ($1 \leq t \leq n, 1 \leq m \leq n-t$). Examples can be found in Section VI.

Construction Method A: Let C be a code of length n with $d_2 \geq 2t+1$ $(1 \leq t \leq n)$. Then we construct codes D_i $(i = 0,1,\cdots,3t)$ of length n by expurgating the code C as follows:

$$D_i = \{\boldsymbol{c} \in C \mid w(\boldsymbol{c}) \equiv i (\text{mod } 3t+1) \vee w(\boldsymbol{c}) \equiv i+1 (\text{mod } 3t+1) \vee \cdots \vee w(\boldsymbol{c}) \equiv i+t (\text{mod } 3t+1)\}$$

for $i = 0,1,\cdots,3t$.

Theorem 11: Each code D_i $(i = 0,1,\cdots,3t)$, obtained by applying Construction Method A to a code C of length n correcting up to t asymmetric errors, is able to correct up to t unidirectional errors.

Proof: Let $\boldsymbol{a}, \boldsymbol{b} \in D_i$, $\boldsymbol{a} \neq \boldsymbol{b}$, $w(\boldsymbol{a}) \geq w(\boldsymbol{b})$. Then either $w(\boldsymbol{a}) - w(\boldsymbol{b}) \leq t$ or $w(\boldsymbol{a}) - w(\boldsymbol{b}) \geq 2t+1$.

a) The case $w(\boldsymbol{a}) - w(\boldsymbol{b}) \leq t$: Since $\boldsymbol{a}, \boldsymbol{b} \in C$, it follows that $d_2(\boldsymbol{a},\boldsymbol{b}) \geq 2t+1$. Suppose $N(\boldsymbol{a},\boldsymbol{b}) = 0$ or $N(\boldsymbol{b},\boldsymbol{a}) = 0$, then

$$d_2(\boldsymbol{a},\boldsymbol{b}) = 2|w(\boldsymbol{a}) - w(\boldsymbol{b})| \leq 2t < 2t+1.$$

This contradicts $d_2(\boldsymbol{a},\boldsymbol{b}) \geq 2t+1$. Hence $N(\boldsymbol{a},\boldsymbol{b}) > 0$ and $N(\boldsymbol{b},\boldsymbol{a}) > 0$, and thus $d_3(\boldsymbol{a},\boldsymbol{b}) = d_2(\boldsymbol{a},\boldsymbol{b}) \geq 2t+1$.

b) The case $w(\boldsymbol{a}) - w(\boldsymbol{b}) \geq 2t+1$: In this case

$$d_3(\boldsymbol{a},\boldsymbol{b}) \geq d_1(\boldsymbol{a},\boldsymbol{b}) \geq w(\boldsymbol{a}) - w(\boldsymbol{b}) \geq 2t+1.$$

From a) and b) it follows that each code D_i corrects t or fewer unidirectional errors. □

Corollary 1: $A_3(n,t) \geq ((t+1)/(3t+1))A_2(n,t)$ for $n \geq t \geq 1$.

Proof: Let C be a code of length n with $d_2 \geq 2t+1$, containing $A_2(n,t)$ codewords. From Theorem 11 it follows that each code D_i $(i = 0,1,\cdots,3t)$, obtained by applying Construction Method A to this code C, is able to correct up to t unidirectional errors. Further, it is easy to see that each codeword of C is also a codeword of exactly $t+1$ codes D_i $(|\{i|\boldsymbol{c} \in D_i\}| = t+1$ for all $\boldsymbol{c} \in C)$. Hence

$$(t+1)A_2(n,t) = (t+1)|C| = \sum_{i=0}^{3t} |D_i| \leq (3t+1)A_3(n,t).$$

□

Note that we can also write Corollary 1 as

$$A_2(n,t) \leq \frac{3t+1}{t+1}A_3(n,t) = \left(3 - \frac{2}{t+1}\right)A_3(n,t), \qquad \text{for } n \geq t \geq 1.$$

Hence

$$A_3(n,t) \leq A_2(n,t) < 3A_3(n,t), \qquad \text{for } n \geq t \geq 1.$$

For $t = 1$, Corollary 1 coincides with Theorem 6, as could be expected:

$$A_2(n,1) \leq 2A_1(n,1) = 2A_3(n,1), \qquad \text{for } n \geq 1.$$

Corollary 2:

a) $A_3(n,t) \geq A_2(n,t) - 2$ for $2t+4 \leq n \leq 3t+2$ and $t = 2,3,4,\cdots$.

b) $A_3(3t+3,t) \geq A_2(3t+3,t) - 5$ for $t = 1,2,3,\cdots$.

c) $A_3(3t+4,t) \geq A_2(3t+4,t) - 8$ for $t = 1,2,3,\cdots$.

Proof: Let C be a code of length n with $d_2 \geq 2t+1$ and size $A_2(n,t)$. Kløve [9] has shown that in this code $A_0 + A_1 + \cdots + A_t = 1$ and $A_{n-t} + A_{n-t+1} + \cdots + A_n = 1$.

a) Considering the code D_{t+1} obtained from C $(2t+4 \leq n \leq 3t+2)$ by applying Construction Method A, we can conclude that

$$\begin{aligned} A_3(n,t) &\geq |D_{t+1}| \geq A_{t+1} + A_{t+2} + \cdots + A_{2t+1} \\ &\geq A_{t+1} + A_{t+2} + \cdots + A_{n-t-1} = A_2(n,t) - 2. \end{aligned}$$

b) Consider the code D_{t+2} obtained from C $(n = 3t+3)$ by applying Construction Method A. Since the number of codewords in C of weight $t+1$ is upper bounded by $A(3t+3, 2t+2, t+1) = 3$, we can conclude that

$$\begin{aligned} &A_3(3t+3,t) \\ &\quad \geq |D_{t+2}| \geq A_{t+2} + A_{t+3} + \cdots + A_{2t+2} \\ &\quad = A_2(3t+3,t) - (A_0 + A_1 + \cdots + A_t) - A_{t+1} \\ &\qquad - (A_{2t+3} + A_{2t+4} + \cdots + A_{3t+3}) \\ &\quad \geq A_2(3t+3,t) - 1 - A(3t+3, 2t+2, t+1) - 1 \\ &\quad = A_2(3t+3,t) - 1 - 3 - 1 = A_2(3t+3,t) - 5. \end{aligned}$$

c) Considering the code D_{t+2} obtained from C $(n = 3t+4)$ by applying Construction Method A, we can conclude that

$$\begin{aligned} &A_3(3t+4,t) \\ &\quad \geq |D_{t+2}| \geq A_{t+2} + A_{t+3} + \cdots + A_{2t+2} \\ &\quad = A_2(3t+4,t) - (A_0 + A_1 + \cdots + A_t) - A_{t+1} \\ &\qquad - A_{2t+3} - (A_{2t+4} + A_{2t+5} + \cdots + A_{3t+4}) \\ &\quad \geq A_2(3t+4,t) - 1 - A(3t+4, 2t+2, t+1) \\ &\qquad - A(3t+4, 2t+2, 2t+3) - 1 \\ &\quad = A_2(3t+4,t) - 1 - 3 - 3 - 1 = A_2(3t+4,t) - 8. \end{aligned}$$ □

Construction Method B: Let X be a code of length n with $d_1 \geq 2t+1$ $(1 \leq t \leq n)$. Let m be an integer such that $1 \leq m \leq n - t$, and let $\boldsymbol{u} = (\boldsymbol{u}', \boldsymbol{u}'')$ be the $(n-m, m)$ partition of any $\boldsymbol{u} \in (\mathrm{GF}(2))^n$. Define

$$T_i(\boldsymbol{s}) = \{\boldsymbol{x} \in X | w(\boldsymbol{x}') = i;\ \boldsymbol{x}'' = \boldsymbol{s}\}$$

for $i = 0,1,\cdots,n-m$ and $\boldsymbol{s} \in (\mathrm{GF}(2))^m$. We define a code Y of length n by

$$Y = \bigcup_{i=0}^{n-m} T_i(\boldsymbol{a}_i)$$

where $\boldsymbol{a}_i \in (\mathrm{GF}(2))^m$ for $i = 0,1,\cdots,n-m+2t$ such that

1) $d_1(\boldsymbol{a}_j, \boldsymbol{a}_{j+1}) \leq 1$, for all $0 \leq j \leq n-m+2t-1$

2) $\boldsymbol{a}_j = \boldsymbol{a}_{j+2t}$, for all $0 \leq j \leq n-m$.

Code Z of length $n-m$ is now formed by taking all the codewords of Y and then deleting the last m coordinates of each codeword.

Theorem 12: Each code Z of length $n-m$, obtained by applying Construction Method B to a code X of length n correcting up to t symmetric errors corrects up to t unidirectional errors.

Proof: Let $\boldsymbol{u}, \boldsymbol{v} \in Z$, $\boldsymbol{u} \neq \boldsymbol{v}$, $w(\boldsymbol{v}) \geq w(\boldsymbol{u})$. Since $d_1(\boldsymbol{a}_j, \boldsymbol{a}_{j+1}) \leq 1$ for all $0 \leq j \leq n-m+2t-1$, it follows that $d_1(\boldsymbol{a}_{w(\boldsymbol{v})}, \boldsymbol{a}_{w(\boldsymbol{u})}) \leq w(\boldsymbol{v}) - w(\boldsymbol{u})$. We now distinguish between two cases: A) $N(\boldsymbol{v},\boldsymbol{u}) > 0$, and B) $N(\boldsymbol{v},\boldsymbol{u}) = 0$.

A) The case $N(\boldsymbol{v},\boldsymbol{u}) > 0$: Since $w(\boldsymbol{v}) \geq w(\boldsymbol{u})$, it follows that $N(\boldsymbol{u},\boldsymbol{v}) \geq N(\boldsymbol{v},\boldsymbol{u}) > 0$, and thus

$$\begin{aligned} d_3(\boldsymbol{v},\boldsymbol{u}) &= d_2(\boldsymbol{v},\boldsymbol{u}) = d_1(\boldsymbol{v},\boldsymbol{u}) + w(\boldsymbol{v}) - w(\boldsymbol{u}) \\ &\geq 2t+1 - d_1(\boldsymbol{a}_{w(\boldsymbol{v})}, \boldsymbol{a}_{w(\boldsymbol{u})}) + w(\boldsymbol{v}) - w(\boldsymbol{u}) \\ &\geq 2t+1 - (w(\boldsymbol{v}) - w(\boldsymbol{u})) \\ &\qquad + w(\boldsymbol{v}) - w(\boldsymbol{u}) = 2t+1. \end{aligned}$$

B) The case $N(\boldsymbol{v},\boldsymbol{u}) = 0$: In this case $d_3(\boldsymbol{v},\boldsymbol{u}) = d_1(\boldsymbol{v},\boldsymbol{u}) = w(\boldsymbol{v}) - w(\boldsymbol{u}) \geq 2t+1-m$. Suppose $w(\boldsymbol{v}) - w(\boldsymbol{u}) = 2t+1-k$ with $k \in \{1,2,\cdots,m\}$; then

$$\begin{aligned} k &\leq d_1(\boldsymbol{a}_{w(\boldsymbol{v})}, \boldsymbol{a}_{w(\boldsymbol{u})}) = d_1(\boldsymbol{a}_{w(\boldsymbol{u})}, \boldsymbol{a}_{w(\boldsymbol{u})+2t+1-k}) \\ &\leq d_1(\boldsymbol{a}_{w(\boldsymbol{u})}, \boldsymbol{a}_{w(\boldsymbol{u})+2t}) + d_1(\boldsymbol{a}_{w(\boldsymbol{u})+2t}, \boldsymbol{a}_{w(\boldsymbol{u})+2t+1-k}) \\ &\leq 0 + |1-k| = k-1 \end{aligned}$$

(contradiction). Hence $d_3(\boldsymbol{v},\boldsymbol{u}) = w(\boldsymbol{v})w(\boldsymbol{u}) \geq 2t+1$. □

Note that in applying Construction Method B on a code X we only have to give m and the vectors $\boldsymbol{a}_i$ for $i =$

TABLE II
Codewords of P_8, P_9, Q_{11}, Q_{12}, R_{13}, R_{14} and R_{15}

	P_8	P_9	Q_{11}	Q_{12}
c_1	00100100	000000011	11000000000	000001100000
c_2	01001001	111000000	00111100000	111100000000
c_3	11110000	000111000	10100011100	000000001111
c_4	10001110	100100110	01010010011	000111010001
c_5	00111011	010010101	10001101011	011011001010
c_6	11010111	110011010	01111001110	010100110110
c_7		101110001	11011111101	101101000111
c_8		011110110		110111011100
c_9		110101101		001110111011
c_{10}		101011111		111011110111

	R_{13}	R_{14}	R_{15}
c_1	1110000000000	11000000000000	111110000000000
c_2	0001111100000	00111110000000	000001111100000
c_3	1001000011110	10100001111000	100001000011110
c_4	0110110011001	01010001000111	011000110011001
c_5	1100101100111	10011100110110	000110001110101
c_6	0111011111111	01101010101101	110100101101010
c_7		00110111011011	011011010100110
c_8		11001111111111	100111110001101
c_9			101010011111011
c_{10}			011101101010111

$0,1,\cdots,2t-1$, bearing in mind that $d_1(\boldsymbol{a}_j, \boldsymbol{a}_{j+1}) \leq 1$ for all $0 \leq j \leq 2t-2$ and $d_1(\boldsymbol{a}_0, \boldsymbol{a}_{2t-1}) \leq 1$. We define

$$S_i(\boldsymbol{s}) = \bigcup_{j=0}^{\left\lfloor \frac{n-m-i}{2t} \right\rfloor} T_{i+2tj}(\boldsymbol{s})$$

for $\boldsymbol{s} \in (\mathrm{GF}(2))^m$ and $i = 0,1,\cdots,2t-1$. Then

$$|Z| = |Y| = \left| \bigcup_{i=0}^{n-m} T_i(\boldsymbol{a}_i) \right| = \left| \bigcup_{i=0}^{2t-1} S_i(\boldsymbol{a}_i) \right| = \sum_{i=0}^{2t-1} |S_i(\boldsymbol{a}_i)|$$

It is easy to prove that we can choose the $\boldsymbol{a}_i$ in Construction Method B in such a way that $|Z| \geq 2^{-m}|X|$. For $t > 1$ this inequality is mostly strict.

VI. Constructions

In this section we apply the construction methods of the previous section to obtain codes correcting up to t unidirectional errors, containing more codewords than the best known corresponding codes of the same length correcting up to t symmetric errors.

A. Codes Correcting Up to Two Unidirectional Errors

In this subsection we construct codes P_i of length i correcting up to two unidirectional errors for $i = 8$, 9, 10, 11, 12, 13, 14, 16, 17, 18, 21, 22.

In Table II we list the codewords of the code P_8 of size 6 and the code P_9 of size 10, both found by trial and error.

Let H_1 be the code of length 11, size 24, and Hamming distance 5, containing the all-zero vector, the all-one vector, and the 11 cyclic shifts of both

$$\boldsymbol{a} = 11011100010$$

and its complement $\bar{\boldsymbol{a}}$. We apply Construction Method B with $X = H_1$ and $m = 1$. Table III shows the cardinalities of the sets $T_i(\boldsymbol{s})$ and $S_i(\boldsymbol{s})$, and a choice for the vectors $\boldsymbol{a}_i$,

TABLE III
Construction Method B Applied to H_1

$X = H_1$ $n = 11$ $m = 1$ $t = 2$							
i	$\lvert T_i(0)\rvert$	$\lvert T_i(1)\rvert$	$\lvert S_i(0)\rvert$	$\lvert S_i(1)\rvert$	$\boldsymbol{a}_i$	$\lvert T_i(\boldsymbol{a}_i)\rvert$	$\lvert S_i(\boldsymbol{a}_i)\rvert$
0	1	0	1	5	1	0	5
1	0	0	6	6	0	0	6
2	0	0	5	1	0	0	5
3	0	0	0	0	0	0	0
4	0	5			1	5	
5	6	6			0	6	
6	5	0			0	5	
7	0	0			0	0	
8	0	0			1	0	
9	0	0			0	0	
10	0	1			0	0	
Σ	12	12	12	12		$\lvert Z\rvert = 16$	$\lvert Z\rvert = 16$

giving a code $Z = P_{10}$ with the largest possible size (16) for a code of length 10 obtained from H_1 by this construction method. If we apply Construction Method B with $X = H_1$, $m = 2$, and the $\boldsymbol{a}_i$ as shown in Table IV, we obtain a code Z of size 8.

Let RM be the Reed–Muller code of length 16, dimension 5, and Hamming distance 8, having generator matrix

$$\begin{bmatrix} 1111111111111111 \\ 0000000011111111 \\ 0000111100001111 \\ 0011001100110011 \\ 0101010101010101 \end{bmatrix}.$$

We can now construct the Nordstrom–Robinson code NR_{16} of length 16, size 256, and Hamming distance 6, by shifting RM over the following eight vectors $\boldsymbol{b}_i$ ($\mathrm{NR}_{16} = \bigcup_{i=0}^{7}\{\boldsymbol{c} + \boldsymbol{b}_i | \boldsymbol{c} \in \mathrm{RM}\}$):

$$\boldsymbol{b}_0 = 0000 \quad 0000 \quad 0000 \quad 0000$$
$$\boldsymbol{b}_1 = 0011 \quad 0101 \quad 1001 \quad 0000$$
$$\boldsymbol{b}_2 = 0101 \quad 1001 \quad 0011 \quad 0000$$
$$\boldsymbol{b}_3 = 1001 \quad 0011 \quad 0101 \quad 0000$$
$$\boldsymbol{b}_4 = 1000 \quad 0100 \quad 0010 \quad 1110$$
$$\boldsymbol{b}_5 = 0100 \quad 0010 \quad 1000 \quad 1110$$
$$\boldsymbol{b}_6 = 0010 \quad 1000 \quad 0100 \quad 1110$$
$$\boldsymbol{b}_7 = 0001 \quad 0001 \quad 0001 \quad 1110.$$

Deleting the last column of NR_{16} we obtain a code NR_{15} of length 15, size 256, and Hamming distance 5. The weight distributions of NR_{15}, NR_{16}, and RM are shown in Table V. We now apply Construction Method B with $X = \mathrm{NR}_{15}$ and $m = 1$. The cardinalities of $T_i(0)$ and $T_i(1)$ are also shown in Table V. Choosing $\boldsymbol{a}_0 = 1$, $\boldsymbol{a}_1 = 0$, $\boldsymbol{a}_2 = 0$, $\boldsymbol{a}_3 = 0$ gives a code $Z = Z_1$ containing 176 codewords. Choosing $\boldsymbol{a}_0 = 1$, $\boldsymbol{a}_1 = 0$, $\boldsymbol{a}_2 = 0$, $\boldsymbol{a}_3 = 1$ gives a code $Z = Z_2$ also containing 176 codewords. Note that the Hamming distance of any two distinct codewords of weight 8 in NR_{16} is at least 8 since these codewords are also contained in RM. From Table V it follows that NR_{16} contains no codewords of weight 7 or 9. Hence the Hamming distance of any two distinct codewords of weight 7 or 8 in NR_{15} is at least 7. We can now easily check that $Z_1 \cup Z_2$ is a code

TABLE IV

THE VECTORS $\boldsymbol{a}_i$ IN THE EXAMPLES OF CONSTRUCTION METHOD B

	$t=2$							$t=3$					$t=4$			
	$X=H_1$		$X=\mathrm{SRC}$			$X=W_1$		$X=\mathrm{BCH}$			$X=G_1$		$X=H_2$			$X=T_{23}$
	$m=1$	$m=2$	$m=1$	$m=2$	$m=3$	$m=1$	$m=2$	$m=1$	$m=2$	$m=3$	$m=1$	$m=2$	$m=1$	$m=2$	$m=3$	$m=1$
i	$\boldsymbol{a}_i$	$\boldsymbol{a}_i$	$\boldsymbol{a}_i$	$\boldsymbol{a}_i$	$\boldsymbol{a}_i$	$\boldsymbol{a}_i$	$\boldsymbol{a}_i$	$\boldsymbol{a}_i$	$\boldsymbol{a}_i$	$\boldsymbol{a}_i$	$\boldsymbol{a}_i$	$\boldsymbol{a}_i$	$\boldsymbol{a}_i$	$\boldsymbol{a}_i$	$\boldsymbol{a}_i$	$\boldsymbol{a}_i$
0	1	01	1	01	001	1	01	1	01	001	0	00	1	10	001	1
1	0	00	0	00	000	0	00	0	01	001	0	01	0	10	000	0
2	0	00	0	00	000	0	00	0	00	000	0	01	0	00	000	0
3	0	00	1	01	001	0	00	0	01	001	0	11	0	10	001	0
4								0	01	001	1	01	0	10	011	1
5								0	11	011	0	01	0	10	111	1
6													0	10	111	0
7													0	11	011	0

TABLE V

WEIGHT DISTRIBUTIONS OF RM, NR_{16}, AND NR_{15}

	RM	NR_{16}	NR_{15}		
i	A_i	A_i	A_i	$\lvert T_i(0)\rvert$	$\lvert T_i(1)\rvert$
0	1	1	1	1	0
1	0	0	0	0	0
2	0	0	0	0	0
3	0	0	0	0	0
4	0	0	0	0	14
5	0	0	42	28	28
6	0	112	70	42	7
7	0	0	15	8	8
8	30	30	15	7	42
9	0	0	70	28	28
10	0	112	42	14	0
11	0	0	0	0	0
12	0	0	0	0	0
13	0	0	0	0	0
14	0	0	0	0	1
15	0	0	1		
16	1	1			
Σ	$\lvert\mathrm{RM}\rvert=32$	$\lvert\mathrm{NR}_{16}\rvert=256$	$\lvert\mathrm{NR}_{15}\rvert=256$	128	128

with $d_3 \geq 5$. The size of $Z_1 \cup Z_2 = P_{14}$ is $|Z_1|+|Z_2 \setminus Z_1| = |Z_1|+|T_7(1)| = 176+8 = 184$. Let $\boldsymbol{u} = (\boldsymbol{u}'_m, \boldsymbol{u}''_m)$ denote the $(14-m, m)$ partition of any $\boldsymbol{u} \in (\mathrm{GF}(2))^{14}$ for $m = 1, 2, \cdots, 12$. We define

$$K_m(\boldsymbol{s}) = \{\boldsymbol{c}'_m | \boldsymbol{c} \in P_{14} \wedge \boldsymbol{c}''_m = \boldsymbol{s}\}$$

for $\boldsymbol{s} \in (\mathrm{GF}(2))^m$ and $m = 1, 2, \cdots, 12$. In Table VI we give the cardinality of $K_5(\boldsymbol{s})$ for $\boldsymbol{s} \in (\mathrm{GF}(2))^5$. From this table it follows that $K_3(010) = P_{11}$ is a code of size 26, $K_2(10) = P_{12}$ is a code of size 52, and $K_1(0) = P_{13}$ is a code of size 92.

Sloane *et al.* [17] have constructed codes of length 19, size 2048, and Hamming distance 5, by dividing the Hamming code H_4 ($n=15$, $|H_4| = 2048$, $d_1 = 3$) into eight cosets of the Preparata code K_4 ($n=15$, $|K_4| = 256$, $d_1 = 5$), and then attaching a different codeword of the even-weight code E_4 ($n=4$, $|E_4| = 8$, $d_1 = 2$) to each coset. Let SRC be a code obtained in this way ($\boldsymbol{0} \in \mathrm{SRC}$). We apply Construction Method B with $X = \mathrm{SRC}$, $m = 1, 2, 3$, and the $\boldsymbol{a}_i$ as shown in Table IV. In this way we obtain a code $Z = P_{18}$ of size 1216 for $m=1$, a code $Z = P_{17}$ of size 640 for $m = 2$, and a code $Z = P_{16}$ of size 352 for $m = 3$.

Wagner [19] has constructed a linear code W of length 23, dimension 14, and Hamming distance 5. We consider a code W_1 which is equivalent to W. W_1 has generator matrix

$$\left[\begin{array}{c|c} & 111000011 \\ & 100110011 \\ & 101010110 \\ & 010111001 \\ & 100001011 \\ & 010100011 \\ & 001000111 \\ I_{14} & 100100110 \\ & 010001101 \\ & 101011000 \\ & 110110100 \\ & 111101010 \\ & 011011111 \\ & 101111101 \end{array}\right].$$

TABLE VI

CARDINALITIES OF $K_5(\boldsymbol{s})$ AND $L_5(\boldsymbol{s})$

$\boldsymbol{s}$	$\lvert K_5(\boldsymbol{s})\rvert$	$\lvert L_5(\boldsymbol{s})\rvert$
00000	4	35
10000	4	47
01000	6	47
11000	6	44
00100	6	47
10100	6	44
01100	4	44
11100	4	53
00010	6	38
10010	6	53
01010	8	53
11010	6	44
00110	6	53
10110	8	44
01110	6	44
11110	6	47
00001	6	47
10001	6	44
01001	6	44
11001	8	53
00101	8	44
10101	6	53
01101	6	53
11101	6	38
00011	4	53
10011	4	44
01011	6	44
11011	6	47
00111	6	44
10111	6	47
01111	4	47
11111	4	35
Σ	184	1474

We apply Construction Method B with $X = W_1$, $m = 1, 2$, and the $\boldsymbol{a}_i$ as shown in Table IV. In this way we obtain a code $Z = P_{22}$ of size 8448 for $m = 1$, and a code $Z = P_{21}$ of size 4224 for $m = 2$.

B. Codes Correcting Up to Three Unidirectional Errors

In this subsection we construct codes Q_i of length i correcting up to three unidirectional errors for $i = 11$, 12, 13, 14, 16, 17, 18, 19, 20, 21, 22.

In Table II we list the codewords of the code Q_{11} of size 7 and the code Q_{12} of size 10, both found by trial and error.

Let BCH be the BCH code of length 15, dimension 5, and Hamming distance 7, having generator matrix

$$\begin{bmatrix} 111011001010000 \\ 011101100101000 \\ 001110110010100 \\ 000111011001010 \\ 000011101100101 \end{bmatrix}$$

We apply Construction Method B with $X = \text{BCH}$, $m = 1$, 2, 3, and the $\boldsymbol{a}_i$ as shown in Table IV. In this way we obtain a code $Z = Q_{14}$ of size 22 for $m = 1$, a code $Z = Q_{13}$ of size 14 for $m = 2$, and a code Z of size 7 for $m = 3$.

We consider a code G_1 which is equivalent to the famous Golay code [11, ch. 2] of length 23, dimension 12, and Hamming distance 7. G_1 has generator matrix

$$\left[\begin{array}{cc} & 11011100010 \\ & 01110110001 \\ & 10101111000 \\ & 01011011100 \\ & 00110101110 \\ & 00001110111 \\ I_{12} & 10010011011 \\ & 11000101101 \\ & 11100010110 \\ & 01101001011 \\ & 10111000101 \\ & 11111111111 \end{array}\right].$$

We apply Construction Method B with $X = G_1$, $m = 1$, 2, and the $\boldsymbol{a}_i$ as shown in Table IV. In this way we obtain a code $Z = Q_{22}$ of size 2588 for $m = 1$, and a code $Z = Q_{21}$ of size 1474 for $m = 2$. Let $\boldsymbol{u} = (\boldsymbol{u}'_m, \boldsymbol{u}''_m)$ denote the $(21 - m, m)$ partition of any $\boldsymbol{u} \in (\text{GF}(2))^{21}$ for $m = 1, 2, \cdots, 18$. We define

$$L_m(\boldsymbol{s}) = \{\boldsymbol{c}'_m | \boldsymbol{c} \in Q_{21} \wedge \boldsymbol{c}''_m = \boldsymbol{s}\}$$

for $\boldsymbol{s} \in (\text{GF}(2))^m$ and $m = 1, 2, \cdots, 18$. In Table VI we give the cardinality of $L_5(\boldsymbol{s})$ for $\boldsymbol{s} \in (\text{GF}(2))^5$. From this table it follows that $L_5(01010) = Q_{16}$ is a code of size 53, $L_4(1010) = Q_{17}$ is a code of size 97, $L_3(010) = Q_{18}$ is a code of size 188, $L_2(10) = Q_{19}$ is a code of size 376, and $L_1(0) = Q_{20}$ is a code of size 737.

C. Codes Correcting Up to Four Unidirectional Errors

In this subsection we construct codes R_i of length i correcting up to four unidirectional errors for $i = 13$, 14, 15, 16, 17, 18, 22.

Table II lists the codewords of the code R_{13} of size 6, the code R_{14} of size 8, and the code R_{15} of size 10. These codes were found by trial and error.

Let H_2 be the code of length 19, size 40, and Hamming distance 9, containing the all-zero vector, the all-one vector, and the 19 cyclic shifts of both

$$\boldsymbol{b} = 1100111101010000110$$

and its complement $\bar{\boldsymbol{b}}$. We apply Construction Method B with $X = H_2$, $m = 1, 2, 3$, and the $\boldsymbol{a}_i$ as shown in Table IV. In this way we obtain a code $Z = R_{18}$ of size 28 for $m = 1$, a code $Z = R_{17}$ of size 18 for $m = 2$, and a code $Z = R_{16}$ of size 11 for $m = 3$.

In [18] van Tilborg constructed a code T_{24} of length 24, dimension 7, and Hamming distance 10, having generator matrix

$$\begin{bmatrix} 001101101011011001000000 \\ 101010111111101101100000 \\ 010100011110100111110000 \\ 000111101101010010111000 \\ 000010010101111000011100 \\ 001001001011100100001110 \\ 000001101110110011000111 \end{bmatrix}.$$

Deleting the last column of T_{24} we obtain a code T_{23} of length 23, dimension 7, and Hamming distance 9. We apply Construction Method B with $X = T_{23}$, $m = 1$, and the $\boldsymbol{a}_i$ as shown in Table IV. The code $Z = R_{22}$ obtained in this way contains 82 codewords.

D. Final Remark

Further investigation may tell us how to rearrange the columns of the codes X in Construction Method B to obtain the largest codes Z. For instance, the method applied to the Wagner code W of length 23, dimension 14, and Hamming distance 5 as stated in [19] and [5] ($X = W, m = 1, \boldsymbol{a}_0 = 1, \boldsymbol{a}_1 = 0, \boldsymbol{a}_2 = 0, \boldsymbol{a}_3 = 0$) gives a code Z ($n = 22, d_3 \geq 5$) of size 8320, while the method applied to the equivalent code W_1 as stated in Section VI-A of this paper ($X = W_1, m = 1, \boldsymbol{a}_0 = 1, \boldsymbol{a}_1 = 0, \boldsymbol{a}_2 = 0, \boldsymbol{a}_3 = 0$) gives a code Z_1 ($n = 22, d_3 \geq 5$) of size 8448.

VII. Tables and Summary

In Tables VII–X we give bounds on $A_i(n, t)$ for $i = 1, 2, 3$, $1 \leq t \leq 4$, $t \leq n \leq 23$. The bounds on $A_2(n, t)$ are taken from [21]. The bounds on $A_1(n, t)$ are taken from [15], except for the lower bounds for $t = 1$ and $16 \leq n \leq 18$. Recently, van Os [13] has shown that $A_1(18, 1) \geq 10496$ (hence $A_1(17, 1) \geq 5248$), and Romanov [16] has shown that $A_1(16, 1) \geq 2720$. The bounds on $A_3(n, t)$ follow from the bounds and constructions obtained in this paper. We now summarize these results. The letters correspond to the

TABLE VII

BOUNDS ON $A_i(n,1)$ FOR $i=1, 2, 3$, AND $1 \le n \le 23$

n	$A_1(n,1) = A_3(n,1)$	$A_2(n,1)$
1	1	1
2	1	2
3	2	2
4	2	4
5	4	6
6	8	12
7	16	18
8	20	36
9	40	62
10	72–79	108–117
11	144–158	174–210
12	256	316–410
13	512	586–786
14	1024	1096–1500
15	2048	2048–2828
16	2720–3276	3856–5430
17	5248–6552	7296–10374
18	10496–13104	13798–19898
19	20480–26208	26216–38008
20	36864–43690	49940–73174
21	73728–87380	95326–140798
22	147456–173784	182362–271953
23	294912–344636	349536–523586

TABLE VIII

BOUNDS ON $A_i(n,2)$ FOR $i=1, 2, 3$, AND $2 \le n \le 23$

n	$A_1(n,2)$	$A_3(n,2)$	$A_2(n,2)$
2	1	[a]1[a]	1
3	1	[a]1[a]	2
4	1	[b]2[b]	2
5	2	[b]2[b]	2
6	2	[b]2[b]	4
7	2	[c]4[c]	4
8	4	[p]6[m]	7
9	6	[p]10[s]	12
10	12	[p]16–18[j]	18
11	24	[p]26–32[j]	30–32
12	32	[p]52–61[k]	54–63
13	64	[p]92–114[j]	98–114
14	128	[p]184–218[j]	186–218
15	256	[e]256–340[m]	266–398
16	256–340	[p]352–680[m]	364–739
17	512–680	[p]640–1277[k]	647–1279
18	1024–1288	[p]1216–2372[m]	1218–2380
19	2048–2372	[e]2048–4096[m]	2050–4242
20	2560–4096	[e]2560–6942[m]	2564–8069
21	4096–6942	[p]4224–13774[m]	4251–14374
22	8192–13774	[p]8448–24106[m]	8450–26679
23	16384–24106	[e]16384–48212[l]	16388–50200

TABLE IX

BOUNDS ON $A_i(n,3)$ FOR $i=1, 2, 3$, AND $3 \le n \le 23$

n	$A_1(n,3)$	$A_3(n,3)$	$A_2(n,3)$
3	1	[a]1[a]	1
4	1	[a]1[a]	2
5	1	[b]2[b]	2
6	1	[b]2[b]	2
7	2	[b]2[b]	2
8	2	[b]2[b]	4
9	2	[c]4[c]	4
10	2	[f]4[m]	6
11	4	[q]7[s]	8
12	4	[q]10–11[k]	12
13	8	[q]14–18[j]	18
14	16	[q]22–34[j]	30–34
15	32	[e]32–50[j]	44–50
16	36–37	[q]53–90[j]	66–90
17	64–72	[q]97–168[j]	122–168
18	128–144	[q]188–320[j]	234–320
19	256–279	[q]376–616[j]	450–616
20	512	[q]737–1142[k]	860–1144
21	1024	[q]1474–2134[j]	1628–2134
22	2048	[q]2588–4114[k]	3072–4116
23	4096	[e]4096–7346[j]	4096–7346

TABLE X

BOUNDS ON $A_i(n,4)$ FOR $i=1, 2, 3$, AND $4 \le n \le 23$

n	$A_1(n,4)$	$A_3(n,4)$	$A_2(n,4)$
4	1	[a]1[a]	1
5	1	[a]1[a]	2
6	1	[b]2[b]	2
7	1	[b]2[b]	2
8	1	[b]2[b]	2
9	2	[b]2[b]	2
10	2	[b]2[b]	4
11	2	[c]4[c]	4
12	2	[c]4[j]	4
13	2	[r]6[j]	6
14	4	[r]8[j]	8
15	4	[r]10–12[j]	12
16	6	[r]11–16[j]	16
17	10	[r]18–26[j]	26
18	20	[r]28–44[j]	36–44
19	40	[e]40–76[j]	46–76
20	40–48	[e]40–134[j]	54–134
21	48–88	[e]48–229[j]	62–229
22	64–150	[r]82–423[j]	88–423
23	128–280	[e]128–745[j]	133–745

references in the tables:

a) $A_3(n,t) = 1$ for $t \le n \le t+1$ and $t = 1,2,3,\cdots$ Section IV, Theorem 10;
b) $A_3(n,t) = 2$ for $t+2 \le n \le 2t+2$ and $t = 1,2,3,\cdots$ Section IV, Theorem 10;
c) $A_3(n,t) = 4$ for $n = 2t+3$ and $t = 1,2,3,\cdots$ Section IV, Theorem 10;
d) $A_3(n,t) = A_1(n,t)$ for $n \ge t = 1$ Section I
e) $A_3(n,t) \ge A_1(n,t)$ for $n \ge t \ge 1$ Section I
f) $A_3(n,t) \ge A_2(n,t) - 2$ for $2t+4 \le n \le 3t+2$ and $t = 2,3,4,\cdots$ Section V, Corollary 2;
g) $A_3(n,t) \ge A_2(n,t) - 5$ for $n = 3t+3$ and $t = 1,2,3,\cdots$ Section V, Corollary 2;
h) $A_3(n,t) \ge A_2(n,t) - 8$ for $n = 3t+4$ and $t = 1,2,3,\cdots$ Section V, Corollary 2;
i) $A_3(n,t) \ge ((t+1)/(3t+1))A_2(n,t)$ for $n \ge t \ge 1$ Section V, Corollary 1;
j) $A_3(n,t) \le A_2(n,t)$ for $n \ge t \ge 1$ Section I
k) $A_3(n,t) \le J_U(n,t)$ for $n \ge t \ge 1$ Section II, Theorem 5;
l) $A_3(n,t) \le tA_1(n,t)$ for $n \ge t \ge 1$ Section III, Theorem 8;

m) $A_3(n,t) \le A_1(n+t-1,t)$ for $n \ge t \ge 1$ — Section III, Theorem 9;

n) Construction Method A, a method in which codes of length n correcting up to t unidirectional errors are obtained by expurgating a code of length n correcting up to t asymmetric errors ($n \ge t \ge 1$) — Section V;

o) Construction Method B, a method in which a code of length $n-m$ correcting up to t unidirectional errors is obtained by expurgating and puncturing a code of length n correction up to t symmetric errors ($n \ge t \ge 1$, $1 \le m \le n-t$) — Section V;

p) codes P_i for $i = 8, 9, 10, 11, 12, 13, 14, 16, 17, 18, 21, 22$ (codes correcting up to two unidirectional errors) — Section VI-A;

q) codes Q_i for $i = 11, 12, 13, 14, 16, 17, 18, 19, 20, 21, 22$ (codes correcting up to three unidirectional errors) — Section VI-B;

r) codes R_i for $i = 13, 14, 15, 16, 17, 18, 22$ (codes correcting up to four unidirectional errors) — Section VI-C;

s) sharpened integer programming bound — Appendix II.

Acknowledgment

The authors would like to thank one of the anonymous referees for constructing the code Q_{12} in Section VI-B and his/her helpful comments.

Appendix I
Proof of Theorem 1c)

In this appendix we give a proof of a necessary and sufficient condition for a code to be unidirectional error correcting; the condition was originally derived by Bose and Rao [4].

Theorem 1c): A code C of length n can correct t or fewer unidirectional errors if and only if $d_3 \ge 2t+1$.

Proof: Define

$$S_0(\boldsymbol{x}) = \{\boldsymbol{a} \in V | \boldsymbol{a} \ge \boldsymbol{x} \wedge w(\boldsymbol{a}) - w(\boldsymbol{x}) \le t\}, \quad \text{for } \boldsymbol{x} \in V$$

$$S_1(\boldsymbol{x}) = \{\boldsymbol{a} \in V | \boldsymbol{x} \ge \boldsymbol{a} \wedge w(\boldsymbol{x}) - w(\boldsymbol{a}) \le t\}, \quad \text{for } \boldsymbol{x} \in V$$

$$S(\boldsymbol{x}) = S_0(\boldsymbol{x}) \cup S_1(\boldsymbol{x}), \quad \text{for } \boldsymbol{x} \in V.$$

Let $\boldsymbol{c} \in C$, then $S(\boldsymbol{c})$ is the set of all vectors obtained from the codeword $\boldsymbol{c}$ suffering t or fewer unidirectional errors. Hence C can correct t or fewer unidirectional errors if and only if $S(\boldsymbol{c}_1) \cap S(\boldsymbol{c}_2) = \varnothing$ for any $\boldsymbol{c}_1, \boldsymbol{c}_2 \in C, \boldsymbol{c}_1 \ne \boldsymbol{c}_2$. Thus we have to prove

$$S(\boldsymbol{c}_1) \cap S(\boldsymbol{c}_2) = \varnothing, \text{ for all } \boldsymbol{c}_1, \boldsymbol{c}_2 \in C \ (\boldsymbol{c}_1 \ne \boldsymbol{c}_2)$$

$$\Leftrightarrow d_3(\boldsymbol{c}_1, \boldsymbol{c}_2) \ge 2t+1, \text{ for all } \boldsymbol{c}_1, \boldsymbol{c}_2 \in C (\boldsymbol{c}_1 \ne \boldsymbol{c}_2).$$

"$\Rightarrow$": Let $\boldsymbol{c}_1, \boldsymbol{c}_2 \in C$, $\boldsymbol{c}_1 \ne \boldsymbol{c}_2$, $S(\boldsymbol{c}_1) \cap S(\boldsymbol{c}_2) = \varnothing$, $w(\boldsymbol{c}_1) \ge w(\boldsymbol{c}_2)$. Suppose $d_3(\boldsymbol{c}_1, \boldsymbol{c}_2) \le 2t$. We distinguish between two cases: A) $N(\boldsymbol{c}_1, \boldsymbol{c}_2) = 0$, and B) $N(\boldsymbol{c}_1, \boldsymbol{c}_2) > 0$.

A) The case $N(\boldsymbol{c}_1, \boldsymbol{c}_2) = 0$: Without loss of generality we may assume that the codewords $\boldsymbol{c}_1$ and $\boldsymbol{c}_2$ look like

$$\begin{array}{cccc} \boldsymbol{c}_1: & 11\cdots1 & 11\cdots1 & 00\cdots0 \\ \boldsymbol{c}_2: & 11\cdots1 & 00\cdots0 & 00\cdots0 \\ & \leftrightarrow & \leftrightarrow & \leftrightarrow \\ & a & b & c \end{array}$$

where $a+b+c=n$ and $b = d_1(\boldsymbol{c}_1, \boldsymbol{c}_2) = d_3(\boldsymbol{c}_1, \boldsymbol{c}_2) \le 2t$. Define $\boldsymbol{a} = 1^v 0^{n-v}$ with $v = a + \lfloor b/2 \rfloor$. Then $\boldsymbol{a} \in S_0(\boldsymbol{c}_2)$ since $\boldsymbol{a} \ge \boldsymbol{c}_2$ and $w(\boldsymbol{a}) - w(\boldsymbol{c}_2) = \lfloor b/2 \rfloor \le t$. Furthermore, $\boldsymbol{a} \in S_1(\boldsymbol{c}_1)$ since $\boldsymbol{c}_1 \ge \boldsymbol{a}$ and $w(\boldsymbol{c}_1) - w(\boldsymbol{a}) = b - \lfloor b/2 \rfloor = \lceil b/2 \rceil \le t$. Hence $S(\boldsymbol{c}_1) \cap S(\boldsymbol{c}_2) \ne \varnothing$ (contradiction).

B) The case $N(\boldsymbol{c}_1, \boldsymbol{c}_2) > 0$: Without loss of generality we may assume that the codewords $\boldsymbol{c}_1$ and $\boldsymbol{c}_2$ look like

$$\begin{array}{ccccc} \boldsymbol{c}_1: & 11\cdots1 & 11\cdots1 & 00\cdots0 & 00\cdots0 \\ \boldsymbol{c}_2: & 11\cdots1 & 00\cdots0 & 11\cdots1 & 00\cdots0 \\ & \leftrightarrow & \leftrightarrow & \leftrightarrow & \leftrightarrow \\ & a & b & c & d \end{array}$$

where $a+b+c+d=n$, and $1 \le c = N(\boldsymbol{c}_1, \boldsymbol{c}_2) \le b = N(\boldsymbol{c}_2, \boldsymbol{c}_1) = d_2(\boldsymbol{c}_1, \boldsymbol{c}_2)/2 = d_3(\boldsymbol{c}_1, \boldsymbol{c}_2)/2 \le t$. Define $\boldsymbol{a} = 1^a 0^{n-a}$. Then $\boldsymbol{a} \in S_1(\boldsymbol{c}_2)$, since $\boldsymbol{c}_2 \ge \boldsymbol{a}$ and $w(\boldsymbol{c}_2) - w(\boldsymbol{a}) = c \le t$. Furthermore, $\boldsymbol{a} \in S_1(\boldsymbol{c}_1)$, since $\boldsymbol{c}_1 \ge \boldsymbol{a}$ and $w(\boldsymbol{c}_1) - w(\boldsymbol{a}) = b \le t$. Hence $S(\boldsymbol{c}_1) \cap S(\boldsymbol{c}_2) \ne \varnothing$ (contradiction).

From A) and B) it follows that $d_3(\boldsymbol{c}_1, \boldsymbol{c}_2) \ge 2t+1$.

"$\Leftarrow$": Let $\boldsymbol{c}_1, \boldsymbol{c}_2 \in C$, $\boldsymbol{c}_1 \ne \boldsymbol{c}_2$, $d_3(\boldsymbol{c}_1, \boldsymbol{c}_2) \ge 2t+1$, $w(\boldsymbol{c}_1) \ge w(\boldsymbol{c}_2)$. Suppose $S(\boldsymbol{c}_1) \cap S(\boldsymbol{c}_2) \ne \varnothing$, so $\exists \boldsymbol{a} \in V$: $\boldsymbol{a} \in S(\boldsymbol{c}_1) \cap S(\boldsymbol{c}_2)$. We distinguish between two cases: A) $N(\boldsymbol{c}_1, \boldsymbol{c}_2) = 0$, and B) $N(\boldsymbol{c}_1, \boldsymbol{c}_2) > 0$.

A) The case $N(\boldsymbol{c}_1, \boldsymbol{c}_2) = 0$: In this case

$$d_3(\boldsymbol{c}_1, \boldsymbol{c}_2) = d_1(\boldsymbol{c}_1, \boldsymbol{c}_2) \le d_1(\boldsymbol{c}_1, \boldsymbol{a}) + d_1(\boldsymbol{a}, \boldsymbol{c}_2) \le t + t = 2t$$

since $\boldsymbol{a} \in S(\boldsymbol{c}_1) \cap S(\boldsymbol{c}_2)$. This contradicts $d_3(\boldsymbol{c}_1, \boldsymbol{c}_2) \ge 2t+1$.

B) The case $N(\boldsymbol{c}_1, \boldsymbol{c}_2) > 0$: Without loss of generality we may assume the codewords $\boldsymbol{c}_1$ and $\boldsymbol{c}_2$ look like

$$\begin{array}{ccccc} \boldsymbol{c}_1: & 11\cdots1 & 11\cdots1 & 00\cdots0 & 00\cdots0 \\ \boldsymbol{c}_2: & 11\cdots1 & 00\cdots0 & 11\cdots1 & 00\cdots0 \\ & \leftrightarrow & \leftrightarrow & \leftrightarrow & \leftrightarrow \\ & a & b & c & d \end{array}$$

where $a+b+c+d=n$, and $1 \le c = N(\boldsymbol{c}_1, \boldsymbol{c}_2) \le b = N(\boldsymbol{c}_2, \boldsymbol{c}_1)$.

1) Suppose $\boldsymbol{a} \in S_0(\boldsymbol{c}_1) \cap S_0(\boldsymbol{c}_2)$. Then $\boldsymbol{a} \ge \boldsymbol{c}_1$, $\boldsymbol{a} \ge \boldsymbol{c}_2$, $c \le w(\boldsymbol{a}) - w(\boldsymbol{c}_1) \le t$, and $b \le w(\boldsymbol{a}) - w(\boldsymbol{c}_2) \le t$. Hence $d_3(\boldsymbol{c}_1, \boldsymbol{c}_2) = d_2(\boldsymbol{c}_1, \boldsymbol{c}_2) = 2\max\{b, c\} \le 2t$. This contradicts $d_3(\boldsymbol{c}_1, \boldsymbol{c}_2) \ge 2t+1$.

2) Suppose $\boldsymbol{a} \in S_1(\boldsymbol{c}_1) \cap S_1(\boldsymbol{c}_2)$. Then $\boldsymbol{c}_1 \ge \boldsymbol{a}$, $\boldsymbol{c}_2 \ge \boldsymbol{a}$, $b \le w(\boldsymbol{c}_1) - w(\boldsymbol{a}) \le t$, and $c \le w(\boldsymbol{c}_2) - w(\boldsymbol{a}) \le t$. Hence $d_3(\boldsymbol{c}_1, \boldsymbol{c}_2) = d_2(\boldsymbol{c}_1, \boldsymbol{c}_2) = 2\max\{b, c\} \le 2t$. This contradicts $d_3(\boldsymbol{c}_1, \boldsymbol{c}_2) \ge 2t+1$.

3) Suppose $\boldsymbol{a} \in S_0(\boldsymbol{c}_1) \cap S_1(\boldsymbol{c}_2)$. Then $\boldsymbol{c}_2 \ge \boldsymbol{a} \ge \boldsymbol{c}_1$, and thus $b = 0$. This contradicts $b \ge 1$.

4) Suppose $\boldsymbol{a} \in S_1(\boldsymbol{c}_1) \cap S_0(\boldsymbol{c}_2)$. Then $\boldsymbol{c}_1 \ge \boldsymbol{a} \ge \boldsymbol{c}_2$, and thus $c = 0$. This contradicts $c \ge 1$.

From A) and B) it follows that $S(\boldsymbol{c}_1) \cap S(\boldsymbol{c}_2) = \varnothing$.

Appendix II
Sharpening of the Integer Programming Bound

Substituting z_i by A_i in the constraints of the integer programming problem stated in Theorem 5, we obtain some restrictions on the weight distribution $A_0, A_1, \cdots, A_n$ of a code C of length n with $d_3 \geq 2t+1$. Sometimes we can sharpen these restrictions using some simple arguments. This will be made clear by two illustrative examples.

If $n=9$ and $t=2$ we obtain $A_0 + A_1 + A_2 \leq 1$, $A_3 \leq 3$, $A_4 \leq 3$, $A_3 + A_4 \leq 5$, all from constraint 2a). Hence $A_0 + A_1 + A_2 + A_3 + A_4 \leq 1+5=6$. Suppose $A_0 + A_1 + A_2 + A_3 + A_4 = 6$; then $A_0 + A_1 + A_2 = 1$ and $A_3 + A_4 = 5$. Since $A_3 = 3$ forces $A_4 = 0$, we have $A_3 = 2$ and $A_4 = 3$. Without loss of generality we may assume the codewords of weight 3 and 4 look like

$$c_1 = 111000000$$

$$c_2 = 000111000$$

$$c_3 = 100100011$$

$$c_4 = 010010101$$

$$c_5 = 001001110.$$

Let c be the codeword of weight less than 3. Then $|\{i | c_i = u_i = 1\}| = 0$ for $u = c_1, c_2$. Hence $\exists j \in \{3,4,5\}$: $c_j \geq c$, and thus $d_3(c_j, c) = d_1(c_j, c) \leq 4$, which contradicts $d_3 \geq 5$. In conclusion, $A_0 + A_1 + A_2 + A_4 \leq 5$ and (of course) $A_5 + A_6 + A_7 + A_8 + A_9 \leq 5$. Hence $A_3(9,2) \leq 5+5=10$, which improves the integer programming bound $J_U(9,2)=12$.

If $n=11$ and $t=3$, we obtain $A_0 + A_1 + A_2 + A_3 \leq 1$, $A_8 + A_9 + A_{10} + A_{11} \leq 1$, $A_4 \leq 2$, $A_5 \leq 2$, $A_6 \leq 2$, $A_7 \leq 2$, $A_4 + A_5 \leq 3$, $A_6 + A_7 \leq 3$, $A_4 + A_5 + A_6 \leq 4$, $A_5 + A_6 + A_7 \leq 4$, all from constraint 2a). Hence $A_0 + A_1 + \cdots + A_{11} \leq 1+3+3+1=8$. Suppose $A_0 + A_1 + \cdots + A_{11} = 8$; then $A_0 + A_1 + A_2 + A_3 = 1$, $A_8 + A_9 + A_{10} + A_{11} = 1$, $A_4 = A_7 = 2$, $A_5 = A_6 = 1$. Without loss of generality, we may assume the codewords of weight 4 and 5 look like

$$c_1 = 11110000000$$

$$c_2 = 00001111000$$

$$c_3 = 10001000111.$$

Again, we can easily check that there can be no vector c of weight less than 4, which satisfies $d_3(c, c_i) \geq 7$ for $i = 1, 2, 3$. This contradicts $A_0 + A_1 + A_2 + A_3 = 1$. Hence $A_3(11,3) \leq 7$, which improves the integer programming bound $J_U(11,3) = 8$.

References

[1] M. R. Best, A. E. Brouwer, F. J. MacWilliams, A. M. Odlyzko, and N. J. A. Sloane, "Bounds for binary codes of length less than 25," *IEEE Trans. Inform. Theory*, vol. IT-24, pp. 81–93, Jan. 1978.

[2] M. Blaum and H. C. A. van Tilborg, "On t-error correcting/all unidirectional error detecting codes," *IEEE Trans. Comput.*, to be published.

[3] B. Bose and D. K. Pradhan, "Optimal unidirectional error detecting/correcting codes," *IEEE Trans. Comput.*, vol. C-31, pp. 564–568, June 1982.

[4] B. Bose and T. R. N. Rao, "Theory of unidirectional error correcting/detecting codes," *IEEE Trans. Comput.*, vol. C-31, pp. 521–530, June 1982.

[5] A. E. Brouwer, P. Delsarte, and P. Piret, "On the (23,14,5) Wagner code," *IEEE Trans. Inform. Theory*, vol. IT-26, pp. 742–743, Nov. 1980.

[6] P. Delsarte and P. Piret, "Bounds and constructions for binary asymmetric error-correcting codes," *IEEE Trans. Inform. Theory*, vol. IT-27, pp. 125–128, Jan. 1981.

[7] I. Ya. Goldbaum, "Estimate for the number of signals in codes correcting nonsymmetric errors," *Automat. Telemekh.*, vol. 32, pp. 94–97, 1971 (in Russian); English translation: *Automat. Rem. Control*, vol. 32, pp. 1783–1785, 1971.

[8] R. L. Graham and N. J. A. Sloane, "Lower bounds for constant weight codes," *IEEE Trans. Inform. Theory*, vol. IT-26, pp. 37–43, Jan. 1980.

[9] T. Kløve, "Upper bounds on codes correcting asymmetric errors," *IEEE Trans. Inform. Theory*, vol. IT-27, pp. 128–131, Jan. 1981.

[10] ——, "Error correcting codes for the asymmetric channel," Dept. Mathematics, Univ. of Bergen, Bergen, Norway, Rep. 18-09-07-81, July 1981.

[11] F. J. MacWilliams and N. J. A. Sloane, *The Theory of Error-Correcting Codes*. Amsterdam, The Netherlands: North-Holland, 1977.

[12] D. Nikolos, N. Gaitanis, and G. Philokyprou, "Systematic t-error correcting/all unidirectional error detecting codes," *IEEE Trans. Comput.*, vol. C-35, pp. 394–402, May 1986.

[13] E. van Os, "Packing density of codes," M.Sc. Thesis, Department of Mathematics and Informatics, Delft University of Technology, Delft, The Netherlands, May 1987 (in Dutch).

[14] D. K. Pradhan, "A new class of error-correcting/detecting codes for fault-tolerant computer application," *IEEE Trans. Comput.*, vol. C-29, pp. 471–481, June 1980.

[15] C. L. M. van Pul, "On bounds on codes," M.Sc. Thesis, Department of Mathematics and Computing Science, Eindhoven University of Technology, Eindhoven, The Netherlands, Aug. 1982.

[16] A. M. Romanov, "New binary codes of minimal distance 3," *Probl. Peredach. Inform.*, vol. 19, pp. 101–102, 1983 (in Russian).

[17] N. J. A. Sloane, S. M. Reddy, and C. L. Chen, "New binary codes," *IEEE Trans. Inform. Theory*, vol. IT-18, pp. 503–510, July 1972.

[18] H. C. A. van Tilborg, "The smallest length of binary 7-dimensional linear codes with prescribed minimum distance," *Discrete Math.*, vol. 33, pp. 197–207, 1981.

[19] T. J. Wagner, "A search technique for quasi-perfect codes," *Inform. Contr.*, vol. 9, pp. 94–99, 1966.

[20] J. H. Weber, C. de Vroedt, and D. E. Boekee, "New upper bounds on the size of codes correcting asymmetric errors," *IEEE Trans. Inform. Theory*, vol. IT-33, pp. 434–437, May 1987.

[21] ——, "Bounds and constructions for binary codes of length less than 24 and asymmetric distance less than 6," *IEEE Trans. Inform. Theory*, vol. IT-34, pp. 1321–1331, Sept. 1988.

Some New Binary Codes Correcting Asymmetric/Unidirectional Errors

YUICHI SAITOH, STUDENT MEMBER, IEEE,
KAZUHIKO YAMAGUCHI, MEMBER, IEEE,
AND HIDEKI IMAI, SENIOR MEMBER, IEEE

Abstract —**We give a tabulation of the numbers of codewords in new binary codes with the asymmetric/unidirectional error correcting capabilities 3, 4, 5, 6 for lengths 14, 15, ⋯, 23.**

The difference between the probability of mistaking a 1 for a 0 and vice-versa can be large in certain digital systems, such as optical communications and optical disks. Practically, we can assume that only one type of error, either $1 \to 0$ or $0 \to 1$, can occur in those systems. These errors are called asymmetric errors. Further, the most likely faults in some of the recently developed VLSI chips cause unidirectional errors,. for which both $1 \to 0$ and $0 \to 1$ errors can occur, but they do not occur simultaneously in a single data word.

We may use ordinary codes that correct both $1 \to 0$ and $0 \to 1$ errors. However, if codes correcting asymmetric/unidirectional errors are used, more efficient coding systems will be realized. For this purpose, codes correcting asymmetric/unidirectional errors have been studied actively [1]–[4]. In this correspondence, some new codes with more efficiency than the known codes are presented.

We use the following notation

X, Y: binary n-tuples.

$N(X,Y)$: number of $1 \to 0$ crossovers from X to Y, that is, for $X = [x_1 x_2 \cdots x_n]$ and $Y = [y_1 y_2 \cdots y_n]$, where x_i and y_i are 0 or 1,

$$N(X,Y) = |\{i \mid x_i = 1 \wedge y_i = 0\}|.$$

$D(X,Y)$: Hamming distance between X and Y.

$\Delta(X,Y)$: asymmetric distance between X and Y, that is

$$\Delta(X,Y) = \max(N(X,Y), N(Y,X)).$$

$D_U(X,Y)$: unidirectional distance between X and Y, that is

$$D_U(X,Y) = \begin{cases} D(X,Y), & \text{if } N(X,Y) = 0 \text{ or } N(Y,X) = 0 \\ 2\Delta(X,Y), & \text{otherwise.} \end{cases}$$

$\Delta(C)$: minimum asymmetric distance of a code C, that is, for all distinct $X, Y \in C$

$$\Delta(C) = \min(\Delta(X,Y)).$$

$D_U(C)$: minimum unidirectional distance of a code C, that is, for all distinct $X, Y \in C$

$$D_U(C) = \min(D_U(X,Y)).$$

The following two theorems are well known [1], [2].

Theorem 1: A code C can correct t or fewer asymmetric errors iff $\Delta(C) \geq t+1$.

Theorem 2: A code C can correct t or fewer unidirectional errors iff $D_U(C) \geq 2t+1$.

Manuscript received May 8, 1989; revised October 25, 1989.
Y. Saitoh and H. Imai are with the Division of Electrical and Computer Engineering, Faculty of Engineering, Yokohama National University, Yokohama, 240 Japan.
K. Yamaguchi is with the Department of Computer Science and Information Mathematics, the University of Electro-Communications, Chofu, 182 Japan.
IEEE Log Number 8933980.

We constructed asymmetric/unidirectional error-correcting codes using two programs based on a greedy algorithm. Fig. 1 gives a block diagram of the first program (Program 1). In Fig. 1, $b_{w,i}$, $i = 1, 2, \cdots, \binom{n}{w}$, is a binary n-tuple of Hamming weight w, where we arrange its suffix such as $b_{w,i} < b_{w,j}$ for $i < j$ regarding $b_{w,i}$ and $b_{w,j}$ as binary numbers, and w_j, $j = 1, 2, \cdots, n-2t+1$, is determined as shown in Table I. Program 1 examines n-tuples of weight around $n/2$ at first. The "asymmetric" version of Program 1 includes an examined n-tuple in the code if its distance to the code satisfies Theorem 1, and the "unidirectional" version of Program 1 includes an examined n-tuple in the code if its distance to the code satisfies Theorem 2. The second program (Program 2) is the same as Program 1 except that w_j is determined as shown in Table II and the n-tuple with a smaller distance to the code is chosen preferentially.

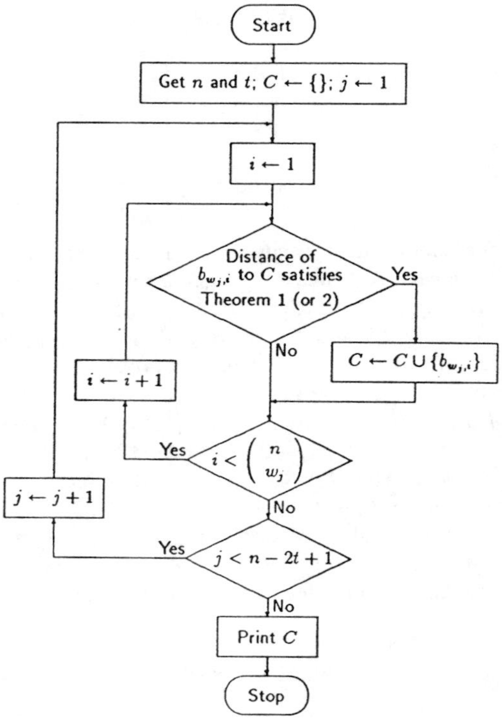

Fig. 1. Block diagram of Program 1.

TABLE I
w_j IN PROGRAM 1

j	Asymmetric Version	Unidirectional Version
1	0	$\lfloor n/2 \rfloor$
2	$\lfloor n/2 \rfloor$	$\lfloor n/2 \rfloor - 1$
3	$\lfloor n/2 \rfloor - 1$	$\lfloor n/2 \rfloor - 2$
4	$\lfloor n/2 \rfloor - 2$	$\lfloor n/2 \rfloor - 3$
⋯	⋯	⋯
$\lfloor n/2 \rfloor - t$	$t+2$	$t+1$
$\lfloor n/2 \rfloor - t + 1$	$t+1$	$\lfloor n/2 \rfloor + 1$
$\lfloor n/2 \rfloor - t + 2$	$\lfloor n/2 \rfloor + 1$	$\lfloor n/2 \rfloor + 2$
$\lfloor n/2 \rfloor - t + 3$	$\lfloor n/2 \rfloor + 2$	$\lfloor n/2 \rfloor + 3$
⋯	⋯	⋯
$n - 2t - 1$	$n - t - 2$	$n - t - 1$
$n - 2t$	$n - t - 1$	1
$n - 2t + 1$	n	$n - 1$

0-8186-4182-7/93 $3.00 © 1990 IEEE

TABLE II
w_j IN PROGRAM 2

j	Asymmetric Version	Unidirectional Version
1	0	$t+1$
2	$t+1$	$t+2$
3	$t+2$	$t+3$
4	$t+3$	$t+4$
...	...	...
$\lfloor n/2 \rfloor - t$	$\lfloor n/2 \rfloor - 1$	$\lfloor n/2 \rfloor$
$\lfloor n/2 \rfloor - t + 1$	$\lfloor n/2 \rfloor$	$n-t-1$
$\lfloor n/2 \rfloor - t + 2$	$n-t-1$	$n-t-2$
$\lfloor n/2 \rfloor - t + 3$	$n-t-2$	$n-t-3$
...	...	...
$n-2t-1$	$\lfloor n/2 \rfloor + 2$	$\lfloor n/2 \rfloor + 1$
$n-2t$	$\lfloor n/2 \rfloor + 1$	1
$n-2t+1$	n	$n-1$

TABLE III
20 CODEWORDS IN THE 5-ASYMMETRIC ERROR CORRECTING CODE OF LENGTH 20

0 0 0 0 0 0 0 0 0 0 0 0 0 0 0 0 0 0 0 0
0 0 0 0 0 0 0 0 0 0 1 1 1 1 1 1 1 1 1 1
0 0 0 0 1 1 1 1 1 1 0 0 0 0 0 0 1 1 1 1
0 0 1 1 0 0 1 1 1 1 0 0 1 1 1 1 0 0 0 0
0 1 1 1 1 1 0 0 0 1 1 1 0 0 0 1 0 0 0 1
1 0 0 0 1 1 0 1 1 0 1 1 0 1 1 0 0 0 0 0
1 0 1 1 0 1 1 0 0 0 0 1 1 0 0 0 0 1 1 0
0 1 0 0 0 0 1 0 1 1 1 1 1 0 0 0 1 0 0 0
0 1 0 1 0 1 0 1 0 0 0 0 0 0 1 1 1 0 1 0
0 1 1 0 1 0 0 1 0 0 0 0 1 1 0 0 0 1 0 1
1 0 0 0 0 0 0 0 1 1 0 0 0 0 1 1 0 1 0 1
0 0 0 0 0 1 1 0 0 0 1 0 0 1 0 0 0 0 1 1
1 1 0 1 0 1 0 1 0 1 1 0 1 1 0 0 1 1 0 0
1 1 0 1 1 0 1 0 1 0 0 1 0 0 1 1 1 1 0 0
0 1 0 1 0 1 1 1 1 0 1 1 1 0 1 0 0 0 1 1
1 0 1 0 0 1 1 0 1 1 1 1 0 1 0 1 1 0 1 0
1 0 1 1 1 0 0 1 0 1 0 1 0 1 1 0 0 1 1 1
0 1 1 0 1 0 0 1 1 1 1 0 1 0 1 1 1 1 0 1
0 1 0 1 1 1 1 0 0 1 0 1 1 1 0 1 1 1 1 1
1 1 1 1 1 1 1 1 1 1 1 1 1 1 1 1 1 1 1 1

As examples of codes constructed by Program 1, the two codes are shown in Tables III and IV.

We call the number of codewords the size of the code. Maximal values of sizes of codes obtained by Programs 1 and 2 and the known methods [1], [2], [4] are shown in Tables V and VI. In these tables, n is the length of a code, and t is the asymmetric or unidirectional error correcting capability. We mark "^{a}" and "^{b}" ("*" and "**") when the sizes of codes obtained by Programs 1 and 2 are greater than (or equal to) those of the known codes [1], [2], [4] and the repetition code $\{00\cdots0, 11\cdots1\}$. Nothing is marked when the sizes of codes obtained by the above programs are less than those of the known codes or the repetition of them.

By these programs, we have constructed some new codes with greater sizes than the known codes for $14 \le n \le 23$ and $3 \le t \le 6$.

TABLE IV
34 CODEWORDS IN THE 4-UNIDIRECTIONAL ERROR CORRECTING CODE OF LENGTH 18

0 0 0 0 0 0 0 0 0 1 1 1 1 1 1 1 1 1	1 0 1 0 0 0 1 0 1 0 1 0 1 0 0 0 1 1
0 0 0 0 1 1 1 1 1 0 0 0 0 0 1 1 1 1	1 1 0 0 0 1 0 1 0 0 0 1 0 1 0 0 1 1
0 0 0 1 0 1 1 1 1 0 1 1 1 1 0 0 0 0	0 0 0 0 0 0 0 1 1 0 0 1 1 0 0 1 0 1
0 1 1 0 1 0 0 1 1 1 0 0 1 1 0 0 0 1	0 0 0 0 0 1 1 0 0 0 1 0 0 1 1 0 1 0
0 1 1 0 1 1 1 0 0 1 1 1 0 0 0 0 1 0	0 0 1 1 1 0 1 0 1 1 0 0 0 0 0 0 0 0
1 0 1 1 0 0 0 1 1 1 0 1 0 0 0 1 1 0	1 1 0 0 0 0 0 0 0 1 0 0 0 0 0 1 1 0
1 0 1 1 0 1 1 0 0 1 0 0 0 1 1 0 0 1	0 1 0 1 1 1 0 1 0 1 0 1 0 1 1 1 0 0
1 1 0 1 1 0 0 0 1 0 1 0 0 1 1 0 1 0	0 1 1 1 0 0 1 1 0 0 1 0 0 1 0 1 1 1
1 1 0 1 1 0 1 0 0 0 0 1 1 0 0 1 0 1	0 1 1 1 0 1 0 0 1 0 0 1 1 0 1 0 1 1
1 1 1 0 0 1 0 1 0 0 1 0 1 0 1 1 0 0	1 0 0 1 1 1 0 1 0 1 1 0 1 0 0 0 1 1
0 0 1 1 1 0 0 1 0 0 1 1 0 0 1 0 0 1	1 0 1 0 1 0 1 1 0 0 0 1 1 1 1 0 1 0
0 0 1 1 1 1 0 0 0 0 0 0 1 1 0 1 1 0	1 0 1 0 1 1 0 0 1 0 1 1 0 1 0 1 0 1
0 1 0 1 0 0 1 1 0 1 0 0 1 0 1 0 1 0	1 1 0 0 0 0 1 1 1 1 1 1 0 0 1 0 0 1
0 1 0 1 0 1 0 0 1 1 1 0 0 0 0 1 0 1	0 0 0 1 1 0 1 1 1 1 1 0 1 1 1 1 0 1
0 1 1 0 0 0 1 0 1 0 0 1 0 1 1 1 0 0	0 1 1 0 0 1 0 1 1 1 1 1 1 1 0 1 1 0
1 0 0 0 1 0 1 1 0 1 1 0 0 1 0 1 0 0	1 1 0 1 1 1 1 0 1 1 0 1 0 1 0 0 1 1
1 0 0 0 1 1 0 0 1 1 0 1 1 0 1 0 0 0	1 0 1 0 1 1 1 0 0 1 1 1 1 0 1 1 1 1

TABLE V
LOWER BOUNDS ON MAXIMAL SIZES OF ASYMMETRIC ERROR CORRECTING CODES

n	$t=3$	$t=4$	$t=5$	$t=6$
14	30	**8	*,**4	*,**4
15	*44	12	**6	*,**4
16	^{a}72	**16	7	*,**4
17	122	26	*,**8	*,**4
18	234	^{a}37	*,**12	**6
19	450	^{a}51	^{a,b}14	**7
20	860	^{b}69	^{a,b}20	9
21	1628	^{b}101	^{b}30	12
22	3072	^{b}151	^{a}46	^{b}14
23	4096	^{b}234	^{a}64	^{b}19

^{a}New code obtained by Program 1.
^{b}New code obtained by Program 2.

TABLE VI
LOWER BOUNDS ON MAXIMAL SIZES OF UNIDIRECTIONAL ERROR CORRECTING CODES

n	$t=3$	$t=4$	$t=5$	$t=6$
14	^{a}24	8	^{a}4	*,**2
15	^{a}42	10	^{a,b}4	^{a,b}3
16	^{a}62	^{b}13	^{b}5	^{a}4
17	^{a}98	*18	^{a,b}6	^{a}4
18	188	^{a}34	^{a,b}10	^{a,b}4
19	376	^{a}48	^{a}12	^{b}5
20	737	^{a}63	^{a}18	^{b}6
21	1474	^{a}96	^{a}27	^{a}8
22	2588	^{a}144	^{a}44	^{b}12
23	4096	^{a}216	^{a}62	^{a}16

^{a}New code obtained by Program 1.
^{b}New code obtained by Program 2.

For example, the size of the code with the length 22 and the asymmetric error-correcting capability 4 is 151, whereas that of the known code with the same length and the same capability is only 88. Further, the size of the code with length 22 and the unidirectional error-correcting capability 4 is 144, whereas that of the known code with the same length and the same capability is only 82.

REFERENCES

[1] J. H. Weber, C. de Vroedt, and D. E. Boekee, "Bounds and constructions for binary codes of length less than 24 and asymmetric distance less than 6," *IEEE Trans. Inform. Theory*, vol. 34, pp. 1321–1331, Sept. 1988.

[2] J. H. Weber, C. de Vroedt, and D. E. Boekee, "Bounds and constructions for codes correcting unidirectional errors," *IEEE Trans. Inform. Theory*, vol. 35, pp. 797–810, July 1989.

[3] Y. Saitoh, K. Yamaguchi, and H. Imai, "A construction method for efficient t-error correcting and all unidirectional error detecting codes" (in Japanese), *Trans. Inst. Electron. Inform. Commun. Eng., Part A*, vol. J72-A, no. 7, pp. 1125–1130, July 1989.

[4] C. Helgesen, "Asymmetriske koder med minimal blokklengde, og vektopptelleren for en klasse asymmetriske koder," Master's thesis, Department of Mathematics, University of Bergen, Bergen, Norway, 1983.

New Lower Bounds for Asymmetric and Unidirectional Codes

Tuvi Etzion, *Member, IEEE*

Abstract —New lower bounds on the sizes of asymmetric codes and unidirectional codes are presented. Various methods are used, three of them of special interest. The first is the partitioning method that is a modification of a method used to construct constant weight codes. The second is the combining codes method that is used to obtain a new code from a few others. The third method is shortening by weights that is applied on symmetric codes or on codes generated by the combining codes method. Tables for the sizes of codes of length $n \leq 23$ are presented.

Index Terms —Asymmetric codes, combining codes, constant weight codes, Golay code, partitions, shortening codes, unidirectional codes.

I. Introduction

The main goal of this correspondence is to present new lower bounds for asymmetric and unidirectional codes of length $n \leq 23$, and some new constructive methods for these codes. Let $\boldsymbol{u} = (u_1, u_2, \cdots, u_n)$ and $\boldsymbol{v} = (v_1, v_2, \cdots, v_n)$ be two binary vectors. Let $N(\boldsymbol{u},\boldsymbol{v})$ denote the number of coordinates where $\boldsymbol{u}$ is 0 and $\boldsymbol{v}$ is 1. The well known Hamming distance is defined by

$$d_h(\boldsymbol{u},\boldsymbol{v}) = N(\boldsymbol{u},\boldsymbol{v}) + N(\boldsymbol{v},\boldsymbol{u}).$$

The asymmetric distance is defined by

$$d_a(\boldsymbol{u},\boldsymbol{v}) = \max\{N(\boldsymbol{u},\boldsymbol{v}), N(\boldsymbol{v},\boldsymbol{u})\}.$$

A code C with minimum asymmetric distance Δ is capable of correcting $\Delta - 1$ or fewer asymmetric errors.

The unidirectional distance is defined by

$$d_u(\boldsymbol{u},\boldsymbol{v}) = d_h(\boldsymbol{u},\boldsymbol{v}), \qquad \text{if } d_a(\boldsymbol{u},\boldsymbol{v}) = d_h(\boldsymbol{u},\boldsymbol{v})$$

and

$$d_u(\boldsymbol{u},\boldsymbol{v}) = 2d_a(\boldsymbol{u},\boldsymbol{v}) - 1, \qquad \text{if } d_a(\boldsymbol{u},\boldsymbol{v}) \neq d_h(\boldsymbol{u},\boldsymbol{v}).$$

This definition came from the fact that was proved by Bose and Rao [1]. A code C is capable of correcting t or fewer unidirectional errors iff the following condition holds. For all distinct $\boldsymbol{u},\boldsymbol{v} \in C$, $d_h(\boldsymbol{u},\boldsymbol{v}) = d_a(\boldsymbol{u},\boldsymbol{v}) \geq 2t+1$ or $d_h(\boldsymbol{u},\boldsymbol{v}) \neq d_a(\boldsymbol{u},\boldsymbol{v}) \geq t+1$. Hence, a code is able to correct up to t unidirectional errors iff its minimum unidirectional distance is at least $2t+1$. The interest in these codes is due to the fact that for certain applications in optical communication and VLSI we need asymmetric and unidirectional channels [1], [12].

We denote by (n,M,d) *code*, a code of length n, minimum Hamming distance d, and M codewords. An $cw(n,d,w)$ *code* is

Manuscript received April 3, 1990; revised January 17, 1991. This work was supported in part by the Technion V.P.R. Fund—Albert Einstein Research Fund. This work was presented in part at the IEEE International Symposium on Information Theory, San Diego, CA, January 14–19, 1991.

The author is with the Computer Science Department, The Technion —Israel Institute of Technology, Haifa 32000, Israel.

IEEE Log Number 9102257.

0-8186-4182-7/93 $3.00 © 1991 IEEE

a code of length n, constant weight w, and minimum Hamming distance d. An *$a(n,\Delta)$ code* is a code of length n and minimum asymmetric distance Δ. An *$u(n,2t+1)$ code* is a code of length n and minimum unidirectional distance $2t+1$. Following Weber *et al.* [12] we denote by $A_2(n,t)$ the maximum number of codewords in a code of length n correcting t or fewer asymmetric errors. $A_3(n,t)$ denote the maximum number of codewords in a code of length n correcting t or fewer unidirectional errors. The known lower bounds on $A_2(n,t)$ and $A_3(n,t)$ are well documented in Weber *et al.* [12] with some improvements given by Saitoh *et al.* [6]. In Tables IV and V, we present the new best known bounds for codes of length less than 24 that are capable of correcting at most four errors. We present various methods to obtain new lower bounds on $A_2(n,t)$ and $A_3(n,t)$. In Section II, we present the partitioning method which is used to attain $a(n,2)$ codes. In Section III, we present the combining code methods. We also use the properties of the preparata code to construct $a(n,3)$ codes with $n \leq 23$. In Section IV, we present the variations of shortening by weights. In Section V, we discuss less systematic methods to construct codes with higher distances. In Section VI, we extend some of the methods to obtain new lower bound on $A_3(n,t)$ and we present the tables of all the known lower bounds for $n \leq 23$. Throughout this correspondence, we will represent binary codewords in hexadecimal notation.

II. The Partitioning Method

The first method is a modification of the partitioning method for constant weight codes of van Pul and Etzion [9]. A set of codes will be called *disjoint* if the intersection of any two different members of the set is empty. Let F^n denote the set of all binary n-tuples. A *partition* $\Pi^{as}(n)$ of F^n is a set of k subsets, $A_1, A_2, \cdots, A_k$, such that each set A_i is an $a(n,2)$ code, $A_i \cap A_j = \varnothing$ for $i \neq j$, $|A_i| \geq |A_{i+1}|$ for $1 \leq i \leq k-1$, and $\cup_{i=1}^{k} A_i = F^n$. Each partition has an *index vector*, *INDEX* $(\Pi^{as}(n)) = (i_1, i_2, \cdots, i_k)$ of length k, with $i_j = |A_j|$. Similarly we define a *partition* $\Pi(n,w)$ of the set of all n-tuples with weight w into disjoint $cw(n,4,w)$ codes. This partition has its own index vector. Let $\Pi(n) = \cup_{w=0}^{n} \Pi(n,w)$ be a partition of F^n into constant weight codes. The correctness of the following lemmas can be easily verified.

Lemma 1: If A_i and B_i, $1 \leq i \leq k$, are disjoint $cw(n_1,4,w_1)$ codes and disjoint $a(n_2,2)$ codes, respectively, then $\cup_{i=1}^{k}(A_i \times B_i)$ is an $a(n_1+n_2,2)$ code.

Lemma 2: Let A_1 be an $cw(n_1,4,w_1)$ code, A_2 and A_3 be disjoint $cw(n_1,4,w_1+k), k \geq 2$, codes. Let B_1 and B_2 be disjoint $a(n_2,2)$ codes, then $(A_1 \times B_1) \cup (A_2 \times B_1) \cup (A_3 \times B_2)$ is an $a(n_1+n_2,2)$ code.

Lemma 3: If A_i and B_j, $1 \leq i \leq k_1$, $1 \leq j \leq k_2$, are disjoint $cw(n_1,4,w_1)$ codes and disjoint $a(n_2,2)$ codes, respectively, then $\cup_{i,j}(A_i \times B_j)$ can be partitioned into $k_3 = \max(k_1,k_2)$ disjoint $a(n_1+n_2,2)$ codes.

Construction A: Take partitions $\Pi(n_1)$ of F^{n_1} and $\Pi^{as}(n_2)$ of F^{n_2}. Maximize the size of the code obtained by using a combination of Lemmas 1 and 2.

We apply Construction A by choosing $w = 0$ or 1, and applying Lemma 1 to $\Pi(n_1, w+2r)$ and $\Pi^{as}(n_2)$ for all $0 \leq r \leq \lfloor n_1/2 \rfloor$. Partitions of F^n into disjoint $a(n,2)$ codes can be obtained by the following method.

Construction B: Let $\Pi(n_1)$ and $\Pi^{as}(n_2)$ be two partitions. Let $\Pi^{as}(n_1+n_2)$ be the partition obtained from $\cup_{i,j}(A_i \times B_j)$, where $A_i \in \Pi(n_1)$ and $B_j \in \Pi^{as}(n_2)$ by using combinations of Lemmas 2 and 3.

The following table presents the parameters for the partitions of asymmetric codes that we found either by use of combinatorial and heuristic methods or by applying Construction B. Appendix A presents these partitions.

n	*INDEX* $(\Pi^{as}(n))$
4	(4,3,3,3,3)
5	(6,6,6,6,4,4)
6	(12,10,10,10,8,8,6)
7	(18,18,18,18,18,18,16,4)
8	(36,34,34,34,32,31,25,16,14)
9	(62,62,62,62,56,56,52,43,28,21,7,1)
10	(108,106,106,106,106,92,90,90,80,80,34,14,8,4)
11	(180,180,176,176,168,168,168,168,168,168,164,164)

The partitions for $n = 4$, 5, and 6, were generated by hand. The partitions for $n = 7$, 8, and 9, were generated by using some combinatorial arguments and computer search. $\Pi^{as}(10)$ was generated by using some combinatorial arguments. $\Pi^{as}(11)$ was generated by using Construction B.

A partition Π with *INDEX* $(\Pi) = (i_1, \cdots, i_k)$ is called *optimal* if for each other partition for n with index vector $(j_1, \cdots, j_r)$, we have $r \geq k$, and for each m, $m \leq k$, $\Sigma_{t=1}^{m} i_t \geq \Sigma_{t=1}^{m} j_t$. It is clear that an $a(4,2)$ code of size 4 must include one word of weight 0, two of weight 2, and one of weight 4. Hence, $\Pi^{as}(4)$ is optimal. It is known [2] that $\Pi(6,3)$ with index vector $(4,4,4,4,2,2)$ is optimal. Based on this fact, we will prove that our $\Pi^{as}(5)$ and $\Pi^{as}(6)$ are optimal. For $n = 5$ we have the number of words with weight two and three in the codes of the partition is not better than 4,4,4,4,2,2, since it can be used to obtain $\Pi(6,3)$. To each code we can add at most one word of weight less than two and at most one word of weight more than three. Hence, $\Pi^{as}(5)$ with index vector $(6,6,6,6,4,4)$ is optimal. For $n = 6$, note that an $a(6,2)$ code contains four codewords of weight less than 3 (more than 3), if and only if it contains three words of weight two (four) and one word of weight zero (six). Since there is one word of weight zero (six) the total number of words with weight 0, 1, 2, 4, 5, and 6, in the codes of the partition is not better than 8,6,6,6,6,6,6. Combining these words with the words of the optimal $\Pi(6,3)$, we have that $\Pi^{as}(6)$ with index vector $(12,10,10,10,8,8,6)$ is optimal.

The following table presents the parameters for the partitions of constant weight codes that were used and were obtained by [2], [9]. These partitions are documented in [2].

(n,w)	*INDEX*$(\Pi(n,w))$
(6,3)	(4,4,4,4,2,2)
(8,4)	(14,14,12,12,10,8)
(10,4)	(30,30,30,30,30,22,22,12,2,2)
(10,4)	(30,30,30,30,26,25,22,15,2)
(12,4)	(51,51,51,51,49,48,48,42,42,40,15,7)
(12,4)	(51,51,51,51,49,48,48,45,39,36,22,4)
(12,4)	(51,51,51,51,49,48,48,45,41,32,22,6)
(12,6)	(132,132,120,120,110,94,90,76,36,14)
(12,6)	(132,132,120,120,110,94,90,72,42,12)

We also used the well known facts about optimal partitions. $\Pi(n,0)$ consists of one codeword, $\Pi(n,1)$ consists of n codes of size 1, $\Pi(n,2)$ consists of $n-1$ codes of size $n/2$ for even n, and $INDEX(\Pi(n,w)) = INDEX(\Pi(n,n-w))$. Using these partitions we obtain the following bounds by Construction A.

1) $A_2(11,1) \geq 180$ by considering $\Pi(6)$ and $\Pi^{as}(5)$.
2) $A_2(12,1) \geq 336$ by considering $\Pi(8)$ and $\Pi^{as}(4)$.
3) $A_2(13,1) \geq 652$ by considering $\Pi(8)$ and $\Pi^{as}(5)$.
4) $A_2(14,1) \geq 1228$ by considering $\Pi(8)$ and $\Pi^{as}(6)$.
5) $A_2(15,1) \geq 2288$ by considering $\Pi(8)$ and $\Pi^{as}(7)$.
6) $A_2(16,1) \geq 4280$ by considering $\Pi(10)$ and $\Pi^{as}(6)$.
7) $A_2(17,1) \geq 8308$ by considering $\Pi(10)$ and $\Pi^{as}(7)$.
8) $A_2(18,1) \geq 15762$ by considering $\Pi(10)$ and $\Pi^{as}(8)$.
9) $A_2(19,1) \geq 29236$ by considering $\Pi(10)$ and $\Pi^{as}(9)$.
10) $A_2(20,1) \geq 56144$ by considering $\Pi(12)$ and $\Pi^{as}(8)$.
11) $A_2(21,1) \geq 107212$ by considering $\Pi(12)$ and $\Pi^{as}(9)$.
12) $A_2(22,1) \geq 198336$ by considering $\Pi(12)$ and $\Pi^{as}(10)$.
13) $A_2(23,1) \geq 353512$ by considering $\Pi(12)$ and $\Pi^{as}(11)$.

Note, that the cartezian products that we used are from $\Pi(2k) \times \Pi^{as}(i)$ for $4 \leq k \leq 6$ and $2k-4 \leq i \leq 2k-1$. We do not have any explanation for this phenomenon. As an illustration we construct the code showing that $A_2(14,1) \geq 1228$.

From $\Pi(8,0)$ and $\Pi^{as}(6)$ we have $1 \cdot 12 = 12$ codewords.
From $\Pi(8,2)$ and $\Pi^{as}(6)$ we have $4 \cdot 12 + 4 \cdot 10 + 4 \cdot 10 + 4 \cdot 10 + 4 \cdot 8 + 4 \cdot 8 + 4 \cdot 6 = 256$ codewords.
From $\Pi(8,4)$ and $\Pi^{as}(6)$ we have $14 \cdot 12 + 14 \cdot 10 + 12 \cdot 10 + 12 \cdot 10 + 10 \cdot 8 + 8 \cdot 8 = 692$ codewords.
From $\Pi(8,6)$ and $\Pi^{as}(6)$ we have $4 \cdot 12 + 4 \cdot 10 + 4 \cdot 10 + 4 \cdot 10 + 4 \cdot 8 + 4 \cdot 8 + 4 \cdot 6 = 256$ codewords.
From $\Pi(8,8)$ and $\Pi^{as}(6)$ we have $1 \cdot 12 = 12$ codewords.
The total is $12 + 256 + 692 + 256 + 12 = 1228$ codewords.

The same method was found independently by Darwish and Bose [4]. Our partitions and bounds improve on their partitions and bounds.

III. Combining Codes

The second method is a modification of the method of Sloane, Reddy, and Chen [8] for combining codes. We can view the partitioning method as a special case of combining codes. The asymmetric version has two variants.

Combining Codes 1: Suppose we are given $k+2$ codes: an (n_1, M_1, d_1) code C_1, an $(n_1, M_2 = kM_1, d_2)$ code C_2, and k pairwise disjoint $a(n_3, \Delta_3)$ codes $B_0, B_1, \cdots, B_{k-1}$, with the properties that 1) C_2 is a union of k disjoint cosets of C_1:

$$C_2 = C_1 \cup (x_1 + C_1) \cup (x_2 + C_1) \cup \cdots \cup (x_{k-1} + C_1),$$

for suitable vectors $x_1, \cdots, x_{k-1}$ (let x_0 be the all-zero vector), and 2) the union of the kB_i's is an (n_3, M_4, d_4) code. Then the new code C consists of all the vectors

$$|x_i + u|v|, \qquad i = 0, \cdots, k-1, \qquad u \in C_1, \qquad v \in B_i,$$

i.e., the vectors of the ith coset of C_1 in C_2 are appended to the vectors of the ith asymmetric code B_i in all possible ways.

Theorem 1: The new code C has length $n_1 + n_3$, size $M_1 M_4$ and asymmetric distance

$$\Delta \geq \min\left\{\left\lceil \frac{d_1}{2} \right\rceil, \Delta_3, \left\lceil \frac{d_2 + d_4}{2} \right\rceil\right\}.$$

The proof is simple and similar to the one in Sloane *et al.* [8].

Combining Codes 2: Suppose we are given $2k+1$ codes, k pairwise disjoint $a(n_1, \Delta_1)$ codes $A_0, A_1, \cdots, A_{k-1}$ and k pairwise disjoint $a(n_3, \Delta_3)$ codes $B_0, B_1, \cdots, B_{k-1}$, with the properties that 1) the union of the kA_i's is an (n_1, M_2, d_2) code, and 2) the union of the kB_i's is an (n_3, M_4, d_4) code. Then the new code C consists of all the vectors

$$|u|v|, \qquad u \in A_i, v \in B_i, \qquad i = 0, \cdots, k-1,$$

Theorem 2: The new code C has length $n_1 + n_3$, size $\sum_{i=0}^{k-1} |A_i||B_i|$, and asymmetric distance

$$\Delta \geq \min\left\{\Delta_1, \Delta_3, \left\lceil \frac{d_2 + d_4}{2} \right\rceil\right\}.$$

The proof is similar to the one of Theorem 1. Applications of the two constructions are also similar to the ones in [8]. The only difference is that we have to find the appropriate asymmetric codes. Note, that combining codes 1 is a special case of combining codes 2. We made a separation between the two methods especially since one of the next methods, namely Shortening by Weights, can be applied on all codes obtained from combining codes 1, but not on all codes obtained from combining codes 2.

Another asymmetric code is obtained by shuffling codes.

Theorem 3: Let C_1 be a code of length n, with minimum Hamming distance $2d$, such that C_2 is a code with minimum Hamming distance $2d-2$ and form as a union of disjoint cosets of C_1, i.e.,

$$C_2 = C_1 \cup (x_1 + C_1) \cup (x_2 + C_1) \cup \cdots \cup (x_{k-1} + C_1),$$

for suitable vectors $x_1, \cdots, x_{k-1}$. Then the code Y defined by

$$Y = \bigcup_{i=0}^{\lfloor \frac{n}{2} \rfloor} W_{2i},$$

where W_j are all the codewords of weight j from one of the cosets of C_1, has asymmetric distance $\Delta \geq d$.

Proof: It is obvious that we only have to show that for $a_1 \in W_{2j}$ and $a_2 \in W_{2j+2r}$, $d > 2r \geq 2$, $d_a(a_1, a_2) \geq d$. This is an immediate result from the facts that $d_h(a_1, a_2) \geq 2d - 2$ and $2d_a(a_1, a_2) = d_h(a_1, a_2) + |w(a_2) - w(a_1)| \geq 2d - 2 + 2r \geq 2d$. □

Theorem 3 can be modified to the case where C_1 has minimum Hamming distance $2d-1$ and C_2 has minimum Hamming distance $2d-3$.

Theorem 4: Let C_1 be a code of length n, with minimum Hamming distance $2d-1$, such that C_2 is a code with minimum Hamming distance $2d-3$ and form as a union of disjoint cosets of C_1, i.e.,

$$C_2 = C_1 \cup (x_1 + C_1) \cup (x_2 + C_1) \cup \cdots \cup (x_{k-1} + C_1),$$

for suitable vectors $x_1, \cdots, x_{k-1}$. Then the code Y defined by

$$Y = \bigcup_{i=0}^{n} W_i,$$

where W_j is defined as in Theorem 3, and $|W_j| = 0$ or $|W_{j+1}| = 0$ for $0 \leq j \leq n-1$, has asymmetric distance $\Delta \geq d$.

Examples of codes with the properties of C_1 and C_2 in our constructions are given in [8]. A special interest we have in the following theorem.

Theorem 5 [8]: The extended Hamming code of length 2^n is a union of disjoint cosets of the Preparata code of length 2^n for any even integer $n \geq 4$.

Now, we give some applications of Theorems 1–5. For length 16, the Preparata code coincides with the Kerdock code and the Nordstrom–Robinson code [5]. We generate this code from the extended Golay code with the following generator matrix [5]

1 0 0 0 0 0 0 1 0 0 0 0 0 1 1 0 1 1 0 0 0 1 0 1
0 1 0 0 0 0 0 1 0 0 0 0 0 0 1 1 0 1 1 0 0 0 1 1
0 0 1 0 0 0 0 1 0 0 0 0 0 1 0 1 1 0 1 1 0 0 0 1
0 0 0 0 0 0 0 0 1 0 0 0 0 0 1 0 1 1 1 1 1 0 0 1
0 0 0 1 0 0 0 1 0 0 0 0 0 0 0 1 0 1 0 1 1 1 0 1
0 0 0 0 1 0 0 1 0 0 0 0 0 0 0 0 1 0 1 0 1 1 1 1
0 0 0 0 0 0 0 0 0 1 0 0 0 1 0 0 0 1 1 1 0 1 1 1
0 0 0 0 0 1 0 1 0 0 0 0 0 1 1 0 0 0 0 1 1 0 1 1
0 0 0 0 0 0 0 0 0 0 1 0 0 1 1 1 0 0 1 0 1 1 0 1
0 0 0 0 0 0 0 0 0 0 0 1 0 0 1 1 1 0 0 1 0 1 1 1
0 0 0 0 0 0 0 0 0 0 0 0 1 1 0 1 1 1 0 0 1 0 1 1
0 0 0 0 0 0 1 1 0 0 0 0 0 1 1 1 1 1 1 1 1 1 1 0

by taking columns 9 through 24 of codewords where in columns 1 through 7 the weight of the codewords is less than 2. We take translates by adding the following vectors

$$x_1 = 0\ 0\ 0\ 0\ 0\ 0\ 0\ 0\ 0\ 0\ 0\ 1\ 0\ 1\ 1\ 1$$

$$x_2 = 0\ 0\ 0\ 0\ 0\ 0\ 0\ 0\ 0\ 1\ 1\ 0\ 0\ 1\ 1\ 0$$

$$x_3 = 0\ 0\ 0\ 0\ 0\ 0\ 0\ 0\ 0\ 1\ 1\ 1\ 0\ 0\ 0\ 1$$

$$x_4 = 0\ 0\ 0\ 0\ 0\ 0\ 1\ 0\ 1\ 0\ 0\ 0\ 0\ 1\ 1\ 0$$

$$x_5 = 0\ 0\ 0\ 0\ 0\ 0\ 1\ 0\ 1\ 0\ 0\ 1\ 0\ 0\ 0\ 1$$

$$x_6 = 0\ 0\ 0\ 0\ 0\ 0\ 1\ 0\ 1\ 1\ 1\ 0\ 0\ 0\ 0\ 0$$

$$x_7 = 0\ 0\ 0\ 1\ 0\ 0\ 0\ 1\ 0\ 1\ 1\ 0\ 0\ 0\ 0\ 0.$$

The weight distribution of the cosets is the same and it is given with the weight distribution of the Preparata code in the following table.

w	Preparata Code	Coset
0	1	
4		20
6	112	48
8	30	120
10	112	48
12		20
16	1	
Total	256	256

We take from the Preparata code the codewords of weight 0, 6, 10, and 16 and from the first coset the codewords with weights 4, 8, and 12. By Theorem 3 these codewords form an $a(16,3)$ code A_0, and hence, $A_2(16,2) \geq 386$.

The codewords of weight 6 of the seven cosets are partitioned into five $a(16,3)$ codes of sizes 96, 80, 64, 48, and 48 [2]. The same partition is applied on the codewords of weight 10. Applying a similar argument as in Theorem 3 implies that we can obtain the $a(16,3)$ codes $A_0, A_1, \cdots, A_7$ with the following distribution table.

w	A_0	A_1	A_2	A_3	A_4	A_5	A_6	A_7
0	1							
4	20	20	20	20	20	20	20	
6	112	96	80	64	48	48		
8	120	120	120	120	120	120	120	30
10	112	96	80	64	48	48		
12	20	20	20	20	20	20	20	
16	1							
Total	386	352	320	288	256	256	160	30

Let $B_0 = \{0\}$ and $B_1 = \{1\}$. By applying combining codes 2 with A_0 and A_1, we obtain $A_2(17,2) \geq 738$.

Let $B_0 = \{00\}$, $B_1 = \{01\}$, $B_2 = \{10\}$, and $B_1 = \{11\}$. By applying combining codes 2 with A_0, A_1, A_2, and A_3, and adding the word 00007, we obtain $A_2(18,2) \geq 1347$.

Let $B_0, B_1, \cdots, B_6$ the following seven $a(3,3)$ codes:

$$B_0 = \{000, 111\}, \quad B_1 = \{001\}, \quad B_2 = \{110\},$$
$$B_3 = \{010\}, \quad B_4 = \{101\}, \quad B_5 = \{100\}, \quad B_6 = \{011\}.$$

By applying combining codes 2 with $A_0, A_1, \cdots, A_6$, we obtain $A_2(19,2) \geq 2404$.

Let $B_0, B_1, \cdots, B_7$ the following eight $a(4,3)$ codes:

$$B_0 = \{0000, 1111\}, \quad B_1 = \{0001, 1110\}, \quad B_2 = \{0010, 1101\},$$
$$B_3 = \{0100, 1011\}, \quad B_4 = \{1000, 0111\}, \quad B_5 = \{1010\},$$
$$B_6 = \{1100\}, \quad B_7 = \{0110\}.$$

By applying combining codes 2 with $A_0, A_1, \cdots, A_7$, we obtain $A_2(20,2) \geq 3650$.

Let $B_0, B_1, \cdots, B_7$ the following eight $a(6,3)$ codes:

$$B_0 = \{101010, 010101\}, \quad B_1 = \{000001, 111000, 110111\},$$
$$B_2 = \{000100, 110010, 111101\}, \quad B_3 = \{000010, 110001, 111110\},$$
$$B_4 = \{001000, 000111, 111011\}, \quad B_5 = \{100000, 010011, 101111\},$$
$$B_6 = \{010000, 100011, 011111\}, \quad B_7 = \{110100, 001011\}.$$

We apply combining codes 1 with the shortened Preparata codes and its seven cosets. We add to the constructed code 202 words, given in Appendix B, using the compressed form of Section V, to obtain $A_2(21,2) \geq 5834$.

Let D_0 be the code defined by taking columns 9–24 of codewords from the extended Golay code, where in the first eight coordinates there are either two ONES in columns 1 and 2, or four ONES in the first four coordinates. To D_0 we add the codewords 0000, 0DCB, 635A, 6E91, 916E, 9CA5, F234, FFFF, to obtain $A_2(16,3) \geq 72$. A code with the same size was found by the computer search of Saitoh *et al.* [6].

Let D_1 be the code defined by taking columns 9–24 of codewords from the extended Golay code where in the first coordinates there are either two ONES in columns 1 and 3 or four ONES in the columns 1, 2, 3, and 5. D_0 and D_1 are two disjoint $a(16,4)$ codes and $D_0 \cup D_1$ is a $(16,128,6)$ code.

Let $B_0 = \{0\}$ and $B_1 = \{1\}$. By applying combining codes 2 with D_0 and D_1, and adding the all-zero and the all-one words, we obtain $A_2(17,3) \geq 130$.

IV. Shortening by Weights

The third method is *shortening by weights* was first presented by Shiozaki [7] and generalized by Weber *et al.* [11]. The method is applied on codes of length n and Hamming distance at least $2d-1$ to obtain $a(n-m,d)$ codes. We modify the method in a way that it can be applied on asymmetric codes which are constructed by combining codes 1. First, we describe the method as appeared in Weber *et al.* [11]. Let $x = (x', x'')$ be the $(m, n-m)$ partition of any $x \in (\mathrm{GF}(2))^n$. Let C_1 be a code of length n and Hamming distance at least $2d-1$. Define

$$T_w(s) = \{u \in C_1 \colon u' = s; w(u'') = w\}$$

for $w = 0, 1, \cdots, n-m$ and $s \in (\mathrm{GF}(2))^m$, where $w(x)$ is the weight of x. We define a code Y of length n by

$$Y = \bigcup_{w=0}^{n-m} T_w(a_w),$$

TABLE I
APPLYING SHORTENING BY WEIGHTS ON THE $(23, 2^{14}, 5)$ WAGNER CODE

w	a_w	$T_w(a_w)$
0	0	1
4	1	20
5	0	64
6	0	188
7	0	320
8	1	660
9	0	960
10	0	1308
11	0	1408
12	1	1308
13	0	960
14	0	660
15	0	320
16	1	188
17	0	64
18	0	20
22	1	1
Total		8450

where $a_i \in (\mathrm{GF}(2))^m$ for $i = 0, 1, \cdots, n-m$ are such that

$$d_h(a_j, a_{j+1}) \le 1, \qquad \text{for } 0 \le j \le n-m-1.$$

The code C_2 of length $n-m$ is now formed by taking all the codewords of Y and then deleting the first m coordinates of each codeword. Weber *et al.* [11] proved the following theorem.

Theorem 6 [11]: C_2 has asymmetric distance $\Delta \ge d$.

The same method can be applied on the asymmetric codes constructed by combining codes 1 if $\Delta = \min\{\lceil d_1/2 \rceil, \Delta_3, \lceil d_2 + d_4/2 \rceil\}$. We just have to make sure that in $x = (x', x'')$ the x'' part will contain the part of the asymmetric code. Now, let Δ be the asymmetric distance of the code C of Theorem 1. To analyze the asymmetric distance of C_2, let $a_1, a_2 \in C_2$ formed from $b_1 = |x_i + u_1|\nu_1|$ and $b_2 = |x_j + u_2|\nu_2|$ by deleting the first m columns. If ν_1 and ν_2 belong to different asymmetric codes then $d_a(a_1, a_2) \ge \lceil d_2 + d_4/2 \rceil \ge \Delta$ with the same proof as was given by Weber *et al.* [11]. If $\nu_1 = \nu_2$ then $d_a(a_1, a_2) \ge \lceil d_1/2 \rceil \ge \Delta$ with the same proof as for shortening by weights [11]. If ν_1 and ν_2 belong to the same asymmetric code, but they are different then $d_a(\nu_1, \nu_2) \ge \Delta_3 \ge \Delta$ and hence, $d_a(a_1, a_2) \ge \Delta$.

The $(23, 2^{14}, 5)$ Wagner code [10] can be formed with the following generator matrix

$$\begin{array}{ccccccccccccccccccccccc}
0&1&0&0&0&0&0&0&0&0&0&0&0&0&1&1&1&1&1&0&0&0&0\\
0&0&1&0&0&0&0&0&0&0&0&0&0&0&1&1&1&0&0&1&1&0&0\\
0&0&0&1&0&0&0&0&0&0&0&0&0&0&1&0&1&0&1&0&1&0&1\\
0&0&0&0&1&0&0&0&0&0&0&0&0&0&0&1&0&1&0&1&1&1&0\\
1&0&0&0&0&0&0&0&0&0&0&0&0&0&1&1&1&0&0&0&0&1&0\\
0&0&0&0&0&1&0&0&0&0&0&0&0&0&1&1&0&1&0&1&0&0&0\\
0&0&0&0&0&0&1&0&0&0&0&0&0&0&1&1&0&0&1&0&0&0&1\\
0&0&0&0&0&0&0&1&0&0&0&0&0&0&1&0&1&0&0&1&0&0&1\\
0&0&0&0&0&0&0&0&1&0&0&0&0&0&0&1&0&1&0&0&0&1&1\\
0&0&0&0&0&0&0&0&0&1&0&0&0&0&0&0&1&0&1&0&1&1&0\\
0&0&0&0&0&0&0&0&0&0&1&0&0&0&0&0&1&1&0&1&1&0&1\\
0&0&0&0&0&0&0&0&0&0&0&1&0&0&1&0&1&1&1&1&0&1&0\\
0&0&0&0&0&0&0&0&0&0&0&0&1&0&1&1&0&1&1&0&1&1&1\\
0&0&0&0&0&0&0&0&0&0&0&0&0&1&0&1&1&0&1&1&1&1&1
\end{array}.$$

We add to this code the 33 words 010A00, 440008, 025000,

TABLE II
APPLYING SHORTENING BY WEIGHTS ON THE GOLAY CODE

w	a_w	$T_w(a_w)$	a_w	$T_w(a_w)$
0	00000	1	0000	1
5			1110	12
6	11111	18		
7	11110	30	1111	48
8	11100	42	1110	72
9	11000	46	1100	88
10	10000	42	1000	88
11	00000	30	0000	72
12	00000	18	0000	48
14			1000	12
18	11111	1		
19			1111	1
Total		228		442

00A080, 128010, 01001A, 000460, 103C11, 140201, 00C300, 404044, 080005, 0A0140, 080828, 300002, 092400, 046010, 201110, 041402, 202204, 02040C, 05C061, 131106, 420021, 008806, 102120, 000851, 204C00, 2400C0, 581000, 019001, 2A4A40, 0000B4, and their complements to obtain $A_2(23, 2) \ge 16450$.

By applying the shortening by weights on the $(23, 2^{14}, 5)$ Wagner code we obtain the code of Weber *et al.* [11], with the distribution given in Table I. We add the 166 words, given in Appendix B, using the compressed form of Section V, to obtain $A_2(22, 2) \ge 8616$.

For $\Delta \ge 4$ we use shortening by weights on the Golay code, constructed by deleting the last coordinate of the extended Golay code, and the weight distribution is given in Table II. We obtain the following codes.

We use the shortening by weights on the first five columns of the Golay code and add the ten words 02650, 06120, 08284, 0DFFE, 11408, 20842, 26FF9, 33EDF, 3E9BF, 3F775, to obtain $A_2(18, 3) \ge 238$.

We use the shortening by weights on the first four columns of the Golay code and add the 16 words 000A5, 03108, 04812, 079FF, 0824B, 12A44, 212D0, 3EFF9, 44360, 5F6FE, 6FFC7, 71F7F, 78000, 7B1ED, 7C8F7, 7F95A, to obtain $A_2(19, 3) \ge 458$.

V. CODES WITH ASYMMETRIC DISTANCE GREATER THAN FOUR

For $\Delta \ge 5$ the codes have even less mathematical structure than for $\Delta = 4$. To obtain a lower bound for $A_2(n, \Delta - 1)$ we can start with a good $cw(n+1, 2\Delta, \lceil n+1/2 \rceil)$ code [2]. We delete its last column and try to add as many codewords as we succeed when we are adding them weight by weight. Using this method we obtain $A_2(18, 4) \ge 39$, $A_2(19, 4) \ge 54$, $A_2(20, 4) \ge 71$, $A_2(21, 4) \ge 104$, $A_2(22, 4) \ge 160$, and $A_2(23, 4) \ge 240$.

All the codes with asymmetric distance 5 are presented in Appendix C, in a compressed form mentioned in Brouwer *et al.* [2]. We generalize this form to represent words added to a code C. In Appendix C, the code C is empty. The words added to the code C are first sorted into lexicographic order, yielding a sequence of words $c_1, c_2, \cdots, c_M$. The compressed notation for these words is $\alpha_1, \alpha_2, \cdots, \alpha_M$. To find $\alpha_i (1 \le i \le M)$, let $u_1, u_2, \cdots$ be the list of all vectors, arranged in lexicographic order and following c_{i-1} in the lexicographic order, that have distance $\ge d$ from the subcode $C \cup \{c_1, \cdots, c_{i-1}\}$. If $c_i = u_r$ we set $\alpha_i = r - 1$. Informally, given $C, c_1, \cdots, c_{i-1}$, we must skip α_i lexicographic words to get c_i. We also abbreviate $a, a, \cdots, a$ (k times) by a^k.

VI. Lower Bounds for Unidirectional Codes

Weber *et al.* [12] proved that $A_3(n,1)$ is the same as the maximum number of codewords in a code of length n and minimum Hamming distance 3. The most updated table on these bounds is given by Brouwer *et al.* [2]. For other unidirectional distances the codes have some similarity to the asymmetric codes. The combining codes methods and the shortening by weights method can also be applied to obtain unidirectional codes. We have to perform the following modifications.

In combining codes 1, we take $ku(n_3, 2t_3+1)$ codes instead of $ka(n_3, \Delta_3)$ codes. This method will be called combining codes 1′. We obtain the following theorem.

Theorem 1′: The new code C has length n_1+n_3, size M_1M_4 and unidirectional distance $2t+1 \geq \min\{d_1, 2t_3+1, d_2+d_4\}$.

In combining codes 2 we take $k\,u(n_1, 2t_1+1)$ codes $U_0, U_1, \cdots, U_{k-1}$, and $ku(n_3, 2t_3+1)$ codes instead of the asymmetric codes. This method will be called combining codes 2′. We obtain the following theorem.

Theorem 2′: The new code C has length n_1+n_3, size $\sum_{i=0}^{k-1}|U_i||B_i|$, and unidirectional distance $2t+1 \geq \min\{2t_1+1, 2t_3+1, d_2+d_4\}$.

Some more specific variants of combining codes can also be used here. Shuffling codes, Theorems 3 and 4 will have the following form.

Theorem 3′: Let C_1 be a code of length n, with minimum Hamming distance $2d$, such that C_2 is a code with minimum Hamming distance $2d-2$ and form as a union of disjoint cosets of C_1, i.e.,

$$C_2 = C_1 \cup (x_1 + C_1) \cup (x_2 + C_1) \cup \cdots \cup (x_{k-1} + C_1),$$

for suitable vectors $x_1, \cdots, x_{k-1}$. Then the code Y defined by

$$Y = \bigcup_{i=0}^{\left\lfloor \frac{n}{2} \right\rfloor} W_{2i},$$

where W_j is defined as in Theorem 3 and W_{2i} and $W_{2i+2d-2}$ are codewords from the same coset, has unidirectional distance $2t+1 \geq 2d-1$.

Theorem 4′: Let C_1 be a code of length n, with minimum Hamming distance $2d-1$, such that C_2 is a code with minimum Hamming distance $2d-3$ and form as a union of disjoint cosets of C_1, i.e.,

$$C_2 = C_1 \cup (x_1 + C_1) \cup (x_2 + C_1) \cup \cdots \cup (x_{k-1} + C_1),$$

for suitable vectors $x_1, \cdots, x_{k-1}$. Then the code Y defined by

$$Y = \bigcup_{i=0}^{n} W_i,$$

where W_j is defined as in Theorem 3, $|W_j| = 0$ or $|W_{j+1}| = 0$ for $0 \leq j \leq n-1$, and also W_{2i} and $W_{2i+2d-2}$ are codewords from the same coset, has unidirectional distance $2t+1 \geq 2d-1$.

The shortening by weights is defined similarly with the equations [12]

$$Y = \bigcup_{w=0}^{n-m} T_w(a_w),$$

where $a_i \in (\mathrm{GF}(2))^m$ for $i = 0, 1, \cdots, n-m+2t$ are such that

$$d_h(a_j, a_{j+1}) \leq 1, \qquad \text{for } 0 \leq j \leq n-m+2t-1$$

$$a_j = a_{j+2t}, \qquad \text{for } 0 \leq j \leq n-m.$$

Theorem 6′ [12]: If C_1 has Hamming distance $\geq 2t+1$ then C_2 has unidirectional distance $\geq 2t+1$.

Again, the same method can be applied on the unidirectional codes constructed by combining codes 1′.

Let U_0 be the $u(16,5)$ code constructed from the codewords with weights 6 and 10 from the Preparata code and weights 4, 8, and 12 from the first coset. $|U_0| = 384$ and therefore, $A_3(16,2) \geq 384$. We can also take $U_i = A_i$, $1 \leq i \leq 6$, and U_7 as A_7 with the all-zero and all-one words, since the A_i's, $1 \leq i \leq 6$, are $u(16,5)$ codes.

Similarly to the lower bounds, $A_2(17,2)$ and $A_2(18,2)$, of Section III we obtain $A_3(17,2) \geq 736$ and $A_3(18,2) \geq 1344$.

A *lexicode with hint* [2], [3] with length n and distance (Hamming, asymmetric, unidirectional) is a code with initial set of vectors (the "hint"). Then we consider all binary vectors of length n in lexicographic order and add them to the code if they are in the desired distance from it.

Let B_1, B_2, B_3, B_4 the following four $u(4,5)$ codes:

$$B_1 = \{0001, 1110\}, \quad B_2 = \{0010, 1101\},$$

$$B_3 = \{0100, 1011\}, \quad B_4 = \{1000, 0111\}.$$

We apply combining codes 1′ with the first four cosets of the shortened Preparata code. The constructed code is considered as a "hint," we add 32 words, and obtain a lexicode with hint and $A_3(19,2) \geq 2080$.

The 32 that are added are derived from the codewords of the punctured first-order Reed–Muller codes with the generator matrix

0 0 0 0 1 1 0 1 1 1 0 0 1 0 1
0 0 0 1 1 1 1 0 0 1 0 1 1 1 0
0 0 1 0 0 1 1 1 0 0 1 0 1 1 0
0 1 0 0 0 1 0 0 0 1 1 1 0 1 1
1 0 0 0 0 0 1 0 1 1 1 1 1 0 0

by adding the tail 0000 to codewords of weight 7 and 15, and the tail 1111 to codewords of weight 0 and 8. Note, that the Preparata code contains the codewords of the first-order Reed–Muller code, which is also U_7 in our case.

Let $B_0, B_1, \cdots, B_7$ the following eight $u(4,5)$ codes:

$$B_0 = \{1110, 0001\}, \quad B_1 = \{0010, 1101\}, \quad B_2 = \{0100, 1011\},$$

$$B_3 = \{1000, 0111\}, \quad B_4 = \{1100\}, \quad B_5 = \{1010\},$$

$$B_6 = \{0110\}, \quad B_7 = \{0000\}.$$

We apply combining codes 2′ with $U_0, U_1, \cdots, U_7$. The constructed code is considered as a "hint," we add 31 words, and obtain a lexicode with hint and $A_3(20,2) \geq 3423$. Instead of these 31 words, we can add the 31 codewords of U_7 (the Reed–Muller code), which have ZEROS, replace in each codeword an arbitrary ZERO by a ONE, and attach the tail 1111.

The following matrix is a generator matrix of a $(22, 2^{13}, 5)$ code:

1 0 0 0 0 0 0 0 0 0 0 0 0 1 1 0 0 1 1 0 0 1
0 1 0 0 0 0 0 0 0 0 0 0 0 1 1 0 1 1 0 1 0 0
0 0 1 0 0 0 0 0 0 0 0 0 0 1 0 0 1 0 0 1 1 0
0 0 0 1 0 0 0 0 0 0 0 0 0 1 0 1 1 0 1 1 1 1
0 0 0 0 1 0 0 0 0 0 0 0 0 0 1 1 1 0 0 1 0 0
0 0 0 0 0 1 0 0 0 0 0 0 0 1 0 1 0 0 1 1 0 0
0 0 0 0 0 0 1 0 0 0 0 0 0 1 1 1 1 1 1 1 1 0
0 0 0 0 0 0 0 1 0 0 0 0 0 0 0 0 1 1 1 0 1 0
0 0 0 0 0 0 0 0 1 0 0 0 0 0 1 0 0 1 1 1 0 0
0 0 0 0 0 0 0 0 0 1 0 0 0 0 1 1 1 0 1 0 1 1
0 0 0 0 0 0 0 0 0 0 1 0 0 0 1 0 0 0 0 1 1 1
0 0 0 0 0 0 0 0 0 0 0 1 0 0 0 1 0 1 0 0 1 1
0 0 0 0 0 0 0 0 0 0 0 0 1 1 1 1 0 0 0 0 0 1.

We take the coset obtained by adding

000000000000000000001

to each codeword. By applying shortening by weight on this coset we obtain the distribution given in Table III. To this code we add 321 words, given in Appendix B, using the compressed form of Section V, to obtain $A_3(21,2) \geq 4672$.

We take the 8448 codewords of weights 4–18 from the $a(22,3)$ code defined in Section IV. This code is considered as a "hint," we add 96 words, and obtain a lexicode with hint and $A_3(22,2) \geq 8544$.

Let V_0 be the code defined by taking the words of weights 6, 8, and 10, after deleting the first eight coordinates of the extended Golay code, where in the first eight coordinates there are either two ONES in columns 1 and 2, or four ONES in the first four coordinates.

Let $V_1(V_2)$ be the code defined by taking the words of weights 6, 8, and 10, after deleting the first eight coordinates of the extended Golay code where in the first eight coordinates there are either two ONES in columns 1 (2) and 3, or four ONES in columns 1, 2, 3, and 5 (6).

Let V_3 be the code defined by taking the words of weights 4, 8, and 12, after deleting the first eight coordinates of the extended Golay code where in the first eight coordinates there are four ONES in columns 1, 2, 3, and 7.

V_0, V_1, V_2, and V_3, are disjoint $u(16,4)$ codes of sizes 56, 56, 56, and 32, respectively, and $\cup_{i=0}^{3} V_i$ is a $(16,200,6)$ code.

Let $B_0 = \{0\}$ and $B_1 = \{1\}$. By applying combining codes 2′ with V_0 and V_1, and adding the words 00071 and 1FF6A, we obtain $A_3(17,3) \geq 114$.

Let $B_0 = \{01\}$, $B_1 = \{10\}$, $B_2 = \{11\}$, and $B_3 = \{00\}$. By applying combining codes 2′ with V_0, V_1, V_2, V_3, and adding the word 30203, we obtain $A_3(18,3) \geq 201$.

All the other codes that we have constructed are given in Appendix D using the compressed form of Section V.

Tables IV and V summarize all the bounds that we have obtained.

Acknowledgment

The author wishes to thank N. J. A. Sloane for supplying partitions for constant weight codes. He also thanks the referees for their helpful comments.

Appendix A

This appendix gives the partitions into disjoint asymmetric codes. The notation is as in Brouwer *et al.* [2]. We ordered the n-tuples in lexicographic order and the disjoint $a(n,2)$ codes are numbered by 1, 2, 3, 4, 5, 6, 7, 8, 9, A, B, and so on. If

$\Pi^{as}(4)$:
1253412434155231

then there are 16 4-tuples in the partitions. The first 4-tuple (namely 0000) is in code 1, the second (namely 0001) in code 2, the third (namely 0010) in code 5, and so on.

$\Pi^{as}(5)$:
52436412315423611521364342361425.
$\Pi^{as}(6)$:
1641375223751431756321464214632552364314614226571421573235731461.
$\Pi^{as}(7)$:
314673126574263457326541421357252651427731256413146723567531467712653723548145662154167763423154734651321653724532
1864242765138.
$\Pi^{as}(8)$:
8364591935224755473672416415832724716538164329135124965235617436125734249136184826816513497236594362517582546327143
4286214517927148269653813279157351372644156532571424613546564312674852839173671543627429519432572471631842812846351
317627835762153643956241.
$\Pi^{as}(9)$:
A6419874379541867532179384A7254154A32562621438579851467473621A368368A6275B43721429158462618638731A769138852143
6232435719945721452A5662351821A372437451A69253648781477413563521486528329A471459B27592184134685635A637235475411
268235465261279841781654871362AAB9419875BA12362943861463257581473627625134641736214A4398123268148574234C5931657
812973211645423B5781571224513845763A6574326813A694233413862475461753279245393175261A92615872842735A113466485923
8734B175326823124A765483712768943952463A13945163B2852712563945711768.
$\Pi^{as}(10)$:
BA887929671A5B379B56BD18D2412564153BA7638496784249738A5CA619B326214593743A87A653C8A469B6972834187612352152
481952431A68349657A43A2C184A549639714639A78278A364B572145138B35225978526431A1749A86E95726413213A562813542976
5871A93D6859741A964325671A2853723154128543623C91A8748A2A7489A63369B751465B2841A213553781359214648276A9378251
465413318AB13754292A58967C3A7865938241A42596143251753218B6B153752462491736241538A7516A298DE897A265741381426A
15428925B351A47618A5298754317A29361453421526923BA187457986A31496CA39B8643745225473468B93AC69B13A689744785A1
23962512415416395A7132578923A8467CA153B529824114A624183257563A798DE894A6357A832142657194261257351B6B81235715
244269524A1538391687A4476984A29135731BA853214564215287C9A671846352953187254312A1482B563217596346A9847ABA8478
19C3263458214513573582A476521469A1279386EC9A37824679215318465A31251462759D68A9371A52462587942153B831541274156
BA87387A936427936945A481C2A33A72691386A1542593847251453216785B4837962964A8C316A78A3473954126143926ACBA8379
425876948367AB3514652142D81DB65B973B5A176929788AB1.

TABLE III
APPLYING SHORTENING BY WEIGHTS ON THE $(22, 2^{13}, 5)$ CODE

w	a_w	$T_w(a_w)$
4	1	16
5	1	49
6	0	115
7	0	256
8	1	448
9	1	617
10	0	731
11	0	736
12	1	592
13	1	411
14	0	241
15	0	96
16	1	32
17	1	11
Total		4351

TABLE IV
LOWER BOUNDS ON $A_2(n, t)$

n	$t = 1$	$t = 2$	$t = 3$	$t = 4$
5	6*	2*	2*	2*
6	12*	4*	2*	2*
7	18*	4*	2*	2*
8	36*	7*	4*	2*
9	62*	12*	4*	2*
10	108	18*	6*	4*
11	180^{x}	30	8*	4*
12	336^{x}	54	14*	4*
13	652^{x}	98	18*	6*
14	1228^{x}	186	30	8*
15	2288^{x}	266	44	12*
16	4280^{x}	386^{x}	72	16*
17	8308^{x}	738^{x}	130^{x}	26*
18	15762^{x}	1347^{x}	238^{x}	39^{x}
19	29236^{x}	2404^{x}	458^{x}	54^{x}
20	56144^{x}	3650^{x}	860	71^{x}
21	107212^{x}	5834^{x}	1628	104^{x}
22	198336^{x}	8616^{x}	3072	160^{x}
23	353512^{x}	16450^{x}	4096	240^{x}

*Tight bounds.
^{x}New bounds.

APPENDIX B

Words added to obtain $A_2(21,2) \geq 5834$:
$0, 21, 4, 0, 1, 0, 5, 2, 1, 0, 3, 2, 1, 3, 0^{2}, 6, 3, 0^{3}, 1^{2}, 4, 0, 2, 1, 3, 1, 0, 1, 0^{3}, 1, 4, 0, 2, 0^{2}, 1,$
$0^{5}, 1, 0, 1, 0^{2}, 6, 2, 1, 8, 3, 1, 0^{4}, 2, 0^{2}, 1, 2, 0^{2}, 2, 0^{5}, 1, 0^{2}, 1, 0^{4}, 1, 0^{2}, 1, 0^{7}, 2, 0^{3}, 1, 0^{2},$
$1, 0^{2}, 1^{3}, 0, 1, 0, 1, 0, 2, 0, 2, 1, 0^{3}, 2, 3, 0^{2}, 2, 0^{2}, 1, 0, 5, 2, 0^{6}, 1, 0, 1^{2}, 0, 2, 0^{2}, 1, 0, 1, 0^{2},$
$1, 0, 3, 0^{3}, 1, 0^{5}, 1^{2}, 4, 0^{2}, 2, 0^{10}, 1, 0^{4}, 1, 0^{11}, 1, 0^{8}.$

Words added to obtain $A_2(22,2) \geq 8616$:
$1, 3, 5, 1, 0, 4, 0^{2}, 1, 0^{4}, 1^{2}, 0^{4}, 1, 0^{5}, 1, 0^{2}, 1, 0^{4}, 2, 0^{8}, 1, 0^{3}, 2, 0^{5}, 1^{2}, 0, 1, 0^{8}, 1, 0^{3}, 1,$
$0^{4}, 1, 0^{24}, 1, 0^{5}, 1, 0^{9}, 4, 0^{8}, 1^{3}, 0^{3}, 1, 0^{5}, 1, 0^{3}, 1, 0^{8}, 1, 0^{4}, 1, 2, 0^{3}, 2^{2}, 0^{6}.$

Words added to obtain $A_3(21,2) \geq 4672$:
$0^{3}, 1, 0^{2}, 1, 0, 1, 2^{2}, 1, 0, 2, 0^{2}, 2, 0^{2}, 1, 0^{5}, 1, 0^{3}, 1, 0, 2, 0^{2}, 2, 1, 0, 2, 0^{2}, 2, 0^{11}, 1, 0, 1, 0,$
$1, 0^{3}, 2, 1, 0, 1, 0^{3}, 2, 1, 0^{5}, 1, 0^{5}, 1, 0, 2, 0^{2}, 2, 1, 0, 1, 0^{3}, 2, 0^{11}, 2, 0^{2}, 1^{2}, 14, 0^{2}, 4, 0^{2}, 8,$
$0^{2}, 2, 1, 3^{2}, 0^{4}, 1, 8, 0, 10, 0^{3}, 5, 14, 3, 0, 3, 8, 1^{2}, 0^{2}, 2, 1, 15, 3^{2}, 0, 3, 0, 2, 1, 0, 2, 0^{2}, 2, 1,$
$4, 3, 0^{3}, 13, 0, 1, 3, 0, 3, 2, 0, 1, 0^{3}, 3^{2}, 2, 0, 7, 0, 5, 0^{3}, 1, 0^{4}, 2, 1, 0, 9, 0^{7}, 1, 0^{2}, 1, 0^{3}, 4, 0,$
$3, 0, 2, 1, 0, 3, 1, 5, 0^{2}, 2, 0^{4}, 1, 2, 0^{2}, 4, 0, 6, 1^{2}, 2, 4, 0^{2}, 9, 0, 3, 5, 2^{2}, 0^{3}, 4, 1, 0, 2, 1, 2,$
$1, 0^{2}, 1^{2}, 0^{3}, 3, 1, 2, 0, 1, 0^{2}, 3, 9, 0, 1, 0, 1, 0, 4, 2, 0^{2}, 2^{2}, 0^{3}, 7, 0, 1^{2}, 8, 0^{2}, 2, 1^{3}, 0^{2}, 2^{2},$
$0, 3, 0^{3}, 2, 5, 6, 0^{3}, 2, 1, 0^{8}.$

TABLE V
LOWER BOUNDS ON $A_3(n, t)$

n	$t = 2$	$t = 3$	$t = 4$
9	10	4*	2*
10	16	4*	2*
11	26	7*	4*
12	52	10	4*
13	92	16^{x}	6*
14	184	24	8*
15	256	42	10
16	384^{x}	62	14^{x}
17	736^{x}	114^{x}	24^{x}
18	1344^{x}	201^{x}	37^{x}
19	2080^{x}	376	51^{x}
20	3423^{x}	737	69^{x}
21	4672^{x}	1474	102^{x}
22	8544^{x}	2588	154^{x}
23	16384	4096	229^{x}

*Tight bounds.
^{x}New bounds.

APPENDIX C

$A_2(18,4) \geq 39$:
0, 2394, 3106, 1215, 609, 624, 898, 552, 162, 98, 127, 14, 33, 39, 22, 2, 14, 1, 0, 8, 3, 19, 6,
$5, 7, 1, 0^{3}, 11, 7, 64, 22, 46, 0, 1, 0^{2}, 3.$

$A_2(19,4) \geq 54$:
0, 4256, 7835, 1019, 789, 3180, 72, 616, 676, 374, 292, 335, 46, 263, 63, 3, 125, 226, 18, 7,
51, 139, 0, 1, 0, 40, 4, 75, 1, 13, 40, 24, 17, 9, 3, 8, 0, 42, 96, 7, 26, 56, 3, 21, 77, 83, 39, 82,
0, 19, 32, 30, 91, 31.

$A_2(20,4) \geq 71$:
0, 7098, 8342, 25626, 3226, 6677, 1202, 3661, 39, 1138, 1069, 1464, 19214, 1006, 2143,
789, 462, 109, 4684, 10488, 494, 3392, 12515, 493, 767, 141, 306, 96, 1, 75, 11, 12, 7, 0,
$54, 0^{2}, 3, 13, 4, 0, 2, 0^{2}, 38, 0^{2}, 4, 0^{3}, 1, 1, 0^{2}, 1, 6, 1, 0^{2}, 6, 1, 0, 2, 0, 4, 0, 18, 0^{2}, 20.$

$A_2(21,4) \geq 104$:
0, 637, 338, 16, 3498, 258, 1755, 989, 20, 1372, 1787, 1368, 576, 323, 29, 391, 151, 12, 38,
258, 214, 175, 34, 336, 89, 267, 521, 305, 161, 5, 128, 335, 123, 117, 524, 42, 436, 173,
285, 1416, 1507, 913, 2000, 0, 611, 2715, 439, 44, 17, 32, 679, 599, 648, 129, 529, 1325,
$640, 220, 931, 2052, 195, 374, 75, 116, 21, 11, 3, 8, 3, 2, 0^{7}, 7, 2^{2}, 0^{5}, 1, 0^{2}, 5, 7, 17, 23,$
$62, 0^{5}, 4, 2, 32, 0, 40, 65.$

$A_2(22,4) \geq 160$:
0, 2523, 8398, 1773, 9887, 8139, 1573, 22197, 6817, 1308, 1797, 5100, 2039, 3110, 22,
3313, 416, 1117, 707, 236, 743, 3035, 1101, 514, 628, 659, 355, 254, 531, 727, 721, 83,
243, 304, 21, 140, 61, 112, 69, 58, 537, 103, 342, 21, 172, 16, 78,

177, 243, 107, 12, 211,
1073, 122, 285, 280, 3, 2, 83, 57, 135, 244, 0, 70, 2, 126, 3, 14, 139, 182, 1, 17, 18, 11, 38,
323, 10, 0, 4, 122, 69, 94, 48, 43, 65, 8, 20, 3, 2, 34, 19, 7, 5, 14, 67, 12, 23, 0, 2, 0, 36, 3,
13, 2, 74, 1, 52, 10, 66, 23, 31, 70, 101, 30, 22, 7, 37, 26, 1^3, 8, 1, 0, 15, 0, 2, 23, 4, 27, 26,
1^2, 13, 3, 4, 0, 20, 0^8, 15, 5, 8, 0^3, 6, 23, 0^3, 18, 22, 1.

$A_2(23,4) \geq 240$:

0, 31472, 32163, 11212, 23438, 3403, 2035, 7607, 17759, 2735, 3222, 2933, 2490, 61,
4098, 2376, 2547, 1507, 1772, 1209, 7139, 4686, 77, 4696, 2249, 3577, 176, 3215, 784,
198, 1959, 1605, 400, 7518, 67, 931, 2429, 412, 1266, 1845, 4, 325, 2306, 1101, 217, 2398,
712, 578, 1708, 51, 117, 108, 237, 695, 2368, 2, 729, 71, 3, 0, 8, 214, 1217, 728, 6, 30, 727,
110, 29, 9, 40, 58, 157, 187, 39, 3, 27, 51, 114, 96, 215, 1, 13, 14, 706, 12, 92, 320, 353, 40,
223, 336, 147, 13, 89, 0^2, 295, 59, 19, 13, 60, 49, 295, 29, 1, 21, 25, 0, 63, 10, 30, 23, 2, 4,
18, 3, 25, 2, 25, 351, 3, 45, 18, 5, 14, 311, 27, 190, 128, 13, 141, 399, 34, 25, 2, 13, 15, 6,
186, 211, 100, 0, 17, 244, 3, 6, 9, 5, 7, 5, 2, 0, 6, 5, 217, 54, 71, 0, 2, 5, 4, 16, 6, 0, 6, 148, 2,
0^2, 1, 10, 0, 3, 8, 12, 50, 0, 2, 3, 2, 1, 6, 8, 0^2, 1, 0, 2, 1^2, 0, 3, 5, 2, 0^2, 1, 0, 1, 7, 0, 8, 0^2,
55, 48, 0^3, 1, 0^3, 1, 0^6, 1, 0, 1, 0, 2, 0, 10, 15, 13, 0^2, 2, 5, 3, 20, 0, 29, 0, 5.

Appendix D

$A_3(13,3) \geq 16$:

229, 132, 96, 25, 30, 4, 0^2, 5, 1, 5, 8, 2, 0^3.

$A_3(16,4) \geq 14$:

626, 4258, 126, 470, 588, 6, 44, 13, 78, 32, 17, 7, 3, 0.

$A_3(17,4) \geq 24$:

626, 1409, 929, 662, 156, 63, 21, 42, 16, 15, 3, 0, 32, 0, 16, 13, 7^2, 3, 0^5.

$A_3(18,4) \geq 37$:

10006, 1743, 681, 268, 228, 326, 375, 178, 80, 210, 41, 54, 50, 35, 0, 3, 2, 0, 26, 15, 15, 8,
1^4, 0^2, 2, 1, 3, 0^2, 1, 0^3.

$A_3(19,4) \geq 51$:

5260, 7763, 951, 739, 3183, 71, 456, 541, 321, 188, 265, 226, 5, 19, 2, 161, 251, 23, 35, 13,
21, 19, 3, 4, 12, 0, 95, 0, 16, 18, 14, 1, 22, 0, 2^2, 5, 17, 1, 3^2, 4, 0^2, 8, 0, 7, 0^2, 1, 0.

$A^3(20,4) \geq 69$:

8191, 784, 3842, 1108, 13408, 7384, 1111, 3313, 1294, 960, 1393, 4546, 9852, 841, 7,
2700, 445, 111, 4170, 10008, 128, 2730, 10431, 699, 93, 278, 96, 1, 69, 9, 11, 8, 0, 5, 2, 0,
4, 1^2, 3, 0^5, 4, 0^4, 1, 0^2, 1, 0, 1, 0, 1, 0, 1, 2, 0^8.

$A_3(21,4) \geq 102$:

1023, 2084, 8883, 5119, 3030, 110, 5474, 175, 53, 455, 2796, 446, 175, 7, 21, 153, 26, 7,
10, 665, 33, 237, 2, 194, 14, 51, 29, 117, 157, 39, 25, 120, 189, 158, 240, 36, 277, 2238,
178, 261, 325, 821, 1612, 1009, 92, 147, 23, 14, 12, 554, 348, 247, 508, 949, 839, 21, 1882,
507, 79, 322, 64, 101, 27, 13, 10, 8, 0, 1, 3, 0^2, 2, 0^6, 2, 0^4, 1, 2, 0^4, 1^2, 0^2, 2, 3, 0^7.

$A_3(22,4) \geq 154$:

15243, 15783, 12153, 1383, 1002, 9789, 6404, 361, 14930, 1324, 3815, 4737, 521, 1356,
12, 943, 4676, 1490, 246, 1162, 1531, 736, 811, 2108, 222, 781, 357, 49, 924, 229, 168,
474, 6, 54, 446, 73, 204, 7, 50, 81, 1241, 276, 79, 12, 63, 83, 104, 623, 35, 416, 2, 65, 36,
98, 9, 86, 175, 20, 7, 129, 7, 10, 79, 2, 103, 2, 1, 30, 7, 6, 102, 16, 27, 0, 2, 155, 19, 63, 69,
81, 8, 10, 34, 8, 5^2, 1, 18, 21, 7, 9, 44, 28, 2^2, 16, 19, 1, 12, 14, 1, 11, 1, 12, 2, 26, 7^2, 22,
10, 11, 0, 1, 0, 24, 15, 0^4, 5, 1, 12, 15, 4^2, 1^3, 0^2, 1, 0^2, 1, 0, 1, 0^2, 2, 0^{14}.

$A_3(23,4) \geq 229$:

14357, 50448, 12388, 22442, 4151, 2743, 5782, 1127, 14198, 3768, 970, 1676, 2374, 1572,
2583, 7901, 8850, 1426, 2006, 35, 1762, 913, 550, 9, 71, 1531, 27, 616, 240, 1922, 123,
1451, 4251, 1222, 27, 2484, 254, 510, 687, 2, 295, 826, 257, 102, 20, 1155, 219, 456, 59,
46, 83, 158, 262, 198, 25, 33, 170, 41, 458, 550, 449, 433, 429, 29, 2, 80, 212, 182, 23, 12,
72, 10, 31, 271, 2, 17, 26, 87, 9, 143, 11, 24, 71, 9, 50, 258, 16, 124, 4^2, 453, 5, 80, 39, 46,
59, 71, 114, 6, 2, 7, 1, 16, 26, 25, 1, 20, 1, 2, 9, 15, 94, 39, 666, 3, 70, 35, 19, 49, 11, 0, 35,
21, 27, 8, 0, 4, 77, 1, 3, 4, 19, 2, 1, 22, 0, 6, 0^3, 15, 33, 7, 0, 32, 47, 7, 0, 2, 5, 106, 25, 3, 7,
57, 57, 6, 1, 15, 0, 22, 4, 0, 3^2, 7, 0, 27, 0, 14, 63, 5, 0^4, 4, 0^5, 2, 1, 2, 1, 0^8, 2, 0, 4, 0^8, 2, 0,
2, 1, 3, 0^5, 1^2, 0^4, 2, 0^7.

References

[1] B. Bose and T. R. N. Rao, "Theory of unidirectional error-correcting/detecting codes," *IEEE Trans. Comput.*, vol. C-31, pp. 521–530, June 1982.

[2] A. E. Brouwer, J. B. Shearer, N. J. A. Sloane, and W. D. Smith, "A new table of constant weight codes," *IEEE Trans. Inform. Theory*, vol. 36, pp. 1334–1380, Nov. 1990.

[3] J. H. Conway and N. J. A. Sloane, "Lexicographic codes: error-correcting codes from game theory," *IEEE Trans. Inform. Theory*, vol. IT-342, pp. 337–348, May 1986.

[4] N. Darwish and B. Bose, "New lower bounds for single asymmetric error correcting codes," preprint.

[5] F. J. MacWilliams and N. J. A. Sloane, *The Theory of Error-Correcting Codes*. Amsterdam, The Netherlands: North-Holland, 1977.

[6] Y. Saitoh, K. Yamaguchi, and H. Imai, "Some new binary codes correcting asymmetric/unidirectional errors," *IEEE Trans. Inform. Theory*, vol. 36, pp. 645–647, May 1990.

[7] A. Shiozaki, "Construction for binary asymmetric error-correcting codes," *IEEE Trans. Inform. Theory*, vol. IT-28, pp. 787–789, Sept. 1982.

[8] N. J. A. Sloane, S. M. Reddy, and C. L. Chen, "New binary codes," *IEEE Trans. Inform. Theory*, vol. IT-18, pp. 503–510, July 1972.

[9] C. L. M. van Pul and T. Etzion, "New lower bounds for constant weight codes," *IEEE Trans. Inform. Theory*, vol. 35, pp. 1324–1329, Nov. 1989.

[10] T. J. Wagner, "A search technique for quasi-perfect codes," *Inform. Contr.*, vol. 9, pp. 94–99, 1966.

[11] J. H. Weber, C. de Vroedt, and D. E. Boekee, "Bounds and constructions for binary codes for length less than 24 and asymmetric distance less than 6," *IEEE Trans. Inform. Theory*, vol. 34, pp. 1321–1331, Sept. 1988.

[12] ——, "Bounds and constructions for codes correcting unidirectional errors," *IEEE Trans. Inform. Theory*, vol. 35, pp. 797–810, July 1989.

CHAPTER 4: CODES FOR CORRECTING *T*-SYMMETRIC ERRORS AND DETECTING ALL UNIDIRECTIONAL ERRORS

Chapter 4 provides results on codes correcting t symmetric errors and detecting d unidirectional errors when $d>t$. The first three papers present constructions and bounds on t-error-correcting/all-unidirectional-error-detecting (EC/AUED) codes. These codes can correct up to t (symmetric) errors and detect any number of unidirectional errors when the number of unidirectional errors exceeds t. Much literature on unidirectional errors focuses on these codes; in part, because they can be used for detecting faults in VLSI systems suffering many changes in polarity (as described above) and, at the same time, for correcting a few symmetric errors without invoking the error detection protocol. In addition, t-EC/AUED codes have a simple mathematical description, making them a natural object for investigation.

In effect, given two binary vectors **X** and **Y** of length n, denote by $N(\mathbf{X},\mathbf{Y})$ the number of locations where **X** is 1 and **Y** is 0; for instance, if **X** = 10011 and **Y** = 01010, $N(\mathbf{X},\mathbf{Y})=2$, and $N(\mathbf{Y},\mathbf{X})=1$. Notice that $d_H(\mathbf{X},\mathbf{Y})=N(\mathbf{X},\mathbf{Y})+N(\mathbf{Y},\mathbf{X})$, where $d_H(\mathbf{X},\mathbf{Y})$ denotes the Hamming distance between **X** and **Y**; also, $\mathbf{X} \subseteq \mathbf{Y}$ if (and only if) $N(\mathbf{X},\mathbf{Y})=0$; now, C is a t-EC/AUED code if (and only if) $N(\mathbf{X},\mathbf{Y}) \geq t+1$ for any $\mathbf{X},\mathbf{Y} \in C$, $\mathbf{X} \neq \mathbf{Y}$. Pradhan provided us with a proof of this result in Chapter 1 of this volume. In the case $t=0$ (that is, pure detection of unidirectional errors), we obtain the condition that code words have to be unordered (as seen in Chapter 2). Consequently, finding a t-EC/AUED code of maximal size is a natural extension of Sperner's lemma. However, for $t \geq 1$, this problem remains unsolved. Lin and Bose have provided a partial extension of Sperner's lemma,[53] in which the authors prove that if C is a 1-EC/AUED code of length n, then

$$|C| \leq \frac{2}{n}\binom{n}{\lfloor n/2 \rfloor}.$$

Elsewhere, Zhang and Xia present deeper results involving t-EC/AUED codes.[25,26]

In practice, however, we want systematic codes; that is, we want to add a tail of n-k bits to k information bits such that resulting codes are t-EC/AUED. Most authors prefer to encode the information bits first into a t-EC code. Then, they add a tail — generally a function of the vector weight (à la Berger), such that the resulting code satisfies necessary and sufficient conditions. Blaum and van Tilborg obtained some of the best results with this procedure — as shown in this chapter's first paper, in which the authors introduce the technique that applies asymmetric error-correcting codes to the tail that is added to the error-correcting code. However, please beware; Tables 1 and 2 in this paper have been permuted. In other words, Table 1 gives the parameters of 2-EC/AUED codes, and Table 2 gives the parameters of 1-EC/AUED codes.

Böinck and van Tilborg present further improvements for small values of k together with lower bounds. Our references provide more sophisticated lower bounds.[25,26]

Bruck and Blaum offer two new techniques that further improve the Blaum/van Tilborg construction. The first involves using control vectors to reduce the spread of weights. The second extends matrices used for redundancy by Blaum and van Tilborg. In a recent paper, Zhang and Tu improve several upper bounds on the redundancy of systematic EC/AUED for $t=1$ and $t=2$.[29] Moreover, Yoshida, Jinushi, and Sakaniwa improve the Blaum/van Tilborg construction for certain parameters.[54] Research has been active in the EC/AUED codes area; consequently, our references cite considerable relevant work.[21,22,48,55-66]

Lin and Bose give constructions of codes that can correct up to t symmetric errors and detect up to d ($d>t$) unidirectional errors. Construction of these codes involves a technique resembling the construction of t-EC/AUED codes; the information bits are encoded first into a t-EC code. However, the subsequent tail does not depend on the number of information bits, but only on t and d. Therefore, if enough information bits exist, these codes will have less redundancy than corresponding t-EC/AUED codes.

Nikolos concludes our chapter with constructions of codes that can (1) correct up to t (symmetric) errors, (2) detect up to d (symmetric) errors, and (3) detect any number of unidirectional errors. Nikolos also extends results to codes that can correct up to t errors, detect up to k errors, and detect up to d unidirectional errors, where $t<k<d$.[67,68]

On t-Error Correcting/All Unidirectional Error Detecting Codes

MARIO BLAUM, MEMBER, IEEE, AND HENK VAN TILBORG, SENIOR MEMBER, IEEE

Abstract—**We present families of binary systematic codes that can correct t random errors and detect more than t unidirectional errors. As in recent papers, we start by encoding the k information symbols into a codeword of an $[n', k, 2t + 1]$ error correcting code. The second step of our construction involves adding more bits to this linear error correcting code in order to obtain the detection capability of all unidirectional errors. Asymmetric error correcting codes turn out to be a powerful tool in our construction. The resulting codes sensibly improve previous results. Asymptotic estimates and decoding algorithms are presented.**

Index Terms—**Asymmetric errors, decoder, encoder, error correcting codes, information symbols, redundant symbols, systematic code, t-error correcting/all unidirectional error detecting codes, unidirectional errors.**

I. Introduction

ERROR correcting/detecting codes are essential in most devices that store digital information. A lot has been written about error correcting/detecting codes [8]. These codes deal with symmetric errors; i.e., errors of type $0 \rightarrow 1$ and $1 \rightarrow 0$ occur with the same probability in a codeword. However, in many types of VLSI circuits the error statistics are different and they exhibit a high incidence of unidirectional errors [1], [2], [11]. Also, certain faults in digital devices can cause unidirectional errors, i.e., all the errors in a codeword are either of type $0 \rightarrow 1$ or $1 \rightarrow 0$.

Some of the digital units that produce unidirectional errors as a consequence of internal failure are data transmission systems, magnetic recording mass memories, and LSI/VLSI circuits such as ROM memories. The number of random faults caused by these failures is usually limited, while the number of unidirectional errors can be large. For that reason, it is useful to have codes that are capable of correcting a relatively small number of random errors and detecting any number of unidirectional errors. Considerable attention was paid in recent literature to this problem [1]-[3], [10]-[12].

The purpose of this paper is to provide techniques to construct systematic codes that are able to correct t random errors and detect all unidirectional errors. The requirement that the codes are systematic allows simple encoding and decoding procedures that are similar to the ones described by other authors. Our construction uses the best symmetric and asymmetric error correcting codes available. As long as better codes are found, our codes will improve accordingly. Most of the codes obtained with our construction improve previous results for t-error correcting/all unidirectional error detecting (t-EC/AUED) codes.

The basic definitions and properties of t-EC/AUED codes are given in this section. In the next sections, we describe the constructions of the codes, we give encoding and decoding procedures, and we provide tables that compare our codes to previously known results.

Assume we have two binary vectors of length n, say $\boldsymbol{x}$ and $\boldsymbol{y}$. We say that $\boldsymbol{x}$ is covered by $\boldsymbol{y}$ ($\boldsymbol{x} \subseteq \boldsymbol{y}$) iff the set of coordinates where $\boldsymbol{x}$ is 1 is contained in the set of coordinates where $\boldsymbol{y}$ is 1. For instance, 1 1 0 0 is covered by 1 1 1 0 but not by 1 0 1 0.

Assume we transmit a vector $\boldsymbol{x}$ and we receive a vector $\hat{\boldsymbol{x}}$. We say that $\boldsymbol{x}$ has suffered unidirectional errors if either $\boldsymbol{x} \subseteq \hat{\boldsymbol{x}}$ or $\hat{\boldsymbol{x}} \subseteq \boldsymbol{x}$ (i.e., the errors are either transitions $0 \rightarrow 1$ or transitions $1 \rightarrow 0$).

Let $\boldsymbol{x}$ and $\boldsymbol{y}$ be two vectors of length n. We denote by $N(\boldsymbol{x}, \boldsymbol{y})$ the number of coordinates where $\boldsymbol{x}$ is 1 and $\boldsymbol{y}$ is 0.

Example: Let $\boldsymbol{x} = 0\,0\,1\,1\,0$, $\boldsymbol{y} = 0\,1\,0\,1\,1$, then $N(\boldsymbol{x}, \boldsymbol{y}) = 1$ and $N(\boldsymbol{y}, \boldsymbol{x}) = 2$.

Notice that the Hamming distance $d(\boldsymbol{x}, \boldsymbol{y})$ satisfies $d(\boldsymbol{x}, \boldsymbol{y}) = N(\boldsymbol{x}, \boldsymbol{y}) + N(\boldsymbol{y}, \boldsymbol{x})$. The following theorem [3], [12] gives necessary and sufficient conditions for a code to be t-EC/AUED.

Theorem 1.1: A code $\mathcal{C}$ is t-EC/AUED iff $N(\boldsymbol{x}, \boldsymbol{y}) \geq t + 1$ for any $\boldsymbol{x}, \boldsymbol{y} \in \mathcal{C}$, $\boldsymbol{x} \neq \boldsymbol{y}$.

II. Construction of the Codes

In this section, we shall describe a construction of a systematic t-EC/AUED code that for larger dimensions gives codes with lower redundancy than the known constructions [1]-[3], [11], [12]. As in [11], we use a linear $[n', k, 2t + 1]$ code $\mathcal{C}'$ as a first step to encode the k information symbols. Before we proceed, let us see what can be said about $N(\boldsymbol{c}, \boldsymbol{d})$ and $N(\boldsymbol{d}, \boldsymbol{c})$ for $\boldsymbol{c} \in \mathcal{C}'$ and $\boldsymbol{d} \in \mathcal{C}'$. ($\lceil x \rceil$ denotes the smallest integer, greater than or equal to x and $w(\boldsymbol{c})$ the weight of $\boldsymbol{c}$.)

Theorem 2.1: Let $\mathcal{C}'$ be an $[n', k, 2t + 1]$ code. Let $\boldsymbol{c} \in \mathcal{C}'$ and $\boldsymbol{d} \in \mathcal{C}'$ with $w(\boldsymbol{c}) = i \leq j = w(\boldsymbol{d})$. Then

$$N(\boldsymbol{d}, \boldsymbol{c}) \geq t + 1 \tag{2.1}$$

Manuscript received April 1, 1987; revised October 7, 1987 and February 6, 1988.

M. Blaum is with IBM Research, Almaden Research Center, San Jose, CA 95120.

H. van Tilborg is with the Eindhoven University of Technology, 5600 MB Eindhoven, The Netherlands.

IEEE Log Number 8930840.

0-8186-4182-7/93 $3.00 © 1989 IEEE

$$N(\boldsymbol{c}, \boldsymbol{d}) \geq \max\left\{0,\ t+1-\left\lceil\frac{j-i}{2}\right\rceil\right\}. \tag{2.2}$$

Proof: Without loss of generality $\boldsymbol{c}$ and $\boldsymbol{d}$ can be assumed to look like

$$\begin{aligned} \boldsymbol{c} &= \overbrace{1\,1\cdots1}^{x}\ \ \overbrace{1\,1\cdots1}^{y}\ \ \overbrace{0\,0\cdots0}^{z}\ \ \overbrace{0\,0\cdots0}^{u} \\ \boldsymbol{d} &= 1\,1\cdots1\ \ 0\,0\cdots0\ \ 1\,1\cdots1\ \ 0\,0\cdots0. \end{aligned}$$

Of course, $x + y + z + u = n'$, but also

$$x+y=i,\ x+z=j \tag{2.3}$$

$$y+z=d(\boldsymbol{c}, \boldsymbol{d}) \geq 2t+1 \tag{2.4}$$

$$y=i-x \leq j-x=z. \tag{2.5}$$

If follows from (2.4) and (2.5) that $2N(\boldsymbol{d}, \boldsymbol{c}) = 2z \geq y + z \geq 2t + 1$. This proves (2.1).

By (2.3) $z = j - x = y + j - i$. From (2.4) we can now deduce that $2y + j - i = y + z \geq 2t + 1$. Hence,

$$N(\boldsymbol{c}, \boldsymbol{d}) = y \geq \left\lceil\frac{2t+1-j+1}{2}\right\rceil = t+1-\left\lceil\frac{j-i}{2}\right\rceil. \qquad \square$$

Theorem 2.1 can be obtained as a corollary of Lemma 1 in [11] if we choose the maximum value of l satisfying $q < 2t + 1 - 2l$ in that lemma.

We now want to construct a t-EC/AUED code $\mathcal{C}$ from the $[n', k, 2t + 1]$-code $\mathcal{C}'$. In view of 1.1, we need to add a tail $\boldsymbol{t}_c$ to each codeword $\boldsymbol{c}$ in $\mathcal{C}'$, with the property that for each $\boldsymbol{c} \in \mathcal{C}'$ and $\boldsymbol{d} \in \mathcal{C}'$, $\boldsymbol{c} \neq \boldsymbol{d}$, $N(\boldsymbol{t}_c, \boldsymbol{t}_d) \geq t + 1 - N(\boldsymbol{c}, \boldsymbol{d})$. Let $w(\boldsymbol{c}) = i \leq j = w(\boldsymbol{d})$. According to Theorem 2.1 it would suffice if

$$\begin{aligned} N(\boldsymbol{t}_c, \boldsymbol{t}_d) &\geq t+1-\max\left\{0,\ t+1-\left\lceil\frac{j-i}{2}\right\rceil\right\} \\ &\geq \min\left\{t+1,\ \left\lceil\frac{j-i}{2}\right\rceil\right\}. \end{aligned}$$

To keep the complexity of the encoding and decoding algorithm low, we shall make the tail $\boldsymbol{t}_c$ only dependent on the weight of $\boldsymbol{c}$ (as in [11]). So, instead of writing $\boldsymbol{t}_c$ we can now write $\boldsymbol{t}_i$ with $i = w(\boldsymbol{c})$.

Definition 2.2: A *descending tail matrix of strength* t + 1 is an $m \times r$ $\{0, 1\}$-matrix with rows $\boldsymbol{t}_i$, $0 \leq i \leq m - 1$, such that for all $0 \leq i \leq j \leq m - 1$,

$$N(\boldsymbol{t}_i, \boldsymbol{t}_j) \geq \min\left\{t+1,\ \left\lceil\frac{j-i}{2}\right\rceil\right\}. \tag{2.6}$$

We shall denote this matrix by $T(m, r; t + 1)$. In view of the preceding, the following theorem is now obvious.

Theorem 2.3: Let $\mathcal{C}'$ be an $[n', k, 2t + 1]$ linear systematic code and let T be a descending tail matrix $T(n' + 1, r; t + 1)$ with rows $\boldsymbol{t}_i$, $0 \leq i \leq n'$. Then

$$\mathcal{C} = \{(\boldsymbol{c}, \boldsymbol{t}_{w(\boldsymbol{c})}) : \boldsymbol{c} \in \mathcal{C}'\}$$

is a t-EC/AUED code of length $n = n' + r$ which is systematic on k positions.

Construction 2.4: Let T_u be the $2u \times u$ $\{0, 1\}$-matrix defined recursively by $T_1 = \binom{1}{0}$

$$T_{u+1} = \left(\begin{array}{c|c} 1\ 1\cdots1 & 1 \\ \hline & 0 \\ & 1 \\ & 0 \\ T_u & \cdot \\ & \cdot \\ & \cdot \\ & 1 \\ \hline 0\ 0\cdots0 & 0 \end{array}\right).$$

Then for every value of t, T_u is a descending tail matrix $T(2u, u; t + 1)$.

The proof by induction is straightforward and will be omitted. The first four matrices T_u are

$$T_1 = \begin{pmatrix}1\\0\end{pmatrix},\quad T_2 = \begin{pmatrix}1&1\\1&0\\0&1\\0&0\end{pmatrix},\quad T_3 = \begin{pmatrix}1&1&1\\1&1&0\\1&0&1\\0&1&0\\0&0&1\\0&0&0\end{pmatrix},$$

$$T_4 = \begin{pmatrix}1&1&1&1\\1&1&1&0\\1&1&0&1\\1&0&1&0\\0&1&0&1\\0&0&1&0\\0&0&0&1\\0&0&0&0\end{pmatrix}.$$

Example 2.5: Let $k = 4$ and $t = 1$. The shortest 1-error correcting code with dimension 4 is the Hamming code of length $n' = 7$. As descending tail matrix $T(8, r; 2)$ we can take T_4. By Theorem 2.3, we have found a 1-EC/AUED code of length 11 which is systematic on four positions.

T_u will be an efficient descending tail matrix only for very small values of n' (in terms of small r). For larger values of n' we shall need much more advanced constructions. To this end we recall the definition of asymmetric error correcting codes [4]–[7], [9], [13], [15].

Definition 2.6: A binary word is said to have suffered asymmetric errors iff all errors are transitions $1 \to 0$ (resp. $0 \to 1$).

Notice that the difference between asymmetric and unidirectional errors is that in the former case we have "*a priori*" knowledge of what the transitions are going to be.

The *asymmetric minimum distance* Δ of a binary code A is defined as

$$\Delta = \min_{\substack{a,b \in \mathcal{A} \\ a \neq b}} \Delta(\boldsymbol{a}, \boldsymbol{b}) \tag{2.7}$$

TABLE I

BOUNDS ON THE CARDINALITY OF ASYMMETRIC ERROR CORRECTING CODES

n	Δ=2	Δ=3	Δ=4	Δ=5
5	6	2	2	2
6	12	4	2	2
7	18	4	2	2
8	36	7	4	2
9	62	12	4	2
10	108-117	18	6	4
11	174-210	30-32	8	4
12	316-410	54-63	12	4
13	586-786	98-114	18	6
14	1096-1500	186-218	30-34	8
15	2048-2828	266-398	44-50	12
16	3856-5430	364-739	66-90	16
17	7296-10374	647-1279	122-168	26
18	13798-19898	1218-2380	234-320	36-44
19	26216-38008	2050-4242	450-616	46-76
20	49940-73174	2564-8069	860-1144	54-134
21	95326-140798	4251-14374	1628-2134	62-229
22	182362-271953	8450-26679	3072-4116	88-423
23	349536-523586	16388-50200	4096-7346	133-745

where

$$\Delta(\boldsymbol{a}, \boldsymbol{b}) = \max\{N(\boldsymbol{a}, \boldsymbol{b}), N(\boldsymbol{b}, \boldsymbol{a})\}.$$

The code $\mathcal{C}$ can correct any t asymmetric errors in a codeword iff $\Delta \geq t + 1$. For further background on asymmetric error correcting codes we refer the reader to the articles listed above, in particular to the excellent survey by Kløve [7]. In [15], one can find the constructions of the asymmetric error correcting codes listed in Table I. Table I also contains upper bounds on their size.

Construction 2.7: Let $\mathcal{C}$ be an asymmetric error correcting code of length r, cardinality $|\mathcal{C}|$, and asymmetric minimum distance Δ. Let A by an $|\mathcal{C}| \times r$ matrix whose rows are the codewords of $\mathcal{C}$ in order of nonascending weight. Then A is a descending tail matrix $T(|\mathcal{C}|, r; \Delta)$.

Proof: Compare the rows $\boldsymbol{a}_i$ and $\boldsymbol{a}_j$, $i < j$, in A. Without loss of generality, they look like

$$\begin{aligned} \boldsymbol{a}_i &= \overbrace{1\,1\cdots 1}^{x}\ \overbrace{1\,1\cdots 1}^{y}\ \overbrace{0\,0\cdots 0}^{z}\ \overbrace{0\,0\cdots 0}^{u} \\ \boldsymbol{a}_j &= 1\,1\cdots 1\ \ 0\,0\cdots 0\ \ 1\,1\cdots 1\ \ 0\,0\cdots 0. \end{aligned}$$

Since $\mathcal{C}$ has asymmetric minimum distance Δ, we know that $\max\{y, z\} \geq \Delta$. But $i \leq j$, so $x + y = w(\boldsymbol{a}_i) \geq w(\boldsymbol{a}_j) = x + z$. Hence, $y \geq z$ and thus $N(\boldsymbol{a}_i, \boldsymbol{a}_j) = y = \max\{y, z\} \geq \Delta$. So (2.6) holds when $t + 1 = \Delta$. □

Example 2.8: $k = 29$, $t = 1$. According to [14], there exists a [35, 29, 3]-code (but not a [34, 29, 3]-code). So $n' = 35$. Construction 2.4 gives a 1-EC/AUED code with $r = 18$. However, Construction 2.7 and Table I imply the existence of a descending tail matrix $T(36, 8; 2)$. This gives $r = 8$.

Note that $N(\boldsymbol{a}_i, \boldsymbol{a}_{i+1}) \geq \Delta$ in Construction 2.7, while by (2.6) we only need that $N(\boldsymbol{a}_i, \boldsymbol{a}_{i+1}) \geq 1$. Hence, it should not come as a surprise to the reader that Construction 2.7 in conjunction with Theorem 2.3 will not yield our best construction of t-EC/AUED codes.

For encoding and decoding of t-EC/AUED codes obtained by Construction 2.7 and Theorem 2.3, one needs (in general) to store the $|\mathcal{C}| \times r$ matrix A. Suppose that $\mathcal{C}$ is the largest asymmetric error correcting code with asymmetric distance Δ that one is willing to use in a particular application. Then the direct product $\mathcal{C} \times \mathcal{C} = \mathcal{C}^2$ is also an asymmetric error correcting code with the same asymmetric minimum distance Δ and so is $\mathcal{C}^3$, $\mathcal{C}^4$, etc. So we can use $\mathcal{C}^l$ with $l = \lceil \log_{|\mathcal{C}|}(n' + 1) \rceil$ to construct a suitable descending tail matrix for an $[n', k, 2t + 1]$-code. The length of this tail is given by

$$r^* = r\lceil \log_{|\mathcal{C}|}(n'+1)\rceil \approx \frac{r}{\log_2 |\mathcal{C}|}\log_2(n'+1). \quad (2.8)$$

Example 2.9: Let $\mathcal{C}$ be the asymmetric error correcting code mentioned in Example 2.8. So $|\mathcal{C}| = 36$, $r = 8$, $\Delta = 2$, $t = 1$. Then (2.8) reduces to

$$r^* \approx \frac{8}{\log_2 36}\log_2(n'+1) \approx 1.547 \log_2(n'+1).$$

By the Gilbert Varshamov bound [8] there are t-error correcting codes whose length tends to ∞ and whose rate tends to 1. In particular, these codes also correct asymmetric errors. Hence, the rate of maximal size asymmetric error correcting codes with fixed asymmetric minimum distance Δ tends to 1 when their length tends to ∞. So $r/\log_2 |\mathcal{C}|$ in (2.8) will tend to 1 for $r \rightarrow \infty$. The reader should compare this to [11, formula (1)], where the tail has an approximate length

$$\sum_{i=1}^{t+1}\left\lceil \log_2 \frac{n'+1}{2i-1}\right\rceil \approx (t+1)\log_2(n'+1) - \log_2(2t+1)!!.$$

[Notation: $(2t + 1)!! = 1.3 \cdots (2t - 1) \cdot (2t + 1)$].

Let A be the descending tail matrix corresponding to code $\mathcal{C}$ and A^l be the matrix corresponding to $\mathcal{C}^l$. The way we order the $|\mathcal{C}|^l$ rows in matrix A^l is as follows: consider row i, $0 \leq i$

$\leq |\mathcal{A}|^l - 1$. Then write i on base $|\mathcal{A}|$, i.e., $i = j_0 + j_l|\mathcal{A}| + \cdots + j_{l-1}|\mathcal{A}|^{l-1}$. If

$$A = \begin{pmatrix} a_0 \\ a_1 \\ \vdots \\ a_{|\mathcal{A}|-1} \end{pmatrix},$$

then row i in $\mathcal{A}^l$ is given by $(a_{j0}, a_{j1}, \cdots, a_{jl-1})$ (the comma denotes concatenation). In this way, when we combine Theorem 2.3 with matrix A^l, we only need to store matrix A and build circuits that compute i on base $|\mathcal{A}|$.

The next construction combines Constructions 2.4 and 2.7.

Construction 2.10: Let $\mathcal{A}$ be an asymmetric error correcting code of length r with minimum asymmetric distance $\Delta = t + 1$. Let A be the $|\mathcal{A}| \times r$ matrix whose rows a_i, $1 \leq i \leq |\mathcal{A}|$, are the codewords of $\mathcal{A}$ in order of nonascending weight. Let t_j, $1 \leq j \leq 2u$, be the rows of T_u for some fixed value of u. Then the $(2u|\mathcal{A}| \times (r + u)$ matrix

$$A \times T_u = \begin{pmatrix} a_1 \times T_u \\ a_2 \times T_u \\ \vdots \\ a_{|\mathcal{A}|} \times T_u \end{pmatrix}$$

where $a_i \times T_u$ stands for

$$\begin{pmatrix} a_i, t_1 \\ a_i, t_2 \\ \vdots \\ a_i, t_{2u} \end{pmatrix}$$

is a descending tail matrix $T(2u|\mathcal{A}|, r + u; t + 1)$.

Proof: Compare a_i, t_u with a_j, t_v. If $i < j$ then $N(a_i, a_j) \geq t + 1$. If $i = j$ and $u < v$, then

$$N(t_u, t_v) \geq \left\lceil \frac{v-u}{2} \right\rceil \geq \min\left\{t+1, \left\lceil \frac{v-u}{2} \right\rceil\right\}. \qquad \square$$

When using Theorem 2.3 and Construction 2.10 to find t-EC/AUED codes, one, of course, wants to minimize the redundancy in the code. Suppose that one wants to construct a t-EC/AUED code that is systematic on k positions. We give a step by step construction procedure.

Construction 2.11:

1. Construct an $[n', k, 2t + 1]$-code with n' minimal (to this end, the table in [14] is very useful).
2. Find an asymmetric t-error correcting code $\mathcal{A}$ of length s and $|\mathcal{A}| = m$, and a tail matrix T_u such that $2um \geq n' + 1$ and $s + u$ is minimal. $\mathcal{A}$ can be found using Table I which comes from [15] and $A(m, s, t + 1)$ denotes the matrix corresponding to A.
3. Construct the t-EC/AUED code using Theorem 2.3 and Construction 2.10.

We illustrate this step by step construction with an example.

Example 2.12: Assume we want to construct a 1-EC/AUED code that is systematic on 16 positions. The first step is finding an $[n', 16, 3]$-code with n' as small as possible. We can take a [21, 16, 3] (shortened) Hamming code, i.e., $n' = 21$. In the second step, we have to find an asymmetric 1-error-correcting code $\mathcal{A}$ of length s and $|\mathcal{A}| = m$, and a tail matrix T_u such that $2um \geq 22$ and $s + u$ is minimal. Using Table I, we readily see that this choice is given by $A(6, 5; 2) \times T_2$, whose first 22 rows are a descending tail matrix $T(22, 7; 2)$. Applying Theorem 2.3 to the [21, 16, 3]-code and this $T(22, 7; 2)$ descending tail matrix, we obtain a 1-EC/AUED of length 28 which is systematic on 16 positions. Notice that the 1-EC/AUED code with $k = 16$ in Table VI of [11] has $n = 29$, i.e., the proposed method gives a redundant bit less.

The first code in each column of Table I (not shown) is the repetition code, whose corresponding matrix is $A(2, t + 1; t + 1)$. Note that one never needs to use a tail matrix T_u with $u \geq 2(t + 1)$ since $A(2, t + 1; t + 1) \times T_{\lceil u/2 \rceil}$ has $4\lceil u/2 \rceil \geq 2u$ rows (the number of rows in T_u), but $t + 1 + \lceil u/2 \rceil \leq u$ columns. The reader should always keep in mind that $A(m_1, s_1; t + 1) \times A(m_2, s_2; t + 1)$ gives an $A(m_1 m_2, s_1 + s_2; t + 1)$ matrix.

The fact that we require $s + u$ to be minimal in step 2 on Construction 2.11 makes this construction more efficient than the combination of Construction 2.7 with Theorem 2.3. If we use Construction 2.7 in Example 2.12, we need to find an asymmetric 1-error correcting code $\mathcal{A}$ of length s and $|\mathcal{A}| = m$ such that $m \geq 22$. Looking at Table I, we see that there is a code with 36 codewords, which gives a matrix $A(36, 8, 2)$. The first 22 rows of this matrix are a descending tail matrix $T(22, 8; 2)$, while in Example 2.12 we had a $T(22, 7; 2)$ matrix. As we see, Construction 2.10 provides a better choice than Constructions 2.4 and 2.7.

III. Tables and Comparisons

The way Tables II–V are made is as follows: for a given r^*, we use Table I to find an $A(m, s; t + 1)$ such that $A(m, s: t + 1) \times T_{r*-s}$ has maximal size, i.e., such that $2(r^* - s)m$ is maximal. With this choice of s we can apply Construction 2.10 to $[n', k, 2t + 1]$-codes whenever $n' + 1 \leq 2(r^* - s)m$. This explains the upper bound $2(r^* - s)m - 1$ on n'. The lower bound on n' is simply one more than the upper bound on n' for redundancy $r^* - 1$. The range of k that corresponds with the range of n' can be determined from the table on $[n', k, 2t + 1]$-codes in [14]. So the k-range is obtained from the n-range and not the other way around. For instance, if $2t + 1 = 9$, the n'-range 28–31 in Table V gives rise to the k-range 11–12, since a [31, 12, 9]-code exists and a [31, 13, 9]-code is not known. It is quite possible that a [31, 13, 9] and even a [31, 14, 9]-code will be found. In that case the k-range will have to be adapted. All these codes can be extended with the same descending tail matrix to form a 4-EC/AUED code.

Tables VI and VII compare Tables II–V with the results in [11].

IV. Decoding

The decoding algorithm of a t-EC/AUED code constructed by Theorem 3.2 is basically as complex as the decoding algorithm of the $[n', k, 2t + 1]$-code $\mathcal{C}'$ used, plus the complexity of the encoding procedure added to it.

The decoding algorithm works as follows. Let $(c, t_{w(c)})$ be the transmitted codeword, where $c \in \mathcal{C}'$ and $t_{w(c)}$ is the corresponding row from the descending tail matrix. Suppose that (r_1, r_2) is the received vector. Then proceed as follows.

TABLE II
1-EC/AUED CODES

k-range	n'-range	r*	Construction
1	5 (4-5)	3	T_3
–	(6-7)	4	T_4
2	8 (8-9)	5	T_5
3-4	10-11	6	$A(2,3;3) \times T_3$ or T_6
5-7	12-15	7	$A(2,3;3) \times T_4$
8-10	16-19	8	$A(2,3;3) \times T_5$
11-14	20-23	9	$A(2,3;3) \times A(2,3;3) \times T_3$ or $A(2,3;3) \times T_6$
15-21	24-31	10	$A(2,3;3) \times A(2,3;3) \times T_4$
22-35	32-47	11	$A(12,9;3) \times T_2$
36-58	48-71	12	$A(18,10;3) \times T_2$ or $A(12,9;3) \times T_3$
59-105	72-119	13	$A(30,11;3) \times T_2$
106-199	120-215	14	$A(54,12;3) \times T_2$
200-373	216-391	15	$A(98,13;3) \times T_2$

TABLE III
2-EC/AUED CODES

k range	n' range	r* (add to n')	Construction
1	3 (2-3)	2	T_2
2	5 (4-5)	3	T_3
3-4	6-7	4	$A(2,2;2) \times T_2$
5-7	8-11	5	$A(2,2;2) \times T_3$
8-11	12-15	6	$A(2,2;2) \times A(2,2;2) \times T_2$
12-18	16-23	7	$A(2,2;2) \times A(2,2;2) \times T_3$ or $A(6,5;2) \times T_2$
19-41	24-47	8	$A(12,6;2) \times T_2$
42-64	48-71	9	$A(12,6;2) \times T_3$ or $A(18,7;2) \times T_2$
65-135	72-143	10	$A(36,8;2) \times T_2$
136-239	144-247	11	$A(62,9;2) \times T_2$
240-422	248-431	12	$A(108,10;2) \times T_2$

TABLE IV
3-EC/AUED CODES

k-range	n'-range	r*	Construction
1	7 (6-7)	4	T_4
–	– (8-9)	5	T_5
2	11 (10-11)	6	T_6
3	13 (12-13)	7	T_7
4-5	14-15	8	$A(2,4;4) \times T_4$ or T_8
6-8	16-19	9	$A(2,4;4) \times T_5$
9-12	20-23	10	$A(2,4;4) \times T_6$
13-14	24-27	11	$A(2,4;4) \times T_7$
15-16	28-31	12	$A(2,4;4) \times A(2,4;4) \times T_4$ or $A(2,4;4) \times T_8$
17-23	32-39	13	$A(2,4;4) \times A(2,4;4) \times T_5$
24-31	40-47	14	$A(2,4;4) \times A(2,4;4) \times T_6$
32-52	48-71	15	$A(18,13;4) \times T_2$
53-98	72-119	16	$A(30,14;4) \times T_2$
99-155	120-179	17	$A(30,14;4) \times T_3$
156-236	180-263	18	$A(44,15;4) \times T_3$ or $A(66,16;4) \times T_2$
237-460	264-487	19	$A(122,17;4) \times T_2$

Step 1: Apply the decoding algorith of $\mathcal{C}'$ to r_1. If the algorithm fails to find a codeword $\hat{c}$ in $\mathcal{C}'$ at distance $\le t$ from r_1, then more than t errors have occurred in r_1 and *a fortiori* in (r_1, r_2). Declare a unidirectional error and stop. If the algorithm finds a codeword $\hat{c}$ in $\mathcal{C}'$ with $d(\hat{c}, r_1) \le t$, then proceed with step 2.

Step 2: Compute $\hat{t} = t_{w(c)}$. If $d((r_1, r_2), (\hat{c}, \hat{t})) \le t$, then declare $(\hat{c}, \hat{t})$ to be the transmitted codeword (note that $(\hat{c}, \hat{t}) = (c, t_{w(c)})$ if $\le t$ errors have occurred during the transmission). If $d((r_1, r_2), (\hat{c}, \hat{t})) \ge t + 1$ then declare a unidirectional error.

It follows from Theorem 2.3 and Construction 2.10 that in the event that less than or equal than t errors have occurred or that more than t unidirectional errors have occurred, the Decoding Algorithm will either correctly decode the errors or correctly declare a unidirectional error.

We end this section with an example that shows how the encoding and decoding works.

Example 4.1: Consider the 1-EC/AUED with $k = 16$ given in Example 2.12. The $T(22, 7; 2)$ tail matrix is given by the first 22 rows of the matrix $A(6, 5; 2) \times T_2$, where

$$A(6, 5; 2) = \begin{pmatrix} 1 & 1 & 1 & 1 & 1 \\ 0 & 0 & 1 & 1 & 1 \\ 1 & 1 & 0 & 0 & 1 \\ 1 & 0 & 1 & 0 & 0 \\ 0 & 1 & 0 & 1 & 0 \\ 0 & 0 & 0 & 0 & 0 \end{pmatrix}$$

and

$$T_2 = \begin{pmatrix} 1 & 1 \\ 1 & 0 \\ 0 & 1 \\ 0 & 0 \end{pmatrix}.$$

The first step is encoding the 16 information symbols into a systematic [21, 16, 3] (shortened) Hamming code. As parity check matrix of this code we may take

$$H = \begin{pmatrix} 0&0&0&0&0&0&0&0&0&0&0&1&1&1&1&1&1&0&0&0&0 \\ 0&0&0&0&1&1&1&1&1&1&1&0&0&0&0&0&0&1&0&0&0 \\ 0&1&1&1&0&0&0&1&1&1&1&0&0&0&1&1&0&0&1&0&0 \\ 1&0&1&1&0&1&1&0&0&1&1&0&1&1&0&1&0&0&0&1&0 \\ 1&1&0&1&1&0&1&0&1&0&1&1&0&1&1&0&0&0&0&0&1 \end{pmatrix}$$

TABLE V
4-ED/AUED CODES

k-range	n'-range	r*	Construction
1	9 (8-9)	5	T_5
–	– (10-11)	6	T_6
–	– (12-13)	7	T_7
2	14 (14-15)	8	T_8
3	17 (16-17)	9	T_9
4	19 (18-19)	10	$A(2,5;5) \times T_5$ or T_{10}
5-7	20-23	11	$A(2,5;5) \times T_6$
8-10	24-27	12	$A(2,5;5) \times T_7$
11-12	28-31	13	$A(2,5;5) \times T_8$
13-15	32-35	14	$A(2,5;5) \times T_9$
16-19	36-39	15	$A(2,5;5) \times A(2,5;5) \times T_5$ or $A_2(2,5;5) \times T_{10}$
20-25	40-47	16	$A(2,5;5) \times A(2,5;5) \times T_6$
26-31	48-55	17	$A(2,5;5) \times A(2,5;5) \times T_7$
32-47	56-71	18	$A(12,15;5) \times T_3$
48-75	72-103	19	$A(26,17;5) \times T_2$
76-123	104-155	20	$A(26,17;5) \times T_3$
124-183	156-215	21	$A(36,18;5) \times T_3$
184-251	216-287	22	$A(36,18;5) \times T_4$
252-331	288-367	23	$A(46,19;5) \times T_4$

which gives the generator matrix

$$G = \left(\begin{array}{cccccccccccccccccccc c}
1 & & & & & & & & & & & & & & & & 0 & 0 & 0 & 1 & 1 \\
 & 1 & & & & & & & & & & & & & & & 0 & 0 & 1 & 0 & 1 \\
 & & 1 & & & & & & & & & & & & & & 0 & 0 & 1 & 1 & 0 \\
 & & & 1 & & & & & & & & & & & & & 0 & 0 & 1 & 1 & 1 \\
 & & & & 1 & & & & & & & & & & & & 0 & 1 & 0 & 0 & 1 \\
 & & & & & 1 & & & & & & & & & & & 0 & 1 & 0 & 1 & 0 \\
 & & & & & & 1 & & & & & & & & & & 0 & 1 & 0 & 1 & 1 \\
 & & & & & & & 1 & & & & & & & & & 0 & 1 & 1 & 0 & 0 \\
 & & & & & & & & 1 & & & & & & & & 0 & 1 & 1 & 0 & 1 \\
 & & & & & & & & & 1 & & & & & & & 0 & 1 & 1 & 1 & 0 \\
 & & & & & & & & & & 1 & & & & & & 0 & 1 & 1 & 1 & 1 \\
 & & & & & & & & & & & 1 & & & & & 1 & 0 & 0 & 0 & 1 \\
 & & & & & & & & & & & & 1 & & & & 1 & 0 & 0 & 1 & 0 \\
 & & & & & & & & & & & & & 1 & & & 1 & 0 & 0 & 1 & 1 \\
 & & & & & & & & & & & & & & 1 & & 1 & 0 & 1 & 0 & 1 \\
 & & & & & & & & & & & & & & & 1 & 1 & 0 & 1 & 1 & 0
\end{array}\right).$$

TABLE VI
COMPARISON FOR $t = 1$ OF [11] WITH TABLE II

k range	n'-range	r^* from [11]	r^* from Table II	Gain in bits
8-11	12-15	6	6	–
12-16	17-21	8	7	1
20-26	25-31	8	8	–
28-32	34-38	10	8	2
52-57	58-63	10	9	1
62-64	69-71	12	9	3
112-120	119-127	12	10	2

TABLE VII
COMPARISON OF SOME RESULTS OF [11] WITH TABLES III–V

k	n'	t	r^* from [11]	r^* from Tables III, IV, V	Gain in bits
12	21	2	11	9	2
51	63	2	14	12	2
113	127	2	17	14	3
12	23	3	13	10	3
16	31	3	13	12	1
46	63	3	17	15	2
231	255	3	25	18	7
39	63	4	20	18	2
99	127	4	25	20	5
223	255	4	30	22	8

Assume we want to encode the information vector

$$u = 1\ 0\ 0\ 1\ 1\ 1\ 0\ 1\ 0\ 0\ 0\ 1\ 0\ 1\ 1\ 0.$$

Using the generator matrix G, this vector is encoded as

$$c = 1\ 0\ 0\ 1\ 1\ 1\ 0\ 1\ 0\ 0\ 0\ 1\ 0\ 1\ 1\ 0\ 1\ 1\ 1\ 0\ 0.$$

Finally, $w(c) = 11$, so we have to append as $t_{w(c)}$ the 12th row in $T(22, 7; 2)$, which is 1 1 0 0 1 0 0. The encoded codeword is finally

$$v = 1\ 0\ 0\ 1\ 1\ 1\ 0\ 1\ 0\ 0\ 0\ 1\ 0\ 1\ 1\ 0\quad 1\ 1\ 1\ 0\ 0\quad 1\ 1\ 0\ 0\ 1\ 0\ 0.$$

This example shows that the encoding is very simple; essentially, it is as complex as the encoder of the 1-error correcting code plus a tail that is a function of the weight of the codeword.

Now, assume we receive $r = (r_1, r_2)$

$$r = 1\ 0\ 0\ 1\ 0\ 1\ 0\ 1\ 0\ 0\ 0\ 1\ 0\ 1\ 1\ 0\quad 1\ 1\ 1\ 0\ 0\quad 1\ 1\ 0\ 0\ 1\ 0\ 0.$$

By step 1 of the algorithm, we have to apply the decoding algorithm of the [21, 16, 3] 1-error correcting code to r_1. The syndrome is given by

$$Hr_1 = \begin{pmatrix} 0 \\ 1 \\ 0 \\ 0 \\ 1 \end{pmatrix}$$

which corresponds to the fifth column of H, i.e., the decoder gives

$$\hat{c} = 1\ 0\ 0\ 1\ 1\ 1\ 0\ 1\ 0\ 0\ 0\ 1\ 0\ 1\ 1\ 0\quad 1\ 1\ 1\ 0\ 0.$$

In step 2 of the decoding algorithm, we must compute $\hat{t} = t_{w(\hat{c})}$, which gives 1 1 0 0 1 0 0.

We observe that $d((r_1, r_2), (\hat{c}, \hat{t})) = 1$, so we declare $(\hat{c}, \hat{t})$ to be the transmitted codeword.

Now, assume we receive $r = (r_1, t_2)$,

$$r = 1\ 0\ 0\ 0\ 0\ 0\ 0\ 0\ 0\ 0\ 0\ 0\ 1\ 0\ 0\ 1\ 0\quad 1\ 0\ 1\ 0\ 0\quad 0\ 0\ 0\ 0\ 1\ 0\ 0.$$

Repeating the procedure, in step 1, the syndrome is

$$Hr_1 = \begin{pmatrix} 1 \\ 0 \\ 0 \\ 1 \\ 1 \end{pmatrix}$$

which corresponds to the 14th column in H. Hence, r_1 is decoded as

$$\hat{c} = 1\,0\,0\,0\,0\,0\,0\,0\,0\,0\,0\,0\,1\,0\,1\,1\,0 \quad 1\,0\,1\,0\,0.$$

Since $w(\hat{c}) = 6$, in step 2 we obtain $\hat{t} = 0\,0\,1\,1\,1\,0\,1$ [the seventh row in $T(22, 7; 2)$]. Clearly, $d((r_1, r_2), (\hat{c}, \hat{t})) = 4 > 1$, so, the decoder declares an uncorrectable error. In this example, this might have happened, for instance, if the vector v obtained at the beginning of this example,

$$v = 1\,0\,0\,1\,1\,1\,0\,1\,0\,0\,0\,1\,0\,1\,1\,0 \quad 1\,1\,1\,0\,0 \quad 1\,1\,0\,0\,1\,0\,0$$

has been transmitted and the vector

$$r = 1\,0\,0\,0\,0\,0\,0\,0\,0\,0\,0\,1\,0\,0\,1\,0 \quad 1\,0\,1\,0\,0 \quad 0\,0\,0\,0\,1\,0\,0$$

has been received. Notice that in this case a unidirectional error of type $1 \to 0$ has occurred.

V. Conclusions

We have presented codes that can correct t errors and detect more than t unidirectional errors. Our construction starts with a t-error correcting code and then strongly uses asymmetric t-error correcting codes. We used the best available random error correcting and asymmetric error correcting codes. If these codes are improved, our construction will be improved too. We give asymptotic results, tables with the relevant parameters, comparison tables with previous constructions in literature, and a decoding algorithm. A specific example has been discussed in detail. A lower bound on the redundancy of a systematic t-EC/AUED code is provided in [2]. The codes presented in this paper have higher redundancy than this bound. If the bound is tight, then there must exist t-EC/AUED codes with lower redundancy than the code proposed here.

References

[1] B. Bose, "On systematic SEC/MUED code," in *Proc. FTCS*, vol. 11, June 1981, pp. 265–267.

[2] B. Bose and D. K. Pradhan, "Optimal unidirectional error detecting/correcting codes," *IEEE Trans. Comput.*, vol. C-31, pp. 564–568, June 1982.

[3] B. Bose and T. R. N. Rao, "Theory of unidirectional error correcting/detecting codes," *IEEE Trans. Comput.*, vol. C-31, pp. 521–530, June 1982.

[4] S. D. Constantin and T. R. N. Rao, "On the theory on binary asymmetric error correcting codes," *Inform. Contr.*, vol. 40, pp. 20–36, 1979.

[5] P. Delsarte and P. Piret, "Bounds and constructions for binary symmetric error correcting codes," *IEEE Trans. Inform. Theory*, vol. IT-27, no. 1, pp. 125–128, Jan. 1981.

[6] T. Kløve, "Upper bounds on codes correcting asymmetric errors," *IEEE Trans. Inform. Theory*, vol. IT-27, no. 1, pp. 128-131, Jan. 1981.

[7] ——, "Error-correcting codes for the asymmetric channel," Rep. in Informatics, Univ. of Bergen, Bergen, Norway.

[8] F. J. MacWilliams and N. J. A. Sloane, *The Theory of Error-Correcting Codes*. Amsterdam, The Netherlands: North-Holland, 1978.

[9] R. J. McEliece, "A comment on 'A class of codes for asymmetric channels and a problem from the additive theory of numbers'," *IEEE Trans. Inform. Theory*, p. 137, 1973.

[10] N. Nikolos, N. Gaitanis, and G. Philokyprou, "t-error correcting all unidirectional error detecting codes starting from cyclic AN codes," in *Proc. 1984 Int. Conf. Fault-Tolerant Comput.*, Kissimmee, FL, pp. 318-323.

[11] ——, "Systematic t-error correcting/all unidirectional error detecting codes," *IEEE Trans. Comput.*, vol. C-35, no. 5, pp. 394–402, May 1986.

[12] D. K. Pradhan, "A new class of error-correcting/detecting codes for fault-tolerant computer application," *IEEE Trans. Comput.*, vol. C-29, pp. 471–481, June 1980.

[13] R. R. Varshamov, "A class of codes for asymmetric channels and a problem from the additive theory of numbers," *IEEE Trans. Inform. Theory*, pp. 92–95, 1973.

[14] T. Verhoeff, "An updated table of minimum distance bounds for binary linear codes," *IEEE Trans. Inform. Theory*, vol. IT-33, no. 5, pp. 665–680, Sept. 1987.

[15] J. H. Weber, C. de Vroedt, and D. E. Boekee, "Bounds and constructions for binary code of length less than 24 and asymmetric distance less than 6," *IEEE Trans. Inform. Theory*, vol. IT-34, no. 5, pp. 1321-1331, Sept. 1988.

Mario Blaum (S'84–M'85) was born in Buenos Aires, Argentina, on September 16, 1951. He received the degree of Licenciado from the University of Buenos Aires in 1977, the M.Sc. degree from the Israel Institute of Technology in 1981, and the Ph.D. degree from the California Institute of Technology in 1984, all in mathematics.

From January to June 1985, he was a Research Fellow at the Department of Electrical Engineering at Caltech. In August, 1985, he joined the IBM Research Division at the Almaden Research Center, San Jose, were he is presently a Research Staff Member. His research interests include error correcting codes, combinatorics, and neural networks.

Henk van Tilborg (M'79–SM'83) was born in Tilburg, The Netherlands, on September 1, 1947. He received the M.Sc. and Ph.D. degrees from the Eindhoven University of Technology, Eindhoven, The Netherlands in 1971 and 1976, respectively.

He spent the first four months of 1971 at the Jet Propulsion Laboratories, Pasadena, CA. During the next three months of 1971 he visited Bell Laboratories, Murray Hill, NJ. During the academic year 1976–1977 he worked again in the Communications Systems Research Section at the Jet Propulsion Laboratory and gave a course in coding theory at the California Institute of Technology, Pasadena, as a Visiting Assistant Professor. During the academic year 1982–1983, he was a Visiting Professor in mathematics at the Catholic University of Leuven, Belgium. During the first two terms of the academic year 1984–1985, he was a Visiting Associate Professor in Electrical Engineering at the California Institute of Technology and during the summer of 1986 he worked as a Visiting Scientist at the IBM Almaden Research Center in San Jose, CA. Since 1972 he has been with the Department of Mathematics in Eindhoven, University of Technology, The Netherlands. His main interests are coding theory, cryptology, and discrete mathematics.

Constructions and Bounds for Systematic tEC/AUED Codes

FRANK J. H. BÖINCK AND HENK C. A. VAN TILBORG, SENIOR MEMBER, IEEE

Abstract —Several methods of constructing systematic t-error correcting/all unidirectional error-detecting codes are described. These codes can be constructed by adding a tail to a linear t-error correcting code, but other constructions presented here are more of an ad hoc nature. These codes will often be found as suitably chosen subsets of nonsystematic tEC/AUED codes. Further bounds on the word length of systematic tEC/AUED codes are derived, and extensive tables are given.

I. Introduction

In recently developed types of VLSI memories error patterns of a unidirectional nature sometimes occur. These are error patterns in which all the erroneous transitions are in the same direction. So only errors of the $0 \to 1$ type or of the $1 \to 0$ type occur. These kinds of error patterns also occur in some data transmission systems and magnetic recording mass memories. Apart from these rather catastrophic unidirectional error patterns occasional random error may also sometimes occur. In this context it is quite natural to look for codes that can correct up to t errors and that can detect any number of unidirectional errors [1]–[8] and [14]–[16].

Before we can define these codes we need some definitions. A vector $\boldsymbol{a}$ is said to be *covered* by a vector $\boldsymbol{b}$, if

$$\forall_{1 \le i \le n}[a_i = 1 \Rightarrow b_i = 1]. \tag{1}$$

Definition 1.1: Let $\boldsymbol{a}$ be a transmitted word and $\boldsymbol{b}$ the received word. Then we shall say that *unidirectional errors* have occurred if either $\boldsymbol{a}$ is covered by $\boldsymbol{b}$ or $\boldsymbol{b}$ by $\boldsymbol{a}$.

Let $\boldsymbol{a}$ and $\boldsymbol{b}$ be two vectors of length n. Then $N(\boldsymbol{a},\boldsymbol{b})$ is defined by

$$N(\boldsymbol{a},\boldsymbol{b}) = |\{1 \le i \le n | a_i = 1 \wedge b_i = 0\}|. \tag{2}$$

For example if $\boldsymbol{a} = 00110$ and $\boldsymbol{b} = 01011$, then $N(\boldsymbol{a},\boldsymbol{b}) = 1$ and $N(\boldsymbol{b},\boldsymbol{a}) = 2$. Note that the Hamming distance $d(\boldsymbol{a},\boldsymbol{b})$ satisfies $d(\boldsymbol{a},\boldsymbol{b}) = N(\boldsymbol{a},\boldsymbol{b}) + N(\boldsymbol{b},\boldsymbol{a})$.

As stated before we are interested in codes that can detect error patterns of the unidirectional type, but are also able to correct error patterns consisting of up to t random errors.

Manuscript received January 1989; revised October 1989. This work was presented in part at the 1990 IEEE Information Theory Symposium, San Diego, CA, January 14–19, 1990.

The authors are with the Department of Mathematics and Computing Science, Eindhoven University of Technology, P.O. Box 513, Eindhoven, The Netherlands.

IEEE Log Number 9036752.

Definition 1.2: A code C is called t-error-correcting/all unidirectional error detecting, denoted by tEC/AUED, if it can correct up to t random errors and is also capable of detecting all error patterns of the unidirectional type.

The following theorem gives a necessary and sufficient condition for a code to be tEC/AUED. Although the proof can be found in the literature [4], [16] we give it here for the sake of completeness.

Theorem 1.3: A code C is tEC/AUED iff

$$\forall_{\boldsymbol{a},\boldsymbol{b} \in C, \boldsymbol{a} \ne \boldsymbol{b}}[N(\boldsymbol{a},\boldsymbol{b}) \ge t+1]. \tag{3}$$

Proof:

$\Leftarrow$ Clearly C is t-error-correcting. Moreover if at most t errors have been made in a transmitted word $\boldsymbol{a}$, the received vector $\boldsymbol{u}$ will still satisfy $N(\boldsymbol{u},\boldsymbol{b}) \ge 1$ and $N(\boldsymbol{b},\boldsymbol{u}) \ge 1$ when compared with any other codeword $\boldsymbol{b}$. So $\boldsymbol{u}$, which is at distance $\le t$ from the codeword $\boldsymbol{a}$, can not also be the result of a unidirectional error pattern having occurred in a codeword $\boldsymbol{b}$, $\boldsymbol{b} \ne \boldsymbol{a}$.

$\Rightarrow$ If $N(\boldsymbol{a},\boldsymbol{b}) = s \le t$, then the vector $\boldsymbol{u}$, obtained from $\boldsymbol{a}$ by changing the s coordinates, where $\boldsymbol{a}$ is one and $\boldsymbol{b}$ is zero, into zero, is at distance s, $s \le t$ to $\boldsymbol{a}$ and is at the same time the result of $N(\boldsymbol{b},\boldsymbol{a})$ unidirectional errors in $\boldsymbol{b}$. So C is not tEC/AUED. □

Many natural questions come up in relation to tEC/AUED codes. How large can they be? Find tEC/AUED codes, which are easy to encode and decode. Find efficient tEC/AUED codes that are also systematic. How large can systematic tEC/AUED codes be? Etcetera.

In one case the answer is known. Indeed by Sperner's Lemma [18] one knows that the largest size of a tEC/AUED code of length n for $t = 0$ is given by $\binom{n}{\lfloor n/2 \rfloor}$. Sperner's Lemma also says that such a code must consist of all weight-w words, where $w = \lfloor n/2 \rfloor$ or $w = \lceil n/2 \rceil$. In view of this Lemma it is maybe not so surprising that the questions, just raised, are not completely answered. In [12] efficient algorithms can be found to encode k information bits into words of weight $\lfloor n/2 \rfloor$ and length n and decode them back again.

The rest of this paper consists of three parts. In the next section bounds on the length of systematic tEC/AUED codes will be given. In Section III constructions of systematic tEC/AUED codes will be presented,

0-8186-4182-7/93 $3.00 © 1990 IEEE

that make use of (nonsystematic) t'EC/AUED codes. In Section IV systematic tEC/AUED codes are constructed by adding a tail to the codewords from a tEC linear code.

II. Bounds on tEC/AUED Codes

In this section we shall derive bounds on tEC/AUED codes. A tEC/AUED code of length n, that has cardinality M, will often be described as an (n, M)–tEC/AUED code. In the sequel we shall need the following lemma.

Lemma 2.1: Let C be a tEC/AUED code that is equidistant with distance $2t+2$. Then C is a constant weight code.

Proof: It follows from the assumptions that any two codewords, say $\boldsymbol{a}$ and $\boldsymbol{b}$, satisfy $d(\boldsymbol{a}, \boldsymbol{b}) = 2t+2$, but also $N(\boldsymbol{a}, \boldsymbol{b}) \geq t+1$ and $N(\boldsymbol{b}, \boldsymbol{a}) \geq t+1$. This implies that $N(\boldsymbol{a}, \boldsymbol{b}) = N(\boldsymbol{b}, \boldsymbol{a}) = t+1$ and thus that $\boldsymbol{a}$ and $\boldsymbol{b}$ have the same weight. □

Theorem 2.2: Let C be a tEC/AUED code with length n and of cardinality M. Let $m = \lceil M/2 \rceil$. Then

$$mn \geq 2(2m-1)(t+1). \tag{4}$$

If (4) holds with equality, then C is a constant weight code. If in this case $M \equiv 0 \pmod 4$, then $t+1$ must be divisible by m.

Proof: We follow the standard derivation of the Plotkin bound. So let A be an $M \times n$ matrix with the codewords of C as rows. Let c_i be the number of ones in the ith column of A. Then we have the following two inequalities for S, defined as the sum of the distances between all pairs of codewords,

$$S = \sum_{i=1}^{n} c_i(M - c_i) \leq m(M-m)n \tag{5}$$

and

$$S \geq (2t+2)\binom{M}{2}. \tag{6}$$

It follows from (5) and (6) that

$$M(M-1)(t+1) \leq m(M-m)n, \tag{7}$$

which can be rewritten as (4) by substituting $M = 2m$ or $M = 2m-1$ in (7).

Assume that equality holds in (4). Then equality also holds in (7) and thus also in (5) and (6). So all pairs of codewords have the same distance $2t+2$. From Lemma 2.1 we conclude that C is a constant weight code.

Now assume that $M \equiv 0 \pmod 4$ (so m is even) and that equality in (4) holds. From (4) it follows that m divides $2(t+1)$. So $2(t+1) = vm$ for some integer v. Suppose that v is odd, say $v = 2u+1$. Equality in (5) implies that all columns have weight m. Since C is a constant weight code, we conclude that all codewords must have weight $n/2$. But $n/2 = (t+1)(2m-1)/m = (2m-1)v/2 = (2m-1)((2u+1)/2$, which is not an integer. From this contradiction we conclude that v is even and thus that m divides $(t+1)$. □

The next bound says something about the possible weights in a tEC/AUED code.

Theorem 2.3: Let C be a nontrivial tEC/AUED code of length n and cardinality M. Let w be the weight of a codeword, then $w \geq t+1$ and

$$n \geq w + n(A, t), \tag{8}$$

where

$$A = \left\lceil \frac{M-1}{\sum_{i=0}^{w-t-1} \binom{w}{i}} \right\rceil$$

and $n(A, t)$ denotes the minimal length of a tEC/AUED code with cardinality at least A.

Proof: It follows from (3) that a codeword in a tEC/AUED code with at least two codewords must have weight at least $t+1$.

Let $\boldsymbol{a}$ be a codeword of weight w, $w \geq t+1$. Without loss of generality the first w coordinates of $\boldsymbol{a}$ are one and the others zero. Any codeword $\boldsymbol{b}$, different from $\boldsymbol{a}$, has at most $w-(t+1)$ ones on its first w positions. So there are $\sum_{i=0}^{w-t-1}\binom{w}{i}$ possible restrictions of $\boldsymbol{b}$ to the first w coordinates. By the pigeonhole principle there are at least A codewords with the same pattern on the first w coordinates. On their last $n-w$ coordinates they form a tEC/AUED code of cardinality at least A. Hence $n - w \geq n(A, t)$. □

We shall now derive a lower bound on the length n of a systematic tEC/AUED codes. If such a code, say C, is systematic on k positions, we shall speak of the $[n, k]$–tEC/AUED code C. In the sequel we shall always assume that $k \geq 2$ and that C is systematic on the first k positions.

Definition 2.4: The number $n[k, t]$ is the minimal length of all $[n, k]$–tEC/AUED codes.

By shortening an $[n, k+1]$–tEC/AUED code on one of its "systematic" positions one obtains the following inequality:

$$n[k+1, t] \geq n[k, t] + 1. \tag{9}$$

When $n \leq 4t+4$ Theorem 2.2 provides a good bound on $n[k, t]$. In this case $M = 2^k$, $k \geq 2$, and $m = 2^{k-1}$. Rewriting (4) as

$$n \geq 4t + 4 - \lfloor (t+1)/2^{k-2} \rfloor,$$

one obtains the following theorem.

Theorem 2.5: The number $n[k, t]$ satisfies

$$n[k, t] \geq 4t + 4 - \left\lfloor \frac{t+1}{2^{k-2}} \right\rfloor, \qquad \text{if } t+1 \not\equiv 2^{k-2} \pmod{2^{k-1}}, \tag{10}$$

$$n[k, t] \geq 4t + 5 - \frac{t+1}{2^{k-2}}, \qquad \text{if } t+1 \equiv 2^{k-2} \pmod{2^{k-1}}. \tag{11}$$

The idea of the bound, that we shall derive next, will be to take a subset of the codewords of an $[n,k]$–tEC/AUED code, such that their restrictions to the last $n-k$ coordinates satisfy special conditions. We then apply bounds on this collection of tails and obtain in this way a bound on the original $[n,k]$–tEC/AUED code.

So let C be an $[n,k]$–tEC/AUED code that is systematic on the first k positions. We write every codeword $\boldsymbol{c}$ as $(\boldsymbol{a},\boldsymbol{b})$, where $\boldsymbol{a}$ has length k and $\boldsymbol{b}$ has length $n-k$.

Definition 2.6: Let C be an $[n,k]$–tEC/AUED code that is systematic on the first k positions. Let u be an integer satisfying $0 \le u \le t$ and $2u+1 \le k$. Then $C^{(u)}$ is defined as the set of codewords $\boldsymbol{c}=(\boldsymbol{a},\boldsymbol{b})$ such that one of the following conditions holds:

1) $\boldsymbol{a}$ has weight at most u or at least $k-u$,
2) $\boldsymbol{a}$ starts with i zeros and has exactly u zeros in the remaining $k-i$ positions of $\boldsymbol{a}$, for some i, $1 \le i \le k-(2u+1)$.

Since the words of type 2 have weight w, $u+1 \le w \le k-1-u$ on the first k coordinates, they must be different from the words of type 1. The number of codewords of the first type is $2\sum_{i=0}^{u}\binom{k}{i}$, while the number of type 2 codewords is

$$\sum_{i=1}^{k-(2u+1)}\binom{k-i}{u}=\sum_{j=2u+1}^{k-1}\binom{j}{u}=\binom{k}{u+1}-\binom{2u+1}{u}.$$

Both numbers only depend on the value of k and u. Their sum will be denoted by $D(k,u)$. So

$$D(k,u) := |C^{(u)}| = 2\sum_{i=0}^{u}\binom{k}{i}+\binom{k}{u+1}-\binom{2u+1}{u}. \quad (12)$$

Lemma 2.7: Let $(\boldsymbol{a}_1,\boldsymbol{b}_1)$ and $(\boldsymbol{a}_2,\boldsymbol{b}_2)$ be two codewords in $C^{(u)}$, $0 \le u \le t$. Then

$$\min\{N(\boldsymbol{a}_1,\boldsymbol{a}_2),N(\boldsymbol{a}_2,\boldsymbol{a}_1)\} \le u, \quad (13)$$

and

$$\max\{N(\boldsymbol{b}_1,\boldsymbol{b}_2),N(\boldsymbol{b}_2,\boldsymbol{b}_1)\} \ge t+1-u. \quad (14)$$

Proof: Assume that one of the pairs $(\boldsymbol{a}_1,\boldsymbol{b}_1)$ and $(\boldsymbol{a}_2,\boldsymbol{b}_2)$ is of type 1, say $(\boldsymbol{a}_1,\boldsymbol{b}_1)$. Then $\boldsymbol{a}_1$ has at most u ones, in which case $N(\boldsymbol{a}_1,\boldsymbol{a}_2)\le u$, or $\boldsymbol{a}_1$ has at most u zeros, in which case $N(\boldsymbol{a}_2,\boldsymbol{a}_1)\le u$. So (13) holds under this assumption.

Now suppose that both $(\boldsymbol{a}_1,\boldsymbol{b}_1)$ and $(\boldsymbol{a}_2,\boldsymbol{b}_2)$ are of type 2, that $\boldsymbol{a}_1$ starts with i_1 zeros and that $\boldsymbol{a}_2$ starts with i_2 zeros. Without loss of generality $i_1 \le i_2$. Then $\boldsymbol{a}_1$ has at most u zeros at those coordinates, where $\boldsymbol{a}_2$ has ones. So $N(\boldsymbol{a}_2,\boldsymbol{a}_1)\le u$, which again proves (13).

Inequality (14) now follows directly from (3). □

Codes that satisfy (14) for all pairs of distinct codewords are called *asymmetric error correcting codes*, denoted by AsEC. Let Δ be equal to the right-hand side of (14). Then Δ is called the asymmetric distance of the code.

Theorem 2.8: Let $Z(r,\Delta)$ denote the maximum number of codewords in any AsEC code of length r and asymmetric distance at least Δ, $1 \le \Delta \le t+1$, and let $u=t+1-\Delta$. Then

$$Z(r,\Delta) \ge 2\sum_{i=0}^{u}\binom{k}{i}+\binom{k}{u+1}-\binom{2u+1}{u}. \quad (15)$$

Taking $u=t$ in (15) we obtain

$$2^r = Z(r,1) \ge 2\sum_{i=0}^{t}\binom{k}{i}+\binom{k}{t+1}-\binom{2t+1}{t}, \quad (16)$$

a result that can be found in [5].

Lemma 2.9: Let C be an $[n,k]$–tEC/AUED code with redundancy $r=n-k$. Let $C^{(u)}$ be defined by Definition 2.6. Let the set of elements of $\{\boldsymbol{b}|(\boldsymbol{a},\boldsymbol{b})\in C^{(u)}\}$ be denoted by $C^{(u)}(r,\Delta,t)$. Then we have the following.

1) $C^{(u)}(r,\Delta,t)$ contains no codewords of weight less than t or more than $r-t$.
2) $C^{(u)}(r,\Delta,t)$ contains at most one codeword of weight t and at most one codeword of weight $r-t$ (corresponding with $\boldsymbol{a}=\mathbf{1}$, resp. $\boldsymbol{a}=\mathbf{0}$).

Proof: We know that words $\boldsymbol{c}_0=(\mathbf{0},\boldsymbol{b}_0)$ and $\boldsymbol{c}_1=(\mathbf{1},\boldsymbol{b}_1)$ exist in $C^{(u)}$, for some value of $\boldsymbol{b}_0$ and $\boldsymbol{b}_1$. Therefore each vector $\boldsymbol{b}\in C^{(u)}(r,\Delta,t)$, from a vector $\boldsymbol{c}=(\boldsymbol{a},\boldsymbol{b})$, $\boldsymbol{c}\ne\boldsymbol{c}_0$ or $\boldsymbol{c}_1$, must have at least $t+1$ zeros and at least $t+1$ ones, since $N(\boldsymbol{c}_0,\boldsymbol{c})\ge t+1$ and $N(\boldsymbol{c},\boldsymbol{c}_1)\ge t+1$ must hold. Furthermore $\boldsymbol{b}_0$ must have at least t zeros, since $(\boldsymbol{e}_1,\boldsymbol{b})$ with $\boldsymbol{e}_1=(1,0,\cdots,0)$ is in $C^{(u)}$ and similarly $\boldsymbol{b}_1$ must have at least t ones. □

From Lemma 2.9 one easily derives a small improvement of inequality (16).

Theorem 2.10: Let C be an $[n,k]$–tEC/AUED code with redundancy $r=n-k$ and let both k and r be greater than or equal to $2t+1$. Then

$$2^r \ge 2\sum_{i=0}^{t}\binom{k}{i}+\binom{k}{t+1}-\binom{2t+1}{t}+2\sum_{i=1}^{t}\binom{r}{i}. \quad (17)$$

Proof: Take $u=t$. Then $\Delta=1$ and $|C^{(t)}(r,1,t)|$ is on one hand given by $|C^{(t)}|$, and thus by (12) with $u=t$. But on the other hand by Lemma 2.9 $|C^{(t)}(r,1,t)|$ is a subset of all words of length r and of weight in between t and $r-t$, with at most one word of weight t and at most one of weight $r-t$, i.e., $|C^{(t)}(r,1,t)| \le 2^r - 2(\sum_{i=0}^{t}\binom{r}{i}-1) = 2^r - 2\sum_{i=1}^{t}\binom{r}{i}$. Combining these two observations results in (17). □

To obtain more powerful bounds from Lemma 2.9 we shall derive two theorems, the first of which can be found in [9]. Let $A(n,d,w)$ denote, as usual, the maximum number of words of length n, weight w and mutual distance at least d. For values of $A(n,d,w)$ we refer the reader to Appendix A, Section 4 in [13] or improvements that can be found in [10] and [17].

TABLE I

Lower Bounds on $r = n - k$ for $[n,k]$–tEC/AUED Codes, $t \le 5$

$t=1$		$t=2$		$t=3$		$t=4$		$t=5$	
k-range	$r \ge$	k-range	$r \ge$	k-range	$r \ge$	k-range	$r \ge$	k-range	$r \ge$
2	4	2–4	8	2	10	2	14	2	16
3	5	5–9	9	3	11	3 –8	15	3–10	19
4–8	6	10–13	10	4–9	12	9–11	16	11–14	20
9–13	7	14–18	11	10–13	13	12–16	17	15–19	21
14–20	8	19–26	12	14–19	14	17–23	18	20–27	22
21–30	9	27–35	13	20–24	15	24–28	19	28–32	23
31–43	10	36–44	14	25–30	16	29–35	20	33–38	24
44–62	11	45–56	15	31–38	17	36–42	21	39–45	25
63–88	12	57–72	16	39–48	18	43–49	22	46–54	26
89–126	13	73–91	17	49–58	19	50–58	23	55–61	27
127–179	14	92–115	18	59–70	20	59–69	24	62–70	28
180–254	15	116–145	19	71–83	21	70–82	25	71–80	29
		146–183	20	84–99	22	83–95	26	92–104	31
				100–118	23	96–109	27	105–120	32

Theorem 2.11: Let $A_i^{(u)}(r,\Delta,t)$ be the number of codewords of weight i in $C^{(u)}(r,\Delta,t)$, $\Delta > 1$, as defined in Lemma 2.9. Then for any w and any s, $0 \le s \le w$,

$$\sum_{i=w-s}^{w} A_i^{(u)}(r,\Delta,t) \le A((r+s),2\Delta,w). \qquad (18)$$

Proof: To every codeword $\boldsymbol{b}$ of $C^{(u)}(r,\Delta,t)$ of weight in between $w-s$ and w we juxtapose a vector $\boldsymbol{b}'$ of length s in such a way that the length $(r+s)$-vector $\boldsymbol{b}^* = (\boldsymbol{b},\boldsymbol{b}')$ has total weight w. In this way one obtains $\sum_{i=w-s}^{w} A_i^{(u)}(r,\Delta,t)$ vectors of weight w and length $r+s$. Since $\max\{N(\boldsymbol{b}_1,\boldsymbol{b}_2), N(\boldsymbol{b}_2,\boldsymbol{b}_1)\} \ge \Delta$ by (14) and the words, previously obtained all have the same weight, we conclude that $N(\boldsymbol{b}_1^*,\boldsymbol{b}_2^*) = N(\boldsymbol{b}_2^*,\boldsymbol{b}_1^*) \ge \Delta$ for any pair $\boldsymbol{b}_1^*$ and $\boldsymbol{b}_2^*$ of them. So their mutual distance is at least 2Δ and their total number is bounded from above by $A(r+s,2\Delta,w)$. □

Theorem 2.12: The numbers B_w defined below give an upper bound for the number of codewords of weight less than or equal to w in $C^{(u)}(r,\Delta,t)$.

$$B_w = \begin{cases} 0, & \text{if } 0 \le w \le t-1, \\ 1, & \text{if } w = t \\ F(w,t,r), & \text{if } t+1 \le w \le r-t-1, \\ \min\{B_{r-t-1}+1, & \text{if } w = r-t, \\ \quad F(r-t,t,r)\}, & \\ B_{r-t}, & \text{if } r-t+1 \le w \le r, \end{cases}$$

where

$$F(w,t,r) = \min_{0 \le s \le w-t} (B_{w-s-1} + A(r+s,2\Delta,w)).$$

Proof: For $w < t$ and $w > r-t$ the previous assertions follow from 1) in Lemma 2.9, while these assertions for $w = t$ and $w = r-t$ follow from 2) in Lemma 2.9.

For $t+1 \le w \le r-t-1$ we proceed by induction. So assume that B_{w-s-1} is an upper bound for the number of codewords of weight at most $w-s-1$ in $C^{(u)}(r,\Delta,t)$, where $0 \le s \le w-t$. Then $B_{w-s-1} + \sum_{i=w-s}^{w} A_i(r,\Delta,t)$ is an upper bound for the number of codewords of weight at most w in $C^{(u)}(r,\Delta,t)$. By Theorem 2.11 $B_{w-s-1} + A(r+s,2\Delta,w)$ is also an upper bound for this number. □

The use of the lemmas and theorems above will be demonstrated in the following example, which will also explain how many entries in Table I have been made.

Example: Suppose that $t=2$ and that we want to determine the range of values for k for which the redundancy of an $[n,k]$–tEC/AUED code is at least nine. To this end we need to determine upper bounds on k for $[n,k]$–tEC/AUED codes with redundancy eight and nine. First let the redundancy $r = n-k$ be equal to 8. Because of Lemma 2.9 we need to derive upper bounds for the cardinality of $C^{(u)}(8,\Delta,2)$, where $u = t+1-\Delta = 3-\Delta$, for $\Delta = 1$, 2, and 3.

Let us consider the case that $\Delta = 3$. From Theorem 2.12 we get $B_0 = B_1 = 0$ and $B_2 = 1$. Further $B_3 = \min\{B_{2-s} + A(8+s,6,3) | 0 \le s \le 1\} = \min\{1+2,3\} = 3$, where we have used known values (or bounds) of $A(n,d,w)$. Similarly $B_4 = 4$, $B_5 = 6$, $B_6 = B_7 = B_8 = 7$. So $|C^{(0)}(8,3,2)| \le 7$. In exactly the same way one can derive that $|C^{(2)}(8,1,2)| \le 184$ and that $|C^{(1)}(8,2,2)| \le 28$. From Definition 2.6 we know that the number of selected codewords $D(k,u)$ as defined in (12) is bounded from above by $|C^{(u)}(r,\Delta,t)|$, with $\Delta = t+1-u$. So we have the three inequalities $D(k,2) \le |C^{(2)}(8,1,2)| \le 184$, $D(k,1) \le |C^{(1)}(8,2,2)| \le 28$ and $D(k,0) \le |C^{(0)}(8,3,2)| \le 7$. The values of $D(k,u)$ can be evaluated from (12). One gets the inequalities $k \le 9$, $k \le 6$ and $k \le 6$ respectively. So $r = 8$ and $t = 2$ together imply that k satisfies $k \le 6$.

Similarly $r = 9$ and $t = 2$ imply that $k \le 9$. So for $k = 7$, 8, or 9 our conclusion will be that the redundancy is at least 9, or, in other words, for $t = 2$ and $k = 7$, 8, or 9 the length n of an $[n,k]$–tEC/AUED code will satisfy $n \ge k+9$.

In this way many entries in Table I have been generated. For the generation of most of the other entries in Table I, we have made use of Theorem 2.5. One upper bound for a particular AsEC code in [20] in combination with Theorem 2.8 resulted in $r \ge 23$, when $k = 50$ and $t = 4$. Further we needed the following result of which we omit the proof [2], since it involves too many details.

Theorem 2.13: Let $n[k,t]$ be defined as in Definition 2.4. Then $n[4,1] \geq 10$ and $n[5,2] \geq 14$.

Readers that are interested in constructions and tables of nonsystematic EC/AUED codes are referred to [2].

III. Ad Hoc Systematic EC/AUED Codes

A first obvious way of obtaining systematic EC/AUED codes is the following construction.

Construction 3.1: Let C' be a good nonsystematic $(n,M)-t$EC/AUED code. Take a subset of 2^k codewords of C', such that a systematic $[n,k]-t$EC/AUED code C is obtained. If all the chosen codewords in C are identical on a particular coordinate, then puncture that coordinate.

Of course the codes previously constructed do not necessarily have a nice structure, in the sense that encoding is easy for instance, but it will turn out that many of them are optimal. The values of the constructions in this section will appear as upper bounds in Table II.

TABLE II
Bounds on $n[k,t]$, $t \leq 15$, $2 \leq k \leq 6$

t/k	2	3	4	5	6
1	6	8	10	11–12	12–14
2	10	11	12	14–17	15–18
3	12	14′	16	17–18	
4	16	18	19–20	20–21	
5	18	22	23	24	
6	22	25	27	28	
7	24	28	30′	32	
8	28	32	34–35	35–36	36–38
9	30	36	38	39–40	40–43
10	34	39	42	43	44
11	36	42	46	47–48	
12	40	46	49	51–52	
13	42	50	53	55–56	56–59
14	46	53	57	59	60
15	48	56	60	62′	64

Example 3.2: A $(7,7)-1$EC/AUED can be made by the seven cyclic shifts of the vector $\boldsymbol{p}_7 = (0110100)$. This vector has ones at the coordinates 1, 2 and 4, which are exactly the quadratic residues modulo 7. The following four shifts of $\boldsymbol{p}_7$ are systematic on the first two coordinates: (0110100), (1101000), (0011010), and (1000110). By puncturing the last coordinate one has obtained a $[6,2]-1$EC/AUED code.

Now extend the seven cyclic shifts of (1101000) with a one and take as row eight the vector (11100100), which is the complement of one of the seven vectors. These eight vectors form an $[8,3]-1$EC/AUED code, that is systematic on the first three coordinates. They are a subset of a possible construction of an $(8,14)-1$EC/AUED code (by means of Hadamard 3-designs).

Similarly $\boldsymbol{p}_{11} = (01011100010)$ gives rise to the following codes: an $[11,3]-2$EC/AUED code, a $[10,2]-2$EC/AUED code and a $[12,4]-2$EC/AUED code. From $\boldsymbol{p}_{23} =$ (11110101100110010100000) one gets a $[22,3]-5$EC/AUED code, a $[23,4]-5$EC/AUED code and a $[24,5]-5$EC/AUED code. The vector $\boldsymbol{p}_{43}$, with ones at the quadratic residues modulo 43, yields a $[43,5]-10$EC/AUED code and a $[44,6]-10$EC/AUED code, and $\boldsymbol{p}_{59}$, with ones at the quadratic residues modulo 59, yields a $[59,5]-14$EC/AUED code and a $[60,6]-14$EC/AUED code. With the quadratic residues in $GF(3^3)$ one can form (a 2-(27,13,6) block design and) a $(27,27)-6$EC/AUED code, from which a $[27,4]-6$EC/AUED code and a $[28,5]-6$EC/AUED code can be made. The sixteen cyclic shifts of (1111001101000010) form a $[16,4]-3$EC/AUED code, as one can easily check. Finally the eight cyclic shifts of (11100010) form an $[8,3]-1$EC/AUED code.

Some $(n,M)-t$EC/AUED codes contain two disjoint subsets of codewords that each form an $[n,k]-t$EC/AUED code. By extending the codewords of one subset with a zero and the others with a one, one obtains a $[n+1,k+1]-t$EC/AUED code. This idea can even be generalized and is exactly the motivation of the following definition.

Definition 3.3: A code C is called s-systematic on k positions if on these k positions each possible k-vector occurs at least s times as the restriction of a codeword in C.

Theorem 3.4: Let C be an $(n,M)-t$EC/AUED code that is s-systematic on k coordinates and let $u = \lfloor \log_2 s \rfloor$. Then a well-chosen subset of the codewords of C can be extended to an $[n+u,k+u]-t$EC/AUED code, that is systematic on $k+u$ coordinates.

Proof: Select 2^u pairwise disjoint subsets of C, that are each systematic on the same k coordinates. By Definition 3.3 this can be done. Extend the words of each of the 2^u chosen subsets with different tails of length u. □

Example 3.5: Let P_{19} be the circulant (Paley matrix) with top row $\boldsymbol{p}_{19}$. The rows of P_{19} form a $(19,19)-4$EC/AUED code, which is 2-systematic on any three consecutive coordinates. By Theorem 3.4 we have a $[20,4]-4$EC/AUED code.

By extending P_{19} with ones and adding to the set of rows the complements of all these rows, one can in the same way obtain a $[21,5]-4$EC/AUED code. Also all rows in P_{19} beginning with a zero form a $(19,10)-4$EC/AUED code, in which every binary three-tuple occurs at least once at any given set of three consecutive coordinates. By puncturing the first coordinate and removing two appropriate words one can obtain a $[18,3]-4$EC/AUED code.

The set of 136 words of length 17, weight 8 and minimal distance 6, as described in [11] turns out to be 2-systematic at each five consecutive coordinates. By Theorem 3.4 an $[18,6]-2$EC/AUED code can be constructed.

The codewords of weight twelve in the extended binary Golay code form a $(24,2576)-3$EC/AUED code that is 16-systematic on six positions and 280-systematic on three positions [13, Theorem 26]. With Theorem 3.4 one can construct a $[28,10]-3$EC/AUED code and a

$[32,11]$–3EC/AUED code. The same procedure applied to the support vectors of the weight-six vectors in the extended ternary Golay code [13, Ch. 20, §1] yields a $[12,5]$–1EC/AUED code and a $[14,6]$–1EC/AUED code.

The Hadamard matrix of order 36 and its complement give rise to a $[35,4]$–8EC/AUED code, a $[36,5]$–8EC/AUED code and a $[38,6]$–8EC/AUED code.

Take the $[8,3]$–1EC/AUED code or the $[16,4]$–3EC/AUED code, described just after Example 3.2. Put 10 in front of every codeword and add to these words their complements. It is not difficult to check that in this way a $[10,4]$–1EC/AUED code and an $[18,5]$–3EC/AUED code are obtained. By deleting the last column in the $[18,5]$–3EC/AUED code one obtains a $[17,5]$–2EC/AUED code. The $[10,4]$–1EC/AUED code, previously found, is optimal by Theorem 2.13.

A last idea in this section will be the following.

Construction 3.6: Let C_1 be an $[n_1,k]$–t_1EC/AUED code and C_2 an (n_2,M)–t_2EC/AUED code with $M \geq 2^k$. Extend each codeword from C_1 with a unique codeword from C_2. In this way one obtains an $[n_1+n_2,k]$–(t_1+t_2+1)EC/AUED code.

If C_1 is 2-systematic on k coordinates and if C_2 has a coordinate on which the symbol 0 appears at least 2^k times and also the symbol 1 occurs at least 2^k times, even an $[n_1+n_2,k+1]$–(t_1+t_2+1)EC/AUED code can be obtained.

Example 3.7: Let C_1 be a 4EC/AUED code which is 2-systematic on three positions (see Example 3.5), obtained from P_{19}. Let C_2 be a code, obtained from the same P_{19} by selecting sixteen rows in such a way that some column has weight 8. Applying Construction 3.6 results in a $[38,4]$–9EC/AUED code, which is optimal by Theorem 2.5.

Applying Construction 3.6 to the union of all rows of P_{19}, extended with a one, together with all their complements yields in the same way a $[40,5]$–9EC/AUED code.

The next lemma and theorem shows that Construction 3.6 often gives rise to codes with parameters that are optimal or nearly optimal. For $k=2$ and $k=3$ one can always obtain optimal codes.

Lemma 3.8: Let C_1 be a $[2(2^k-1)s,k]$–$(2^{k-1}s-1)$EC/AUED code, $k \geq 2$, $s \geq 1$, and let C_2 be an $(n_2, \geq 2^k)$–t_2EC/AUED code, such that the bounds on n in Theorem 2.2 with $M = 2^k$ hold with equality. So

$$n_2 = 4t_2+4-\lfloor (t_2+1)/2^{k-2} \rfloor, \quad \text{if } t_2+1 \not\equiv 2^{k-2} \pmod{2^{k-1}}, \tag{19}$$

$$n_2 = 4t_2+5-\lfloor (t_2+1)/2^{k-2} \rfloor, \quad \text{if } t_2+1 \equiv 2^{k-2} \pmod{2^{k-1}}. \tag{20}$$

Then Construction 3.6 yields an optimal $[2(2^k-1)s + n_2, k]$–$(2^{k-1}s+t_2)$EC/AUED code.

Proof: This is a direct consequence of Construction 3.6 and the inequalities (10) and (11). □

Theorem 3.9: Optimal $[n,k]$–tEC/AUED codes with the following sets of parameters can be obtained from Lemma 3.8:

1) $k=2$ and $k=3$ for all t,
2) $k=4$ and all t, except possibly if $t=4$ or if $8|t$,
3) $k=5$ and $t \equiv 5$, 6, 7, 10, 14 or 15 mod 16.

Proof: For the proof we need the $[2(2^k-1),k]$–$(2^{k-1}-1)$EC/AUED code C, that will be described right after Construction 4.1 in the next section. Apply Construction 3.6 $s-1$ times recursively to C. In this way a $[2(2^k-1)s,k]$–$(2^{k-1}s-1)$EC/AUED code will be obtained. Lemma 3.8 implies that if for all t_2, $t_0 \leq t_2 \leq t_0 + 2^{k-1}-1$, $(n_2, \geq 2^k)$–t_2EC/AUED codes exist such that (10) or (11) holds with equality then optimal $[n,k]$–tEC/AUED codes exist for all t, $t \geq t_0$.

1) $k=2$ and $k=3$. It suffices to know the existence of $(n_2, \geq 2^k)$–t_2EC/AUED codes, that meet (10) or (11) with equality, for the parameter sets $(n_2,k,t_2)=(6,2,1)$ and $(10,2,2)$ in the $k=2$ case and for $(8,3,1)$, $(11,3,2)$, $(14,3,3)$ and $(18,3,4)$ in the $k=3$ case. These codes have been described before, except for the $(14,3,3)$ code, which will appear in Construction 4.1. That these codes satisfy (19) or (20) can easily be checked by hand.
2) $k=4$. This time we have codes satisfying (19) or (20) with $(n_2,k,t_2)=(12,4,2)$, $(16,4,3)$, $(23,4,5)$, $(27,4,6)$, $(30,4,7)$, and $(38,4,9)$. So 2) is proved for all t with $t \not\equiv 0 \pmod 4$. However by taking for C_1 the $[30,4]$–7EC/AUED code (Table III) and for C_2 sixteen rows of P_{19} we obtain an optimal $[49,4]$–12EC/AUED code and recursively also optimal codes with $k=4$ for all t, with $t \equiv 4 \pmod 8$ and $t \geq 12$.

TABLE III
$[n,k]$–tEC/AUED Codes Obtained by Construction 4.1

t/k	2	3	4	5	6	7	8	9	10	11	12	13	14	15
1	6	8	10	12	14	16								
2						22								
3					22	24								
4					28	30	32	34	38	40				
5					30	32	34	36	40	42	44	46	48	52

3) $k=5$. Now we have only the following optimal codes at our disposal: $(n_2, k, t_2) = (24, 5, 5)$, $(28, 5, 6)$, $(32, 5, 7)$, $(43, 5, 10)$, $(59, 5, 14)$, and $(62, 5, 15)$. Apply Construction 3.6 with the $[62,5]$–15EC/AUED code as C_1 described just below Construction 4.1. □

In the next two examples more codes will be constructed in the previous way, but their optimality is unclear.

Example 3.10: Let C_1 be a $[30,4]$–7EC/AUED code and let C_2 be the $[35,4]$–8EC/AUED code, that can be constructed from a $[16,4]$–3EC/AUED code and sixteen rows of P_{19}. In this way codes can be constructed with parameters $k=4$, $t=8l$ and $n=30l+5$.

Example 3.11: By taking a [24,5]–5EC/AUED code as C_1 as well as C_2 one obtains a [48,5]–11EC/AUED code. By taking a [28,5]–6EC/AUED code as C_1 and a [24,5]–5EC/AUED code as C_2 one obtains a [52,5]–12EC/AUED code. By taking a [28,5]–6EC/AUED code as C_1 as well as C_2 one obtains a [56,5]–13EC/AUED code.

In Table II all the values, obtained in this section, appear as upper bounds on $n[k,t]$. The values indexed with a prime come from Construction 4.1. The lower bounds on $n[k,t]$ come from (9), (10), (11), and Table I.

IV. Adding Tails to Linear Codes

In the literature the standard way of obtaining systematic EC/AUED codes has been to add a tail to each codeword of an $[n',k]$–tEC code C', in such a way that the new codewords form an $[n,k]$–tEC/AUED code C.

Construction 4.1: Let C' be a $[n',k]$EC code with minimum distance d'. Then the code C, obtained from C' by adding to each codeword its complement, is a $[2n',k]$–$(d'-1)$EC/AUED code.

Construction 4.1 follows from the fact that code C, constructed in that way, is a constant weight code with minimum distance $2d'$. Although it is hardly worthy of carrying the name "construction," Construction 4.1 does give rise to some nice classes of EC/AUED codes.

For instance the even weight $[n',n'-1,2]$ EC code C' yields a $[2n',n'-1]$–1EC/AUED code C, which for $k=2$, 3 and 4 is optimal. The $[2^k-1,k]$ Simplex code C' with minimum distance 2^{k-1}, results similarly in a $[2(2^k-1),k]$–$(2^{k-1}-1)$EC/AUED code C. The first order Reed–Muller codes yield $[2^k,k]$–$(2^{k-2}-1)$EC/AUED codes.

Construction 4.1 has been applied to existing linear $[n,k,d]$EC codes, as tabulated in [19]. In those cases that the resulting systematic $[2n,k]$–$(d-1)$EC/AUED code improves or equals earlier results we have listed the parameters in Table III.

In [1] it is observed, as one can easily check oneself, that if $\boldsymbol{x}$ and $\boldsymbol{y}$ are two codewords in a $[n',k,2t+1]$EC code, and $w(\boldsymbol{x})=i\le j=w(\boldsymbol{y})$, then

$$N(\boldsymbol{y},\boldsymbol{x})\ge t+1, \tag{21}$$

$$N(\boldsymbol{x},\boldsymbol{y})\ge \max\{0,t+1-\lceil (j-i)/2\rceil\}. \tag{22}$$

So in [1] it is proposed to add a tail $\boldsymbol{t}_c$ of length $n-n'$ to each codeword $\boldsymbol{c}$ of an $[n',k,2t+1]$EC code C', in such a way that the resulting code C is an $[n,k]$–tEC/AUED code. It is quite natural (but a restriction of the generality) to give codewords of the same weight, say i, also the same tail, which we shall denote by $\boldsymbol{t}_i$.

Lemma 4.2: Let C be the code obtained from an $[n',k,2t+1]$EC code C' by adding a tail $\boldsymbol{t}_i$ to each codeword of weight i, $0\le i\le n'$. Then C is an $[n,k]$–tEC/AUED code if for every two codewords $\boldsymbol{c}$ and $\boldsymbol{d}$ in C' of weight i resp. j with $i\le j$ one has

$$\begin{aligned}N(\boldsymbol{t}_i,\boldsymbol{t}_j)&\ge t+1-\max\{0,t+1-\lceil (j-i)/2\rceil\}\\ &=\min\{t+1,\lceil (j-i)/2\rceil\}.\end{aligned} \tag{23}$$

Proof: This is a direct consequence of (3), (21), and (22). □

The matrix with $\boldsymbol{t}_i$ as the ith row is called a descending tail matrix in [1] and the extension technique, previously described, gives rise to many codes [1]. What we will do here is slightly different. We first extend the $[n',k,2t+1]$EC code C' with an overall parity check equation to an $[n'',k,2t+2]$EC code C'' and then add tails to the various codewords. Because only even weights occur in C'' it is sufficient if the tails satisfy

$$N(\boldsymbol{T}_i,\boldsymbol{T}_j)\ge \min\{t+1,j-i\}, \tag{24}$$

for $i\le j$, where T_i now is the tail attached to the words of weight $2i$.

We shall present now a number of so called *descending tail matrices* $T'(L,u,t)$ of this second type, that have size $L\times u$, of which the first row will be the tail of the all-zero codeword in C'', the second row the tail of all codewords of weight $2t+2$ in C'', the third row will be the tail of all codewords of weight $2t+4$, etc. So the last row will be the tail of the words of weight $2t+2L-2$. So n' should satisfy $2\lfloor (n'+1)/2\rfloor\le 2t+2L-2$. This explains the value of $n'_{\max}$ that is listed in the subsequent tables. Note that u will be equal to $n-n''$.

Descending Tail Matrix 4.3: For $u=2t+2+s$ with $t\ge 2s$, $s\ge 0$, one gets $n'_{\max}=6t+6+4s$ with the following descending tail matrix $T'(L,u,t)$:

w					$\underline{T}_w$					
	←	t+1		→	←	s	→	←	t+1	→
0	1	1	⋯	1	1	⋯	1	1	⋯	⋯	1
2t+2	0	0	⋯	0	1	⋯	⋯	⋯	⋯	⋯	1
2t+4	1	0			⋱	⋱					⋮
⋮	⋮	⋱	⋱			⋱	⋱				⋮
⋮	⋮		⋱	⋱			⋱	⋱			⋮
⋮	⋮			⋱	⋱			⋱	⋱		⋮
⋮	⋮				⋱	⋱			⋱	⋱	⋮
⋮	⋮					⋱	⋱			0	1
4t+4+2s	1	⋯	⋯	⋯	⋯	⋯	1	0	⋯	0	0
4t+6+2s	0	1	⋯	⋯	⋯	⋯	1	0	⋯	⋯	0
⋮	⋮	⋱	⋱				⋮	⋮			⋮
⋮	⋮		⋱	⋱			⋮	⋮			⋮
⋮	⋮			⋱	⋱		⋮	⋮			⋮
⋮	⋮				⋱	⋱	⋮	⋮			⋮
6t+4+4s	0					0	1	0	⋯	⋯	0
6t+6+4s	0	⋯	⋯	⋯	⋯	⋯	0	0	⋯	⋯	0

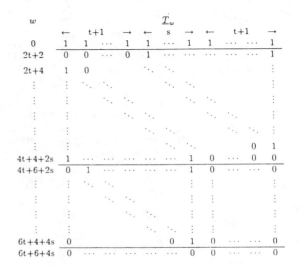

Example 4.4: $u = 4$, $t = 1$, $s = 0$: $n'_{\max} = 12$ with $T'(6, 4, 1)$ given by

w	T_w
0	1111
4	0011
6	1001
8	1100
10	0100
12	0000

.

The descending tail matrices that now follow for $u = 2t + 2 + s$ with $t < 2s$ all are found by ad hoc methods.

Descending Tail Matrix 4.5: $u = 5$, $t = 1$: $n'_{\max} = 18$ with $T'(9, 5, 1)$ given by

w	T_w
0	11111
4	00111
6	10011
8	11001
10	11100
12	10100
14	01010
16	00001
18	00000

.

Descending Tail Matrix 4.6: $u = 2t + 4$, $t = 1, 2, 3$.

w	T_w	w	T_w	w	T_w
0	111111	0	11111111	0	1111111111
4	001111	6	00011111	8	0000111111
6	100111	8	10001111	10	1000011111
8	110011	10	11000111	12	1100001111
10	111001	12	11100011	14	1110000111
12	111100	14	11110001	16	1111000011
14	101010	16	11111000	18	1111100001
16	011010	18	01111000	20	1111110000
18	010110	20	01001001	22	0111110000
20	010101	22	00101001	24	0011110000
22	110000	24	00100101	26	0011011000
24	100100	26	10100100	28	0011001100
26	001100	28	10010100	30	0010001100
28	001001	30	10010010	32	0000001100
30	000011	32	00010010	34	0000000100
32	000010	34	00000010	36	0000000000
34	000000	36	00000000		

$t = 1$, $n'_{\max} = 34$; $t = 2$, $n'_{\max} = 36$; $t = 3$, $n'_{\max} = 36$

Descending Tail Matrix 4.7: $u = 2t + 5$, $t = 1, 2, 3, 4, 5$.

w	T_w	w	T_w	w	T_w	w	T_w	w	T_w
0	1111111	0	111111111	0	11111111111	0	1111111111111	0	111111111111111
4	0011111	6	000111111	8	00001111111	10	0000011111111	12	000000111111111
6	1001111	8	100011111	10	10000111111	12	1000001111111	14	100000011111111
8	1100111	10	110001111	12	11000011111	14	1100000111111	16	110000001111111
10	1110011	12	111000111	14	11100001111	16	1110000011111	18	111000000111111
12	1111001	14	111100011	16	11110000111	18	1111000001111	20	111100000011111
14	1111100	16	111110001	18	11111000011	20	1111100000111	22	111110000001111
16	1010101	18	111111000	20	11111100001	22	1111110000011	24	111111000000111
18	0110101	20	011111000	22	11111110000	24	1111111000001	26	111111100000011
20	0101101	22	011011100	24	01111110000	26	1111111100000	28	111111110000001
22	0101011	24	011001100	26	01110111000	28	1111011100000	30	111111111000000
24	1101010	26	101001100	28	01010111000	30	0111011100000	32	111011111000000
26	1011010	28	101100100	30	01010101010	32	0011101110000	34	110011111000000
28	1110000	30	100100110	32	10011001100	34	0011100111000	36	100011111000000
30	0111000	32	100110010	34	00011001100	36	0011100011000	38	001110011100000
32	0011100	34	110010010	36	00011000110	38	0010110011000	40	000111001110000
34	0001110	36	010010011	38	10001010001	40	1000110011000	42	000111000111000
36	0000111	38	010010001	40	00100010011	42	1000110001100	44	000101000111000
38	1000011	40	000011001	42	10100100000	44	1000110000100	46	000101000011000
40	1001001	42	000101001	44	10100000000	46	1000010000100	48	000100000011000
42	1001000	44	000101000	46	01000000000	48	1000000000100	50	000000000011000
44	1000100	46	000100000	48	00000000000	50	0000000000100	52	000000000001000
46	0100100	48	000000000			52	0000000000000	54	000000000000000
48	0100010								
50	0010010								
52	0010001								
54	0000001								
56	0000000								

$t = 1$, $n'_{\max} = 56$; $t = 2$, $n'_{\max} = 48$; $t = 3$, $n'_{\max} = 48$; $t = 4$, $n'_{\max} = 52$; $t = 5$, $n'_{\max} = 54$

Descending Tail Matrix 4.8: $u = 2t + 6$, $t = 1, 2$.

w	T_w	w	T_w	w	T_w	w	T_w
0	11111111	0	1111111111	46	00111100	48	1100110000
4	00111111	6	0001111111	48	01100110	50	0010110001
6	10011111	8	1000111111	50	00110011	52	0000111001
8	11001111	10	1100011111	52	10011001	54	0010001101
10	11100111	12	1110001111	54	10010010	56	0100001011
12	11110011	14	1111000111	56	01010010	58	0100000011
14	11111001	16	1111100011	58	01001010	60	1000000011
16	11111100	18	1111110001	60	01001001	62	0000010110
18	11101100	20	1111111000	62	00101001	64	0000010100
20	10101101	22	0111111000	64	00100101	66	0001000000
22	10110101	24	0111101100	66	10100100	68	0000000000
24	10110110	26	0110110110	68	11000000		
26	11010110	28	0110100110	70	01100000		
28	11011010	30	1010100110	72	00110000		
30	01011011	32	1010101010	74	00011000		
32	01101011	34	1010011010	76	00001100		
34	00001111	36	1001011010	78	00000110		
36	10000111	38	1001011100	80	00000011		
38	11000011	40	1001010101	82	00000001		
40	11100001	42	0101010101	84	00000000		
42	11110000	44	1111000000		$t = 1$		$t = 2$
44	01111000	46	1101100000		$n'_{\max} = 84$		$n'_{\max} = 68$

With descending tail matrices 4.3, 4.5–4.8 one can find systematic $[n, k]$–tEC/AUED codes that are often better than those in [1], as the following examples may make clear.

Example 4.9 $t = 1$, $k = 8$: The shortest $[n', k, 2t + 1]$EC code with these parameters is a $[12, 8, 3]$EC code. Extending this code yields a $[13, 8, 4]$EC code. The descending tail matrix with four columns of Example 4.4 can be used to obtain a $[17, 8]$–1EC/AUED code. This code has redundancy 9 instead of 10, as the best $[n, 8]$–1EC/AUED code in [1] does.

Example 4.10 $t = 6$, $k = 16–19$: In the range of $k =$ 16–19 we know from [19] that $[n', k, 2t + 1]$EC codes exist with redundancy 31. Extending these codes yields $[k + 32, k, 14]$EC codes. Descending tail matrix 4.3 (with $s = 2$) has 16 columns and sufficient rows. In this way one obtains $[n, k]$–tEC/AUED codes with $t = 6$, k in the range 16–19 and $n = k + 48$, so n in the range 64–67.

TABLE IV
UPPER AND LOWER BOUNDS ON $r = n - k$ FOR $[n, k]$–tEC/AUED CODES

$t = 1$		$t = 2$		$t = 3$		$t = 4$		$t = 5$	
k-range	r	k-range	r	k-range	r	k-range	r	k-range	r
4	6	4	8	4	12	4–5	15–16	4–5	19
5	6–7	5–6	9–12	5	12–13	6	15–22	6	19–24
6	6–8	7–9	9–15	6	12–16	7	15–23	7	19–25
7–8	6–9	10–13	10–17	7–9	12–17	8	15–24	8	19–26
9–11	7–10	14	11–18	10	13–18	9	16–25	9	19–27
12–13	7–11	15–18	11–19	11–12	13–20	10	16–28	10	19–30
15–20	8–12	19–22	12–19	13	13–23	11	16–29	11	20–31
21–26	9–12	23–25	12–20	14	14–23	12	17–29	12	20–32
27–28	9–13	26	12–21	15–16	14–25	13–15	17–31	13	20–33
29–30	9–14	27–30	13–21	17–20	14–26	16	17–33	14	20–35
31–43	10–14	31–35	13–22	21–24	15–28	17–18	18–33	15–17	21–37
44–50	11–14	36	14–22	25–30	16–28	19–21	18–34	18–19	21–38
51–57	11–15	37–44	14–23	31	17–28	22–23	18–35	20–21	22–38
58–62	11–16	45–53	15–23	32–33	17–29	24	19–35	22–24	22–39
63–77	12–16	54–55	15–24			25	19–36	25–27	22–43
						26–28	19–37		
						29	20–37		

In Table IV a number of lower and upper bounds on $r = n - k$ are listed for $[n, k]$–tEC/AUED codes. The upper bounds come from Construction 4.1 (see also Table III) and from descending tail matrices 4.3, 4.5–4.8. The lower bounds come from Table I.

References

[1] M. Blaum and H. C. A. van Tilborg, "On t-error correcting/all unidirectional error detecting codes," *IEEE Trans. Comput.*, vol. C-38, pp. 1493–1501, Nov. 1989.

[2] F. J. H. Böinck, "On t-error correcting and all unidirectional error detecting codes," M.S. thesis, Dept. of Math. and Comput. Sci., Eindhoven Univ. of Technology, Eindhoven, The Netherlands, 1988.

[3] B. Bose, "On systematic SEC/MUED code," *Proc. FTCS*, vol. 11, June 1981, pp. 265–267.

[4] B. Bose and T. R. N. Rao, "Theory of unidirectional error correcting/detecting codes," *IEEE Trans. Comput.*, vol. C-31, pp. 521–530, June 1982.

[5] B. Bose and D. K. Pradhan, "Optimal unidirectional error detecting/correcting codes," *IEEE Trans. Comput.*, vol. C-31, pp. 564–568, June 1982.

[6] J. Bruck and M. Blaum, "Some new EC/AUED codes," *Proc. Nineteenth Int. Symp. Fault-Tolerant Comput.*, Chicago, IL, 1989, pp. 208–215.

[7] ——, "New techniques for constructing EC/AUED codes," IBM Research Report, RJ 6818 (65352), May 1989.

[8] L. Chen, "A note on systematic tEC-MUED code," *Chinese J. Comput.*, vol. 7, pp. 306–312, 1984.

[9] P. Delsarte and P. Piret, "Bounds and constructions for binary asymmetric error correcting codes," *IEEE Trans. Inform. Theory*, vol. IT-27, pp. 125–128, Jan. 1981.

[10] R. L. Graham and N. J. A. Sloane, "Lower bounds for constant weight codes," *IEEE Trans. Inform. Theory*, vol. IT-26, pp. 37–43, Jan. 1980.

[11] R. E. Kibler, "Some new constant weight codes," *IEEE Trans. Inform. Theory*, vol. IT-26, pp. 364–365, May 1980.

[12] D. E. Knuth, "Efficient balanced codes," *IEEE Trans. Inform. Theory*, vol. IT-32, pp. 51–53, Jan. 1986.

[13] F. J. MacWilliams and N. J. A. Sloane, *The Theory of Error-Correcting Codes*. Amsterdam: North Holland, 1977.

[14] D. Nikolos, N. Gaitanis, and G. Philokyprou, "t-error correcting all unidirectional error detecting codes starting from cyclic AN codes," in *Proc. 1984 Int. Conf. Fault-Tolerant Comput.*, Kissimmee, FL, pp. 318–323.

[15] ——, "Systematic t-error correcting/all unidirectional error detecting codes," *IEEE Trans. Comput.*, vol. C-35, pp. 394–402, May 1986.

[16] D. K. Pradhan, "A new class of error-correcting/detecting codes for fault-tolerant computer application," *IEEE Trans. Comput.*, vol. C-29, pp. 471–481, June 1980.

[17] C. L. M. Pul, "On bounds on codes," M.S. thesis, Dept. Math. Comput. Sci., Eindhoven Univ. of Technol., Eindhoven, The Netherlands, 1982.

[18] E. Sperner, "Ein Satz über Untermengen einer endlichen Menge," *Math. Zeitschrift*, vol. 27, pp. 544–548, 1928.

[19] T. Verhoeff, "An updated table of minimum distance bounds for binary linear codes," *IEEE Trans. Inform. Theory*, vol. IT-33, pp. 665–680, Sept. 1987.

[20] J. H. Weber, C. de Vroedt, and D. E. Boekee, "Bounds and constructions for binary codes of length less than 24 and asymmetric distance less than 6," *IEEE Trans. Inform. Theory*, vol. IT-34, pp. 1321–1331, Sept. 1988.

New Techniques for Constructing EC/AUED Codes

Jehoshua Bruck and Mario Blaum

***Abstract*—The most common method to construct a *t*-error correcting/all unidirectional error detecting (EC/AUED) code is to choose a *t*-error correcting (EC) code and then to append a tail in such a way that the new code can detect more than *t* errors when they are unidirectional. The tail is a function of the weight of the codeword.**

We present two new techniques for constructing *t*-EC/AUED codes. The first technique modifies the *t*-EC code in such a way that the weight distribution of the original code is reduced. So, a smaller tail is needed. Frequently, this technique gives less overall redundancy than the best available *t*-EC/AUED codes.

The second technique improves the parameters of the tails with respect to previous results.

***Index Terms*—Coset, decoding, descending tail matrix, encoding, error-correcting codes, redundancy, unidirectional errors, unidirectional error detecting codes.**

I. Introduction

The problem of finding error correcting/all unidirectional error detecting codes (EC/AUED) has received wide attention in recent literature [1]–[10]. The reader can find good discussions about the practical applications of EC/AUED codes in most of the references cited above.

In this paper, we concentrate on the mathematical aspects of the codes. Given two binary vectors $\boldsymbol{u}$ and $\boldsymbol{v}$ of length n, denote by $N(\boldsymbol{u},\boldsymbol{v})$ the number of $1 \rightarrow 0$ transitions from $\boldsymbol{u}$ to $\boldsymbol{v}$. (For example, if $\boldsymbol{u} = 10101$ and $\boldsymbol{v} = 00011$, then $N(\boldsymbol{u},\boldsymbol{v}) = 2$ and $N(\boldsymbol{v},\boldsymbol{u}) = 1$). Clearly, $d_H(\boldsymbol{u},\boldsymbol{v}) = N(\boldsymbol{u},\boldsymbol{v}) + N(\boldsymbol{v},\boldsymbol{u})$, where d_H denotes Hamming distance.

We say that $\boldsymbol{u}$ is contained in $\boldsymbol{v}$ ($\boldsymbol{u} \subseteq \boldsymbol{v}$) if $N(\boldsymbol{u},\boldsymbol{v}) = 0$.

Assume that $\boldsymbol{u}$ is transmitted but $\hat{\boldsymbol{u}}$ is received. We say that $\boldsymbol{u}$ has suffered unidirectional errors if either $\boldsymbol{u} \subseteq \hat{\boldsymbol{u}}$ or $\hat{\boldsymbol{u}} \subseteq \boldsymbol{u}$.

We are interested in codes that can correct up to t errors and detect all unidirectional errors when the number of unidirectional errors is greater than t. In other words, when more than t errors occur and those errors are unidirectional, we do not want the received word to fall into a sphere of radius t whose center is a codeword. The next theorem [4], [5] gives necessary and sufficient conditions for a code to be t-EC/AUED.

Theorem 1.1: Let C be a subset of $\{0,1\}^n$. Then C is a t-EC/AUED code if and only if, for any pair of vectors $\boldsymbol{u} \in C$ and $\boldsymbol{v} \in C$, $N(\boldsymbol{u},\boldsymbol{v}) \geq t+1$ and $N(\boldsymbol{v},\boldsymbol{u}) \geq t+1$.

Given k information bits, the way most authors construct a t-EC/AUED code C of length n is as follows: first the information bits are encoded into a t-EC (error-correcting) code C' of length n', with n' as small as possible. Usually but not necessarily, this code is systematic. Choosing a good $[n', k, 2t+1]$ code is not a problem. There is a vast literature on the subject. For instance, we can use the tables in [11] to choose, given k and t, the best k-dimensional t-EC code known.

Manuscript received May 15, 1989; revised July 10, 1990.
The authors are with IBM Research Division, Almaden Research Center, San Jose, CA 95120.
IEEE Log Number 9103101.

The second step involves adding a tail of length r as further redundancy. The length of the code is then $n = n' + r$, and the total redundancy is $n' - k + r$. The tail is a function of the weight of the vector. The goal is to obtain a tail with r as small as possible.

For the sake of completeness, we give a general construction for t-EC/AUED codes. We need a definition first. We denote by $\lceil x \rceil$ ($\lfloor x \rfloor$) the smallest (largest) integer j such that $j \geq x$ ($j \leq x$).

Definition 1.1: A descending tail matrix of strength s is an $m \times r$ $\{0,1\}$-matrix with rows $\boldsymbol{t}_i$, $0 \leq i \leq m-1$, such that for all $0 \leq i \leq j \leq m-1$,

$$N(\boldsymbol{t}_i, \boldsymbol{t}_j) \geq \min\{s, \lceil (j-i)/2 \rceil\}.$$

An $m \times r$ matrix of strength s is denoted $T(m, r; s)$.

Construction 1.1: Let C' be a t-EC of length n' and let T be a $T(n'+1, r; t+1)$ descending tail matrix with rows $\boldsymbol{t}_0, \boldsymbol{t}_1, \cdots, \boldsymbol{t}_{n'}$. Let C be the following code of length $n' + r$:

$$C = \{(\boldsymbol{v}, \boldsymbol{t}_{w(\boldsymbol{v})}) : v \in C'\}$$

where $w(\boldsymbol{v})$ denotes the Hamming weight of $\boldsymbol{v}$. Then C is a t-EC/AUED code.

Proving that C is a t-EC/AUED is relatively easy using Theorem 1.1 [1].

Some of the best descending tail matrices are given in [1]. As said before, the goal is to make r as small as possible. The construction in [1] heavily depends on the best asymmetric error-correcting codes available.

In this paper, we propose two different techniques to reduce the redundancy of t-EC/AUED codes. The two methods can be used together. The first one involves using t-EC codes that contain the all-1 vector (for instance, BCH codes and the Golay code have this property). When choosing a codeword, we take either a codeword or its complement, according to which of the two has smaller weight. We have to pay a bit for this operation, but the weight distribution is reduced by half. We then append a tail in the way described by Construction 1.1. Overall, we will often gain in redundancy.

The construction will be described in detail in Section II. We then discuss the problems of encoding and decoding in Section III. Although the new codes are not strictly systematic, they are very close to being so. We will see that encoding and decoding are nearly as simple as in the systematic case. In Section IV, we provide tables and examples.

Section V can be read independently of the rest of the paper. There, we provide some techniques to improve upon the tail matrices given in [1].

II. Construction

As stated in the Introduction, the construction in [1] depends on a tail that is appended to each codeword in a t-EC code. This tail is a function of the weight of the codeword and it is obtained from a descending tail matrix of strength s (Definition 1.1). Table I gives a list of parameters for the descending tail matrices obtained in [1].

The next construction is the main result in this seciton. It can be viewed as a modification of Construction 1.1.

0-8186-4182-7/93 $3.00 © 1992 IEEE

TABLE I
PARAMETERS OF SOME DESCENDING TAIL MATRICES $T(m, r; t+1)$

t	r	m	t	r	m	t	r	m	t	r	m
1	2	4	2	3	6	3	4	8	4	5	10
1	3	6	2	4	8	3	5	10	4	6	12
1	4	8	2	5	10	3	6	12	4	7	14
1	5	12	2	6	12	3	7	14	4	8	16
1	6	16	2	7	16	3	8	16	4	9	18
1	7	24	2	8	20	3	9	20	4	10	20
1	8	48	2	9	24	3	10	24	4	11	24
1	9	72	2	10	32	3	11	28	4	12	28
1	10	144	2	11	48	3	12	32	4	13	32
1	11	248	2	12	72	3	13	40	4	14	36
1	12	432	2	13	120	3	14	48	4	15	40
			2	14	216	3	15	72	4	16	48
			2	15	392	3	16	120	4	17	56
						3	17	180	4	18	72
						3	18	264	4	19	104
						3	19	488	4	20	156
									4	21	216
									4	22	288

Construction 2.1: Let k be the number of information bits. Assume that we want to construct a t-EC/AUED code. Then:

1) Choose an $[n', k+1, d]$ EC code ($d \geq 2t+1$) C' containing the all-1 vector with n' as small as possible.
2) Choose a $T(\lfloor n'/2 \rfloor + 1, r; t+1)$ descending tail matrix T with rows $\boldsymbol{t}_i$, $0 \leq i \leq \lfloor n'/2 \rfloor$ and r as small as possible.
3) Let C be the code

$$C = \{(\boldsymbol{c}, \boldsymbol{t}_{w(\boldsymbol{c})}) : \boldsymbol{c} \in C', w(\boldsymbol{c}) \leq n'/2\}.$$

The code C obtained in the previous construction is t-EC/AUED since the subset of codewords of weight $\leq \lfloor n/2 \rfloor$ is still a t-EC code. According to Construction 1.1, the tail makes it t-EC/AUED.

Example 2.1: Assume $k = 3$ and $t = 1$. According to Construction 2.1, we consider the [7, 4, 3] Hamming code whose generator matrix is

$$G = \begin{pmatrix} 1 & 0 & 0 & 0 & 0 & 1 & 1 \\ 0 & 1 & 0 & 0 & 1 & 0 & 1 \\ 0 & 0 & 1 & 0 & 1 & 1 & 0 \\ 0 & 0 & 0 & 1 & 1 & 1 & 1 \end{pmatrix}.$$

We easily see that the codewords of weight ≤ 3 are

$$c_0 = 0000000$$
$$c_1 = 1000011$$
$$c_2 = 0100101$$
$$c_3 = 0010110$$
$$c_4 = 1001100$$
$$c_5 = 0101010$$
$$c_6 = 0011001$$
$$c_7 = 1110000.$$

According to [1], we can use the $T(4, 2; 2)$ matrix

$$T = \begin{pmatrix} 1 & 1 \\ 1 & 0 \\ 0 & 1 \\ 0 & 0 \end{pmatrix}.$$

The code is then given by the following set of codewords:

$$\boldsymbol{v}_0 = 0000000 \quad 11$$
$$\boldsymbol{v}_1 = 1000011 \quad 00$$
$$\boldsymbol{v}_2 = 0100101 \quad 00$$
$$\boldsymbol{v}_3 = 0010110 \quad 00$$
$$\boldsymbol{v}_4 = 1001100 \quad 00$$
$$\boldsymbol{v}_5 = 0101010 \quad 00$$
$$\boldsymbol{v}_6 = 0011001 \quad 00$$
$$\boldsymbol{v}_7 = 1110000 \quad 00.$$

Notice that we have 3 information bits and 6 redundant bits. If we use the construction in [1], we need 7 redundant bits.

Sometimes, taking a coset instead of the code itself may be convenient to reduce the span of the weight distribution.

III. ENCODING AND DECODING

In the previous section we described a t-EC/AUED code but we did not explain how to encode the data. This is very easily done, as we will see.

Assume we want to encode k bits into a t-EC/AUED code C. Choose an $[n', k+1, 2t+1]$ code C' containing the all-1 vector (with n' as small as possible) and a $T(\lfloor n'/2 \rfloor + 1, r, t+1)$ descending tail matrix T (with r as small as possible). The symbol $\oplus$ denotes "exclusive-OR" and 1 denotes the all-1 vector. Then proceed as follows:

Algorithm 3.1 (Encoding Algorithm) Let $\boldsymbol{u} = (u_1, u_2, \cdots, u_k)$ be the vector of information bits. Then:

1) Encode $(\boldsymbol{u}, 0) = (u_1, u_2, \cdots, u_k, 0)$ into a vector $\boldsymbol{c}$ in C'.
2) If $w(\boldsymbol{c}) > \lfloor n'/2 \rfloor$ then $\boldsymbol{c} \leftarrow \boldsymbol{c} \oplus 1$.
3) Let $\boldsymbol{v} = (\boldsymbol{c}, t_{w(\boldsymbol{c})})$ be the output of the encoder, where $\boldsymbol{t}_i$, $0 \leq i \leq \lfloor n'/2 \rfloor$, are the rows of T.

Observe that code C' is not required to be systematic. However, if that is the case, the t–EC/AUED code C will be practically systematic, in the sense that the first k bits in codeword $\boldsymbol{v}$ will either be the information bits or their complements.

Example 3.1: Consider code C in Example 2.1. Assume that we want to encode $\boldsymbol{v} = 010$. The first step is to encode $(\boldsymbol{v}, 0) = 0100$ into the [7, 4] Hamming code. This gives $\boldsymbol{c} = 0100101$. Since $w(\boldsymbol{c}) = 3$, $\boldsymbol{t}_{w(\boldsymbol{c})} = 00$. The encoded vector is then $\boldsymbol{v} = (\boldsymbol{c}, \boldsymbol{t}_3) = 010010100$.

Similarly, assume that we want to encode $\boldsymbol{u} = 110$. The encoding of $(\boldsymbol{u}, 0) = 1100$ into C' gives $\boldsymbol{c} = 1100110$. Since $w(\boldsymbol{c}) = 4 > 3 = \lfloor n'/2 \rfloor$, then $\boldsymbol{c} = 1111111 \oplus 1100110 = 0011001$. As before, the encoded vector is $\boldsymbol{v} = (\boldsymbol{c}, \boldsymbol{t}_3) = 001100100$.

The decoding is also very simple. Essentially, it works as in [1], with the extra step of taking complements when necessary.

Algorithm 3.2 (Decoding Algorithm) Let C be the EC/AUED obtained from Construction 2.1. Let $\hat{\boldsymbol{v}}$ be the received word and $\hat{\boldsymbol{c}}$ the first n' bits of $\hat{\boldsymbol{v}}$. Then:

1) Decode $\hat{\boldsymbol{c}}$ with respect to C'. If more than t errors, declare an uncorrectable error. Else let $\boldsymbol{c}$ be the corrected word.
2) Let $\boldsymbol{v} = (\boldsymbol{c}, \boldsymbol{t}_{w(\boldsymbol{c})})$. If $d_H(\hat{\boldsymbol{v}}, \boldsymbol{v}) > t$ (d_H denotes Hamming distance), then declare an uncorrectable error.
3) Else, let $u_1, u_2, \cdots, u_{k+1}$ be the $k+1$ information bits from codeword $\boldsymbol{c} \in C'$. Then, the output of the decoder is given by the vector of length k

$$\boldsymbol{u} = (u_1 \oplus u_{k+1}, u_2 \oplus u_{k+1}, \cdots, u_k \oplus u_{k+1}).$$

TABLE II
PARAMETERS OF SOME 1-EC/AUED CODES

k	n'	$\lfloor n'/2 \rfloor$	r	$n-k$	$n-k$ from [1]	EC-Code
3	7	3	2	6	7	Hamming
10	15	7	4	9	10	Hamming
22	28	14	6	12	13	Hamming_s
25	31	15	6	12	13	Hamming
87	95	47	8	16	17	Hamming_s
246	255	127	10	19	20	Hamming
277	287	143	10	20	21	Hamming_s

TABLE III
PARAMETERS OF SOME 2-EC/AUED CODES

k	n'	$\lfloor n'/2 \rfloor$	r	$n-k$	$n-k$ from [1]	EC-Code
6	15	7	4	13	15	BCH
15	26	13	7	18	20	BCH_s
20	31	15	7	18	20	BCH
45	58	29	10	23	24	BCH_s
50	63	31	10	23	24	BCH
107	122	61	12	27	28	BCH_s
112	127	63	12	27	28	BCH
222	239	119	13	30	31	BCH_s

Example 3.2: Again consider the code of Examples 2.1 and 3.1.

1) Assume we receive $\hat{\boldsymbol{v}} = 100101110$. According to the Decoding Algorithm, we first consider $\hat{c} = 1001011$. The parity check matrix of C' is
$$H = \begin{pmatrix} 0 & 1 & 1 & 1 & 1 & 0 & 0 \\ 1 & 0 & 1 & 1 & 0 & 1 & 0 \\ 1 & 1 & 0 & 1 & 0 & 0 & 1 \end{pmatrix}.$$
So, we obtain the syndrome $\boldsymbol{s} = \hat{c}H^T = 111$ which corresponds to the fourth column of H, hence $\hat{c}$ is decoded as $\boldsymbol{c} = 1000011$. Now, $\boldsymbol{v} = (\boldsymbol{c}, \boldsymbol{t}_{w(\boldsymbol{c})}) = 100001100$, hence $d_H(\hat{\boldsymbol{v}}, \boldsymbol{v}) = 2 > 1 = t$. Thus, the decoder declares an uncorrectable error.
2) Assume we receive $\hat{\boldsymbol{v}} = 011011000$. As before, $\hat{c} = 0110110$, and $\boldsymbol{s} = \hat{c}H^T = 101$, which corresponds to the second column of H. Hence, $\hat{c}$ is decoded as $\boldsymbol{c} = 0010110$. So, $\boldsymbol{v} = (\boldsymbol{c}, \boldsymbol{t}_{w(\boldsymbol{c})}) = 001011000$ and $d_H(\hat{\boldsymbol{c}}, \boldsymbol{c}) = 1$. Since $u_4 = 0$, the output of the decoder is $\boldsymbol{u} = 001$.
3) Assume we receive $\hat{\boldsymbol{v}} = 001110100$. Now $\hat{c} = 0011101$, and $\boldsymbol{s} = \hat{c}H^T = 100$, which corresponds to the fifth column of H. Hence $\hat{c}$ is decoded as $\boldsymbol{c} = 0011001$. So, $\boldsymbol{v} = (\boldsymbol{c}, \boldsymbol{t}_{w(\boldsymbol{c})}) = 001100100$ and $d_H(\hat{\boldsymbol{c}}, \boldsymbol{c}) = 1$. Since $u_4 = 1$, the output of the decoder is $\boldsymbol{u} = 001 \oplus 111 = 110$.

IV. TABLES AND COMPARISONS

We have seen in Example 2.1 that we gained one bit with our construction with respect to [1]. In this section, we show that this is not an isolated case.

As stated in Section II, Table I contains the parameters of some descending tail matrices $T(m, r; t+1)$ obtained from [1].

Construction 2.1 ties the results from [1] in most cases, but quite often it also improves them, as shown in Tables II–V.

The tables have seven columns. The first column contains the number of information bits k. The second column gives the length n' of the EC-code. Column 3 contains $\lfloor n'/2 \rfloor$. Column 4 gives the number of extra bits r that we have to add to the EC-code in order

TABLE IV
PARAMETERS OF SOME 3-EC/AUED CODES

k	n'	$\lfloor n'/2 \rfloor$	r	$n-k$	$n-k$ from [1]	EC-Code
4	15	7	4	15	18	BCH
11	23	11	6	18	21	Golay
15	31	15	8	24	26	BCH
37	56	28	12	31	32	BCH_s
44	63	31	12	31	32	BCH
105	127	63	15	37	38	BCH
214	239	119	16	41	42	BCH_s
483	511	255	18	46	47	BCH

TABLE V
PARAMETERS OF SOME 4-EC/AUED CODES

k	n'	$\lfloor n'/2 \rfloor$	r	$n-k$	$n-k$ from [1]	EC-Code
38	63	31	13	38	42	BCH
98	127	63	18	47	48	BCH
222	255	127	20	53	54	BCH

to obtain a t-EC/AUED code (Construction 2.1). Column 5 gives the total redundancy $n - k = n' - k + r$ used in the Construction. Column 6 gives the total redundancy obtained using the codes in [1]. Finally, column 7 indicates the EC-code used (containing the all-1 vector). The subscript "s" indicates a shortened code.

Notice that we use only BCH codes and the Golay code, which are easy to decode, while in [1] the best codes of [11] have been chosen. Sometimes no efficient decoder is known for the best possible code.

In order to shorten a code containing the all-1 vector in such a way that the shortened code also contains the all-1 vector, we use the following lemma.

Lemma 4.1: Let $\mathcal{C}$ be an $[n, k, d]$ EC code with parity-check matrix H. Assume that the all-1 vector is in $\mathcal{C}$. Let $\boldsymbol{c}$ be a codeword in $\mathcal{C}$ such that its nonzero components are $i_1, i_2, \cdots, i_w$, $1 \le i_1 < i_2 < \cdots < i_w \le n$. Let $\tilde{H}$ be the matrix obtained by deleting columns $i_1, i_2, \cdots, i_2$ from H. Let $\tilde{\mathcal{C}}$ be the $[n-w, k-w, d]$ code whose parity check matrix is $\tilde{H}$. Then the all-1 vector is in $\tilde{\mathcal{C}}$.

Proof: The all-1 vector is in $\tilde{\mathcal{C}}$ if and only if the sum (modulo 2) of all the columns in $\tilde{H}$ gives the zero column.

Since the all-1 vector $\mathbf{1}$ is in $\mathcal{C}$, then $\mathbf{1} \oplus \boldsymbol{c}$ is also in $\mathcal{C}$. This vector has zero components $i_1, i_2, \cdots, i_w$. Summing the columns corresponding to the nonzero components, we obtain the zero column. But these columns correspond to the columns in $\tilde{H}$. □

Example 4.1: Consider the [7, 4] Hamming code of Example 2.1. Take codeword $\boldsymbol{c} = 1110000$. In order to obtain matrix $\tilde{H}$ according to Lemma 4.1, we have to delete the first three columns of matrix H of Example 3.2. This gives
$$\tilde{H} = \begin{pmatrix} 1 & 1 & 0 & 0 \\ 1 & 0 & 1 & 0 \\ 1 & 0 & 0 & 1 \end{pmatrix}.$$
The shortened Hamming code has length 4 and dimension 1. The all-1 vector is in the shortened code.

We use this procedure to shorten several of the codes presented in Tables II–V.

V. IMPROVEMENTS ON THE TAIL MATRIX

In this section we show some methods to improve upon the parameters given in Table I. Basically, fixing r and t, we want to obtain a descending tail matrix $T(m, r; t+1)$ such that m is larger

TABLE VI

PARAMETERS OF IMPROVED DESCENDING TAIL MATRICES $T(m, r; t+1)$

t	r	m	t	r	m	t	r	m	t	r	m
1	2	4	2	3	6	3	4	8	4	5	10
1	3	6	2	4	8	3	5	10	4	6	12
1	4	$9^{(5)}$	2	5	10	3	6	12	4	7	14
1	5	12	2	6	12	3	7	14	4	8	16
1	6	$18^{(5)}$	2	7	16	3	8	16	4	9	18
1	7	$29^{(6)}$	2	8	20	3	9	20	4	10	20
1	8	$50^{(5)}$	2	9	24	3	10	$26^{(2)}$	4	11	24
1	9	$74^{(5)}$	2	10	32	3	11	28	4	12	28
1	10	$146^{(5)}$	2	11	$52^{(1)}$	3	12	32	4	13	32
1	11	$250^{(5)}$	2	12	$76^{(1)}$	3	13	40	4	14	36
1	12	$434^{(5)}$	2	13	$124^{(1)}$	3	14	$56^{(1)}$	4	15	40
			2	14	$220^{(1)}$	3	15	$80^{(1)}$	4	16	48
			2	15	$396^{(1)}$	3	16	$128^{(1)}$	4	17	$60^{(1)}$
						3	17	$184^{(1)}$	4	18	$80^{(3)}$
						3	18	$272^{(1)}$	4	19	$116^{(1)}$
						3	19	$496^{(1)}$	4	20	$164^{(3)}$
									4	21	$224^{(3)}$
									4	22	$292^{(4)}$

1. From Construction 5.1
2. From Example 5.1
3. From Construction 5.2
4. From Construction 5.3
5. From Construction 5.4
6. From Example 5.2

than the one given in Table I. The parameters in Table I come from [1]. Table VI improves on Table I based on the results of this section. The superindexes in Table VI denote the entries from Table I that have been improved and the method (to be described later in this section) used in the improvement.

Let us recall briefly how the descending tail matrices were obtained in [1].

Let A be an $m \times r$ matrix with rows $\boldsymbol{a}_1, \boldsymbol{a}_2, \cdots, \boldsymbol{a}_m$ and B an $m' \times r'$ matrix with rows $\boldsymbol{b}_1, \boldsymbol{b}_2, \cdots, \boldsymbol{b}_{m'}$. Then, we denote by $A \times B$ (also called external or Kronecker product) the $(mm') \times (r + r')$ matrix whose $(i-1)m' + j$ row, $1 \le i \le m, 1 \le j \le m'$ is vector $\boldsymbol{a}_i, \boldsymbol{b}_j$. Given $j \ge 1$, let T_j be the matrix constructed inductively as follows:

$$T_1 = \begin{pmatrix} 1 \\ 0 \end{pmatrix} \quad \text{and} \quad T_{j+1} = \left(\begin{array}{ccc|c} 1 & 1 & \ldots & 1 \\ \hline & & & 0 \\ & & & 1 \\ & & T_j & \vdots \\ & & & 0 \\ & & & 1 \\ \hline 0 & 0 & \ldots & 0 \end{array}\right).$$

For example,

$$T_2 = \begin{pmatrix} 1 & 1 \\ 1 & 0 \\ 0 & 1 \\ 0 & 0 \end{pmatrix} \quad \text{and} \quad T_3 = \begin{pmatrix} 1 & 1 & 1 \\ 1 & 1 & 0 \\ 1 & 0 & 1 \\ 0 & 1 & 0 \\ 0 & 0 & 1 \\ 0 & 0 & 0 \end{pmatrix}.$$

Given r and t, let $\mathcal{A}$ be an asymmetric t-error correcting code of length $r' < r$ and cardinality $|\mathcal{A}| = m'$. Let $A(m', r'; t+1)$ be the matrix obtained by ordering the elements of $\mathcal{A}$ in descending weight order. Then, the matrix $A(m', r'; t+1) \times T_{r-r'}$ is a descending tail matrix $T(m, r; t+1)$, where $m = 2(r - r')m'$ [1]. We call a matrix of this type a Blaum-van Tilborg (BT) descending tail matrix of strength $t + 1$. The construction is optimized over the best asymmetric t-error correcting codes available and the matrices T_j in order to obtain m as large as possible. Results concerning good asymmetric error correcting codes can be found in [12].

Example 5.1: Let $\mathcal{A}$ be the 3-asymmetric error correcting code of length 8. The rows of the corresponding matrix $A(4, 8; 4)$ are

$$\boldsymbol{a}_1 = 11111111$$
$$\boldsymbol{a}_2 = 00001111$$
$$\boldsymbol{a}_3 = 11110000$$
$$\boldsymbol{a}_4 = 00000000.$$

The BT matrix $T(16, 10; 4)$ is then

$$A(4,8;4) \times T_2 = \left|\begin{array}{c|c} 11111111 & \begin{array}{c}11\\10\\01\\00\end{array} \\ \hline 00001111 & \begin{array}{c}11\\10\\01\\00\end{array} \\ \hline 11110000 & \begin{array}{c}11\\10\\01\\00\end{array} \\ \hline 00000000 & \begin{array}{c}11\\10\\01\\00\end{array} \end{array}\right| = \left|\begin{array}{c} 11111111 \times T_2 \\ \hline 00001111 \times T_2 \\ \hline 11110000 \times T_2 \\ \hline 00000000 \times T_2 \end{array}\right|$$

We show next how we can construct a descending tail matrix T by inserting some rows in $A(4, 8; 4) \times T_2$. The new matrix is

$$T = \left|\begin{array}{c} 11111111 \times T_2 \\ \hline 01111111\ 01 \\ 00111111\ 10 \\ 00111111\ 01 \\ 00011111\ 10 \\ \hline 00001111 \times T_2 \\ \hline 11001100\ 10 \\ 11001100\ 01 \\ \hline 11110000 \times T_2 \\ \hline 01110000\ 01 \\ 00110000\ 10 \\ 00110000\ 01 \\ 00010000\ 10 \\ \hline 00000000 \times T_2 \end{array}\right|$$

It is easy to verify that the new matrix is a $T(26, 10; 4)$ descending tail matrix. In Table I, we can see that our best result was $m = 24$. This example shows the potential of the method. In the discussion that follows, whenever we have a matrix $A(m, r'; t+1)$ with rows $\boldsymbol{a}_1, \boldsymbol{a}_2, \cdots, \boldsymbol{a}_m$, we make the following assumption: $\boldsymbol{a}_1 = 11 \cdots 1, \boldsymbol{a}_2 = \overbrace{00 \cdots 0}^{t+1} 11 \cdots 1, a_{m-1} = \overbrace{11 \cdots 1}^{t+1} 00 \cdots 0$ and $\boldsymbol{a}_m = 00 \cdots 0$. This is not entirely correct, though. We can make the assumption on $\boldsymbol{a}_2$ and on $\boldsymbol{a}_{m-1}$ separately by an adequate permutation of the columns of $A(m, r'; t+1)$. In general, there is not necessarily a permutation that can take $\boldsymbol{a}_2$ and $\boldsymbol{a}_{m-1}$ to the form described above simultaneously. However, this fact is not very relevant in the construction that follows. The real assumption is $\boldsymbol{a}_2 = \overbrace{00 \cdots 0}^{t+1} 11 \cdots 1$, and a_{m-1} is a permutation of $\overbrace{11 \cdots 1}^{t+1} 00 \cdots 0$.

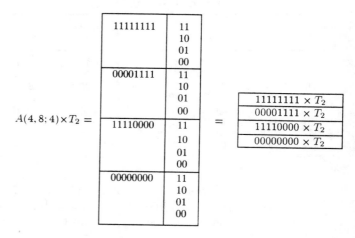

The next construction partially generalizes Example 5.1.

Construction 5.1: Let $A(m, r-2; t+1) \times T_2$ be a BT descending tail matrix $T(4m, r; t+1)$, where $t \geq 2$ and $m \geq 3$. Denote the rows of $A(m, r-2; t+1)$ $\boldsymbol{a}_1, \boldsymbol{a}_2, \cdots, \boldsymbol{a}_m$. Let B and B' be the following $T(2(t-1), r; t+1)$ descending tail matrices:

$$B = \begin{array}{|l|c|}\hline \overbrace{01111\ldots1}^{t+1}\,11\ldots1 & 01 \\ \overbrace{00111\ldots1}^{t+1}\,11\ldots1 & 10 \\ \overbrace{00111\ldots1}^{t+1}\,11\ldots1 & 01 \\ \overbrace{00011\ldots1}^{t+1}\,11\ldots1 & 10 \\ \overbrace{00011\ldots1}^{t+1}\,11\ldots1 & 01 \\ \cdots & \cdots \\ \overbrace{00\ldots011}^{t+1}\,11\ldots1 & 10 \\ \overbrace{00\ldots011}^{t+1}\,11\ldots1 & 01 \\ \overbrace{00\ldots001}^{t+1}\,11\ldots1 & 10 \\ \hline \end{array} \quad \text{and} \quad B' = \begin{array}{|l|c|}\hline \overbrace{01111\ldots1}^{t+1}\,00\ldots0 & 01 \\ \overbrace{00111\ldots1}^{t+1}\,00\ldots0 & 10 \\ \overbrace{00111\ldots1}^{t+1}\,00\ldots0 & 01 \\ \overbrace{00011\ldots1}^{t+1}\,00\ldots0 & 10 \\ \overbrace{00011\ldots1}^{t+1}\,00\ldots0 & 01 \\ \cdots & \cdots \\ \overbrace{00\ldots011}^{t+1}\,00\ldots0 & 10 \\ \overbrace{00\ldots011}^{t+1}\,00\ldots0 & 01 \\ \overbrace{00\ldots001}^{t+1}\,00\ldots0 & 10 \\ \hline \end{array}$$

Then, the following matrix T is a $T(4m + 4(t-1), r; t+1)$ descending tail matrix:

$$T = \begin{array}{|c|}\hline \boldsymbol{a}_1 \times T_2 \\ \hline B \\ \hline \boldsymbol{a}_2 \times T_2 \\ \boldsymbol{a}_3 \times T_2 \\ \cdots \\ \boldsymbol{a}_{m-1} \times T_2 \\ \hline B' \\ \hline \boldsymbol{a}_m \times T_2 \\ \hline \end{array}$$

We prove that matrix T above is a $T(4m + 4(t-1), r; t+1)$ descending tail matrix in the Appendix.

Example 5.2: Applying Construction 5.1 to the $T(16, 10, ; 4)$ BT matrix $A(4, 8; 4) \times T_2$ in Example 5.1, we obtain

$$T' = \begin{array}{|l|}\hline 11111111 \times T_2 \\ \hline 01111111\ 01 \\ 00111111\ 10 \\ 00111111\ 01 \\ 00011111\ 10 \\ \hline 00001111 \times T_2 \\ \hline 11110000 \times T_2 \\ \hline 01110000\ 01 \\ 00110000\ 10 \\ 00110000\ 01 \\ 00010000\ 10 \\ \hline 00000000 \times T_2 \\ \hline \end{array}$$

Matrix T' is a $T(24, 10, 4)$ descending tail matrix. In Example 5.1, we had obtained a $T(26, 10; 4)$ descending tail matrix T. Construction 5.1 only shows how to insert rows between blocks 1 and 2 and between blocks $m-1$ and m. However, in individual cases, depending on the asymmetric code used, it is possible to insert rows between the middle blocks, as shown in Example 5.1. Table VI shows improvements over Table I using Construction 5.1 together with other constructions to be presented in this section. However, the reader can improve further on Table VI by taking individual cases and inserting rows between the middle blocks.

A BT descending tail matrix $A(m, r'; t+1) \times T_j$ can be considered as a sequence of m blocks $\boldsymbol{a}_1 \times T_j, \boldsymbol{a}_2 \times T_j, \cdots, \boldsymbol{a}_m \times T_j$. Construction 5.1 gives a way of inserting extra rows between blocks 1 and 2 and between blocks $m-1$ and m when $t \geq 2$, $m \geq 3$ and $j = 2$. In [1], most of the constructions involve $j = 2, j = 3$, and $j = 4$. The next two constructions show how to insert rows between blocks 1 and 2 and between blocks $m-1$ and m when $t = 4$ and $j = 3$ or $j = 4$. The proofs that the new matrices are still descending tail matrices of strength $t+1$ are similar to the case $j = 2$ and will be omitted.

Construction 5.2: Assume that we have a BT $(6m, r; 5)$ descending tail matrix $A(m, r-3; 5) \times T_3 (m \geq 3)$. Let B and B' be the following $4 \times r$ matrices:

$$B = \begin{array}{|l|c|}\hline 011111\ldots1 & 010 \\ 001111\ldots1 & 001 \\ 000111\ldots1 & 110 \\ 000011\ldots1 & 101 \\ \hline \end{array} \quad \text{and } B' = \begin{array}{|l|c|}\hline 0111100\ldots0 & 010 \\ 0011100\ldots0 & 001 \\ 0001100\ldots0 & 110 \\ 0000100\ldots0 & 101 \\ \hline \end{array}$$

Then, the following matrix T is a $T(6m + 8, r; 5)$ descending tail matrix:

$$T = \begin{array}{|c|}\hline \boldsymbol{a}_1 \times T_3 \\ \hline B \\ \hline \boldsymbol{a}_2 \times T_3 \\ \hline \boldsymbol{a}_3 \times T_3 \\ \hline \vdots \\ \hline \boldsymbol{a}_{m-1} \times T_3 \\ \hline B' \\ \hline \boldsymbol{a}_m \times T_3 \\ \hline \end{array}$$

Construction 5.3: Assume that we have a BT $T(8m, r; 5)$ descending tail matrix $A(m, r-4; 5) \times T_4 (m \geq 3)$. Let B and B' be the following $2 \times r$ matrices:

$$B = \begin{array}{|l|c|}\hline 001111\ldots1 & 0011 \\ 000111\ldots1 & 1100 \\ \hline \end{array} \quad \text{and} \quad B' = \begin{array}{|l|c|}\hline 0011100\ldots0 & 0011 \\ 0001100\ldots0 & 1100 \\ \hline \end{array}$$

Then, the following matrix T is a $T(8m + 4, r; 5)$ descending tail matrix:

$$T = \begin{array}{|c|}\hline \boldsymbol{a}_1 \times T_4 \\ \hline B \\ \hline \boldsymbol{a}_2 \times T_4 \\ \hline \boldsymbol{a}_3 \times T_4 \\ \hline \vdots \\ \hline \boldsymbol{a}_{m-1} \times T_4 \\ \hline B' \\ \hline \boldsymbol{a}_m \times T_4 \\ \hline \end{array}$$

Up to now, we have analyzed codes with $t \geq 2$. Let us turn now our attention to the case $t = 1$.

We have that $T_2 = \begin{pmatrix} 1 & 1 \\ 1 & 0 \\ 0 & 1 \\ 0 & 0 \end{pmatrix}$. Similarly, we can define $T_2' = \begin{pmatrix} 1 & 1 \\ 0 & 1 \\ 1 & 0 \\ 0 & 0 \end{pmatrix}$.

The next construction shows how to modify a BT $T(4m, r; 2)$ descending tail matrix in such a way that a $T(4m+2, r; 2)$ descending tail matrix is obtained. The proof will be omitted.

Construction 5.4: Consider an $A(m, r-2; 2)$ matrix. Then, if m is even, the following matrix is a $T(4m+2, r; 2)$ descending tail matrix:

$T =$

$\boldsymbol{a}_1 \times T_2$
0111...1 01
$\boldsymbol{a}_2 \times T_2'$
$\boldsymbol{a}_3 \times T_2$
...
$\boldsymbol{a}_{m-1} \times T_2$
0100...0 01
$\boldsymbol{a}_m \times T_2'$

If m is odd, the same is true for the following matrix:

$T =$

$\boldsymbol{a}_1 \times T_2$
0111...1 01
$\boldsymbol{a}_2 \times T_2'$
$\boldsymbol{a}_3 \times T_2$
...
$\boldsymbol{a}_{m-1} \times T_2'$
0100...0 10
$\boldsymbol{a}_m \times T_2$

Example 5.3: Let $r = 7$ and $t = 2$. Then, the following is a BT $T(24, 7; 2)$ descending tail matrix:

$A(6, 5; 2) \times T_2 =$

$11111 \times T_2$
$11100 \times T_2$
$10011 \times T_2$
$00101 \times T_2$
$01010 \times T_2$
$00000 \times T_2$

According to Construction 5.4, the following is a $T(26, 7; 2)$ descending tail matrix:

$T =$

$11111 \times T_2$
11110 01
$11100 \times T_2'$
$10011 \times T_2$
$00101 \times T_2'$
$01010 \times T_2$
01000 01
$00000 \times T_2'$

However, we can improve further and obtain a $T(29, 7; 2)$ descending tail matrix by adding more rows as follows:

$T =$

$11111 \times T_2$
11110 01
$11100 \times T_2'$
11001 10
$10011 \times T_2$
00111 01
$00101 \times T_2'$
00110 10
$01010 \times T_2$
01000 01
$00000 \times T_2'$

It is straightforward to verify that T' is indeed a $T(29, 7; 2)$ descending tail matrix.

As Example 5.3 shows, we can improve on Table VI by taking separately each individual case and inserting more rows in an ad hoc way that depends on the asymmetric error correcting code considered.

VI. Conclusions

Some new methods for constructing t-EC/AUED codes have been presented. In the first method, the information bits are encoded first into a t-EC code containing the all-1 vector. Since most codes used in applications have this property (BCH, shortened BCH, Golay), this is a natural assumption. The key idea in the construction is reducing the weight distribution of the t-EC code used. Our codes have frequently less redundancy than the best EC/AUED codes previously known. The encoding and decoding procedures are as simple as those of known codes.

The second procedure improves the tail matrices obtained by a previously known method. The results of the new method, together with some ad hoc constructions given in examples, are tabulated in Table VI. Table VI should not be taken as a new record on m. The reader should be able to improve upon Table VI by ad hoc methods similar to the ones given in the examples.

Appendix

Lemma: The matrix T obtained in Construction 5.1 is a $T(4m + 4(t-1), r; t+1)$ descending tail matrix.

Proof: We have to prove that the rows corresponding to B and B' in T comply with Definition 1.1. Denote the rows of T as $\boldsymbol{t}_j, 1 \le j \le 4m + 4(t-1)$. Notice that the rows corresponding to B are rows t_j, $5 \le j \le 2(t+1)$ in T, while the rows corresponding to B' are rows t_j, $4(m-1)+2(t-1)+1 \le j \le 4(m-1)+4(t-1)$ in T. Take the first $r-2$ elements of any row of B. We obtain a vector of length $r-2$ that contains $\boldsymbol{a}_2$, denote it by v. Since $N(\boldsymbol{a}_2, \boldsymbol{a}_j) \ge t+1$ for all $j \ge 3$, also $N(\boldsymbol{v}, \boldsymbol{a}_j) \ge t+1$. Now take the first $r-2$ elements of any row in B', call the resulting vector $\boldsymbol{v}'$. Since $\boldsymbol{v}'$ is contained in $\boldsymbol{a}_{m-1}$, it is also clear that $N(\boldsymbol{v}, \boldsymbol{v}') \ge t+1$. So, it is enough to compare the rows of B with the rows of $\boldsymbol{a}_1 \times T_2$ and of $\boldsymbol{a}_2 \times T_2$. Similarly, it is enough to compare the rows of B' with the rows of $\boldsymbol{a}_{m-1} \times T_2$ and of $\boldsymbol{a}_m \times T_2$.

Take the first element of B in T, i.e., $\boldsymbol{t}_5 = 011...1\ 01$. We have the following:

$$N(\boldsymbol{t}_1, \boldsymbol{t}_5) = N(11...1\ 11,\ 011...1\ 01) = 2$$

$$N(\boldsymbol{t}_2, \boldsymbol{t}_5) = N(11...1\ 10,\ 011...1\ 01) = 2$$

$$N(\boldsymbol{t}_3, \boldsymbol{t}_5) = N(11...1\ 01,\ 011...1\ 01) = 1$$

$$N(\boldsymbol{t}_4, \boldsymbol{t}_5) = N(11...1\ 00,\ 011...1\ 01) = 1.$$

So, Definition 1.1 is satisfied for $\boldsymbol{t}_j$, $1 \leq j \leq 4$ with respect to $\boldsymbol{t}_5$. Also, notice that

$$N\left(\boldsymbol{t}_5, \boldsymbol{t}_{2(t+1)+1}\right) = N\left(011...1\ 01,\ \overbrace{00...0}^{t+1}11...1\ 11\right) = t$$

$$N\left(\boldsymbol{t}_5, \boldsymbol{t}_{2(t+1)+2}\right) = N\left(011...1\ 01,\ \overbrace{00...0}^{t+1}11...1\ 10\right) = t+1$$

$$N\left(\boldsymbol{t}_5, \boldsymbol{t}_{2(t+1)+3}\right) = N\left(011...1\ 01,\ \overbrace{00...0}^{t+1}11...1\ 01\right) = t$$

$$N\left(\boldsymbol{t}_5, \boldsymbol{t}_{2(t+1)+4}\right) = N\left(011...1\ 01,\ \overbrace{00...0}^{t+1}11...1\ 00\right) = t+1.$$

So, Definition 1.1 is satisfied for $\boldsymbol{t}_j$, $2(t+1)+1 \leq j \leq 2(t+1)+4$ with respect to $\boldsymbol{t}_5$. Similarly, we verify Definition 1.1 with respect to $\boldsymbol{t}_{2(t+1)}$.

Let us consider now the rows $\boldsymbol{t}_j$, $6 \leq j \leq 2t-1$. Take $\boldsymbol{t}_{6+2l} = \overbrace{00...0}^{l+2}11...1\ 10$, $0 \leq l \leq t-3$. Notice that

$$N(\boldsymbol{t}_1, \boldsymbol{t}_{6+2l}) = N\left(11...1\ 11, \overbrace{00...0}^{l+2}11...1\ 10\right) = l+3$$

$$N(\boldsymbol{t}_2, \boldsymbol{t}_{6+2l}) = N\left(11...1\ 10, \overbrace{00...0}^{l+2}11...1\ 10\right) = l+2$$

$$N(\boldsymbol{t}_3, \boldsymbol{t}_{6+2l}) = N\left(11...1\ 01, \overbrace{00...0}^{l+2}11...1\ 10\right) = l+3$$

$$N(\boldsymbol{t}_4, \boldsymbol{t}_{6+2l}) = N\left(11...1\ 00, \overbrace{00...0}^{l+2}11...1\ 10\right) = l+2$$

satisfying Definition 1.1 on block $\boldsymbol{a}_1 \times T_2$ with respect to $\boldsymbol{t}_{6+2l}$. Similarly,

$$N\left(\boldsymbol{t}_{6+2l}, \boldsymbol{t}_{2(t+1)+1}\right) = N(\overbrace{00...0}^{l+2}11...1\ 10,\ \overbrace{00...0}^{t+1}11...1\ 11) = t-l-1$$

$$N\left(\boldsymbol{t}_{6+2l}, \boldsymbol{t}_{2(t+1)+2}\right) = N(\overbrace{00...0}^{l+2}11...1\ 10,\ \overbrace{00...0}^{t+1}11...1\ 10) = t-l-1$$

$$N\left(\boldsymbol{t}_{6+2l}, \boldsymbol{t}_{2(t+1)+3}\right) = N(\overbrace{00...0}^{l+2}11...1\ 10,\ \overbrace{00...0}^{t+1}11...1\ 01) = t-l$$

$$N\left(\boldsymbol{t}_{6+2l}, \boldsymbol{t}_{2(t+1)+4}\right) = N(\overbrace{00...0}^{l+2}11...1\ 10,\ \overbrace{00...0}^{t+1}11...1\ 00) = t-l$$

showing that Definition 1.1 is satisfied on block $\boldsymbol{a}_2 \times T_2$ with respect to $\boldsymbol{t}_{6+2l}$. We show analogously that Definition 1.1 is satisfied with respect to elements $\boldsymbol{t}_{6+2l+1}$.

Similarly, we verify Definition 1.1 on blocks $\boldsymbol{a}_{m-1} \times T_2$ and $\boldsymbol{a}_m \times T_2$ with respect to the rows of B', completing the proof.

References

[1] M. Blaum and H. van Tilborg, "On t-error correcting/all unidirectional error detecting codes," *IEEE Trans. Comput.*, vol. 38, no. 11, pp. 1493–1501, Nov. 1989.

[2] F. J. H. Boinck and H. van Tilborg, "Constructions and bounds for systematic t EC/AUED codes," *IEEE Trans. Inform. Theory*, vol. IT-36, pp. 1381–1390, Nov. 1990.

[3] B. Bose, "On systematic SEC/MUED codes," in *Proc. FTCS*, vol. 11, June 1981, pp. 265–267.

[4] B. Bose and D. K. Pradhan, "Optimal unidirectional error detecting/correcting codes," *IEEE Trans. Comput.*, vol. C-32, pp. 521–530, June 1982.

[5] B. Bose and T. R. N. Rao, "On the theory of unidirectional error correcting/detecting codes," *IEEE Trans. Comput.*, vol. C-31, pp. 521–530, June 1982.

[6] S. Kundu, "Design of testable CMOS circuits for TSC systems," Ph.D. dissertation, Univ. of Iowa, May 1988.

[7] D. Nikolos, N. Gaitanis, and G. Philokyprou, "t-error correcting all unidirectional error detecting codes starting from cyclic AN codes," in *Proc. Int. Conf. Fault-Tolerant Comput.*, Kissimmee, FL 1984, pp. 318–323.

[8] ——, "Systematic t-error correcting/all unidirectional error detecting codes," *IEEE Trans. Comput.*, vol. C-35, pp. 394–402, May 1986.

[9] D. K. Pradhan, "A new class of error-corrrecting/detecting codes for fault-tolerant computer applications," *IEEE Trans. Comput.*, vol. C-29, pp. 471–481, June 1980.

[10] D. L. Tao, C. R. P. Hartmann, and P. K. Lala, "An efficient class of unidirectional error detecting/correcting codes," *IEEE Trans. Comput.*, vol. C-37, pp. 879–882, July 1988.

[11] T. Verhoeff, "An updated table of minimum-distance bounds for binary linear codes," *IEEE Trans. Inform. Theory*, vol. IT-33, pp. 665–680, Sept. 1987.

[12] J. H. Weber, C. de Vroedt, and D. E. Boekee, "Bounds and constructions for binary codes of length less than 24 and asymmetric distance less than 6," *IEEE Trans. Inform. Theory*, vol. IT-34, pp. 1321–1331, Sept. 1988.

Theory and Design of t-Error Correcting and $d(d > t)$-Unidirectional Error Detecting (t-EC d-UED) Codes

DER JEI LIN, MEMBER, IEEE, AND BELLA BOSE, MEMBER, IEEE

Abstract—**The fundamental theory of t-error correcting and $d(d > t)$-unidirectional error detecting (t-EC d-UED) codes are given. Many construction methods for t-EC d-UED codes are developed. The encoding/decoding methods for these codes are described. The optimality of these codes are also considered.**

Index Terms—**Decoding, encoding, error correction, error detecting, symmetric errors, unidirectional errors.**

I. Introduction

The importance and benefits of error control codes for computer and communication systems are well recognized. Error correcting/detecting codes that are effective against both symmetric and unidirectional errors are useful in providing protection against transient, intermittent, and permanent faults [1]–[8]. In the case of symmetric errors, both $1 \rightarrow 0$ and $0 \rightarrow 1$ errors can occur with equal probability in a data word whereas in the case of unidirectional errors even though both $1 \rightarrow 0$ and $0 \rightarrow 1$ errors are possible, the errors in any particular data word are of the same type. Transient faults are likely to cause a limited number of symmetric errors or multiple unidirectional errors [5], [7]. Also, intermittent faults, because of short duration, are expected to cause a limited number of errors [9]. On the other hand, permanent faults cause either symmetric or unidirectional errors, depending on the nature of the faults [7], [10], [11]. The most likely faults in some of the recently developed LSI/VLSI, ROM, and RAM memories (such as the faults that affect address decoders, word lines, power supply, and stuck-fault in a serial bus, etc. [1], [7], [11], [12]), cause unidirectional errors. The number of symmetric errors is usually limited while the number of unidirectional errors, caused by the above mentioned faults, can be fairly large.

In the past, researchers have designed codes which correct all patterns of t to fewer symmetric errors and detect all (t + 1 or more) unidirectional errors [1], [3], [4], [13], [14], [16]. In all these papers, it is assumed that the number of unidirectional errors due to the above mentioned faults can be unlimited (i.e., up to n' where n' is the number of bits in the data word). However, in many cases, it is reasonable to assume that the number of unidirectional errors, even though large, is also limited. For example, in a byte/chip memory organization, if a chip failure occurs, then the number of unidirectional errors can be at most one byte length. Thus, in this paper, we are interested in studying the theory and design of codes capable of correcting t or fewer symmetric errors and detecting up to a fixed number $d(d > t)$, instead of all, unidirectional errors. Some preliminary results on t-EC d-UED codes are given in [15]. The codes given here are much superior.

The codes presented in this paper have the following characteristics.

1) The codes are designed by appending an appropriate check symbol CH_X to each codeword X that belongs to a distance $2t + 2$ systematic code C. Thus, the t-EC d-UED codes presented here are also systematic.

2) The number of check bits needed for CH_X depends only on t and d but independent of the length n of the code C. On the other hand, the systematic t-EC AUED codes presented so far in the literature [1], [3], [4], [13], [14] are designed by appending $t + 1$ check symbols, $CH_1, CH_2, \cdots, CH_{t+1}$, to a distance $2t + 1(2t + 2$ in [14]) code C and the number of check bits needed for each of the symbols CH_i, $i = 1, 2, \cdots, t + 1$, depends on t and n. Thus, the number of check bits required for the t-EC d-UED codes is fewer than that of t-EC AUED codes.

3) The t-EC d-UED codes are equivalent to t-unidirectional error correcting and $d(d > t)$-unidirectional error detecting codes, i.e., the necessary and sufficient conditions required for error correction and detection are the same in both cases as shown in Theorems 2.1 and 2.2

4) For the t-EC d-UED codes presented here, the number of check bits required is less than that of the corresponding t-symmetric error correcting and d-symmetric error detecting codes.

5) Many codes are close to optimal.

6) The encoding/decoding complexity of the t-EC d-UED codes presented here is comparable to that of the distance $2t + 2$ codes.

The paper is organized as follows. Section II describes the necessary and sufficient conditions for a code to be t-EC and d-UED. Three different methods of constructing systematic t-EC d-UED codes are given in Section III. The encoding/decoding methods are discussed in Section IV. In Section V, a lower bound on the number of check bits for systematic t-EC d-UED codes is developed and from this lower bound, the

Manuscript received May 25, 1987; revised December 10, 1987. This work was supported by the National Science Foundation under Grant DMC-8421104.

The authors are with the Department of Computer Science, Oregon State University, Corvallis, OR 97331.

IEEE Log Number 8719326.

Reprinted from *IEEE Transactions on Computers*, April 1988, pp. 433-439.

0-8186-4182-7/93 $3.00 © 1988 IEEE

optimality of the codes given here are discussed. Section VI gives some concluding remarks.

The following notations are used in this paper.

$N(X, Y)$: number of $1 \to 0$ crossovers from X to Y.
$D(X, Y)$: Hamming distance between X and Y.
$D(C)$: minimum distance of a code C.
$W(X)$: weight or the number of 1's in X.

II. The Basic Theorems of t-EC d-UED Code

Let $N(X, Y)$ represent the number of $1 \to 0$ crossovers from X to Y. For example, if $X = 1011$ and $Y = 0110$, then $N(X, Y) = 2$ and $N(Y, X) = 1$. The Hamming distance $D(X, Y)$ between two words is the number of positions in which they differ. In other words, $D(X, Y) = N(X, Y) + N(Y, X)$.

The following two fundamental theorems describe the necessary and sufficient conditions for error correction and detection.

Theorem 2.1: A code C is capable of correcting t unidirectional errors and detecting $d(d > t)$ unidirectional errors if and only if it satisfies the following condition:

for all $X, Y \in C$ with $X \neq Y$ either $t + d + 1 \leq D(X, Y)$ or $t + 1 \leq N(X, Y)$ and $t + 1 \leq N(Y, X)$.

A slightly stronger result, when the code satisfies the above conditions, is given in the following theorem. The proof for Theorem 2.1 is similar to that of the one given for Theorem 2.2.

Theorem 2.2: A code C is t-EC d-UED if and only if it satisfies the following condition:

for all $X, Y \in C$ with $X \neq Y$ either $t + d + 1 \leq D(X, Y)$ or $t + 1 \leq N(X, Y)$ and $t + 1 \leq N(Y, X)$.

Proof: Since for all $X, Y \in C$ either $2t + 2 \leq N(X, Y) + N(Y, X)$ or $t + d + 1 \leq D(X, Y)$, all t or fewer errors can be corrected. Now assume that the codeword X has suffered t_1, $t < t_1 \leq d$, unidirectional errors and we receive X'. We have to show that $t + 1 \leq D(X', Y)$ for all codewords $Y \neq X$. Without loss of generality, assume that the errors are $0 \to 1$ type. If $t + 1 \leq N(X, Y)$ and $t + 1 \leq N(Y, X)$, then $D(X', Y) \geq N(X', Y) \geq N(X, Y) \geq t + 1$. If $t + d + 1 \leq D(X, Y)$, then $D(X', Y) = N(X', Y) + N(Y, X') \geq N(X, Y) + N(Y, X) - t_1 \geq t + d + 1 - t_1 \geq t + 1$. This proves the sufficient condition.

To prove the necessary condition, let $N(X, Y) = t_1 \leq t$ and $D(X, Y) = t_1 + t_2 \leq t + d$. Without loss of generality, we can assume that

$$\begin{aligned} X &= 11 \cdots 1 \quad \overbrace{11 \cdots 1}^{N(X,Y)} \quad \overbrace{00 \cdots 0}^{N(Y,X)} \quad 00 \cdots 0 \\ Y &= 11 \cdots 1 \quad 00 \cdots 0 \quad 11 \cdots 1 \quad 00 \cdots 0. \end{aligned}$$

Let $t_3 = \min \ (t_2, d)$ and

$$Z = 11 \cdots 1 \quad \overbrace{00 \cdots 0}^{N(X,Y)} \quad \overbrace{\underbrace{0 \cdots 0}_{t_3}1 \cdots 1}^{N(Y,X)} \quad 00 \cdots 0.$$

Note that Z can be obtained in two ways—as a result of t_1 $1 \to 0$ errors in X or as a result of t_3 $1 \to 0$ errors in Y. This contradicts the fact that C is t-EC d-UED. //

From a practical application point of view, we expect that the single error correcting and d-unidirectional error detecting (SEC d-UED) codes will be more important among all t-EC d-UED codes. So when $t = 1$, Theorem 2.2 is restated as the following corollary.

Corollary 2.3: A code C is SEC d-UED if and only if it satisfies the following condition:

for all $X, Y \in C$ with $X \neq Y$ either $d + 2 \leq D(X, Y)$ or $2 \leq N(X, Y)$ and $2 \leq N(Y, X)$.

III. Systematic Code Construction for t-EC d-UED ($1 \leq t$) Code

In this section, three different methods of constructing systematic t-EC d-UED ($1 \leq t$) code will be developed. To construct a systematic t-EC d-UED code, some bits are appended to a t symmetric error correcting and $t + 1$ symmetric error detecting code (i.e., a systematic parity check code with Hamming distance $2t + 2$). Let C be a systematic parity check code with $D(C) = 2t + 2$, then the t-EC d-UED code constructed from C, denoted as C', will have the form

$$C' = \{X\mathrm{CH}_X | X \in C \text{ and } \mathrm{CH}_X \text{ is the appended symbol}\},$$

where CH_X may be simply denoted as CH if there is no ambiguity.

How large d can be will depend on the choice of the symbol CH and the number of bits in CH. The description of CH will be discussed in three cases.

Method A: If there exists a set of s-bit symbols, called S, such that $D(S) = m$ and $(2t + m + 2)/2 \leq |S|$, then use s-bit symbols for CH to construct a t-EC $(t + m + 1)$-UED code.

Method B: Use s bits, where $t + 3 \leq s$, for CH to construct a t-EC $(2s - t - 1)$-UED code.

Method C: If there exists a t-EC AUED code S with length s such that $s \leq |S|$, then use the codewords of S for CH to construct a t-EC $(2|S| - t - 1)$-UED code.

Before describing the code design, we prove the following two lemmas which give some properties of distance $2t + 2$ codes. These properties are useful in proving the error correcting and detecting capabilities of the codes designed in this paper.

Lemma 3.1: Let C be a distance $2t + 2$ code with length n. Then there exists a code C' having even weight codewords, $|C'| = |C|$, and same minimum distance and length as C.

Proof: Delete the least significant bit of C. Then the resultant codewords will have minimum distance at least $2t + 1$. Now append an even parity bit to these codewords. The resultant codewords C' will have even number of 1's, minimum distance $2t + 2$, and $|C'| = |C|$. //

Thus, we can always assume that the weight of each codeword in a distance $2t + 2$ code is even. The following lemma can be obtained from Lemma 1 in [4]. Here we give another proof for this special case.

Lemma 3.2: Let C be a code with $D(C) = 2t + 2$. For any

$X, Y \in C$, let $q = W(X) - W(Y)$. (We assume that $0 \leq q$.) Note that q is an even number.

a) If $2t + 2 \leq q$, then $q \leq N(X, Y)$ and $0 \leq N(Y, X)$.
b) If $0 \leq q \leq 2t$, then $(2t + 2 + q)/2 \leq N(X, Y)$ and $(2t + 2 - q)/2 \leq N(Y, X)$.

Proof: Since $0 \leq q$, we can find q positions where X has 1's and Y has 0's. And, in the remaining $n - q$ positions the numbers of crossovers from X to Y and from Y to X are equal. That is,

$$N(X, Y) = q + N(Y, X). \tag{3.1}$$

Also, recall that $D(C) = 2t + 2$. Therefore, by (3.1), we have

$$2t+2 \leq D(X, Y) = N(X, Y) + N(Y, X) = q + 2N(Y, X). \tag{3.2}$$

a) If $2t + 2 \leq q$, it is obvious that $q \leq N(X, Y)$ and $0 \leq N(Y, X)$.
b) If $0 \leq q \leq 2t$, by (3.2), we have $2t + 2 - q \leq 2N(Y, X)$, or equivalently $(2t + 2 - q)/2 \leq N(Y, X)$.

And hence, by (3.1), we also have

$$\frac{2t+2+q}{2} = \frac{2t+2-q}{2} + q \leq N(Y, X) + q = N(X, Y). \quad //$$

Method A

Theorem 3.3: Let S be a set of s-bit symbols such that $D(S) = m$ and $(2t + m + 2)/2 \leq |S|$. Also, let the elements of S be indexed as $S = \{Z_0, Z_1, \cdots, Z_{|S|-1}\}$. Define a function f from $\{0, 1, \cdots, |S| - 1\}$ to S as $f(i) = Z_i$. If CH_X is assigned as $CH_X = f(W(X)/2 \bmod |S|)$ for all $X \in C$, then C' is t-EC $(t + m + 1)$-UED.

Proof: Let $X' = XCH_X$ and $Y' = YCH_Y$ be any two codewords in C', and $q = W(X) - W(Y)$. (We assume $0 \leq q$.) By Lemma 3.2, we have the following results.

a) If $2t + m + 2 \leq q$, then $2t + m + 2 \leq D(X, Y)$, and hence $2t + m + 2 \leq D(X', Y')$.
b) If $q = 0$, then $t + 1 \leq N(X, Y)$ and $t + 1 \leq N(Y, X)$, and hence $t + 1 \leq N(X', Y')$ and $t + 1 \leq N(Y', X')$.
c) If $2 \leq q \leq 2t + m + 1$, then $2t + 2 \leq D(X, Y)$. In this case, since $2 \leq q \leq 2t + m + 1$ and $(2t + m + 2)/2 \leq |S|$, we have $CH_X \neq CH_Y$. Thus, $m \leq D(CH_X, CH_Y)$ and hence $2t + m + 2 \leq D(X', Y')$.

Therefore, by Theorem 2.2, C' is t-EC $(t + m + 1)$-UED. //

Let us consider the special case $m = 1$ in Theorem 3.3. Let $s = \lceil \log_2 (t + 2) \rceil$, then the set S of all s-bit symbols always satisfies $D(S) = 1$ and $(2t + 1 + 2)/2 \leq t + 2 \leq |S| = 2^s$. Therefore, we have the following corollary.

Corollary 3.4: Let $s = \lceil \log_2(t + 2) \rceil$. Define a function f from $\{0, 1, \cdots, 2^s - 1\}$ to s-bit symbols as $f(i)$ = the binary representation of i in s bits. If CH_X is assigned as $CH_X = f(W(X)/2 \bmod 2^s)$ for all $X \in C$, then C' is t-EC $(t + 2)$-UED.

By Corollary 3.4, an SEC 3-UED code can be constructed from the extended Hamming code by merely adding two bits to each codeword.

Corollary 3.5: There exists a systematic SEC 3-UED code with code length 2 bits longer than the extended Hamming code.

Now, consider the set $S = \{001, 010, 100\}$ or $\{000, 011, 101, 110\}$. S satisfies $D(S) = 2$ and $(2 \cdot 1 + 2 + 2)/2 \leq |S|$. Thus, by Theorem 3.3, we have the following corollary.

Corollary 3.6: There exists an SEC 4-UED code using 3 bits for CH.

Method B

Theorem 3.7: Let $t + 3 \leq s$. Define

$$Z_0 = 0 \cdots 01 \cdots 1 \left(\text{there are } \left\lceil \frac{s}{2} \right\rceil \text{ 1's and } \left\lfloor \frac{s}{2} \right\rfloor \text{ 0's in } Z_0\right)$$

and

$$S = \{Z_i \mid i = 0, 1, \cdots, s-1 \text{ and } Z_{j+1} \text{ is 1 bit (circular) left shift of } Z_j,\ 0 \leq j \leq s-2\}.$$

(e.g., if $t = 1$ and $s = 4$, then $Z_0 = 0011$, $Z_1 = 0110$, $Z_2 = 1100$, and $Z_3 = 1001$).

Also, define a function f from $\{0, 1, \cdots, s - 1\}$ to S as $f(i) = Z_i$. If CH_X is assigned as $CH_X = f(W(X)/2 \bmod s)$ for all $X \in C$, then C' is t-EC $(2s - t - 1)$-UED. (*Note*: If $s < t + 3$, then Method A gives better code.)

Proof: First, notice that f has the following properties.

1) $N(f(i), f(j)) = m$, if $|i - j| = m$ or $s - m$, where $m = 0, 1, \cdots, \min(t, \lfloor s/2 \rfloor)$,
2) $N(f(i), f(j)) \geq t + 1$, otherwise. (3.3)

Let X', Y', and q be the same notations as in the proof of Theorem 3.3. By Lemma 3.2, we have the following results.

a) If $2s \leq q$, then $2s \leq D(X, Y)$, and hence $2s \leq D(X', Y')$.
b) If $q = 0$, then $t + 1 \leq N(X, Y)$ and $t + 1 \leq N(Y, X)$, and hence $t + 1 \leq N(X', Y')$ and $t + 1 \leq N(Y', X')$.
c) If $2 \leq q \leq 2t$, then $(2t + 2 + q)/2 \leq N(X, Y)$ and $(2t + 2 - q)/2 \leq N(Y, X)$.
d) If $2t + 2 \leq q \leq 2s - 2$, then $q \leq N(X, Y)$ and $0 \leq N(Y, X)$.

Thus, we need to prove the theorem for q in the range $2 \leq q \leq 2s - 2$. Let $i = W(X)/2 \bmod s$ and $j = W(Y)/2 \bmod s$. Then, when $2 \leq q \leq 2s - 2$, we have

$$i - j = \frac{q}{2} \text{ or } -\left(s - \frac{q}{2}\right). \tag{3.4}$$

The discussion will be divided into two cases, according to the value of s.

Case a): $t + 3 \leq s \leq 2t + 1$.

In this case, $\min(t, \lfloor s/2 \rfloor) = \lfloor s/2 \rfloor$). Now, the discussion will be done on two subintervals $2 \le q \le s$ and $s + 1 \le q \le 2s - 2$.

i) $2 \le q \le s$.

By (3.3) and (3.4), we have

$$\frac{q}{2} \le N(CH_X, CH_Y) \text{ and } \frac{q}{2} \le N(CH_Y, CH_X). \quad (3.5)$$

Combine (3.5) with c), we have

$$t+1 \le N(X', Y') \text{ and } t+1 \le N(Y', X').$$

ii) $s + 1 \le q \le 2s - 2$.

The condition of q implies

$$s - \frac{s-1}{2} \le \frac{q}{2} = s - \left(s - \frac{q}{2}\right) \le s - 1 \text{ and } 1 \le s - \frac{q}{2} \le \frac{s-1}{2}.$$

Thus, by (3.3) and (3.4), we have

$$s - \frac{q}{2} \le N(CH_X, CH_Y) \text{ and } s - \frac{q}{2} \le N(CH_Y, CH_X). \quad (3.6)$$

Then, combine (3.6) with c) and d), we have

$$D(X', Y') = N(X, Y) + N(Y, X) + N(CH_X, CH_Y) + N(CH_Y, CH_X) \ge 2s.$$

Therefore, when $t + 3 \le s \le 2t + 1$, the condition in Theorem 2.2 is satisfied for the situation $2 \le q \le 2s - 2$.

Case b): $2t + 2 \le s$.

In this case, $\min(t, \lfloor s/2 \rfloor) = t$. Similar to Case a), the discussion will be on three subintervals $2 \le q \le 2t$, $2t + 2 \le q \le 2s - 2t - 2$, and $2s - 2t \le q \le 2s - 2$.

i) $2 \le q \le 2t$.

The condition of q implies $1 \le q/2 \le t$. Thus, by (3.3) and (3.4), we have

$$\frac{q}{2} \le N(CH_X, CH_Y) \text{ and } \frac{q}{2} \le N(CH_Y, CH_X). \quad (3.7)$$

Combine (3.7) with c), we have

$$t+1 \le N(X', Y') \text{ and } t+1 \le N(Y', X').$$

ii) $2t + 2 \le q \le 2s - 2t - 2$.

The condition of q implies $t + 1 \le q/2 \le s - (t + 1)$. Thus, by (3.3) and (3.4), we have

$$t+1 \le N(CH_X, CH_Y) \text{ and } t+1 \le N(CH_Y, CH_X).$$

Hence, $t + 1 \le N(X', Y')$ and $t + 1 \le N(Y', X')$.

iii) $2s - 2t \le q \le 2s - 2$.

The condition of q implies

$$t+2 \le s - t \le \frac{q}{2} = s - \left(s - \frac{q}{2}\right) \le s - 1 \text{ and } 1 \le s - \frac{q}{2} \le t.$$

Thus, by (3.3) and (3.4), we have

$$s - \frac{q}{2} \le N(CH_X, CH_Y) \text{ and } s - \frac{q}{2} \le N(CH_Y, CH_X). \quad (3.8)$$

Combine (3.8) with d), we have $2s \le D(X', Y')$. Therefore, when $2t + 2 \le s$, the condition in Theorem 2.2 is satisfied for the situation $2 \le q \le 2s - 2$, too.

Thus, the proof of the theorem is completed. //

Method C

Theorem 3.8: Let S be a t-EC AUED code of length s. Also, let the elements of S be indexed as $S = \{Z_0, Z_1, \cdots, Z_{|S|-1}\}$.

Define a function f from $\{0, 1, \cdots, |S| - 1\}$ to S as $f(i) = Z_i$. If CH_X is assigned as $CH_X = f(W(X)/2 \bmod |S|)$ for all $X \in C$, then C' is t-EC $(2|S| - t - 1)$-UED.

(*Note:* If we use this method, we must choose S as large as possible and s as small as possible. Also, we must have $s \le |S|$; otherwise Method B is better).

Proof: Let X', Y', and q be the same notations as in the proof of Theorem 3.3. Since S is t-EC AUED, we have

$$t+1 \le N(Z_i, Z_j) \qquad \text{for any } i \ne j. \quad (3.9)$$

By Lemma 3.2, we have the following results.

a) If $2|S| \le q$, then $2|S| \le q \le N(X, Y)$, and hence $2|S| \le D(X', Y')$.

b) If $q = 0$, then $t + 1 \le N(X, Y)$ and $t + 1 \le N(Y, X)$, and hence $t + 1 \le N(X', Y')$, and $t + 1 \le N(Y', X')$.

c) If $2 \le q \le 2|S| - 2$, then $CH_X \ne CH_Y$ and hence by (3.9) $t + 1 \le N(X', Y')$ and $t + 1 \le N(Y', X')$.

Therefore, by Theorem 2.2, C' is t-EC $(2|S| - t - 1)$-UED. //

Remarks (on Methods A, B, and C)

1) Notice that when $t = 1$ and $8 \le s$, from Bose–Rao codes [14], [16], it can be seen that there always exists an SEC AUED code S with length s such that $s \le |S|$. Thus, when $8 \le s$, Method C is the best method among all three methods to construct an SEC d-UED code.

Table I shows the number of unidirectional errors d that can be detected by the proposed methods for $t = 1, \cdots, 6$, using s bits in CH.

Key to Table I:

a) $t = 1$: See Corollaries 3.5 and 3.6 for $s = 2, 3$. See Method B for $4 \le s \le 7$. Method C is used for $8 \le s \le 18$ with S chosen from the following codes: Bose–Rao codes for $s = 8, 18$ [14]; a conference matrix code for $s = 9$ [17]; Steiner systems $S(4, 5, 11)$ and $S(5, 6, 12)$ for $s = 11, 12$ [17]; Brouwer codes for $13 \le s \le 16$ [18]; Kibler code for $s = 17$ [19].

b) $t = 2$: See Corollary 3.4 for $s = 2$. See Method B for $5 \le s \le 11$. Method A is used for $s = 4$ with $S = \{0001, 0010, 0100, 1000\}$. Method C is used for $12 \le s \le 15$ with S chosen from the following codes: a Hadamard matrix code for $s = 12$; a cyclic code for $s = 13$; 3-design 3-(16, 6, 4) (Nordstrom–Robinson code) for $s = 14, 15$ [17].

c) $t = 3$: See Corollary 3.4 for $s = 3$. See Method B for $6 \le s \le 15$. Method A is used for $s = 4$ with $S = \{0001, 0010, 0100, 1000, 1111\}$. Method C is used for $16 \le s \le 18$

TABLE I
THE VALUES OF d USING s BITS FOR CH IN t-EC d-UED CODES ($t = 1, \cdots, 6$)

t = 1		t = 2		t = 3		t = 4		t = 5		t = 6	
s	d	s	d	s	d	s	d	s	d	s	d
2	3	2	4	3	5	3	6	3	7	3	8
3	4	4	5	4	6	4	7	4	8	5	9
4	6	5	7	6	8	6	8	6	9	7	10
5	8	6	9	7	10	8	11	7	10	8	11
6	10	7	11	8	12	9	13	9	12	10	13
7	12	8	13	9	14	10	15	10	14	11	15
8	26	9	15	10	16	11	17	11	16	12	17
9	34	10	17	11	18	12	19				
11	130	11	19	12	20	13	21				
12	262	12	41	13	22	14	23				
13	314	13	49	14	24	15	25				
14	630	14	81	15	26	16	27				
15	1162	15	137	16	56	17	29				
16	2326			17	64	18	31				
17	2990			18	92	19	33				
18	5418					20	71				

with S chosen from a Hadamard matrix code for $s = 16$, from a conference matrix code for $s = 17$, and from [24, 12, 8] Golay code for $s = 18$ [17].

d) $t = 4$: See Corollary 3.4 for $s = 3$. See Method B for $8 \leq s \leq 19$. Method A is used for $s = 4, 6$ with $S = \{0011, 0101, 1001, 0110, 1010, 1100\}$ and $S = \{001111, 010110, 011001, 100101, 101010, 110011, 111100\}$ (from Hamming code), respectively. Method C is used for $s = 20$ with S a Hadamard matrix code.

e) $t = 5$: See Corollary 3.4 for $s = 3$. Method A is used for $s = 4, 6, 7$ with $S = \{0000, 0011, 0101, 1001, 0110, 1010, 1100\}$, $S = \{000000, 001111, 010110, 011001, 100101, 101010, 110011, 111100\}$ (from Hamming code), and $S = \{0000000, 0011110, 0101101, 0110011, 1001011, 1010101, 1100110, 1111000\}$ (from Hamming code), respectively. Method B is used for $s = 9, 10, 11$.

f) $t = 6$: See Corollary 3.4 for $s = 3$. Method A is used for $s = 5, 7, 8$ with $S = \{00011, 00101, 01001, 10001, 00110, 01010, 10010, 01100\}$, $S =$ the Hamming (7, 4) code, and $S =$ the extended Hamming (8, 4) code, respectively. Method B is used for $s = 10, 11, 12$.

2) The number of bits used for CH is independent of n, the code length of C, in contrast to the number of bits used for $CH_1, CH_2, \cdots, CH_{t+1}$, which are dependent on n, in t-EC AUED code constructed in papers [1], [3], [4], [13], and [14]. The proposed t-EC d-UED codes use fewer check bits than the t-EC AUED codes.

For instance, if $n = 64$, the best SEC AUED code needs 10 bits for CH_1 and CH_2 [14]. But, if we need to detect only up to 34 errors, the proposed SEC d-UED code uses fewer bits for CH. (See Table I.) Similarly, if $n = 128$, the 2-EC AUED codes given in [4], [13], and [14] need at least 15 bits for CH_1, CH_2, and CH_3. But, if we need to detect only up to 81 errors the proposed 2-EC d-UED code uses fewer bits for CH. (See Table I.)

3) The number of bits used for CH may be reduced for some special code C. For instance, if C is the extended Hamming (8, 4) code, then the codewords in C have only three different weights, 0, 4, and 8. Thus, if we use CH $= 0$ for weight zero codeword and weight eight codeword and CH $= 1$ for all weight four codewords, then C' is indeed SEC 3-UED. But, in general, reducing the number of bits in CH may not always be feasible. Here, we would like to show that, to extend the extended Hamming (16, 11) code to SEC 3-UED, SEC 4-UED, and SEC 5-UED code we need at least 2, 3, and 4 bits, respectively, in CH.

Let C be the extended Hamming (16, 11) code with the parity check matrix

$$H = \begin{bmatrix} 0&0&0&0&1&1&1&1&1&1&1&1&0&0&0&0 \\ 0&1&1&1&0&0&0&1&1&1&1&0&1&0&0&0 \\ 1&0&1&1&0&1&1&0&0&1&1&0&0&1&0&0 \\ 1&1&0&1&1&0&1&0&1&0&1&0&0&0&1&0 \\ 1&1&1&1&1&1&1&1&1&1&1&1&1&1&1&1 \end{bmatrix}.$$

Then

$$\begin{aligned} X_1 &= 1\ 1\ 1\ 0\ 0\ 0\ 0\ 0\ 0\ 0\ 0\ 0\ 0\ 0\ 0\ 1, \\ X_2 &= 1\ 1\ 0\ 1\ 0\ 0\ 0\ 1\ 1\ 0\ 0\ 0\ 0\ 0\ 0\ 1, \\ X_3 &= 1\ 1\ 1\ 0\ 0\ 0\ 0\ 1\ 1\ 1\ 0\ 0\ 0\ 0\ 0\ 1, \\ X_4 &= 1\ 1\ 0\ 1\ 0\ 1\ 1\ 1\ 1\ 1\ 1\ 0\ 0\ 0\ 0\ 1, \text{ and} \\ X_5 &= 1\ 1\ 1\ 0\ 1\ 1\ 1\ 1\ 1\ 1\ 1\ 1\ 0\ 0\ 0\ 1 \end{aligned}$$

are codewords in C with

$$N(X_{i+1}, X_i) = 3,\ N(X_i, X_{i+1}) = 1, \qquad \text{for } i = 1, 2, 3, 4,$$

and

$$N(X_{i+2}, X_i) = 4,\ N(X_i, X_{i+2}) = 0, \qquad \text{for } i = 1, 2, 3.$$

Case a): at least two bits are needed for CH to extend C to SEC 3-UED.

In order to extend C to an SEC 3-UED code, X_1, X_2, and X_3 must have distinct CH. Therefore, at least 2 bits are needed for CH.

Case b): at least three bits are needed for CH to extend C to SEC 4-UED.

Suppose C can be extended to an SEC 4-UED code by using two bits for CH. Now, consider CH_{X_3}. If $CH_{X_3} = 00$ then CH_{X_4} has to be 11. But $CH_{X_4} = 11$ forces $CH_{X_2} = 00$ which is impossible, since CH_{X_2} cannot be same as CH_{X_3}. Also, $CH_{X_3} = 11$ forces $CH_{X_1} = 00$ and $CH_{X_2} = 00$ which is impossible, since CH_{X_1} and CH_{X_2} have to be distinct. If $CH_{X_3} = 01$, then $CH_{X_1} = 10$. Thus, no proper symbol can be assigned to CH_{X_2}. By the same reason, $CH_{X_3} = 10$ is also impossible. Therefore, in order to extend C to SEC 4-UED, at least three bits are needed for CH.

Case c): at least four bits are needed for CH to extend C to SEC 5-UED.

Suppose C can be extended to an SEC 5-UED code by using 3 bits for CH. Similar to Case b), let us consider all possibilities of CH_{X_3}. If $CH_{X_3} = 000$, then both CH_{X_4} and

CH_{X_5} must have to be 111 which is impossible. Similarly, $CH_{X_3} = 111$ forces both CH_{X_1} and CH_{X_2} to 000 which is impossible. If $CH_{X_3} = 001$, then $CH_{X_5} = 110$. Thus, no proper symbol can be assigned to CH_{X_4}. Similarly, CH_{X_3} cannot be 010 or 100. If $CH_{X_3} = 011$, then $CH_{X_1} = 100$. So, no proper symbol can be assigned to CH_{X_2}. Similarly, CH_{X_3} cannot be 101 or 110.

Therefore, at least four bits are needed to extend C to an SEC 5-UED code. //

IV. Decoding Algorithm

Since all three Methods A, B, and C in Section III use the same principle, except using different set S for the check symbol CH, only the decoding algorithm for Method C is developed in this section. In fact, the algorithm developed here can be applied to all three methods, except the proof of the validity needs slight modification.

Let $X^* = XCH_X$ be an error-free transmitted codeword in the proposed t-EC d-UED code and $(X^*)' = X'(CH_X)'$ be the received word with some errors in X^*.

Decoding Algorithm:

1) Compute the syndrome of X' as usual in code C. Let m be the multiplicity of errors corresponding to the syndrome.
2) If $t < m$, then signal "errors detected" and stop.
3) Decode X' using a decoding algorithm in code C to get X'' and compute $CH_{X''}$ for X''.
4) If $m + D((CH_X)', CH_{X''}) \leq t$, then output $X'' CH_{X''}$ and stop; else signal "errors detected" and stop.

End(of Decoding Algorithm).

Theorem 4.1: The Decoding Algorithm described above is valid.

Proof: To prove the validity of the algorithm, we need to prove that

a) if t or fewer errors have occurred in the received word, then the algorithm outputs the correct codeword,

and

b) if more then t but no more than $d(=2|S| - t - 1)$ unidirectional errors have occurred in the received word, then the algorithm should signal "errors detected." Let m_1 and m_2 be the numbers of errors that have occurred in X and CH_X, respectively.

Case a): t or fewer errors.

By the structure of C, $m_1 \leq t$ implies $m = m_1$ and $X'' = X$ in steps 1) and 3). Then, in step 4), $m + D((CH_X)', CH_{X''}) = m_1 + m_2 \leq t$. Therefore, the algorithm outputs the correct codeword $X'' CH_{X''} = XCH_X$.

Case b): more than t but no more than d unidirectional errors.

If $t < m$, then step 2) does the job. So, we need to consider the only case $m \leq t$. What we need to show is that $t < m + D((CH_X)', CH_{X''})$ for this case.

Two subcases will be discussed here.

Subcase 1): $m_1 \leq t$.

The proof is same as in Case a), i.e., in step 4) $m + D((CH_X)', CH_{X''}) = m_1 + m_2$. Since $t < m_1 + m_2$, the algorithm signals "errors detected."

Subcase 2): $t < m_1$.

By the structure of S (being t-EC AUED) and the characteristic of unidirectional errors from CH_X to $(CH_X)'$, it is easy to see that if $CH_{X''} \neq CH_X$, then $t < D((CH_X)', CH_{X''})$. It will be shown that under the condition $t < m_1 \leq d$ and $m \leq t$, $CH_{X''} \neq CH_X$ always holds.

If $m = 0$, then $X'' = X' = X + Y$ with $W(Y) = m_1$. That is, $D(X'', X) = m_1$. Since $t < m_1 \leq d = 2|S| - t - 1$, according to the definition of CH, $CH_{X''} \neq CH_X$.

If $0 < m \leq t$, then $X'' = X' + A$ with $W(A) = m$. On the other hand, $X' = X + B$ with $W(B) = m_1$. Thus, $X'' = X + A + B$, and hence

$$m_1 - m \leq D(X'', X) = W(A+B) \leq m_1 + m. \qquad (4.1)$$

Since $t < m_1 \leq d = 2|S| - t - 1$ and $0 < m \leq t$, we have

$$m_1 + m \leq 2|S| - 1, \qquad (4.2)$$

and

$$1 \leq m_1 - m. \qquad (4.3)$$

In (4.3), $m_1 - m = 1$ happens only when $m = t$ and $m_1 = t+1$. But since C is a t-error correcting and $(t + 1)$-error detecting code, this will never occur. Thus, (4.3) can be rewritten as

$$2 \leq m_1 - m. \qquad (4.4)$$

Now, combining (4.1), (4.2), with (4.4), we have

$$2 \leq D(X'', X) \leq 2|S| - 1.$$

Thus, by the definition of CH, $CH_{X''} \neq CH_X$. Therefore, the algorithm signals "errors detected." //

V. On the Number of Check Bits and the Optimality of the Code

When new codes are developed, it is important to know how close are these codes compared to the possible optimal codes in terms of the number of check bits. In this direction, a lower bound on the number of check bits in a t-EC d-UED code is developed.

Theorem 5.1: For any systematic t-EC d-UED code ($1 \leq t$) with k information bits and r check bits, r must satisfy the following condition:

$$\log_2 \left[\sum_{i=0}^{t} \binom{k}{i} + \binom{k}{t+1} - \binom{k-d+t}{t+1} \right] \leq r.$$

Proof: Consider the following sets of k-tuple information symbols.

$$B_0 = \{I = (i_0, \cdots, i_{k-1}) | W(I) \leq t\}, \text{ and}$$

$$B_j = \{I = (i_0, \cdots, i_{k-1}) | i_s = 1, \quad \text{for } 0 \leq s \leq j-1, \text{ and } W(I) = t+j\}, \text{ for } 1 \leq j \leq d-t.$$

Now, define

$$S = \bigcup_{i=0}^{d-t} B_i.$$

By Theorem 2.2, it is easy to see that all information symbols in S need distinct check symbols. And

$$|S| = \sum_{i=0}^{t} \binom{k}{i} + \sum_{i=1}^{d-t} \binom{k-i}{t}$$

$$= \sum_{i=0}^{t} \binom{k}{i} + \binom{k}{t+1} - \binom{k-d+t}{t+1}.$$

Therefore, the condition holds. //

For $t = 1$, the lower bound in the theorem is $\log_2((d(2k - d + 1) + 2)/2)$; which is approximately equal to $\log_2(k) + \log_2(d)$.

The number of check bits used in the SEC d-UED code described in Section III is approximately equal to $\log_2(k) + (1 + s)$, where s = the length of CH in the proposed code. Thus, in Method C, if $s \ll |S|$, the code is close to optimal.

VI. Conclusion

We have presented, first, the fundamental theory of t-EC d-UED codes and then given many code designs. The codes are designed by appropriately appending check symbols to the codewords of a distance $2t + 2$ code C. Any efficient distance $2t + 2$ systematic code can be used for C. We have also presented the encoding/decoding algorithms. The optimality of these codes are also considered. When the error nature is of unidirectional type, which is the case in many VLSI systems, these codes are very useful.

Acknowledgment

The authors wish to thank Dr. M. Blaum and the referees, in particular, the referees C and D, for their valuable comments.

References

[1] B. Bose and D. K. Pradhan, "Optimal unidirectional error detecting/correcting codes," *IEEE Trans. Comput.*, vol. C-31, pp. 564–568, June 1982.

[2] B. Bose and T. R. N. Rai, "Unidirectional error codes for shift register memories," *IEEE Trans. Comput.*, vol. C-33, pp. 575–578, June 1984.

[3] D. Nikolos, N. Gaitanis, and G. Philokyprou, "t-Error Correcting all unidirectional error detecting codes starting from cyclic AN codes," in *Dig. Papers. 14th Int. Symp. Fault-Tolerant Comput.*, June 1984, pp. 318–323.

[4] ——, "Systematic t-error correcting/all unidirectional error detecting codes," *IEEE Trans. Comput.*, vol. C-35, pp. 394–402, May 1986.

[5] D. K. Pradhan, "A new class of error correcting/detecting codes for fault tolerant computer applications," *IEEE Trans. Comput.*, vol. C-29, pp. 471–481, June 1980.

[6] D. K. Pradhan and S. M. Reddy, "Fault tolerant failsafe logic networks," in *Proc. IEEE COMPCON*, Mar. 1977, pp. 361–363.

[7] D. K. Pradhan and J. J. Stiffler, "Error-correcting codes and self-checking circuits," *IEEE Computer*, vol. 13, pp. 27–37, Mar. 1980.

[8] J. F. Wakerly, "Detection of unidirectional multiple errors using low-cost arithmetic codes," *IEEE Trans. Comput.*, vol. C-24, pp. 210–212, Feb. 1975.

[9] D. Tasar and V. Tasar, "A study of intermittent faults in digital computers," in *Proc. AFIPS Conf.*, 1977, pp. 807–811.

[10] M. Goto, "Rates of unidirectional 2-column errors detectable by arithmetic codes," in *Dig. Papers, 10th Int. Symp. Fault-Tolerant Comput.*, Oct. 1980, pp. 21–25.

[11] B. Parhami and A. Avizienis, "Detection of storage errors in mass memories using low-cost arithmetic error codes," *IEEE Trans. Comput.*, vol. C-27, pp. 302–308, Apr. 1978.

[12] R. W. Cook, W. H. Sisson, T. F. Storey, and W. N. Toy, "Design of self-checking microprogram control," *IEEE Trans. Comput.*, vol. C-22, pp. 255–262, Mar. 1973.

[13] D. L. Tao, C. R. P. Hartmann, and P. K. Lala, "An efficient class of unidirectional error detecting/correcting codes," to be published.

[14] D. J. Lin, "Unidirectional error correcting/detecting codes," Ph.D. dissertation, Oregon State Univ., Corvallis, OR, July 1987.

[15] B. Bose, "Unidirectional error correction/detection for VLSI memory," in *Dig. Papers, 11th Int. Symp. Comput. Architecture.*, June 1984, pp. 242–244.

[16] B. Bose and T. R. N. Rao, "Theory of unidirectional error correcting/detecting codes," *IEEE Trans. Comput.*, vol. C-31, pp. 521–530, June 1982.

[17] F. J. MacWilliams and N. J. A. Sloane, *The Theory of Error-Correcting Codes*. Amsterdam, The Netherlands: North-Holland, 1977.

[18] A. E. Brouwer, "A few new constant weight codes," *IEEE Trans. Inform. Theory*, vol. IT-26, p. 366, May 1980.

[19] R. E. Kibler, "Some new constant weight codes," *IEEE Trans. Inform. Theory*, vol. IT-26, pp. 364–365, May 1980.

Der Jei Lin (S'86–M'88) received the B.S. and M.A. degrees in mathematics and the Ph.D. degree in computer science from Fu-Jen University, Taipei, Taiwan, Oakland University, Rochester, MI, and Oregon State University, Corvallis, in 1967, 1973, and 1987, respectively.

His research interests include coding theory, combinatorics, algorithm analysis, and cryptography.

Dr. Lin is a member of the Association for Computing Machinery.

Bella Bose (S'78, M'79) received the B.E. degree in electrical engineering from Madras University, Madras, India, in 1973, the M.E. degree in electrical engineering from the Indian Institute of Science, Bangalore, in 1975, and the M.S. and Ph.D. degrees in computer science and engineering from Southern Methodist University, Dallas, TX in 1979 and 1980, respectively.

Since 1980 he has been with the Department of Computer Science, Oregon State University, Corvallis. At present, he is an Associate Professor in this department. He was a Visiting Associate Professor at Stanford University from January 1987 to September 1987. His current research interests include error control codes, fault-tolerant computing, algorithm analysis, and VLSI.

Dr. Bose is a member of the Association for Computing Machinery.

Theory and Design of t-Error Correcting/ d-Error Detecting ($d > t$) and All Unidirectional Error Detecting Codes

Dimitris Nikolos

Abstract—**In this paper, the fundamental theory of t-error correcting/ d-error detecting ($d > t$) and all unidirectional error detecting (t-EC/d-ED/AUED) codes is given. A method for construction of systematic t-EC/d-ED/AUED codes is presented. The encoding/decoding algorithms for these codes and their implementation are also described.**

Index Terms—**Error correction, error detection, parity check codes, permanent faults, random errors, transient faults, unidirectional errors.**

I. Introduction

A VARIETY of error control codes has been proposed and many of them have been used to enhance the reliability of computer systems. Of special interest are the error detecting and correcting codes that are effective against transient, intermittent, and permanent faults [1]–[3].

Transient faults are likely to cause a limited number of symmetric errors (both $1 \to 0$ and $0 \to 1$ errors are equally likely to occur in a data word) or multiple unidirectional errors (both $1 \to 0$ and $0 \to 1$ errors can occur but in any particular word all errors are of the same type) [1], [2]. Also, intermittent faults, because of short duration [4], are expected to cause a limited number of errors. On the other hand, permanent faults cause either symmetric or unidirectional errors, depending on the nature of the faults [1], [2], [6]. The most likely faults in some of the recently developed LSI/VLSI ROM and RAM memories (such as the faults that affect address decoders, word lines, power supply, and stuck-fault in a serial bus, etc., [1], [2], [5]–[7]) cause unidirectional errors. The number of symmetric errors is usually limited while the number of unidirectional errors, caused by the above mentioned faults, can be fairly large. Taking into account the above and the fact that many of the symmetric errors stem from transient and intermittent faults as well as the fact that error correction is the best way to cope with transient and intermittent faults, t-EC/AUED codes have been designed [2], [3], [8]–[14], [25]. Recently, t-EC/d-UED codes with $d > t$ have been designed [26] for the cases in which the number of unidirectional errors, even though large, is also limited.

Apart from the effectiveness of an error control code in combating errors, its suitability for use in a computer system heavily depends also on the existence of simple and fast encoder and decoder circuits [1], [16]. Unless the hardware needed to generate and check the code is relatively simple compared to the hardware monitored, a fault-prone decoder could increase rather than decrease the likelihood of erroneous information propagation. Also even a delay of one microsecond in handling critical-path information in a computer could be intolerable. Unfortunately, both the decoder complexity and the decoding delay tend to increase rapidly with the number of errors to be corrected [15]. In practice we usually correct a very small number of errors in order to keep the decoder complexity low and the decoding delay small. Then, to prevent some symmetric errors to pass undetected, we should be able to detect a greater number of symmetric errors. Thus, in this paper, we propose the use of t-EC/d-ED/AUED codes, with $t < d$, instead of t-EC/AUED codes which have already been proposed. t-EC/d-ED/AUED codes stand for codes which are capable of correcting all errors with multiplicity (Hamming weight) less than or equal to t, detecting all errors with multiplicity greater than t and less than or equal to d, and also detecting all ($d + 1$ or more) errors if they are unidirectional. To this end we give the necessary and sufficient conditions for a code to be t-EC/d-ED/AUED, with $t < d$, as well as a general method for designing such codes. Some preliminary results on t-EC/d-ED/AUED codes are given in [17]. The codes given here are superior.

As we will show in Section II some methods which have already been given for designing t-EC/AUED codes can be used also for designing t-EC/d-ED/AUED codes with $d > t$. However, the method presented in this paper gives much superior codes.

The paper is organized as follows. In Section II, the necessary and sufficient conditions for a code to be t-EC/d-ED/AUED, with $d > t$, are given. A method for the construction of systematic t-EC/d-ED/AUED codes is described in Section III. Also in this section the implementation of these codes is discussed. In Section IV, we present the error detection/correction algorithm. In Section V, we give t-EC/d-ED/AUED codes with $d > t + 1$, for various values of the parameters t and d.

The following notations are used in this paper.

$N(X, Y)$: number of $1 \to 0$ crossovers from X to Y.

$D(X, Y)$: Hamming distance between X and Y.

$D(C)$: minimum distance of a code C.

$W(X)$: weight or number of 1's in X.

$L(X)$: number of 0's in X.

$\Delta(X, Y) = \max\{N(X, Y), N(Y, X)\}$: asymmetric distance between X and Y.

$\Delta = \min_{X, Y \in A, X \neq Y} \Delta(X, Y)$: minimum asymmetric distance of a code A.

$|A|$: the cardinality of a code A.

$\lfloor Z \rfloor$: the largest integer less than or equal to Z.

$\lceil Z \rceil$: the smallest integer greater than or equal to Z.

II. Necessary and Sufficient Conditions for t-EC/d-ED/AUED Codes with $d > t$

Let X and Y be two binary n-tuples. Then by $N(X, Y)$ we denote

Manuscript received September 8, 1988; revised August 1, 1989.

The author was with the Computers Laboratory, University of Athens, Athens, Greece. He is now with the Department of Computer Engineering and Informatics, University of Patras, 26500 Rio, Patras, Greece.

IEEE Log Number 9041276.

0-8186-4182-7/93 $3.00 © 1991 IEEE

the number of $1 \to 0$ crossovers from X to Y. For example, let $X = 110100$ and $Y = 100001$; then $N(X,Y) = 2$ and $N(Y,X) = 1$. The Hamming distance $D(X,Y)$ between two words is the number of positions in which they differ. It is obvious that $D(X,Y) = N(X,Y) + N(Y,X)$.

The following theorem [2], [10] gives the necessary and sufficient conditions for a code to be t-EC/AUED.

Theorem 1: A code C is t-EC/AUED iff it satisfies the following condition: for all $X, Y \in C$ with $X \neq Y$, $N(X,Y) \geq t+1$ and $N(Y,X) \geq t+1$.

A stronger result for a code C is given in the following theorem [8], [10].

Theorem 2: For all distinct $X, Y \in C$ if $N(X,Y) \geq t+1$ and $N(Y,X) \geq t+1$, then C is capable of correcting t or fewer symmetric errors, detecting $t+1$ symmetric errors, and also detecting all ($t+2$ or more) unidirectional errors.

The following theorem gives the necessary and sufficient conditions for a code to be t-EC/d-ED/AUED, with $d > t+1$.

Theorem 3: A code C is t-EC/d-ED/AUED with $d > t+1$ if and only if it satisfies the following conditions: for all distinct $X, Y \in C$, $D(X,Y) \geq t+d+1$, $N(X,Y) \geq t+1$ and $N(Y,X) \geq t+1$.

The proof of Theorem 3 is given in the Appendix.

We remind that in the methods given in [3], [13], and [14] for designing t-EC/AUED codes, the first step was the encoding of the information in a systematic t-error correcting parity check code. Therefore, Theorem 3 implies that the methods mentioned in [3], [13] (only the first method of this reference), and [14] can be used also for the construction of t-EC/d-ED/AUED codes with $d > t+1$ provided in the first step the information to be encoded in a systematic t error correcting and d error detecting parity check code. However, the methods which are presented in this paper give significantly more efficient codes.

III. Design of Systematic t-EC/d-ED/AUED Codes with $d > t$

In this section, we will develop a method for constructing systematic t-EC/d-ED/AUED codes, with $d > t$. To this end we will use systematic t-error correcting and d-error detecting parity check codes, as well as codes with minimum asymmetric distance Δ greater than or equal to one.

The minimum asymmetric distance Δ of a binary code A is defined as

$$\Delta = \min_{\substack{X,Y \in A \\ X \neq Y}} \Delta(X,Y)$$

where $\Delta(X,Y) = \max\{N(X,Y), N(Y,X)\}$.

Let F be a systematic t-error correcting and d-error detecting parity check code with length n'. Also, let $A_1, A_2, \ldots, A_k$, with $1 \leq k \leq t+1$, be codes with lengths $r_1, r_2, \ldots, r_k$ and asymmetric distances $\Delta_1, \Delta_2, \cdots, \Delta_k$ such that $\sum_{f=1}^{k} \Delta_f = t+1$.

As a code A_j with asymmetric distance $\Delta_j = 1$ we will use the binary representation of the numbers $0, 1, 2, \cdots, 2^{\lceil \log(n'+1) \rceil - a_j} - 1$, where the value of a_j is such that $2^{a_j} \leq d - t + 1 + 2 \cdot \sum_{f=1}^{j-1} \Delta_f < 2^{a_j+1}$. Then the cardinality of the code will be $|A_j| = 2^{\lceil \log(n'+1) \rceil - a_j}$ and its length $r_j = \lceil \log(n'+1) \rceil - a_j$. The cardinality of any code A_i with $\Delta_i > 1$ is $|A_i| \geq \left\lceil (n'+1) / \left(d - t + 1 + 2 \cdot \sum_{f=1}^{i-1} \Delta_f \right) \right\rceil$.

For any code A_i with $\Delta_i > 1$ consider the $|A_i| \times r_i$ matrix M_i whose rows are the codewords of A_i in the order of nondescending weights. Also, for any code A_j with $\Delta_j = 1$ consider the $|A_j| \times r_j$ matrix M_j whose row m is the binary representation of m.

Code Construction Technique

The codewords in the proposed t-EC/d-ED/AUED code, $d > t$, have the following form

$$X R_{1,i_1} R_{2,i_2} \cdots R_{k,i_k}$$

i.e., each codeword is the concatenation of $X, R_{1,i_1}, R_{2,i_2}, \cdots, R_{k,i_k}$. X represents the encoding of the given information bits into a codeword in a systematic t-error correcting and d-error detecting parity check code. For $\Delta_j \neq 1$ R_{j,i_j} is the row i_j of matrix M_j with $i_j = \left\lfloor L(X) / \left(d - t + 1 + 2 \cdot \sum_{f=1}^{j-1} \Delta_f \right) \right\rfloor$, where $L(X)$ denotes the number of 0's in X. While for $\Delta_j = 1$ R_{j,i_j} is the row i_j of the matrix M_j with $i_j = \lfloor L(X)/2^{a_j} \rfloor$, where the value of a_j satisfies the relation $2^{a_j} \leq d - t + 1 + 2 \cdot \sum_{f=1}^{j-1} \Delta_f < 2^{a_j+1}$.

We note that for any pair of values of t and d, the above method constructs a family of t-EC/d-ED/AUED codes. For example, for $t = 2$ and $d = 8$ the above method gives four different 2-EC/8-ED/AUED codes:

one 2-EC/8-ED/AUED code with codewords of the form

$$X R_{1,i_1} \quad \text{where } R_{1,i_1} \in A_1 \quad \text{and} \quad \Delta_1 = 3,$$

two 2-EC/8-ED/AUED codes with codewords of the form

$$X R_{1,i_1} R_{2,i_2} \quad \text{where } R_{1,i_1} \in A_1, \; R_{2,i_2} \in A_2 \quad \text{and} \quad \Delta_1 = 1, \; \Delta_2 = 2 \quad \text{or} \quad \Delta_1 = 2 \quad \text{and} \quad \Delta_2 = 1,$$

one 2-EC/8-ED/AUED code with codewords of the form

$$X R_{1,i_1} R_{2,i_2} R_{3,i_3} \quad \text{where } R_{j,i_j} \in A_j \quad \text{and} \quad \Delta_j = 1 \quad \text{for } j = 1, 2, 3.$$

As the value of t increases the number of different t-EC/d-ED/AUED codes, with specific values of t and d, which can be constructed by the above method increases too.

For example for $t = 3$ and $d = 8$ our method gives eight different 3-EC/8-ED/AUED codes:

one 3-EC/8-ED/AUED code with codewords of the form

$$X R_{1,i_1} \quad \text{where } R_{1,i_1} \in A_1 \quad \text{and} \quad \Delta_1 = 4,$$

three 3-EC/8-ED/AUED codes with codewords of the form

$$X R_{1,i_1} R_{2,i_2} \quad \text{where } R_{1,i_1} \in A_1, \; R_{2,i_2} \in A_2 \quad \text{and} \quad \Delta_1 = 1, \; \Delta_2 = 3 \quad \text{or} \quad \Delta_1 = 3, \; \Delta_2 = 1 \quad \text{or} \quad \Delta_1 = \Delta_2 = 2,$$

three 3-EC/8-ED/AUED codes with codewords of the form

$$X R_{1,i_1} R_{2,i_2} R_{3,i_3} \quad \text{where } R_{1,i_1} \in A_1, \; R_{2,i_2} \in A_2, \; R_{3,i_3} \in A_3 \quad \text{and} \quad \Delta_1 = \Delta_2 = 1, \; \Delta_3 = 2 \quad \text{or} \quad \Delta_1 = 1, \; \Delta_2 = 2, \; \Delta_3 = 1 \quad \text{or} \quad \Delta_1 = 2 \quad \text{and} \quad \Delta_2 = \Delta_3 = 1,$$

one 3-EC/8-ED/AUED code with codewords of the form

$$X R_{1,i_1} R_{2,i_2} R_{3,i_3} R_{4,i_4} \quad \text{where } R_{j,i_j} \in A_j \quad \text{and} \quad \Delta_j = 1 \quad \text{for } j = 1, 2, 3, 4.$$

As we will see later, the above codes do not need the same number of check bits.

In the following, we illustrate the code construction technique.

TABLE I

BOUNDS OF THE CARDINALITY OF ASYMMETRIC ERROR/CORRECTING CODES [23]

n	Δ=2	Δ=3	Δ=4	Δ=5
5	6	2	2	2
6	12	4	2	2
7	18	4	2	2
8	36	7	4	2
9	62	12	4	2
10	108-117	18	6	4
11	174-210	30-32	8	4
12	316-410	54-63	12	4
13	586-786	98-114	18	6
14	1096-1500	186-218	30-34	8
15	2048-2828	266-398	44-50	12
16	3856-5430	364-739	66-90	16
17	7296-10374	647-1279	122-168	26
18	13798-19898	1218-2380	234-320	36-44
19	26216-38008	2050-4242	450-616	46-76
20	49940-73174	2564-8069	860-1144	54-134
21	95326-140798	4251-14374	1628-2134	62-229
22	182362-271953	8450-26679	3072-4116	88-423
23	349536-523586	16388-50200	4096-7346	133-745

Consider the systematic parity check code F with generator matrix

$$G = \begin{bmatrix} 1 & 0 & 0 & 0 & 0 & 0 & 0 & 0 & 0 & 1 & 1 & 1 & 1 & 1 & 1 & 1 \\ 0 & 1 & 0 & 0 & 0 & 0 & 1 & 1 & 1 & 1 & 1 & 1 & 0 & 0 & 0 & 1 \\ 0 & 0 & 1 & 1 & 1 & 1 & 1 & 1 & 1 & 0 & 0 & 0 & 0 & 0 & 0 & 1 \end{bmatrix}.$$

F has 3 information bits and for all distinct $X, Y \in F$ $D(X,Y) \geq 8$. We will use the parity check code F in order to construct 2-EC/5-ED/AUED codes. According to our method we can construct four different 2-EC/5-ED/AUED codes. Each of these codes is constructed in one of the following four examples.

Example 1: In this example, we will construct a 2-EC/5-ED/AUED code with codewords of the form XR_{1,i_1} where $R_{1,i_1} \in A_1$ and $\Delta_1 = 3$.

The cardinality of A_1 should be $|A_1| \geq \lceil (n'+1)/(d-t+1) \rceil = 5$. Table I contains bounds on the cardinality of asymmetric error correcting codes [23]. From Table I we can see that a code with five codewords and $\Delta \geq 3$ will have length greater than or equal to 8. We will use the code with codewords (00000000), (00000111), (00111000),(00111111), and (11110100). Then the matrix M_1 will be

$$M_1 = \begin{bmatrix} 0 & 0 & 0 & 0 & 0 & 0 & 0 & 0 \\ 0 & 0 & 0 & 0 & 0 & 1 & 1 & 1 \\ 0 & 0 & 1 & 1 & 1 & 0 & 0 & 0 \\ 1 & 1 & 1 & 1 & 0 & 1 & 0 & 0 \\ 0 & 0 & 1 & 1 & 1 & 1 & 1 & 1 \end{bmatrix}.$$

In Table II we present all the codewords of the 2-EC/5-ED/AUED code.

Example 2: In this example, we will construct a 2-EC/5-ED/AUED code with codewords of the form $XR_{1,i_1}R_{2,i_2}$, where $R_{1,i_1} \in A_1$ and $R_{2,i_2} \in A_2$ with $\Delta_1 = 1$ and $\Delta_2 = 2$.

TABLE II

2-EC/5-ED/AUED CODE OF EXAMPLE 1

X		R_{1,i_1}
0 0 1	1 1 1 1 1 1 0 0 0 0 0 0 1	0 0 1 1 1 0 0 0
0 1 0	0 0 0 1 1 1 1 1 1 0 0 0 1	0 0 1 1 1 0 0 0
1 0 0	0 0 0 0 0 0 1 1 1 1 1 1 1	0 0 1 1 1 0 0 0
0 0 0	0 0 0 0 0 0 0 0 0 0 0 0 0	0 0 1 1 1 1 1 1
0 1 1	1 1 1 0 0 0 1 1 1 0 0 0 0	0 0 1 1 1 0 0 0
1 0 1	1 1 1 1 1 1 1 1 1 1 1 1 0	0 0 0 0 0 0 0 0
1 1 0	0 0 0 1 1 1 0 0 0 1 1 1 0	0 0 1 1 1 0 0 0
1 1 1	1 1 1 0 0 0 0 0 0 1 1 1 1	0 0 0 0 0 1 1 1

TABLE III

2-EC/5-ED/AUED CODE OF EXAMPLE 2

X		R_{1,i_1}	R_{2,i_2}
0 0 1	1 1 1 1 1 1 0 0 0 0 0 0 1	0 1 0	0 0 1 1
0 1 0	0 0 0 1 1 1 1 1 1 0 0 0 1	0 1 0	0 0 1 1
1 0 0	0 0 0 0 0 0 1 1 1 1 1 1 1	0 1 0	0 0 1 1
0 0 0	0 0 0 0 0 0 0 0 0 0 0 0 0	1 0 0	1 1 1 1
0 1 1	1 1 1 0 0 0 1 1 1 0 0 0 0	0 1 0	0 0 1 1
1 0 1	1 1 1 1 1 1 1 1 1 1 1 1 0	0 0 0	0 0 0 0
1 1 0	0 0 0 1 1 1 0 0 0 1 1 1 0	0 1 0	0 0 1 1
1 1 1	1 1 1 0 0 0 0 0 0 1 1 1 1	0 0 1	0 0 1 1

According to our method the cardinality of A_1 will be $|A_1| = 2^{\lceil \log(n'+1) \rceil - a_1}$, where the value of a_1 is such that $2^{a_1} \leq d - t + 1 < 2^{a_1+1}$.

Therefore, $a_1 = 2$ and $|A_1| = 8$. Then the matrix M_1 will be

$$M_1 = \begin{bmatrix} 0 & 0 & 0 \\ 0 & 0 & 1 \\ 0 & 1 & 0 \\ 0 & 1 & 1 \\ 1 & 0 & 0 \\ 1 & 0 & 1 \\ 1 & 1 & 0 \\ 1 & 1 & 1 \end{bmatrix}.$$

The cardinality of A_2 will be $|A_2| \geq \lceil (n'+1)/(d-t+1+2) \rceil = 3$. As A_2 we will use the code with codewords (1 1 1 1), (0 0 1 1), and (0 0 0 0).

Then the matrix M_2 will be

$$M_2 = \begin{bmatrix} 0 & 0 & 0 & 0 \\ 0 & 0 & 1 & 1 \\ 1 & 1 & 1 & 1 \end{bmatrix}.$$

In Table III we present all the codewords of the 2-EC/5-ED/AUED code.

TABLE IV
2-EC/5-ED/AUED CODE OF EXAMPLE 3

	X	R_{1,i_1}	R_{2,i_2}
0 0 1	1 1 1 1 1 1 0 0 0 0 0 0 1	1 1 0 0 0	0 1
0 1 0	0 0 0 1 1 1 1 1 1 0 0 0 1	1 1 0 0 0	0 1
1 0 0	0 0 0 0 0 0 1 1 1 1 1 1 1	1 1 0 0 0	0 1
0 0 0	0 0 0 0 0 0 0 0 0 0 0 0 0	1 1 1 1 1	1 0
0 1 1	1 1 1 0 0 0 1 1 1 0 0 0 0	1 1 0 0 0	0 1
1 0 1	1 1 1 1 1 1 1 1 1 1 1 1 0	0 0 0 0 0	0 0
1 1 0	0 0 0 1 1 1 0 0 0 1 1 1 0	1 1 0 0 0	0 1
1 1 1	1 1 1 0 0 0 0 0 0 1 1 1 1	0 0 0 1 1	0 0

Example 3: Here we will construct a 2-EC/5-ED/AUED code with codewords of the form $XR_{1,i_1}R_{2,i_2}$, where

$$R_{1,i_1} \in A_1 \quad \text{and} \quad R_{2,i_2} \in A_2$$
$$\text{with } \Delta_1 = 2 \quad \text{and} \quad \Delta_2 = 1.$$

According to our method the cardinality of A_1 should be $|A_1| \geq \lceil (n'+1)/(d-t+1) \rceil = 5$. As A_1 we will use the code with codewords (0 0 0 0 0), (0 0 0 1 1), (0 1 1 1 0), (1 1 0 0 0), and (1 1 1 1 1). Then the matrix M_1 will be

$$M_1 = \begin{bmatrix} 0 & 0 & 0 & 0 & 0 \\ 0 & 0 & 0 & 1 & 1 \\ 1 & 1 & 0 & 0 & 0 \\ 0 & 1 & 1 & 1 & 0 \\ 1 & 1 & 1 & 1 & 1 \end{bmatrix}.$$

The cardinality of A_2 will be $|A_2| = 2^{\lceil \log(n'+1) \rceil - a_2}$, where the value of a_2 is such that $2^{a_2} \leq d - t + 1 + 2 \cdot 2 < 2^{a_2+1}$. Therefore, $a_2 = 3$ and $|A_2| = 4$. Then the matrix M_2 will be

$$M_2 = \begin{bmatrix} 0 & 0 \\ 0 & 1 \\ 1 & 0 \\ 1 & 1 \end{bmatrix}.$$

In Table IV we present all the codewords of this 2-EC/5-ED/AUED code.

Example 4: In this example we will construct a 2-EC/5-ED/AUED code with codewords of the form

$$XR_{1,i_1}R_{2,i_2}R_{3,i_3} \quad \text{where } R_{j,i_j} \in A_j \quad \text{and}$$
$$\Delta_j = 1 \qquad \text{for } j = 1, 2, 3.$$

According to our method the cardinality of A_j will be $|A_j| = 2^{\lceil \log(n'+1) \rceil - a_j}$, where the values of a_j are such that $2^{a_j} \leq d - t + 1 + 2 \cdot \sum_{f=1}^{j-1} \Delta_f < 2^{a_j+1}$. Therefore, $a_1 = 2$, $a_2 = 2$, $a_3 = 3$ and $|A_1| = 8$, $|A_2| = 8$, $|A_3| = 4$. Then

$$M_1 = M_2 = \begin{bmatrix} 0 & 0 & 0 \\ 0 & 0 & 1 \\ 0 & 1 & 0 \\ 0 & 1 & 1 \\ 1 & 0 & 0 \\ 1 & 0 & 1 \\ 1 & 1 & 0 \\ 1 & 1 & 1 \end{bmatrix} \qquad M_3 = \begin{bmatrix} 0 & 0 \\ 0 & 1 \\ 1 & 0 \\ 1 & 1 \end{bmatrix}.$$

TABLE V
2-EC/5-ED/AUED CODE OF EXAMPLE 4

	X	R_{1,i_1}	R_{2,i_2}	R_{3,i_3}
0 0 1	1 1 1 1 1 1 0 0 0 0 0 0 1	0 1 0	0 1 0	0 1
0 1 0	0 0 0 1 1 1 1 1 1 0 0 0 1	0 1 0	0 1 0	0 1
1 0 0	0 0 0 0 0 0 1 1 1 1 1 1 1	0 1 0	0 1 0	0 1
0 0 0	0 0 0 0 0 0 0 0 0 0 0 0 0	1 0 0	1 0 0	1 0
0 1 1	1 1 1 0 0 0 1 1 1 0 0 0 0	0 1 0	0 1 0	0 1
1 0 1	1 1 1 1 1 1 1 1 1 1 1 1 0	0 0 0	0 0 0	0 0
1 1 0	0 0 0 1 1 1 0 0 0 1 1 1 0	0 1 0	0 1 0	0 1
1 1 1	1 1 1 0 0 0 0 0 0 1 1 1 1	0 0 1	0 0 1	0 0

In Table V we present all the codewords of this 2-EC/5-ED/AUED code.

We can see that the redundancy of the codes of Tables III and IV is 1 bit lower than the redundancy of the codes of Tables II and V. In the majority of cases, the difference of redundancy between the various t-EC/d-ED/AUED codes which are constructed by the method proposed here, for specific values of t and d, is greater than 1. We should note that the form of the code with the least redundancy depends on the values of t and d, and the length of the systematic t-error correcting and d-error detecting parity check code which is used in the construction.

The proposed code construction method implies that encoding in one of the t-EC/d-ED/AUED codes is straightforward and simple. The encoder consists of a t-error correcting and d-error detecting parity check code encoder and a circuit calculating the values of R_{j,i_j} for $j = 1, 2, \cdots, k$.

According to our method the values of R_{j,i_j} depend only on the number of zeros in X, $L(X)$. Therefore, the circuit for the calculation of R_{j,i_j} can be composed from a circuit calculating $L(X)$ [21], [22] (Berger code generator) and a ROM (or a RAM) which accepts the value of $L(X)$ as address and the contents of this address are the values of $R_{1,i_1}, R_{2,i_2}, \cdots, R_{k,i_k}$. Note that the value of $L(X)$ is very small, $L(X) \leq n'$, thus, a ROM with very small number of words, $n' + 1$ words, is enough. Let, for example, a parity check code C with $n' = 255$ and $D(C) = 11$ be used in the construction of a 2-EC/8-ED/AUED code. Then $n' + 1 = 256$ and a ROM of 256 words is enough. (From Table VII we can see that the number of extra check bits is 12. Thus, we need a 256 × 12 bit ROM.) Further reduction can be obtained if we substitute the ROM with a PLA in order to take into account the fact that many different ROM locations contain identical words.

Depending on the form of the code, the encoder can be done simpler. If the codewords of the code have the form

$$XR_{1,i_1}R_{2,i_2} \cdots R_{t+1,i_{t+1}} \quad \text{with } R_{j,i_j} \in A_j \quad \text{and}$$
$$\Delta_j = 1 \qquad \text{for } j = 1, 2, \cdots, t+1$$

the value of R_{j,i_j} can be obtained from the binary representation of the number of zeros in X by discarding the a_j least significant bits. Hence, the values of R_{j,i_j} for $j = 1, 2, \cdots, t+1$ are derived using only a Berger code generator. Therefore, encoding in codes of this form can be carried out faster and with less hardware than the codes of the other forms. The codes with codewords of the form $XR_{1,i_1}R_{2,i_2} \cdots R_{k,i_k}$ where for some values $j_1, j_2, \cdots, j_m$ with $1 \leq j_1, j_2, \cdots, j_m \leq k$ we have $R_{j_f,i_{j_f}} \in A_{j_f}$ with $\Delta_{j_f} = 1$ for $f = 1, 2, \cdots, m$ constitute, with respect to the implementation, intermediate situations. In these cases, the values of $R_{j_f, i_{j_f}}$ can be derived by discarding the a_{j_f} least significant bits of the binary representation of the number of zeros in X. Then, the word length of the ROM will be smaller because the values of $R_{j_f, i_{j_f}}$ for $f = 1, 2, \cdots, m$ will not be stored in the ROM.

The following lemmas are necessary in order to prove that the codes which are constructed by our method are indeed t-EC/d-ED/AUED codes. We can easily see that the following Lemma 1 is equivalent to Lemma 1 in [13] (Theorem 2.1 in [14] constitutes a special case of Lemma 1 in [13] as well as of the following lemma.) We give an independent proof for sake of completeness.

Lemma 1: Let C' be a parity check code with minimum Hamming distance $D(C') = t + d + 1$, where $d \geq t$. If $X, Y \in C'$, $X \neq Y$ and $W(X) - W(Y) = q \geq 0$ then $N(X,Y) \geq t + 1$ and $N(Y,X) \geq \max\{0, t + 1 - \left\lceil \frac{q-(d-t)}{2} \right\rceil\}$.

Proof: Without loss of generality we can assume that

$$\begin{array}{ccccc} & m & N(X,Y) & N(Y,X) & \\ X = & 11\cdots1 & 11\cdots1 & 00\cdots0 & 00\cdots0 \\ Y = & 11\cdots1 & 00\cdots0 & 11\cdots1 & 00\cdots0. \end{array}$$

Since

$$W(X) = N(X,Y) + m \quad (1)$$
$$W(Y) = N(Y,X) + m \quad (2)$$

and the relation $W(X) \geq W(Y)$ implies that $N(X,Y) \geq N(Y,X)$. Then taking into account that

$$N(X,Y) + N(Y,X) \geq D(C') = t + d + 1 \quad \text{with } d \geq t \quad (3)$$

we get $2N(X,Y) \geq t + d + 1$, therefore $N(X,Y) \geq t + 1$. From (1) and (2) we get $W(X) - W(Y) = N(X,Y) - N(Y,X)$ or equivalently $N(X,Y) = W(X) - W(Y) + N(Y,X)$. Then from (3) we get $2N(Y,X) + W(X) - W(Y) \geq t + d + 1$ or equivalently $2N(Y,X) \geq 2t + 1 - (W(X) - W(Y) - (d - t))$ which implies that $N(Y,X) \geq t + 1 - \left\lceil \frac{W(X) - W(Y) - (d-t)}{2} \right\rceil$.

Lemma 2: Let A be a code of length r, cardinality $|A|$, and minimum asymmetric distance $\Delta \geq 1$. Let M be an $|A| \times r$ matrix whose rows are the codewords of A in the order of nondescending weights. Then for any pair of rows a_i, a_j, $i > j$, of the matrix M we have $N(a_i, a_j) \geq \Delta$.

Proof: Consider the rows a_i and a_j of M with $i > j$. Without loss of generality we can assume that

$$\begin{array}{ccccc} & m & N(a_i,a_j) & N(a_j,a_i) & \\ a_i = & 11\cdots1 & 11\cdots1 & 00\cdots0 & 00\cdots0 \\ a_j = & 11\cdots1 & 00\cdots0 & 11\cdots1 & 00\cdots0. \end{array}$$

Since the rows of M constitute a code with minimum asymmetric distance Δ we have

$$\max\{N(a_i,a_j), N(a_j,a_i)\} \geq \Delta. \quad (4)$$

Then since $i > j$ we have $W(a_i) \geq W(a_j)$ or equivalently $m + N(a_i,a_j) \geq m + N(a_j,a_i)$ or equivalently $N(a_i,a_j) \geq N(a_j,a_i)$. Then, from (4), we get $N(a_i,a_j) \geq \Delta$.

Theorem 4: The proposed code C is t-EC/d-ED/AUED.

Proof: According to Theorem 3 we have to prove that for all distinct $S, S' \in C$ $D(S,S') \geq t + d + 1$, $N(S,S') \geq t + 1$ and $N(S',S) \geq t + 1$. Let $S, S' \in C$ with $S = XR_{1,i_1}R_{2,i_2} \cdots R_{k,i_k}$, $S' = YR_{1,j_1}R_{2,j_2} \cdots R_{k,j_k}$ and $L(Y) \geq L(X)$. Then according to the code construction method, X and Y belong to C', where C' is a t-error correcting and d-error detecting parity check code, therefore $D(X,Y) \geq t + d + 1$ and thus $D(S,S') \geq t + d + 1$.

Also since $W(X) \geq W(Y)$ from Lemma 1 we conclude that $N(X,Y) \geq t + 1$, therefore $N(S,S') \geq t + 1$.

In order to prove that $N(S',S) \geq t + 1$ we will consider the following cases.

Case a: $i_m = j_m$ for $m = 1, 2, \cdots, k$.

We consider two subcases.

Subcase a.1: The asymmetric distance of A_1 is $\Delta_1 = 1$.

Since $i_1 = j_1$ from the code construction method we conclude that $\lfloor L(Y)/2^{a_1} \rfloor = \lfloor L(X)/2^{a_1} \rfloor$ or equivalently $L(Y) - L(X) \leq 2^{a_1} - 1$ for a value of a_1 such that $2^{a_1} \leq d - t + 1 < 2^{a_1+1}$. Therefore,

$$L(Y) - L(X) < d - t + 1. \quad (5)$$

Subcase a.2: The asymmetric distance of A_1 is $\Delta_1 > 1$.

Since $i_1 = j_1$ from the code construction method we conclude that $\lfloor L(X)/(d-t+1) \rfloor = \lfloor L(Y)/(d-t+1) \rfloor$ which implies that

$$L(Y) - L(X) < d - t + 1. \quad (6)$$

We can see that relations (5) and (6) are identical, therefore, for both subcases a.1 and a.2 we have $L(Y) - L(X) < d - t + 1$ or equivalently $n' - W(Y) - (n' - W(X)) < d - t + 1$ or $W(X) - W(Y) = q < d - t + 1$ which implies that

$$q \leq d - t. \quad (7)$$

From Lemma 1 we get $N(Y,X) \geq \max\{0, t + 1 - \left\lceil \frac{q-(d-t)}{2} \right\rceil\}$.

Then from (7) we get $N(Y,X) \geq t + 1$, therefore, $N(S', S) \geq t + 1$.

Case b: $i_m \neq j_m$ for $m = 1, 2, \cdots, v$ with $v < k$ and $i_{v+1} = j_{v+1}$.

Since $L(Y) \geq L(X)$ and $i_m \neq j_m$ for $m = 1, 2, \cdots, v$ with $v < k$ we get $j_m > i_m$ for $m = 1, 2, \cdots, v$ with $v < k$. Then Lemma 2 implies $N(R_{m,j_m}, R_{m,i_m}) > \Delta_m$ for $m = 1, 2, \cdots, v$ with $v < k$, therefore

$$N(R_{1,j_1}R_{2,j_2} \cdots R_{v,j_v}R_{1,i_1}R_{2,i_2} \cdots R_{v,i_v}) \geq \sum_{m=1}^{v} \Delta_m. \quad (8)$$

We consider two subcases.

Subcase b.1: The asymmetric distance of A_{v+1} is $\Delta_{v+1} = 1$.

Since $i_{v+1} = j_{v+1}$ from the code construction method we conclude that $\lfloor L(Y)/2^{a_{v+1}} \rfloor = \lfloor L(X)/2^{a_{v+1}} \rfloor$ or equivalently $L(Y) - L(X) < 2^{a_{v+1}}$ for a value of a_{v+1} such that $2^{a_{v+1}} \leq d - t + 1 + 2 \cdot \sum_{m=1}^{v} \Delta_m < 2^{a_{v+1}+1}$.

Therefore,

$$L(Y) - L(X) < d - t + 1 + 2 \cdot \sum_{m=1}^{v} \Delta_m. \quad (9)$$

Subcase b.2: The asymmetric distance of A_{v+1} is $\Delta_{v+1} > 1$.

Since $i_{v+1} = j_{v+1}$ from the code construction method we conclude that $\lfloor L(X)/(d - t + 1 + 2 \cdot \sum_{m=1}^{v} \Delta_m) \rfloor = \lfloor L(Y)/(d - t + 1 + 2 \cdot \sum_{m=1}^{v} \Delta_m) \rfloor$ which implies that

$$L(Y) - L(X) < d - t + 1 + 2 \cdot \sum_{m=1}^{v} \Delta_m. \quad (10)$$

TABLE VI
1-EC/d-ED/AUED Codes

k	n′	d	n	
			$XR_{1,i_1}R_{2,i_2}$ $\Delta_1 = \Delta_2 = 1$	XR_{1,i_1} $\Delta_1 = 2$
6	15	4	19*	19
5	15	5	19*	19
20	31	4	37*	37
16	31	5	37*	37
11	31	9	35*	35
5	31	14	34*	35
50	63	4	71	70*
45	63	5	71	70*
39	63	7	70	69*
38	63	8	69 *	69
36	63	9	69 *	69
23	63	14	68 *	68
112	127	4	137	135*
106	127	5	137	135*
99	127	7	136	135*
98	127	8	135	134*
92	127	9	135	134*
77	127	14	134	133*
238	255	4	267	265*
231	255	5	267	264*
223	255	7	266	264*
222	255	8	265	263*
215	255	9	265	263*
198	255	14	264	263*

We can see that relations (9) and (10) are identical, therefore, for both subcases b.1 and b.2 we have $L(Y) - L(X) < d - t + 1 + 2 \cdot \sum_{m=1}^{v} \Delta_m$ or equivalently $W(X) - W(Y) = q < d - t + 1 + 2 \cdot \sum_{m=1}^{v} \Delta_m$ and thus $q - d + t < 2 \cdot \sum_{m=1}^{v} \Delta_m + 1$ or equivalently

$$q - (d - t) \leq 2 \cdot \sum_{m=1}^{v} \Delta_m. \tag{11}$$

Lemma 1 implies that $N(Y, X) \geq \max\left\{0, t + 1 - \left\lceil \frac{q-(d-t)}{2} \right\rceil\right\}$ thus taking into account (11) we get $N(Y, X) \geq \max\left\{0, t + 1 - \left\lceil \frac{2 \cdot \sum_{m=1}^{v} \Delta_m}{2} \right\rceil\right\}$ or equivalently

$$N(Y, X) \geq t + 1 - \sum_{m=1}^{v} \Delta_m. \tag{12}$$

From (8) and (12) we get $N(YR_{1,j_1}R_{2,j_2} \cdots R_{k,j_k}), XR_{1,i_1} R_{2,i_2} \cdots R_{k,i_k} \geq t + 1$, therefore $N(S', S) \geq t + 1$.

Case c: $i_m \neq j_m$ for $m = 1, 2, \cdots, k$. Since $L(Y) \geq L(X)$ we conclude that $j_m > i_m$ for $m = 1, 2, \cdots, k$. Then from Lemma 2 we get $N(R_{m,j_m}, R_{m,i_m}) \geq \Delta_m$ for $m = 1, 2, 3, \cdots, k$, therefore $N(R_{1,j_1}R_{2,j_2} \cdots R_{k,j_k}, R_{1,i_1}R_{2,i_2} \cdots R_{k,i_k}) \geq \sum_{m=1}^{k} \Delta_m$ and taking into account that $\sum_{m=1}^{k} \Delta_m \geq t + 1$ (see the code construction method) we get $N(S', S) \geq t + 1$.

TABLE VII
2-EC/d-ED/AUED Codes

k	n′	d	n			
			$XR_{1,i1}R_{2,i2}R_{3,i3}$	$XR_{1,i1}R_{2,i2}$		$XR_{1,i1}$
			$\Delta_1 = \Delta_2 = \Delta_3 = 1$	$\Delta_1=1, \Delta_2=2$	$\Delta_1=2, \Delta_2=1$	$\Delta_1=3$
4	15	5	20*	21	20	21
15	31	5	39*	39	39	40
11	31	8	38*	38	38	39
44	63	5	74	73*	73	73
36	63	8	73	73	72*	72
30	63	10	72	71*	72	72
105	127	5	141	140	139*	139
92	127	8	140	139	139	138*
85	127	10	139	137*	138	137
230	255	5	272	270	270	268*
215	255	8	271	269	269	267*
207	255	10	270	268	268	266*

IV. Error Detection/Correction Algorithm for the t-EC/d-ED/AUED Codes

Let $Q = XR_{1,i_1}R_{2,i_2} \cdots R_{k,i_k}$ be an error free codeword in the proposed t-EC/d-ED/AUED code and let $Q' = X'R'_{1,i_1}R'_{2,i_2} \cdots R'_{k,i_k}$ be the resulting vector after some errors in Q.

Error Detection/Correction Algorithm:

Step 1. Compute the syndrome S of X' in the parity check code. Let S correspond to g multiplicity error. If $g > t$ then note that the error is only detectable and stop. While if $g \leq t$ correct X' using the correction procedure in the parity check code obtaining X'' as the resulting word.

Step 2. Compute the values of R''_{j,i_j} for $j = 1, 2, \cdots, k$ which correspond to X''. Call Q'' the word $X''R''_{1,i_1}R''_{2,i_2} \cdots R''_{k,i_k}$. If $D(Q', Q'') \leq t$ then the word Q'' is the correct codeword R. End. Else an only detectable error with multiplicity greater than t has occurred. End.

The following example illustrates how the error detection and correction algorithm is applied.

Example 5:[1] We consider the 2-EC/5-ED/AUED code of Example 1. The parity check matrix which corresponds to the generator matrix G is

$$H = \begin{bmatrix}
0&0&1&1&0&0&0&0&0&0&0&0&0&0&0&0\\
0&0&1&0&1&0&0&0&0&0&0&0&0&0&0&0\\
0&0&1&0&0&1&0&0&0&0&0&0&0&0&0&0\\
0&1&1&0&0&0&1&0&0&0&0&0&0&0&0&0\\
0&1&1&0&0&0&0&1&0&0&0&0&0&0&0&0\\
0&1&1&0&0&0&0&0&1&0&0&0&0&0&0&0\\
1&1&0&0&0&0&0&0&0&1&0&0&0&0&0&0\\
1&1&0&0&0&0&0&0&0&0&1&0&0&0&0&0\\
1&1&0&0&0&0&0&0&0&0&0&1&0&0&0&0\\
1&0&0&0&0&0&0&0&0&0&0&0&1&0&0&0\\
1&0&0&0&0&0&0&0&0&0&0&0&0&1&0&0\\
1&0&0&0&0&0&0&0&0&0&0&0&0&0&1&0\\
1&1&1&0&0&0&0&0&0&0&0&0&0&0&0&1
\end{bmatrix}.$$

Consider the following codeword belonging to the above mentioned 2-EC/5-ED/AUED code

[1] In this example, G^T denotes the transposition matrix of G.

TABLE VIII
3-EC/d-ED/AUED CODES

k	n'	d	n							
			$XR_{1,i1}R_{2,i2}R_{3,i3}R_{4,i4}$	$XR_{1,i1}R_{2,i2}R_{3,i3}$			$XR_{1,i1}R_{2,i2}$			$XR_{1,i}$
			$\Delta_1=\Delta_2=\Delta_3=\Delta_4=1$	$\Delta_1=1, \Delta_2=2$ $\Delta_3=2$	$\Delta_1=\Delta_3=1$ $\Delta_2=2$	$\Delta_1=2$ $\Delta_2=\Delta_3=1$	$\Delta_1=1$ $\Delta_2=3$	$\Delta_1=3$ $\Delta_2=1$	$\Delta_1=\Delta_2=2$	$\Delta_1=4$
11	31	7	41*	41	41	41	42	41	41	42
6	31	11	39*	39	39	39	39	39	39	39
39	63	5	79	78	78	78	78	77*	77	77
38	63	6	77	77	76*	76*	76	76	76	76
30	63	9	76	75	76	75	76	75	74*	75
24	63	11	75	74*	74*	75	74	75	74	74
99	127	5	147	146	145	145	144	143	144	142*
98	127	6	145	144	144	143	143	143	142	141*
85	127	9	144	142	143	143	142	142	141*	141*
78	127	11	143	141	141	142	143	141	140*	140*
223	255	5	279	277	276	276	275	273	274	271*
222	255	6	277	275	275	275	273	273	273	271*
207	255	9	276	274	274	274	272	272	272	270*
199	255	11	275	273	273	273	271	271	271	269*

$$Q = \underbrace{1\,0\,0 \quad 0\,0\,0\,0\,0\,0\,1\,1\,1\,1\,1\,1\,1}_{X} \quad \underbrace{0\,0\,1\,1\,1\,0\,0\,0}_{R_{1,2}}$$

Suppose that two symmetric errors have occurred in the above codeword, in the positions marked with *, as shown below. Let the received word be

$$Q' = \underbrace{1\,\overset{*}{1}\,0 \quad 0\,0\,0\,0\,0\,0\,1\,1\,1\,1\,1\,1\,1}_{X'} \quad \underbrace{0\,0\,\overset{*}{0}\,1\,1\,0\,0\,0}_{R'_{1,2}}.$$

Error Detection/Correction Algorithm:

Step 1. We compute the syndrome S of X' in the parity check code.

$$S = H \cdot X'^T = [0\,0\,0\,1\,1\,1\,1\,1\,1\,1\,0\,0\,0\,1]^T.$$

Since the syndrome S is equal to the second column of the parity check matrix H we conclude that a single error has occurred in the second position of X'. The error is corrected and the resulting word is

$$X'' = (1\,0\,0 \quad 0\,0\,0\,0\,0\,0\,1\,1\,1\,1\,1\,1\,1).$$

Step 2. We consider the value of R''_{1,i_1} which corresponds to X''. Since $L(X) = 8$ we have $i_1 = \lfloor L(X)/(d-t+1) \rfloor = \lfloor 8/(5-2+1) \rfloor = 2$, therefore $R''_{1,i_1} = R_{1,2} = (0\,0\,1\,1\,1\,0\,0\,0)$.

Then $$Q'' = \underbrace{1\,0\,0 \quad 0\,0\,0\,0\,0\,0\,1\,1\,1\,1\,1\,1\,1}_{X''} \quad \underbrace{0\,0\,1\,1\,1\,0\,0\,0}_{R''_{1,i_1}}$$

Since $D(Q', Q'') = 2 \leq t = 2$ the word Q'' is the correct word Q.

Next, we consider the occurrence of a symmetric error with multiplicity five in the same word Q.

Let the received word be

$$Q' = \underbrace{\overset{*}{0}\,\overset{*}{0}\,1 \quad 0\,0\,\overset{*}{1}\,0\,0\,0\,\overset{*}{1}\,0\,1\,1\,1\,1\,1}_{X'} \quad \underbrace{0\,0\,1\,1\,1\,0\,\overset{*}{1}\,0}_{R'_{1,2}}.$$

Step 1. We compute the syndrome S of X' in the parity check code.

$$S = H \cdot X'^T = [1\,1\,0\,1\,1\,1\,1\,0\,1\,1\,1\,1\,0]^T.$$

Since the syndrome is not equal to a column of H or to the sum of two columns of H, more than two errors have occurred in X' and hence in Q. Therefore, the error is only detectable.

Finally, we consider the occurrence of a unidirectional error with multiplicity greater than five in the same word Q. Let the received word be

$$Q' = \underbrace{1\,0\,0 \quad 0\,0\,0\,0\,0\,0\,\overset{*}{0}\,\overset{*}{0}\,\overset{*}{0}\,\overset{*}{0}\,\overset{*}{0}\,\overset{*}{0}\,\overset{*}{0}}_{X'} \quad \underbrace{0\,0\,1\,\overset{*}{0}\,\overset{*}{0}\,0\,0\,0}_{R'_{1,2}}.$$

TABLE IX
4-EC/d-ED/AUED CODES
(*Continued on next page*)

k	n'	d	n							
			$XR_{1.i_1}R_{2.i_2}R_{3.i_3}R_{4.i_4}R_{5.i_5}$	$XR_{1.i_1}R_{2.i_2}R_{3.i_3}R_{4.i_4}$				$XR_{1.i_1}R_{2.i_2}R_{3.i_3}$		
			$\Delta_i = 1$ for $i=1,2,3,4,5$	$\Delta_1=\Delta_2=\Delta_3=1$ $\Delta_4=2$	$\Delta_1=\Delta_2=\Delta_4=1$ $\Delta_3=2$	$\Delta_1=\Delta_3=\Delta_4=1$ $\Delta_2=2$	$\Delta_2=\Delta_3=\Delta_4=1$ $\Delta_1=2$	$\Delta_1=\Delta_2=1$ $\Delta_3=3$	$\Delta_1=\Delta_3=1$ $\Delta_2=3$	$\Delta_2=\Delta_3=1$ $\Delta_1=3$
10	31	7	43*	43	43	43	43	43	44	44
6	31	10	42*	42	42	42	42	42	42	43
35	63	7	80	80	80	79	79	80	79	79
24	63	10	79	78	78	79	78	78	79	78
91	127	7	149	148	148	148	147	147	147	147
78	127	10	148	146	146	147	147	145	146	146
214	255	7	282	280	280	280	280	279	278	278
199	255	10	281	279	279	279	279	277	277	277

Step 2. We compute the syndrome S of X' in the parity check code.

$$S = H \cdot X'^T = [0\ 0\ 0\ 0\ 0\ 0\ 1\ 1\ 1\ 1\ 1\ 1\ 1]^T.$$

Since the syndrome S is equal to the first column of the parity check matrix H we conclude that a single error has occurred in the first position of X'. The error is corrected and the resulting word is

$$X'' = (0\ 0\ 0\ 0\ 0\ 0\ 0\ 0\ 0\ 0\ 0\ 0\ 0\ 0\ 0\ 0].$$

Step 3. We compute the value of $R''_{1.i_1}$ which corresponds to X''. Since $L(X) = 16$ we have $i_1 = \lfloor L(X)/(d-t+1)\rfloor = \lfloor 16/(5-2+1)\rfloor = 4$, therefore $R''_{1,i_1} = R_{1.4} = 0\ 0\ 1\ 1\ 1\ 1\ 1\ 1$. Then

$$Q'' = 0\ 0\ 0\quad \underbrace{0\ 0\ 0\ 0\ 0\ 0\ 0\ 0\ 0\ 0\ 0\ 0\ 0}_{X''}\quad \underbrace{0\ 0\ 1\ 1\ 1\ 1\ 1\ 1}_{R''_{1.i_1}}$$

Since $D(Q', Q'') = 6 > t = 2$ we conclude that only detectable error has occurred.

V. t-EC/d-ED/AUED CODES WITH $d > t + 1$

In Tables VI–IX we present systematic t-EC/d-ED/AUED codes for various values of the parameters t and d, with $d > t + 1$. n denotes the length and k the number of information bits of the t-EC/d-ED/AUED code. By n' we denote the length of the systematic t-error correcting and d-error detecting code which has been used to construct the t-EC/d-ED/AUED code. In our constructions (Tables VI–IX) as t-error correcting and d-error detecting codes we have used BCH codes [18], [19], [24].

In some cases, one information bit of a BCH code was replaced from a parity bit in order to get a code with even Hamming distance. In Tables VI–IX the best t-EC/d-ED/AUED code, for specific values of t and d, is marked by an asterisk. For the characterization of a code as the best we have taken into account the redundancy. In the cases in which more than one t-EC/d-ED/AUED code have the same redundancy we have taken into account the cost of implementation and the speed of encoding and decoding of the candidate t-EC/d-ED/AUED codes.

From Tables VI–IX we can see that for small code lengths the codes with codewords of the form $XR_{1.i_1}R_{2.i_2}\cdots R_{t+1.i_{t+1}}$ with $\Delta_j = 1$ for $j = 1, 2, \cdots, t+1$ are superior, while for large code lengths the codes with codewords of the form $XR_{1.i_1}$ with $\Delta_1 = t + 1$ are superior.

We have to note that, depending on the weight distribution [24] of the t-error correcting and d-error detecting parity check code, which is used in the construction of a t-EC/d-ED/AUED code, the number of different values which the expression $\left\lfloor L(X)/\left(d-t+1+2\cdot\sum_{f=1}^{j-1}\Delta_f\right)\right\rfloor$ (or $\lfloor L(X)/2^{a_j}\rfloor$) takes may be much smaller than the value of the expression $\left\lceil (n'+1)/\left(d-t+1+2\cdot\sum_{f=1}^{i-1}\Delta_f\right)\right\rceil$. In these cases, the redundancy of the t-EC/d-ED/AUED codes can be further reduced.

TABLE IX
(Continued)

n							
$XR_{1,i_1}R_{2,i_2}$		$XR_{1,i_1}R_{2,i_2}R_{3,i_3}$			$XR_{1,i_1}R_{2,i_2}$		XR_{1,i_1}
$\Delta_1=1,\ \Delta_2=4$	$\Delta_1=4, \Delta_2=1$	$\Delta_1=1, \Delta_2=\Delta_3=2$	$\Delta_1=\Delta_3=2,\ \Delta_2=1$	$\Delta_1=\Delta_2=2, \Delta_3=1$	$\Delta_1=3,\ \Delta_2=2$	$\Delta_1=2,\ \Delta_2=3$	$\Delta_1=5$
44	44	43	43	43	44	43	45
42	43	42	42	43	43	42	44
79	79	79	79	78*	79	78*	79
78	78	77*	77*	77	77	77	78
146	145*	146	146	145	146	145	145
145	145	145	145	144*	144*	144*	144
276*	276	278	278	276	276	277	277
275	275	277	277	275	275	275	274*

For instance, we refer to the code of Example 1 (Table II). We can see that the codewords contain 2, 6, 8, or 16 zeros, that is $L(X)$ is equal to 2, 6, 8, or 16. Then the value of the expression $\lfloor L(X)/4 \rfloor$ is equal to 0, 1, 2, or 4. Therefore, what is needed is a code A_1' with asymmetric distance $\Delta_1 = 3$ and cardinality $|A_1'| = 4$. Then from Table I we can see that the length of A_1' will be six and its words can be (0 0 0 0 0 0), (0 0 0 1 1 1), (1 1 1 0 0 0), and (1 1 1 1 1 1). Therefore,

$$M_1' = \begin{bmatrix} 0 & 0 & 0 & 0 & 0 & 0 \\ 0 & 0 & 0 & 1 & 1 & 1 \\ 1 & 1 & 1 & 0 & 0 & 0 \\ 1 & 1 & 1 & 1 & 1 & 1 \end{bmatrix}.$$

In Table X we give all the codewords of the 2-EC/5-ED/AUED code derived using A_1'. We can see that this code has 2 check bits less than the code of Table II. For the same reasons, in Example 2 instead of the code A_1 we can use the code A_1' with codewords (00), (01), (10), (11), and

$$M_1' = \begin{bmatrix} 0 & 0 \\ 0 & 1 \\ 1 & 0 \\ 1 & 1 \end{bmatrix}.$$

Then we can easily see that, the code which is derived requires one check bit less than the code of Example 2. Also, in Example 3 instead of the code A_1 we can use a code A_1' with $\Delta_1' = 2$ and $|A_1'| = 4$. Considering as A_1' the code with codewords (0 0 0 0), (1 1 0 0), (0 0 1 1), and (1 1 1 1) we can see that the 2-EC/5-ED/AUED code which is derived here has one check bit less than that of Example 3. Finally in Example 4 instead of A_1 and A_2 we can use the codes A_1' and A_2' with codewords (00), (01), (10), and (11). Then, the code which is constructed has two bits less than that of Example 4.

TABLE X
2-EC/5-ED/AUED CODE

X		R_{1,i_1}
0 0 1	1 1 1 1 1 1 0 0 0 0 0 0 1	1 1 1 0 0 0
0 1 0	0 0 0 1 1 1 1 1 1 0 0 0 1	1 1 1 0 0 0
1 0 0	0 0 0 0 0 0 1 1 1 1 1 1 1	1 1 1 0 0 0
0 0 0	0 0 0 0 0 0 0 0 0 0 0 0 0	1 1 1 1 1 1
0 1 1	1 1 1 0 0 0 1 1 1 0 0 0 0	1 1 1 0 0 0
1 0 1	1 1 1 1 1 1 1 1 1 1 1 1 0	0 0 0 0 0 0
1 1 0	0 0 0 1 1 1 0 0 0 1 1 1 0	1 1 1 0 0 0
1 1 1	1 1 1 0 0 0 0 0 0 1 1 1 1	0 0 0 1 1 1

VI. CONCLUSION

In this paper, we have presented the fundamental theory of t-EC/d-ED/AUED codes, with $d > t$. Also we have given a method for construction of systematic t-EC/d-ED/AUED codes, with $d > t$, as well as encoding/decoding algorithms and their implementation. For any pair of values of the parameters t and d, with $d > t$, the proposed method gives a family of t-EC/d-ED/AUED codes. These codes differ with respect to the redundancy, the speed of encoding and decoding, and the cost of their implementation.

Appendix

Here we will give the proof of Theorem 3.

In the following discussion, T_Z refers to the set of vectors obtained from Z due to m_1 $(0 \le m_1 \le t)$ symmetric errors in Z, Q_Z refers to the set of vectors obtained from Z due to m_2 $(m_2 \ge d + 1)$ unidirectional errors in Z, and M_Z refers to the set of vectors obtained from Z due to m_3 $(t + 1 \le m_3 \le d)$ symmetric errors in Z.

Lemma A1 is similar to Lemma 2.16 in [9].

Lemma A1: For a pair of vectors X and Y, if $N(X,Y) \ge t + 1$ and $N(Y,X) \ge t + 1$ then

$$T_X \cap Q_X = \emptyset \tag{A1}$$

and

$$T_X \cap Q_Y = \emptyset. \tag{A2}$$

Proof: For any $Y' \in Q_Y$, if Y' is obtained from Y due to m $(m \ge d + 1)$ $1 \rightarrow 0$ errors, then taking into account that $N(X,Y) \ge t + 1$ we conclude that $N(X,Y') \ge t + 1$; while, if Y' is obtained from Y due to m $(m \ge d + 1)$ $0 \rightarrow 1$ errors, then taking into account that $N(Y,X) \ge t + 1$ we conclude that $N(Y',X) \ge t + 1$. Hence, in both cases we have $D(X,Y') \ge t + 1$.

For all $X' \in T_X$, $D(X,X') \le t$. Therefore, if $Y' \in Q_Y$ then $Y' \notin T_X$ which implies $T_X \cap Q_Y = \emptyset$.

Equation (A1) is obvious by definition of T_X and Q_X.

Proof of Theorem 3: Let M be the set of vectors obtained from all codewords in C due to m_3 $(t + 1 \le m_3 \le d)$ symmetric errors, i.e.,

$$\begin{aligned} M &= M_X \bigcup M_Y \cdots \\ &= \bigcup_{Z \in C} M_Z. \end{aligned}$$

Also let Q be the set of vectors obtained from all codewords in C due to $d + 1$ or more unidirectional errors, i.e.,

$$\begin{aligned} Q &= Q_X \bigcup Q_Y \cdots \\ &= \bigcup_{Z \in C} Q_Z. \end{aligned}$$

We have to prove that for arbitrary $X \in C$. $T_X \cap M = \emptyset$ and $T_X \cap Q = \emptyset$. Since for all distinct $X.Y \in C$, $D(X.Y) \ge t + d + 1$, we conclude that $T_X \cap M_Y = \emptyset$. Also by definition of T_X and M_X we have $T_X \cap M_X = \emptyset$. Then taking into account that $T_X \cap M = (T_X \cap M_X) \cup (T_X \cap M_Y) \cdots$ we conclude that $T_X \cap M = \emptyset$.

Since $T_X \cap Q = (T_X \cap Q_X) \cup (T_X \cap Q_Y) \cdots$ and Lemma A1 implies that each term of the form $T_X \cap Q_Z$ is empty we have $T_X \cap Q = \emptyset$. The above prove that the conditions are sufficient.

In order to prove that the conditions are necessary suppose that C is a t-EC/d-ED/AUED code, with $d > t + 1$, and that there exist $X, Y \in C$ such that:

a) $D(X,Y) < t + d + 1$, $N(X,Y) \ge t + 1$ and $N(Y,X) \ge t + 1$ or

b) $D(X,Y) \ge t + d + 1$, $N(X,Y) < t + 1$ and $N(Y,X) \ge t + 1$ or

c) $D(X,Y) < t + d + 1$, $N(X,Y) < t + 1$ and $N(Y,X) \ge t + 1$.

Case a: We consider that there exist $X.Y \in C$ such that $D(X,Y) < t + d + 1$, $N(X,Y) \ge t + 1$ and $N(Y,X) \ge t + 1$.

Since $d > t + 1$ the conditions $N(X,Y) \ge t + 1$ and $N(Y,X) \ge t + 1$ do not contradict the condition $D(X,Y) < t + d + 1$. Since $D(X,Y) < t + d + 1$ or equivalently $D(X,Y) \le t + d$ there always exists at least one word Z such that $D(X,Z) = t_1 \le t$ and $D(Z,Y) = t_2 \le d$. Therefore, Z can be obtained in two ways, as a result of t_1 errors in X, where $t_1 \le t$, or as a result of t_2 errors in Y, where $t_2 \le d$. This contradicts the fact that C is a t-error correcting and d-error detecting code with $d > t$.

Case b: We consider that there exist $X.Y \in C$ such that $D(X,Y) \ge t + d + 1$, $N(X,Y) = t_1 < t + 1$ and $N(Y,X) \ge t + 1$.

Then $N(Y,X) = D(X,Y) - N(X,Y) \ge t + d + 1 - t = d + 1$. Without loss of generality we can assume that

$$\begin{array}{rcccc} & & N(X,Y) & N(Y.X) & \\ X = & 11\cdots1 & 11\cdots1 & 00\cdots0 & 00\cdots0 \\ Y = & 11\cdots1 & 00\cdots0 & 11\cdots1 & 00\cdots0. \end{array}$$

Let

$$\begin{array}{rcccc} & & N(X,Y) & N(Y,X) & \\ Z = & 11\cdots1 & 00\cdots0 & 00\cdots0 & 00\cdots0. \end{array}$$

Note that Z can be obtained in two ways, as a result of $N(X,Y) = t_1 \le t$ $1 \rightarrow 0$ errors in X or as a result of $N(Y,X) = d + 1$ $1 \rightarrow 0$ errors in Y. This contradicts the fact that C is a t-error correcting and all unidirectional error detecting code.

Case c: We consider that there exist $X. Y \in C$ such that $D(X,Y) < t + d + 1$, $N(X,Y) < t + 1$ and $N(Y,X) \ge t + 1$.

The proof is the same with the proof of case a.

References

[1] D. K. Pradhan and J. J. Stiffler, "Error correcting codes and self-checking circuits," *IEEE Comput. Mag.*, vol. 13, Mar. 1980.

[2] D. K. Pradhan, "A new class of error-correcting/detecting codes for fault-tolerant computer applications," *IEEE Trans. Comput.*, vol. C-29, pp. 471–481, June 1980.

[3] B. Bose and D. K. Pradhan, "Optimal unidirectional error detecting codes," *IEEE Trans. Comput.*, vol. C-31, pp. 564–568, June 1982.

[4] D. Tasar and V. Tasar, "A study of intermittent faults in digital computers," in *Proc. AFIPS Conf.*, 1977, pp. 807–811.

[5] R. W. Cook, W. H. Sisson, T. F. Storey, and W. W. Toy, "Design of a self-checking microprogram control," *IEEE Trans. Comput.*, vol. C-22, pp. 255–262, Mar. 1973.

[6] B. Parhami and A. Avizienis, "Detection of storage errors in mass memories using low-cost arithmetic codes," *IEEE Trans. Comput.*, vol. C-27, pp. 302–308, Apr. 1978.

[7] J. F. Wakerly, "Detection of unidirectional multiple errors using low cost arithmetic codes," *IEEE Trans. Comput.*, vol. C-24, pp. 210–212, Feb. 1975.

[8] D. K. Pradhan and S. M. Reddy, "Fault-tolerant failsafe logic networks," in *Proc. IEEE COMPCON*, San Francisco, CA, Mar. 1977, p. 363.

[9] B. Bose, "Theory and design of unidirectional error codes," Ph.D. dissertation, Dep. Comput. Sci. Eng., Southern Methodist Univ., Dallas, TX, May 1980.

[10] B. Bose and T. R. N. Rao, "Theory of unidirectional error correcting/detecting codes," *IEEE Trans. Comput.*, vol. C-31, pp. 521–530, June 1982.
[11] B. Bose, "On systematic SEC/MUED code," in *Proc. FTCS*, vol. 11, June 1981, pp. 265–267.
[12] D. Nikolos, N. Gaitanis, and G. Philokyprou, "t-error correcting all unidirectional error detecting codes starting from cyclic AN codes," in *Proc. 1984 Int. Conf. Fault-Tolerant Comput.*, Kissimmee, FL, pp. 318–323.
[13] ——, "Systematic t-error correcting/all unidirectional error detecting codes," *IEEE Trans. Comput.*, vol. C-35, pp. 394–402, May 1986.
[14] M. Blaum and H. van Tilborg, "On t-error correcting/all unidirectional error detecting codes," *IEEE Trans. Comput.*, vol. 38, pp. 1493–1501, Nov. 1989.
[15] J. J. Stiffler, "Coding for random-access memories," *IEEE Trans. Comput.*, vol. C-27, pp. 526–531, June 1978.
[16] P. Golan, "Fast decoder for double-error correction in main memories," in *Proc. 7th Int. Conf. Fault-Tolerant Syst. Diagnostics*, Brno, Czechoslovakia, 1984, pp. 64–70.
[17] D. Nikolos, "A class of error detecting/correcting codes for semiconductor memory systems," in *Proc. VIII Int. Conf. Fault-Tolerant Syst. Diagnostics*, Katowice, Poland, Sept. 10–12, 1985, pp. 197–202.
[18] W. W. Peterson and E. J. Weldon, *Error Correcting Codes.* Cambridge, MA: M.I.T. Press, 1972.
[19] F. J. Mac Williams and N. J. A. Sloane, *The Theory of Error-Correcting Codes.* Amsterdam, The Netherlands: North-Holland, 1978.
[20] J. F. Wakerly, *Error Detecting Codes, Self-Checking Circuits and Applications.* Amsterdam, The Netherlands: North-Holland, 1978.
[21] T. O. Anderson, "Modular switching network for generating the weight of a binary vector," *Comput. Design*, vol. 2, pp. 106–110, Apr. 1972.
[22] M. A. Marouf and A. D. Friedman, "Design of self-checking checkers for Berger codes," in *Dig. 1978, Int. Symp. Fault-Tolerant Comput.*, Tolouse, France, June 1978, pp. 179–184.
[23] J. H. Weber, C. de Vroedt, and D. E. Boekee, "Bounds and constructions for binary codes of length less than 24 and asymmetric distance less than 6," *IEEE Trans. Inform. Theory*, submitted for publication.
[24] S. Lin and D. J. Costello, Jr., *Error Control Coding: Fundamentals and Applications.* Englewood Cliffs, NJ: Prentice Hall, 1983.
[25] D. L. Tao, C. R. P. Hartmann, and P. K. Lala, "An efficient class of unidirectional error detecting/correcting codes," *IEEE Trans. Comput.*, vol. 37, pp. 879–882, July 1988.
[26] D. J. Lin and B. Bose, "Theory and design of t-error correcting and $d(d > t)$-unidirectional error detecting (t-EC d-UED) codes," *IEEE Trans. Comput.*, vol. 37, pp. 433–439, Apr. 1988.

Dimitris Nikolos was born in Arta, Greece. He received the B.Sc. degree in physics in 1979, the M.Sc. degree in electronics in 1981, and the Ph.D. degree in computer science in 1985, all from the University of Athens, Greece.

During the period November 1981–June 1985 he was working in the Computer Department of N.R.C. "Democritos" under scholarship from the Hellenic Atomic Energy Commission. Since June 1985 he has cooperated with the Computers Laboratory of the University of Athens and the Institute of Telecommunications and Informatics of N.R.C.P.S. "Democritos". In April 1989, he joined the Department of Computer Engineering and Informatics, University of Patras, as a Lecturer. His main research interests are fault-tolerant computing, computer architecture, database systems, parallel processing, and bus conformance testing.

Chapter 5: Codes for Correcting and Detecting Combinations of Symmetric and Unidirectional Errors

This chapter presents results on different combinations for correcting and detecting symmetric and unidirectional errors. First, Berger gives the construction of a code that detects a burst of symmetric errors, and also detects any number of unidirectional (or asymmetric) errors. Al-Bassam, Bose, and Venkatesan have proven that Berger's construction is optimal.[69]

Weber, de Vroedt, and Boekee give necessary and sufficient conditions for codes dealing with errors of different types — useful information for researchers and engineers needing different combinations for correcting and detecting symmetric, unidirectional, and asymmetric errors. The authors present a table with necessary and sufficient conditions for many code types, together with the proofs that the conditions are in fact necessary and sufficient. Again, our references provide additional reading in this area.[70]

Blaum and Bruck conclude by studying constructions of unordered codes with minimum distance $t+1$. As shown by Weber, de Vroedt and Boekee in this chapter — and by Nikolos in the preceding chapter — these codes can detect up to t (symmetric) errors and any number of unidirectional errors. We find another application in parallel asynchronous communications;[71] constructions given in this paper naturally generalize the Berger construction, and also consider optimality issues regarding the number of redundant bits.

A Note on Burst Detecting Sum Codes

Jay M. Berger

I.B.M. Corporation, Advanced Systems Development Division, Yorktown Heights, New York

A new burst error detecting code is described which has the form of the sum codes in that the check bits are determined from the algebraic sum of suitably weighted information bits. With the use of approximately $k + \log_2 (n/k)$ redundancy bits,where n is the number of information bits, the resultant code will detect all bursts of errors of length k or less in any channel and will also be a perfect error detection code in a completely asymmetric channel.

A simple extension of the sum codes described in a previous paper (Berger, 1961) can be made which will allow the detection of bursts of errors of any desired length and which will still detect all possible errors in a completely asymmetric channel. These codes will have all of the features of the simple sum code and will have considerably less redundancy than would be required if the sum code and a cyclic code were superposed. That is, if there are n information bits in the sum code word and one wishes in addition to detect bursts of length k, then the superposition of the two codes that would be perfectly error detecting in a completely asymmetric channel and detect all bursts of length k or less in an arbitrary channel would require about $k + \log_2 n$ check bits.[1] The code to be described that will accomplish these same objectives as a single simple code will be shown to require about $k + \log_2 (n/k)$ check bits. This code is a sum code in which the weights associated with the information bit positions are chosen to accomplish the desired burst error detection. As was shown in I for the previously described sum code, the resultant code is separable between the information bits and check bits, and the check bits are complemented before transmission to attain the detection properties in the asymmetric channel.

[1] In this case the sum code would not detect errors in the k check bits that are added for the burst detection, although bursts could be detected over the entire encoded word. For minimum redundancy and maximum effectiveness, both codes might be considered to be applied independently to the information bits only.

Reprinted from *Information and Control*, Vol. 4, 1961, pp. 297-299.

DESCRIPTION OF THE BURST DETECTING SUM CODE

Given an n bit binary word, W, that one wishes to encode in order that upon receipt after transmission all bursts of errors of length k or less in any channel, and also all errors if the channel was completely asymmetric can be detected, the following procedure may be employed. For the purpose of this description, consider that the rightmost digit of W is transmitted first and that the check bits follow W with the least significant bit of the check bits sent first. Then, proceeding from left to right, the first digit of W is weighted by 2^{k-1}, the next by 2^{k-2}, and so on down to 2^0. This pattern of weights is repeated until all digits of W are exhausted. The check sum is formed by simple addition of the weights corresponding to the bit positions occupied by "1" 's and conversion of that sum to a binary form. Before transmission, each bit position of the check sum is complemented and then recomplemented at the receiver to compare with the sum of the weights derived from the received information bits. As may be seen from I, the structure of the sum codes is such that if any set of nonzero weights is used on the information bits, together with complementation of the sum to form the transmitted check bits, one will always obtain perfect error detection in a completely asymmetric channel. Therefore, it remains only to demonstrate that this choice of weights results in the desired burst detection properties.

Note first that the check bits themselves are effectively weighted since they are the binary representation of the formed sum. Thus the last k check bits are weighted by the first of the repeated patterns of weights. Secondly, one observes that any burst of length k or less spans bits which each have a distinct power of two as weights. Thus no burst pattern of length k or less can occur such that compensating contributions to the sums will be made in order that no error will be detected. A simple example will clarify these arguments. Let the number of information bits $n = 12$, and for convenience, label these bits i_1 through i_{12}. Consider bursts of length 3 so that the weights used will be 4, 2, and 1. Thus 5 check bits will be required which are labeled C_1 through C_5, with C_5 the least significant bit. A received code word after recomplementation, with the weights indicated above the digits, would have the following appearance:

$$C_1 C_2 C_3 C_4 C_5 \overset{4}{i_1} \overset{2}{i_2} \overset{1}{i_3} \overset{4}{i_4} \overset{2}{i_5} \cdots \overset{1}{i_{12}}$$

Now, clearly, any burst of length 3 or less occurring only in the information bits will change the value of the formed sum, thus causing a mismatch with the check sum. For example, if i_2, i_3, i_4 were respectively 100 before transmission and a burst changed them to 011, then the formed sum would be increased by 3. Similarly, the same argument applies if the burst occurred only in the check bits. (Note that C_1 and C_2 have effective weights of 16 and 8, respectively.) In fact, all bursts of length up to and including the full number of check bits that occur entirely within the check bits will be detected. Finally, if the burst spans a part of the check bits and a part of the information bits, both sums will change, but they cannot both be changed by the same amount. For example, if the burst is over C_4, C_5, i_1, then since C_4 has effective weight 2 and C_5 effective weight 1, the check sum can change by ± 1, ± 2, or ± 3 while the formed sum can change by only ± 4.

As with the cyclic codes, many of the bursts greater than length k will also be detected. Thus, in the example above, there are 224 possible interior bit patterns of length 4 and of these only 40 can be altered by a burst of length 4 and go undetected. Similarly, multiple independent errors are more likely to be detected than in the case of the simple sum codes because of the presence of the weights.

The number of redundancy bits required in this code is clearly equal to the smallest integer containing the $\log_2$ of the sum of all of the possible weights on the information bits. Expressing the number of information bits n, and the maximum burst length k in terms of the division algorithm as $n = qk + r$, $0 \leq r < k$, the required number of redundancy bits, R, is readily seen to be equal to the smallest integer greater than $\log_2 [q(2^k - 1) + 2^k(1 - 2^{-r})]$. In most cases, the approximate formula $R \cong [k + \log_2 (q + 1)]$ is sufficiently accurate, where the square brackets, [ ], indicate the largest integer contained within. Thus, compared to a cyclic code which requires k check bits, approximately only the relatively small number, $\log_2 (n/k)$, of additional check bits are required to achieve perfect error detection in the completely asymmetric channel.

RECEIVED: May 22, 1961

REFERENCE

BERGER, J. M. (1961). A note on error detection codes for asymmetric channels. *Information and Control* **4**, 68, hereinafter referred to as I.

Necessary and Sufficient Conditions on Block Codes Correcting/Detecting Errors of Various Types

J. H. Weber, C. de Vroedt, and D. E. Boekee

Abstract— **Necessary and sufficient conditions are given for a block code to be capable of correcting up to t_1 symmetric errors, up to t_2 unidirectional errors, and up to t_3 asymmetric errors, as well as detecting from t_1+1 up to d_1 symmetric errors that are not of the unidirectional type, from t_2+1 up to d_2 unidirectional errors that are not of the asymmetric type, and from t_3+1 up to d_3 asymmetric errors. Many known conditions on block codes concerning error correction and/or detection appear as special cases of this general result. Further, some codes turn out to have stronger error correcting/detecting capabilities than they were originally designed for.**

Index Terms— **Asymmetric errors, error correction, error detection, symmetric errors, unidirectional errors.**

I. Introduction

We consider discrete channels with an (input and output) alphabet $\mathcal{A}=\{0,1,\cdots,a-1\}(a\geq 2)$. For reliable transmission of data over such a channel we can use a block code C of length n over the alphabet $\mathcal{A}$, i.e., $C\subseteq\mathcal{A}^n$. Most block codes have been designed to correct and/or detect errors with a symmetric nature, such as the errors caused by the *a-ary symmetric channel* (cf. [7]), on which $P(y\mid x)=\epsilon$ if $x\neq y$ and $P(y\mid x)=1-(a-1)\epsilon$ if $x=y$ (with $0\leq\epsilon\leq 1/(a-1)$), where $P(y|x)$ denotes the probability of receiving the symbol $y\in\mathcal{A}$ when the symbol $x\in\mathcal{A}$ is sent. However, in some applications, such as optical communications, the errors have a highly asymmetric nature. Channels causing this kind of error can often be modeled by the *a-ary asymmetric channel* (cf. [4]), on which $P(y|x)=0$ for all $y>x$. Further, in some recently developed memory systems, the errors appear to be of a unidirectional nature. These memory systems can be modeled by an *a-ary unidirectional channel* (cf. [1]), that behaves for a certain codeword either like the a-ary asymmetric channel or like the inverted a-ary asymmetric channel, on which $P(y|x)=0$ for all $y<x$.

Based on the preceding statements, we shall now formally define the error types that will be considered in this paper. First we define

$$N(\underline{u},\underline{v})=|\{i|u_i<v_i\}|,$$

$$d(\underline{u},\underline{v})=N(\underline{u},\underline{v})+N(\underline{v},\underline{u})=|\{i|u_i\neq v_i\}|\ \text{(Hamming distance)},$$

for $\underline{u}=(u_1,u_2,\cdots,u_n),\underline{v}=(v_1,v_2,\cdots,v_n)\in\mathcal{A}^n$. The vector $\underline{u}$ is said to cover the vector $\underline{v}$ ($\underline{u}\geq\underline{v}$) if $N(\underline{u},\underline{v})=0$. When sending a codeword $\underline{c}\in C$ and receiving a vector $\underline{y}\in\mathcal{A}^n$, we say that $\underline{c}$ has suffered t *asymmetric errors* if $\underline{c}$ covers $\underline{y}$ and $d(\underline{c},\underline{y})=t$, that $\underline{c}$ has suffered t *unidirectional errors* if $\underline{c}$ covers or is covered by $\underline{y}$ and $d(\underline{c},\underline{y})=t$, and that $\underline{u}$ has suffered t *symmetric errors* if $d(\underline{c},\underline{y})=t$.

In accordance with the three error types, we define three kinds of spheres with radius r for each $\underline{x}\in\mathcal{A}^n$:

$$S_{Sy}(\underline{x},r)=\{\underline{y}\in\mathcal{A}^n\mid d(\underline{x},\underline{y})\leq r\},$$

$$S_U(\underline{x},r)=\{\underline{y}\in\mathcal{A}^n\mid d(\underline{x},\underline{y})\leq r\wedge(\underline{x}\geq\underline{y}\vee\underline{y}\geq\underline{x})\},$$

$$S_{As}(\underline{x},r)=\{\underline{y}\in\mathcal{A}^n\mid d(\underline{x},\underline{y})\leq r\wedge\underline{x}\geq\underline{y}\}.$$

For the sake of convenience we also define a super-sphere

$$S(\underline{x},r_1,r_2,r_3)=S_{Sy}(\underline{x},r_1)\cup S_U(\underline{x},r_2)\cup S_{As}(\underline{x},r_3)$$

for each $\underline{x}\in\mathcal{A}^n$ and $0\leq r_1\leq r_2\leq r_3$. Each sphere $S_X(\underline{c},t)$ contains the vectors that can be received when codeword $\underline{c}$ is sent suffering t or less errors of type X (with X =Sy(mmetric), X =U(nidirectional), or X =As(ymmetric), respectively). Hence we say that a code C can *correct* up to t errors of type X if the spheres $S_X(\underline{c},t)$ are disjoint for any two distinct codewords. On the other hand, we say that a code can *detect* up to d errors of type X if the sphere $S_X(\underline{c},d)$ does not contain other codewords than $\underline{c}$ for all $\underline{c}\in C$. Necessary and sufficient conditions are known for a code to be capable of correcting or detecting errors of each of the three types. But sometimes a combination of correction and detection is required, or even simultaneous correction and/or detection of errors of various types. For example, some authors (see, e.g., [1], [2], [9]) have considered codes correcting up to t symmetric errors and detecting all ($t+1$ or more) unidirectional errors, since it was observed that in some memory systems the number of unidirectional errors can be unlimited, whereas the number of symmetric errors is limited with high probability. A necessary and sufficient condition for this case was derived in [2]. To be able to deal with such cases it is interesting to look for necessary and sufficient conditions for all combinations of correction and detection for the three error types considered here.

We call a code t_1-SyEC t_2-UEC t_3-AsEC d_1-SyED d_2-UED d_3-AsED ($0\leq t_1\leq t_2\leq t_3, 0\leq d_1\leq d_2\leq d_3, t_i\leq d_i$) if it can correct up to t_1 symmetric errors, up to t_2 unidirectional errors, and up to t_3 asymmetric errors, as well as detect from t_1+1 up to d_1 symmetric errors that are not of the unidirectional type, from t_2+1 up to d_2 unidirectional errors that are not of the asymmetric type, and from t_3+1 up to d_3 asymmetric errors. In the context of the spheres this means that

$$S(\underline{x},t_1,t_2,t_3)\cap S(\underline{y},d_1,d_2,d_3)=\emptyset$$

for any two distinct codewords $\underline{x}$ and $\underline{y}$.

In Section II we derive necessary and sufficient conditions for a code to be t_1-SyEC t_2-UEC t_3-AsEC d_1-SyED d_2-UED d_3-AsED. Hence we can obtain necessary and sufficient conditions for correction and/or detection of any combination of symmetric/unidirectional/asymmetric errors by making appropriate choices for t_i and d_i. Some important cases are considered in Section III. Many existing results appear as special cases of the general result. In Section IV we pay attention to another error criterion. Finally, concluding remarks are found in Section V.

II. General Conditions

In literature (see, e.g., [2], [3], [5], [6], [8], [10]) various necessary and sufficient conditions were derived on block codes to have certain error correcting and/or detecting capabilities. Since in each derivation the same kinds of techniques were used, we have tried to obtain general conditions covering all combinations of symmetric, unidirectional, and asymmetric errors. The result is given in Theorem 1.

Manuscript received September 10, 1990; revised September 16, 1991.

J. H. Weber and D. E. Boekee are with the Department of Electrical Engineering, Information Theory Group, Delft University of Technology, 2600 GA Delft, The Netherlands.

C. de Vroedt is with the Department of Mathematics and Informatics, Delft University of Technology, 2600 AJ Delft, The Netherlands.

IEEE Log Number 9103100.

Reprinted from *IEEE Transactions on Computers*, September 1992, pp. 1189-1193.

0-8186-4182-7/93 $3.00 © 1992 IEEE

Theorem 1: A code C is t_1-SyEC t_2-UEC t_3-AsEC d_1-SyED d_2-UED d_3-AsED (with $0 \le t_1 \le t_2 \le t_3, 0 \le d_1 \le d_2 \le d_3, t_i \le d_i$) if and only if all $\underline{a}, \underline{b} \in C$ with $\underline{a} \ne \underline{b}$ and $N(\underline{a}, \underline{b}) \ge N(\underline{b}, \underline{a})$ satisfy

$$\begin{cases} d(\underline{a}, \underline{b}) \ge t_2 + d_3 + 1 \wedge d(\underline{a}, \underline{b}) \\ \quad \ge t_3 + d_2 + 1 & \text{if } N(\underline{b}, \underline{a}) = 0 \\ d(\underline{a}, \underline{b}) \ge t_3 + d_1 + 1 \wedge d(\underline{a}, \underline{b}) \\ \quad \ge t_1 + d_3 + 1 \wedge N(\underline{a}, \underline{b}) \ge d_3 + 1 & \text{if } 1 \le N(\underline{b}, \underline{a}) \le t_3 \\ d(\underline{a}, \underline{b}) \ge t_3 + d_1 + 1 & \text{if } N(\underline{b}, \underline{a}) \ge t_3 + 1. \end{cases}$$

Proof: From the definition of a t_1-SyEC t_2-UEC t_3-AsEC d_1-SyED d_2-UED d_3-AsED code it follows that we have to prove that for all $\underline{a}, \underline{b} \in C$ with $\underline{a} \ne \underline{b}$ and $N(\underline{a}, \underline{b}) \ge N(\underline{b}, \underline{a})$:

$$S(\underline{a}, t_1, t_2, t_3) \cap S(\underline{b}, d_1, d_2, d_3) = \varnothing$$

$$\text{and } S(\underline{b}, t_1, t_2, t_3) \cap S(\underline{a}, d_1, d_2, d_3) = \varnothing$$

$$\Leftrightarrow$$

$$\begin{cases} d(\underline{a}, \underline{b}) \ge t_2 + d_3 + 1 \wedge d(\underline{a}, \underline{b}) \\ \quad \ge t_3 + d_2 + 1 & \text{if } N(\underline{b}, \underline{a}) = 0 \\ d(\underline{a}, \underline{b}) \ge t_3 + d_1 + 1 \wedge d(\underline{a}, \underline{b}) \\ \quad \ge t_1 + d_3 + 1 \wedge N(\underline{a}, \underline{b}) \ge d_3 + 1 & \text{if } 1 \le N(\underline{b}, \underline{a}) \le t_3 \\ d(\underline{a}, \underline{b}) \ge t_3 + d_1 + 1 & \text{if } N(\underline{b}, \underline{a}) \ge t_3 + 1. \end{cases}$$

Without loss of generality we may assume that $\underline{a}$ and $\underline{b}$ satisfy

$$\begin{cases} a_i = b_i & \text{for } 1 \le i \le \alpha \\ a_i > b_i & \text{for } \alpha + 1 \le i \le \alpha + \beta \\ a_i < b_i & \text{for } \alpha + \beta + 1 \le i \le \alpha + \beta + \gamma = n \end{cases}$$

with $\alpha = |\{i \mid a_i = b_i\}|$, $\beta = |\{i \mid a_i > b_i\}|$, and $\gamma = |\{i \mid a_i < b_i\}|$.

"$\Rightarrow$" Define $\underline{z} \in \mathcal{A}^n$ as

$$\begin{cases} z_i = a_i & \text{for } 1 \le i \le \alpha \\ z_i = b_i & \text{for } \alpha + 1 \le i \le \alpha + \beta \\ z_i = a_i & \text{for } \alpha + \beta + 1 \le i \le \alpha + \beta + \mu \\ z_i = b_i & \text{for } \alpha + \beta + \mu + 1 \le i \le \alpha + \beta + \gamma = n \end{cases}$$

where μ will be filled in in accordance with the case under consideration. We next consider three different cases.

1) The case $N(\underline{b}, \underline{a}) = 0$. Suppose $d(\underline{a}, \underline{b}) \le t_2 + d_3$ or $d(\underline{a}, \underline{b}) \le t_3 + d_2$.

   i) If $d(\underline{a}, \underline{b}) \le t_2 + d_3$, then $\underline{z}$(with $\mu = \min\{N(\underline{a}, \underline{b}), d_3\}$) $\in S_U(\underline{a}, t_2) \cap S_{As}(\underline{b}, d_3)$.

   ii) If $d(\underline{a}, \underline{b}) \le t_3 + d_2$, then $\underline{z}$(with $\mu = \min\{N(\underline{a}, \underline{b}), t_3\}$) $\in S_U(\underline{a}, d_2) \cap S_{As}(\underline{b}, t_3)$.

2) The case $1 \le N(\underline{b}, \underline{a}) \le t_3$. Suppose $d(\underline{a}, \underline{b}) \le t_3 + d_1$ or $d(\underline{a}, \underline{b}) \le t_1 + d_3$ or $N(\underline{a}, \underline{b}) \le d_3$.

   i) If $d(\underline{a}, \underline{b}) \le t_3 + d_1$ and $t_3 \le N(\underline{a}, \underline{b})$, then $\underline{z}$(with $\mu = t_3$) $\in S_{Sy}(\underline{a}, d_1) \cap S_{As}(\underline{b}, t_3)$.

   ii) If $d(\underline{a}, \underline{b}) \le t_3 + d_1$ and $t_3 > N(\underline{a}, \underline{b})$, then $\underline{z}$(with $\mu = N(\underline{a}, \underline{b})$) $\in S_{As}(\underline{a}, t_3) \cap S_{As}(\underline{b}, t_3)$.

   iii) If $d(\underline{a}, \underline{b}) \le t_1 + d_3$ and $d_3 \le N(\underline{a}, \underline{b})$, then $\underline{z}$(with $\mu = d_3$) $\in S_{Sy}(\underline{a}, t_1) \cap S_{As}(\underline{b}, d_3)$.

   iv) If $d(\underline{a}, \underline{b}) \le t_1 + d_3$ and $d_3 > N(\underline{a}, \underline{b})$, then $\underline{z}$(with $\mu = N(\underline{a}, \underline{b})$) $\in S_{As}(\underline{a}, t_3) \cap S_{As}(\underline{b}, d_3)$.

   v) If $N(\underline{a}, \underline{b}) \le d_3$, then $\underline{z}$(with $\mu = N(\underline{a}, \underline{b})$) $\in S_{As}(\underline{a}, t_3) \cap S_{As}(\underline{b}, d_3)$.

3) The case $N(\underline{b}, \underline{a}) \ge t_3 + 1$. Suppose $d(\underline{a}, \underline{b}) \le t_3 + d_1$.

   i) If $d(\underline{a}, \underline{b}) \le t_3 + d_1$, then $\underline{z}$(with $\mu = t_3$) $\in S_{Sy}(\underline{a}, d_1) \cap S_{As}(\underline{b}, t_3)$.

Hence we have shown that $\underline{z}$ is in $S(\underline{a}, t_1, t_2, t_3) \cap S(\underline{b}, d_1, d_2, d_3)$ or $S(\underline{b}, t_1, t_2, t_3) \cap S(\underline{a}, d_1, d_2, d_3)$ for each case, which contradicts the assumption that these two intersections of sets are both empty.

"$\Leftarrow$" Suppose there exists a $\underline{z} \in \mathcal{A}^n$ such that $\underline{z} \in S(\underline{a}, t_1, t_2, t_3) \cap S(\underline{b}, d_1, d_2, d_3)$ or $\underline{z} \in S(\underline{b}, t_1, t_2, t_3) \cap S(\underline{a}, d_1, d_2, d_3)$. Again, we shall find a contradiction for each case. This will only be shown for $\underline{z} \in S(\underline{a}, t_1, t_2, t_3) \cap S(\underline{b}, d_1, d_2, d_3)$, since it can be shown in a completely analogous way for $\underline{z} \in S(\underline{b}, t_1, t_2, t_3) \cap S(\underline{a}, d_1, d_2, d_3)$. We again consider three cases.

1) The case $N(\underline{b}, \underline{a}) = 0$.

   i) If $N(\underline{a}, \underline{z}) = 0$, then $d(\underline{a}, \underline{b}) = N(\underline{a}, \underline{b}) \le N(\underline{z}, \underline{b}) \le d(\underline{z}, \underline{b}) \le d_3$.

   ii) If $N(\underline{a}, \underline{z}) \ge 1$, then $d(\underline{a}, \underline{b}) \le d(\underline{a}, \underline{z}) + d(\underline{z}, \underline{b}) \le t_2 + d_3$.

2) The case $1 \le N(\underline{b}, \underline{a}) \le t_3$.

   i) If $N(\underline{a}, \underline{z}) \ge 1$ and $N(\underline{z}, \underline{a}) \ge 1$, then $d(\underline{a}, \underline{b}) \le d(\underline{a}, \underline{z}) + d(\underline{z}, \underline{b}) \le t_1 + d_3$.

   ii) If $N(\underline{a}, \underline{z}) = 0$, then $N(\underline{a}, \underline{b}) \le N(\underline{z}, \underline{b}) \le d(\underline{z}, \underline{b}) \le d_3$.

   iii) If $N(\underline{z}, \underline{a}) = 0$ and $N(\underline{z}, \underline{b}) \ge 1$ and $N(\underline{b}, \underline{z}) \ge 1$, then $d(\underline{a}, \underline{b}) \le d(\underline{a}, \underline{z}) + d(\underline{z}, \underline{b}) \le t_2 + d_1$.

   iv) If $N(\underline{z}, \underline{a}) = 0$ and $N(\underline{z}, \underline{b}) = 0$, then $N(\underline{a}, \underline{b}) \le N(\underline{a}, \underline{z}) \le d(\underline{a}, \underline{z}) \le t_2$.

   v) If $N(\underline{z}, \underline{a}) = 0$ and $N(\underline{b}, \underline{z}) = 0$, then $N(\underline{b}, \underline{a}) \le N(\underline{b}, \underline{z}) = 0$.

3) The case $N(\underline{b}, \underline{a}) \ge t_3 + 1$.

   i) If $N(\underline{b}, \underline{z}) \ge 1$ and $N(\underline{z}, \underline{b}) \ge 1$, then $d(\underline{a}, \underline{b}) \le d(\underline{a}, \underline{z}) + d(\underline{z}, \underline{b}) \le t_3 + d_1$.

   ii) If $N(\underline{z}, \underline{b}) = 0$, then $N(\underline{b}, \underline{a}) \le N(\underline{a}, \underline{b}) \le N(\underline{a}, \underline{z}) \le d(\underline{a}, \underline{z}) \le t_3$.

   iii) If $N(\underline{b}, \underline{z}) = 0$, then $N(\underline{b}, \underline{a}) \le N(\underline{z}, \underline{a}) \le d(\underline{z}, \underline{a}) \le t_3$. □

Sometimes a code turns out to have stronger error correcting/detecting capabilities than it was originally designed for, as can be seen from the next theorem.

Theorem 2: Any t_1-SyEC t_2-UEC t_3-AsEC d_1-SyED d_2-UED d_3-AsED code (with $0 \le t_1 \le t_2 \le t_3, 0 \le d_1 \le d_2 \le d_3, t_i \le d_i$) is also a t'_1-SyEC t'_2-UEC t'_3-AsEC d'_1-SyED d'_2-UED d'_3-AsED code with

$$t'_1 = \max\{t_1, t_3 + d_1 - d_3\},$$
$$t'_2 = \max\{t_2, t_3 + d_2 - d_3\}, t'_3 = t_3,$$
$$d'_1 = \max\{d_1, \min\{t_3 + 1, t_1 + d_3 - t_3\}\},$$
$$d'_2 = \max\{d_2, t_2 + d_3 - t_3\}, d'_3 = d_3.$$

Proof: First, observe that $t'_2 + d_3 = t_3 + d'_2$. Next, since

$$0 \le t_1 \le t'_1 = \max\{t_1, t_3 + d_1 - d_3\} \le \max\{t_2, t'_2 - d'_2 + d_1\}$$
$$\le t'_2 = \max\{t_2, t_3 + d_2 - d_3\} \le t_3 = t'_3,$$
$$0 \le d_1 \le d'_1 \le \max\{d_1, d_3 + t_1 - t_3\} \le \max\{d_2, d'_2 - t'_2 + t_1\}$$
$$\le d'_2 = \max\{d_2, d_3 + t_2 - t_3\} \le d_3 = d'_3,$$
$$t'_1 = \max\{t_1, t_3 + d_1 - d_3\} \le d_1 \le d'_1, t'_2$$
$$= \max\{t_2, t_3 + d_2 - d_3\} \le d_2 \le d'_2, t'_3 = t_3 \le d_3 = d'_3,$$

we may apply Theorem 1 to obtain necessary and sufficient conditions for a code to be t'_1-SyEC t'_2-UEC t'_3-AsEC d'_1-SyED d'_2-UED d'_3-AsED. Finally, we show that these conditions are implied by the necessary and sufficient conditions for a code to be t_1-SyEC t_2-UEC t_3-AsEC d_1-SyED d_2-UED d_3-AsED.

1) The case $N(\underline{b},\underline{a}) = 0$.

i) If $t_3 + d_2 \geq t_2 + d_3$, then $d(\underline{a},\underline{b}) \geq t_3 + d_2 + 1 = t'_3 + d'_2 + 1 = t'_2 + d'_3 + 1$.

ii) If $t_3 + d_2 < t_2 + d_3$, then $d(\underline{a},\underline{b}) \geq t_2 + d_3 + 1 = t'_2 + d'_3 + 1 = t'_3 + d'_2 + 1$.

2) The case $1 \leq N(\underline{b},\underline{a}) \leq t_3$.

i) If $t_3 + d_1 \geq t_1 + d_3$, then $d(\underline{a},\underline{b}) \geq t_3 + d_1 + 1 = t'_3 + d'_1 + 1 = t'_1 + d'_3 + 1$ and $N(\underline{a},\underline{b}) \geq d_3 + 1 = d'_3 + 1$.

ii) If $t_3 + d_1 < t_1 + d_3$, then $d(\underline{a},\underline{b}) \geq t_1 + d_3 + 1 = t'_1 + d'_3 + 1 \geq t'_3 + d'_1 + 1$ and $N(\underline{a},\underline{b}) \geq d_3 + 1 = d'_3 + 1$.

3) The case $N(\underline{b},\underline{a}) \geq t_3 + 1$.

i) If $t_3 + 1 \leq d_1$ or $t_1 + d_3 \leq t_3 + d_1$, then $d(\underline{a},\underline{b}) \geq t_3 + d_1 + 1 = t'_3 + d'_1 + 1$.

ii) If $t_3 + 1 > d_1$ and $t_1 + d_3 > t_3 + d_1$, then $d(\underline{a},\underline{b}) \geq 2t_3 + 2 \geq t'_3 + d'_1 + 1$. □

III. Special Cases

In this section we consider some important t_1-SyEC t_2-UEC t_3-AsEC d_1-SyED d_2-UED d_3-AsED codes (with $0 \leq t_1 \leq t_2 \leq t_3, 0 \leq d_1 \leq d_2 \leq d_3, t_i \leq d_i$). Many known results on error correcting/detecting codes will appear as special cases of the general theorem, and also some interesting new results will show up.

If we want to restrict ourselves to *correction* only, we substitute $d_i = t_i (i = 1, 2, 3)$ into Theorem 1. Hence a code C is t_1-SyEC t_2-UEC t_3-AsEC if and only if all $\underline{a},\underline{b} \in C$ with $\underline{a} \neq \underline{b}$ and $N(\underline{a},\underline{b}) \geq N(\underline{b},\underline{a})$ satisfy

$$\begin{cases} d(\underline{a},\underline{b}) \geq t_2 + t_3 + 1 & \text{if } N(\underline{b},\underline{a}) = 0 \\ d(\underline{a},\underline{b}) \geq t_1 + t_3 + 1 \wedge N(\underline{a},\underline{b}) \geq t_3 + 1 & \text{if } N(\underline{b},\underline{a}) \geq 1. \end{cases}$$

If we want to restrict ourselves to *detection* only, we substitute $t_i = 0 (i = 1, 2, 3)$ into Theorem 1. Hence a code C is d_1-SyED d_2-UED d_3-AsED if and only if all $\underline{a},\underline{b} \in C$ with $\underline{a} \neq \underline{b}$ and $N(\underline{a},\underline{b}) \geq N(\underline{b},\underline{a})$ satisfy

$$\begin{cases} d(\underline{a},\underline{b}) \geq d_3 + 1 & \text{if } N(\underline{b},\underline{a}) = 0 \\ d(\underline{a},\underline{b}) \geq d_1 + 1 & \text{if } N(\underline{b},\underline{a}) \geq 1. \end{cases}$$

From this (and also from Theorem 2) it follows that any d_1-SyED d_2-UED d_3-AsED code is also a d_1-SyED d_3-UED d_3-AsED code. Thus we only have to consider d_1-SyED d_2-UED codes.

When considering combinations of *correction and detection*, it is interesting (also from a practical point of view) to look at t_1-SyEC t_2-UEC d_2-UED codes. By substituting $t_3 = t_2, d_1 = t_1$, and $d_3 = d_2$ into Theorem 1, we find that a code C is t_1-SyEC t_2-UEC d_2-UED if and only if all $\underline{a},\underline{b} \in C$ with $\underline{a} \neq \underline{b}$ and $N(\underline{a},\underline{b}) \geq N(\underline{b},\underline{a})$ satisfy

$$\begin{cases} d(\underline{a},\underline{b}) \geq t_2 + d_2 + 1 & \text{if } N(\underline{b},\underline{a}) = 0 \\ d(\underline{a},\underline{b}) \geq t_1 + d_2 + 1 & \\ \quad \wedge N(\underline{a},\underline{b}) \geq d_2 + 1 & \text{if } 1 \leq N(\underline{b},\underline{a}) \leq t_2. \end{cases}$$

By substituting $t_1 = 0, t_2 = t$, and $d_2 = d$ into the previous result, we find that a code C is t-UEC d-UED if and only if all $\underline{a},\underline{b} \in C$ with $\underline{a} \neq \underline{b}$ and $N(\underline{a},\underline{b}) \geq N(\underline{b},\underline{a})$ satisfy

$$d(\underline{a},\underline{b}) \geq t + d + 1 \vee (N(\underline{b},\underline{a}) \geq 1 \wedge N(\underline{a},\underline{b}) \geq d + 1) \vee N(\underline{b},\underline{a}) \geq t + 1.$$

Note that this is a correction of a result presented earlier by Lin and Bose in [5] (Theorem 2.1), in which they claim that a binary $(q = 2)$ code C is t-UEC d-UED if and only if all $\underline{a},\underline{b} \in C$ with $\underline{a} \neq \underline{b}$ and $N(\underline{a},\underline{b}) \geq N(\underline{b},\underline{a})$ satisfy

$$d(\underline{a},\underline{b}) \geq t + d + 1 \vee N(\underline{b},\underline{a}) \geq t + 1.$$

This condition is indeed sufficient for a code to be t-UEC d-UED, but *not* necessary. The latter can be seen from the code $C = \{10000, 01111\}$ which is 2-UEC 3-UED, but does not satisfy the condition of Lin and Bose.

Next we consider codes *detecting all errors* of a certain type. To this end we first investigate t_1-SyEC t_2-UEC t_3-AsEC d_1-SyED d_2-UED AAsED (all asymmetric error detecting) codes. By substituting $d_3 = n$ into Theorem 1, we find that a code C is t_1-SyEC t_2-UEC t_3-AsEC d_1-SyED d_2-UED AAsED if and only if all $\underline{a},\underline{b} \in C$ with $\underline{a} \neq \underline{b}$ and $N(\underline{a},\underline{b}) \geq N(\underline{b},\underline{a})$ satisfy

$$d(\underline{a},\underline{b}) \geq t_3 + d_1 + 1 \wedge N(\underline{b},\underline{a}) \geq t_3 + 1.$$

From this it follows that any t_1-SyEC t_2-UEC t_3-AsEC d_1-SyED d_2-UED AAsED code is also a t_3-SyEC t_3-UEC t_3-AsEC $(\max\{d_1, t_3 + 1\})$-SyED AUED AAsED code. Hence we can restrict ourselves to t-SyEC d-SyED AUED codes, which are characterized by the necessary and sufficient condition

$$d(\underline{a},\underline{b}) \geq t + d + 1 \wedge N(\underline{b},\underline{a}) \geq t + 1$$

for all $\underline{a},\underline{b} \in C$ with $\underline{a} \neq \underline{b}$ and $N(\underline{a},\underline{b}) \geq N(\underline{b},\underline{a})$. Note that any t-SyEC AUED code is also a t-SyEC $(t + 1)$-SyED AUED code.

Finally, the results of this section are summarized in Table I, which also contains a few other interesting results. In this table, all conditions for a code C to have the denoted error correcting/detecting capability must hold for all $\underline{a},\underline{b} \in C$ with $\underline{a} \neq \underline{b}$ and $N(\underline{a},\underline{b}) \geq N(\underline{b},\underline{a})$. The values of t_i and d_i denote the substitutions that must be made to derive the relevant condition from Theorem 1.

IV. Another Error Criterion

In this paper the number of errors when sending a codeword $\underline{c}$ and receiving a vector $\underline{y}$ has been defined to be the number of coordinates in which the two vectors differ:

$$|\{i \mid c_i \neq y_i\}|.$$

How much these coordinates differ is not important in this definition. If one wishes to take into account the magnitude of each symbol error, a suitable and widely used (cf. [4]) definition for the number of errors is

$$\sum |c_i - y_i|.$$

Note that there is no difference between these two definitions in the binary case $(q = 2)$.

All the results on t_1-SyEC t_2-UEC t_3-AsEC d_1-SyED d_2-UED d_3-AsED codes derived in this paper while counting the number of errors as $|\{i|c_i \neq y_i\}|$ are also valid when counting the number of errors as $\sum |c_i - y_i|$, if we adapt the definitions of $N(\underline{a},\underline{b})$ and $d(\underline{a},\underline{b})$ for the latter case as follows:

$$N(\underline{a},\underline{b}) = \sum \max\{b_i - a_i, 0\},$$
$$d(\underline{a},\underline{b}) = N(\underline{a},\underline{b}) + N(\underline{b},\underline{a}) = \sum |b_i - a_i|.$$

Another thing we must adapt is the vector $\underline{z}$ in the "⇒" part of the

TABLE I

NECESSARY AND SUFFICIENT CONDITIONS ON ERROR CORRECTING/DETECTING CODES

EC/ED capability	t_1	t_2	t_3	d_1	d_2	d_3	condition
t-SyEC	t	t	t	t	t	t	$d(\underline{a},\underline{b})\geq 2t+1$
t-UEC	0	t	t	0	t	t	$d(\underline{a},\underline{b})\geq 2t+1 \vee (N(\underline{b},\underline{a})\geq 1 \wedge N(\underline{a},\underline{b})\geq t+1)$
t-AsEC	0	0	t	0	0	t	$N(\underline{a},\underline{b})\geq t+1$
t_1-SyEC t_2-UEC	t_1	t_2	t_2	t_1	t_2	t_2	$d(\underline{a},\underline{b})\geq 2t_2+1 \vee (N(\underline{b},\underline{a})\geq 1 \wedge N(\underline{a},\underline{b})\geq t_2+1 \wedge d(\underline{a},\underline{b})\geq t_1+t_2+1)$
t_1-SyEC t_3-AsEC	t_1	t_1	t_3	t_1	t_1	t_3	$d(\underline{a},\underline{b})\geq t_1+t_3+1 \wedge N(\underline{a},\underline{b})\geq t_3+1$
t_2-UEC t_3-AsEC	0	t_2	t_3	0	t_2	t_3	$N(\underline{a},\underline{b})\geq t_2+t_3+1 \vee (N(\underline{b},\underline{a})\geq 1 \wedge N(\underline{a},\underline{b})\geq t_3+1)$
t_1-SyEC t_2-UEC t_3-AsEC	t_1	t_2	t_3	t_1	t_2	t_3	$N(\underline{a},\underline{b})\geq t_2+t_3+1 \vee (N(\underline{b},\underline{a})\geq 1 \wedge N(\underline{a},\underline{b})\geq t_3+1 \wedge d(\underline{a},\underline{b})\geq t_1+t_3+1)$
d-SyED	0	0	0	d	d	d	$d(\underline{a},\underline{b})\geq d+1$
d-UED	0	0	0	0	d	d	$d(\underline{a},\underline{b})\geq d+1 \vee N(\underline{b},\underline{a})\geq 1$
d_1-SyED d_2-UED	0	0	0	d_1	d_2	d_2	$d(\underline{a},\underline{b})\geq d_2+1 \vee (N(\underline{b},\underline{a})\geq 1 \wedge d(\underline{a},\underline{b})\geq d_1+1)$
t-SyEC d-SyED	t	t	t	d	d	d	$d(\underline{a},\underline{b})\geq t+d+1$
t-SyEC d-UED	t	t	t	t	d	d	$d(\underline{a},\underline{b})\geq t+d+1 \vee N(\underline{b},\underline{a})\geq t+1$
t-UEC d-UED	0	t	t	0	d	d	$d(\underline{a},\underline{b})\geq t+d+1 \vee N(\underline{b},\underline{a})\geq t+1 \vee (N(\underline{b},\underline{a})\geq 1 \wedge N(\underline{a},\underline{b})\geq d+1)$
t_1-SyEC t_2-UEC d-UED	t_1	t_2	t_2	t_1	d	d	$d(\underline{a},\underline{b})\geq t_2+d+1 \vee N(\underline{b},\underline{a})\geq t_2+1 \vee (N(\underline{b},\underline{a})\geq 1 \wedge N(\underline{a},\underline{b})\geq d+1 \wedge d(\underline{a},\underline{b})\geq t_1+d+1)$
t-AsEC d-AsED	0	0	t	0	0	d	$N(\underline{a},\underline{b})\geq d+1 \vee N(\underline{b},\underline{a})\geq t+1$
AUED	0	0	0	0	n	n	$N(\underline{b},\underline{a})\geq 1$
t-SyEC AUED	t	t	t	t	n	n	$N(\underline{b},\underline{a})\geq t+1$
d-SyED AUED	0	0	0	d	n	n	$N(\underline{b},\underline{a})\geq 1 \wedge d(\underline{a},\underline{b})\geq d+1$
t-SyEC d-SyED AUED	t	t	t	d	n	n	$N(\underline{b},\underline{a})\geq t+1 \wedge d(\underline{a},\underline{b})\geq t+d+1$

proof of Theorem 1:

$$\begin{cases} z_i = a_i & \text{for } 1 \leq i \leq \alpha \\ z_i = b_i & \text{for } \alpha+1 \leq i \leq \alpha+\beta \\ z_i = a_i & \text{for } \alpha+\beta+1 \leq i \leq \alpha+\beta+\mu \\ z_i = b_i - (\lambda - \sum_{k=\alpha+\beta+1}^{\alpha+\beta+\mu} |b_k - a_k|) & \text{for } i = \alpha+\beta+\mu+1 \\ & \text{provided that } \mu \leq \gamma - 1 \\ z_i = b_i & \text{for } \alpha+\beta+\mu+2 \leq i \leq \alpha+\beta+\gamma = n \end{cases}$$

with

$$\mu = \max\{j \mid 0 \leq j \leq \gamma \wedge \sum_{k=\alpha+\beta+1}^{\alpha+\beta+j} |b_k - a_k| \leq \lambda\}$$

and

$$\lambda = \begin{cases} t_3 & \text{in the cases 1) ii). 2) i). 3) i)} \\ d_3 & \text{in the cases 1) i). 2) iii).} \\ n(a-1) & \text{in the cases 2) ii). 2) iv). 2) v).} \end{cases}$$

Finally, in order to obtain the results on t-SyEC d-SyED AUED codes, d_2 and d_3 must be substituted by $n(a-1)$ in stead of n.

V. CONCLUSION

In this paper we have given general necessary and sufficient conditions for codes to correct and/or detect errors of three different types. This covers earlier results as well as new interesting results. Some codes turn out to have stronger error correcting/detecting capabilities than they were originally designed for. An extension has also been given to another error criterion.

REFERENCES

[1] B. Bose and D. K. Pradhan, "Optimal unidirectional error detecting/correcting codes," *IEEE Trans. Comput.*, vol. C-31, pp. 564–568, June 1982.

[2] B. Bose and T. R. N. Rao, "Theory of unidirectional error correcting/detecting codes," *IEEE Trans. Comput.*, vol. C-31, pp. 521–530, June 1982.

[3] S. D. Constantin and T. R. N. Rao, "On the theory of binary asymmetric error-correcting codes," *Inform. Contr.*, vol. 40, pp. 20–36, 1979.

[4] T. Kløve, "Error correcting codes for the asymmetric channel," Rep. 18–09–07–81, Dep. Mathematics, Univ. Bergen, July 1981.
[5] D. J. Lin and B. Bose, "Theory and design of t-error correcting and d ($d > t$) unidirectional error detecting (t-EC d-UED) codes," *IEEE Trans. Comput.*, vol. C-37, pp. 433–439, Apr. 1988.
[6] F. J. MacWilliams and N. J. A. Sloane, *The Theory of Error-Correcting Codes.* Amsterdam, The Netherlands: North-Holland, 1977.
[7] R. J. McEliece, *The Theory of Information and Coding.* Reading, MA: Addison-Wesley, 1977.
[8] D. Nikolos, "Theory and design of t-error correcting/d-error detecting ($d > t$) and all unidirectional error detecting codes," *IEEE Trans. Comput.*, vol. C-40, pp. 132–142, Feb. 1991.
[9] D. Nikolos, N. Gaitanis, and G. Philokyprou, "Systematic t-error correcting/all unidirectional error detecting codes," *IEEE Trans. Comput.*, vol. C-35, pp. 394–402, May 1986.
[10] D. K. Pradhan and S. M. Reddy, "Fault-tolerant failsafe logic networks," in *Proc. IEEE COMPCON*, San Francisco, CA, Mar. 1977, p. 363.

Unordered Error-Correcting Codes and their Applications

Mario Blaum and Jehoshua Bruck
IBM Research Division
Almaden Research Center
San Jose, CA 95120

Abstract

We give efficient constructions for error correcting unordered (ECU) codes, i.e., codes such that any pair of codewords are at a certain minimal distance apart and at the same time they are unordered. These codes are used for detecting a predetermined number of (symmetric) errors and for detecting all unidirectional errors. We also give an application in parallel asynchronous communications.

1 Introduction

Given a binary vector of length n, we say that the *support* of a vector is the set of non-zero coordinates. We say that two vectors are unordered if their supports are unordered as sets, i.e., none of them contains the other. For instance, let $\underline{u} = 11001$, $\underline{v} = 01100$ and $\underline{w} = 11000$. The supports of $\underline{u}$, $\underline{v}$ and $\underline{w}$ are respectively $\{1,2,5\}$, $\{2,3\}$ and $\{1,2\}$. We easily see that $\underline{u}$ and $\underline{v}$ and $\underline{v}$ and $\underline{w}$ are unordered, while $\underline{u}$ and $\underline{w}$ are not unordered. In fact, since the support of $\underline{w}$ is contained in the support of $\underline{v}$, we say that $\underline{w}$ is *contained* in $\underline{v}$.

We say that a code C is unordered if every pair of codewords in C is unordered. Unordered codes are important in several applications. Among them, let us point out protecting a WOM (write only memory) against hostile overwrites [9], parallel asynchronous communications [14, 2] (see also Section 4) and detection of asymmetric and unidirectional errors in computer memories [1].

A natural question is what is the maximal size of an unordered code of length n? This question was answered by Sperner [12] in 1928: the maximal size is $\binom{n}{\lceil n/2 \rceil}$ and the code is obtained by taking all the binary vectors of length n and weight (i.e., number of 1's) $\lceil n/2 \rceil$ (by $\lceil x \rceil$ we denote the smallest integer larger or equal than x and by $\lfloor x \rfloor$ the largest integer smaller or equal than x).

Sperner codes, though, are difficult to implement when n is large. Except for look-up tables, there are no efficient encoders. Most encoders used in practice are systematic, i.e., given any k information bits, the encoder adds a tail of r redundant bits. In our case, we want to add a tail such that the resulting code is unordered. An optimal solution to this problem was found by Berger [1] in 1962. Berger's encoder works as follows: given an information vector of length k and weight w, add a tail to this information vector that consists of the binary representation of $k - w$. For instance, if $k = 5$ and we want to encode the information vector 10110, since $k - w = 2$ whose binary representation is 010, we have to append this tail to 10110. It is not difficult to show that the resulting code is unordered. Moreover, the code is optimal in the sense that r is the length of the shortest tail that needs to be appended to the information part in order to obtain an unordered code [7].

In this paper, we study unordered codes having error correcting capability. Namely, any two codewords are unordered and are at distance at least $t + 1$ apart, where t is a prescribed number. Among the applications of error correcting unordered (ECU) codes are codes that can detect up to t symmetrical errors and detect all unidirectional errors [10, 17]. Such codes are useful in semiconductor computer memories, in which faults affecting a large number of bits tend to be of unidirectional type.

Another interesting application is in parallel asynchronous communications. In effect, consider a communication channel that consists of several sub-channels transmitting simultaneously and asynchronously [14]. As an example of this scheme, we can consider a board with several chips. The sub-channels represent wires connecting between the chips where differences in the lengths of the wires might result in asynchronous reception. In current technology, the receiver acknowledges reception of the message before the transmitter sends the following message. Namely, pipelined utilization of the channel is not possible.

We developed a scheme that enables to transmit without an acknowledgement of the message allowing for pipelined communication and providing a higher bandwidth [2]. Moreover, our scheme allows for a certain number of transitions from a second message to arrive before reception of the current message has been completed, a condition that we call skew. We have derived necessary and sufficient conditions for codes that can detect skew as well as they can correct the skew and allow continuous operation. It turns out that ECU codes satisfy the necessary and sufficient conditions.

Our main contribution in this paper is the construc-

Reprinted from *Proceedings FTCS-22*, 1992, pp. 486-493.

0-8186-4182-7/93 $3.00 © 1992 IEEE

tion of efficient ECU codes. We present 3 possible constructions of error-correcting unordered (ECU) codes and compare between them. Our first construction, (also the most general one), is as follows: we first encode the information bits into an error-correcting code, and then we add a tail in such a way that the resulting code is unordered. Although such a construction is not globally optimal, it has the advantage that the resulting code is systematic when the error-correcting code is systematic. Our construction generalizes the Berger construction. In fact, Berger codes are a particular case of our construction when the underlying error-correcting codes have minimum distance 1. We also prove that our codes are optimal when the error-correcting code is an extended Hamming code, and also for certain BCH codes. Our second construction works for the case in which the minimum distance is either 3 or 4 and has the advantage that it is systematic and easy to implement. Our third construction is based on Sperner's result. We first encode the information into a balanced vector and then encode the balanced vector into an error correcting code. While this construction is more efficient for large n it has the disadvantages that it is not systematic and that encoding is difficult.

The paper is organized as follows: in the next section we present our three constructions together with tables that compare their efficiencies. In Section 3 we prove that our first construction adds the optimal tail for certain important families of codes. Finally, in Section 4 we review the important application of ECU codes to parallel asynchronous communications.

2 Construction of ECU codes

We start this Section giving a generalization of the Berger construction.

Construction 2.1 Assume that we want to construct an ECU code $\mathcal{C}$ with minimum distance d and dimension k. Choose an $[n', k, d]$ error correcting (EC) code $\mathcal{C}'$. Let $\underline{u}$ be an information vector of length k. Then proceed as follows:

1. Encode $\underline{u}$ into a vector $\underline{v} \in \mathcal{C}'$.
2. Let j be the (Hamming) weight of $\underline{v}$. Then append to $\underline{v}$ the complement of the binary representation of $\lfloor j/d \rfloor$.

The code obtained with this encoding procedure is ECU with minimum distance d.

Before proving that the code is ECU, we observe the following:

1. The code $\mathcal{C}$ has length $n' + \lceil \log_2 \lceil (n'+1)/d \rceil \rceil$.
2. The Berger construction corresponds to the special case in which $\mathcal{C}'$ is the $[k, k, 1]$ code.
3. The code $\mathcal{C}$ is systematic if the code $\mathcal{C}'$ is systematic.
4. We may sometimes make the construction more efficient when the all-1 vector is in $\mathcal{C}'$ by taking a coset of this code. The construction is analogous but we have less than $n' + 1$ different weights in the coset [5].
5. For a table with the best error-correcting codes, see [15, 16].

Lemma 2.1 The code $\mathcal{C}$ obtained in Construction 2.1 is ECU with minimum distance d.

Proof: It is clear that the minimum distance is d. Assume that we have two codewords $\underline{u}$ and $\underline{v}$ in $\mathcal{C}'$ with weights i and j respectively, where $i \le j$. Notice that $N(\underline{v}, \underline{u}) > 0$. Let $\underline{t_u}$ and $\underline{t_v}$ be the tails when we encode using Construction 2.1. We will prove that $N\left((\underline{u}, \underline{t_u}), (\underline{v}, \underline{t_v})\right) > 0$.

We have two possibilities: either $\lfloor i/d \rfloor = \lfloor j/d \rfloor$ or $\lfloor i/d \rfloor \ne \lfloor j/d \rfloor$.

If $\lfloor i/d \rfloor = \lfloor j/d \rfloor$, then $j - i \le d - 1$. If $\underline{u} \subseteq \underline{v}$, then $d_H(\underline{u}, \underline{v}) = j - i \le d - 1$, a contradiction. So, in particular, $(\underline{u}, \underline{t_u})$ and $(\underline{v}, \underline{t_v})$ are unordered.

If $\lfloor i/d \rfloor \ne \lfloor j/d \rfloor$, then, in particular, $\lfloor i/d \rfloor < \lfloor j/d \rfloor$. According to Construction 2.1, $\underline{t_u}$ as a binary number is larger than $\underline{t_v}$ as a binary number. This means, $N(\underline{t_u}, \underline{t_v}) > 0$. Since we had that $N(\underline{v}, \underline{u}) > 0$, it follows that $(\underline{u}, \underline{t_u})$ and $(\underline{v}, \underline{t_v})$ are unordered. □

Example 2.1 Assume that we want to construct an ECU code with minimum distance 4 and dimension 57 using Construction 2.1. We first encode the 57 information bits into a $[64, 57, 4]$ extended Hamming code. Then we add a tail of length $\lceil \log_2 \lceil 65/4 \rceil \rceil = 5$ bits. This gives a total of 12 redundant bits. If we take a coset of the $[64, 57, 4]$ code, then the weight distribution goes from 1 to 63, so we have 63 different weights. Now, $\lceil \log_2 \lceil 63/4 \rceil \rceil = 4$ bits, so we save one bit in the total redundancy.

The next construction gives a very simple method to obtain ECU codes with minimum distance $d = 3$.

Construction 2.2 Let $(u_0, u_1, \ldots, u_{k-1})$ be an information vector. Then proceed as follows:

1. Add a parity bit $u_k = \bigoplus_{i=0}^{k-1} u_i$.
2. Let $\{i_1, i_2, \ldots, i_j\}$ be the set where $(u_0, u_1, \ldots, u_k)$ is zero (i.e., the complement of the support). Let $\underline{r}$ be the binary representation of $\sum_{l=1}^{j} i_l$. Appending $\underline{r}$ to $(u_0, u_1, \ldots, u_k)$ completes the encoding.

The code obtained with this encoding procedure is ECU with minimum distance 3.

Before proving that Construction 2.2 gives an ECU code with minimum distance 3, let us illustrate it with an example.

Example 2.2 Assume that we want to construct an ECU code with minimum distance 3 and dimension 5 using Constructions 2.1 and 2.2. Let us start with Construction 2.1. Assume that we want to encode (1 0 0 1 1). By using the parity check matrix

$$H = \begin{pmatrix} 1 & 1 & 1 & 0 & 0 & 1 & 0 & 0 & 0 \\ 1 & 0 & 0 & 1 & 1 & 0 & 1 & 0 & 0 \\ 0 & 1 & 0 & 1 & 0 & 0 & 0 & 1 & 0 \\ 0 & 0 & 1 & 0 & 1 & 0 & 0 & 0 & 1 \end{pmatrix},$$

the vector is encoded into

$$(1\,0\,0\,1\,1 \quad 1\,1\,1\,1).$$

We finally have to add a tail that is the complement of the binary representation of $\lceil 7/3 \rceil = 3$. Since this is the possible maximum number, it is enough with two bits to represent this tail, i.e., we have to add 0 0. The final encoded vector is

$$(1\,0\,0\,1\,1 \quad 1\,1\,1\,1 \quad 0\,0),$$

so we need 6 redundant bits with Construction 2.1.

Let us encode the same vector using Construction 2.2. We first add a parity bit, so we obtain

$$(1\,0\,0\,1\,1 \quad 1).$$

The set of zeros is $\{1, 2\}$. Since the possible maximum is 15, we need 4 extra redundant bits. Now, 1+2=3, which represented in binary with 4 bits is 0 0 1 1. The final encoded vector is

$$(1\,0\,0\,1\,1 \quad 1 \quad 0\,0\,1\,1).$$

As we can see, we need now 5 redundant bits, so we have saved a bit with respect to Construction 2.1. However, this is not always the case. The choice of one construction over the other depends on the parameter k being considered. Moreover, by looking at Table 1, this appears to be the only case in which Construction 2.2 performs better than Construction 2.1.

Observe that, given k information bits, Construction 2.2 adds $\lceil \log_2 k + \log_2(k+1) \rceil$ redundant bits.

Decoding ECU codes when used for detection of t (symmetric) errors and detection of all unidirectional errors is very simple: we reencode the information bits, and we check if the obtained redundancy coincides with the received redundancy. If they coincide, then no errors are detected, otherwise we conclude that errors have occurred.

Let us prove now that Construction 2.2 gives in fact an ECU code with minimum distance 3.

Lemma 2.2 The code $\mathcal{C}$ obtained in Construction 2.2 is ECU with minimum distance 3.

Proof: Consider two codewords $\underline{v}_1 = (\underline{u}_1, \underline{r}_1)$ and $\underline{v}_2 = (\underline{u}_2, \underline{r}_2)$, where $\underline{u}_1$ and $\underline{u}_2$ are the information vectors plus the extra parity check bits. In particular, $d_H(\underline{u}_1, \underline{u}_2) \geq 2$.

Assume first that $\underline{u}_1$ and $\underline{u}_2$ are unordered. If $d_H(\underline{u}_1, \underline{u}_2) > 2$, we are done, so let $d_H(\underline{u}_1, \underline{u}_2) = 2$. Since, in particular, $\underline{v}_1$ and $\underline{v}_2$ are also unordered, we have to show that $\underline{r}_1 \neq \underline{r}_2$, which will make $d_H(\underline{v}_1, \underline{v}_2) \geq 3$.

Since $d_H(\underline{u}_1, \underline{u}_2) = 2$ and $\underline{u}_1$ and $\underline{u}_2$ are unordered, let j be the location where $\underline{u}_1$ is 0 and $\underline{u}_2$ is 1 and l the location where $\underline{u}_1$ is 1 and $\underline{u}_2$ is 0. Without loss of generality, assume that $j > l$. Therefore, $\underline{r}_1$ will be larger than $\underline{r}_2$ as a binary number. In particular, they are different, so $d(\underline{v}_1, \underline{v}_2) \geq 3$.

Assume next that $\underline{u}_1$ and $\underline{u}_2$ are not unordered. Without loss of generality, assume that $\underline{u}_1 \leq \underline{u}_2$. In particular, the set of zeros of $\underline{u}_2$ is contained into the set of zeros of $\underline{u}_1$, thus, $\underline{r}_1$ is larger than $\underline{r}_2$ as a binary number. Therefore $\underline{r}_1$ is not contained in $\underline{r}_2$, proving that $\underline{v}_1$ and $\underline{v}_2$ are unordered. We can also easily see that $d_H(\underline{v}_1, \underline{v}_2) \geq 3$. In effect, since $\underline{u}_1 \leq \underline{u}_2$, $d_H(\underline{u}_1, \underline{u}_2) \geq 2$, and since, in particular, $\underline{r}_1 \neq \underline{r}_2$, this completes the proof. □

We give a third construction, that is quite natural but it is not systematic. The encoding is giving by a look-up table, so this construction is not very practical when k is large. Essentially, we reverse the order of Construction 2.1: we first encode the k information symbols into m symbols such that $2^k \leq \binom{m}{\lceil m/2 \rceil}$ and m is as small as possible. We then add r redundant bits is such a way that we obtain an error-correcting code with minimum distance d. It is clear that the resulting construction gives an ECU code with minimum distance d and length $m + r$. Formally:

Construction 2.3 Let $\underline{u} = (u_0, u_1, \ldots, u_{k-1})$ be an information vector. Let f be a 1-1 assignment from the 2^k information vectors to balanced vectors of length m and weight $\lceil m/2 \rceil$, where m is the minimum such that $2^k \leq \binom{m}{\lceil m/2 \rceil}$. Let $\mathcal{C}'$ be an $[n, m, d]$ error-correcting code. Then proceed as follows:

1. Obtain $\underline{v} = f(\underline{u})$.
2. Encode $\underline{v}$ into a vector $\underline{w} \in \mathcal{C}'$.

The code obtained with this encoding procedure is ECU with minimum distance d.

Example 2.3 Assume that we want to encode $\underline{u} = (1\ 0\ 0\ 1\ 1)$ as in Example 2.2 to obtain an ECU code with minimum distance 3, but this time using Construction 2.3. The smallest m such that $2^5 = 32 \leq \binom{m}{\lceil m/2 \rceil}$ is 7, so we have to encode $\underline{u}$ into a vector of length 7 and weight 3 (or 4). We can use lexicographic order. The vector $\underline{u}$ taken as a binary number corresponds to 19. The 19th vector of length 7 and weight 3 is $\underline{v} = (0\ 1\ 1\ 1\ 0\ 0\ 0)$. Now, we can use an $[11, 7, 3]$ Hamming code, say, the one whose parity check matrix is

$$H = \begin{pmatrix} 1 & 1 & 1 & 0 & 0 & 0 & 1 & 1 & 0 & 0 & 0 \\ 1 & 0 & 0 & 1 & 1 & 0 & 1 & 0 & 1 & 0 & 0 \\ 0 & 1 & 0 & 1 & 0 & 1 & 1 & 0 & 0 & 1 & 0 \\ 0 & 0 & 1 & 0 & 1 & 0 & 1 & 0 & 0 & 0 & 1 \end{pmatrix}.$$

Vector $\underline{u}$ is then encoded into

$$(0\,1\,1\,1\,0\,0\,0\ \ 0\,1\,0\,1).$$

As we can see, we need 6 redundant bits with Construction 2.3.

In order to obtain an ECU code with minimum distance $d = 4$ using Construction 2.2 or Construction 2.3, we simply add a parity bit to the a code with $d = 3$. When Construction 2.1 is used, sometimes codes with minimum distance 4 tie the redundancy of codes with minimum distance 3.

Table 1 gives the total redundancy we have to add to k information bits (for some values of k) to obtain ECU codes with $d = 3$ and $d = 4$ using the different constructions.

Table 2 gives the total redundancy we have to add to k information bits (for some values of k) to obtain ECU codes with $d = 5$, 6, 7, 8, 9 and 10 using Construction 2.1. For the first 4 rows of the table, we used the tables given in [15, 16]. For $k = 128$ and $k = 256$, since they are beyond the scope of the table, we used BCH codes [18].

In Table 3, we do the same thing with respect to Construction 2.3. Not surprisingly, the reader can observe that Construction 2.1 performs better than Construction 2.3 for relatively small values of k and large values of d.

In the next section, we deal with the issues of optimality of ECU codes.

3 Optimality of ECU Codes

In this section, we prove the optimality of Construction 2.1 for extended Hamming codes and for certain BCH codes in the following sense: the tail added to the error correcting code has minimal length, i.e., it is impossible to find a shorter tail making the code unordered.

We begin by defining the concept of a *chain* of vectors.

Definition 3.1 A set of binary vectors $\{V_1, V_2, \ldots, V_m\}$ is a chain of length m if any two vectors in the set are ordered.

The idea in proving the optimality of our constructions is to exhibit a long enough chain of codewords in the error correcting code. The following lemma gives the key:

Lemma 3.1 Let $\{C_1, C_2, \ldots, C_m\}$ be a chain of vectors, each being a codeword in a given code $\mathcal{C}$. Then the length of the a tail that we have to add to $\mathcal{C}$ to make it unordered is at least $\lceil \log_2 m \rceil$ bits.

Proof: Since all the codewords in the chain are ordered, we need to have a different tail for every one of them to make them unordered. Hence, we need at least m different tails. □

We prove the optimality of some of our constructions by exhibiting chains of length $\lceil n/d \rceil + 1$ in an $[n, k, d]$ code. First we prove the optimality of our construction for the extended Hamming code by exhibiting a chain of $2^{m-2} + 1$ codewords in a code of length 2^m.

Proposition 3.1 The $[2^m, 2^m - m - 1, 4]$ extended Hamming code contains a chain of $2^{m-2}+1$ codewords.

Proof: The columns of the parity check matrix of a $(2^m, 2^m - m - 1, 4)$ extended Hamming code are:

$$\{(v_1, v_2, \ldots, v_m, 1)^T \ : \ (v_1, v_2, \ldots, v_m) \in \{0,1\}^m\}.$$

Note that we can arrange the columns in the parity check matrix in pairs such that the first m bits are complementary. Namely, column $(v_1, v_2, \ldots, v_m, 1)^T$ is paired with $(\bar{v}_1, \bar{v}_2, \ldots, \bar{v}_m, 1)^T$. Hence, the sum of a pair of columns in this arrangement gives the vector $(1, 1, \ldots, 1, 0)^T$ and the sum of 2 pairs (4 columns) is the all-0 vector. We call this matrix H_m. For example,

$$H_3 = \begin{pmatrix} 0 & 1 & 0 & 1 & 0 & 1 & 0 & 1 \\ 0 & 1 & 0 & 1 & 1 & 0 & 1 & 0 \\ 0 & 1 & 1 & 0 & 0 & 1 & 1 & 0 \\ 1 & 1 & 1 & 1 & 1 & 1 & 1 & 1 \end{pmatrix}.$$

Consider the extended Hamming code that corresponds to the matrix H_m. It follows from the construction of H_m that the following set of $2^{m-2} + 1$ codewords is a chain:

$$\{(1111)^i 0^{2^m - 4i} \ : \ 0 \leq i \leq 2^{m-2}\}$$

where S^i, S a binary vector, is a vector obtained by concatenating S i times. □

The second result is related to BCH codes. We prove that in many cases we can exhibit chains of codewords that show the optimality of our construction. The key to exhibiting long chains is the following lemma [6]:

Lemma 3.2 Consider a binary t-error-correcting BCH code defined in a standard way, i.e., as a cyclic code of length $2^m - 1$. Let a and b be two integers such that

$$a \cdot b = 2^m - 1$$

and

$$a \geq 2t + 1.$$

Then the following b polynomials correspond to codewords:

$$z_1(X) = 1 + X^b + X^{2b} + \cdots + X^{(a-1)b}$$

and for $2 \leq i \leq b$,

$$z_i(X) = X^{i-1} z_1(X).$$

Using this lemma we can prove the following:

Proposition 3.2 Given a t-error correcting BCH code of length $2^m - 1 = a \cdot b$ where a and b are integers, and $a \geq 2t + 1$, we can exhibit a chain of length $b + 1$.

Proof: The proof follows from lemma 3.2. The chain consists of the all-0 vector and the set of b vectors that correspond to partial sums of the polynomials from Lemma 3.2 as follows:

$$\left\{ \sum_{i=1}^{j} z_i \ : \ 1 \leq j \leq b \right\}.$$

□

Example 3.1 Consider the case $t = 2$, namely $2t + 1 = 5$. We can exhibit a chain of $((2^m - 1)/5) + 1$ codewords in all the cases in which $2^m - 1 \equiv 0 (\text{mod } 5)$. For example, for $m = 4$ we can exhibit a chain of length 4. In general, we can exhibit a long chain whenever $m \equiv 0(\text{mod } 4)$ (by Fermat's Theorem). Similarly, for $2t + 1 = 7$, we can exhibit a long chain for all all the cases in which $m \equiv 0(\text{mod } 6)$.

4 Application to Parallel Asynchronous Communications

In this section, we give an application of ECU unordered codes to parallel asynchronous communications.

Consider a communication channel that consists of several sub-channels transmitting simultaneously. Namely, we would like to transmit a binary vector of length n using n parallel channels/wires. Every wire can carry only one bit of information. Each wire represents a coordinate of the vector to be transmitted. The propagation delay in the wires varies. The problem is to find an efficient communication scheme that will be delay-insensitive.

Since the signals do not arrive at the same time, a natural question is: how does the receiver know that the reception is complete? This problem is studied in [14]. There, the forgoing physical model is described as a scheme in which the sender communicates with the receiver via parallel tracks by rolling marbles (that correspond to a logical 1) in the tracks. Although the marbles are sent in parallel, the channels are asynchronous. This means that marbles are received randomly and at different instants.

Let us introduce some notation. The tracks are represented with the numbers $1, 2, \ldots, n$. After the m-th marble has arrived, the receiver obtains a sequence $X_m = x_1, x_2, \ldots, x_m$, where $1 \leq x_i \leq n$, the number x_i meaning that the i-th marble was received at the x_i-th track. The set $\{x_1, x_2, \ldots, x_m\}$ is the support (i.e., the set of non-zero coordinates) of a vector and determines uniquely a binary vector. From now on, the sequence $X_m = x_1, x_2, \ldots, x_m$ will denote either the sequence as defined above, or a binary vector as defined by its support. Also, X may denote either a vector or its support. This abuse of notation should be clear from the context.

For example, let a vector $X = 0110$ and a vector $Y = 0100$. In the language of sets we have $X = \{2, 3\}$ and $Y = \{2\}$. Clearly, when the receiver gets a marble in track number 2, it is not clear whether he just received Y or he should wait to get a marble in track number 3 (this will correspond to receiving X).

So, we have the following situation: assuming that a vector X is transmitted, once reception has been completed, the receiver acknowledges receipt of the message. The next message is sent by the sender only after the receipt of the acknowledgement. The problem is finding a code C whose elements are messages such that the receiver can identify when transmission has been completed. It is easy to see, as proved in [14], that the codes having the right property are unordered codes.

One of the disadvantages of using the asynchronous type of communication is the fact that the channel is not fully utilized. Namely, there is at most one vector in the wires at any given time. This becomes very critical when the transmission rates are getting higher and lines are getting longer, so it is desirable to have a scheme that enables a pipelined utilization of the channel. In addition, our scheme has the important feature of not using a handshake (acknowledgement) mechanism. Hence, there is no need of communication between receiver and sender.

We note that if one is ready to pay in performance, then a possible strategy, if acknowledgment of messages is not allowed, is that the sender will wait long enough between messages. So, if the sender sends a codeword X followed by a codeword Y, it will be very unlikely that a marble from Y will arrive before the reception of X has been completed. With this scheme, we can again use unordered codes as in [14].

So, we would like to study parallel asynchronous pipelined communication without acknowledgement. The main difficulty in this scheme is that a certain number of marbles from the second message might arrive before reception of the current message has been completed, a condition that we call *skew*.

It turns out that skew should be defined using two parameters. Assume that we transmit a vector X followed by a vector Y. In general, since X is transmitted first, the marbles from X will tend to arrive before the marbles from Y. Also, if a marble in Y arrives before the transmission of X has been completed, it is very likely that few marbles remain in X. Let us call t_1 the maximum number of marbles that may remain in X when a marble from Y arrives. Also, we do not expect too many marbles from Y to arrive before the transmission of X has been completed. Let us call t_2 the maximum number of marbles from Y that may arrive before the completion of X.

Our approach to dealing with skew is to use coding theory methodology and to try to identify the properties of a family of vectors (a code) that can handle the skew. In some applications, we might merely want to detect that skew has occurred, and then invoke a protocol that will halt transmission and allow for retransmission. Codes detecting skew are called *skew-detecting* codes. Formally:

Definition 4.1 We say that a code $\mathcal{C}$ is (t_1, t_2)-skew-detecting if, for any pair of codewords $X, Y \in \mathcal{C}$ such that codeword X is transmitted followed by codeword Y, and the skew between X and Y is limited by the following two conditions:

1. at most t_1 marbles may still be missing from X when a marble from Y arrives; and
2. at most t_2 marbles from Y may arrive before all the marbles from X have arrived;

then $\mathcal{C}$ will correctly decode X when there is no skew between X and Y, and will detect at a certain point the presence of skew provided it does not exceed the t_1 and t_2 constraints.

In other applications, we might want to go further and correct the skew, since this will allow for continuous operation. Codes capable of correcting skew are called *skew-tolerant* codes. Formally,

Definition 4.2 We say that a code $\mathcal{C}$ is (t_1, t_2)-skew-tolerant if, for any pair of codewords $X, Y \in \mathcal{C}$ such that codeword X is transmitted followed by codeword Y, and the skew between X and Y is limited by the following two conditions:

1. at most t_1 marbles may still be missing from X when a marble from Y arrives; and
2. at most t_2 marbles from Y may arrive before all the marbles from X have arrived;

then $\mathcal{C}$ will correctly decode X when the skew between X and Y does not exceed the t_1 and t_2 constraints.

Before stating the necessary and sufficient conditions for skew tolerant and skew detecting codes, we give some notation. Given two binary vectors X and Y of length n, we denote by $N(X,Y)$ the number of coordinates in which X is 1 and Y is 0. For example, if $X = 10110$ and $Y = 00101$, we have $N(X,Y) = 2$ and $N(Y,X) = 1$. Notice that $N(X,Y) + N(Y,X) = d_H(X,Y)$, where d_H denotes Hamming distance.

The following theorem gives necessary and sufficient conditions for a code to be (t_1, t_2)-skew-detecting.

Theorem 4.1 Let $\mathcal{C}$ be a code and, given two positive integers t_1 and t_2, let $t = \min\{t_1, t_2\}$ and $T = \max\{t_1, t_2\}$. Then, code $\mathcal{C}$ is (t_1, t_2)-skew-detecting if and only if, for any pair of codewords X and Y in $\mathcal{C}$, at least one of the following two conditions occurs:

(a) $\min\{N(X,Y), N(Y,X)\} \geq t + 1$

or

(b) $\min\{N(X,Y), N(Y,X)\} \geq 1$ and $\max\{N(X,Y), N(Y,X)\} \geq T + 1$.

The following corollary is clear from the necessary and sufficient conditions.

Corollary 4.1 A code $\mathcal{C}$ is (t, t)-skew-detecting if and only if, for any $X, Y \in \mathcal{C}$, $\min\{N(X,Y), N(Y,X)\} \geq 1$ and $\max\{N(X,Y), N(Y,X)\} \geq t + 1$.

The following theorem gives necessary and sufficient conditions for a code to be (t_1, t_2)-skew-tolerant.

Theorem 4.2 Let $\mathcal{C}$ be a code, t_1 and t_2 two positive integers and $t = \min\{t_1, t_2\}$. Then, code $\mathcal{C}$ is (t_1, t_2)-skew-tolerant if and only if, for any pair of codewords X and Y in $\mathcal{C}$, at least one of the following two conditions occurs:

(a) $\min\{N(X,Y), N(Y,X)\} \geq t + 1$

or

(b) $\min\{N(X,Y), N(Y,X)\} \geq 1$ and $\max\{N(X,Y), N(Y,X)\} \geq t_1 + t_2 + 1$.

For a proof of Theorems 4.1 and 4.2 together with decoding algorithms, the reader is referred to [2].

The connection between ECU codes and (t_1, t_2)-skew-detecting and tolerant codes is given by the following lemma:

Lemma 4.1 Let t_1 and t_2 be positive integers and $t = \min\{t_1, t_2\}$. Then:

1. Let $\mathcal{C}$ be an ECU with minimum distance $\geq t_1 + t_2 + 1$. Then $\mathcal{C}$ is (t_1, t_2)-skew-detecting.

2. Let $\mathcal{C}$ be an ECU with minimum distance $\geq t_1 + t_2 + t + 1$. Then $\mathcal{C}$ is (t_1, t_2)-skew-tolerant.

Proof:

1. Let $t = \min\{t_1, t_2\}$ and $T = \max\{t_1, t_2\}$. Let $X, Y \in \mathcal{C}$, and assume that condition (a) is violated, say, $N(X,Y) \leq t$. The codewords are unordered, and also, $N(Y,X) = d_H(X,Y) - N(X,Y) \geq t_1 + t_2 + 1 - t = T + 1$. Hence, X and Y satisfy condition (b), proving that the code is (t_1, t_2)-skew-detecting.

2. Let $X, Y \in \mathcal{C}$, and assume that condition (a) is violated, say, $N(X,Y) \leq t$. The codewords are unordered, and also $N(Y,X) = d_H(X,Y) - N(X,Y) \geq t_1 + t_2 + 1$. Hence, X and Y satisfy condition (b), proving that the code is (t_1, t_2)-skew-tolerant.

□

In the particular case in which $t_1 = t_2 = t$, an ECU code with minimum distance $2t + 1$ gives a (t, t)-skew-detecting code, while an ECU with minimum distance $3t + 1$ gives a (t, t)-skew-tolerant code.

We also notice that, given t_1 and t_2, $t = \min\{t_1, t_2\}$, a t-error correcting/all unidirectional error detecting (EC/AUED) code [11] is (t_1, t_2)-skew-detecting and (t_1, t_2)-skew-tolerant, since it satisfies the first of the necessary and sufficient conditions in Theorems 4.1 and 4.2. For efficient constructions of t-EC/AUED codes, the reader is referred to [3, 4, 5, 13].

In general, constructions using ECU codes have less redundancy than constructions using EC/AUED codes, unless there is a large imbalance between t_1 and t_2 [2].

Let us point out that some of the constructions of (t_1, t_2) skew-tolerant codes were improved in a recent paper [8].

References

[1] J. M. Berger, "A note on error detecting codes for asymmetric channels," Information and Control, Vol. 4, pp. 68-73, March 1961.

[2] M. Blaum and J. Bruck, "Coding for Skew-Tolerant Parallel Asynchronous Communications," IBM Research Report, RJ 8268 (75629), July 1991.

[3] M. Blaum and H. van Tilborg, "On t-Error Correcting/All Unidirectional Error Detecting Codes," IEEE Trans. on Computers, vol. C-38, pp. 1493-1501, November 1989.

[4] F. J. H. Boinck and H. van Tilborg, "Constructions and bounds for systematic tEC/AUED codes," IEEE Trans. on Information Theory, vol. IT-36, No. 6, pp. 1381-1390, November 1990.

[5] J. Bruck and M. Blaum, "New Techniques for Constructing EC/AUED Codes," IBM Research Report, RJ 6818 (65352), May 1989, to appear in IEEE Trans. on Computers.

[6] R. H. Deng and M. A. Herro, "DC-Free Coset Codes," IEEE Trans. on Information Theory, vol. IT-34, pp. 786-792, July 1988.

[7] C. V. Freiman, "Optimal Error Detecting Codes for Completely Asymmetric Binary Channels," Information and Control, Vol. 5, pp. 64-71, March 1962.

[8] L. H. Khachatrian, "Construction of (t_1, t_2)-tolerant Codes," to appear in Proceedings of Dilijan Conference, Sept. 1991.

[9] E. L. Leiss, "Data Integrity in Digital Optical Disks," IEEE Trans. on Computers, Vol. C-33, No. 9, pp. 818-827, Sept. 1984.

[10] D. Nikolos, "Theory and Design of t-Error Correcting/d-Error Detecting $(d > t)$ and All Unidirectional Error Detecting Codes," IEEE Trans. on Computers, Vol. C-40, No. 2, pp. 132-142, Feb. 1991.

[11] D. K. Pradhan, "A new class of error-correcting detecting codes for fault-tolerant computer application," IEEE Trans. on Computers, vol. C-29, pp. 471-481, June 1980.

[12] E. Sperner, "Ein Satz über Untermengen einer endlichen Menge," Math. Z. **27**, 544-548, 1928.

[13] D. L. Tao, C. R. P. Hartmann and P. K. Lala, "An Efficient Class of Unidirectional Error Detecting/Correcting Codes," IEEE Trans. on Computers, vol. C-37, pp. 879-882, July 1988.

[14] T. Verhoeff, "Delay-insensitive codes - an overview," Distributed Computing, 3:1-8, 1988.

[15] T. Verhoeff, "An Updated Table of Minimum Distance Bounds for Binary Linear Codes," IEEE Trans. on Information Theory, vol. IT-33, pp. 665-680, Sept. 1987.

[16] T. Verhoeff, "An Updated Table of Minimum Distance Bounds for Binary Linear Codes," updated January 1989, preprint.

[17] J. H. Weber, C. de Vroedt and D. E. Boekee, "Necessary and Sufficient Conditions on Block Codes Correcting/Detecting Errors of Various Types," Proceedings of the Tenth Symposium on Information Theory in the Benelux, Houthalen, Belgium, May 25-26, 1989, pp. 31-36, to appear in IEEE Trans. on Computers.

[18] W. Wesley Peterson and E. J. Weldon, "Error-Correcting Codes," Second Edition, MIT Press, 1984.

	Construction 2.1		Construction 2.2		Construction 2.3	
k	$d=3$	$d=4$	$d=3$	$d=4$	$d=3$	$d=4$
4	5	6	5	6	6	7
5	6	7	5	6	6	7
6	6	7	6	7	6	7
7	6	7	6	7	7	8
8	7	7	7	8	7	8
9	7	7	7	8	8	9
10	7	7	7	8	8	9
11	7	8	8	9	8	9
12	8	9	8	9	8	9
13	8	9	8	9	8	9
14	8	9	8	9	8	9
15	8	9	8	9	8	9
16	8	9	9	10	8	9
22	9	9	9	10	8	9
23	9	9	10	11	8	9
26	9	10	10	11	9	10
32	10	11	11	12	9	10
64	12	13	13	14	11	12
128	14	15	15	16	12	13
256	16	17	17	18	14	15

Table 1: Parameters of some codes using Constructions 2.1, 2.2 and 2.3

k	$d=5$	$d=6$	$d=7$	$d=8$	$d=9$	$d=10$
4	5	6	5	6	6	7
10	11	12	13	14	19	20
20	13	14	18	19	23	24
32	15	15	20	21	27	28
64	17	18	23	24	31	32
128	20	21	29	30	37	38
256	24	25	33	34	42	42

Table 2: Parameters of some codes using Construction 2.1.

k	$d=5$	$d=6$	$d=7$	$d=8$	$d=9$	$d=10$
4	5	6	5	6	6	7
10	12	13	16	17	21	22
20	13	14	19	20	24	25
32	14	15	20	21	27	28
64	17	18	23	24	32	33
128	20	21	28	29	36	37
256	23	24	32	33	41	42

Table 3: Parameters of some codes using Construction 2.3.

Chapter 6: Codes for Detecting and/or Correcting Unidirectional Burst Errors

This chapter identifies constructions of codes for detecting and correcting bursts of unidirectional errors; such codes have applications in computer memories where unidirectional errors tend to occur in clusters.

Similar to the Berger construction in Chapter 2's first paper, Bose begins with the construction of a code that detects a single unidirectional burst. He also presents a lower bound for single unidirectional-burst-detecting codes, a construction of *b* adjacent unidirectional error-detecting codes, and totally self-checking checker design methods for codes.

Using a different approach, Blaum improves upon Bose's result. However, Bose's lower bound is not met and the construction's optimality is still an open problem. Jha proposes totally self-checking checks for the Bose and Blaum codes (and also for the Bose/Lin code found in Chapter 2 of this volume).[72]

Davydov, Dzodzuashvili, and Tenegol'ts conclude by constructing a code that corrects a single unidirectional burst of errors. The authors present their results for asymmetric errors; although this paper was published in 1972, when the unidirectional-errors concept was unknown, it is valid for unidirectional errors. Moreover, using the Park/Bose bound,[73] we can prove that the Davydov/Dzodzuashvili/Tenegol'ts code is optimal. Our references identify additional relevant reading.[74]

Burst Unidirectional Error-Detecting Codes

BELLA BOSE

***Abstract*—Systematic codes capable of detecting burst unidrectional errors of length up to 2^{r-1} using r check bits where $r \geq 3$ are presented. Moreover, b-adjacent unidirectional error-detecting codes using $\lceil \log_2(b + 1) \rceil$ check bits are also described. These codes are shown to be optimal or near optimal. The encoding/decoding and the totally self-checking checker design methods for these codes are also given.**

***Index Terms*—Burst errors, decoder, encoder, self-checking checker, unidirectional errors.**

I. Introduction

The use of error control codes to achieve the high reliability requirement of modern computer systems is becoming an important design technique. Error-detecting and correcting codes are extensively used in modern computer systems, especially in memory units.

In the past three to four decades, the theory of symmetric error codes has been well developed, for example, refer to [1] and [2] where "*symmetric error*" means that both $1 \rightarrow 0$ and $0 \rightarrow 1$ errors can occur in a data word. However, the most likely errors in some of the recently developed VLSI memory systems are of the unidirectional type [3], [4]; in *unidirectional type errors,* even though both $1 \rightarrow 0$ and $0 \rightarrow 1$ errors are possible, in a single data word all errors are of the same type. For example, a failure due to address decoder would result in multiple data access most of the time, including the correct data word. In this case, the errors in the output data word are of unidirectional type because the output data word is bit-by-bit AND/OR of many words including the correct word. In addition, the power supply failure will result in changing the received word to all 0 or all 1. Furthermore, a single stuck-at fault in a shift register memory or in a serial bus will result in the output of constant 1's or 0's. These errors can be modeled as unidirectional errors.

The present paper describes systematic codes capable of detecting burst unidirectional errors. A *burst error* of length l means that the error bits are within a cluster of l-adjacent bits. In this definition, we assume that the leftmost bit is adjacent to the rightmost bit in a codeword. It is obvious that any t-unidirectional error-detecting code is also capable of detecting a burst unidirectional error of length up to t. Thus, one can use a t-unidirectional error-detecting code given in [5] for burst unidirectional error detection. However, the burst unidirectional error-detecting capability of the codes presented in this paper is better than that of codes mentioned in the above paper. The proposed code detects a burst unidirectional error of length up to 2^{r-1} using r check bits, whereas the best systematic unidirectional error-detecting code presented in [5] can detect up to $5 \cdot 2^{r-4} + r - 4$ errors using $r \geq 4$ check bits. Note that in the case of symmetric errors, any code that detects a burst of length up to t needs at least t check bits [1]. Thus, when the error nature in a system is of unidirectional burst type, the proposed code is very cost effective.

In [6], it is proved that the set of codewords with weight $\lfloor n/2 \rfloor$ modulo $(t + 1)$ where n is the length of the codewords forms the optimal t-unidirectional error-detecting code. Obviously, these codes also detect a burst unidirectional error of length up to t and the information rate of these codes is slightly better than that of the codes given in this paper. However, codes given in [6] are non-systematic, and thus we need to develop complex encoding/decoding methods for these codes. On the other hand, the systematic codes designed in this paper are optimal or close to optimal and need simple encoding/decoding circuits.

The paper is organized as follows. In Section II, the code format and error-detecting capabilities of the proposed codes are described. The application of these burst unidirectional error-detecting codes for byte per card memory organization is given in Section III. Following the notation used in [7], we call these codes b-adjacent unidirectional error-detecting codes. The b-adjacent codes are shown to be optimal. The design of a "totally self-checking (TSC)" checker, which detects not only system errors but also its own errors for the proposed codes, is given in Section IV.

Research in the direction of unidirectional error correction and detection is discussed in [8]–[12].

The following notations are used in this paper.

k: Number of information bits.

r: Number of check bits.

$n = k + r$: Length of the code.

I_0: Number of 0's in the information part.

I_1: Number of 1's in the information part.

In the rest of this paper, unidirectional errors will be referred to as, simply, errors unless otherwise specified.

Manuscript received December 1, 1985; revised December 10, 1985. This work was supported by NSF Grant DMC-8421104.

The author is with the Department of Computer Science, Oregon State University, Corvallis, OR 97331.

IEEE Log Number 8607585.

II. Code Construction

As we mentioned before, the proposed code can detect a burst errors of length up to 2^{r-1} using r check bits. When $r = 2$, the code can detect a burst error of length 2, which is not interesting because there are codes [5] which can detect 2-(random) unidirectional errors using 2 check bits. Moreover, using 2 check bits, we can design codes capable of detecting burst symmetric errors of length up to 2 [1]. Therefore, we assume that the number of check bits r is greater than 2. Furthermore, we assume that the number of information bits k is at least 2^r (i.e., $k \geq 2^r$); when $k < 2^r$, we can use Berger–Freiman codes [13], [14] which can detect all unidirectional errors.

When all 2^k information symbols do not occur, the codes proposed in [15] need fewer check bits than the Berger–Freiman codes. This code also detects all unidirectional errors. However, in this paper, we assume that all 2^k information symbols do occur in the code.

Code Format

Let $(a_k, a_{k-1}, \cdots, a_1)$ be the given information symbol with k bits where $a_i \in \{0, 1\}$ for $i = 1, 2, \cdots, k$. The check CS is given by

$$CS \equiv I_0(\text{mod } 2^r) \equiv \sum_{i=1}^{k} \overline{a}_i \text{ mod } 2^r$$

where I_0 is the number of 0's in the information part and r is the number of check bits.

In other words, take the check symbol as the binary representation of the number of 0's (modulo 2^r) found in the information symbol where r is the number of check bits.

Let $(b_{r-1}, b_{r-2}, \cdots, b_0)$ be the check obtained using the above rule where $b_i \in \{0, 1\}$ for $i = 0, 1, \cdots, r - 1$. Instead of concatenating the check symbol to the information symbol, the bits of the codeword are arranged as shown in Fig. 1.

0-8186-4182-7/93 $3.00 © 1986 IEEE

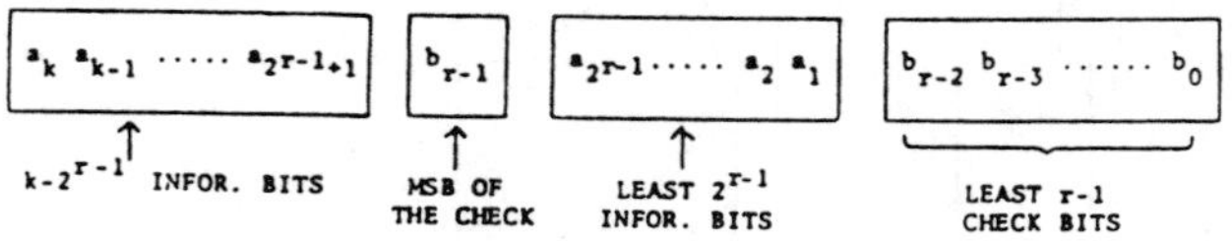

Fig. 1. Code format of burst error-detecting code.

The most significant bit b_{r-1} of the check is placed in between the information bits $a_{2^{r-1}+1}$ and $a_{2^{r-1}}$, and the other check bits $(b_{r-2}, b_{r-3}, \cdots, b_0)$ are placed after the information bit a_1. By this way, for a burst unidirectional error of length at most 2^{r-1}, the MSB b_{r-1} of the check and some other check bit cannot be simultaneously in error. The importance of this concept will be explained shortly in the proof of Theorem 2.1. Before that, an example is given below to explain the code construction technique.

Example 2.1: Let $k = 12$, $r = 3$, and the given information symbol be 1100 0100 0000. Since there are nine zeros in the information part, the check is given by $9 \bmod 2^3 \equiv 9 \bmod 8 \equiv 1 \equiv 001_2$. Thus, the code word will be as follows.

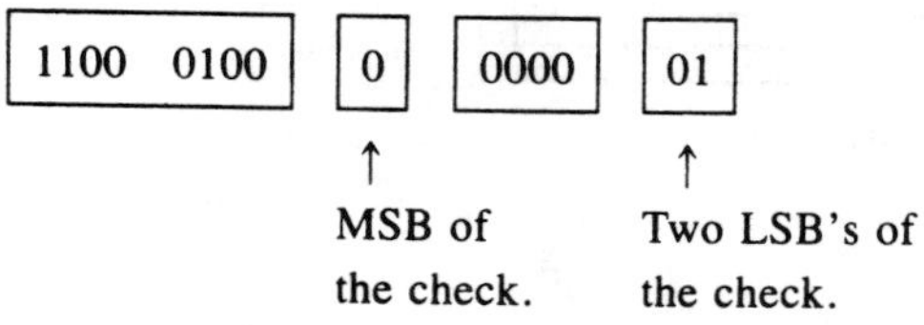

The code can detect a burst unidirectional error of length up to $2^{3-1} = 4$.

In order to verify whether the received word is error free or not, a new check symbol is generated from the received information symbol and this check symbol is compared to the received check symbol. If they agree, then there is no burst unidirectional error of length $\le 2^{r-1}$; if they do not, there must be some error(s) in the received word.

The following theorem establishes the burst error-detecting capabilities of the code.

Theorem 2.1: The above proposed code can detect any single burst errors of length up to 2^{r-1} using r check bits.

Proof: By our design rule, the check symbol CS is given by $CS = I_0 \bmod 2^r$ where I_0 is the number of 0's in the information part. Let $(b_{r-1}, b_{r-2}, \cdots, b_0)$ be the binary representation of $I_0 \bmod 2^r$. Let I_0' and CS' be, respectively, the number of 0's in the information part and check part of the received codeword. When $CS' - I_0' \equiv 0 \bmod 2^r$, there is no error and when $CS' - I_0' \not\equiv 0 \bmod 2^r$, there is some error. The theorem is proved using three cases.

Case 1: (Errors only in the information part.) Let there be l-unidirectional errors in the information part where $1 \le l \le 2^{r-1}$. Then $I_0' \equiv I_0 \pm l$ and $CS' = CS$. Now $CS' - I_0' \equiv CS - (I_0 \pm l) \equiv I_0 - (I_0 \pm l) \equiv \pm l \bmod 2^r$. But $\pm l \bmod 2^r \not\equiv 0$ because $1 \le l \le 2^{r-1}$. Thus, these errors can be detected.

Case 2: (Errors only in the check part.) In this case, $I_0' = I_0$ and $CS' = CS \pm a$ where $1 \le a \le 2^{r-1}$. Now $CS' - I_0' \equiv (CS \pm a) - CS \equiv \pm a \not\equiv 0 \bmod 2^r$. Again, these errors can be detected.

Case 3: (Errors both in the check and the information parts.) Since the MSB and some other bit of the check cannot be in error simultaneously, we can take the following two subcases.

Case 3a: (Errors only in the MSB of the check and some other information bits.) Let l information bits be in error where $1 \le l \le 2^{r-1} - 1$. Thus, for $1 \to 0$ errors, $I_0' = I_0 + l$ and $CS' = CS - 2^{r-1}$, and for $0 \to 1$ errors, $I_0' = I_0 - l$ and $CS' = CS + 2^{r-1}$. Therefore, $CS' - I_0' \equiv \pm(2^{r-1} + l) \not\equiv 0 \bmod 2^r$. Thus, these types of errors are detected.

Case 3b: (Errors only in some of the least $(r - 1)$ check bits and some information bits.) $CS' = CS + a$ and $I_0' = I_0 - l$ for $0 \to 1$ errors and $CS' = CS - a$ and $I_0' = I_0 + l$ for $1 \to 0$ errors where $1 \le a \le 2^{r-1} - 1$ and $1 \le l \le 2^{r-1} - 1$. Thus, $CS' - I_0' \equiv \pm(a + l) \not\equiv 0 \bmod 2^r$. Again, these errors are detected.

The above theorem shows that the code can detect a single unidirectional burst of length at most 2^{r-1}. This is the maximum possible for this code. In other words, the code cannot detect all unidirectional bursts of length $2^{r-1} + 1$. For example, consider the codeword given in Example 2.1. Let there be a burst $0 \to 1$ errors of length 5, one in the MSB of the check and the other four in the least significant bits of the information part. Then the erroneous word will be [11 00 0100] [1] [1111] [01]. The new check symbol calculated from the erroneous information part is $5 = 101_2$, which is same as the erroneous check symbol. Therefore, this error cannot be detected. In general, when the MSB of check and some 2^{r-1} information bits adjacent to the MSB of the check are in error, this burst error of length $2^{r-1} + 1$ is not detected.

This brings up the next important question—what is the maximum length of the burst error that can be detected using r check bits? In the next few paragraphs, we try to attack this problem. First we need the following definitions.

A word $X = (x_1, x_2, \cdots, x_n)$ is said to *cover* another word $Y = (y_1, y_2, \cdots, y_n)$ if, whenever $y_i = 1$, $x_i = 1$ for $i = 1, 2, \cdots, n$. When neither word covers the other, they are called *unordered*. For example, $X = (11011)$ covers $Y = (10001)$, whereas $Z = (00111)$ and X are unordered. X covers Y is written as $Y \le X$.

Furthermore, a set of n distinct words $X1, X2, \cdots, Xn$ is called a *maximal cover* of length n whenever $Xi \le X(i + 1)$ and there exists no Y which is distinct from Xi and $X(i + 1)$ such that $Xi \le Y \le X(i + 1)$ for $i = 1, 2, \cdots, n - 1$. For example, the set $\{0000, 0001, 0011, 0111, 1111\}$ is a maximal cover of length 5.

Theorem 2.2: Let C be a code with $k \ge (r - 1)2^{r-1}$ information bits. If C can detect a burst error of length up to 2^{r-1}, then the number of check bits in C must be at least r.

Proof: Suppose C has only $r - 1$ check bits. Since we assumed that $k \ge (r - 1)2^{r-1}$ and the leftmost bit is adjacent to the rightmost bit in a codeword, there must be a cluster of 2^{r-1} information bits with no check bit placed in between any two information bits. Using these 2^{r-1} information bits, we can construct a maximal cover of length $2^{r-1} + 1$. We can assign some fixed constant to the other information bits in this maximal cover. Since the code is capable of detecting a burst error of length up to 2^{r-1}, the check symbols for the above set of maximal cover information symbols must all be distinct. Thus, there must be at least $2^{r-1} + 1$ distinct check symbols. However, using $r - 1$ check bits, we can have a maximum of 2^{r-1} distinct check symbols. This gives a contradiction. Therefore, C must have at least r check bits. □

Since the proposed code detects a burst error of length up to 2^{r-1} using r check bits, the code is optimal for detecting a burst error of this length if $k \ge (r - 1)2^{r-1}$. However, we do not know whether there exists an r check bit code which can detect a burst error of length up to l where $2^{r-1} + 1 \le l \le 2^r - 1$. Note that for this burst error length, it can be proved (similarly to Theorem 2.2) that a minimum of r check bits are needed, whereas the proposed code uses $r + 1$ check bits.

Encoding and Decoding Circuit Design

At the encoder side, the number of zeros in the information part is counted under modulo 2^r operation and this number in binary form gives the check symbol. Similarly, at the decoder side, again the number of zeros in the received (output) information part is counted under modulo 2^r operation and this check symbol is compared to the received check symbol for error detection. Thus, in both encoder and decoder sides, we need to count the number of zeros in the information part. In a sequential encoder/decoder circuit design, all we need is an r-bit counter at the encoder side and an r-bit counter and an r-bit comparator at the decoder side. The r-bit counter is incremental for every input 0 information bit. Whenever a carry occurs from the MSB (i.e., the number is $\ge 2^r$), this carry can be ignored.

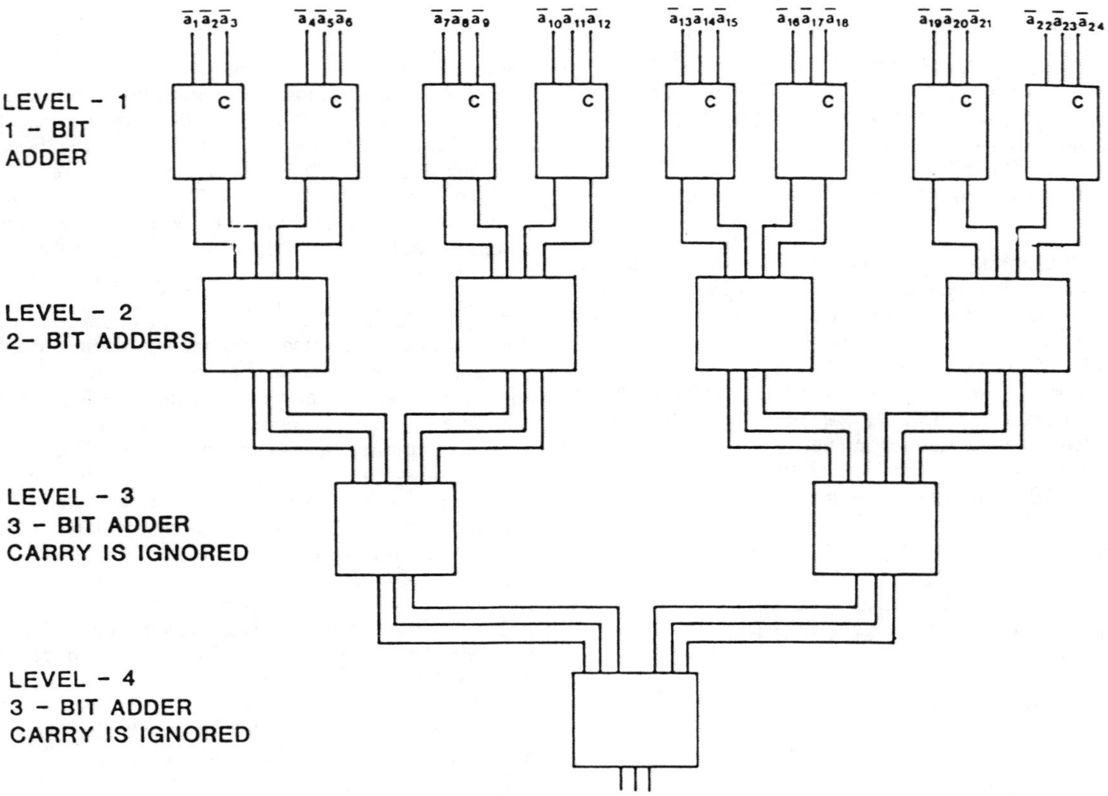

Fig. 2. Zero mod 8 generator.

The sequential encoding/decoding method is very slow. In a computer system where the throughput rate is on the order of hundreds of kilobits per second, we need to design fast encoding/decoding methods.

Instead of using a modulo 2^r counter for counting the number of zeros in the information part, we can use a tree of adder circuits as discussed in [5]. A modulo 8 zero counter tree circuit using 2's complement adders is shown in Fig. 2. Here we assume that the number of input bits is 24 and all the bits are in complemented form. The first and second levels contain, respectively, 1-bit and 2-bit adder circuits, and from the third level on, the circuit contains 3-bit adders all the way down. In general, a modulo 2^r zero counter can be designed using a tree-type circuit which contains i-bit adders at level i where $i = 1, 2, \cdots, r - 1$ and r-bit adders in the remaining levels.

III. *b*-Adjacent Unidirectional Error-Detecting Codes

The advent of VLSI has pushed the idea of bit per card to a cluster of b bits (byte) per card memory organization. If a failure occurs, the resultant information read out from the memory is likely to have a block of b-adjacent bits in error, and these errors, as discussed in Section I, are most likely of the unidirectional type.

We assume that the information bits are clustered into s groups of b-adjacent bits where $s \geq 1$. Thus, the number of information bits k will be sb. The proposed code needs $r = \lceil \log_2(b + 1) \rceil$ check bits to detect b-adjacent errors, and we assume that these r check bits are clustered as a single byte. Thus, the check byte length is smaller than that of the information bytes. Furthermore, we assume that at most one byte is in error. For byte lengths in the range $2^r + 1 \leq b \leq 2^{r+1} - 1$, the proposed code needs one less bit compared to the b-burst error-detecting code discussed in Section II.

The check symbol generation method is same as that of the previously discussed burst error-detecting code. Let r be equal to $\lceil \log_2(b + 1) \rceil$ where b is the byte length. The check symbol generation rule is as follows.

Take the check symbol CS as the binary representation of the number of 0's (modulo 2^r), found in the information symbol, i.e.,

$$CS \equiv I_0 \text{ MOD } 2^r \equiv \sum_{i=1}^{K} \bar{a}_i \bmod 2^r$$

where I_0 is the number of 0's in the information part. Alternatively, we can take $CS \equiv I_1$ MOD 2^r where I_1 is the number of 1's in the information part. However, the former scheme is preferred, because the code designed using this method also detects many other unidirectional errors.

Now we consider the error-detecting capability of the code. Let CS' and I_0' be, respectively, the check symbol and the number of 0's in the information symbol of the received word. Since we assumed that at most a single byte can be in error, we need to consider only the following two cases. 1) (Only some information byte in error.) When some t where $1 \leq t \leq b$ errors occur in some information byte, $CS' - I_0' \equiv CS - (I_0 \pm t) \equiv \pm t \not\equiv 0 \bmod 2^r$. 2) (Errors only in the check part.) We can write $CS' = CS \pm a$ where $1 \leq a < 2^r$. Then $CS' - I_0' \equiv (CS \pm a) - I_0 \equiv \pm a \not\equiv 0 \bmod 2^r$. Therefore, the code can detect all b-adjacent errors.

The proposed code is optimal for all byte lengths b. This can be seen from the following argument. Consider a single information byte, which as mentioned before, is b bits long. By choosing the appropriate bit patterns in these b bits and some fixed constant values for all other bits, we can construct a maximal cover of $b + 1$ information symbols. For a code to be capable of detecting b-adjacent errors, the check symbols for these maximal cover information symbols must all be distinct. Thus, the code must have at least $b + 1$ distinct check symbols or $\lceil \log_2(b + 1) \rceil$ check bits. Since the code uses exactly this many check bits, the code is optimal.

Note that a b-adjacent symmetric error-detecting code needs b check bits. This code can be constructed using interlacing scheme by which the ith bit in each of s bytes is used to calculate the ith parity bit, giving a total of b parity check bits. On the other hand, the proposed b-adjacent unidirectional code needs only $\lceil \log_2(b + 1) \rceil$ check bits.

The encoding/decoding circuits for the b-adjacent unidirectional error-detecting codes are same as the one discussed in the previous section.

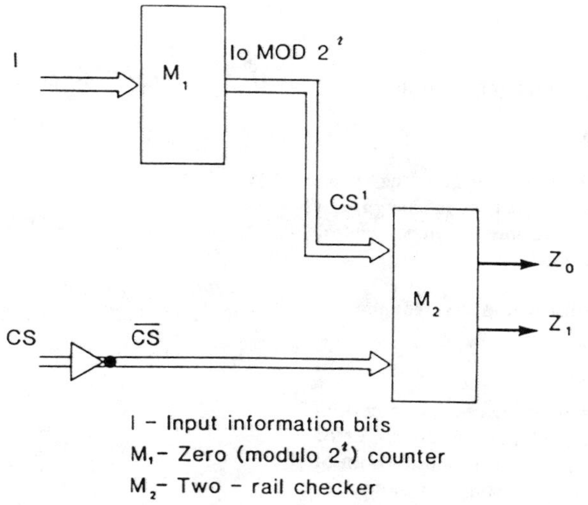

Fig. 3. TSC checker for burst and b-adjacent error-detecting codes.

IV. Totally Self-Checking Checker Design

In a conventional fault-tolerant system, using error-detecting codes, the checker forms the "hardcore," meaning that any error in the checker will result in disaster. In order to alleviate this problem, the concept and design of a "totally self-checking (TSC)" checker, which detects not only the system errors but also its own errors, are introduced [16], [17]. A TSC checker must satisfy three properties—self testing, fault secure, and code disjoint, which are defined below. In the following definitions, C, $\overline{C}$, A, $\overline{A}$, and F represent, respectively, the input code space, input noncode space, output code space, output noncode space, and fault set for the checker. Furthermore, Z represents the output function of the checker.

Self Testing: A circuit is self testing for the fault set F if, for every $f \in F$, the circuit produces a noncode space output for at least one code space input, i.e., for all $f \in F$, there exists a $c \in C$ such that $Z(c,f) \in \overline{A}$.

Fault Secure: A circuit is fault secure for a fault set F if, for every fault $f \in F$ and for all $c \in C$, either $Z(c,f) = Z(c)$ or $Z(c,f) \in \overline{A}$.

Code Disjoint: A circuit is code disjoint if it maps the input code space to the output code space and input noncode space to the output noncode space, i.e., for all $c \in C$, $Z(c) \in A$ and for all $x \in \overline{C}$, $Z(x) \in \overline{A}$.

It is assumed that the system and the checker are not faulty simultaneously.

The block diagram for the TSC checker for the proposed code is shown in Fig. 3. The bitwise complement of the received check symbol $\overline{CS}$ and the check symbol CS' generated from the received information symbol form a two-rail code. The TSC checker for a two-rail code is given using random logic in [16] where the set of single stuck-type faults forms the fault set. In [18], the PLA implementation of a TSC checker for a two-rail code is given. The fault set in this implementation is the single faults of the following types—stuck-at faults, crosspoint defects, and shorts between lines. Either one of the designs can be used for the block M_2 in Fig. 3. Since the check part of the code contains all possible 2^r binary r tuples, following the theory given in [19], it can be shown that the checker satisfies the TSC checker properties.

V. Summary

Burst unidirectional error-protecting codes are designed in this paper. These codes need fewer check bits than that of the corresponding burst symmetric error-protecting codes. Furthermore, the encoding/decoding circuits and the TSC checker for these codes are easy to implement. The b-adjacent unidirectional error-detecting codes are also presented. These codes can be successfully used in byte per card memory organizations and byte-wide communication systems.

References

[1] W. W. Peterson and E. J. Weldon, *Error Correcting Codes.* Cambridge, MA: M.I.T. Press, 1972.

[2] E. R. Berlekamp, Algebraic Coding Theory. New York: McGraw-Hill, 1968.

[3] R. W. Cook *et al.*, "Design of self-checking microprogram control," *IEEE Trans. Comput.*, vol. C-22, pp. 255–262, Mar. 1973.

[4] D. K. Pradhan and J. J. Stiffler, "Error correcting codes and self-checking circuits in fault tolerant computers," *Computer*, pp. 27–37, Mar. 1980.

[5] B. Bose and D. J. Lin, "Systematic unidirectional error detecting codes," in *Dig. Papers, 14th Int. Conf. Fault Tolerant Comput.*, June 1984, pp. 94–99.

[6] J. M. Borden, "Optimal asymmetric error detecting codes," *Inform. Contr.*, Apr. 1984.

[7] D. C. Bossen, "b-adjacent error correction," *IBM J. Res. Develop.*, vol. 14, pp. 402–408, July 1970.

[8] D. K. Pradhan, "A new class of error correcting/detecting codes for fault-tolerant computer applications," *IEEE Trans. Comput.*, vol. C-29, pp. 471–481, June 1980.

[9] B. Bose and T. R. N. Rao, "Theory of unidirectional error correcting/detecting codes," *IEEE Trans. Comput.*, vol. C-31, pp. 521–530, June 1982.

[10] B. Bose, "On systematic SEC-MUED codes," in *Dig. Papers, 11th Int. Symp. Fault Tolerant Comput.*, June 1981, pp. 265–267.

[11] B. Bose and D. K. Pradhan, "Optimal unidirectional error detecting codes," *IEEE Trans. Comput.*, vol. C-31, pp. 564–568, June 1982.

[12] D. Nikolos, N. Gaitaris, and G. Philokyprou, "Systematic error correcting and all unidirectional error detecting codes starting from cyclic AN codes," in *Dig. Papers, 14th Int. Conf. Fault Tolerant Comput.*, June 1984, pp. 318–323.

[13] J. M. Berger, "A note on error detecting codes for asymmetric channels," *Inform. Contr.*, vol. 4, pp. 60–73, Mar. 1961.

[14] C. V. Freiman, "Optimal error detection codes for completely asymmetric binary channels," *Inform. Contr.*, vol. 5, pp. 64–71, Mar. 1962.

[15] J. E. Smith, "On separable unordered codes," *IEEE Trans. Comput.*, vol. C-33, pp. 741–743, Aug. 1984.

[16] W. C. Carter and P. R. Schneider, "Design of dynamically checked computers," in *Proc. IFIP'68, Vol. 2*, Edinburgh, Scotland, Aug. 1968, pp. 878–883.

[17] D. A. Anderson and G. Metze, "Design of totally self-checking check circuits for m-out-of-n codes," *IEEE Trans. Comput.*, vol. C-22, pp. 263–269, Mar. 1973.

[18] S. L. Wang and A. Avizienis, "The design of totally self-checking circuits using programmable logic arrays," in *Proc. 9th Int. Symp. Fault Tolerant Comput.*, June 1979, pp. 173–180.

[19] M. Ashjee and S. M. Reddy, "On totally self-checking checkers for separable codes," *IEEE Trans. Comput.*, vol. C-26, pp. 737–744, Aug. 1977.

Systematic Unidirectional Burst Detecting Codes

MARIO BLAUM

Abstract—**Families of systematic unidirectional burst detecting codes are presented. When the number of information bits is large enough, the new codes can detect longer bursts than previously known codes. Encoding and decoding procedures are indicated.**

Index Terms—**Bursts, decoder, encoder, information bits, redundancy, systematic code, unidirectional errors.**

I. Introduction

Consider a binary block code, i.e., each codeword has a certain length n. We say that a codeword has suffered a unidirectional error when all errors are either transitions $0 \to 1$ or $1 \to 0$ but not both of them at the same time. It has been reported that in some VLSI circuits the errors are of unidirectional type [1], [10], [14]. The theoretical and practical aspects of unidirectional error correcting/detecting codes have aroused considerable interest in recent literature [2], [4]–[9], [11]–[16].

In certain semiconductor computer memory architectures, the unidirectional errors tend to be confined in a burst, i.e., a cluster of adjacent bits up to a certain length is affected (assuming that the rightmost bit is adjacent to the leftmost bit). In the rest of this paper, a burst of unidirectional errors will be called a burst. In applications, it is important to implement codes that are capable of detecting bursts of a certain length using a minimum of redundancy. Conversely, given a certain number of redundant bits, we want to detect bursts as long as possible. We want the codes to have very easy encoding and decoding procedures. To that end, they have to be systematic (i.e., if $\vec{c}$ denotes the information bits, the encoded vector has the form $(\vec{c}, \vec{r})$, where $\vec{r}$ denotes the redundant bits). Moreover, as in previous results [2], [5], [7], the redundant bits will be a function of the weight (i.e., number of 1's) of the information part.

In [5], Bose presents a family of systematic codes that can detect any burst of length up to 2^{r-1}, $r \geq 3$ being the number of redundant bits (the number of information bits is $k \geq 2^r$).

Given a sufficiently large number k of information bits and r redundant bits, denote by $b(r)$ the maximum length of a burst that a systematic code can detect. It was proved in [5] that $b(r) \leq 2^r - 1$. An open question in [5] was if $b(r) > 2^{r-1}$.

The purpose of this paper is providing an affirmative answer to this question. In Section II we give some theoretical results that set the problem in a combinatorial context. In Section III, for each integer r, we construct a code (according to the guidelines of Section II) that can detect a burst of length up to $c(r)$, where $c(r) > 2^{r-1}$ when $r \geq 4$. An estimate for $c(r)$ is given, and it is shown that $c(r)$ is asymptotically equal to 2^r. In Section IV, encoding and decoding procedures are given.

II. General Construction and Combinatorial Properties

In this section, we present a general method to construct a burst detecting code. In the next one, we give a specific construction.

Let $r \geq 1$. Denote by $\mathbb{Z}_{2^r}$ the integers mod 2^r. Let $f: \mathbb{Z}_{2^r} \to \{0, 1\}^r$ be 1 - 1. From now on, $\{0, 1\}^r$ is considered as a directed cycle with the cyclic structure induced by f, i.e.,

$$f(i) \to f(i+1), \qquad i \in \mathbb{Z}_{2^r}. \tag{2.1}$$

We say that a binary m-tuple $\vec{x} = (x_1, x_2, \cdots, x_m)$ *covers* another binary m-tuple $\vec{y} = (y_1, y_2, \cdots, y_m)$ if $x_j = 1$ whenever $y_j = 1$ (notation: $\vec{y} \leq \vec{x}$). We call the weight of $\vec{x} = (x_1, x_2, \cdots, x_m)$ the number of 1's in $\vec{x}$, i.e., wt $(\vec{x}) = \sum_{j=1}^{m} x_j$.

Let $i \in \mathbb{Z}_{2^r}$. We define

$$c(i, f; r) = \min \{ j : 1 \leq j \leq 2^r, f(i) \leq f(i+j \bmod 2^r), \text{wt}(f(i+j \bmod 2^r)) - \text{wt} f(i)) \leq 1 \} \tag{2.2}$$

and

$$c(f; r) = \min_i c(i, f; r). \tag{2.3}$$

Example 2.1: Let $r = 3$ and $f: \mathbb{Z}_8 \to \{0, 1\}^3$ given by Table I. In the third column, we write the values of $c(i, f; 3)$ according to definition (2.2). Taking the minimum on the values of this column, we obtain $c(f; 3)$, which in this case is 4.

TABLE I
$r = 3$, $c(f; 3) = 4$

i	f(i)	c(i,f;3)
0	1 1 1	8
1	0 1 1	7
2	1 0 1	6
3	1 1 0	5
4	0 0 1	5
5	0 1 0	4
6	1 0 0	4
7	0 0 0	5

Given $r \geq 1$ and $f: \mathbb{Z}_{2^r} \to \{0, 1\}^r$, we can now construct a code that can detect bursts of length up to $c(f; r)$.

Construction 2.2: Let $k \geq r.\ (c(f; r) - 1)$ be the number of information bits. Let $\vec{a} = (a_1, a_2, \cdots, a_k)$ be the information vector. The parity vector $\vec{b} = (b_{r-1}, b_{r-2}, \cdots, b_0)$ is defined as

$$\vec{b} = f(\text{wt}(\vec{a}) \bmod 2^r). \tag{2.4}$$

For simplicity, call $c = c(f; r)$. The bits in a codeword $\vec{v}$ are arranged as follows:

$$\vec{v} = a_1 a_2 \cdots a_{c-1} b_{r-1} a_c a_{c+1} \cdots a_{2(c-1)} b_{r-2} a_{2(c-1)+1} a_{2(c-1)+2} \cdots a_{3(c-1)} b_{r-3} \cdots b_2 a_{(r-2)(c-1)+1} \cdots a_{(r-1)(c-1)} b_1 a_{(r-1)(c-1)+1} \cdots a_k b_0. \tag{2.5}$$

We denote $C(f; r)$ the code obtained by this construction.

Example 2.3: Let $k = 9$. Consider $C(f; 3)$ when f is the function defined by Table I. Some codewords are listed below.

$$\vec{v}_1 = 101\ \ 0\ \ 001\ \ 1\ \ 110\ \ 0$$

$$\vec{v}_2 = 011\ \ 0\ \ 101\ \ 1\ \ 001\ \ 0$$

$$\vec{v}_3 = 111\ \ 0\ \ 101\ \ 0\ \ 110\ \ 0.$$

The first two information vectors have weight 5. According to Table I and (2.4), the parity vector is 0 1 0. Similarly, the third information vector has weight 7, so the parity vector is 0 0 0. The parity and information bits are distributed according to (2.5).

We can now prove our main result.

Theorem 2.4: The code $C(f; r)$ can detect any burst of length up to $c(f; r)$.

Proof: Assume a burst of length l, $1 \leq l \leq c(f; r)$ occurs. Without loss, the burst may be considered of type $0 \to 1$, so the weigth of a codeword increases l', where $1 \leq l' \leq l$. According to (2.5), a burst of length up to $c(f; r)$ either does not affect the parity bits or affects exactly one parity bit. We treat the two cases separately.

Case I: No parity bits are affected.

Let $\vec{a}\vec{b}$ be the transmitted codeword, where $\vec{a}$ denotes the information bits and $\vec{b}$ denotes the parity bits. Since no parity bits are affected, the received word has the form $\vec{a}'\ \vec{b}$, $\vec{a}'$ being a corrupted version of $\vec{a}$. The burst will *not* be detected only if $\vec{a}'\vec{b}$ is a codeword in $C(f; r)$. If this is the case, by (2.4),

Manuscript received May 10, 1987; revised November 12, 1987.
The author is with the IBM Almaden Research Center, San Jose, CA 95120.
IEEE Log Number 8719341.

$$\vec{b} = f\,(\text{wt}\,(\vec{a}')\bmod 2^r)$$

$$= f\,(\text{wt}\,(\vec{a}) + l' \bmod 2^r),$$

but also

$$\vec{b} = f\,(\text{wt}\,(\vec{a})\bmod 2^r).$$

Since f is 1-1, we must have $l' \equiv 0 \bmod 2^r$, so $l' \geq 2^r$, a contradiction (notice that $c(f;\,r) < 2^r$).

Case II: Exactly one parity bit is affected.

TABLE II
$r = 4,\ c(f;\,4) = 9$

i	f(i)	c(i,f;4)
0	1 1 1 1	16
1	0 1 1 1	15
2	1 0 1 1	14
3	1 1 0 1	13
4	1 1 1 0	12
5	0 0 1 1	12
6	0 1 0 1	11
7	0 1 1 0	10
8	1 0 0 1	10
9	1 0 1 0	9
10	1 1 0 0	9
11	0 0 0 1	10
12	0 0 1 0	9
13	0 1 0 0	9
14	1 0 0 0	10
15	0 0 0 0	12

TABLE III
$r = 5,\ c(f;\,5) = 19$

i	f(i)	c (i,f;5)
0	1 1 1 1 1	32
1	0 1 1 1 1	31
2	1 0 1 1 1	30
3	1 1 0 1 1	29
4	1 1 1 0 1	28
5	1 1 1 1 0	27
6	0 0 1 1 1	27
7	0 1 0 1 1	26
8	0 1 1 0 1	25
9	0 1 1 1 0	24
10	1 0 0 1 1	24
11	1 0 1 0 1	23
12	1 0 1 1 0	22
13	1 1 0 0 1	22
14	1 1 0 1 0	21
15	1 1 1 0 0	21
16	0 0 0 1 1	22
17	0 0 1 0 1	21
18	0 0 1 1 0	20
19	0 1 0 0 1	20
20	0 1 0 1 0	19
21	0 1 1 0 0	19
22	1 0 0 0 1	20
23	1 0 0 1 0	19
24	1 0 1 0 0	19
25	1 1 0 0 0	20
26	0 0 0 0 1	22
27	0 0 0 1 0	21
28	0 0 1 0 0	21
29	0 1 0 0 0	22
30	1 0 0 0 0	24
31	0 0 0 0 0	27

Let $\vec{a}\vec{b}$ be the transmitted codeword and $\vec{a}'\,\vec{b}'$ be the received word. Now we have $\text{wt}\,(\vec{a}') = \text{wt}\,(\vec{a}) + l' - 1$ and $\text{wt}\,(\vec{b}') = \text{wt}\,(\vec{b}) + 1$. As before, assume that the burst is undetected so $\vec{a}'\,\vec{b}'$ is a codeword. By (2.4), we have

$$\vec{b}' = f\,(\text{wt}\,(\vec{a}')\bmod 2^r)$$

$$= f\,(\text{wt}\,(\vec{a}) + l' - 1 \bmod 2^r). \tag{2.6}$$

Also $\vec{b} = f(\,\text{wt}\,(\vec{a})\bmod 2^r)$. Since $\text{wt}\,(\vec{b}') - \text{wt}\,(\vec{b}) = 1$ and $\vec{b} \leq \vec{b}'$, (2.2) and (2.6) imply

$$l' - 1 \geq c\,(\text{wt}\,(\vec{a}),\, f;\, r) \geq c(f;\, r).$$

Since $l' \leq c(f;\,r)$, this is a contradiction. □

Example 2.5: Consider Tables I–IV. When $r = 3$ (Table I), according to Theorem 2.4, the code obtained from Construction 2.2

TABLE IV
$r = 6,\ c(f;\,6) = 41$

i	f(i)	c(i,f;6)	i	f(i)	c(i,f;6)
0	1 1 1 1 1 1	64	32	1 0 0 0 1 1	44
1	0 1 1 1 1 1	63	33	1 0 0 1 0 1	43
2	1 0 1 1 1 1	62	34	1 0 0 1 1 0	42
3	1 1 0 1 1 1	61	35	1 0 1 0 0 1	42
4	1 1 1 0 1 1	60	36	1 0 1 0 1 0	41
5	1 1 1 1 0 1	59	37	1 0 1 1 0 0	41
6	1 1 1 1 1 0	58	38	1 1 0 0 0 1	42
7	0 0 1 1 1 1	58	39	1 1 0 0 1 0	41
8	0 1 0 1 1 1	57	40	1 1 0 1 0 0	41
9	0 1 1 0 1 1	56	41	1 1 1 0 0 0	42
10	0 1 1 1 0 1	55	42	0 0 0 0 1 1	44
11	0 1 1 1 1 0	54	43	0 0 0 1 0 1	43
12	1 0 0 1 1 1	54	44	0 0 0 1 1 0	42
13	1 0 1 0 1 1	53	45	0 0 1 0 0 1	42
14	1 0 1 1 0 1	52	46	0 0 1 0 1 0	41
15	1 0 1 1 1 0	51	47	0 0 1 1 0 0	41
16	1 1 0 0 1 1	51	48	0 1 0 0 0 1	42
17	1 1 0 1 0 1	50	49	0 1 0 0 1 0	41
18	1 1 0 1 1 0	49	50	0 1 0 1 0 0	41
19	1 1 1 0 0 1	49	51	0 1 1 0 0 0	42
20	1 1 1 0 1 0	48	52	1 0 0 0 0 1	44
21	1 1 1 1 0 0	48	53	1 0 0 0 1 0	43
22	0 0 0 1 1 1	49	54	1 0 0 1 0 0	43
23	0 0 1 0 1 1	48	55	1 0 1 0 0 0	44
24	0 0 1 1 0 1	47	56	1 1 0 0 0 0	46
25	0 0 1 1 1 0	46	57	0 0 0 0 0 1	49
26	0 1 0 0 1 1	46	58	0 0 0 0 1 0	48
27	0 1 0 1 0 1	45	59	0 0 0 1 0 0	48
28	0 1 0 1 1 0	44	60	0 0 1 0 0 0	49
29	0 1 1 0 0 1	44	61	0 1 0 0 0 0	51
30	0 1 1 0 1 0	43	62	1 0 0 0 0 0	54
31	0 1 1 1 0 0	43	63	0 0 0 0 0 0	58

can detect bursts of length up to 4. This ties the performance of the code described in [5]. When $r = 4$ (Table II), however, the code $C(f;\,4)$ can detect any burst of length up to 9 while the code in [5] can detect any burst of length up to 8.

The difference is more dramatic in Tables III and IV. $C(f;\,5)$ and $C(f;\,6)$ have burst-detecting capability 19 and 41, respectively, while the codes in [5], for the same redundancy, have burst-detecting capability 16 and 32, respectively.

Of course, the functions f described in Tables I–IV have not been taken at random (there is a slight abuse of notation by calling f these four functions, but this should not lead to confusion). We describe them in the next section together with an estimate for $c(f;\,r)$.

III. A Particular Construction

In this section, we generalize the functions f given in Tables I–IV.

Given a binary r-tuple $\vec{v} = (v_{r-1}, v_{r-2}, \cdots, v_1, v_0)$ we call the ***support*** of $\vec{v}$ (denoted supp $(\vec{v})$) the set of coordinates where $\vec{v}$ is nonzero, i.e.,

$$\text{supp}\,(\vec{v}) = \{k : 0 \leq k \leq r-1,\ v_k = 1\}.$$

Clearly $|\mathrm{supp}\,(\vec{v})| = \mathrm{wt}\,(\vec{v})$.

Assume $\mathrm{supp}\,(\vec{v}) = \{j_1, j_2, \cdots, j_i\}$, where $0 \le j_1 < j_2 < \cdots < j_i \le r-1$. Since a binary r-tuple is uniquely determined by its support, we denote $\vec{v} = [j_1, j_2, \cdots, j_i]$ (if $\vec{v} = \vec{0}$, we consider $i = 0$).

Define the following 1-1 function

$$f: \mathbb{Z}_{2^r} \to \{0, 1\}^r$$

$$[j_1, j_2, \cdots, j_i] \xrightarrow{f^{-1}} \sum_{k=0}^{r-i-1} \binom{r}{k} + \sum_{k=1}^{i} \binom{j_k}{k}. \tag{3.1}$$

Several remarks have to be made regarding the definition of f. We are assuming the following conventions: $\binom{m}{n} = 0$ when $n > m$ and $\sum_{k=1}^{0} \binom{j_k}{k} = 0$.

It is not difficult to prove that f is 1-1, but we omit the proof. The reader can verify that the function f defined by (3.1) corresponds to the function defined in Tables I–IV when $r = 3$, 4, 5 and 6, respectively.

Another way of describing the function f is as follows: observe that in Tables I–IV we are ordering the 2^r-binary r-tuples in a certain way. First we write the only vector of weight r; then the r vectors of weight $r-1$ in increasing order when considered as binary numbers; then the $\binom{r}{2}$ vectors of weight $r-2$. In general, if we have written the $\binom{r}{k}$ vectors of weight k, then we write the $\binom{r}{k-1}$ vectors of weight $k-1$ in increasing order as binary numbers. The last vector is the all zero vector.

Given an r-tuple, say $f(i)$, we want to find the r-tuple $f(i + j \bmod 2^r)$, $1 \le j \le 2^r$ such that $f(i) \le f(i + j \bmod 2^r)$, $\mathrm{wt}\,(f(i + j \bmod 2^r)) - \mathrm{wt}\,(f(i)) \le 1$ and j is minimum with these properties [see (2.2)]. If $i = 0$, $f(0) = (1\,1 \cdots 1)$, $j = 2^r$ and $f(0 + j) = f(j)$. If $i = 2^r - 1$, $f(2^r - 1) = (0\,0 \cdots 0)$, and $f(2^r - 1 + j) = (0\,0 \cdots 0\,1)$.

In general, if $f(i) = [j_1, j_2, \cdots, j_k]$, $1 \le k \le r-1$, we want to find the first r-tuple $f(i + j)$ of weight $k + 1$ covering $f(i)$. Let l be the first index such that $j_l > l - 1$ (i.e., $j_\alpha = \alpha - 1$ for $1 \le \alpha < l$). Then

$$f(i) = [0, 1, \cdots l-2, j_l, j_{l+1}, \cdots j_k] \tag{3.2}$$

and

$$f(i + j \bmod 2^r) = [0, 1, \cdots l-2, l-1, j_l, j_{l+1}, \cdots j_k]. \tag{3.3}$$

Applying (3.1) to (3.2) and (3.3), we obtain

$$i = \sum_{\alpha=0}^{r-k-1} \binom{r}{\alpha} + \sum_{\alpha=l}^{k} \binom{j_\alpha}{\alpha} \tag{3.4}$$

$$i + j \bmod 2^r = \sum_{\alpha=0}^{r-k-2} \binom{r}{\alpha} + \sum_{\alpha=l}^{k} \binom{j_\alpha}{\alpha+1}. \tag{3.5}$$

Taking the difference between (3.5) and (3.4) and adding 2^r to the right-hand side, we have

$$j = 2^r - \binom{r}{k+1} + \sum_{\alpha=l}^{k} \binom{j_\alpha}{\alpha+1} - \binom{j_\alpha}{\alpha}. \tag{3.6}$$

Since this j is the minimum with this property, $j = c(i, f; r)$. Also, the sum in (3.6) can start at $\alpha = 1$. We summarize our results in the following lemma.

Lemma 3.1: Consider f: $\mathbb{Z}_{2^r} \to \{0, 1\}^r$ defined by (3.1) and $c(i, f; r)$ defined by (2.2). Then if $f(i) = [j_i, j_2, \cdots, j_k]$,

$$c(i, f; r) = 2^r - \binom{r}{k+1} + \sum_{\alpha=1}^{k} \binom{j_\alpha}{\alpha+1} - \binom{j_\alpha}{\alpha}. \tag{3.7}$$

Example 3.2: Consider Table IV. Here, $r = 6$. Since $f(63) = (0\,0\,0\,0\,0\,0)$, $k = 0$, and according to (3.7), $c(63, f; 6) = 2^6 - 6 = 58$, confirming the result in the table. Also $f(0) = (1\,1\,1\,1\,1\,1) = [0, 1, 2, 3, 4, 5]$. Here, $k = 6$ so (3.7) gives

$$c(0, f; 6) = 2^6 - \binom{6}{7} + \sum_{\alpha=1}^{6} \binom{\alpha-1}{\alpha+1} - \binom{\alpha-1}{\alpha} = 64.$$

For a less pathological example, consider $f(26) = (0\,1\,0\,0\,1\,1)$. The first r-tuple (as a binary number) of weight 4 covering $(0\,1\,0\,0\,1\,1)$ is $(0\,1\,0\,1\,1\,1) = f(8)$. Hence, $c(26, f; 6) = 64 + 8 - 26 = 46$. We also have $f(26) = [0, 1, 4]$, $k = 3$. Applying (3.7), we obtain

$$c(26, f; 6)$$
$$= 64 - \binom{6}{4} + \binom{0}{2} - \binom{0}{1} + \binom{1}{3} - \binom{1}{2} + \binom{4}{4} - \binom{4}{3}$$
$$= 64 - 15 + 1 - 4 = 46,$$

confirming formula (3.7).

TABLE V

r	2^{r-1}	c(f;r)
3	4	4
4	8	9
5	16	19
6	32	41
7	64	85
8	128	178
9	256	364
10	512	750
11	1024	1522
12	2048	3108
13	4096	6280
14	8192	12756
15	16384	25708
16	32768	52041
17	65536	104707
18	131072	211469
19	262144	424993
20	524288	856903

We want now to find

$$c(f; r) = \min_i c(i, f; r).$$

From an observation of Tables I–IV, we conclude that this minimum is obtained at several values. However, it is enough to identify one of those values.

In Table I, the minimum is achieved at $(0\,1\,0)$, in Table II at $(1\,0\,1\,0)$, in Table III at $(0\,1\,0\,1\,0)$, and in Table IV at $(1\,0\,1\,0\,1\,0)$. This tends to suggest that in general, the minimum is achieved at ($\lfloor x \rfloor$ denotes the integer part of x).

$$(\cdots\,1\,0\,1\,0) = \left[1, 3, 5, \cdots, 2\left\lfloor \frac{r}{2} \right\rfloor - 1\right].$$

For $f(i) = (\cdots\,1\,0\,1\,0)$, according to (3.7), we have

$$c(i, f; r) = 2^r - \binom{r}{\left\lfloor \frac{r}{2} \right\rfloor + 1} + \sum_{\alpha=1}^{\lfloor r/2 \rfloor} \binom{2\alpha-1}{\alpha+1} - \binom{2\alpha-1}{\alpha}.$$

Notice that for $r = 3$, 4, 5 and 6, this formula gives the values of $c(f; 3)$, $c(f; 4)$, $c(f; 5)$, and $c(f; 6)$, respectively. We want to prove the result in general.

Theorem 3.3: Consider f: $\mathbb{Z}_{2^r} \to \{0, 1\}^r$ defined by (3.1) and $c(f; r)$ defined by (2.3). Then

$$c(f;\, r) = 2^r - \binom{r}{\left\lfloor \frac{r}{2} \right\rfloor + 1} - \sum_{\alpha=1}^{\lfloor r/2 \rfloor} \binom{2\alpha - 1}{\alpha} - \binom{2\alpha - 1}{\alpha + 1}. \tag{3.8}$$

The proof of (3.8) is given in [3].

The next lemma, also proved in [3], gives an easier expression for (3.8).

Lemma 3.4: Consider f: $\mathbb{Z}_{2^r} \rightarrow \{0, 1\}^r$ defined by (3.1) and $c(f;\, r)$ defined by (2.3), then

$$c(f;\, r) = 2^r - \sum_{\alpha=0}^{r-1} \binom{\alpha}{\left\lfloor \frac{\alpha}{2} \right\rfloor}. \tag{3.9}$$

In Table V, we compare $c(f;\, r)$ to 2^{r-1}, the burst detecting capability of the codes described in [5]. We have made r range from 3 to 20. Observe that the difference widens as r increases. In [5], it was shown that an upper bound of the burst detecting capability of a systematic code is $2^r - 1$. In Table VI, we exhibit several quotients $c(f;\, r)/2^r$. Observe that this quotient approaches 1 as r increases. The table suggests that $c(f;\, r)$ is asymptotically equal to 2^r. We state this result in the following theorem.

TABLE VI

r	$\frac{c(f,r)}{2^r}$
5	.594
6	.641
10	.732
15	.784
20	.817
30	.852
50	.886
70	.904
80	.910
100	.920
120	.927
150	.935
170	.939
200	.943
210	.945

Theorem 3.5: Let $c(f;\, r)$ be given by (3.8), then

$$\lim_{r \rightarrow \infty} \frac{c(f;\, r)}{2^r} = 1.$$

Again, the proof of Theorem 3.5 can be found in [3]. We have increased the lower bound on the maximum burst detecting capability $b(r)$ of a systematic code. Finding the exact value of $b(r)$ is still an open problem.

IV. Encoding and Decoding

The encoding proceeds as follows: given the k information symbols $\vec{a} = (a_1, a_2 \cdots a_k)$, determine their weight modulo 2^r using a counter of 1's or by any other means (such that $k \geq (c(f;\, r) - 1)r$). Write this weight in binary, it is described by an r-tuple $\vec{u} = (u_{r-1}, u_{r-2}, \cdots, u_0)$. Then enter $\vec{u}$ as input in a PROM. The PROM is programmed in such a way that its output is the r-tuple $\vec{b} = (b_{r-1}, b_{r-2}, \cdots, b_0) = f(\text{ wt } (\vec{a}) \bmod 2^r)$. Then we append the vector $\vec{b}$ to $\vec{a}$ in the way described by (2.5).

An alternative approach for the encoding is to obtain the Boolean equations for each entry of the output based in the input vector $\vec{u}$. To this end, we may use the tables of the function f. For instance, if r = 3 and the weight modulo 8 input vector is given by the 3-tuple (A, B, C), from Table I, we verify that the output is (b_2, b_1, b_0), where

$$b_2 = \bar{A}B + \bar{A}\bar{C} + B\bar{C}$$

$$b_1 = \bar{A}\bar{B} + \bar{A}C + \bar{B}C$$

$$b_0 = \bar{A}\bar{B} + \bar{A}\bar{C} + \bar{B}\bar{C}.$$

Similarly, if r = 4 and the weight modulo 16 of $\vec{a}$ is represented by the r-tuple (A, B, C, D), from Table IV, the output is given by (b_3, b_2, b_1, b_0), where

$$b_3 = A\bar{B}\bar{C} + \bar{A}\bar{B}C + \bar{A}\bar{C}\bar{D} + AC\bar{D}$$

$$b_2 = A\bar{B}C\bar{D} + ABC\bar{D} + \bar{A}\bar{B}\bar{C} + \bar{A}B\bar{D} + \bar{A}CD$$

$$b_1 = \bar{A}B + \bar{A}\bar{C} + \bar{A}\bar{D} + B\bar{C}\bar{D}$$

$$b_0 = \bar{B}\bar{C}\bar{D} + \bar{A}C\bar{D} + \bar{A}\bar{C}D + \bar{B}CD.$$

The decoder uses the same circuits as the encoder. A comparator is added at the end. Say that $\vec{a}\,\vec{b}$ was transmitted and $\vec{a}'\ \vec{b}'$ is received. The comparator compares $f(\text{ wt } (\vec{a}'))$ to $\vec{b}'$. If $f(\text{ wt } (\vec{a}')) = \vec{b}'$, the decoder decides that no errors have occurred. If $f(\text{ wt } (\vec{a}')) \neq \vec{b}'$, the decoder declares that a burst has occurred.

V. Conclusions

We have presented a family of systematic codes $C(f;\, r)$, where $r \geq 3$ is the number of redundant bits and f: $\mathbb{Z}_{2^r} \rightarrow \{0, 1\}^r$ is 1-1. If the information bits are given by a vector $\vec{a} = (a_1, a_2, \cdots, a_k)$, the redundant bits $\vec{b} = (b_{r-1}, b_{r-2}, \cdots, b_0)$ are obtained as $\vec{b} = f(\text{wt } (\vec{a}) \bmod 2^r)$. These redundant bits are then distributed in a particular way. We gave a specific family of functions f. The burst detecting capability of a code $C(f;\, r)$ is $c(f;\, r)$, where an explicit formula for $c(f;\, r)$ was given. If we call $b(r)$ the maximum burst detecting capability of a systematic code with r redundant bits, it was known that $2^{r-1} \leq b(r) \leq 2^r - 1$. We showed that $2^{r-1} < c(f;\, r) \leq b(r) \leq 2^r - 1$ when $r \geq 4$ and that $c(f;\, r)$ and 2^r (and, hence, $b(r)$ and 2^r) are asymptotically equal. Finally, simple encoding and decoding procedures were indicated. Note that the codes normally used for burst error detection, like CRC, can only detect bursts of length up to r, r being the number of redundant bits. So, knowing that the errors are of unidirectional type allows the design of codes a lot more powerful for burst error detection.

Acknowledgment

The author wants to thank T. Howell and P. Siegel for useful discussions. Lemma 3.4 was pointed out by T. Howell.

References

[1] D. A. Anderson and G. Metze, "Design of totally self-checking circuits for *m*-out-of-*n* codes," *IEEE Trans. Comput.*, vol. C-22, pp. 263–269, Mar. 1973.

[2] J. M. Berger, "A note on error detecting codes for asymmetric channels," *Inform. Contr.*, vol. 4, pp. 68–73, Mar. 1961.

[3] M. Blaum, "Systematic unidirectional burst detecting codes," IBM RJ 5662 (57161), May 1987.

[4] M. Blaum and H. van Tilborg, "On t-error correcting/all unidirectional error-detecting codes," IBM RJ 5566 (56685), Mar. 1987.

[5] B. Bose, "Burst unidirectional error-detecting codes," *IEEE Trans. Comput.*, vol. C-35, pp. 350–353, Apr. 1986.

[6] ——,, "On systematic SEC/MUED code," in *Proc. FTCS*, vol. 11, June 1981, pp. 265–267.

[7] B. Bose and D. J. Lin, "Systematic unidirectional error-detecting codes," *IEEE Trans. Comput.*, vol. C-34, pp. 1026–1032, Nov. 1985.

[8] B. Bose and D. K. Pradhan, "Optimal unidirectional error-detecting/correcting codes," *IEEE Trans. Comput.*, vol. C-31, pp. 564–568, June 1982.

[9] B. Bose and T. R. N. Rao, "Theory of unidirectional error-correcting/detecting codes," *IEEE Trans. Comput.*, vol. C-31, pp. 521–530, June 1982.

[10] R. W. Cook *et al.*, "Design of self-checking microprogram control," *IEEE Trans. Comput.*, vol. C-22, pp. 255–262, Mar. 1973.

[11] N. Nikolos, N. Gaitanis, and G. Philokyprou," t-error correcting all unidirectional error detecting codes starting from cyclic AN codes," in *Proc. 1984 Int. Conf. Fault-Tolerant Comput.*, Kissimmee, FL, pp. 318–323.

[12] ——,, "Systematic t-error correcting/all unidirectional error detecting codes," *IEEE Trans. Comput.*, vol. C-35, pp. 394–402, May 1986.

[13] D. K. Pradhan, "A new class of error-correcting/detecting codes for fault-tolerant computer application," *IEEE Trans. Comput.*, vol. C-29, pp. 471-481, June 1980.

[14] D. K. Pradhan and J. J. Stiffler, "Error-correcting codes and self-checking circuits in fault-tolerant computers," *IEEE Computer*, vol. 13, pp. 27–37, Mar. 1980.

[15] J. E. Smith, "On separable unordered codes," *IEEE Trans. Comput.*, vol. C-33, pp. 741–743, Aug. 1984.

[16] D. L. Tao, C. R. P. Hartmann, and P. K. Lala, "An efficient class of unidirectional error-detecting/correcting codes," *IEEE Trans. Comput.*, to be published.

COMPUTING TECHNIQUES IN AUTOMATIC CONTROL

CODE CORRECTING NONSYMMETRICAL BURSTS OF ERRORS DURING DATA EXCHANGE BETWEEN COMPUTERS

A. A. Davydov, A. G. Dzodzuashvili, and G. M. Tenegol'ts

UDC 681.32.041.5

A code is proposed which corrects burst-type errors of computer words upon exchange of data between computers in the case when the errors are of a nonsymmetrical nature. This code admits an uncomplicated programming realization in computers.

In connection with the growth of complex information systems including computers joined by communication lines, in conjunction with increasingly high standards of reliability of the data transmitted and processed by these systems, it is a real problem now to develop special error-correcting codes admitting simple realization by computer programs [1].

Codes were constructed in [2] which correct repeated independent errors upon exchange of information between computers, and which have uncomplicated programming realizations.

In the present paper we consider a code which corrects errors of the burst type in computer words when data is transferred between computers in the case when the communications channel is nonsymmetric, i.e., when the probability of the transition $0 \to 1$ is essentially larger than the probability of a distortion of the type $1 \to 0$ (or the converse).

1. Code Correcting Bursts of Computer-Word Errors in the Case of a Completely Asymmetrical Channel

As is customary, we understand by a completely asymmetrical binary channel one in which errors of only one type can occur: $0 \to 1$ (or, alternatively, $1 \to 0$). In the sequel we shall consider, for definiteness, only channels with errors of the form $0 \to 1$.

A code correcting errors of the type of bursts of computer words of length b for a completely asymmetrical channel is specified in the following way. The computer data words $\alpha^{(1)}, \alpha^{(2)}, \ldots, \alpha^{(k)}$, each of which has the form $\alpha^{(l)} = \alpha_{n-1}^{(l)} \alpha_{n-2}^{(l)} \ldots \alpha_0^{(l)}$, where $\alpha_j^{(l)} = 0, 1$ $(l = \overline{1, k};\ j = \overline{0, n-1})$, give rise to two groups of control words. The first group of control words is defined by:

$$\alpha^{(k+b-j)} = \sum_{\substack{i=0 \\ k-j-ib\geqslant 1}}^{]\frac{k}{b}[-1} {}_{(\mathrm{mod}\ 2)}\ \alpha^{(k-j-ib)} \quad (j = \overline{0, b-1}),$$

where $\Sigma_{(\mathrm{mod}\ 2)}$ is the sign of mod 2 addition. To find the control words of the second group, we define a number B by the formula

$$B = \mathrm{res} \sum_{i=1}^{]\frac{k}{b}[} i \sum_{j=0}^{b-1} a^{(k-j-(i-1)b)} \pmod{P},$$

Moscow. Translated from Avtomatika i Telemekhanika, Vol. 33, No. 7, pp. 178-184, July, 1972. Original article submitted June 17, 1971.

TABLE 1

Program characteristics		Program purpose		
		Coding	Decoding	
			no errors	error burst of length $\leq b$
Total time of program execution, in seconds, t(k, b)		$k\left(160+\frac{196}{b}\right)\cdot 10^{-6}$	$(48k+144b)\cdot 10^{-6}$	$\left[k\left(184+\frac{148}{b}\right)+144b\pm 2000\right]\cdot 10^{-6}$
Number of computer operations	On one binary symbol $\frac{t(k,\, b)}{24\cdot 10^{-6}k}$	$6,7+\frac{8,2}{b}$	$2+6\frac{b}{k}$	$7,7+\frac{6,2}{b}+6\frac{b}{k}$
	On one information word $\frac{t(k,\, b)}{45\cdot 24\cdot 10^{-6}k}$	$0,15+\frac{0,18}{b}$	$0,044+0,133\frac{b}{k}$	$0,17+\frac{0,14}{b}+0,133\frac{b}{k}$
Total volume (in cells)		30	70	

where res A (mod P) denotes the least non-negative residue of A modulo P, $a^{(l)}$ is a number derived from the computer word

$$\alpha^{(l)}=\alpha_{n-1}^{(l)}\alpha_{n-2}^{(l)}\ldots\alpha_{0}^{(l)}\qquad(\alpha_i^{(l)}=0,1;\quad i=\overline{0,n-1})$$

by the rule

$$a^{(l)}=\sum_{i=0}^{n-1}2^i\alpha_i^{(l)},$$

and n is the length of a computer word, with l varying from l to k.

The modulus P is defined as the least power of two satisfying the inequality:

$$P\geqslant 2^m\geqslant 2(q-1)k+1, \tag{1}$$

where $q = 2^n$.

The second group of control words $\alpha^{(b+k+1)}, \alpha^{(b+k+2)}, \ldots, \alpha^{(N)}$ are the binary forms of the number $B = \beta_{m-1}\ldots\beta_0$ ($\beta_i = 0,1$; $i=\overline{0,\ m-1}$), with $\alpha_{n-1}^{(b+k+1)} = \beta_{m-1}$, $\alpha_{n-2}^{(b+k+1)} = \beta_{m-2}, \ldots$, while, in the least significant bit of word $\alpha^{(N)}$, there appears the logical negation of symbol β_{m-1}, i.e., $\alpha_0^{(N)} = \bar{\beta}_{m-1}$.

In decoding one first checks the equation

$$\alpha_{n-1}^{(b+k+1)'}=\alpha_0^{(N)'} \tag{2}$$

(here and later the prime on a symbol means that the element in question belongs to the received message). Violation of (2) indicates the presence of an error in one of the symbols $\alpha_{n-1}^{(b+k+1)'}$ or $\alpha_0^{(N)'}$. In this case there are no errors in the information words. If (2) is met we then compute the expressions

$$L_j=\sum_{i=0}^{n-1}2^i l_i^{(j)}\qquad(j=\overline{0,\,b-1}),$$

where

$$l^{(j)}=\sum_{\substack{i=0\\ k+b-j-ib\geqslant 1}}^{]\frac{k}{b}[}{}_{(\mathrm{mod}\ 2)}\ \alpha^{(k+b-j-ib)'}\qquad(j=\overline{0,\,b-1}),$$

and

$$L_b = \overline{\text{res}}\left[\sum_{i=1}^{]\frac{k}{b}[} i \sum_{j=0}^{b-1} a^{(k-j-(i-1)b)'} - B'\right] \quad (\text{mod } P),$$

where res A (mod P) denotes the least residue in absolute value of expression A modulo P, and B' is the number whose binary representation is incorporated in the words $\alpha^{(b+k+1)'}$, $\alpha^{(b+k+2)'}$, ..., $\alpha^{(N)'}$.

If $L_0 = L_1 = \ldots L_{b-1} = 0$, then there is no error in the information part. If at least one component $L_j \neq 0$ $(j = \overline{0, b-1})$, then there are errors in the information words if and only if $L_b > 0$. We now prove this.

Indeed, the following three situations are possible: 1) there are errors only in the first group of control words; 2) some of the words of the second group are distorted; 3) there are errors in the information words. In case 1 it is obvious that $L_b = 0$. In case 2 errors are possible in the words of the first control group but there are no information words with errors. Therefore $L_b \equiv -h_b (\text{mod } P)$, where $h_B = B' - B > 0$. Since the leading bit β'_{m-1} of number B' is not distorted, then $|-h_B| < P/2$ and $L_B = -h_B < 0$.

Finally, in case 3 number B' is correct, and errors are possible in the information words and in the first group of control words. Let a burst of errors distort the words $\alpha^{(k+b-ib-(r+1))'}$, $\alpha^{(k+b-ib-(r+2))'}$, ..., $\alpha^{(k+b-ib-(b-1))'}$, $(i = 0,]\frac{k}{b}[, r = \overline{0, b-1})$. $\alpha^{(k+b-(i+1)b)'}$, $\alpha^{(k+b-(i+1)b-1)'}$, ..., $\alpha^{(k+b-(i+1)b-r)'}$.

Then,

$$L_B \equiv (i+1)\ (L_0 + L_1 + \ldots + L_r) + i(L_{r+1} + L_{r+2} + \ldots + L_{b-1}),$$
$$(\text{mod } P) \equiv i(L_0 + L_1 + \ldots + L_{b-1}) + (L_0 + L_1 + \ldots + L_r)\ (\text{mod } P).$$

And since the errors are of the type $0 \to 1$ then

$$0 < i(L_0 + L_1 + \ldots + L_{b-1}) + (L_0 + L_1 + \ldots + L_r) < P/2$$

in view of the choice of P (cf., (1)).

Consequently, in case 3

$$L_b = i(L_0 + L_1 + \ldots + L_{b-1}) + (L_0 + \ldots + L_r) > 0, \qquad (3)$$

which also proves the aforementioned conditions for observing errors in the information words. From (3), since $\sum_{j=0}^{b-1} L_j > \sum_{j=0}^{r} L_j$, we simultaneously define $i = \left[L_b \Big/ \sum_{j=0}^{b-1} L_j\right]$ (function [x] is the integer part of x).

The value of r is determined from the condition $\sum_{j=0}^{r} L_j = L_b - i\sum_{j=0}^{b-1} L_j$ by successively comparing the sums of the form $\sum_{j=0}^{r} L_j$ (for r = 1, 2, ..., b−1) with the magnitude of the difference $L_b - i\sum_{j=0}^{b-1} L_j$. If $L_b - i\sum_{j=0}^{b-1} L_j = 0$, then r = 0, and all the errors are lumped in the group of computer words multiplied, for the computation of B, by i = 1. If i = 0, then the errors are located in the first group of control words. Correction of the distorted words is performed by the formula $\alpha^{(k-j-tb)} = \alpha^{(k-j-tb)'} \oplus l^{(j)}$, where $\oplus$ denotes bitwise addition mod 2, t = i for $j = \overline{0, r}$; t = i − 1 for $j = \overline{r+1, b-1}$. The block diagram of the decoding algorithm is shown on Fig. 1.

We now estimate the redundancy of the code in question.

For the notation of the first group of control words nb bits are required. For writing number B no more than $n + 1 +]\log_2 k[$ bits are necessary. Moreover, one bit is necessary for writing β_{m-1}. The total redundancy is $(b + 1)n + 2 +]\log_2 k[$ bits which, when $k < 2^{n-2}$ (this occurs in practice), makes up b + 2 computer words, and this is significantly less than for codes correcting error bursts in symmetrical channels.

We note that our suggested code is convenient for programmed realization on a computer since, in particular, decoding requires only one division.

Programs were written realizing the procedures of coding and decoding our proposed code for the M-220 computer.

The characteristics of the programs are given in Table 1.

The redundancy of our proposed code can be reduced somewhat if, in the determination of B, we understand by the expression $a^{(l)}$ the quantity of ones in word $\alpha^{(l)}$. Then, P is chosen in the form $P \geq 2^m \geq 2k]\log_2 n[+ 1$.

For decoding we understand by L_j the quantity of ones in word $l^{(j)}$ $(j = \overline{0, b-1})$. The other formulas for decoding remain as before. The redundancy is now $bn + 2 +]\log_2 n[+]\log_2 k[$ bits which, for $k < 2^{n-2}/n$, constitutes $b + 1$ computer words.

We note that our method can be used for constructing codes for a binary asymmetrical channel. Their redundancy would be $r = b + 2 +]\log_2 k[$. It compares favorably with the analogous code considered in [3]. The redundancy of this latter was $r \geq 2b - 1 +]\log_2 k/(2b-1) + 1[$, i.e., when $b \geq 7$, this latter code has the greater redundancy.

2. Code Correcting Errors in Two Neighboring Computer Words for a Completely Asymmetrical Channel

In case $b = 2$, i.e., two neighboring computer words are distorted, we can propose a code with somewhat lower redundancy. It is specified in the following way. Starting from the information-bearing computer words $\alpha^{(1)}$, $\alpha^{(2)}, \ldots, \alpha^{(k)}$, we define numbers B_1 and B_2 in the form $B_1 = \operatorname{res} \sum_{i=1}^{k} a_i \pmod{P_1}$, where $P_1 = 2^{m_1} \geq 2(q-1) + 1$, and $B_2 = \operatorname{res} \sum_{i=1}^{k} i a_i \pmod{P_2}$, where $P_2 = 2^{n_2} \geq 2(q-1)(2k-1) + 1$.

In control word $\alpha^{(k+1)}$ we write the logical negation of the least significant bits of the binary representation of number $B_1 = \beta_n^{(1)}\beta_{n-1}^{(1)} \ldots \beta_0^{(1)}$, i.e., $\alpha^{(k+1)} = \bar{\beta}_{n-1}^{(1)} \ldots \bar{\beta}_0^{(1)}$. In the second group of control words $\alpha^{(k+2)}, \ldots, \alpha^{(N)}$ we embed the binary representation of number $B_2 = \beta_{n_2-1}^{(2)}\beta_{n_2-2}^{(2)} \ldots \beta_0^{(2)}$, with $\alpha_{n-1}^{(k+2)} = \beta_{n_2-1}^{(2)}$, $\alpha_{n-2}^{(k+2)} = \beta_{n_2-2}^{(2)}, \ldots$ while the least significant bits of word $\alpha^{(N)}$ have the form $\alpha_1^{(N)} = \beta_n^{(1)}$, $\alpha_0^{(N)} = \bar{\beta}_{n_2-1}^{(2)}$.

In decoding we check the validity of the equation $\alpha_0^{(N)} = \bar{\alpha}_{n-1}^{(k+2)}$. If it is not true, there are errors in the control part. If the equality does hold, we then turn to the determination of the expressions:

$$L_1 = \operatorname{res} \sum_{i=1}^{k} a_i' - B_1' \pmod{P_1}, \quad L_2 = \overline{\operatorname{res}} \sum_{i=1}^{k} i a_i' - B_2' \pmod{P_2},$$

where $B_1' = \bar{\alpha}_1^{(N)'}\bar{\alpha}_{n-1}^{(k+1)'} \ldots \bar{\alpha}_1^{(k+1)'}\bar{\alpha}_0^{(k+1)'}$, and B_2' is defined starting from control words $\alpha^{(k+2)'}, \ldots, \alpha^{(N)'}$.

It is easy to see that errors in the information words occur if and only if $L_2 > 0$. In this case, all the bits of number B_2' and the most significant bit $\beta_n^{(1)}$ of number B_1' are correct. In the remaining bits of B_1' (written in word $\alpha^{(k+1)'}$) it is possible to have $h_{B_1} = B_1' - B_1$ errors, where $h_{B_1} < 0$ thanks to the twofold inversion entering into the definition of B_1'.

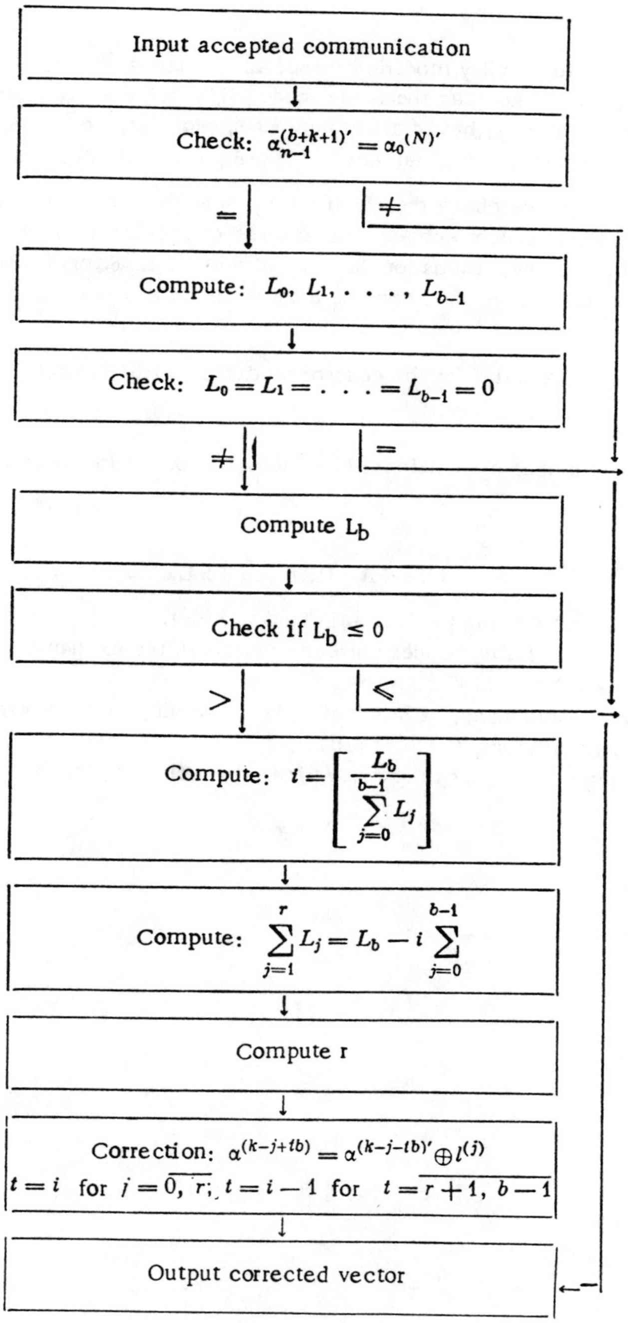

Fig. 1

Let the words $\alpha^{(i+1)'}$, $\alpha^{(i)'}$ $(i = \overline{1, k+1})$ be distorted. Then,

$$L_1 = h_1 + h_2,\ L_2 = ih_1 + (i+1)h_2,$$

where $h_1 = a_i' - a_i$, $h_2 = a_{i+1}' - a_{i+1}$, if $i + 1 \leq k$, and $h_2 = -h_{B_1}$, if $i = k$. Since $h_{B_1} < 0$, it will always be the case that $h_1 > 0$, $h_2 < 0$.

From system (4) we determine $i = [L_2/L_1]$, $h_2 = L_2 - iL_1$, $h_1 = L_1 - h_2$.

In conclusion we mention that for many communications systems, a good model is a channel which is asymmetrical during a communications interchange. In such a channel, both types of error are possible: $0 \to 1$ and $1 \to$. However, during the course of the given interchange, the type of error does not change. The difference from the completely asymmetrical channel is that it is not known beforehand which form the distortions will take in the given communications channel.

The codes considered above are readily modified for use in this latest channel, specifically: modification of the code of the first section amounts to keeping the Berger code [4], detecting any asymmetrical errors, not only of the most significant bit β_{m-1} of number B, but of all of number B. For this, we introduce additional control words in which we embed the binary representation of number $B_1 = N_0(B)$, where $N_0(B)$ is the quantity of zeros in number B.

For decoding, instead of Eq. (2) we check the condition $B_1' = N_0(B')$ which, if not met, indicates the absence of errors in the information part while its correctness indicates the correctness of number B'. In the latter case, we determine the expressions $L_0, L_1, \ldots, L_b$, just as for the code of section 1. Errors in the information part occur if and only if $L_b \neq 0$. With this, if $L_b < 0$, we then have an error of the type $1 \to 0$ while, if $L_b > 0$, the error is of the type $0 \to 1$.

In decoding we use the same formulas for the code of section 1, with the condition that $L_j =$ (sign L_b) $\sum_{i=0}^{n-1} 2^i l_i^{(j)}$ $(j = \overline{0, b-1})$. The number of additional bits necessary for the modified code equals $]\log_2 m[-1$.

LITERATURE CITED

1. S. I. Samoilenko, Noise-Stable Coding [in Russian], Nauka (1966).
2. A. A. Davydov and G. M. Tenengol'ts, "Codes correcting errors in the exchange of data between computers," Tekhnicheskaya Kibernetika, No. 4 (1971).
3. S. Sh. Oganesyan and V. G. Yagdzhyan, "Classes of codes correcting bursts of errors in an asymmetrical channel," Problemy Peredachi Informatsii, 6, No. 4 (1970).
4. G. O. Berger, "On error-detecting codes in asymmetrical channels," in: Coding Theory [Russian translation], Mir (1964).

Chapter 7: Codes for Detecting and/or Correcting Unidirectional Byte Errors

Our concluding chapter deals with detecting and correcting unidirectional byte errors; such codes are useful in page-oriented computer memories. Dunning, Dial, and Varanasi present codes that detect a limited number of unidirectional byte errors, and that simultaneously detect all unidirectional errors. Unidirectional byte errors are unidirectional within a byte. For instance, two different bytes might have been affected by unidirectional errors of opposite direction; one of them may have $0 \rightarrow 1$ type errors, and the other may have $1 \rightarrow 0$ type errors. These authors have conducted other research on this topic.[75]

Rao, Feng, and Kolluru generalize the preceding construction for any number t of bytes that have suffered unidirectional errors. The authors also provide an improved construction for codes that eliminates the need for encoding two syndromes, thereby reducing total redundancy.

Bose and Al-Bassam present constructions of codes correcting single unidirectional byte errors and detecting double unidirectional byte errors. The authors give a lower bound on the redundancy, showing that their unidirectional byte correcting code is close to optimal. The Bose/Al-Bassam code has less redundancy than a symmetric byte-correcting code; as an example, it has less redundancy than Reed-Solomon code. Bose has contributed additional research on this topic.[76]

Our final paper by Saitoh and Imai presents constructions of codes for correcting multiple unidirectional byte errors. The authors also define a unidirectional byte distance and give construction methods for the simultaneous correction and detection of unidirectional byte errors. Interested readers will find additional material in our references.[77-82] Bose, Rao, and Montgomery provide valuable research on correcting unidirectional errors in multitrack memories — magnetic tape, for example.[83-85]

Unidirectional Byte Error Detecting Codes for Computer Memory Systems

LARRY A. DUNNING, GUR DIAL, AND MURALI R. VARANASI

Abstract—**Codes are developed for detecting unidirectional errors in *t* bytes simultaneously (*t*-UBED) while also providing all unidirectional error detection (AUED). These classes of codes differ from purely all unidirectional error detecting codes in that the errors in one byte may be of the form $1 \rightarrow 0$ while in another byte they may be of the form $0 \rightarrow 1$. The codes utilize two bytes for parity check information. As an example, a code providing 3-UBED+AUED protection for up to 12 information bytes of 8 bits each can be constructed.**

Index Terms—**Byte errors, error-detection coding, memory fault tolerance, unidirectional errors.**

I. Introduction

When data in a computer memory are stored in a byte-per-chip or byte-per-card fashion, errors are likely to be confined to one or to a few bytes [12], [15]. Codes have been designed for byte error correction and detection [19], [21], and also to detect and correct byte errors together with random errors [6], [14], [15], [17], [20], [27].

Unidirectional errors are known to be predominant in many computer memory and VLSI circuits [26]. When a unidirectional error occurs, several 1's may be replaced erroneously by 0's or several 0's may be replaced by 1's, but not both. Protection against unidirectional errors can be provided by all unidirectional error detecting (AUED) codes [1], [2], [11], [22] or *t*-unidirectional error detecting codes [9]. Codes have also been designed to protect against combinations of unidirectional and random errors [5], [10], [13], [23]–[25], [28]. Berger [3] has proposed codes which are AUED and burst error detecting.

Given that computer memory data are stored in a byte-per-chip or byte-per-card fashion, it is often probable that when errors occur in multiple bytes the errors will be unidirectional within each individual byte. However, the errors in one byte may be of the form $1 \rightarrow 0$ while in another byte they may be of the form $0 \rightarrow 1$. When a memory word is handled as a whole, unidirectional errors of a single form may occur across the entire word. Fig. 1 contrasts a unidirectional error with a unidirectional byte error affecting 2 bytes.

In this paper, codes are developed which detect some small number t of unidirectional byte errors in computer memory words composed of m information bytes each containing b bits, and the codes will simultaneously detect all unidirectional errors across the entire memory word. The codes will always use two additional b-bit bytes to hold parity check information and will be said to be t-unidirectional byte error detecting and all unidirectional error detecting (t-UBED+AUED) codes. Fig. 2 shows the general form of a codeword including both information and check bytes.

Several investigators have developed codes for somewhat similar situations. Burst unidirectional error detecting codes [4], [7] are available to detect a single burst of unidirectional errors within a codeword. Codes for byte-per-card organizations which are 1-UBED were also developed in [7]. An excellent construction for 1-UBED codes using less than two full check bytes is given in [8]. Codes developed in [16] are for the case in which all bytes are 9 bits in length and each byte contains a parity check bit.

Manuscript received July 6, 1989; revised November 20, 1989. This work supported in part by the Center for Microelectronics Research of the University of South Florida.

L. Dunning is with the Department of Computer Science, Bowling Green State University, Bowling Green, OH 43403.

G. Dial is with the Universidade Federal de Santa Catarina, 88000 Florianopolis, Santa Catarina, Brazil.

M. R. Varanasi is with the Department of Computer Science and Engineering, University of South Florida, Tampa, FL 33620.

IEEE Log Number 8933882.

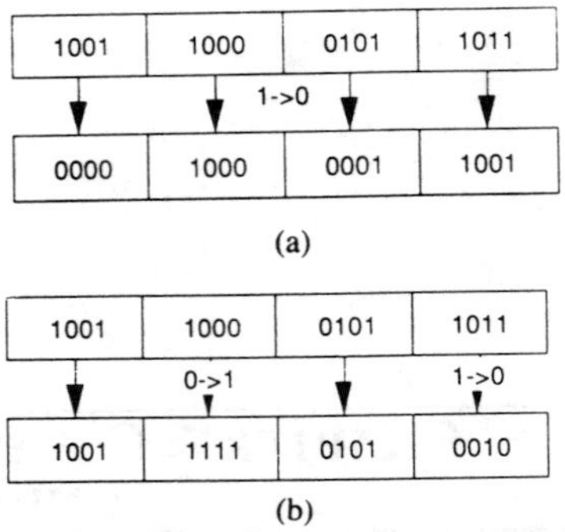

Fig. 1. (a) Unidirectional error example. (b) Two unidirectional byte error example.

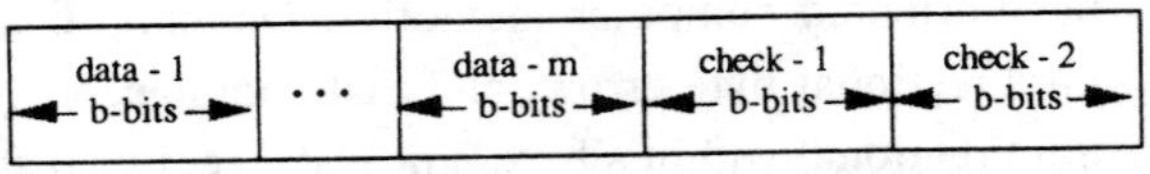

Fig. 2. Memory codeword organization.

TABLE I
Number of 8-Bit Information Bytes by Code Type

Protection Level	information bytes m	length in bytes
2-UBED + AUED	$m \le 47$	$m+2 \le 49$
3-UBED + AUED	$m \le 12$	$m+2 \le 14$

Table I gives the number of information bytes m of the codes constructed for the case $b = 8$ of greatest practical interest. A code can be shortened to give fewer information bytes than listed. For comparison, a higher radix symbol (byte) distance 3 Hamming code requires 2 check bytes to provide detection of double byte errors. However, the higher radix Hamming codes are not capable of AUED protection. When the codes are used for error detection, the efforts required for encoding and decoding, respectively, are equal and reasonably efficient implementation should therefore be possible. Codes which are 2-UBED may be viewed as being unidirectional byte error locating (UBEL). That is, they are capable of detecting and locating, but not correcting, a single unidirectional byte error. This capability could be used for diagnostic purposes in an off-line mode even when these codes are being used operationally as 2-UBED codes.

II. Construction of the Codes

In this section, t-UBED codes are constructed as follows. The weights of the data bytes are encoded into a syndrome using the parity check matrix of a higher radix distance $d = t + 1$ BCH code over $GF(p)$ where p is an appropriate prime. Any change in t or less of the weights will result in a change in the BCH syndrome. The BCH syndrome is combined with a record of the total Hamming weight of all the information bytes to form the overall syndrome of a codeword. The overall syndrome itself is stored in the parity check bytes. The second parity check byte is always chosen to be of constant weight and is therefore immune to unidirectional errors. To guarantee AUED, the first parity check byte must be chosen so that its weight is a nonincreasing function of the total weight of the information bytes. To guarantee that the code is t-UBED, the first parity check byte is chosen in such a fashion that whenever

0-8186-4182-7/93 $3.00 © 1990 IEEE

TABLE II
SPANS OF SOME SELECTED ASCENDING SEQUENCES

b	$s^b_{1,b-1}$	$s^b_{2,b-2}$	$s^b_{3,b-3}$	$s^b_{4,b-4}$
3	1			
4	2	∞		
5	3	6		
6	4	11	∞	
7	5	17	26	
8	6	24	47	∞

two such first parity check bytes differ by a unidirectional error, the information portions of their corresponding codewords will have disparate weights. This causes the two corresponding codewords to differ in a least $t+1$ bytes and the error then falls outside the class of errors under consideration.

We now give a formal description of the codes. First, the sets of possible values taken on by the check bytes will be specified. Then, the parity check matrices of the higher radix BCH codes will be described. Finally, the mappings from information bytes to syndromes and from the collection of syndromes into the parity check bytes are given.

Denote by C^b_k either the sequence of b-bit bytes which have Hamming weight k given in lexicographic order or the set of such bytes, depending on the context. The number of such bytes is the number of combinations of b items taken k at a time denoted $C(b,k)$. The order of the sequence is identical with numerical order in base 2.

The values of the second check byte are chosen from the sequence $V = C^b_{\lfloor b/2 \rfloor}$ of bytes whose Hamming weight is $\lfloor b/2 \rfloor$. The number of such bytes may be abbreviated by $v = C(b, \lfloor b/2 \rfloor)$. The members of the sequence of bytes V may sometimes be referred to explicitly as $V = \boldsymbol{v}_0, \boldsymbol{v}_1, \cdots, \boldsymbol{v}_{v-1}$.

The values of the first check byte are chosen from what will be termed a descending sequence with span s. Let $h(\cdot)$ denote the Hamming weight function.

Definition: An ascending (respectively, descending) sequence with span s and length u is a sequence of b-bit bytes $\boldsymbol{u}_0, \boldsymbol{u}_1, \cdots, \boldsymbol{u}_{u-1}$ such that the following conditions hold for all $0 \le i \le j < u$:

a) $h(\boldsymbol{u}_i) \le h(\boldsymbol{u}_j)$ (respectively, $h(\boldsymbol{u}_i) \ge h(\boldsymbol{u}_j)$)

b) If $\boldsymbol{u}_i$ and $\boldsymbol{u}_j$ differ by a unidirectional error then $j - i - 1 \ge s$.

Condition a) says that the weights of the bytes in such a sequence are nondecreasing (respectively, nonincreasing) in weight. Condition b) guarantees that if two bytes in the sequence differ by a unidirectional error, then there will be at least s intervening bytes in the sequence. The notions of ascending and descending sequences are equivalent since an ascending sequence in reverse order is a descending sequence, and vice versa. The descending sequences to be used in the construction which follows are defined to be the reverse, denoted R, of certain ascending sequences. Let

$$U^b_{k_1,k_2} = \cdot C^b_{k_1} \| \cdots \| C^b_{k_2}$$

where $\|$ denotes concatenation of sequences, and k_1 and k_2 with $k_1 \le k_2$ give the least and greatest weights of bytes to be included in the sequence, respectively. The span of $U^b_{k_1,k_2}$ denoted $s^b_{k_1,k_2}$ is given in Table II for some small values of b, k_1, and k_2. Refer to the Appendix for the method used to obtain these spans.

Example 1: The descending sequence $U = R(U^4_{1,3})$ has length 14, span 2 and is given by

$$\begin{array}{ll} u_{13} = 0001 & u_6 = 1001 \\ u_{12} = 0010 & u_5 = 1010 \\ u_{11} = 0100 & u_4 = 1100 \\ u_{10} = 1000 & u_3 = 0111 \\ u_9 = 0011 & u_2 = 1011 \\ u_8 = 0101 & u_1 = 1101 \\ u_7 = 0110 & u_0 = 1110. \end{array}$$

The syndrome which is recorded in the check bytes described above is formed from the Hamming weights of the information bytes using a parity check matrix H of a BCH code over $GF(p)$, p a prime, having minimum distance $d = t+1$ where the desired resultant code is t-UBED+AUED. The prime p must satisfy $p > b$. The parity check matrix will also be required to have the property that all the entries in its first row are 1's. The number of columns in the parity check matrix H will be equal to the number of information bytes m, and the number of rows of H will be denoted by r. For $t=2$ and $d=3$ one possible parity check matrix is the $r=2$ by $m=p$ matrix

$$H = \begin{pmatrix} 1 & 1 & \cdots & 1 \\ 0 & 1 & \cdots & p-1 \end{pmatrix}. \tag{1}$$

For $t=3$ and $d=4$, an extended $r=3$ by $m=p+1$ BCH parity check matrix [29] is

$$E = \begin{pmatrix} 0 & 1 & 1 & 1 & \cdots & 1 \\ 0 & 0 & 1 & 2 & \cdots & (p-1) \\ 1 & 0 & 1 & 2^2 & \cdots & (p-1)^2 \end{pmatrix}.$$

Assuming $p \ge 3$, let a, $0 < a < p$, be a quadratic nonresidue mod p so that $x^2 \equiv a \bmod p$ has no solutions [18, Theorem 85]. The matrix

$$J = \begin{pmatrix} -a & 0 & 1 \\ 0 & 1 & 0 \\ 0 & 0 & 1 \end{pmatrix}$$

is nonsingular since it is upper triangular. It is easy to verify that the matrix $N = J \cdot E$ is a parity check matrix of a $d=4$ code whose first row contains only nonzero entries. An equivalent parity check matrix H with the first row composed entirely of ones can be obtained by multiplying each column vector in N by the multiplicative inverse of its first entry [16]. For $p = 11$ using $a = 2$ the construction just described results in

$$H = \begin{pmatrix} 1 & 1 & 1 & 1 & 1 & 1 & 1 & 1 & 1 & 1 & 1 & 1 \\ 0 & 0 & 10 & 1 & 2 & 5 & 5 & 6 & 6 & 9 & 10 & 1 \\ 1 & 0 & 10 & 2 & 6 & 9 & 3 & 3 & 9 & 6 & 2 & 10 \end{pmatrix}. \tag{2}$$

Formal specification of the overall syndrome and the mapping which records it in the parity check bytes will complete the description of our method of constructing t-UBED+AUED codes.

Construction 1: For a fixed byte width b, let U be a descending sequence of span s and length u and recall that $V = C^b_{\lfloor b/2 \rfloor}$ is a sequence of $v = C(b, \lfloor b/2 \rfloor)$ bytes. Let $p > b$ be a prime and let H be an $r \times m$ parity check matrix of a linear error detecting code over $GF(p)$ having minimum distance $d = t+1$. To encode a codeword the check bytes $\boldsymbol{c}_1$ and $\boldsymbol{c}_2$ are computed from the data bytes $\boldsymbol{d}_1, \cdots, \boldsymbol{d}_m$ according to the following formulas:

$$z \leftarrow \sum_{i=1}^{m} h(\boldsymbol{d}_i) \tag{3}$$

$$(s_1, s_2, \cdots, s_r)^t \leftarrow H \cdot (h(\boldsymbol{d}_1), \cdots, h(\boldsymbol{d}_m))^t \tag{4}$$

$$n \leftarrow z \cdot p^{r-1} + s_2 \cdot p^{r-2} + \cdots + s_{r-1} \cdot p + s_r \tag{5}$$

$$\boldsymbol{c}_1 \leftarrow \boldsymbol{u}_i \quad \text{where } i = \lfloor n/v \rfloor \tag{6}$$

$$\boldsymbol{c}_2 \leftarrow \boldsymbol{v}_j \quad \text{where } j = n \bmod v. \tag{7}$$

In the above computation, each distinct overall syndrome $(z, s_2, \cdots, s_r)$ is given a sequence number n. Under this sequencing, the syndromes are in order by the overall weight z of their corresponding sets of data bytes. From (6) and (7) it follows that the check byte values are being arranged in a corresponding lexicographic fashion and that

$$n = i \cdot v + j. \tag{8}$$

That is, if the possible pairs of check bytes are considered in the sequence

$$(\boldsymbol{u}_0, \boldsymbol{v}_0), \cdots, (\boldsymbol{u}_0, \boldsymbol{v}_{v-1}), (\boldsymbol{u}_1, \boldsymbol{v}_0), \cdots, (\boldsymbol{u}_1, \boldsymbol{v}_{v-1}), \cdots, (\boldsymbol{u}_{u-1}, \boldsymbol{v}_0), \cdots, (\boldsymbol{u}_{u-1}, \boldsymbol{v}_{v-1})$$

then the nth pair corresponds to the nth overall syndrome. The syndrome s_1 can be computed from z using the formula

$$s_1 = z \bmod p. \tag{9}$$

In order for Construction 1 to be valid and produce a code which is actually t-UBED+AUED, several inequalities must hold.

Theorem 1: Let $w = m \cdot b$ denote the maximum weight of the information bytes of a codeword in Construction 1. Then, Construction 1 yields a t-UBED+AUED code provided that the following inequalities both hold:

a) $(w + 1) \cdot p^{r-1} \leq u \cdot v$

b) $((t - 1) \cdot b + 1) \cdot p^{r-1} \leq (s + 1) \cdot v$.

Before proving Theorem 1, two examples are provided to show that Construction 1 does produce codes with parameters in ranges which could be of practical interest.

Example 2(a): Suppose $b = 8$ and a 2-UBED+AUED code is desired. A code with up to 47 information bytes can easily be constructed. Let $p = 47$ and choose H to be the $r = 2$ by $m = 47$ parity check matrix of a $d = 3$ code as given in (1). Thus, the maximum weight of the information bytes is $w = 8 \cdot 47 = 376$. Let $U = R(U^8_{1,7})$ and it follows that $u = 254$ and $s = s^8_{1,7} = 6$ from Table II. Of course, $v = C(8, 4) = 70$, and the inequalities a) and b) of Theorem 1 are then easily verified.

Example 2(b): Suppose $b = 8$ and a 3-UBED+AUED code is desired. A code with up to 12 information bytes can easily be constructed. Let $p = 11$ and choose H to be the $r = 3$ by $m = 12$ parity check matrix of a $d = 4$ code as given in (2). Thus, the maximum weight of the information bytes is $w = 8 \cdot 12 = 96$. Let $U = R(U^8_{3,5})$ and it follows that $u = C(8, 3) + C(8, 4) + C(8, 5) = 182$ and $s = s^8_{3,5} = 47$ from Table II. Of course, $v = C(8, 4) = 70$, and the inequalities a) and b) of Theorem 1 are then easily verified.

Proof of Theorem 1: The mapping of overall syndromes into the parity check bytes is one-to-one as a result of condition a) of Theorem 1. It may be assumed that the second check byte is always correct since any unidirectional error in this constant weight byte will be detected.

To see that the code is AUED, suppose to the contrary that $\boldsymbol{x} = (\boldsymbol{d}_1, \cdots, \boldsymbol{d}_m, \boldsymbol{c}_1, \boldsymbol{c}_2)$ and $\boldsymbol{x}' = (\boldsymbol{d}'_1, \cdots, \boldsymbol{d}'_m, \boldsymbol{c}'_1, \boldsymbol{c}'_2)$ are two codewords which differ by only unidirectional errors which are assumed w. l.o.g to be entirely of the form $0 \to 1$. Thus, from (3) $z < z'$ and it follows that $n < n'$ where n and n' are computed from $\boldsymbol{x}$ and $\boldsymbol{x}'$, respectively using (5). Since $\boldsymbol{c}_2 = \boldsymbol{c}'_2$ and $n < n'$ it follows that $\boldsymbol{c}_1 \neq \boldsymbol{c}'_1$ and from the decreasing sequence property that $h(\boldsymbol{c}_1) \geq h(\boldsymbol{c}'_1)$. It is not possible that $h(\boldsymbol{c}_1) > h(\boldsymbol{c}'_1)$ since all errors were of the type $0 \to 1$. Thus, $\boldsymbol{c}_1 \neq \boldsymbol{c}'_1$ and $h(\boldsymbol{c}_1) = h(\boldsymbol{c}'_1)$. This would imply the presence of a nonunidirectional error in the first check byte which has been ruled out by assumption and thus proves the code to be AUED.

To see that the code is t-UBED, suppose that the two codewords $\boldsymbol{x} = (\boldsymbol{d}_1, \cdots, \boldsymbol{d}_m, \boldsymbol{c}_1, \boldsymbol{c}_2)$ and $\boldsymbol{x}' = (\boldsymbol{d}'_1, \cdots, \boldsymbol{d}'_m, \boldsymbol{c}'_1, \boldsymbol{c}'_2)$ differ by unidirectional errors in at most t bytes. If the errors are confined to the information bytes, then the vectors $(h(\boldsymbol{d}_1), \cdots, h(\boldsymbol{d}_m))$ and $(h(\boldsymbol{d}'_1), \cdots, h(\boldsymbol{d}'_m))$ differ in at most t positions. The error detecting properties of H then imply that the BCH syndromes $(s_1, s_2, \cdots, s_r)$ and $(s'_1, s'_2, \cdots, s'_r)$ computed by (4) from $\boldsymbol{x}$ and $\boldsymbol{x}'$, respectively, differ. Since z and z' as computed by (3) from $\boldsymbol{x}$ and $\boldsymbol{x}'$, respectively,

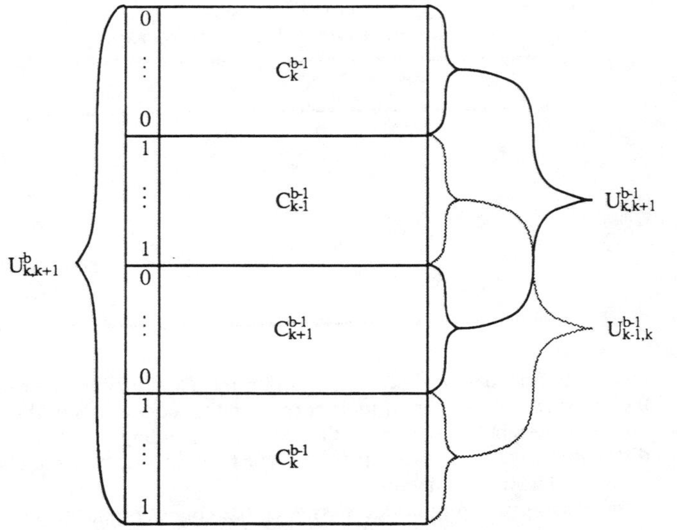

Fig. 3. Recursive construction of ascending sequence.

can be used to recover s_1 and s'_1, by applying (9), it follows that the respective overall syndromes $(z, s_2, \cdots, s_r)$ and $(z', s'_2, \cdots, s'_r)$ of $\boldsymbol{x}$ and $\boldsymbol{x}'$ differ. Thus, n and n' and in turn $\boldsymbol{c}_1$ and $\boldsymbol{c}'_1$ must differ. This implies the existence of an error in a parity check byte contrary to assumption. It remains to prove that $\boldsymbol{x}$ and $\boldsymbol{x}'$ cannot differ by unidirectional errors in t bytes given that $\boldsymbol{c}_1$ and $\boldsymbol{c}'_1$ differ by a unidirectional byte error. If $\boldsymbol{c}_1$ and $\boldsymbol{c}'_1$ differ by a unidirectional error, then their corresponding indexes i and i' as computed in (6) differ by at least $s+1$. That is, since $\boldsymbol{c}_1$ and $\boldsymbol{c}'_1$ are taken from a descending sequence of span s, $|i - i'| \geq s + 1$ must hold. Because $\boldsymbol{c}_2 = \boldsymbol{c}'_2$ from (7) it follows that $j = j'$, and using (8) together with condition b) of Theorem 1, yields that $|n - n'| \geq (s+1) \cdot v \geq ((t-1) \cdot b + 1) \cdot p^{r-1}$. From (5) it follows that $n = z \cdot p^{r-1} + y$ and $n' = z' \cdot p^{r-1} + y'$ for some y, y' satisfying $0 \leq y,\ y' < p^{r-1}$. Now, $p^{r-1} - 1 \geq |y - y'|$ gives $|z - z'| \cdot p^{r-1} + p^{r-1} - 1 \geq |n - n'| \geq ((t-1)b + 1) \cdot p^{r-1}$. Dividing by p^{r-1} yields $|z - z'| + (p^{r-1} - 1)/p^{r-1} \geq (t-1)b + 1$. Since $|z - z'|$ and $(t-1)b + 1$ are integral and $(p^{r-1} - 1)/p^{r-1} < 1$ it is immediate that $|z - z'| \geq (t-1)b + 1$. Thus, unidirectional errors in at least t information bytes must have occurred to account for this change in total Hamming weight. However, since the first check byte was also in error, there must have been errors in at least $t + 1$ bytes. This is contrary to assumption and the code must therefore be t-UBED. □

Appendix

Since the descending sequence used in Construction 1 would probably be stored in ROM in an actual implementation, it would not appear to matter whether a descending sequence has a nice underlying structure. The spans of the ascending sequences presented in Table II have been verified by direct computation and this suffices for verification of the codes presented here. However, it seems appropriate to give a brief sketch of the development which motivated these particular sequences.

Define $s^b_k = s^b_{k,k+1}$. Since C^b_k is always immune to unidirectional errors it follows that $s^b_{k_1,k_2} = \min\{s^b_k | k_1 \leq k \leq k_2\}$. Thus, it suffices to determine s^b_k which will be termed an elementary span. The related sequence $U^b_{k,k+1}$ is depicted in Fig. 3. Inspecting Fig. 3, the following recursion for s^b_k can be obtained:

$$s^b_0 = 0; s^b_{b-1} = 0;$$

$$s^b_k = \min\left\{ s^{b-1}_k + \binom{b-1}{k-1}, s^{b-1}_{k-1} + \binom{b-1}{k+1}, \binom{b-1}{k-1} + \binom{b-1}{k+1} \right\}. \tag{10}$$

TABLE III
VALUES OF SOME ELEMENTARY SPANS

b	s_0^b	s_1^b	s_2^b	s_3^b	s_4^b	s_5^b	s_6^b	s_7^b
1	0							
2	0	0						
3	0	1	0					
4	0	2	2	0				
5	0	3	6	3	0			
6	0	4	11	11	4	0		
7	0	5	17	26	17	5	0	
8	0	6	24	47	47	24	6	0

Inspection of Fig. 3 again shows that $C(b, k) \geq s_k^b$ and that $C(b, k+1) \geq s_k^b$. Substituting $b-1$ for b in these inequalities yields $C(b-1, k-1) \geq s_{k-1}^{b-1}$ and $C(b-1, k+1) \geq s_k^{b-1}$. This allows (10) to be simplified to

$$s_k^b = \min\left\{ s_k^{b-1} + \binom{b-1}{k-1}, s_{k-1}^{b-1} + \binom{b-1}{k+1} \right\}.$$

Table III gives values of s_k^b for small b and k.

REFERENCES

[1] S. Al-Bassam and B. Bose, "Design of efficient balanced codes," in *Proc. 19th Int. Conf. Fault-Tolerant Comput.*, June 1989, pp. 229–236.

[2] J. M. Berger, "A note on error detecting codes for asymmetric channels," *Inform. Contr.*, vol. 4, pp. 68–73, Mar. 1961.

[3] J. M. Berger, "A note on burst detecting sum codes," *Inform. Contr.*, vol. 4, pp. 297–299, 1961.

[4] M. Blaum, "Systematic unidirectional burst detecting codes," *IEEE Trans. Comput.*, vol. C-37, pp. 453–457, Apr. 1988.

[5] M. Blaum and H. van Tilborg, "On *t*-error correcting/all unidirectional error detecting codes," IBM Res. Rep. 5566(56685), Mar. 1987.

[6] J. P. Boly, "On combined symbol and digit error control codes," Master's thesis, Dep. Math. Comput. Sci., Eindhoven Univ. of Technology, Eindhoven, The Netherlands, 1987.

[7] B. Bose, "Burst unidirectional error detecting codes," *IEEE Trans. Comput.*, vol. C-35, pp. 350–353, Apr. 1986.

[8] ——, "Byte unidirectional error correcting codes," in *Proc. 19th Int. Conf. Fault-Tolerant Comput.*, June 1989, pp. 222–228.

[9] B. Bose and D. J. Lin, "Systematic unidirectional error-detecting codes," *IEEE Trans. Comput.*, vol. C-34, pp. 1026–1032, Nov. 1985.

[10] B. Bose and D. K. Pradhan, "Optimal unidirectional error detecting/correcting codes," *IEEE Trans. Comput.*, vol. C-31, pp. 564–568, June 1982.

[11] B. Bose and T. R. N. Rao, "Theory of unidirectional error correcting/detecting codes," *IEEE Trans. Comput.*, vol. C-31, pp. 521–530, 1982.

[12] D. C. Bossen, L. C. Chang, and C. Chen, "Measurement and generation of error correcting codes for package failures," *IEEE Trans. Comput.*, vol. C-27, pp. 201–204, Mar. 1978.

[13] J. Bruck and M. Blaum, "Some new EC/AUED codes," in *Proc. 19th Int. Conf. Fault-Tolerant Comput.*, June 1989, pp. 208–215.

[14] C. L. Chen, "Error correcting codes with byte error detection capability," *IEEE Trans. Comput.*, vol. C-32, pp. 615–621, July 1983.

[15] L. A. Dunning, "SEC-BED-DED codes for error control in byte-organized memory systems," *IEEE Trans. Comput.*, vol. C-34, pp. 557–562, June 1985.

[16] L. A. Dunning, G. Dial, and M. R. Varanasi, "Unidirectional 9-bit byte error detecting codes for computer memory systems," in *Proc. 19th Int. Conf. Fault-Tolerant Comput.*, June 1989, pp. 216–221.

[17] L. A. Dunning and M. R. Varanasi, "A rotational (14·4, 49) SEC-DED-S4ED code for byte organized fault tolerant memory applications," in *Proc. 14th Int. Conf. Fault-Tolerant Comput.*, June 1984, pp. 330–333.

[18] G. H. Hardy and E. M. Wright, *An Introduction to the Theory of Numbers*, 5th ed. London, England: Oxford Univ. Press, 1979.

[19] S. J. Hong and A. M. Patel, "A general class of maximal codes for computer applications," *IEEE Trans. Comput.*, vol. C-21, pp. 1322–1331, Dec. 1972.

[20] S. Kaneda, "A class of odd-weight-column SEC-DED-SbED codes for computer memory applications," *IEEE Trans. Comput.*, vol. C-33, pp. 737–739, Aug. 1984.

[21] S. Kaneda and E. Fujiwara, "Single byte error correcting–double byte error detecting codes for computer memory systems," *IEEE Trans. Comput.*, vol. C-31, pp. 596–602, July 1982.

[22] D. E. Knuth, "Efficient balanced codes," *IEEE Trans. Comput.*, vol. C-32, pp. 51–53, Jan. 1986.

[23] D. J. Lin and B. Bose, "Theory and design of *t*-error correcting and $d(d > t)$-unidirectional error detecting (*t*-EC-*d*-UED) codes," *IEEE Trans. Comput.*, vol. C-37, pp. 433–439, Apr. 1988.

[24] N. Nikolos, N. Gaitanis, and G. Philokyprou, "Systematic *t*-error correcting/all unidirectional error detecting codes," *IEEE Trans. Comput.*, vol. C-35, pp. 394–402, May 1986.

[25] D. K. Pradhan, "A new class of error-correcting/detecting codes for fault tolerant computer applications," *IEEE Trans. Comput.*, vol. C-29, pp. 471–481, June 1980.

[26] D. K. Pradhan and J. J. Stiffler, "Error correcting codes and self-checking circuits in fault-tolerant computers," *IEEE Comput. Mag.*, vol. 13, pp. 27–37, Mar. 1980.

[27] S. M. Reddy, "A class of linear codes for error control in byte-per-card organized digital systems," *IEEE Trans. Comput.*, vol. C-27, pp. 455–459, May 1978.

[28] D. L. Tao, C. R. P. Hartmann, and P. K. Lala, "An efficient class of unidirectional error detecting/error correcting codes," *IEEE Trans. Comput.*, vol. C-37, pp. 879–882, July 1988.

[29] J. K. Wolf, "Adding two information symbols to certain nonbinary BCH codes and some applications," *Bell Syst. Tech. J.*, vol. 48, pp. 2405–2424, Sept. 1969.

Efficient Multiple Unidirectional Byte Error-Detecting Codes for Computer Memory Systems *

T. R. N. Rao, G. L. Feng and M. S. Kolluru
The Center for Advanced Computer Studies
University of Southwestern Louisiana
Lafayette, LA 70504-4330

Abstract

In this paper, a new method of construction of more efficient codes, which can detect t unidirectional byte errors or all unidirectional bit errors (t-UbED/AUED), is presented. In this construction, we generalize and improve the t-UbED/AUED codes proposed by Dunning et al., in such a way that two weight syndromes need not be protected from unidirectional errors when t > 2. Thus, this construction is more efficient and can be applied to all multiple unidirectional byte error-detecting codes.

Keywords: bit unidirectional errors, unidirectional byte errors, memory fault tolerance, error-detection codes.

I. Introduction

In computer memory systems, for data stored in a byte-per-chip or byte-per-card fashion, byte errors tend to occur [1-2]. Codes have been designed for byte-error correction and detection [3-7], and also for their detection and correction together with random errors [8-12].

The faults that occur in many computer memories and VLSI circuits, most likely cause "*unidirectional errors*", for which both $1 \rightarrow 0$ and $0 \rightarrow 1$ errors may occur, though not occurring simultaneously in a single data word. However, the errors in one byte may be of the form $1 \rightarrow 0$ while in another byte they may be the from $0 \rightarrow 1$. When a memory is handled as a whole, unidirectional errors of a single form may occur across the entire word. Figure 1.1 contrasts a unidirectional error with a unidirectional byte error affecting two bytes.

In byte-organized computer memories, transient and permanent faults are apt to cause multiple unidirectional byte errors. Codes that can detect a small number t of unidirectional byte errors in computer memory words, composed of small m information bytes each containing b bits, and which also detect simultaneously, all unidirectional errors across the entire memory word, were developed in [5-6]. These codes are termed t-unidirectional byte error detecting and all unidirectional error detecting (t-UbED/AUED) codes, and always use two additional b-bit bytes to hold the parity check information. Figure 1.2 shows the general form of a codeword including both information and check bytes.

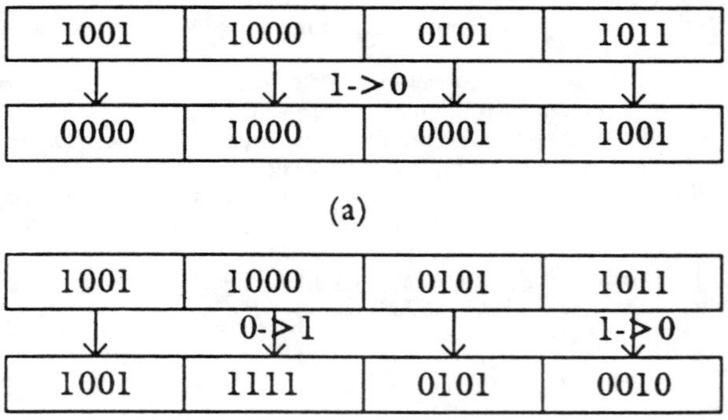

(b)

Fig. 1.1 (a) Unidirectional error example.
(b) 2-Unidirectional byte error example.

In this paper, we generalize the construction of t-UbED/AUED codes in [6] to any t and further improvise the construction for $t \geqslant 3$. The organization of this paper is follows. In the next section, we briefly review the general principle of construction of t-UbED/AUED codes. Then we generalize the construction proposed by

* This work was supported in part by the Office of Naval Research under Grant N00014-91-J-1067.

0-8186-4182-7/93 $3.00 © 1992 IEEE

Dunning et al. for any t and m. In Section III, we give an improved method for construction of t-UbED/AUED codes for any t and m, which eliminates the need to encode the two syndromes (s_{-1} and s_{t-2}). Thus, the constructed t-UbED/AUED codes are found to be more efficient. In the last section, we provide some conclusions.

data - 1	..	data - m	check - h	..	check - 1
← b-bits →		← b-bits →	← b-bits →		← b-bits →

Fig. 1.2 Memory codeword organization.

II. Construction of t-UbED/AUED codes

In this section, we first review a simple construction of t-UbED/AUED codes. Then we give a generalization of the construction of t-UbED/AUED codes proposed by Dunning et al. in [6].

Let us design a t-UbED/AUED code with m information bytes, each byte having b bits. The most simple design is the following.

For convenience, let $p > \max\{ b, m\text{-}1 \}$ be a minimal prime integer. Let

$$H = \begin{bmatrix} 1 & 0 & 1^{-1} & 2^{-1} & \cdots & (p-1)^{-1} \\ 0 & 0 & 1 & 1 & \cdots & 1 \\ 0 & 0 & 1 & 2 & \cdots & (p-1) \\ | & | & | & | & \cdots & | \\ 0 & 1 & 1^{t-2} & 2^{t-2} & \cdots & (p-1)^{t-2} \end{bmatrix} \quad (2.1)$$

Then H is a parity check matrix of an extended Reed-Solomon code over GF(p) with minimum distance t+1. Let H* be a t×m submatrix of H, which consists of the right most (m) columns of H. We can easily see the following:

Lemma 2.1: Let H* be a parity check matrix of a linear code C* (m, m-t) over GF(p), which has a minimum distance t+1 and which can detect any t or fewer errors.

Let H^*_{-1}, H^*_{t-2}, and $H^*_{-1,t-2}$ be submatrices of H^* obtained by deleting the top row, the bottom row, and both, respectively. Then, we have the following:

Lemma 2.2: For $m \leqslant p\text{-}1$, let H^*_{-1}, H^*_{t-2}, and $H^*_{-1,t-2}$ be parity check matrices of linear codes C^*_{-1}, C^*_{t-2}, and $C^*_{-1,t-2}$ codes over GF(p) respectively, which have minimum distances t, t and t-1, and which can detect any t-1, t-1 and t-2 or fewer errors, respectively.

Let information data bytes be $\mathbf{d}_1, \dots, \mathbf{d}_m$ and the Hamming weight of $\mathbf{d}_i$ be $w(\mathbf{d}_i) \leqslant b$. Thus, $w(\mathbf{d}_i) \in GF(p)$. We define syndromes as follows:

$$\begin{bmatrix} s_{-1} \\ s_0 \\ s_1 \\ | \\ s_{t-2} \end{bmatrix} = H^* \cdot \begin{bmatrix} w(\mathbf{d}_1) \\ w(\mathbf{d}_2) \\ | \\ w(\mathbf{d}_{m-1}) \\ w(\mathbf{d}_m) \end{bmatrix} \quad (2.2)$$

From (2.2) and Lemmas 2.1 and 2.2, we obtain the following:

Lemma 2.3: If $\mathbf{d}'_i$ differ from $\mathbf{d}_i$, for i = 1, 2, ... , m, by t or fewer unidirectional byte errors, then $(s_{-1}, s_0, \dots, s_{t-2}) \neq (s'_{-1}, s'_0, \dots, s'_{t-2})$, where s'_j are all obtained by $H^* \cdot (w(\mathbf{d}'_1), \dots, w(\mathbf{d}'_m))^T$. If the information bytes are different by t-1 or fewer unidirectional byte errors, then $(s_0, \dots, s_{t-2}) \neq (s'_0, \dots, s'_{t-2})$ and $(s_{-1}, s_0, \dots, s_{t-3}) \neq (s'_{-1}, s'_0, \dots, s'_{t-3})$. If the information bytes are different by t-2 or fewer unidirectional byte errors, then $(s_0, \dots, s_{t-3}) \neq (s'_0, \dots, s'_{t-3})$.

Construction 1: Let $z = \sum_{i=1}^{m} w(\mathbf{d}_i)$, $n = z \cdot p^{t-1} + s_1 \cdot p^{t-2} + \cdots + s_{t-3} \cdot p^2 + s_{t-2} \cdot p^1 + s_{-1}$, where s_i's are defined by (2.2). Let $v = C^b_{\lfloor \frac{b}{2} \rfloor}$ and let V be a set of all $\lfloor \frac{b}{2} \rfloor$-out-of-b codewords, i.e., $V = \{ \mathbf{v}_0, \mathbf{v}_1, \dots, \mathbf{v}_{v-1} \mid w(\mathbf{v}_i) = \lfloor \frac{b}{2} \rfloor \}$. Suppose $h = \lceil \log_p ((m \cdot b+1) \cdot p^{t-1}) \rceil$. Then, to construct a t-

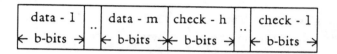

UbED/AUED codeword, the check bytes are determined by the following process:

$$\mathbf{c}_h \leftarrow \mathbf{v}_{i_h} \qquad \text{where } i_h = \lfloor \frac{n}{v^{h-1}} \rfloor$$

$$\mathbf{c}_{h-1} \leftarrow \mathbf{v}_{i_{h-1}} \qquad \text{where } i_{h-1} = \lfloor \frac{n}{v^{h-2}} \rfloor \bmod v$$

...

$$\mathbf{c}_2 \leftarrow \mathbf{v}_{i_2} \qquad \text{where } i_2 = \lfloor \frac{n}{v^1} \rfloor \bmod v$$

$$\mathbf{c}_1 \leftarrow \mathbf{v}_{i_1} \qquad \text{where } i_1 = n \bmod v$$

Theorem 2.1: ($\mathbf{d}_1, \ldots, \mathbf{d}_m, \mathbf{c}_1, \ldots, \mathbf{c}_h$) form a t-UbED/AUED code with m information bytes and h check bytes, each byte having b bits.

Proof: Let $\mathbf{x} = (\mathbf{d}_1, \cdots, \mathbf{d}_m, \mathbf{c}_1, \cdots, \mathbf{c}_h)$ and $\mathbf{x}' = (\mathbf{d}'_1, \cdots, \mathbf{d}'_m, \mathbf{c}'_1, \cdots, \mathbf{c}'_h)$ be two codewords obtained by construction 1. We will prove that it is impossible that $\mathbf{x}'$ differs from $\mathbf{x}$ by only unidirectional errors or at most t unidirectional byte errors.

First we prove that it is impossible that $\mathbf{x}'$ differs from $\mathbf{x}$ by only unidirectional errors. Without loss of generality, suppose there are the unidirectional errors of the form $0 \rightarrow 1$. Let us consider the following two cases:

Case (a1): There are some errors $0 \rightarrow 1$ on $\mathbf{d}_i$ for i = 1, 2, ... , m. Thus, $z < z'$ and $n < n'$. On the other hand, since $\mathbf{c}'_j$ and $\mathbf{c}_j$ are $\lfloor \frac{b}{2} \rfloor$-out-of-b bytes for j = 1, 2, ... , h , there are no $0 \rightarrow 1$ errors on $\mathbf{c}_j$, i.e., $\mathbf{c}'_j = \mathbf{c}_j$. Hence, $n = n'$ from construction 1. This is a contradiction.

Case (a2): No $0 \rightarrow 1$ errors on $\mathbf{d}_i$ for i = 1, 2, ... , m. This implies $\mathbf{d}_i = \mathbf{d}'_i$. Since the check bytes are uniquely determined by their information bytes from construction 1, $\mathbf{c}_j = \mathbf{c}'_j$ for j = 1, 2, ... , h. Therefore, $\mathbf{x} = \mathbf{x}'$, i. e., there are no unidirectional errors on $\mathbf{x}$. This is a contradiction.

Now we prove that it is impossible that $\mathbf{x}'$ differs from $\mathbf{x}$ by ν unidirectional byte errors, where $\nu \leqslant t$. Let us consider the following two cases:

Case (b1): There are no unidirectional byte errors on the check bytes. Thus, $\mathbf{c}'_j = \mathbf{c}_j$ for j = 1, 2, ... , h. This means $z = z'$ and $n = n'$. From the definition of n and $s_0 = z \bmod p$, we have, $s_u = s'_u$ for u = -1, 0, ..., t-2. On the other hand, ν unidirectional byte errors are only on the information bytes, where $1 \leqslant u \leqslant t$, then from Lemma 2.3 $(s_{-1}, s_0, \ldots, s_{t-2}) \neq (s'_{-1}, s'_0, \ldots, s'_{t-2})$. This is a contradiction.

Case (b2): There is at least one unidirectional byte error on the check bytes. Since $\mathbf{c}_j$ and $\mathbf{c}'_j$ are $\lfloor \frac{b}{2} \rfloor$-out-of-b bytes for j = 1, 2, ... , h, there is no unidirectional byte error on $\mathbf{c}_j$, i. e., $\mathbf{c}_j = \mathbf{c}'_j$ which is a contradiction. □

Example 2.1: Suppose a 7-UbED/AUED code, which has m = 32 information bytes with b = 8 bits, is desired. Let p = 31 be a prime integer and choose H* to be 7×32 parity check matrix of a d = 8 code as given in (2.1). Let U be a set of all 4-out-of-8 codewords, then $v = C_4^8 = 70$. Thus, $h = \lceil \log_{70}((32 \cdot 8+1) \cdot (31)^{7-1}) \rceil = 7$. Therefore, by construction 1, seven check bytes are required.

In order to improve the t-UbED/AUED codes, we begin by introducing the following concept, which was first introduced in [6].

Definition 2.1: An ascending (respectively, descending) sequence with spans s and length u is a sequence of b-bit bytes $\mathbf{u}_0, \mathbf{u}_1, \ldots, \mathbf{u}_{u-1}$ such that the following conditions hold for all $0 \leqslant i \leqslant j < u$:

a) $w(\mathbf{u}_i) \leqslant w(\mathbf{u}_j)$ (respectively, $w(\mathbf{u}_i) \geqslant w(\mathbf{u}_j)$)

b) If $\mathbf{u}_i$ and $\mathbf{u}_j$ differ by a unidirectional error then $j - i - 1 \geqslant s$.

In [6], a class of such sequences is given. Let U_{k_1,k_2} be the set of all bytes with b-bits, which have weight $k_1 \leqslant k \leqslant k_2$. For given b, k_1, and k_2, a recursive construction of ascending sequence and a table of the values of some elementary spans are also given in [6].

Using $U^b_{k_1,k_2}$ and $\lfloor \frac{b}{2} \rfloor$-out-of-b code, codes which can detect some small number t of unidirectional byte errors and detect all unidirectional errors simultaneously and use two additional b-bit bytes as check bytes, were developed. However, this construction is suitable only for small t and special m. In this section, we generalize this construction. Then, we give an improved construction in the next section.

Construction 2: For a fixed byte width b, let V be a set of all $\lfloor \frac{b}{2} \rfloor$-out-of-b bytes, and $v = |V|$. Let $p > \max\{ b, m-1 \}$. We choose U to be a descending sequence of span s and length u such that h is as small as possible and the following inequalities hold:

(a) $(m \cdot b + 1) \cdot p^{t-1} \leq u \cdot v^{h-1}$
(b) $((t-1) \cdot b + 1) \cdot p^{t-1} \leq (s + 1) \cdot v^{h-1}$.

To encode a codeword, all check bytes except $\mathbf{c}_h$, are computed from construction 1. But $\mathbf{c}_h \leftarrow \mathbf{u}_{i_h}$ where $i_h = \lfloor \frac{n}{v^{h-1}} \rfloor$.

Theorem 2.2: A code ($\mathbf{d}_1, \ldots, \mathbf{d}_m, \mathbf{c}_1, \ldots, \mathbf{c}_h$) obtained by construction 2 is a t-UbED/AUED code.

Proof: Let $\mathbf{x}$ and $\mathbf{x}'$ be two codewords obtained by construction 2. We will prove that it is impossible that $\mathbf{x}'$ differs from $\mathbf{x}$ by only unidirectional errors or at most t unidirectional byte errors.

First we prove that it is impossible that $\mathbf{x}'$ differs from $\mathbf{x}$ by only unidirectional errors. Without loss of generality, suppose there are the unidirectional errors of the form $0 \rightarrow 1$. Let us consider the following two cases:

Case (a1): There are some $0 \rightarrow 1$ errors on $\mathbf{d}_i$ for $i = 1, 2, \ldots, m$. Thus, $z < z'$ and $n < n'$. Since $\mathbf{c}'_j$ for $j = 1, 2, \ldots, h-1$ are $\lfloor \frac{b}{2} \rfloor$-out-of-b bytes, no $0 \rightarrow 1$ errors occur on $\mathbf{c}_j$, i.e., $\mathbf{c}'_j = \mathbf{c}_j$. Hence, $i_h < i'_h$, where $\mathbf{c}_h = \mathbf{u}_{i_h}$ and $\mathbf{c}'_h = \mathbf{u}_{i'_h}$. But from the decreasing sequence property, it follows that $w(\mathbf{c}_h) > w(\mathbf{c}'_h)$. Thus, there is at least one $1 \rightarrow 0$ error on $\mathbf{c}_h$. This contradicts the initial condition that only $0 \rightarrow 1$ unidirectional errors occur on $\mathbf{x}$.

Case (a2): No $0 \rightarrow 1$ errors occur on $\mathbf{d}_i$ for $i = 1, 2, \ldots, m$. By the same reason as in Case (a2) of the proof of Theorem 2.1, we get a contradiction.

Now we prove that it is impossible that $\mathbf{x}'$ differs from $\mathbf{x}$ by ν unidirectional byte errors, where $\nu \leq t$. Let us consider the following two cases:

Case (b1): There are no unidirectional byte errors on the check bytes. Thus, $\mathbf{c}'_j = \mathbf{c}_j$ for $j = 1, 2, \ldots, h$. This implies $z = z'$ and $n = n'$. From the definition of n and $s_0 = z \bmod p$, we have, $s_u = s'_u$ for $u = -1, 0, \ldots, t-2$. On the other hand, from Lemma 2.3, if ν unidirectional byte errors are on the information bytes, where $1 \leq \nu \leq t$, then $(s_{-1}, s_0, \ldots, s_{t-2}) \neq (s'_{-1}, s'_0, \ldots, s'_{t-2})$. This is a contradiction.

Case (b2): There is at least one unidirectional byte error on the check bytes. Since $\mathbf{c}_j$ and $\mathbf{c}'_j$ are $\lfloor \frac{b}{2} \rfloor$-out-of-b bytes for $j = 1, 2, \ldots, h-1$, there is no unidirectional byte error on $\mathbf{c}_j$, i.e., $\mathbf{c}_j = \mathbf{c}'_j$. If there is a unidirectional byte error on $\mathbf{c}_h$, i.e., $\mathbf{c}_h$ and $\mathbf{c}'_h$ differ by a unidirectional byte error, then from definition 1, $|i_h - i'_h| \geq s + 1$, where i_h and i'_h are their corresponding indices. Since $i_j = i'_j$ for $j = 1, 2, \ldots, h-1$, we have $|n - n'| \geq (s+1) \cdot v^{h-1} \geq ((t-1) \cdot b + 1) \cdot p^{t-1}$. Furthermore, $|z - z'| \cdot p^{t-1} + p^{t-1} - 1 \geq |n - n'| \geq (s+1) \cdot v^{h-1} \geq ((t-1) \cdot b + 1) \cdot p^{t-1}$, i.e., $|z - z'| > (t-1) \cdot b + 1$. Since there are at most t-1 unidirectional byte errors on information bytes, we have $|z - z'| \leq (t-1) \cdot b$. This is a contradiction. □

Since $u > v$, we see that construction 2 is better than construction 1. When $h = 2$, construction 2 is reduced to construction 1 in [6]. We say that construction 2 is a generalization of construction 1 in [6].

Example 2.2: Let us consider Example 2.1 again. Let h = 5, and let U be a set of all 3-out-of-8, 4-out-of-8 and 5-out-of-8 codes, then u = $C_3^8 + C_4^8 + C_5^8 = 182$, and s = 47 from [6]. It is easily checked that:

$(32 \cdot 8+1) \cdot (31)^{7-1} = (2.2808845) \cdot (10)^{11} < (3.058874) \cdot (10)^{11} = (182) \cdot (70)^5$.

$((7\text{-}1) \cdot 8+1) \cdot (31)^{7-1} = (4.348768) \cdot (10)^{10} < (8.06736) \cdot (10)^{10} = (47 + 1) \cdot (70)^5$.

Thus, the conditions (a) and (b) of construction 2 are satisfied for h = 6, u = 182, and s = 47. Therefore, in order to construct this code, *six* check bytes are required from construction 2.

Example 2.3: Suppose a 4-UbED/AUED code, which has m = 60 information bytes with b = 8 bits, is desired. Let p = 61 be a prime integer and choose H to be 4×60 parity check matrix of a d = 5 code as given in (2.1). Let U be a set of all 4-out-of-8 codewords, then v = $C_4^8 = 70$. Since $(m \cdot b+1) \cdot p^{t-1} = (1.09177) \cdot (10)^8 = (318.30029) \cdot (70)^3 = (318.30029) \cdot v^3$ and 318.30029 > u, to construct such a code, by construction 2, (3 + 2) = 5 check bytes are required. Actually, such a 4-UbED/AUED code can also be constructed with 5 check bytes using construction 1.

III. An improved construction of t-UbED/AUED codes

In the previous section, we generalized construction 1 in [6]. We will improve the generalized construction in this section. For convenience, we assume $p < 2^b$ in this section. For the case of $p \geqslant 2^b$, the constructions here can be easily modified. In this section, in order to satisfy Lemma2.2 we always assume that $m \leqslant p\text{-}1$.

When t > 2, we have $s_{-1}, s_0, \dots , s_{t-2}$. It is easily seen that if the top row or the bottom row of H is deleted, the remaining submatrix has minimum distance t. If the top and the bottom rows are both deleted, then the remaining submatrix has minimum distance t-1. Thus, s_{-1} and s_{t-2} need not be encoded in U or V in the construction. We have the following improved construction.

Construction 3: Let b, p, s, v (V), and u (U) be defined in construction 2. Let $b^* = b - \lceil \log_2 p \rceil$, V* be a set of all $\lfloor \frac{b^*}{2} \rfloor$-out-of-b* bytes $\mathbf{v}^*_i$, and $v^* = |V^*|$. Let h be the smallest integer such that the following inequalities hold:

(a) $(m \cdot b + 1) \cdot p^{t-3} \leqslant u \cdot v^{h-3} v^{*2}$.
(b) $((t\text{-}1) \cdot b + 1) \cdot p^{t-3} \leqslant (s + 1) \cdot v^{h-3} v^{*2}$.

To encode a codeword, the check bytes are computed as follows:

z and s_i for i = -1, 0, 1, ... , t-2, are the same as in construction 2.

$$n \leftarrow z \cdot p^{t-3} + s_1 \cdot p^{t-4} + \cdots + s_{t-4} \cdot p + s_{t-3},$$

$\mathbf{c}_h \leftarrow \mathbf{u}_{i_h}$ where $i_h = \lfloor \frac{n}{v^{h-3} v^{*2}} \rfloor$

$\mathbf{c}_{h-1} \leftarrow \mathbf{v}_{i_{h-1}}$ where $i_{h-1} = \lfloor \frac{n}{v^{h-4} v^{*2}} \rfloor \bmod v$

...

$\mathbf{c}_3 \leftarrow \mathbf{v}_{i_3}$ where $i_3 = \lfloor \frac{n}{v^{*2}} \rfloor \bmod v$

$\mathbf{c}_2 \leftarrow (\mathbf{v}^*_{i_2} | s_{t-2})$ where $i_2 = \lfloor \frac{n}{v^*} \rfloor \bmod v^*$

$\mathbf{c}_1 \leftarrow (\mathbf{v}^*_{i_1} | s_{-1})$ where $i_1 = n \bmod v^*$

where $(\mathbf{v}^*_{i_2} | s_{t-2})$ denotes a cascaded byte.

Theorem 3.1: A code $(\mathbf{d}_1, \dots , \mathbf{d}_m, \mathbf{c}_1, \dots, \mathbf{c}_h)$ obtained by construction 2 is a t-UbED/AUED code.

Proof: Let $\mathbf{x}$ and $\mathbf{x}'$ be two codewords obtained by construction 3. We will prove that it is impossible that $\mathbf{x}'$ differs from $\mathbf{x}$ by only unidirectional errors or at most t unidirectional byte errors.

First we prove that it is impossible that $\mathbf{x}'$ differs from $\mathbf{x}$ by only unidirectional errors. Without loss of generality, suppose there are unidirectional errors of the form $0 \rightarrow 1$. Let us consider the following two cases:

Case (a1): There are some $0 \rightarrow 1$ errors on $\mathbf{d}_i$ for i = 1, 2, ... , m. Thus, $z < z'$ and $n < n'$. Since

$\mathbf{c}'_j$ for j = 2, 3, ... , h-1 and $\mathbf{v}^*_{i_\mu}$ for μ = 1, 2 are $\lfloor \frac{b}{2} \rfloor$-out-of-b bytes and $\lfloor \frac{b'}{2} \rfloor$-out-of-$b'$ bytes, respectively, where b' = b - $\lceil \log_2 p \rceil$, there are no 0 → 1 errors on $\mathbf{c}_j$ and $\mathbf{v}^*_{i_\mu}$. Hence, $i_h < i'_h$, where $\mathbf{c}_h = \mathbf{u}_{i_h}$ and $\mathbf{c}'_h = \mathbf{u}_{i'_h}$. By the same reason as in Case (a1) of the proof of Theorem 2.2, it is impossible that there exist 0 → 1 unidirectional errors on $\mathbf{x}$.

Case (a2): No 0 → 1 errors occur on $\mathbf{d}_i$ for i = 1, 2, ... , m. By the same reason as in Case (a2) of the proof of Theorem 2.1, we get a contradiction.

Now we prove that it is impossible that $\mathbf{x}'$ differs from $\mathbf{x}$ by ν unidirectional byte errors, where $1 \leqslant \nu \leqslant t$. Let us consider the following two cases:

Case (b1): There are no unidirectional byte errors on the check bytes. This means that the check bytes of $\mathbf{x}$ are equal to the check bytes of $\mathbf{x}'$, i. e., z = z' and n = n', $s_{-1} = s'_{-1}$, $s_{t-2} = s'_{t-2}$. Also from the definition of n and s_0 = z mod p, we know that $s_u = s'_u$ for u = -1, 0, ..., t-2. However, there are ν unidirectional byte errors on information bytes, where $1 \leqslant \nu \leqslant t$. From Lemma 2.3, we have $(s_{-1}, s_0, \ldots, s_{t-2}) \neq (s'_{-1}, s'_0, \ldots, s'_{t-2})$. This is a contradiction.

Case (b2): There is at least one unidirectional byte error on the check bytes. Since $\mathbf{c}_j$ and $\mathbf{c}'_j$ are $\lfloor \frac{b}{2} \rfloor$-out-of-b bytes for j = 3, ... , h-1, and $\mathbf{v}^*_\mu$ for μ = 1, 2 are $\lfloor \frac{b'}{2} \rfloor$-out-of-$b'$ bytes, there is no unidirectional byte error on these bytes and on $\mathbf{v}^*_\mu$. Let us consider the following subcases:

Subcase i): if $\mathbf{c}_h \neq \mathbf{c}'_h$, i.e., if $\mathbf{c}_h$ and $\mathbf{c}'_h$ differ by a unidirectional byte error, then by the same reason as in the case (b2) of the proof of Theorem 2.2, we get a contradiction.

Subcase ii): if $\mathbf{c}_h = \mathbf{c}'_h$, we have $s_i = s'_i$ for i ≠ -1 and t-2 because $\mathbf{c}_j = \mathbf{c}'_j$ and $\mathbf{v}^*_\mu = \mathbf{v}^{*\prime}_\mu$. We consider the three cases. If $s_{-1} \neq s'_{-1}$ and $s_{t-2} = s'_{t-2}$, then there is one unidirectional byte error on the byte which contains s_{-1}. Thus, there are at most t-1 unidirectional byte errors on other bytes. However, from Lemma 2.3 and $s_i = s'_i$ for i ≠ -1, there are no $1 \leqslant \nu\text{-}1 \leqslant$ t-1 unidirectional byte errors on the information bytes, i.e., $\mathbf{d}_i = \mathbf{d}'_i$ for i = 1, 2, ..., m. On the other hand, s_i and s'_i are uniquely determined by the information bytes. Thus, $s_{-1} = s'_{-1}$, which shows a contradiction. By the same reason, it is impossible that $s_{-1} = s'_{-1}$ and $s_{t-2} \neq s'_{t-2}$. If $s_{-1} \neq s'_{-1}$ and $s_{t-2} \neq s'_{t-2}$, then there are two unidirectional byte errors on the bytes which contain s_{-1} and s_{t-2}, respectively. Thus, there are at most t-2 unidirectional errors on other bytes. However, from Lemma 2.3 and $s_i = s'_i$ for i ≠ -1, t-2, there are no $1 \leqslant \nu\text{-}2 \leqslant$ t-2 unidirectional byte errors on the information bytes. On the other hand, s_i and s'_i are uniquely determined by the information bytes. Thus, $s_i = s'_i$. Again we have a contradiction.□

For b* = b - b', we have $C^{b'}_{\lfloor \frac{b'}{2} \rfloor} \cdot 2^{b^*} > C^{b}_{\lfloor \frac{b}{2} \rfloor}$. Thus, construction 3 is more efficient than construction 2.

Example 3.1: Let us consider Example 2.3 again. Let h = 4, and let U be a set of all 3-out-of-8, 4-out-of-8 and 5-out-of-8 codes. Then u = $C^8_3 + C^8_4 + C^8_5$ = 182, and s = 47 from [6]. From construction 3, b* = 8 - $\lceil \log_2 61 \rceil$ = 2, V* = { 01, 10 }, and v* = 2. It is easily checked that:

$$(60\cdot 8+1)\cdot(61)^{4-3} = 29341 < 50960 = (182)\cdot(2)^2\cdot(70) .$$

$$((4\text{-}1)\cdot 8+1)\cdot(61)^{4-3} = 1525 < 13440 = (47+1)\cdot(2)^2\cdot(70).$$

Therefore the conditions (a) and (b) are satisfied. Such a 4-UbED/AUED code with four check bytes can be constructed using construction 3.

Example 3.2: For b=8,m=60, the 5-UbED/AUED and 6-UbED/AUED codes obtained by construction 3 have *one* check byte less than the codes obtained by constructions 1 and 2.

In error control codes, "*rate*" r is very important. It is defined by

$$r = \frac{number\ of\ information\ bits}{total\ number\ of\ information\ \text{and}\ check\ bits}.$$

To improve the rate of t-UbED/AUED codes further, we propose a new method. The original method is to use all the check bits. If a check byte that can be saved has less than b-1 bits, then in the above condition its rate will be improved. This is achieved by using the saved space for additional information bits. Under the condition stated before, place this check byte in some information byte. This process of saving a check byte is explained below.

Following construction 3, parameters h, u, and s are found. Let u* be maximum value satisfying the conditions (a) and (b) in construction 2. Let δ be the minimum integer satisfying $C^{\delta}_{\lfloor \frac{\delta}{2} \rfloor} \geq \lfloor \frac{(m \cdot b+1) \cdot p^{t-3}}{u^* \cdot v^{h-4} v^{*2}} \rfloor$. If $\frac{\delta}{b} < \frac{m}{m+h}$, then using the following construction, a more efficient t-UbED/AUED code can be obtained.

Construction 4: Let $\mathbf{d}_m = (d_{m,1}, \dots, d_{m,b-\delta}, 0, \dots, 0)$, where $d_{m,k}$ are information bits for k = 1, ..., b-δ. Using construction 3, we find values of $\mathbf{c}_j$ for j = 1, 2, ... , h-2. Let $\hat{v} = C^{\delta}_{\lfloor \frac{\delta}{2} \rfloor}$, and $\hat{V} = \{ \hat{\mathbf{v}}_0, \hat{\mathbf{v}}_1, \dots, \hat{\mathbf{v}}_{\hat{v}-1} \}$ be a set of all $\lfloor \frac{\delta}{2} \rfloor$-out-of-$\delta$ codes. Let $i_{h-1} = \lfloor \frac{n}{v^{h-4} v^{*2}} \rfloor \bmod \hat{v}$, then $\hat{\mathbf{v}}_{i_{h-1}}$ is placed in δ bits in the right part of $\mathbf{d}_m$. Let $i_h = \lfloor \frac{n}{v^{h-4} \hat{v} v^{*2}} \rfloor$, then $\mathbf{c}_h \leftarrow \mathbf{u}^*_{i_h}$, where $\mathbf{u}^*_{i_h}$ is an element of the ascending sequence with span s* and length u*. Thus, one check byte is saved.

The rate r of the original code constructed by construction 3 is $\frac{mb}{(m+h)b} = \frac{m}{m+h}$ and the rate r* of the new code constructed by construction 4 is $\frac{mb-\delta}{(m+h-1)b}$. It can be easily checked that if $\frac{\delta}{b} < \frac{m}{m+h}$ then $r < \hat{r}$.

Example 3.3: Let us consider Example 3.1. After calculation we have u* = 182, s* = 47, δ = 6, which satisfy the condition of construction 4. By construction 4, ($\mathbf{d}_1, \dots, \mathbf{d}_{59}, \hat{\mathbf{d}}_{60}, \mathbf{c}_4, \mathbf{c}_2, \mathbf{c}_1$) is a 4-UbED/AUED code , where $\hat{\mathbf{d}}_{60} = (d_{60,1}, d_{60,2}, 0, 0, 0, 0, 0, 0) + (0, 0, \hat{v}_1, \dots, \hat{v}_6)$ and $(\hat{v}_1, \dots, \hat{v}_6)$ is $\mathbf{c}_3$. The rate $\hat{r}$ of the new code is $\frac{60 \cdot 8-6}{(60+3) \cdot 8} = 0.9404761$ and the rate r of the original code is $\frac{60}{60+4} = 0.9375$. Thus, $r < \hat{r}$.

IV. Conclusions

In this paper, we have proposed a generalized method for the construction of t-UbED/AUED codes for any t and m, and have also improved the construction for t $\geq$ 3. This improved construction is due to the fact that the syndromes s_{-1} and s_{t-2} need not be encoded as explained in this paper. Further improvement over constructions 1, 2, and 3 can be achieved by moving information (data) bits into part of the check byte. Thus, the code rate can be improved. Some examples were presented for each of the constructions.

References

[1] D. C. Bossen, L. C. Chang, and C. Chen, "Measurement and generation of error correcting codes for package failures," *IEEE Trans. Comput.*, vol. C-27, pp. 201-204. Mar. 1978.

[2] L. A. Dunning, "SEC-BED-DED codes for error control in byte-organized memory systems," *IEEE Trans. Comput.*, vol. C-34, pp. 557-562. June 1985.

[3] S. J. Hong and A. M. Patel, "A general class of maximal codes for computer applications," *IEEE Trans. Comput.*, vol. C-21, pp. 1322-1331. Dec. 1972.

[4] S. Kaneda and E. Fujiwara, "Single byte error correcting-double byte error detecting codes for computer memory systems," *IEEE Trans. Comput.,* vol. C-31, pp. 596-602. July 1982.

[5] L. A. Dunning, G. Dial, and M. R. Varanasi, "Unidirectional 9-bit byte error-detecting codes for computer memory systems," in *Proc. 19th Int. Conf. Fault-Tolerant Comput.,* June 1989, pp. 216-221.

[6] L. A. Dunning, G. Dial, and M. R. Varanasi, "Unidirectional byte error-detecting codes for computer memory systems," *IEEE Trans. Comput.,* vol. C-39, pp. 592-595. April 1990.

[7] Y. Saitoh and H. Imai, "Multiple unidirectional byte error-correcting codes," *IEEE Trans. Infor. Theory,* vol. IT-37, pp. 903-908. May 1991.

[8] C. L. Chen, "Error correcting codes with byte error detection capability," *IEEE Trans. Comput.,* vol. C-32, pp. 615-621. July 1983.

[9] S. M. Reddy, "A class of linear codes for error control in byte-per-card organized digital systems," *IEEE Trans. Comput.,* vol. C-27, pp. 455-459. July 1983.

[10] L. A. Dunning and M. R. Varanasi, "A rotational (14·4,49) SEC-DED-S4ED code for byte organized fault tolerant memory applications," in *Proc. 14th Int. Conf. Fault-Tolerant Comput.,* June 1984, pp. 330-333.

[11] S. Kaneda, "A class of odd-weight-column SEC-DED-SbED codes for computer memory applications," *IEEE Trans. Comput.,* vol. C-33, pp. 737-739. Aug. 1984.

[12] T. R. N. Rao and E. Fujiwara, *Error-Control Coding for Computer Systems,* Prentice Hall, 1989.

Byte Unidirectional Error Correcting and Detecting Codes

Bella Bose and Sulaiman Al-Bassam

Abstract—**Efficient byte unidirectional error correcting codes that are better than byte symmetric error correcting codes are presented. The encoding and decoding algorithms are discussed. A lower bound on the number of check bits for byte unidirectional error correcting codes is derived. It is then shown that these codes are close to optimal. Capability of these codes for asymmetric error correction is also described. Codes capable of detecting double byte unidirectional errors are also given.**

Index Terms— **Asymmetric errors, decoding, encoding, error correction, unidirectional errors.**

I. Introduction

Error correcting and detecting codes are used to improve the reliability of modern computer systems. In particular, the importance and benefits of error control codes for memories, whether semiconductor RAM or ROM, disk file, or tape, and for straight data transfer paths, are well recognized.

Increasing speed and system efficiency demands have pushed the bit per card memory organization to byte per card memory organization, where a byte is a cluster of, say, b-adjacent data bits; the data paths transfer the bits of the byte in parallel. A single fault in these systems, either in the memory or in the data path, is likely to cause many bit errors, mostly of unidirectional type in the byte. Unidirectional errors in a particular word can be either $0 \rightarrow 1$ or $1 \rightarrow 0$ type, but not both; the type is not known *a priori.* The causes of these unidirectional errors are many and varied [1], [2]. A decoder failure often results in either no access, in which case the output bits will be all 0's or all 1's, or multiple access, in which case the output will be AND or OR of two or more words, including the intended word. These errors can be modeled as unidirectional errors. Moreover, when the memory system is designed using byte per chip, a single failure in the chip often results in byte unidirectional errors.

Efficient burst and byte unidirectional error detecting codes are designed in [3], [4]. Multiple byte unidirectional errors are considered in [5], where the errors within a single byte are of the same type but some bytes can have $1 \rightarrow 0$ type errors and others $0 \rightarrow 1$ errors. In this paper we consider the problems of designing codes capable of correcting single byte unidirectional errors and codes of detecting double byte unidirectional errors.

Symmetric codes in a data word can be both $0 \rightarrow 1$ and $1 \rightarrow 0$ simultaneously. Byte symmetric error correcting codes are discussed in [6]–[8]. Other codes useful for symmetric error correction and detection in byte oriented systems are described in [9]–[19]. The byte symmetric error correcting Hong–Patel codes [8] can also be used for correcting byte unidirectional errors. However, since unidirectional errors are more restrictive than symmetric errors, one is led to believe that there could be higher efficiency unidirectional codes. Can we design byte unidirectional error correcting codes using fewer check bits than used by byte symmetric error correcting codes?

Manuscript received November 18, 1989, revised August 17, 1990. This work was supported by the National Science Foundation under Grant MIP-9016143.

The authors are with the Department of Computer Science, Oregon State University, Corvallis, OR 97331.

IEEE Log Number 9200321.

As proved later, any byte symmetric error correcting code needs at least $2b$ check bits, where b is the number of bits in a byte. The codes described here require less than $2b$ check bits to correct byte unidirectional errors when the number of information bytes is up to $(p-1)/2$, where p is the largest prime less than 2^b. Thus, in this range of information byte numbers, the codes given here are better than any byte symmetric error correcting code. But when the number of information bytes is greater than 2^{b-1}, it is proved here that, for almost all cases, there are no better unidirectional codes than the symmetric codes.

We also designed codes capable of detecting double byte unidirectional errors. These codes need approximately $1+\log(k)$ check bits, where k is the total number of information bits, and these codes are close to optimal. One the other hand any double symmetric error detecting code needs at least $\max\{2b, b+\log(m)\}$ check bits, where m is the number of bytes, and thus the proposed codes use fewer check bits.

As in [8] we also assume that the check bytes may or may not be b-bits long.

The rest of the paper is organized as follows. The code format and the code construction are given in Section II. The encoding/decoding procedures are explained in Section III. Section IV gives a lower bound on the number of check bits for byte unidirectional error correcting codes. In Section V byte asymmetric error correcting codes are discussed. In Section VI, the proposed codes are compared with byte symmetric error correcting codes. In Section VII, we consider the problem of designing codes for double unidirectional error detection.

We use the following notations:

b	bits per byte.
m	number of information bytes.
r	number of check bits.
k	total number of information bits, i.e. $k = mb$.
$\log(x)$	all logarithms are to base 2 and rounded up to the next integer, i.e. we write $\log(x)$ for $\lceil \log_2(x) \rceil$.

II. Byte Unidirectional Error Correcting (UEC) Code Design

The format of the code is shown in Fig. 1. The code consists of two check symbols: 1) The parity check byte and 2) the arithmetic residue check (ARC) byte. The parity check byte length is the same as that of the information bytes, whereas the arithmetic residue check byte length, s, is less than b. Let x_{ij} represent the jth bit of the ith information byte. The jth parity bit, y_j, of the parity byte is obtained by taking modulo 2 addition of the b-adjacent jth information bits, i.e.,

$$y_j = x_{1j} + x_{2j} + \cdots + x_{mj} \quad \text{for } j = 1, 2, 3, \cdots, b. \tag{2-1}$$

In this equation + indicates the EXOR operation.

The arithmetic residue check (ARC) is obtained as follows. Let p be the smallest prime such that $(p-1)/2 \geq m$ and $p > b$, or $p > \max(2m, b)$. Then the ARC is given by

$$\text{ARC} \equiv -\left(\sum_{i=1}^{m}\sum_{j=1}^{b} x_{ij} * i\right) (\text{mod } p) \equiv -\sum_{i=1}^{m} N_i * i \,(\text{mod } p) \tag{2-2}$$

where N_i is the number of 1's in byte i. The integer value of ARC is represented in binary as $(b_{s-1}b_{s-2}\cdots b_0)$.

0-8186-4182-7/93 $3.00 © 1992 IEEE

$x_{mb} \cdots x_{m1}$	....	$x_{2b} \cdots x_{21}$	$x_{1b} \cdots x_{11}$	$y_b \cdots y_1$	$b_{s-1} \cdots b_0$
IB_m		IB_2	IB_1	PB	ARC

IB_i - Information byte i, i = 1, 2, ... m

PB - Parity Byte

ARC - Arithmetic Residue Check (ARC) byte

Length of IB_i and PB is b

Length of ARC is s where s < b

Number of check bits r = b+s < 2b

Fig. 1. Format of the byte unidirectional error correcting code.

Example 2.1: Suppose a system consists of 6 information bytes with 8 bits per byte. Since $m = 6$ we take the check base of ARC as 13, which is the smallest prime greater than $2m = 12$. For the word given below, there are $4, 4, 2, 7, 8$ and 0 1's in bytes $1, 2, 3, 4, 5$ and 6, respectively. So

$$\begin{aligned} \text{ARC} &\equiv -4*1+4*2+2*3+7*4+8*5+0*6)(\text{mod } 13) \\ &\equiv -8(\text{mod } 13) \equiv 5(\text{mod } 13). \end{aligned}$$

Thus the ARC is 0101. □

0000 0000	1111 1111	1111 1110	0100 0001	0100 0111	1011 1000	1011 1111	0101
IB_6	IB_5	IB_4	IB_3	IB_2	IB_1	PB	ARC

Suppose

$$X' = x'_{mb} \cdots x'_{m1} \cdots x'_{2b} \cdots x'_{21}\, x'_{1b} \cdots x'_{11} y'_b \cdots y'_1 b'_{s-1} \cdots b'_0$$

is the received word. At the received end two syndromes, S_1 and S_2, are calculated as follows:

$$S_1 = (e_b e_{b-1} \cdots e_1) \qquad (2\text{-}3)$$

where $e_i = y'_i + x'_{1i} + x'_{2i} + x'_{3i} + \cdots + x'_{mi}$ for $i = 1, 2, 3, \cdots, b$, and

$$S_2 = \left(\text{ARC}' + \sum_{i=1}^{m} N'_i * i\right)(\text{mod } p). \qquad (2\text{-}4)$$

Here ARC$'$ is the received arithmetic residue check, and N'_i is the number of 1's in the received byte i. The error correcting capability of the code can be analyzed by considering the following four cases.

Case 1 (no error): When there are no error in the data, it is easy to verify that the syndromes will be $S_1 = 0$ and $S_2 = 0$.

Case 2 (parity check byte in error): In this case the syndromes will be $S_1 \neq 0$ and $S_2 = 0$. The error correction is straightforward; i.e. reconstruct the parity from the error free information bytes.

Case 3 (ARC byte in error): It is easy to verify that $S_1 = 0$ and $S_2 \neq 0$ for this case. The correct ARC can be obtained from the received error free information bytes. (Note: We assume that the range of ARC is between 0 and $p - 1$. If the value of the received ARC is greater than or equal to p, then the ARC byte is considered in error.)

Case 4 (one of the information bytes in error): Suppose there are t errors in the jth byte, where $1 \leq t \leq b$ and $1 \leq j \leq m$. The syndrome S_2 will be $S_2 \equiv -tj(\text{mod } p)$ for $1 \to 0$ type errors and $S_2 \equiv +tj$ (mod p) for $0 \to 1$ type errors. The following two conditions must be satisfied in order to carry out the error correction.

1) We need to have both $S_1 \neq 0$ and $S_2 \neq 0$ so that this case is distinguishable from the above three cases. This condition is satisfied because it is easy to verify that $S_1 \neq 0$. In addition, p does not divide $\pm tj$ because $0 < t, j < p$ (and relatively prime to p); thus $S_2 \neq 0$.

TABLE I

Byte Unidirectional Error Correcting Code Parameters With $b = 4, 8$ and 16

b bits/byte	# of bits in ARC	ARC Check (p)	Total # of check bits	max # of infor. bytes
4	3	7	7	3
8	4	13	12	6
	5	31	13	15
	6	61	14	30
	7	127	15	63
16	5	31	21	15
	6	61	22	30
	7	127	23	63
	8	251	24	125
	9	509	25	254
	10	1021	26	510
	11	2039	27	1019
	12	4093	28	2046
	13	8179	29	4089

2) This second condition is required in order to locate the erroneous byte. Note that from S_1 we can find the erroneous bit positions and also the number of bits in error. Thus if we know the byte in error, the error correction can be carried out. The ARC is useful for locating the erroneous byte.

As we mentioned before, when the errors are in byte j, $S_2 \equiv -tj$ (mod p) for $1 \to 0$ type errors, and $S_2 = +tj$ (mod p) for $0 \to 1$ type errors. The syndromes corresponding to errors in different bytes, say byte i and byte j, must be distinct, i.e.

$$ti \not\equiv \pm tj(\text{mod } p) \quad \text{for } i \neq j, 1 \leq i, j \leq m \quad \text{and} \quad 1 \leq t \leq b < p.$$

Since p is a prime and $t \leq b < p$, we need to show that $i \not\equiv \pm j$ (mod$p$) for $i \neq j$ and $i, j = 1, 2, \cdots, m$. We have chosen the number of information bytes m as $m \leq (p-1)/2$, and so i and $j \leq (p-1)/2$. Thus it is easy to verify that $i \not\equiv j$ (mod p) and $i \not\equiv -j$ (mod p), whenever $i \neq j$ for $i, j = 1, 2, \cdots, m$. Therefore the code is capable of correcting byte unidirectional errors. Examples illustrating the above concepts are given in the encoding and decoding section.

In most practical systems the byte length is a power of 2, and Table I shows the code parameters for byte lengths, 4, 8, and 16. For the given number of ARC check bits, s, we have chosen the check base as the largest prime less than 2^s so that the number of information bytes, m, is maximized.

III. Encoding and Decoding of Byte UEC Codes

In this section we discuss the encoding and decoding algorithms of the codes. Encoding corresponds to appending the two checks, the parity check byte and the arithmetic residue check byte, to the given information bytes.

The ith bit of the parity check byte can be obtained by EXORing the b-adjacent ith bits of the information bytes, for $i = 1, 2, \cdots, b$.

Let N_j be the number of 1's in byte j, for $j = 1, 2, \cdots, m$. Then ARC $= -\left(\sum_{j=1}^{m} N_j * j\right)$ (mod p).

The number of 1's in each information byte is counted and multiplied by appropriate j's. (Here the multiplication is mod p multiplication.)

The summation $R = \left(\sum_{j=1}^{m} N_j * j\right)$ (mod p) can be obtained using a tree of modulo p adders. The additive inverse of R (i.e. $p - R$) in binary gives the ARC.

Example 3.1: In the Example 2.1, we have taken the prime 13 as the check base. There are $4, 4, 2, 7, 8,$ and 0

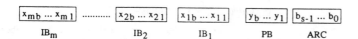

TABLE II
MULTIPLICATIVE INVERSE MODULO 13

t	t^{-1} (mod 13)
1	1
2	7
3	9
4	10
5	8
6	11
7	2
8	5

1's in bytes 1, 2, 3, 4, 5, and 6, respectively. Thus $R = (4*1+4*2+2*3+7*4+8*5+0*6) \pmod{13} = 8 \pmod{13}$. Therefore, ARC $= 13 - 8 = 5$ which in binary is 0101. □

Decoding (Error correction):

At the decoder side the syndromes S_1 and S_2 need to be calculated. S_1 is obtained by EXORing the b-adjacent bits of the information and the parity bytes. S_1 is stored in a parity register, PR.

From the received information bytes a new arithmetic residue check byte is calculated and added to the received arithmetic residue check to get S_2. The circuit to generate the syndrome S_2 is the same as the one that generates the ARC at the encoding section. S_2 can be stored in a modulo p register ARR (arithmetic residue register). When both S_1 and S_2 are equal to zero, there is no error. On the other hand, when both are not equal to zero, it means that some information byte is in error. The number of 1's, t, in S_1 which is stored in PR, is counted and the multiplicative inverse t^{-1} with respect to modulo p is obtained. We assume that the multiplicative inverses are precomputed and stored in a small table. Now t^{-1} is multiplied with the content of the register ARR; (i.e. obtain $t^{-1}S_2 \equiv j \pmod{p}$). If $j \equiv t^{-1}S_2 \pmod{p}$ is less than or equal to m, then the jth information byte is in error; otherwise the $(p-j)$th information byte is in error. Once we know the erroneous information byte j, it is EXORed with PR to get the correct data.

Example 3.1 (continue): We will consider the same example given in Section II. There are six information bytes with eight bits/byte. Table II gives the multiplicative inverse t^{-1} with respect to modulo 13 for a given integer t (≤ 8). Suppose the received word is as shown below.

IB6'	IB5'	IB4'	IB3'	IB2'	IB1'	PB'	ARC'
0001 1111	1111 1111	1111 1110	0100 0001	0100 0111	1011 1000	1011 1111	0101

There are five $0 \rightarrow 1$ errors in the sixth information byte. Then $S_1 = 0001\ 1111$ and $S_2 = 4 \pmod{13}$. From S_1 we know that the number of errors, t, is 5. The multiplicative inverse of 5 is 8, which we get from Table II. Now $8 * S_2 \equiv 6 \pmod{13}$, and thus the byte 6 is in error. The correct data can be obtained by EXORing S_1 with the received sixth information byte.

On the other hand, suppose the received word is

IB6'	IB5'	IB4'	IB3'	IB2'	IB1'	PB'	ARC'
0000 0000	1111 0000	1111 1110	0100 0001	0100 0111	1011 1000	1011 1111	0101

(Here there are four $1 \rightarrow 0$ errors in the fifth information byte.) Then $S_1 = 0000\ 1111$ and $S_2 \equiv -4*5 \equiv -7 \equiv 6 \pmod{13}$. From S_1 we know that $t = 4$. Thus $t^{-1}S_2 \equiv 10*6 \equiv 8 \pmod{13}$. Since $8 > (p-1)/2 = 6$, the erroneous byte is $13 - 8 = 5$. □

IV. OPTIMALITY OF THE BYTE UEC CODES

First we prove a theorem that gives a lower bound on the number of check bits needed for any byte unidirectional error correcting code. The codes described above need check bits close to the number given by this lower bound, and so the codes are close to optimal. In Section VI we also use this theorem to show the following important nonintuitive result: Even though the unidirectional errors are more restrictive than the symmetric errors, in almost all cases there exist no better byte *unidirectional* error correcting codes than the byte *symmetric* error correcting codes, when the number of information bytes, m, is greater than 2^{b-1}.

Theorem 4.1: Let m be the number of information bytes with b bits/byte. Then any code that corrects byte unidirectional errors needs at least $\log(m(2^b - 1) + 1) \approx b + \log(m)$ check bits.

Proof: Consider the following set of $m(2^b - 1) + 1$ information symbols.

0000		....	00	xx.....xx b bits
0000		....	yy.....yy b bits	00.....00
0000		yy.....yy b bits	00.....00	00.....00
yy.....yy b bits	00....	....	....	00

In the above, the symbols x and y stand for either 0 or 1, with $yy \ldots yy \neq \mathbf{0}$. So, $xx \ldots xx$ can be any b-bit binary vector and $yy \cdots yy$ can be any nonzero b-bit binary vector. For a code to be capable of correcting byte unidirectional errors, the check symbols for the above set of information symbols must be all distinct. Suppose the check symbols for two distinct information symbols, say $X1$ and $X2$, are the same. Let the nonzero bits of $X1$ and $X2$ be in byte i and byte j, respectively. Suppose all 1's becomes 0's in byte i of $X1$ and in byte j of $X2$. These are valid byte unidirectional errors. In these two cases the decoder gets the same word; i.e. all zero information bytes with the check byte the same as that of $X1$ ($X2$). Now the decoder cannot decide whether to decode this work to $X1$ or to $X2$. Thus the code needs at least $m(2^b - 1) + 1$ check symbols; i.e. the number of check bits must be at least $\log(m(2^b - 1) + 1) \approx b + \log(m)$ check bits. □

The proposed byte unidirectional error correcting codes require approximately $b + \log(m) + 1$ check bits, and thus they are close to optimal.

V. BYTE ASYMMETRIC ERROR CORRRECTING CODES

In the case of asymmetric errors only one type of error, say $0 \rightarrow 1$ errors, can occur in the system, and the type of errors is known *a priori*. The code described in the previous section can also be used to correct byte asymmetric errors, but for a given check base the number of allowable information bytes can be doubled; i.e. if the check base is a prime p, then the number of information bytes can be up to $p - 1$. This can be seen from the following discussions.

If t asymmetric $(0 \rightarrow 0)$ errors occur in byte j then the syndrome S_2 should not be equal to 0; i.e.

$$S_2 = tj \pmod{p} \neq 0 \qquad \text{for } j = 1, 2, \cdots, (p-1).$$

Since p is prime and $t < p$, it is easy to verify this condition.

In addition, the syndromes corresponding to t errors in different bytes i and j must be distinct; i.e.

$$ti \neq tj (\bmod p) \qquad i, j = 1, 2, \cdots, (p-1).$$

Since p is a prime and $t < p$, this condition is equivalent to $i \neq j (\bmod p)$ for $i \neq j, i, j = 1, 2, \cdots, (p-1)$ and $t \leq b$, and this condition is obviously true.

The encoding/decoding algorithms discussed in the previous section can be easily modified so that they can be applied to asymmetric codes.

Next we consider the optimality of the codes. Suppose the number of information bytes is m. Then it is easy to prove that any byte asymmetric error correcting code needs at least $\log\left(m(2^b-1)+1\right)$ check bits. The proof of this statement is the same as the one given in Theorem 4.1. As we mentioned before, if the check base of the ARC is p, then the number of information bytes can be up to $p-1$. Thus we need at least $\log((p-1)(2^b-1)+1) \approx b + \log(p)$ check bits for this code. Since the code uses exactly this many check bits the code is optimal.

VI. Comparison of Byte UEC Codes with Byte Symmetric EC Codes

The following theorem gives a lower bound on the number of check bits for byte symmetric error correcting codes. This bound is useful in comparing the byte symmetric and unidirectional error correcting codes.

Theorem 6.1: Any byte symmetric error correcting code with $m > 1$ needs at least $2b$ check bits.

Proof: Consider the following set of 2^{2b} information symbols.

$$000\ldots.00 \qquad \underbrace{xx\ldots xx}_{b \text{ bits}} \qquad \underbrace{xx\ldots xx}_{b \text{ bits}}$$

Here x can be 0 or 1. For a code to be capable of correcting byte symmetric errors, the checks for this set of information symbols must be all distinct. Suppose that for two information symbols, X and Y, the checks are equal. Let

$$X = 000\ldots. \qquad x_b x_{b-1} \cdots x_1 \qquad w_b w_{b-1} \cdots w_1$$
$$Y = 000\ldots. \qquad y_b y_{b-1} \cdots y_1 \qquad z_b z_{b-1} \cdots z_1$$

Suppose the decoder receives a word with the check part the same as that of X and Y and the information part the same as Z, where

$$Z = 000\ldots. \qquad x_b x_{b-1} \cdots x_1 \qquad z_b z_{b-1} \cdots z_1$$

Note that Z can be obtained from X due to symmetric errors in the first byte or from Y due to symmetric errors in the second byte. Thus the decoder can not decide whether to decode the received word, Z, to X or to Y. Therefore the code must have at least 2^{2b} distinct check symbols; i.e. the code needs at least $2b$ check bits. □

First we compare the unidirectional and asymmetric codes by taking an 8 bits/byte arrangement and then consider the general case. From the above theorem we know that any byte symmetric error correcting code needs at least $2b$ check bits. Thus in the case of 8 bits/byte, any byte symmetric error correcting code needs at least 16 check bits. Now the largest 7 bit prime is 127, and thus if we take 127 as the check base for ARC, the byte unidirectional code described here can have up to 63 information bytes. Thus, for the 8 bit/byte arrangement when the number of information bytes is less than or equal to 63, unidirectional codes need fewer check bits than byte symmetric error correcting codes. In particular, as shown in Table I, using $3, 4, 5, 6,$ and 7 check bits for ARC (and thus using $11, 12, 13, 14,$ and 15 total check bits), we can have byte unidirectional error correcting codes. For these cases byte symmetric error correcting codes need at least 16 check bits.

However, when the number of information bytes, m, is in the range $128 < m < 255$, Theorem 4.1 shows that any byte unidirectional error correcting code needs at least 16 check bits. But the Hong–Patel byte symmetric error correcting code uses exactly 16 check bits for this range of information bytes. Furthermore, when m is in the range $256 < m < 511$, Theorem 4.1 gives a lower bound of 17 check bits for any byte unidirectional error correcting code, and the Hong–Patel codes use exactly 17 check bits to correct byte symmetric errors. We can extend the above argument and show that, for $m > 128$, in almost all cases there exist no better unidirectional byte error correcting codes than the byte symmetric error correcting codes.

In general, when the number of information bytes is less than or equal to $(p-1)/2$, where p is the largest prime less than 2^b, the byte unidirectional codes described here are better than any byte symmetric error correcting codes. On the other hand, when $m > 2^{b-1}$, Theorem 4.1 says that at least $b + \log(m)$ check bits are needed to correct byte unidirectional errors. However, for these numbers of information bytes, the Hong–Patel codes [8] use exactly this many check bits to correct byte symmetric errors. Thus, when $m > 2^{b-1}$, in almost all cases there exist no better byte unidirectional codes than byte symmetric error correcting codes, and the Hong–Patel codes are close to optimal even for byte unidirectional error correction.

VII. Double Byte Unidirectional Error Detecting Codes

The byte unidirectional error model considered here is the same as the one assumed in [5], i.e.

1) A single byte can be in error and all the errors in this erroneous byte is of the same type.
2) Two bytes can be in error in which case
   a) error in both bytes are of $1 \rightarrow 0$ type,
   b) errors in both bytes are of $0 \rightarrow 1$ type, or
   c) errors in one byte are of $1 \rightarrow 0$ type and the other are $0 \rightarrow 1$ type.

In the case of symmetric error any double byte error detecting code needs at least $\max\{2b, b + \log(m)\}$ check bits as shown in Lemmas 7.1 and 7.2. However the double byte unidirectional error detecting codes described here need only $1 + \log(bm)$ check bits and so are better.

Lemma 7.1: Any double byte symmetric error detecting code needs at least $2b$ check bits.

Proof: Consider the set of information symbols given in the proof of Theorem 6.1. For these 2^{2b} information symbols, the checks must all be distinct. If any two words X and Y in that set have the same check symbol U, then due to single or double byte errors, the transmitted word XU can be received as YU. Thus the code needs at least $\log(2^{2b}) = 2b$ check bits. □

Lemma 7.2: The number of check bits required for any double byte symmetric error detecting code is at least $\log(m(2^b-1)+1)$ which is approximately equal to $b + \log(m)$.

Proof: We can take the set of information symbols given in the proof of Theorem 4.1 and show that the checks must all be distinct. □

The double byte error detecting code designed here consists of two arithmetic checks, ARC1 and ARC2, with different check bases.

ARC1 is obtained as follows:

$$\text{ARC1} \equiv -\sum_{i=1}^{m} N_i (\text{mod } 2b+1) \qquad \text{(7-1)}$$

where N_i is the number of 1's in information byte i. Let p_1 be the smallest prime such that $p_1 > \max(b, m)$. The check base for ARC2 is the largest prime p that can be represented with $\log(p_1)$ bits. The ARC2 value is obtained as

$$\text{ARC2} \equiv -\sum_{i=1}^{m} (iN_i) \bmod p. \qquad \text{(7-2)}$$

Example 7.1: In example 2.1, the number of information bytes $m = 6$ and $b = 8$. The check base for ARC1 is $2b + 1 = 17$. The smallest prime $p_1 > \max(b, m) = 8$ is 11 which needs 4 bits in binary representation. Thus the check base ARC2 is the largest 4 bit prime which is 13. Since the number of 1's in the information bytes is 25 the value of ARC1 is $-25 \bmod 17 \equiv 9 \bmod 17$. So ARC1 = 01001. ARC2, as calculated in example 2.1, is equal to 0100. □

At the received end two syndromes S_1 and S_2 are computed as follows.

$$S_1 \equiv \left(\text{ARC1}' + \sum_{i=1}^{m} N_i'\right) \text{mod}(2b+1) \qquad \text{(7-3)}$$

$$S_2 \equiv \left(\text{ARC2}' + \sum_{i=1}^{m} iN_i'\right) \bmod p \qquad \text{(7-4)}$$

where ARC1$'$ and ARC2$'$ are the received arithmetic checks and N_i' is the number of 1's in the received information byte i.

In order to show that the code is capable of detecting single or double byte unidirectional errors, we need to prove that $S_1 \not\equiv 0$ or $S_2 \not\equiv 0$ when there are such errors. To show this, consider the following cases:

Case 1 (single byte error): Suppose t errors occur in some information byte i, then $S_1 \equiv \pm t \not\equiv 0 \text{ mod}(2b+1)$. If the errors are in ARC1, then again $S_1 \not\equiv 0$ and if the errors are in ARC2 then $S_2 \not\equiv 0$. (If the value of the received ARC1 or ARC2 is greater than the corresponding check base we assume that the check is in error.)

Case 2 (Double byte errors):

a) Both ARC1 and ARC2 in error: It is easy to see that both $S_1 \not\equiv 0$ and $S_2 \not\equiv 0$.

b) ARC1 and one of the information bytes, say byte i, in error: Let the number of errors in information byte i be t. Then $S_2 \equiv \pm ti \bmod p \neq 0$ since $t < p$ and $i < p$.

c) ARC2 and one of the information bytes, say i, in error: Again, let the number of errors in byte i be t. Then $S_1 \equiv \pm t \bmod (2b+1)$.

d) Two information bytes say i and j are in error: Let the number of errors in byte i be t_1, and the byte j be t_2. Suppose the errors are of the same type. Then $S_1 \equiv \pm(t_1 + t_2) \text{ mod}(2b+1) \not\equiv 0$ since $t_1 + t_2 < (2b+1)$. On the other hand, assume that the errors are of different types. If $t_1 \neq t_2$ then $S_1 \equiv \pm(t_1 - t_2) \not\equiv 0 \bmod (2b+1)$. If $t_1 = t_2$ then $S_2 \equiv \pm t_1(i-j) \not\equiv 0 \bmod p$ because $t_1 < p, |i-j| < p$ and p is a prime.

Note: When b is a power of 2, the check base of ARC1 can be taken as $2b$ and that of ARC2 as p, where p is the largest $\log(p_1)$ bit prime where p_1 is the smallest prime such that $p_1 > \max(2m, b)$. In some cases this code is slightly better.

The code described above needs $\log(2b+1) + \log(p)$ which is approximately equal $1 + \log(mb) = 1 + \log(k)$ check bits. The following lower bound theorem shows that the code is close to optimal.

Theorem 7.3: Any double byte unidirectional error detecting code with m information bytes and b-its per byte, needs at least $\max\left(\log(mb+1), \log(b+1)^2\right)$ check bits.

Proof: Let the set D of b elements be $\{00\cdots001, 00\cdots011, 00\cdots111, \cdots, 11\cdots111\}$. And let $S_i = \{x_m \cdots x_2 x_1 | x_i \in D$ and $xj = 00\cdots000$ for $j \neq i\}$; S_0 contains one element (the all zero vector). Let $S = S_0 \cup S_1 \cup S_1 \cdots \cup S_m$. Now, S has $mb+1$ elements as shown below.

Byte m		Byte 2	Byte 1
00 00	. . . .	00 00	00 000
00 00	. . . .	00 00	00 001
00 00	. . . .	00 00	00 011
00 00	. . . .	00 00	00 111
⋮			
00 00	. . . .	00 00	11 111
00 00	. . . .	00 01	00 00
00 00	. . . .	00 11	00 00
⋮			
00 00	. . . .	11 111	00 00
00 01	000	00 00	00 00
00 11	000	00 00	00 00
⋮			
11 111	000	00 00	00 00

For a code to be capable of detecting double byte unidirectional errors, the check symbols of these $mb+1$ information words must be all distinct.

Similarly, the check symbols of the set

$$T = \{x_m \cdots x_2 x_1 | x_1, x_2 \in D \cup 00\cdots000 \text{ and } x_i = 00\cdots000 \text{ for } i > 2\}$$

of $(b+1)^2$ information words must be all distinct. □

VIII. Conclusion

In this paper we have designed efficient byte unidirectional error correcting codes and described efficient encoding and decoding algorithms. The proposed codes require fewer check bits than the optimal byte symmetric error correcting codes and hence, when the error nature in a system is of byte unidirectional type, these codes are cost effective. We derived a lower bound on the number of check bits for byte unidirectional error correcting codes and showed that the codes designed here are most likely the only codes better than byte symmetric error correcting codes. Also we designed double byte unidirectional error detecting codes. Again, we derived a lower bound on the number of check bits for the double byte unidirectional error detecting codes and showed that these codes are close to optimal.

Acknowledgment

The authors would like to thank N. Darwish for his valuable comments and discussions.

References

[1] D. K. Pradhan and S. M. Reddy, "Fault tolerant fail safe logic networks," in *Proc. IEEE COMPCON*, San Francisco, CA, Mar. 1977, p. 363.

[2] D. K. Pradhan and J. J. Stiffler, "Error correcting codes and self-checking circuits," *IEEE Comput. Mag.*, vol. 13, no. 3, pp. 27–37, Mar. 1980.

[3] B. Bose, "Burst unidirectional error-detecting codes," *IEEE Trans. Comput.*, vol. C-35, pp. 350–353, Apr. 1986.

[4] M. Blaum, "Systematic unidirectional burst detecting codes," *IEEE Trans. Comput.*, vol. C-37, pp. 453–457, Apr. 1988.

[5] L. A. Dunning, G. Dial, and M. Varanasi, "Unidirectional 9-bit byte error detection codes for computer memory systems," in *Dig. Papers, 19th Int. Conf. Fault Tolerant Comput.*, June 1989, pp. 88–93.
[6] I. S. Reed and G. Solomon, "Polynomial codes over certain finite fields," *J. Soc. Ind. Appl. Math.*, vol. 8, pp. 300–304, June 1960.
[7] D. C. Bossen, "b-adjacent error correction," *IBM J. Res. Develop.*, vol. 14, pp. 402–408, July 1970.
[8] S. J. Hong and A. M. Patel, "A general class of maximal codes for computer applications," *IEEE Trans. Comput.*, vol. C-21, pp. 1322–1331, Dec. 1972.
[9] D. C. Bossen, L. C. Chang, and C. L. Chen, "Measurement and generation of error correcting codes for package failures," *IEEE Trans. Comput.*, vol. C-27, no. 3, pp. 201–204, Mar. 1978.
[10] S. M. Reddy, "A class of linear codes for error control in byte-per-card organized digital systems," *IEEE Trans. Comput.*, vol. C-27, no. 5, pp. 455–459, May 1978.
[11] S. Kaneda and E. Fujiwara, "Single byte error correcting double byte error detecting codes for memory systems," *IEEE Trans. Comput.*, vol. C-31, no. 7, pp. 596–602, July 1982.
[12] L. A. Dunning and M. R. Varanasi, "Code constructions for error control in byte organized memory systems," *IEEE Trans. Comput.*, vol. C-32, no. 6, pp. 535–542, June 1983.
[13] C. L. Chen, "Error correcting codes with byte error detecting capability," *IEEE Trans. Comput.*, vol. C-32, no. 7, pp. 615–621, July 1983.
[14] C. L. Chen, "Byte-oriented error-correcting codes for semiconductor memory systems," *IEEE Trans. Comput.*, vol. C-35, pp. 646–648, July 1986.
[15] S. Kaneda, "A class of odd-weight-column SEC-DED-SbED codes for memory system applications," in *Dig. Papers, 14th Int. Conf. Fault Tolerant Comput.*, June 1984, pp. 88–93.
[16] L. A. Dunning and M. A. Varanasi, "Code construction for error control in byte organized memory systems." *IEEE Trans. Comput.*, vol. C-32, pp. 535–542, June 1983.
[17] L. A. Dunning, "SEC-BED-DED for error control in byte organized memory systems," *IEEE Trans. Comput.*, vol. C-34, pp. 557–562, June 1985.
[18] T. R. N. Rao and E. Fujiwara, *Error control coding for computer systems.* Englewood Cliffs, NJ: Prentice-Hall, 1989.
[19] D. Burton, *Elementary Number Theory.* Boston, MA: Allyn and Bacon, 1976.

Multiple Unidirectional Byte Error-Correcting Codes

Yuichi Saitoh, *Student Member, IEEE*, and
Hideki Imai, *Senior Member, IEEE*

***Abstract*—Codes correcting/detecting unidirectional byte errors are investigated. It is shown that such codes have the capability of correcting combinations of bidirectional and unidirectional byte errors. This correspondence also gives code constructions. These are derived from the combination of two codes. One is a code for encoding the Hamming weights of data bytes and is used to estimate error-locations. The other is a byte-error-correcting code for error-evaluation. Moreover, we describe a decoding procedure for the codes, correcting combinations of bidirectional and unidirectional byte errors. The constructions provide many efficient codes of short length. For example, when a byte consists of 32 bits, a systematic code can be constructed with 61 information bytes and 3 check bytes that has the capability of correcting a single bidirectional byte error or double unidirectional byte errors, whereas the best known double-byte-error-correcting code requires 4 check bytes.**

***Index Terms*—Byte errors, coding/decoding, error-correction coding, error-detection coding, memory fault tolerance, unidirectional errors.**

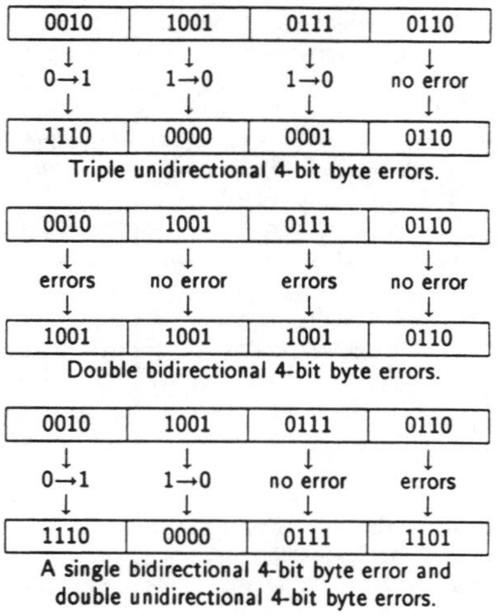

Fig. 1. Examples of unidirectional and bidirectional byte errors.

I. Introduction

In computer memories, when data are stored in a byte-per-chip or byte-per-card fashion, byte errors tend to occur. Therefore byte-error-correcting/detecting codes are useful for protection against them and have been applied in computer systems [9], [15].

The most likely faults in many computer memories and VLSI circuits cause *unidirectional errors*, for which both $1 \to 0$ and $0 \to 1$ errors may occur but they do not occur simultaneously in a single data word [12], [14], [15]. When we consider codes correcting or detecting unidirectional errors, we normally assume that a data word is equivalent to a codeword. The various types of codes for protection of data from unidirectional errors have been provided [15], and several investigations of such codes have been performed recently [1], [2], [4]–[8], [10], [15]–[20].

When both $1 \to 0$ and $0 \to 1$ errors may occur but they do not occur simultaneously in a single byte, the errors are called a *unidirectional byte error* [7], [8], which is a kind of byte error. We refer to a byte error that is not a unidirectional byte error as a bidirectional byte error. Examples of unidirectional and bidirectional byte errors are shown in Fig. 1. (When a byte consists of b bits, a byte error is also called a b-bit byte error.)

Transient and permanent faults in byte-organized computer memories are apt to cause multiple unidirectional byte errors. Because bidirectional byte errors also arise from intermittent faults in such memories, codes correcting and detecting combinations of bidirectional and unidirectional byte errors are very important for protection of byte-organized memories. However, such codes have not been found yet and therefore instead of them we use byte-error-correcting codes, typically Reed–Solomon (RS) codes, which include shortened and lengthened (also called extended) RS codes [3, pp. 220–224].

We abbreviate "t-fold-b-bit-byte-error-correcting (or -detecting)" as t-bEC (or t-bED). Also "t-fold-unidirectional-b-bit-byte-error-correcting (or -detecting)" is written as t-UbEC (or t-UbED). Bose [5] has proposed a class of 1-UbEC codes, and Dunning, Dial, and Varanasi [7], [8] have presented a construction of t-UbED codes.

This correspondence gives a necessary and sufficient condition for t-UbEC codes in terms of a newly defined distance and shows that these codes can correct all combinations of μ bidirectional byte errors and ν unidirectional byte errors for $0 \le 2\mu + \nu \le t$.

Further, we propose a construction method for systematic t-UbEC codes. This is based on the combination of two codes. One is a code for encoding the Hamming weights of data bytes and used to estimate error-locations. This encoding technique has been proposed by Dunning *et al.* [7], [8] for t-UbED codes. The other is a byte-error-correcting code for error-evaluation. We also present a decoding procedure for the t-UbEC codes that can correct all combinations of $\lfloor (t-s)/2 \rfloor$ or less bidirectional byte errors and s or less unidirectional byte errors for $0 \le s \le t$. Such construction and decoding can easily be generalized to the case of t-UbEC/$d(>t)$-UbED codes.

By our construction methods for t-UbEC and t-UbEC/d-UbED codes we obtain more efficient codes than RS codes. For example, in the case where the number of information bytes is 61, the 2-U32EC code has 3 check bytes, whereas the 2-32EC RS code requires 4 check bytes and the RS code with 3 check bytes is only a 3-32ED or 1-32EC/2-32ED code. Further, in the case where the number of information bytes is 56, the 2-U32EC/6-U32ED code has 4 check bytes, whereas the 2-32EC/6-32ED RS code requires 8 check bytes and the RS code with 4 check bytes is only a 4-32ED or 1-32EC/3-32ED or 2-32EC code.

This correspondence also gives a construction method for nonsystematic t-UbEC codes.

Manuscript received July 11, 1990; revised December 14, 1990. This work was presented in part at the meeting of Technical Group on Information Theory, IEICE, Yokohama, Japan, July 21, 1990 and at the 1990 International Symposium on Information Theory and Its Applications, Honolulu, HI, Nov. 27–30, 1990.

The authors are with the Division of Electrical and Computer Engineering, Faculty of Engineering, Yokohama National University, 156 Tokiwadai, Hodogaya-ku, Yokohama, 240 Japan.

IEEE Log Number 9142947.

0-8186-4182-7/93 $3.00 © 1991 IEEE

II. Distance and Error-Correcting Capability

Let x be a concatenation of $x_1, x_2, \cdots, x_n$, that is,

$$x = [x_1 x_2 \cdots x_n],$$

where x_i are binary b-tuples. Similarly, let

$$y = [y_1 y_2 \cdots y_n]$$

and

$$z = [z_1 z_2 \cdots z_n],$$

where y_i and z_i are binary b-tuples.

Consider that x is transmitted and y is received. Assume that a bidirectional byte error has occurred in x_i. Then y_i is in error. We can consider that x_i is turned into z_i by a unidirectional byte error and z_i is turned into y_i by a unidirectional byte error. Thus a bidirectional byte error is resolved into two unidirectional byte errors. Accordingly it may be convenient to define a distance which increases by one for the occurrence of a unidirectional byte error and by two for the occurrence of a bidirectional byte error. Hence we define the unidirectional byte distance as follows.

Definition 1: The function $N(\cdot)$ is defined as

$$N([u_1 u_2 \cdots u_b],[v_1 v_2 \cdots v_b]) = |\{i | u_i = 1 \wedge v_i = 0\}|,$$

where u_i, $v_i = 0$ or 1. Then the unidirectional byte distance $\mathscr{D}(x, y)$ is defined as

$$\mathscr{D}(x,y) = 2|\{i | N(x_i, y_i) \neq 0 \wedge N(y_i, x_i) \neq 0\}| + |\{i | x_i \neq y_i \wedge (N(x_i, y_i) = 0 \vee N(y_i, x_i) = 0)\}|.$$

Example 1: If $b = 4$ and

$$x = [0010 \quad 1001 \quad 0111 \quad 0110],$$

$$y = [1110 \quad 0000 \quad 0100 \quad 1101],$$

then $\mathscr{D}(x, y) = 5$.

It is easily seen that the unidirectional byte distance $\mathscr{D}(x, y)$ is a "metric" function that is a real-valued function satisfying

$$\mathscr{D}(x,y) > 0, \quad \text{for } x \neq y$$

$$= 0, \quad \text{for } x = y, \quad \text{(positive definiteness)}$$

$$\mathscr{D}(x,y) = \mathscr{D}(y,x), \quad \text{(symmetry)}$$

$$\mathscr{D}(x,y) + \mathscr{D}(y,z) \geq \mathscr{D}(x,z), \quad \text{(triangle inequality)}.$$

Let $\mathscr{D}_{\min}(C)$ denote the minimum unidirectional byte distance of a code C, that is,

$$\mathscr{D}_{\min}(C) = \min_{\substack{x,y \in C \\ x \neq y}} \mathscr{D}(x,y).$$

From the definition of the unidirectional byte distance, it is obvious that C is a t-UbEC code if and only if

$$\mathscr{D}_{\min}(C) \geq 2t + 1.$$

With respect to the correction of combinations of bidirectional and unidirectional byte errors, we have the following theorem.

Theorem 1: A t-UbEC code can correct all combinations of μ bidirectional byte errors and ν unidirectional byte errors for $0 \leq 2\mu + \nu \leq t$.

Proof: Let C be a t-UbEC code. Also assume that x in C is transmitted and μ bidirectional byte errors and ν unidirectional byte errors occur. Then the distance between x and the received word y is $\mathscr{D}(x, y) = 2\mu + \nu$. Consider any z in C. Then $\mathscr{D}(y, z) \geq \mathscr{D}(x, z) - \mathscr{D}(x, y) \geq 2t + 1 - t = t + 1$ if $0 \leq 2\mu + \nu \leq t$. Hence the t-UbEC code C, for which $\mathscr{D}_{\min}(C) \geq 2t + 1$, can correct those errors if $0 \leq 2\mu + \nu \leq t$. □

III. Systematic Code Construction

The code proposed here is a systematic code when it is regarded as a binary code. The check bits of the code are divided into two groups: One for estimation of error-locations and the other for error-evaluation. Hereafter, the following notations are used.

$W(x_m)$	Hamming weight of x.
$[ab \cdots]$	Concatenation of $a, b, \cdots$.
b	Number of bits per byte.
C_E	Systematic t-bED code for which no byte includes information bits and check bits simultaneously. This is also a $\lfloor (t-s)/2 \rfloor$-fold-byte-error- and s-fold-byte-erasure-correcting code for $0 \leq s \leq t$ [3, pp. 256–260].
n_E	Number of bytes per codeword of C_E.
k_E	Number of information bytes of C_E.
r_E	Number of check bytes of C_E, that is, $r_E = n_E - k_E$.
C_L	$q(>b)$-ary systematic code having n_E information symbols and correcting up to t errors. This can also be used as a $(t-\epsilon)$-fold-error- and 2ϵ-fold-erasure-correcting code for $0 \leq \epsilon \leq t$ [3, pp. 256–260].
r_L	Number of check symbols of C_L.
C_D	Binary *all-unidirectional-error-detecting* (AUED) code [15, pp. 357–360] with at least q codewords.
l	Length of C_D. We assume $l < b$.

The encoding procedure of the proposed code is sketched as follows: Information bytes are encoded into a codeword y of C_E. Letting the Hamming weights of all bytes in y be the information symbols of C_L, we calculate the r_L check symbols of C_L. We then regard each check symbol as a binary word and encode each word into an l-tuple codeword of C_D. Finally, in order that two or more check symbols may not be lost by a single byte error, each binary l-tuple is buried in the distinct information byte of y. For this purpose we have to reserve l bits in each of r_L information bytes.

The construction of the code is precisely described as follows. A codeword of C_E is represented by

$$[x_1 x_2 \cdots x_{k_E} x_{k_E+1} \cdots x_{n_E}].$$

The symbols x_i for all i are binary b-tuples such as

$$x_i = [x_1^{(i)} x_2^{(i)} \cdots x_b^{(i)}],$$

where $x_j^{(i)} = 0$ or 1 for all j. We use $x_1, \cdots, x_{k_E}$ as information bytes and $x_{k_E+1}, \cdots, x_{n_E}$ as check bytes, but we do not use the first l bits of x_i for $i = 1, 2, \cdots, r_L$. We set $x_j^{(i)} = 0$ for $i = 1, 2, \cdots, r_L$ and $j = 1, 2, \cdots, l$, initially. Let

$$z_i = [x_{l+1}^{(i)} x_{l+2}^{(i)} \cdots x_b^{(i)}], \quad \text{for } i = 1, 2, \cdots, r_L.$$

Then

$$x_i = [0_l z_i], \quad \text{for } i = 1, 2, \cdots, r_L,$$

where 0_l denotes the concatenation of l 0's.

A codeword of C_L is denoted by

$$[u_1 u_2 \cdots u_{n_E} v_1 v_2 \cdots v_{r_L}],$$

where u_i for $i = 1, 2, \cdots, n_E$ and v_j for $j = 1, 2, \cdots, r_L$ are information and check symbols, respectively, and all of them are symbols from $\{0, 1, 2, \cdots, q-1\}$.

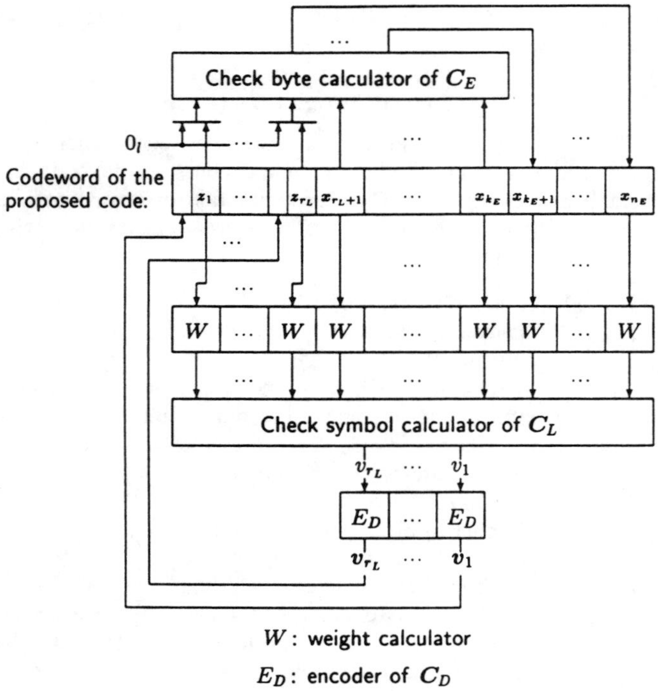

Fig. 2. Encoding of systematic t-UbEC code.

The encoding of the code is performed as follows.

1) Encode $k_E \cdot b - r_L \cdot l$ information bits into $[\boldsymbol{x}_1 \cdots \boldsymbol{x}_{k_E}]$.
2) Calculate check bytes $[\boldsymbol{x}_{k_E+1} \cdots \boldsymbol{x}_{n_E}]$ from $[\boldsymbol{x}_1 \cdots \boldsymbol{x}_{k_E}]$ using $\boldsymbol{C}_E$.
3) Let $u_i = W(\boldsymbol{x}_i)$ for all i.
4) Calculate check symbols $[v_1 \cdots v_{r_L}]$ from $[u_1 \cdots u_{n_E}]$ using C_L.
5) Encode v_i into a codeword $\boldsymbol{v}_i$ of C_D for all i.
6) Let $\boldsymbol{x}_i' = [\boldsymbol{v}_i \boldsymbol{z}_i]$, for $i = 1, 2, \cdots, r_L$. Finally, let the encoded result be

$$[\boldsymbol{x}_1' \boldsymbol{x}_2' \cdots \boldsymbol{x}_{r_L}' \boldsymbol{x}_{r_L+1} \cdots \boldsymbol{x}_{k_E} \boldsymbol{x}_{k_E+1} \cdots \boldsymbol{x}_{n_E}].$$

The encoding procedure is depicted in Fig. 2.

The code has $k_E \cdot b - r_L \cdot l$ information bits and $r_E \cdot b + r_L \cdot l$ check bits. If $r_L \cdot l = m \cdot b$ for an integer m, then the code has $k_E - m$ information bytes and $r_E + m$ check bytes.

The parts of the received word corresponding to $\boldsymbol{x}_i$ for $i = r_L + 1, \cdots, n_E$ and $\boldsymbol{z}_i$ and $\boldsymbol{v}_i$ for $i = 1, \cdots, r_L$ are denoted hereafter by $\bar{\boldsymbol{x}}_i$, $\bar{\boldsymbol{z}}_i$, and $\bar{\boldsymbol{v}}_i$, respectively. Also let $\bar{\boldsymbol{x}}_i = [0_l \bar{\boldsymbol{z}}_i]$ for $i = 1, \cdots, r_L$ and $\bar{u}_i = W(\bar{\boldsymbol{x}}_i)$ for $i = 1, \cdots, n_E$. Furthermore, if no error is detected by the AUED decoding for C_D, then we denote the decoded result of $\bar{\boldsymbol{v}}_i$ by $\bar{v}_i$; otherwise we define $\bar{v}_i$ as an erasure.

Theorem 2: The code encoded by the preceding procedure is a t-UbEC code.

Proof: Suppose that $\sigma(\leq t)$ unidirectional byte errors have occurred and that ϵ unidirectional byte errors are detected at $\bar{\boldsymbol{v}}_i$ of $\bar{\boldsymbol{x}}_i'$. Clearly, $0 \leq \epsilon \leq \sigma$. We know the number ϵ and the locations of erroneous $\bar{\boldsymbol{v}}_i$ from the AUED decoding for C_D. If errors are detected at $\bar{\boldsymbol{v}}_i$, then $\bar{\boldsymbol{x}}_i$ and $\bar{u}_i$ are possibly in error, and we set these $\bar{u}_i$ and $\bar{v}_i$ as erasures. Then the number of the erasures is 2ϵ. Because $u_i \neq \bar{u}_i$ for any unidirectional byte error in $\bar{\boldsymbol{x}}_i$, the number of the other erroneous $\bar{u}_i$ is $\sigma - \epsilon$. Then we can obtain the locations of all erroneous $\bar{u}_i$ from the $(t-\epsilon)$-fold-error- and 2ϵ-fold-erasure-correction decoding for $\boldsymbol{C}_L$ because $\sigma - \epsilon \leq t - \epsilon$. If $\bar{u}_i$ is in error, then the ith byte is in error. Hence considering these erroneous bytes as byte erasures, we can correct all of the σ unidirectional byte errors by σ-fold-byte-erasure-correction decoding for $\boldsymbol{C}_E$ because $\sigma \leq t$. □

Combining Theorems 1 and 2, we have the following corollary.

Corollary 1: The code encoded by the preceding procedure can correct all combinations of $\lfloor (t-s)/2 \rfloor$ or less bidirectional b-bit byte errors and s or less unidirectional b-bit byte errors for $0 \leq s \leq t$.

The code can be decoded as follows.

1) Decode $\bar{\boldsymbol{v}}_i$ using $\boldsymbol{C}_D$ and let $\bar{v}_i(\in \{0, 1, \cdots, q-1\})$ be the decoded result for all i. If errors are detected in $\bar{\boldsymbol{v}}_i$, then set $\bar{v}_i$ as an erasure and $\bar{\boldsymbol{x}}_i$ as a byte erasure. Let the number of the byte erasures be ϵ. If $\epsilon = t$, then set $s = t$ and go to Step 4); otherwise go to the next step.
2) Calculate $\bar{u}_i = W(\bar{\boldsymbol{x}}_i)$ for all i.
3) Decode $[\bar{u}_1 \cdots \bar{u}_{n_E} \bar{v}_1 \cdots \bar{v}_{r_L}]$ by the $(t-\epsilon)$-fold-error- and 2ϵ-fold-erasure-correction decoding for $\boldsymbol{C}_L$. From the result, find locations of errors in $[\bar{u}_1 \cdots \bar{u}_{n_E}]$. If $\bar{u}_i$ is in error, then set $\bar{\boldsymbol{x}}_i$ as a byte erasure. Let s be the number of the byte erasures.
4) Decode $[\bar{\boldsymbol{x}}_1 \bar{\boldsymbol{x}}_2 \cdots \bar{\boldsymbol{x}}_{n_E}]$ by the $\lfloor (t-s)/2 \rfloor$-fold-byte-error- and s-fold-byte-erasure-correction decoding for $\boldsymbol{C}_E$.

Theorem 3: The code from the proposed construction can correct all combinations of $\lfloor (t-s)/2 \rfloor$ or less bidirectional b-bit byte errors and s or less unidirectional b-bit byte errors for $0 \leq s \leq t$ by the preceding decoding procedure.

Proof: The following notations are used in this proof.

τ_1: Number of bidirectional byte errors that cause $u_i = \bar{u}_i$.
τ_2: Number of bidirectional byte errors that cause $u_i \neq \bar{u}_i$.
σ: Number of unidirectional byte errors.

Assume that $0 \leq 2(\tau_1 + \tau_2) + \sigma \leq t$. We know all or a part of the locations of erroneous $\bar{\boldsymbol{v}}_i$ from Step 1) of the decoding procedure. The number of such locations is ϵ. Clearly, $\epsilon \leq \tau_1 + \tau_2 + \sigma \leq 2(\tau_1 + \tau_2) + \sigma \leq t$. If $\epsilon = t$, then we obtain all the locations of the erroneous bytes. Hence we go to Step 4) and can correct the errors. If $\epsilon < t$, then we should perform Steps 2) and 3). In this case, there are $\tau_1 + \tau_2 + \sigma - \epsilon$ byte errors whose locations are unknown. Since $\tau_1 + \tau_2 + \sigma - \epsilon \leq t - \epsilon$, we know the locations of $\tau_2 + \sigma$ byte errors by the $(t-\epsilon)$-fold-error- and 2ϵ-fold-erasure-correction decoding for C_L. Then setting $s = \tau_2 + \sigma$, we can correct all the errors by Step 4) because

$$\tau_1 \leq \left\lfloor \frac{t - 2\tau_2 - \sigma}{2} \right\rfloor \leq \left\lfloor \frac{t-s}{2} \right\rfloor. \qquad \square$$

Similarly, we can construct and decode t-UbEC/d-UbED codes if $\boldsymbol{C}_L$ is a q-ary systematic code of n_E information symbols that corrects t or less errors and detects d or less uncorrectable errors.

It should be mentioned that for the unidirectional-byte-error-correction decoding we need to use only byte-erasure-correction in Step 4) of the decoding algorithm.

Example 2: Let us construct an 8-UbEC code. Correctable errors of this code are shown in Table I. Suppose that $b = 32$ and $q = 251$. Let C_D be an $(l/2)$-out-of-l code [15, p. 358]. Then

TABLE I
CORRECTABLE ERRORS OF AN 8-UbEC CODE

Number of Bidirectional Byte Errors	Number of Unidirectional Byte Errors
0	≤ 8
1	≤ 6
2	≤ 4
3	≤ 2
4	0

TABLE II
PARAMETERS OF t-UbEC CODES

b	l	q	t	k	r	r_{RS}
16	6	19	4	5	7	8
24	8	67	3	4–57	5	6
			6	8–46	10	12
24	10	251	6	7–229	11	12
32	8	67	2	3–61	3	4
			4	6–54	6	8
			6	9–47	9	12
			8	12–40	12	16
32	10	251	8	11–223	13	16
32	12	919	4	5–905	7	8
			8	10–890	14	16
64	8	67	4	7–55	5	8
			8	14–42	10	16
64	12	919	8	13–893	11	16
64	16	12853	2	3–12847	3	4
			4	6–12840	6	8
			6	9–12833	9	12
			8	12–12826	12	16

we must have $l = 10$ from

$$\binom{l}{l/2} \ge q = 251.$$

Let C_L be a (252, 236) RS code over the Galois field GF(251) and let C_E be a (236, 228) RS code over GF(2^{32}). Then the code constructed here has

$$\frac{1}{32}(228\cdot 32 - 16\cdot 10) = 223$$

information bytes and

$$\frac{1}{32}(8\cdot 32 + 16\cdot 10) = 13$$

check bytes, whereas the 8-32EC RS code having 223 information bytes requires 16 check bytes. Also the 4-32EC RS code of the same number of information bytes and check bytes is not capable of correcting eight-fold unidirectional byte errors although it has the capability of detecting nine or less byte errors.

It should be noted that the code obtained by interleaving a (236, 228) RS code over GF(256) four times can also be used as C_E. This code has simpler implementation than the code over GF(2^{32}).

IV. COMPARISON

Tables II and III show the comparison of the codes constructured by the method of the previous section and RS codes. The symbols b, l, and q are defined as before. The symbols k and r denote the number of information bytes and that of check bytes, respectively. Thus they satisfy $k\cdot b = k_E \cdot b - r_L \cdot l$ and $r \cdot b = r_E \cdot b + r_L \cdot l$. The symbol r_{RS} represents the number of check bytes of t-bEC or t-bEC/d-bED RS codes having k information

TABLE III
PARAMETERS OF t-UbEC/d-UbED CODES

b	l	g	t	d	k	r	r_{RS}
8	6	19	1	7	2–5	7	8
16	6	19	1	7	5–8	4	8
			2	6	5–7	5	8
			3	5	5–6	6	8
16	8	67	1	3	2–61	3	4
			1	5	3–58	4	6
			2	4	3–57	5	6
			1	7	4–55	5	8
			2	6	4–54	6	8
			3	5	4–53	7	8
16	10	251	1	7	3–238	6	8
			2	6	3–237	7	8
32	8	67	1	3	3–62	2	4
			1	7	6–57	3	8
			2	6	6–56	4	8
			3	5	6–55	5	8
32	12	919	1	7	5–908	4	8
			2	6	5–907	5	8
			3	5	5–906	6	8

bytes. RS codes are used as C_E and C_L, and $(l/2)$-out-of-l codes are used as C_D. Then

$$k_E \le q + 1 - 3t,$$
$$r_E = t,$$
$$r_L = 2t,$$
$$r = t + \frac{2tl}{b},$$

for the t-UbEC codes and

$$k_E \le q + 1 - 2t - d,$$
$$r_E = t,$$
$$r_L = t + d,$$
$$r = t + \frac{(t+d)l}{b},$$

for the t-UbEC/d-UbED codes. We remark that the RS code over GF(2^b) may be used as C_E, but the implementation is simplified if we use the code obtained by interleaving the RS code over GF($2^{b/i}$) i times, where i is a divisor of b, as mentioned in Example 2. All the proposed codes in Tables II and III are superior to t-bEC or t-bEC/d-bED RS codes.

When RS codes are used as C_E and C_L, the t-UbEC code satisfying

$$2t\left(1 - \frac{l}{b}\right) \le k \le q + 1 - 3t - \frac{2tl}{b}$$

and

$$l \le \frac{1}{2} b$$

is more efficient than the t-bEC RS code. In that case the rate R of the t-UbEC code is given by

$$R = 1 - \frac{t}{k+r}\left(1 + \frac{2l}{b}\right).$$

In addition, if

$$(t+d)\left(1 - \frac{l}{b}\right) \le k \le q + 1 - 2t - d - \frac{(t+d)l}{b}$$

and

$$l \le \frac{d}{t+d} b,$$

then the t-UbEC/d-UbED code is more efficient than the t-bEC/d-bED RS code. In that case the rate R of the t-UbEC/d-UbED code is

$$R = 1 - \frac{1}{k+r}\left\{t + \frac{(t+d)l}{b}\right\}.$$

H. van Tilborg and M. Blaum [19] have presented a construction method for a class of binary t-fold-error-correcting codes, which is called the TB code here. The TB code is obtained by considering $\binom{b}{\lfloor b/2 \rfloor}$ codewords in a $\lfloor b/2 \rfloor$-out-of-b code as symbols in an alphabet and constructing a t-fold-error-detecting code over that alphabet. Although it is not mentioned in [19], the TB code is a nonsystematic t-UbEC code. The TB code of short length is sometimes more efficient than the proposed code. For example, in the case where the code length is 12 bytes and the RS code is used as the t-fold-error-detecting code, the rate of the 4-U16EC TB code is 0.569, whereas that of the proposed 4-U16EC code is 0.417 as shown in Table II. It is easily proved, however, that the TB code is more redundant when the length is long. For instance, in the case where the length is 64 bytes, the rate of the 2-U32EC TB code is 0.883, whereas that of the proposed 2-U32EC code is 0.953.

V. Nonsystematic Code Construction

In this section, we present a construction of nonsystematic t-UbEC codes. The notations are taken from the previous sections except the following symbols.

- C_E (Systematic or nonsystematic) t-bED code.
- n Number of bytes per codeword of C_E.
- M_E Number of codewords in C_E.
- C_L $q(>b)$-ary (systematic or nonsystematic) code of length n and correcting up to t errors.
- M_L Number of codewords in C_L.

The following theorem can be proved in a similar way to Theorem 2.

Theorem 4:

$$\{[x_1 x_2 \cdots x_n] \mid [x_1 x_2 \cdots x_n] \in C_E, \\ [W(x_1)W(x_2)\cdots W(x_n)] \in C_L\}$$

is a t-UbEC code.

This result is easily generalized to t-UbEC/d-UbED codes.

We say that two codes of length N over an alphabet Q are equivalent if one is an image of the other by a bijection from Q^N to Q^N. Clearly, if two codes are equivalent, then one has the same error-correcting capability as the other for ordinary errors. Let C_E' and C_L' be arbitrary equivalent codes of C_E and C_L, respectively. Then it is easily shown that the average number of the codewords in

$$\{[x_1 x_2 \cdots x_n] \mid [x_1 x_2 \cdots x_n] \in C_E', \\ [W(x_1)W(x_2)\cdots W(x_n)] \in C_L'\}$$

is

$$\frac{M_L}{q^n} M_E.$$

This leads to the following theorem.

Theorem 5: Assume that there exist a t-bED code of length n bytes having M_E codewords and a t-fold-error-correcting $q(>b)$-ary code of length n having M_L codewords. Then there exists a code of Theorem 4 such that the number of codewords M satisfies

$$M \ge \frac{M_L}{q^n} M_E.$$

Consider the case where equivalent codes of RS codes are used as C_E and C_L. Then $n \le q+1$ and

$$M \ge \frac{2^{(n-t)b}}{q^{2t}}.$$

Then the rate R_N of the code satisfies

$$R_N = \frac{\log_{2^b} M}{n} \ge 1 - \frac{t}{n}(1 + 2\log_{2^b} q).$$

If $n = k + r \le q + 1 - 2t$, then the rate R_S of the systematic code of Section III satisfies

$$R_S = 1 - \frac{t}{n}\left(1 + \frac{2l}{b}\right) < 1 - \frac{t}{n}\left(1 + \frac{2\log_2 q}{b}\right) \le R_N,$$

and therefore the code of this section is more efficient than the code of Section III of the same length. For example, in the case where $q = 67$ and $n = 64$, the rate of the 2-U32EC code of this section is at least 0.957, whereas that of the code of Section III having the same error-correcting capability is 0.953 as exhibited in Table II.

In general, the following theorem can be proved.

Theorem 6: There exists a code of Theorem 4 of which the rate R_N satisfies

$$R_N > R_S,$$

for the rate R_S of the code of Section III of the same length having the same error-correcting/detecting capability.

Proof: Here C_E and C_L for the coce of Section III and those for the code of Theorem 4 are represented by C_{ES}, C_{LS}, C_{EN}, and C_{LN}, respectively. Assume that

$$k_E' = \log_{2^b} M_E$$

and

$$r_L' = \log_q \frac{q^n}{M_L}.$$

From Theorem 5, R_N satisfies

$$R_N \ge R_N' = \frac{1}{n}\log_{2^b}\frac{M_L}{q^n}M_E = \frac{1}{n}\left(\log_{2^b} M_E - \log_{2^b}\frac{q^n}{M_L}\right) = \frac{1}{n}\left(k_E' - \frac{\log_2 q}{b} r_L'\right).$$

In order to prove this theorem, we only need to show that $R_N > R_S$ in the case where $C_{ES} = C_{EN}$ and C_{LN} is the shortened code of C_{LS}. In such a case, $k_E' = k_E$ and $r_L' = r_L$. Therefore $R_S < R'_N \leq R_N$ because

$$R_S = \frac{1}{n}\left(k_E - \frac{l}{b} r_L\right)$$

and $l > \log_2 q$. Hence by Theorem 4 we can construct the code for which $R_N > R_S$ for any C_{ES} and any C_{LS}. □

VI. Conclusion

This correspondence has given a necessary and sufficient condition for t-UbEC codes using the unidirectional byte distance and has shown that these codes can correct all combinations of μ bidirectional byte errors and ν unidirectional byte errors for $0 \leq 2\mu + \nu \leq t$. Further, we have proposed the construction of systematic t-UbEC codes, and we have shown that, in the case where b is large, these codes are more efficient than RS codes. We have also presented their encoding and decoding procedures. Moreover, this correspondence has given the nonsystematic code construction of such codes, and we have proved that these codes are more efficient than the systematic codes.

References

[1] S. Al-Bassam and B. Bose, "On balanced codes," *IEEE Trans. Inform. Theory*, vol. 36, no. 2, pp. 406–408, Mar. 1990.

[2] ——, "Asymmetric/unidirectional error correcting and detecting codes," presented at *7th Int. Conf. Applied Algebra, Algebraic Algorithms and Error-Correcting Codes*, Toulouse, France, June 1989.

[3] R. E. Blahut, *Theory and Practice of Error Control Codes*. Reading, MA: Addison-Wesley, May 1984.

[4] F. J. H. Böinck and H. C. A. van Tilborg, "Constructions and bounds for systematic tEC/AUED codes," *IEEE Trans. Inform. Theory*, vol. 36, no. 6, pp. 1381–1390, Nov. 1990.

[5] B. Bose, "Byte unidirectional error-correcting codes," in *Dig. Papers 19th Int. Symp. Fault-Tolerant Comput.*, Chicago, IL, June 1989, pp. 222–228.

[6] J. Bruck and M. Blaum, "New techniques for constructing EC/AUED codes," IBM Research Report, RJ6818 (65352), Oct. 1989.

[7] L. A. Dunning, G. Dial, and M. R. Varanasi, "Unidirectional byte error-detecting codes for computer memory systems," *IEEE Trans. Comput.*, vol. 39, pp. 592–595, Apr. 1990.

[8] ——, "Unidirectional 9-bit byte error-detecting codes for computer memory systems," in *Dig. Papers 19th Int. Symp. Fault-Tolerant Comput.*, Chicago, IL, June 1989, pp. 216–221.

[9] H. Imai, Ed., *Essentials of Error-Control Coding Techniques*. San Diego, CA: Academic Press, Apr. 1990.

[10] D. E. Knuth, "Efficient balanced codes," *IEEE Trans. Inform. Theory*, vol. IT-32, no. 1, pp. 51–53, Jan. 1986.

[11] F. J. MacWilliams and N. J. A. Sloane, *The Theory of Error-Correcting Codes*. Amsterdam, The Netherlands: North-Holland, 1977.

[12] B. Parhami and A. Avižienis, "Detection of storage errors in mass memories using low-cost arithmetic error codes," *IEEE Trans. Comput.*, vol. C-27, pp. 302–308, Apr. 1978.

[13] W. W. Peterson and E. J. Weldon, Jr., *Error-Correcting Codes*, 2nd. ed. Cambridge, MA: MIT Press, 1972.

[14] D. K. Pradhan and J. J. Stiffler, "Error-correcting codes and self-checking circuits," *IEEE Comput.*, vol. 13, no. 3, pp. 27–37, Mar. 1980.

[15] T. R. N. Rao and E. Fujiwara, *Error-Control Coding for Computer Systems*. London, UK: Prentice Hall Int., 1989.

[16] T. V. Ramabadran, "A coding scheme for m-out-of-n codes," *IEEE Trans. Commun.*, vol. 38, pp. 1156–1163, Aug. 1990.

[17] Y. Saitoh and H. Imai, "Andrew's t-EC/AUED codes," *Electron. Lett.*, vol. 25, no. 15, pp. 949–950, July 1989.

[18] Y. Saitoh, "Design of asymmetric or unidirectional error control codes," Master's thesis, Division of Elect. and Comput. Eng., Faculty of Eng., Yokohama National Univ., Yokohama, Japan, Feb. 1990.

[19] H. van Tilborg and M. Blaum, "On error-correcting balanced codes," *IEEE Trans. Inform. Theory*, vol. 35, no. 5, pp. 1091–1095, Sept. 1989.

[20] J. H. Weber, "Bounds and constructions for binary block codes correcting asymmetric or unidirectional errors," Ph.D. dissertation, Delft Univ. of Technology, Delft, The Netherlands, Nov. 1989.

REFERENCES

1. R.E. Blahut, *Theory and Practice of Error Control Codes,* Addison-Wesley, Reading, Mass., 1983.

2. S. Lin and D.J. Costello, *Error Control Coding: Fundamentals and Applications,* Prentice-Hall, Englewood Cliffs, N.J., 1983.

3. F.J. MacWilliams and N.J.A. Sloane, *The Theory of Error-Correcting Codes,* Elsevier-North Holland, New York, N.Y., 1978.

4. R.J. McEliece, *The Theory of Information and Coding,* Addison-Wesley, Reading, Mass., 1977.

5. W.W. Peterson and E.J. Weldon, *Error-Correcting Codes,* Second Edition, MIT Press, Cambridge, Mass., 1984.

6. T.R.N. Rao and E. Fujiwara, *Error Control Coding for Computer Systems,* Prentice-Hall, Englewood Cliffs, N.J., 1989.

7. S.D. Constantin and T.R.N. Rao, "On the Theory of Binary Asymmetric Error Correcting Codes," *Information and Control,* Jan. 1979, pp. 20-36.

8. J.M. Borden, "A Low Rate Bound for Asymmetric Error-Correcting Codes," *IEEE Trans. Information Theory,* July 1983, pp. 600-602.

9. B. Bose and S. Cunningham, "Asymmetric Error Correcting Codes," *Methods in Communication, Security, and Computer Science,* Springer-Verlag, New York, N.Y., 1993.

10. P. Delsarte and P. Piret, "Bounds and Constructions for Binary Asymmetric Error-Correcting Codes," *IEEE Trans. Information Theory,* Jan. 1981, pp. 125-131.

11. T. Helleseth and T. Klove, "On Group-Theoretic Codes for Asymmetric Channels," *Information and Control,* Apr. 1981, pp. 1-9.

12. R.J. McEliece, "Comment on 'A Class of Codes for Asymmetric Channels and a Problem from the Additive Theory of Numbers'," *IEEE Trans. Information Theory,* Jan. 1973, p. 137.

13. R.J. McEliece and E.R. Rodemich, "The Constantin-Rao Construction for Binary Asymmetric Error-Correcting Codes," *Information and Control,* Jan. 1980, pp. 187-196.

14. A. Shiozaki, "Single Asymmetric Error-Correcting Cyclic AN Codes," *IEEE Trans. Computers,* June 1982, pp. 554-555.

15. A. Shiozaki, "Construction for Binary Asymmetric Error-Correcting Codes," *IEEE Trans. Information Theory,* Sept. 1982, pp. 787-789.

16. R.R. Varshamov, "On the Theory of Asymmetric Codes," *Doklady Akademiia Nauk USSR,* Vol. 164, Oct. 1965, pp. 757-760.

17. J.H. Weber, C. de Vroedt, and D.E. Boekee, "Bounds and Constructions for Binary Codes of Length Less than 24 and Asymmetric Distance Less than 6," *IEEE Trans. Information Theory,* Sept. 1988, pp. 1321-1331.

18. Z. Zhang and X.G. Xia, "New Lower Bounds for Binary Codes of Asymmetric Distance 2," *IEEE Trans. Information Theory,* Sept. 1992, pp. 1592-1597.

19. J.H. Weber, *Bounds and Constructions for Binary Block Codes Correcting Asymmetric or Unidirectional Errors,* doctoral dissertation, Delft University of Technology, Delft, The Netherlands, Nov. 1989.

20. B. Bose, *Theory and Design of Unidirectional Error Codes,* doctoral dissertation, Southern Methodist University, Dallas, Tex., May 1980.

21. B. Bose and D.K. Pradhan, "Optimal Unidirectional Error Detecting/Correcting Codes," *IEEE Trans. Computers,* June 1982, pp. 564-568.

22. B. Bose and T.R.N. Rao, "On the Theory of Unidirectional Error Correcting/Detecting Codes," *IEEE Trans. Computers,* June 1982., pp. 521-530

23. D.K. Pradhan, "A New Class of Error-Correcting Detecting Codes for Fault-Tolerant Computer Application," *IEEE Trans. Computers,* June 1980., pp. 471-481

24. I. Anderson, *Combinatorics of Finite Sets,* Clarendon Press, Oxford, England, 1987.

25. Z. Zhang and X.G. Xia, "LYM-Type Inequalities for *t*EC/AUED Codes," *IEEE Trans. Information Theory,* Jan. 1993, pp. 232-238.

26. Z. Zhang and X.G. Xia, "LYM-Type Inequalities for *t*-Antichains," submitted to *Discrete Math* (a copy of this paper can be obtained from the author, Zhen Zhang, EEB-508, USC, Los Angeles, CA 90089-2565).

27. Y. Iwadare, E. Fujiwara, and K. Iwasaki, "Coding Theory Applications in Fault Tolerant Computing," *IEICE Trans.,* Feb. 1991, pp. 244-258.

28. A.G. Skolleborg, "Code Control of Symmetric and Unidirectional Errors," tech. report, Delft University of Technology, Delft, The Netherlands, Dec. 1991.

29. Z. Zhang and C. Tu, "On the Construction of Systematic *t*EC/AUED Codes," to appear in *IEEE Trans. Information Theory* (a copy of this paper can be obtained from the author, Zhen Zhang, EEB-508, USC, Los Angeles, CA 90089-2565).

30. E. Sperner, "Ein Satz über Untermengen einer endlichen Menge," *Mathematische Zeitschrift 27,* 1928, pp. 544-548 (in German).

31. H. Dong, "Modified Berger Codes for Detection of Unidirectional Errors," *IEEE Trans. Computers,* June 1984, pp. 572-575.

32. J.E. Smith, "On Separable Unordered Codes," *IEEE Trans. Computers,* Aug. 1984, pp. 741-743.

33. R.R. Varshamov, "A Class of Codes for Asymmetric Channels and a Problem from the Additive Theory of Numbers," *IEEE Trans. Information Theory,* Jan. 1973, pp. 92-95.

34. N.K. Jha, "Separable Codes for Detecting Unidirectional Errors," *IEEE Trans. Computer-Aided Design,* May 1989, pp. 571-574.

35. N.K. Jha and M.B. Vora, "A t-Unidirectional Error Detecting Systematic Code," *Computers and Mathematics with Applications,* Vol. 16, No. 9, 1988, pp. 705-714.

36. B. Parhami and A. Avizienis, "Detection of Storage Errors in Mass Memories Using Low-Cost Arithmetic Codes," *IEEE Trans. Computers,* Apr. 1978, pp. 302-308.

37. J.F. Wakerly, "Detection of Unidirectional Multiple Errors Using Low-Cost Arithmetic Codes," *IEEE Trans. Computers,* Feb. 1975, pp. 210-212.

38. E.L. Leiss, "Data Integrity in Optical Disks," *IEEE Trans. Computers,* Sept. 1984, pp. 818-827.

39. Y. Tohma, R. Sakai, and R. Ohyama, "Realization of Fail-Safe Sequential Machines by Using k-out-of-n Code," *IEEE Trans. Computers,* Nov. 1971, pp. 1270-1275.

40. Y. Takasaki et al., "Optical Pulse Formats for Fiber Optic Digital Communications," *IEEE Trans. Communications,* Apr. 1976, pp. 404-413.

41. A.X. Widmer and P.A. Franaszek, "A DC-Balanced, Partitioned-Block, 8B/10B Transmission Code," *IBM J. Reseach and Development,* Sept. 1983, pp. 440-451.

42. J.F. Tabor, "Noise Reduction Using Low Weight and Constant Weight Coding Techniques," Tech. Report 1232, MIT AI Lab, Cambridge, Mass., 1990.

43. N. Alon, E.E. Bergmann, D. Coppersmith, and A.M. Odlyzko, "Balancing Sets of Vectors," *IEEE Trans. Information Theory,* Jan. 1988, pp. 128-130.

44. B. Bose, "On Unordered Codes," *IEEE Trans. Computers,* Feb. 1991, pp. 125-131.

45. S. Al-Bassam and B. Bose, "Design of Efficient Balanced Codes," *Proc. FTCS-19,* IEEE Computer Society Press, Los Alamitos, Calif., 1989, pp. 229-236.

46. S. Al-Bassam and B. Bose, "On Balanced Codes," *IEEE Trans. Information Theory,* Mar. 1990, pp. 406-408.

47. S. Al-Bassam, G. Ramanathan, and B. Bose, "Improved Construction Methods for Error Correcting Constant Weight Codes," *Proc. FTCS-22,* IEEE Computer Society Press, Los Alamitos, Calif., 1992, pp. 510-517.

48. Y. Saitoh, *Design of Asymmetric or Unidirectional Error Control Codes,* master's thesis, Yokohama National University, Yokohama, Japan, Feb. 1990.

49. H. van Tilborg and M. Blaum, "On Error-Correcting Balanced Codes," *IEEE Trans. Information Theory,* Sept. 1989, pp. 1091-1095.

50. J.H. Weber, C. de Vroedt, and D.E. Boekee, "Bounds on the Size of Codes Correcting Unidirectional Errors," *Proc. Ninth Symp. Information Theory in the Benelux,* Werkgemeenschap voor Informatie en Communicatietheorie, Enschede, The Netherlands, 1988, pp. 9-15.

51. J.H. Weber, C. de Vroedt, and D.E. Boekee, "Codes Correcting Unidirectional Errors," *Proc. Beijing Int'l Workshop Information Theory,* IEEE Service Center, Piscataway, N.J., 1988.

52. G. Fang and H.C. van Tilborg, "New Tables of AsEC and UEC Codes," Tech. Report 91-WSK-02, Department of Mathematics and Computing Science, Eindhoven University of Technology, Eindhoven, The Netherlands, Aug. 1991.

53. D.J. Lin and B. Bose, "On the Maximality of the Group Theoretic SEC-AUED Codes," in *Sequences: Combinatorics, Compression, Security, and Transmission,* R. Capocelli, ed., Springer-Verlag, New York, N.Y., 1990, pp. 506-529.

54. K. Yoshida, H. Jinushi, and K. Sakaniwa, "A New Construction Method for *t*-EC/AUED Codes Based on *t*-EC Codes," *IEEE Int'l Symp. Information Theory,* IEEE Service Center, Piscataway, N.J., 1993, p. 292.

55. R. Andrew, "Construction of *t*-EC/AUED Codes," *Electronic Letters,* Sept. 1988, pp. 1256-1258.

56. B. Bose, "On Systematic SEC/MUED Codes," *Proc. FTCS-11,* IEEE Computer Society Press, Los Alamitos, Calif., 1981, pp. 265-267.

57. J. Bruck and M. Blaum, "Some New EC/AUED Codes," *Proc. FTCS-19,* IEEE Computer Society Press, Los Alamitos, Calif., 1989, pp. 208-215.

58. N.K. Jha, "A New Class of Symmetric Error Correcting/Unidirectional Error Detecting Codes," *Computers and Mathematics with Applications,* Vol. 19, No. 5, 1990, pp. 95-104.

59. S. Kundu, *Design of Testable CMOS Circuits for TSC Systems,* doctoral dissertation, University of Iowa, Iowa City, Ia., 1988.

60. S. Kundu and S.M. Reddy, "On Symmetric Error Correcting All Unidirectional Error Detecting Codes," *IEEE Trans. Computers,* June 1990, pp. 752-761.

61. B.L. Montgomery and B.V.K.V. Kumar, "Systematic Random Error Correcting and All Unidirectional Error Detecting Codes," *IEEE Trans. Computers,* June 1990, pp. 752-761.

62. K. Naemura, "Semidistance Codes and *t*-Symmetric Error Correcting/All Unidirectional Error Detecting Codes," *IEICE Trans. on Information and Systems,* Nov. 1992, pp. 873-883.

63. K. Naemura, "Construction of *m*-out-of-*k*-Systematic *t*-Symmetric Error Correcting/All Unidirectional Error Detecting Codes," *IEICE Trans. Fundamentals,* Sept. 1992, pp. 1128-1133.

64. D. Nikolos, N. Gaitanis, and G. Philokyprou, "*t*-Error Correcting All Unidirectional Error Detecting Codes Starting from Cyclic AN Codes," *Proc. FTCS-14,* IEEE Computer Society Press, Los Alamitos, Calif., 1984, pp. 318-323.

65. D. Nikolos, N. Gaitanis and G. Philokyprou, "Systematic *t*-Error Correcting/All Unidirectional Error Detecting Codes," *IEEE Trans. Computers,* May 1986, pp. 394-402.

66. D.L. Tao, C.R.P. Hartmann, and P.K. Lala, "An Efficient Class of Unidirectional Error Detecting/Correcting Codes," *IEEE Trans. Computers,* July 1988, pp. 879-882.

67. D. Nikolos and A. Krokos, "Theory and Design of *t*-Error Correcting, *k*-Error Detecting and *d*-Unidirectional Error Detecting Codes with $d>k>t$," *IEEE Trans. Computers,* Apr. 1992, pp. 411-419.

68. D. Nikolos, "*t*-Symmetric and *d*-Unidirectional ($d>t$) Error-Detecting Cyclic AN Arithmetic Codes," *Int'l J. Electronics,* Vol. 68, No. 1, 1990, pp. 1-22.

69. S. Al-Bassam, B. Bose, and R. Venkatesan, "Burst and Unidirectional Error Detecting Codes," *Proc. FTCS-21,* IEEE Computer Society Press, Los Alamitos, Calif., 1991, pp. 378-384.

70. K. Sakaniwa, T.N. Ahn, and T.R.N. Rao, "A Note on *t*-Unidirectional Error Correcting and *d* ($d \geq t$)-Unidirectional Error Detecting (*t*-UEC and *d*-UED) Codes," *IEEE Trans. Computers,* Aug. 1991, pp. 987-988.

71. M. Blaum and J. Bruck, "Coding for Skew-Tolerant Parallel Asynchronous Communications," to be published in *IEEE Trans. Information Theory,* Mar. 1993.

72. N.K. Jha, "Totally Self-Checking Checker Designs for Bose-Lin, Bose, and Blaum Codes," *IEEE Trans. Computer-Aided Design Integrated Circuits and Systems,* Jan. 1991, pp. 136-143.

73. S. Park and B. Bose, "Burst Asymmetric/Unidirectional Error Correcting Detecting Codes," *Proc. FTCS-20,* IEEE Computer Society Press, Los Alamitos, Calif., 1990, pp. 273-280.

74. Y. Saitoh and H. Imai, "Constructions of Codes Correcting Burst Asymmetric Errors," *Electronics Letters,* Mar. 1990, pp. 286-287.

75. L.A. Dunning, G. Dial, and M.R. Varanasi, "Unidirectional 9-bit Byte Error-Detecting Codes for Computer Memory Systems," *Proc. FTCS-19,* IEEE Computer Society Press, Los Alamitos, Calif., 1989, pp. 216-221.

76. B. Bose, "Byte Unidirectional Error-Correcting Codes," *Proc. FTCS-19,* IEEE Computer Society Press, Los Alamitos, Calif., 1989, pp. 222-228.

77. Y. Saitoh and H. Imai, "An Application of Unidirectional Byte Error Correcting Codes," IEICE Tech. Report IT91-94, IEICE, Tokyo, Japan, Jan. 1992, pp. 37-40.

78. Y. Saitoh and H. Imai, "Generalized Concatenated Codes for Unidirectional-Byte-Error-Control," IEICE Tech. Report IT92-14, IEICE, Tokyo, Japan, May 1992.

79. Y. Saitoh and H. Imai, "Some Codes for Correcting and Detecting Unidirectional Byte Errors," to be published in *IEEE Trans. Computers* (this paper can be obtained from the author, Yuichi Saitoh, Institute of Industrial Science, University of Tokyo, 22-1, Roppongi 7-chome, Minato-ku, Tokyo, 106 Japan).

80. Y. Saitoh and H. Imai, "Bounds for Unidirectional Byte Error-Correcting Codes," IEICE Tech. Report IT92-64, IEICE, Tokyo, Japan, Aug. 1992.

81. Y. Saitoh and H. Imai, "Runlength-Limited Short-Length Codes for Unidirectional-Byte-Error-Control," *IEICE Trans. Fundamentals Electronics, Communications, and Computer Sciences,* Sept. 1992.

82. Y. Saitoh and H. Imai, "Generalized Concatenated Codes for Channels where Unidirectional Byte Errors are Predominant," to be published in *IEEE Trans. Information Theory* (this paper can be obtained from the author, Yuichi Saitoh, Institute of Industrial Science, University of Tokyo, 22-1, Roppongi 7-chome, Minato-ku, Tokyo, 106 Japan).

83. B. Bose, "Two Dimensional ARC Codes", *Int'l J. Computers and Mathematics with Applications,* Vol. 13, No.5/6, 1987, pp.547-554.

84. B. Bose and T.R.N. Rao, "Unidirectional Error Codes for Shift-Register Memories," *IEEE Trans. Computers,* June 1984, pp. 575-578.

85. B.L. Montgomery, "Efficient Unidirectional Error Codes for Block Memories," *IEEE Trans. Computers,* Nov. 1991, pp. 1257-1259.

About the Author

Mario Blaum was born in Buenos Aires, Argentina. He received his degree of Licenciado from the University of Buenos Aires in 1977, his MSc from the Israel Institute of Technology in 1981, and his PhD from the California Institute of Technology in 1984 — all in mathematics. From January to June, 1985, he was a research fellow at Caltech's Department of Electrical Engineering. In August, 1985, he joined the IBM Research Division at the Almaden Research Center, where he is presently a research staff member. His research interests include error-correcting codes, storage technology, combinatorics, and neural networks. A senior member of the IEEE, he can be reached at IBM Research Division, Almaden Research Center, 650 Harry Road, San Jose, CA 95120; or, via email at <BLAUM(A)ALMADEN.IBM.COM>.

Knowledge-Based Systems: Fundamentals and Tools
Edited by Oscar N. Garcia and Yi-Tzuu Chien
(ISBN 0-8186-1924-4); 512 pages

Local Network Technology (Third Edition)
Edited by William Stallings
(ISBN 0-8186-0825-0); 512 pages

Nearest Neighbor Pattern Classification Techniques
Edited by Belur V. Dasarathy
(ISBN 0-8186-8930-7); 464 pages

Object-Oriented Computing, Volume 1: Concepts
Edited by Gerald E. Petersen
(ISBN 0-8186-0821-8); 214 pages

Object-Oriented Computing, Volume 2: Implementations
Edited by Gerald E. Petersen
(ISBN 0-8186-0822-6); 324 pages

Real-Time Systems Abstractions, Languages, and Design Methodologies
Edited by Krishna M. Kavi
(ISBN 0-8186-3152-X); 550 pages

Reduced Instruction Set Computers (RISC) (Second Edition)
Edited by William Stallings
(ISBN 0-8186-8943-9); 448 pages

Software Design Techniques (Fourth Edition)
Edited by Peter Freeman and Anthony I. Wasserman
(ISBN 0-8186-0514-6); 730 pages

Software Engineering Project Management
Edited by Richard H. Thayer
(ISBN 0-8186-0751-3); 512 pages

Software Maintenance and Computers
Edited by David H. Longstreet
(ISBN 0-8186-8898-X); 304 pages

Software Management (Fourth Edition)
Edited by Donald J. Reifer
(ISBN 0-8186-3342-5); 656 pages

Software Reengineering
Edited by Robert S. Arnold
(ISBN 0-8186-3272-0); 688 pages

Software Reuse — Emerging Technology
Edited by Will Tracz
(ISBN 0-8186-0846-3); 400 pages

Software Risk Management
Edited by Barry W. Boehm
(ISBN 0-8186-8906-4); 508 pages

Standards, Guidelines and Examples on System and Software Requirements Engineering
Edited by Merlin Dorfman and Richard H. Thayer
(ISBN 0-8186-8922-6); 626 pages

System and Software Requirements Engineering
Edited by Richard H. Thayer and Merlin Dorfman
(ISBN 0-8186-8921-8); 740 pages

Systems Network Architecture
Edited by Edwin R. Coover
(ISBN 0-8186-9131-X); 464 pages

Test Access Port and Boundary-Scan Architecture
Edited by Colin M. Maunder and Rodham E. Tulloss
(ISBN 0-8186-9070-4); 400 pages

Visual Programming Environments: Paradigms and Systems
Edited by Ephraim Glinert
(ISBN 0-8186-8973-0); 680 pages

Visual Programming Environments: Applications and Issues
Edited by Ephraim Glinert
(ISBN 0-8186-8974-9); 704 pages

Visualization in Scientific Computing
Edited by G. M. Nielson, B. Shriver, and L. Rosenblum
(ISBN 0-8186-8979-X); 304 pages

Volume Visualization
Edited by Arie Kaufman
(ISBN 0-8186-9020-8); 494 pages

REPRINT COLLECTIONS

Distributed Computing Systems: Concepts and Structures
Edited by A. L. Ananda and B. Srinivasan
(ISBN 0-8186-8975-0); 416 pages

Expert Systems: A Software Methodology for Modern Applications
Edited by Peter G. Raeth
(ISBN 0-8186-8904-8); 476 pages

Milestones in Software Evolution
Edited by Paul W. Oman and Ted G. Lewis
(ISBN 0-8186-9033-X); 332 pages

Object-Oriented Databases
Edited by Ez Nahouraii and Fred Petry
(ISBN 0-8186-8929-3); 256 pages

Validating and Verifying Knowledge-Based Systems
Edited by Uma G. Gupta
(ISBN 0-8186-8995-1); 400 pages

ARTIFICIAL NEURAL NETWORKS TECHNOLOGY SERIES

Artificial Neural Networks — Concept Learning
Edited by Joachim Diederich
(ISBN 0-8186-2015-3); 160 pages

Artificial Neural Networks — Electronic Implementation
Edited by Nelson Morgan
(ISBN 0-8186-2029-3); 144 pages

Artificial Neural Networks — Theoretical Concepts
Edited by V. Rao Vemuri
(ISBN 0-8186-0855-2); 160 pages

SOFTWARE TECHNOLOGY SERIES

Bridging Faults and IDDQ Testing
Edited by Yashwant K. Malaiya and Rochit Rajsuman
(ISBN 0-8186-3215-1); 128 pages

Computer-Aided Software Engineering (CASE) (2nd Edition)
Edited by Elliot Chikofsky
(ISBN 0-8186-3590-8); 184 pages

Fault-Tolerant Software Systems: Techniques and Applications
Edited by Hoang Pham
(ISBN 0-8186-3210-0); 128 pages

Software Reliability Models: Theoretical Development, Evaluation, and Applications
Edited by Yashwant K. Malaiya and Pradip K. Srimani
(ISBN 0-8186-2110-9); 136 pages

MATHEMATICS TECHNOLOGY SERIES

Computer Algorithms
Edited by Jun-ichi Aoe
(ISBN 0-8186-2123-0); 154 pages

Distributed Mutual Exclusion Algorithms
Edited by Pradip K. Srimani and Sunil R. Das
(ISBN 0-8186-3380-8); 168 pages

Genetic Algorithms
Edited by Bill P. Buckles and Frederick E. Petry
(ISBN 0-81862935-5); 120 pages

Multiple-Valued Logic in VLSI Design
Edited by Jon T. Butler
(ISBN 0-8186-2127-3); 128 pages

Offices of the IEEE Computer Society

Headquarters Office
1730 Massachusetts Avenue, N.W.
Washington, DC 20036-1903
Phone: (202) 371-0101 — Fax: (202) 728-9614

Publications Office
P.O. Box 3014
10662 Los Vaqueros Circle
Los Alamitos, CA 90720-1264
Membership and General Information: (714) 821-8380
Publication Orders: (800) 272-6657 — Fax: (714) 821-4010

European Office
13, avenue de l'Aquilon
B-1200 Brussels, BELGIUM
Phone: 32-2-770-21-98 — Fax: 32-3-770-85-05

Asian Office
Ooshima Building
2-19-1 Minami-Aoyama, Minato-ku
Tokyo 107, JAPAN
Phone: 81-3-408-3118 — Fax: 81-3-408-3553

IEEE Computer Society

IEEE Computer Society Press Publications

Monographs: A monograph is an authored book consisting of 100-percent original material.
Tutorials: A tutorial is a collection of original materials prepared by the editors, and reprints of the best articles published in a subject area. Tutorials must contain at least five percent of original material (although we recommend 15 to 20 percent of original material).
Reprint collections: A reprint collection contains reprints (divided into sections) with a preface, table of contents, and section introductions discussing the reprints and why they were selected. Collections contain less than five percent of original material.
Technology series: Each technology series is a brief reprint collection — approximately 126-136 pages and containing 12 to 13 papers, each paper focusing on a subset of a specific discipline, such as networks, architecture, software, or robotics.
Submission of proposals: For guidelines on preparing CS Press books, write the Editorial Director, IEEE Computer Society Press, PO Box 3014, 10662 Los Vaqueros Circle, Los Alamitos, CA 90720-1264, or telephone (714) 821-8380.

Purpose

The IEEE Computer Society advances the theory and practice of computer science and engineering, promotes the exchange of technical information among 100,000 members worldwide, and provides a wide range of services to members and nonmembers.

Membership

All members receive the acclaimed monthly magazine *Computer*, discounts, and opportunities to serve (all activities are led by volunteer members). Membership is open to all IEEE members, affiliate society members, and others seriously interested in the computer field.

Publications and Activities

***Computer* magazine:** An authoritative, easy-to-read magazine containing tutorials and in-depth articles on topics across the computer field, plus news, conference reports, book reviews, calendars, calls for papers, interviews, and new products.

Periodicals: The society publishes six magazines and five research transactions. For more details, refer to our membership application or request information as noted above.

Conference proceedings, tutorial texts, and standards documents: The IEEE Computer Society Press publishes more than 100 titles every year.

Standards working groups: Over 100 of these groups produce IEEE standards used throughout the industrial world.

Technical committees: Over 30 TCs publish newsletters, provide interaction with peers in specialty areas, and directly influence standards, conferences, and education.

Conferences/Education: The society holds about 100 conferences each year and sponsors many educational activities, including computing science accreditation.

Chapters: Regular and student chapters worldwide provide the opportunity to interact with colleagues, hear technical experts, and serve the local professional community.